LEGAL WRITING: GETTING IT RIGHT AND GETTING IT WRITTEN

Seventh Edition

Mary Barnard Ray
Senior Lecturer in Law Emerita
University of Wisconsin Law School

Jill J. Ramsfield
Professor of Law Emerita
Georgetown Law

AMERICAN CASEBOOK SERIES®

WEST ACADEMIC

860 Blue Gentian Road, Suite 350
Eagan, MN 55121
1-877-888-1330

Published in the United States of America

ISBN: 979-8-88786-828-8

To each other, with gratitude for the friendship and professional respect that has brought us happily through four decades and seven editions.

Acknowledgments

Much has changed since 1986, when we began collaborating on the first edition of this book. Writing is done electronically, as is most research. Mail became faxes, which became email, which became instant messaging. Legal research was done exclusively in books, and then electronically with some artificial intelligence built in, and now AI can affect most research and writing decisions. One thing that has not changed, however, is our mutual respect and friendship. So, above all, we must acknowledge that enduring fact.

We warmly thank those who have helped on this seventh edition. University of Wisconsin Law School's Associate Dean for Library and Information Services and Director of the Law Library Bonnie Shucha offered invaluable expertise on current research sources and techniques, including the use of artificial intelligence in research and writing. Professor Steph Tai, also of the University of Wisconsin Law School, gave incisive insights on using artificial intelligence as part of scholarly research and writing, as well as advice on gender and writing. Chris Anzidei suggested care and attention to Power Point presentations, *Reply to All*, and other important challenges legal writers face in practice. Will Ray provided advice on cleansing documents and Mary Ann Polewski, Administrative Director of the Legal Analysis, Advocacy, and Writing Program at the University of Wisconsin, gave the citation entries the benefit of her expertise. Clients, loyal users of earlier editions, and other former students suggested needed additions and changes, for which we are very grateful. Dennis Ray, Gene Vricella, and Judy Mahr, as usual, encouraged, endured, and greatly enhanced this two-year production.

Above all, we acknowledge you, our careful readers, and we look forward to receiving your feedback on this edition.

Introduction

Just when you think you have addressed all the major concerns that legal writers face, another major change appears on the horizon. For this edition, that major change is the use of generative artificial intelligence (AI). To address AI, we have added new entries on ARTIFICIAL INTELLIGENCE AND RESEARCH; ARTIFICIAL INTELLIGENCE AND WRITING; and PROMPTS. However, realizing the breadth of AI's effect on legal writing, we have gone beyond adding these discrete entries. We address AI's uses and hazards throughout the book in the scores of topics where it may come into play. Thus when you turn to a topic in this book, you can be assured that the ongoing effects of AI have been taken into consideration.

As with previous editions, this edition addresses the questions that professional legal writers face as they work. It answers the busy lawyer's questions on the job, the law student's questions at the computer, and all legal writers' questions about the process of researching and writing well under pressure.

A reference with quick, reliable entries, this book answers the questions that arise during research, writing, analyzing, and editing. It addresses questions that occur to all legal writers, such as identifying the writing priorities for Complaints or the proper uses of commas. It also addresses the individual writer's propensities, such as writing blocks and perfectionism. It covers small particulars, such as whether to use *infer* or *imply*, and large issues, such as when to stop researching.

This book helps the legal writer resolve incidental problems, review a document efficiently, and develop an individualized approach to legal writing. In addition to the content of previous editions, this edition includes new entries on such topics as CYBERSECURTY, DISINFORMATION, GENDER IN WRITING, MISINFORMATION, METADATA REMOVAL, and the dangers of REPLY TO ALL. This resource also helps the legal writer develop over time. What sufficed in undergraduate studies can become inadequate in law school and may fail in practice. Year by year, lawyers must achieve more, becoming more prolific, more productive, and perhaps more profound. We hope you find that this edition answers your questions while you are trying to get your legal texts written—and right.

How to Use This Book

This book, combined with your citation reference, should provide you with all the information you need to answer your legal writing questions clearly and quickly. Use this book as a reference, a tutorial text, or an efficient helper. Highlight it, tab it—tailor your use to suit your individual writing process and personality.

This book covers the full range of topics that arise in legal writing, all arranged alphabetically so that you can find them quickly. It addresses little details, like how to handle gender pronouns, when to use *that* or *which*, and why nonverbal cues such as smiley faces can be misinterpreted. It gives you valuable guidance on all sorts of documents lawyers must write, from research memos and appellate briefs to wills and corporate documents. It also addresses process questions, such as how to collaborate successfully on a document, how to find the best structure for your document, and how to manage writers. It also helps you navigate the use of artificial intelligence (AI) in both research and writing.

Finding the Information You Need

To find an answer to any writing question, simply look up your topic, using the term that seems logical to you. You should find either the information you want under that topic or a cross-reference to the entry that does contain the information. For example, if you were facing the task of writing a contract for the first time, you could look up CONTRACTS and find an overview of the writing tasks most important in contract drafting. If you were puzzled about how to start a research project, you could turn to RESEARCH STRATEGY GUIDE and use it to develop your research plan. If you were not sure whether you needed to use commas or semicolons to punctuate a list, you could look under LISTS, PUNCTUATION OF and find the answers you need. For ideas on how to design and structure issues, you can look under ISSUES or BRIEFS.

If you have any trouble finding the information you need, consult the topical list of entries that follows this section to find the term you need or scan the index entries in the back of the book.

Entries are alphabetized by letter, with no regard to spaces or punctuation marks. To avoid a clutter of quotation marks, examples within the text are set off in italics. Longer examples are indented, with good examples in bold type and key terms shaded. In longer entries, subsections are numbered for easier and more precise reference. Citations used in examples are fictitious but conform in format to the Bluebook. Controversial grammatical points have been resolved in favor of the clearer choice for legal writing. When applicable, we have resolved these points according to the Bluebook and the U.S. Government Printing Office Style Manual because these sources are the recognized authorities in legal writing.

Finding Quick Answers

Your favorite way to use this book may be as a quick reference, a place to find answers in a minute and get back to the immediate task. Having the book on your desk frees you from having to remember details. For example, you may be writing a brief and be unsure about whether to use *affect* or *effect*. Rather than guessing which to use, you can look up the entry quickly, fix your text, and move on. Or you might be puzzling too long over the point headings in your argument. To accelerate the process, you can look up POINT HEADINGS, apply the techniques you find there, and move to the next task. Or, if you are having trouble getting started on a tough letter to a client, you can turn to the entries on BAD NEWS, GIVING IT or BAD NEWS, SOFTENING IT and imitate the form to get started, refining it to fit with your own style and your particular situation.

Reviewing Others' Writing

If you are teaching legal writing or managing legal writers, using this text allows you to provide more helpful information quickly. To comment on a usage problem, you can simply highlight the relevant term on the draft, signaling the writer to look up the entry corresponding to the highlighted term. For bigger issues, you can simply write "See [name of entry]." This use of the book as a reference frees you as the reviewer to focus your commenting energy on the substantive and unique issues remaining in the text. By keeping the alphabetical or topical list of entries nearby as you review a text, you can save time as you become more familiar with the entries covering points you often address.

Improving Your Knowledge About Writing

You can also use the book as your personal writing guide, a reference for building your knowledge of and vocabulary for writing in the areas of greatest interest to you. Scan the topical list of entries and note those of particular interest to you. Read the complete group of entries under a topic if you like, or read them in smaller spurts, checking off the entries you have read. Highlight, tab, or mark it as you wish to make it your own.

You may use this book to satisfy your curiosity about all sorts of writing questions, large and small. You can learn more about any topic easily by referring to the other entries or outside sources cross-referenced within the entry. For example, if you are examining memo writing, you may want to read all the entries under MEMOS in the topical index. Inherent in analysis is an approach to organization, so you may want also to assign yourself entries listed under that topic, such as LEGAL

ANALYSIS or REASONING, PRESENTING IT. Typical mistakes occur in briefs, such as a lack of smooth logical flow or shifts in levels of formality, so you may want to consult CONNECTIONS, MAKING THEM or FORMALITY, LEVEL OF. You may encounter a sticky question involving gender reference, so you might want to read GENDER IN WRITING; SEXIST LANGUAGE, WAYS TO AVOID; or S/HE. Plagued by email protocol, you may appreciate EMAIL, REPLAY TO ALL, and TONE.

Improving Your Writing Over Time

You may want to develop your personal plan for improvement with a little less structure than a course, but a more systematic approach than just looking up questions as they arise. One way to do this is to start recording entries you consult as you are writing. Over time, note the entries that you look up the most. You might keep a separate file or mark this book with your own code of tabs to remind yourself periodically of those trouble areas. You might keep a list.

Date	Document Type	Main Problems	Entries

After you have identified these areas, you can begin collecting further feedback. For example, specifically request feedback about those areas from your colleagues or supervisor. You can also read cross-referenced entries, especially those that discuss the related, broader topics. Gradually, after you categorize these areas, read supplemental entries when you are beginning the writing process or when you get to those areas of concern. Consciously build techniques to combat the problems. This way, you may gradually remove weaknesses and develop strengths.

Another way to encourage and guide your own improvement is to set goals for yourself as a writer and work toward those goals over time. Rather than starting with your problem, begin with your interest and read entries that are related to that interest. You can move through the book gradually, in order of importance for you. To help you find related entries of interest to you, consult the Topical List of Entries that follows this section.

Topical List of Entries

Overview of Topics

Law Practice
International Legal Writing
Writing and Technology
Writing Process
- General Concepts
- Working with Other Writers
- Making Preliminary Decisions

Writing Techniques
- Researching
- Citing
- Reasoning
- Persuading
- Organizing
  - Large-Scale Organization
  - Small-Scale Organization
  - Organization in Specific Documents
  - Process of Organization
- Writing
- Structuring Sentences
- Choosing Words
  - Accuracy
  - Legal terms
  - Conciseness
  - Clarity and Readability
  - Specific Wording Techniques
- Tone
- Using Graphic Aids

Legal Documents
- Memos
- Briefs
- Various Legal Documents

Checklists
Grammar Concepts
- Generally
- Nouns
- Verbs
- Modifiers
- Punctuation
- Usage

Topical List

Law Practice

ARTIFICIAL INTELLIGENCE AND RESEARCH ... 39
ARTIFICIAL INTELLIGENCE AND WRITING ... 41
ADJUSTING TO A NEW WRITING SITUATION ... 13
CONDITIONS, STATING THEM ... 132
COUNSELING CLIENTS ... 145
DEADLINES, MEETING THEM ... 151
DISINFORMATION ... 164
EMAIL OR MEMO? ... 181
EXECUTIVE SUMMARY ... 192
GENDER IN WRITING ... 208
GHOST WRITING ... 214
GRACE UNDER FIRE ... 217
INTERVIEWING CLIENTS ... 249
JUDGES, HOW TO ADDRESS ... 262
MANAGING WRITERS ... 289
MISINFORMATION ... 303
MULTI-TASKING ... 308
ORAL PRESENTATIONS ... 341
PRIORITIES WITHIN ONE PROJECT ... 418
PROFESSIONAL LANGUAGE AND PRESENTATION ... 422
PROMPTS ... 425
RECORDS, KEEPING THEM ... 468
REPLY TO ALL ... 472
TIME MANAGEMENT ... 573
TRIAGE ... 588
WRITING BLOCK ... 631

International Legal Writing

ARTIFICIAL INTELLIGENCE AND RESEARCH ... 39
ARTIFICIAL INTELLIGENCE AND WRITING ... 41
COMMUNICATIONS, INTERNATIONAL ... 112
ENGLISH AS A SECOND LANGUAGE ... 187
GRAPHICS AND SYMBOLS IN EMAIL ... 218
PROMPTS ... 425
REASONING, PRESENTING IT ... 459
STARE DECISIS ... 546
SYLLOGISMS ... 558

Writing and Technology

ARTIFICIAL INTELLIGENCE AND RESEARCH ... 39
ARTIFICIAL INTELLIGENCE AND WRITING ... 41
ADJUSTING TO A NEW WRITING SITUATION ... 13
CITATIONS, ELECTRONIC ... 89

CLEANSING ELECTRONIC DOCUMENTS 95
COMMUNICATIONS, ELECTRONIC 111
COMMUNICATIONS, REAL-TIME 118
CYBERSECURITY 149
ELECTRONIC ETIQUETTE 173
EMAIL, HOW TO MANAGE 180
EMOJIS 182
GRAPHICS AND SYMBOLS IN EMAIL 218
HALLUCINATIONS 228
LINK ROT 280
METADATA REMOVAL 301
PAPERLESS PRACTICE 365
PRIVACY 419
PROMPTS 425
SOCIAL MEDIA 541
TEXTING UNDER THE TABLE 565
WORDS SPELLCHECKERS MAY NOT CATCH 625
WRITING AND TECHNOLOGY 628

Writing Process

General Concepts

ADJUSTING TO A NEW WRITING SITUATION 13
ARTIFICIAL INTELLIGENCE AND WRITING 41
AUDIENCE 48
AUDIENCE OR *READER*? 50
DOCUMENT CHECKLIST 164
ELECTRONIC ETIQUETTE 173
GETTING STARTED 212
HABITS, WRITING 227
HELP 230
MULTI-TASKING 308
PAPERLESS PRACTICE 365
PERFECTIONISM 382
POLISHING 394
PREWRITING 408
PRINCIPLES OF GOOD LEGAL WRITING 411
PRIORITIES WITHIN ONE PROJECT 418
PROCESS AND PRODUCT COMPARED 420
PROCRASTINATION 421
PROFESSIONAL POSTURE 424
PURPOSE 432
REASONING, PRESENTING IT 459
RESEARCH AS WRITING 473
RESEARCH STRATEGY GUIDE 476
REVISING 484
REWRITING 487
THESIS SENTENCES 570

TIME MANAGEMENT 573
TRIAGE 588
WRITING 627
WRITING PROCESS 643

Working with Other Writers

CHOICES IN LEGAL WRITING 86
COLLABORATION 96
DEADLINES, MEETING THEM 151
EDITING 168
GHOST WRITING 214
GRACE UNDER FIRE 217
INDEPENDENCE IN LEGAL WRITING 242
INSTRUCTIONS, WRITING THEM 246
MANAGING WRITERS 289
METADATA REMOVAL 301
REPLY TO ALL 472
TIME MANAGEMENT 573
TRIAGE 588
VOICE 612

Making Preliminary Decisions

ARTIFICIAL INTELLIGENCE AND RESEARCH 39
ARTIFICIAL INTELLIGENCE AND WRITING 41
ARGUING IN THE ALTERNATIVE 33
AUDIENCE 48
COMMUNICATIONS, EMAIL 112
DEADLINES, MEETING THEM 151
ELECTRONIC FILINGS 173
GETTING STARTED 212
INTRODUCTIONS 250
ISSUES 255
NOTES 316
ORGANIZE, HOW TO 353
ORGANIZATION FOR THOSE WHO CAN'T OUTLINE 346
PERFECTIONISM 382
PREWRITING 408
PRINCIPLES OF GOOD LEGAL WRITING 411
PROCRASTINATION 421
PROMPTS 425
PURPOSE 432
QUESTIONS PRESENTED 435
READERS 450
REASONING, ANALOGICAL 454
REASONING, DEDUCTIVE 455
REASONING, INDUCTIVE 456
REASONING, MODERN 457

REASONING, OTHER ... 457
REASONING, POSTMODERN ... 458
REASONING, PRESENTING IT ... 459
RESEARCH STRATEGY GUIDE ... 476
SCOPE ... 516
SECONDARY SOURCES ... 517
STANDARD OF REVIEW ... 544
TABLE OF AUTHORITIES ... 562
THEME ... 567
TABLE OF CONTENTS ... 563
THEORY OF THE CASE ... 568
TIME MANAGEMENT ... 573
VOICE ... 612
WRITING, OBJECTIVE ... 633
WRITING, PERSUASIVE ... 634
WRITING PROCESS ... 643
WRITING TO ATTORNEYS ... 645
WRITING TO CLIENTS ... 647

Writing Techniques

Researching

ARTIFICIAL INTELLIGENCE AND RESEARCH ... 39
CYBERSECURITY ... 149
ISSUES ... 255
LEGAL ANALYSIS ... 269
LINK ROT ... 280
MANDATORY AUTHORITY ... 292
NOTES ... 316
PERSUASIVE AUTHORITY ... 387
QUESTIONS PRESENTED ... 435
READERS ... 450
REASONING, PRESENTING IT ... 459
RESEARCH AS WRITING ... 473
RESEARCH STRATEGY GUIDE ... 476
SECONDARY SOURCES ... 517
STANDARD OF REVIEW ... 544
SYNTHESIS ... 560
THEORY OF THE CASE ... 568
TRIAGE ... 588
UPDATING THE LAW ... 593
WHEN TO STOP ... 616

Citing

ALWD GUIDE TO LEGAL CITATION ... 19
BLUEBOOK ... 62
CITATIONS ... 86
CITATIONS, BASIC FORMATS ... 88
CITATIONS, ELECTRONIC ... 89

CITATIONS, PARALLEL 90
CITATIONS, PINPOINT 91
CITATIONS, SIGNALS 91
CITATIONS, STRING 92
CITATIONS, VARYING FORMATS 93
FOOTNOTES 202
PARENTHESES 373
PARENTHETICALS 375
POLISHING 394

Reasoning

REASONING, ANALOGICAL 454
REASONING, DEDUCTIVE 455
REASONING, INDUCTIVE 456
REASONING, MODERN 457
REASONING, POSTMODERN 458
REASONING, PRESENTING IT 459

Persuading

ARGUING IN THE ALTERNATIVE 33
BAD NEWS, GIVING IT 51
BAD NEWS, SOFTENING IT 54
COMMUNICATIONS, PERSUASIVE 115
COMMUNICATIONS, TONE OF 119
COUNTERARGUMENTS, HOW TO HANDLE 145
ISSUES 255
ORGANIZATION, LARGE-SCALE 349
ORGANIZATION, SMALL-SCALE 352
OUTLINES 357
POINT OF VIEW, OBJECTIVE TO PERSUASIVE 393
POSITIONS OF EMPHASIS 397
PRECISION 401
PROMPTS 425
READERS 450
REASONING, ANALOGICAL 454
REASONING, DEDUCTIVE 455
REASONING, INDUCTIVE 456
REASONING, MODERN 457
REASONING, POSTMODERN 458
REASONING, PRESENTING IT 459
SENTENCE LENGTH 520
SENTENCE STRUCTURE 525
SHORT SENTENCES 536
STARE DECISIS 546
STYLE 551
TONE IN LETTERS AND EMAIL 582
TOUGH, SOUNDING THAT WAY 583
VOICE 612

WRITING, PERSUASIVE 634
WRITING TO ATTORNEYS 645
WRITING TO CLIENTS 647

Organizing

Large-Scale Organization

HEADINGS 229
LEGAL ANALYSIS 269
ORGANIZATION, CHRONOLOGICAL 346
ORGANIZATION FOR THOSE WHO CAN'T OUTLINE 346
ORGANIZATION, TOPICAL 353
ORGANIZATION, LARGE-SCALE 349
REASONING, ANALOGICAL 454
REASONING, DEDUCTIVE 455
REASONING, INDUCTIVE 456
REASONING, MODERN 457
REASONING, OTHER 457
REASONING, POSTMODERN 458
REASONING, PRESENTING IT 459
TOPICAL ORGANIZATION 582

Small-Scale Organization

CONNECTIONS, MAKING THEM 135
LISTS, STRUCTURE OF 281
LOGICAL LINKS 288
ORGANIZATION, SMALL-SCALE 352
PARAGRAPHS 369
SENTENCE STRUCTURE 525
SYNTAX 560
TOPIC SENTENCES OR *THESIS SENTENCES*? 583
TRANSITIONS 584

Organization in Specific Documents

ANSWERS TO COMPLAINTS 25
BRIEFS 65
BRIEFS, AMICUS 68
BRIEFS, APPELLATE 69
BRIEFS, PRETRIAL 72
BRIEFS, REPLY 72
BRIEFS, TRIAL 73
COMPLAINTS 124
CONCLUSIONS 130
CONTRACTS 140
DISCUSSION SECTION 162
EMAIL OR MEMO? 181
INTRODUCTIONS 250
JURY INSTRUCTIONS 264
MEMOS 295

PROCEDURAL OR *SUBSTANTIVE*? 420
QUESTIONS PRESENTED 435

Process of Organization
DEADLINES, MEETING THEM 151
HABITS, WRITING 227
NOTES 316
ORGANIZATION FOR THOSE WHO CAN'T OUTLINE 346
ORGANIZATION, SMALL-SCALE 352
OUTLINES 357
POLISHING 394
POWERPOINTS 399
PREWRITING 408
REVISING 484
REWRITING 487
TIME MANAGEMENT 573
WRITING PROCESS 643

Writing
ARTIFICIAL INTELLIGENCE AND WRITING 41
COMMUNICATIONS, CLOSINGS FOR 110
COMMUNICATIONS, ELECTRONIC 111
COMMUNICATIONS, EMAIL 112
COMMUNICATIONS, INTERNATIONAL 112
COMMUNICATIONS, OPENINGS FOR 114
COMMUNICATIONS, PERSUASIVE 115
COMMUNICATIONS, REAL-TIME 118
COMMUNICATIONS, TONE OF 119
DICTATION 159
DRAFTING 167
DRAFTS 167
METADATA REMOVAL 301
WRITING 627
WRITING BLOCK 631
WRITING PROCESS 643
WRITING TO ATTORNEYS 645
WRITING TO CLIENTS 647

Structuring Sentences
AGREEMENT, SUBJECTS AND VERBS 16
CLAUSES 94
COMPLEX SENTENCES 126
COMPOUND SENTENCES 127
CONJUNCTIONS 133
DEPENDENT CLAUSES 157
INTRUSIVE PHRASES 253
PARALLEL STRUCTURE 370
PHRASES 388

SENTENCE FRAGMENTS 520
SENTENCE, PARTS OF 521
SENTENCE STRUCTURE 525
SUBJECT-VERB AGREEMENT 554
SUBORDINATION 556
SYNTAX 560

Choosing Words

Accuracy

ACCURACY 5
AMBIGUITY, WAYS TO AVOID 20
ANTONYMS 27
HOMONYMS 233
OF COURSE 327
PRECISION 401
SYNONYMS 560
THIS 572

Legal Terms

ABOVE 5
AFFECT OR *EFFECT*? 15
AFORESAID 15
ATTORNEY OR *LAWYER*? 48
BLUEBOOK 62
DICTA 159
EQUITY 190
IMPLY OR *INFER*? 241
JARGON 262
JUDGES, HOW TO ADDRESS 262
KEY TERMS 267
LEGALESE 275
MIGHT OR *MAY*? 303
PRECISION 401
PURSUANT TO 433
TERMS OF ART 564
WHETHER 618

Conciseness

AS A MATTER OF FACT 45
AT THIS POINT IN TIME 47
CLEARLY 95
CONCISENESS 127
FACT OF THE MATTER, THE 196
FACT THAT, THE 197
FLOWERY LANGUAGE 200
FOR THE PERIOD OF 208
IN ADVANCE OF 241
IN ORDER TO OR *TO*? 246

IN QUESTION 246
IT IS SAID THAT, IT WOULD SEEM THAT, IT MIGHT BE SAID THAT 261
IT IS . . . THAT 261
JARGON 262
OBVIOUSLY 327
REPETITION 470
THERE IS . . . THAT 570
UNTIL SUCH TIME AS 592
WORDY PHRASES 626

Clarity and Readability

COLLOQUIALISM 100
CONDITIONS, STATING THEM 132
FORMS 206
KEY TERMS 267
JARGON 262
LEGALESE 275
LISTS, STRUCTURE OF 281
LOGICAL LINKS 288
MODIFIERS 304
PRECISION 401
PRIOR TO 419
READABILITY 446
REALLY 454
RESPECTIVELY 483
TERMS OF ART 564
TRANSITIONS 584
UNDOUBTEDLY 590
UTTERLY 594
VARIETY 595
VERY 612

Specific Wording Techniques

ALLITERATION 17
ASSONANCE 46
CLICHÉ 95
EMPHASIS 184
FORMALITY, LEVEL OF 204
GENDER IN WRITING 208
HYPERBOLE 235
IDIOM 238
PERSUASIVE WRITING 387
POSITIONS OF EMPHASIS 397
REPETITION 470
RHYMES 491
TONE 578

VARIETY 595
VOICE 612

Tone
BAD NEWS, SOFTENING IT 54
COMMUNICATIONS, INTERNATIONAL 112
COMMUNICATIONS, TONE OF 119
EMOJIS 182
FORMALITY, LEVEL OF 204
PROFESSIONAL LANGUAGE AND PRESENTATION 422
SOCIAL MEDIA 541
TONE 578
TOUGH, SOUNDING THAT WAY 583

Using Graphic Aids
BOLDFACE TYPE 62
BULLET POINTS 74
CHARTS 85
EMOJIS 182
FONT CHOICES 201
FONT SIZE 202
GRAPHICS, HOW TO USE 218
GRAPHICS, WHICH FORM TO USE 223
ITALICS 259
LISTS, WHEN TO USE 286
POWERPOINTS 399
TYPEFACE SIZE 588
UNDERLINING 589

Legal Documents

Memos
ANALOGOUS CASES 23
APPLICATION 32
BRIEF ANSWERS 64
CAPTIONS 79
CASE BRIEFS 81
CONCLUSIONS 130
CONCLUSORY 132
DISCUSSION SECTION 162
INTRODUCTIONS 250
LEGAL ANALYSIS 269
MEMOS 295
OBJECTIVITY 326
ORGANIZATION, LARGE-SCALE 349
ORGANIZATION, SMALL-SCALE 352
OUTLINES 357
QUESTIONS PRESENTED 435
READERS 450
REASONING, ANALOGICAL 454

REASONING, DEDUCTIVE 455
REASONING, INDUCTIVE 456
REASONING, MODERN 457
REASONING, OTHER 457
REASONING, POSTMODERN 458
REASONING, PRESENTING IT 459
STARE DECISIS 546
STATEMENT OF FACTS 547
WRITING, OBJECTIVE 633
WRITING TO ATTORNEYS 645
WRITING TO CLIENTS 647

Briefs

ARGUING IN THE ALTERNATIVE 33
ARGUMENT SECTION 34
BRIEFS 65
BRIEFS, AMICUS 68
BRIEFS, APPELLATE 69
BRIEFS, PRETRIAL 72
BRIEFS, REPLY 72
BRIEFS, TRIAL 73
CONCLUSIONS 130
COUNTERARGUMENTS, HOW TO HANDLE 145
CREDIBILITY 147
DESIGN 157
ISSUES 255
MEMORANDUM OF POINTS AND AUTHORITIES 295
PERSUASIVE WRITING 387
POINT HEADINGS 392
POINT OF VIEW, OBJECTIVE TO PERSUASIVE 393
READERS 450
REASONING, ANALOGICAL 454
REASONING, DEDUCTIVE 455
REASONING, INDUCTIVE 456
REASONING, MODERN 457
REASONING, OTHER 457
REASONING, POSTMODERN 458
REASONING, PRESENTING IT 459
STANDARD OF REVIEW 544
STARE DECISIS 546
STATEMENT OF THE CASE 548
SUMMARY OF THE ARGUMENT 557
SYLLOGISMS 558
WRITING TO ATTORNEYS 645

Various Legal Documents

ANSWERS TO COMPLAINTS 25
BENCH MEMOS 58

BRIEFS 65
BRIEFS, AMICUS 68
BRIEFS, APPELLATE 69
BRIEFS, PRETRIAL 72
BRIEFS, REPLY 72
BRIEFS, TRIAL 73
CASE BRIEFS 81
COMMUNICATIONS, EMAIL 112
COMPLAINTS 124
CONTRACTS 140
CORPORATE DOCUMENTS 142
INFORMATIVE ARTICLES 243
LEGISLATION 277
MEMORANDUM OF POINTS AND AUTHORITIES 295
MOTIONS 306
NOTICE OF MOTION 319
OPINIONS, JUDICIAL 330
OPINIONS, LEGAL 332
ORDERS 345
PLEADINGS 389
SCHOLARLY WRITING 499
SETTLEMENT LETTERS AND EMAIL 532
VERIFICATION 611
WILLS 620

Checklists

DOCUMENT CHECKLIST 164
POLISHING CHECKLIST 395
PREWRITING CHECKLIST 410
PRINCIPLES OF GOOD LEGAL WRITING 411
RESEARCH PROCESS CHECKLIST 475
RESEARCH STRATEGY GUIDE 476
REVISING CHECKLIST 486
REWRITING CHECKLIST 489
UPDATING THE LAW 593
WHEN TO STOP 616

Grammar Concepts

Generally

BENDING THE RULES 61
GRAMMAR 218
SENTENCE FRAGMENTS 520
SYNTAX 560

Nouns

ABSTRACT NOUNS 5
ANTECEDENTS 27
COLLECTIVE NOUNS 100

NOMINALIZATION 314
NOUNS 322
PROPER NOUNS 431

Verbs

ACTIVE VOICE 8
PASSIVE VOICE 377
PAST PARTICIPLES 379
SPLIT INFINITIVES 543
VERBS, AUXILIARY 595
VERBS, EFFECTIVE USE OF 598
VERBS, IRREGULAR 600
VERBS, LINKING 601
VERBS, MOODS 602
VERBS, PARTICIPLES 604
VERBS, TENSES 605
VERB TENSES, WHICH TO USE? 609
VOICE, ACTIVE OR PASSIVE? 613

Modifiers

ADJECTIVES 11
ADVERBS 14
APPOSITIVE 33
ARTICLES, GRAMMAR 39
MODIFIERS 304
MODIFIERS, DANGLING 305
MODIFIERS, MISPLACED 305
MODIFIERS, SQUINTING 306
NONRESTRICTIVE PHRASES 315
PREPOSITIONAL PHRASES 404
PREPOSITIONS 405
PRONOUNS 427

Punctuation

ABBREVIATING DATES, NAMES, STATES, AND TITLES 1
ABBREVIATIONS IN TEXT 4
ACCURACY 5
APOSTROPHES 28
BRACKETS 63
CAPITALIZATION 77
COLONS 101
COMMA, OXFORD 103
COMMAS 104
DASHES 149
ELLIPSES 175
EM OR EN DASH? 176
EXCLAMATION POINTS 192

HYPHENS 235
LISTS, STRUCTURE OF 281
PERIODS 383
QUESTION MARKS 433
RUN-ON SENTENCES 495
SEMICOLONS 518
SPACING BETWEEN SENTENCES 543

Usage

ABBREVIATING DATES, NAMES,
STATES, AND TITLES 1
ABHORRENCE OF OR *ABHORRENCE FOR?* 5
AFFECT OR *EFFECT?* 15
AGREE TO OR *AGREE WITH?* 16
ALL READY OR *ALREADY?* 18
ALTHOUGH OR *THOUGH?* 18
ALTOGETHER OR *ALL TOGETHER?* 19
A.M. 19
AMONG OR *BETWEEN?* 23
AND/OR 24
AS IF OR *AS THOUGH?* 45
AS OR *LIKE?* 45
AS TO 47
BAD OR *BADLY?* 56
BASED ON 56
BASICALLY 57
B.C. OR *B.C.E.?* 57
BECAUSE OR *SINCE?* 57
BEST OR *BETTER?* 61
BLACK 62
CAN HARDLY OR *CAN'T HARDLY?* 76
CANNOT OR *CAN NOT?* 76
CAN OR *COULD?* 76
CAN OR *MAY?* 76
CERTAIN 85
CLEARLY 95
COLLOQUIALISM 100
COMPLEMENT OR *COMPLIMENT?* 126
COMPOUND WORDS, WHEN TO HYPHENATE 127
CONTACT 136
CONTEND 137
CONTINUAL OR *CONTINUOUS?* 139
CORRESPOND TO OR *CORRESPOND WITH?* 144
COULD CARE LESS OR *COULDN'T CARE LESS?* 144
DIFFERENT FROM OR *DIFFERENT THAN?* 161
EACH 168
ELEGANT VARIATION 175

EMINENT OR *IMMINENT*? 181
END RESULT 187
ETC. 190
EVERYBODY 190
EVERYONE 191
FACT OF THE MATTER, THE 196
FARTHER OR *FURTHER*? 197
FEWER OR *LESS*? 198
FIGURATIVE MEANING 199
FLOWERY LANGUAGE 200
FOREGO OR *FORGO*? 204
GOOD OR *WELL*? 217
HANGED OR *HUNG*? 229
HYPERBOLE 235
IF AND WHEN 239
IMPACT 241
IMPLY OR *INFER*? 241
IN ADVANCE OF 241
JARGON 262
LAWYER OR *ATTORNEY*? 268
LAY OR *LIE*? 269
LEAD OR *LED*? 269
MATHEMATICAL SYMBOLS 293
MAY OR *MIGHT*? 294
MOST IMPORTANTLY 306
OBLIVIOUS OF OR *OBLIVIOUS TO*? 327
OK, *O.K.*, OR *OKAY*? 327
ON LINE, *ONLINE*, OR *ON-LINE*? 328
ORAL OR *VERBAL*? 341
OTHERWISE 357
PADDING 365
PER 381
PERCENT, *%*, OR *PER CENT*? 381
PHENOMENA OR *PHENOMENONS*? 388
PREPOSITION, ENDING A SENTENCE WITH 404
PROCEDURAL OR *SUBSTANTIVE*? 420
REALLY 454
REGARDLESS OR *IRREGARDLESS*? 470
RECUR OR *REOCCUR*? 468
S/HE 535
SOMEDAY OR *SOME DAY*? 542
SOMEONE 542
THEIRS OR *THEIR'S*? 567
THEREFORE OR *THEREFOR*? 570
TO BE 577
UNTO 593
UTTERLY 594

VERY 612
VIRTUALLY 612
VIZ. 612
WE 615
WHEN OR *IF*? 615
WHETHER OR *WHETHER OR NOT*? 619
WHOEVER OR *WHOMEVER*? 619
WHO OR *WHOM*? 620
YET 657

LEGAL WRITING: GETTING IT RIGHT AND GETTING IT WRITTEN

Seventh Edition

ABBREVIATING DATES, NAMES, STATES, AND TITLES

Authorities differ on how to abbreviate titles and names, and these rules are in flux; accommodate your readers' preferences, if they have any. For related information, see ABBREVIATIONS IN TEXT.

1. Academic degrees.

These abbreviations generally appear after the person's name. Currently the standard use includes periods within the abbreviations, with no spaces between the period and the following letter of the abbreviation. There is a trend to omit the periods in abbreviations that use only a single letter for each word, most notably in sources relying on *The Chicago Manual of Style*. Other sources, however, retain the periods. Including the periods also provides a smoother appearance when one of the degrees is a doctorate, which requires the internal period in all sources, but no period at the end. When the title appears at the end of the sentence, do not add an additional period. As in other situations where abbreviations end a sentence, one period is sufficient for both purposes.

Ph.D., B.A., B.S., J.D., M.D.

Do not use a title before the name when including degree information after the name.

Noriko Niko, J.D.

rather than

Ms. Noriko Niko, J.D.

When dealing with an unusual title you have not previously encountered, follow the general rule of capitalizing the first letter of each word and spell out the title rather than abbreviating, because the abbreviation would likely not be understandable to your reader. You are unlikely to be able to abbreviate an unfamiliar title.

Juliana Jones, Ambassador Extraordinary and Plenipotentiary

rather than

Juliana Jones, Amb. Extr. and Plen.

An additional decision here is whether the titles should be included. A good general rule is to include them when they are needed to designate the person's relevant authority or when the AUDIENCE might be offended if they are omitted.

The featured speaker will be ex-Ambassador George Henrich.

rather than

The featured speaker will be George Henrich.

Otherwise, you can usually omit the titles. In some documents, such as academic journals, the author's titles are commonly omitted because the quality of the document, rather than the author's title, is the source of authority.

2. Judicial titles.

When writing about a judge, use *the honorable Judge* [name] for lower court judges and *the honorable Justice* [name] for higher court justices. Always precede the judge's name with *Judge* or *Justice.* This is what the *J.* preceding a judge's name in an opinion represents.

3. Titles for government officials.

Spell out *Senator*, *Representative*, and *President.* In other cases, you may abbreviate the title.

4. Other personal titles.

You may place a title before the name or after it, but do not place titles in both places.

James Maarjberg, Esq.

rather than

Mr. James Maarjberg, Esq.

and

Sarah Levin, M.D., Ph.D.

rather than

Dr. Sarah Levin, Ph.D.

Abbreviations for generations are an exception to this rule.

Dr. Marcus Stonefield, Jr.

Rev. Ambrose Winthrop III

When abbreviating a middle name, use a period when it is an abbreviation but omit the period when the letter does not stand for an abbreviated name.

Dr. M.L. King, Jr.

Harry S Truman

5. Governmental agencies and departments.

Do not abbreviate *Company* or *Corporation* when they are part of the name of units of the Federal Government.

Federal Savings and Loan Corporation

The use of abbreviations otherwise depends on context and audience. For example, you may use *FDA* for *Food and Drug Administration* when your audience will understand the abbreviation immediately and when the document's level of formality allows abbreviations. But if your reader will have to look up *FDLP* to learn that it is the *Federal Depository Library Program*, write the name out in full the first time with the abbreviation in parenthesis after.

Federal Depository Library Program (FDLP)

6. Countries and states.

Spell out *United States* when using it in a sentence, particularly one that includes the name of another country.

Officials of the United States and France concurred on this position when meeting last month.

rather than

Officials of the U.S. and France concurred on this position when meeting last month.

Abbreviate *U.S.* when it precedes another word or title, where it is functioning as an adjective.

Decisions from the U.S. district courts are subject to appellate review and may ultimately reach the U.S. Supreme Court.

Do not abbreviate the names of foreign countries except the former U.S.S.R., because of the length of the written name and the familiarity of the abbreviation.

Spell out the name of a state in text, but abbreviate it when it follows a capitalized geographic term. Use the abbreviations preferred by the relevant citation authority, rather than the two-letter abbreviations without periods, which are used by the post office and most general publications.

Mount Rushmore, located in South Dakota, provided a precedent for creating national monuments within government lands.

but

The structural integrity of this dam, critical to preventing flooding in Fargo, N.D., is currently being evaluated.

7. Company names.

In court documents, follow the style manual that the court's rules designate, whether the *BLUEBOOK, ALWD GUIDE TO LEGAL CITATION*, or another. In other general business writing, you may abbreviate words commonly used and abbreviated in company titles, such as *Co., Corp., Inc., Ltd., &, Bros.*, and *No.* Do not, however, abbreviate *Association* or *Manufacturing* and do not abbreviate *Company* or *Corporation* when these words are part of the name of a federal government entity. In general, write the name as the company does. This includes omitting periods, commas, or other punctuation you might be inclined to include whenever the company does not include it and when no confusion will result.

U.S. News & World Report

Telephone and Data Systems, Inc.

New York State Teachers Association

Standard Oil Co. Inc.

rather than

US News and World Report

TDS, Incorporated

NY State Teachers' Assoc.

Standard Oil Company

8. Days and months.

Do not abbreviate days of the week or months of the year in text.

ABBREVIATIONS IN TEXT

Use abbreviations only in the following situations.

1. Abbreviate the name of a party if the initials are widely recognized, such as *FEMA* or *NBC*.
2. Abbreviate words commonly used and abbreviated when they are part of company titles, such as *Co., Corp., Inc., Ltd., &*, and *No.*, unless the company itself does not abbreviate them in its title.
3. Abbreviate conventional personal titles, such as *Mr.* and *Ms.*
4. In CITATIONS, abbreviate according to the form your AUDIENCE uses.

For related information, see ABBREVIATING DATES, NAMES, STATES, AND TITLES; and INITIALS.

ABHORRENCE OF OR *ABHORRENCE FOR*?

Use *abhorrence of*; *abhorrence for* is incorrect.

ABOVE

Above is equivalent to *supra*. Although you can use *above* to refer the reader to previous text, avoid sending the reader back farther than a few paragraphs. Legal readers like to keep moving.

When using *above* as a preposition, use it to indicate spatial relationships.

The defendant then placed the insecticide in the cabinet above the refrigerator.

Use *over*, rather than *above*, to indicate higher quantities.

The driver was over 21.

rather than

The driver was above the age of 21.

For related information, see LEGALESE.

ABSTRACT NOUNS

Abstract nouns describe ideas or general concepts, in contrast to concrete nouns, which describe tangible items. For example, *justice* and *transportation* are abstract; *courtroom* and *bicycle* are concrete. In general, choose concrete nouns because they are more readable and more memorable. Use abstract nouns when you need them to describe ideas accurately or to deemphasize an unfavorable fact, such as the details of an auto accident caused by your client. In that situation, you might use the abstract noun *accident* rather than the concrete phrase *when the truck hit the car*. For problems related to abstract nouns, see ACCURACY, subsection 1(b); AMBIGUITY, WAYS TO AVOID, subsection 4; and PRECISION, subsection 2. For uses of abstract nouns, see NOUNS; and WRITING, PERSUASIVE, subsection 4(b).

ACCURACY

Accuracy comes into play in every stage in legal writing. For dealing with accuracy in the early stages, see ORGANIZATION, LARGE-SCALE; ORGANIZATION, SMALL-SCALE; and RESEARCH STRATEGY GUIDE.

Even when you are revising for READABILITY and eloquence, do not sacrifice accuracy. The following rules should help you maintain accuracy in all situations, particularly in DRAFTING, where accuracy errors can have significant legal consequences.

1. Accuracy in WORD CHOICE.

(a) Use one term consistently throughout a document to identify each key person, thing, or idea.

Even though the defendant admitted while in custody that he had been using drugs, this admission of impropriety is not relevant to the present case.

The following version, in contrast, leaves the reader guessing about the relationship between *commented* and *admission of impropriety*.

Even though the defendant commented while in custody that he had been using drugs, this admission of impropriety is not relevant to the present case.

Using synonyms is particularly risky with legal readers because they will wonder if you intended to change the meaning, even though you may have only been trying to add variety. For more examples and discussion of this point, see AMBIGUITY, WAYS TO AVOID, subsection 4; REPETITION, subsection 1; and SYNONYMS.

(b) Use the most specific word you can. Often inaccuracies occur because the writer chose an unnecessarily general term and as a result inadvertently broadened the term's reference. For example, do not say *vehicle* when you mean to refer only to *school bus*. For more on this, see PRECISION, subsection 2.

Although you always need to be accurate in legal writing, you may sometimes need to be less specific, even somewhat vague. For discussions of times you may avoid specificity, see EMPHASIS, subsection 2.

(c) Make the meaning of your words clear in context so you avoid unintended innuendo or humor. In the following examples, the first version is not as concise or as interesting as the second, but it is more accurate.

She released him from employment as soon as she was no longer bedridden.

rather than

She let him go as soon as she could get out of bed.

(d) Make sure each pronoun is unambiguous. For example, if only one woman is mentioned in your text, you need not worry about *she* causing inaccuracy. If, however, two or more appear, then *she* is likely to be ambiguous. In this situation, check each *she*.

Ms. Jones did not ask Ms. Wilson to doublecheck the amount, because Ms. Wilson routinely checked all the amounts listed.

rather than

Ms. Jones did not ask Ms. Wilson to doublecheck the amount, because she routinely checked all the amounts listed.

For more on this, see AMBIGUITY, WAYS TO AVOID, subsection 2. For general information, see PRONOUNS.

(e) Make sure each *this* is unambiguous. *This* is the pronoun most likely to cause inaccuracies. *This* can refer to an idea or a thing, one word or a whole sentence; as a result, you must make sure that the reader always knows what *this* means. If there is any question, add the appropriate noun after *this*.

The court reasoned that the difference in the nature of the assault was not the factor determining this issue. This reasoning resulted in . . . .

rather than

The court reasoned that the difference in the nature of the assault was not the factor determining this issue. This resulted in . . . .

For related information, see VARIETY.

2. Accuracy in sentence structure.

Whenever possible, place all modifiers and modifying phrases immediately next to the word modified.

Our client has arranged with other subcontractors to fill the ditches.

rather than

Our client has arranged to fill the ditches with other subcontractors.

and

Only Ms. Sparks suggested filing a suit for adverse possession.

rather than

Ms. Sparks only suggested filing a suit for adverse possession.

For related general information, see MODIFIERS. For related information, see MODIFIERS, DANGLING; and *ONLY*, WHERE TO PLACE.

3. Accuracy in citations.

(a) Make sure all the volume and page numbers are correct. Incorrect citations irritate readers because the reader finds the volume and page, only to find some case having nothing to do with the point.

(b) Use a pinpoint citation to refer to a particular rule, holding, quotation, or proposition in a source. Pinpoint citations designate the exact page or line number. These specific references are greatly appreciated by any reader whose job it is to evaluate the merits of the point being made. Using pinpoint citations routinely also discourages you from using unneeded string citations. See CITATIONS, PINPOINT.

(c) Use correct citation form. Especially watch the spacing, a frequent source of error. Judges in particular find citation errors distracting, so use letter-perfect citations to enhance your credibility.

For details on proper citation form, see CITATIONS; CITATIONS, BASIC FORMATS; CITATIONS, PARALLEL; and CITATIONS, STRING.

For accuracy concerns in content and specific situations, see ARTIFICIAL INTELLIGENCE AND RESEARCH; ARTIFICIAL INTELLIGENCE AND WRITING; BAD NEWS, SOFTENING IT; COMMUNICATIONS, ELECTRONIC; CONTRACTS; HALLUCINATIONS; LEGAL ANALYSIS; LEGISLATION; and OPINIONS, LEGAL. For related writing concerns, see PRECISION and SYNONYMS.

ACTIVE VERBS

See ACTIVE VOICE.

ACTIVE VOICE

Active voice is the grammatical structure in which the sentence's subject performs the action stated by the verb. The sections below explain (1) how active voice works, (2) how to identify it, (3) when to use it, and (4) how to distinguish it from linking verbs.

1. How active voice works.

Because the subject does the acting and the verb describes that action, active voice moves the action with the reader's eye from the left to right.

The boy hit the ball.

The defendant argued that the court should suppress the evidence.

The court decided that freedom of association was not an issue.

This use of active voice prevents the legal reader from having to double back mentally to understand the point.

The ball was hit by the boy.

It was argued by the defendant that the evidence should be suppressed by the court.

It was decided that freedom of association was not an issue.

The passive voice can also create a sentence that is less precise, as in the last example, which makes the reader wonder who *decided.*

Active voice also makes the sentence shorter in most cases.

The court held that the plaintiff could not collect punitive damages.

rather than

It was held by the court that punitive damages could not be collected by the plaintiff.

Therefore, if wordiness is a problem in your writing, read through the draft once just for passive voice. Check each subject and verb and translate from passive to active whenever active is appropriate. For an example of how this step fits in the writing process, see REVISING CHECKLIST. For related information, see CONCISENESS, subsection 6.

2. How to determine whether voice is active or passive.

The quickest way to determine whether you are using passive or active voice is to locate the verb in a sentence or clause and to ask yourself *Who or what did this action?* If the answer to your question is not the same word as the subject of that verb, then you have used passive voice. If you use that answer as your subject, you convert the sentence to active voice. Although a grammar checker on your computer may help locate passive voice, this technique will help you determine how to fix it quickly.

The ball was hit by the boy.

Who did the hitting? The boy, so this is passive voice. The same content in active voice would read as follows.

The boy hit the ball.

Also, active voice can clarify descriptions of cases, as the following revision illustrates.

> It was argued by the defendant that the evidence should be suppressed by the court.

Who did the arguing? The defendant. Who did the suppressing? The court. So the active voice would be as follows.

> **The defendant argued that the court should suppress the evidence.**

Sometimes the actor is unclear, as in the following example.

> It was decided that freedom of association was not an issue.

Who did the deciding? We do not know as it is now worded. To change this sentence to active voice, you would need to identify the entity making the decision.

3. When to use active voice.

Use active voice unless the writing requires the passive for effect. For examples of times when passive is useful, see PASSIVE VOICE.

> **The government's actions violated the plaintiff's right to privacy.**
>
> rather than
>
> The Plaintiff's right to privacy was violated.

When using active voice, avoid canceling its advantages by using vague verbs, such as *consists of, seems, feels, concerns,* or *involves.*

> **The court has presented two inconsistent standards of review in jury misconduct cases.**
>
> rather than
>
> The court seems unsure about the standard of review in these kinds of cases.

4. How active voice compares to linking verbs.

Using active voice rather than passive is not a matter of avoiding any form of the verb *to be. To be* is necessary and useful in legal writing because it is a linking verb that functions as a verbal equals sign. For information about using *to be,* see VERBS, LINKING.

ACTUALLY

Actually means *in fact.* It is an ADVERB used to communicate that the action stated did indeed happen and the writer is communicating literally, not figuratively.

The defendant actually hid the knife by sliding it under the cake.

Because legal writers rarely use figurative speech, they also rarely use *actually*. Therefore, for ACCURACY, avoid using it. For related information, see LITERAL MEANING and FIGURATIVE MEANING.

AD HOC

This Latin phrase means *for a particular, specific purpose*. Usually it applies either to committees that have been created to fulfill a certain function or to situations that are unusual and need particular attention.

The ad hoc committee on zoning enforcement will meet each Thursday for four weeks.

or

The ad hoc solution is to pay the directors less and the workers more.

In legal writing, ad hoc is neither capitalized nor italicized. As with all LATIN PHRASES, use it sparingly; substitute English where possible. For related information, see JARGON; LEGALESE; and READABILITY, subsection 3.

ADJECTIVES

Adjectives modify nouns or pronouns. Use adjectives only when they are needed or, as Mark Twain said, *As to the adjective: when in doubt, strike it out*. If you find yourself writing several adjectives to modify one noun, stop and find the noun that more precisely states your meaning.

Mr. Barnes has frequently testified as an expert witness on bone disease.

rather than

Mr. Barnes is a known, respected, and often-used authority on bone diseases.

Proper adjectives are adjectives derived from proper names. Capitalize most proper adjectives: *American banking system, the Atlantic seaboard, Syrian refugees*. Do not capitalize an adjective derived from a proper name when it has been used frequently and for a long time in the general language: *cesarean operation, india ink, italic type, murphy bed*, or *venetian blinds*. For an extensive list of adjectives derived from proper names, see the most recent version of the *U.S. Government Printing Office Style Manual*.

Predicate adjectives are adjectives that follow linking verbs, such as *is* or *seems*, and describe the subject of those verbs.

The case is relevant.

For related examples and explanation, see ADJECTIVES AFTER A LINKING VERB and MODIFIERS.

ADJECTIVES AFTER A LINKING VERB

When two or more adjectives work together to modify a noun, connect them with hyphens when placed before the subject.

The fear-stricken, guilt-ridden youth could not move from the street.

When the adjectives follow a linking verb, they are predicate adjectives and do not require hyphens. See VERBS, LINKING.

The youth was fear stricken and guilt ridden.

rather than

The youth was fear-stricken and guilt-ridden.

When following this rule, you may sometimes find the text awash in hyphens. If this happens, revise some sentences or reword descriptions to reduce the number of hyphens.

Euphoric after winning a close football game, the 16-year-old driver was laughing with his friends and waving to teammates in another car when he ran a stop sign and hit a heavily loaded dump truck crossing the intersection. The collision resulted in life-threatening injuries to his passengers, who were not wearing seat belts. The airbags and his seat belt, however, prevented serious injury to him. The fear-stricken youth was filled with guilt, to the point that he could not move from the street.

rather than

Punch-drunk with euphoria after winning the close-fought football game, the 16-year-old was laughing with his friends and waving to glee-filled teammates in another car when he ran a stop sign and hit the dirt-filled dump truck in the intersection. The T-bone collision resulted in blunt-force-caused injuries to his passengers, who were not wearing seat belts. Although the airbags deployed and prevented serious injury to him, some of his passengers faced life-threatening injuries. The fear-stricken, guilt-ridden youth could not move from the street.

For the relevant general rules, see HYPHENS.

ADJUSTING TO A NEW WRITING SITUATION

A change in circumstances usually requires some changes in your writing. If you are starting a new job, see tips 1–6 below to help smooth your transition. If you are adjusting to a new technology, see tip 7.

1. Ask about the writing preferences of your new supervising attorneys. Whether it is preferred typeface or what is meant by a *rough draft*, these small bits of knowledge can help speed your adjustment to the new environment. For example, some readers are unbearably distracted by citation errors, even in the roughest draft, while others do not expect full citation form until the later stages. Some readers like a cut-and-paste collection of relevant language from cases in a first draft, while others want clear thesis sentences and full reasoning from the beginning. Accuracy is always needed, but thoroughness can be a greater concern in REWRITING than in WRITING for some writers. For more background, see ACCURACY, THOROUGHNESS, and WRITING PROCESS.

2. Keep track of all deadlines and be sure to meet them. Unlike the academic world, where deadlines may be flexible, deadlines in the legal world are usually firm. It is wiser to turn in a good document on time than a perfect document late.

3. Always make sure your writing is accurate and sufficiently complete first. Adjust your priorities as needed to meet all deadlines. It is natural to want to impress your new employer, but impressing them with well-written documents will not work if those documents are late. After assuring accuracy, if you have time, rewrite for CLARITY and TONE. If time remains, work on other READABILITY touches, such as CONCISENESS. For help prioritizing, see WRITING, WRITING TO ATTORNEYS, WRITING TO CLIENTS, REWRITING, REVISING, POLISHING, and TRIAGE.

4. Put your writing process on paper when you start the new job, so that you can make changes as you learn where PRIORITIES need to be shifted to different stages of writing.

5. Accept all criticism with grace, even though this is hard. When someone criticizes your writing, work to listen to the substance of the criticism. This is valuable feedback, because other readers may well have the same response. Take notes and study the reader response patterns over time. Your lack of defensiveness in response to a critique will earn you respect immediately. Over time, your decisions to adjust your writing as needed will earn you respect and improve your writing, especially if you understand the underlying reasons. If the comments are unclear, ask for clarification and use entries in this book to determine what the real problem is. For example, see ORGANIZE,

HOW TO; PROFESSIONAL LANGUAGE AND PRESENTATION; and TONE. By being professional and open to other ideas, you can gain a reputation for having GRACE UNDER FIRE.

6. Respect the expertise and experience of all the people you work with, for they are crucial contributors to your success. You will gain all sorts of helpful advice, and you can return the favor to those who follow you when you have gained more expertise.

7. Ask about your office's use of artificial intelligence (AI). If your office is using AI, be sure to understand the parameters of the model used. For help on this, see ARTIFICIAL INTELLIGENCE AND RESEARCH, ARTIFICIAL INTELLIGENCE AND WRITING, DISCUSSION SECTION, and PROMPTS.

For related information, see EDITING, GRACE UNDER FIRE, MANAGING WRITERS, PRINCIPLES OF GOOD LEGAL WRITING, and TIME MANAGEMENT.

A.D. OR *C.E.*?

To remain neutral with respect to religion, use *C.E.*, which stands for *common era*. Use periods after the letters with no spaces between; place it after the date.

1620 C.E.

rather than

A.D. 1620

C.E., like the corresponding *B.C.E.*, goes after the date, in contrast to *A.D.* Other designations exist in other religions and in some archeology contexts, but *C.E.* will be the term understood by the broadest audience.

ADVERBS

Adverbs modify verbs, ADJECTIVES, or other adverbs.

The overly cautious Mr. Smith cannot justly be penalized for acting very carefully.

Avoid overusing them; too many adverbs can bog down a sentence while adding a minimum of information.

Mr. Smith should not be penalized for acting carefully.

Three adverbs you can omit readily are *clearly*, *merely*, and *obviously*. Another adverb you can view with suspicion is *very*, because it usually weakens the point rather than strengthening it, as in the example above. For related information, see CONCISENESS, subsection 7, and MODIFIERS.

AFFECT OR *EFFECT*?

In legal writing you usually want *effect* when using the noun and *affect* when using the verb.

This law had a sweeping effect.

but

This law affected police procedures.

This is because *effect* as a noun means *something that was the result of another action*, while *affect* as a noun means a *feeling*. *Affect* as a verb, however, means *to influence*. Occasionally you will need *effect* as a verb if you mean *to cause to come into being*.

Through persistent lobbying, the group effected a change in the inheritance laws.

AFORESAID

When writing to clients, substitute *above*, *mentioned earlier*, *named earlier*, or some other more explanatory phrase. One of the most frequent complaints coming from the general public is that lawyers use LEGALESE, and *aforesaid* is viewed as legalese.

In a legal document written to be read by other lawyers, such as a pleading, you may use *aforesaid*, but you must use it precisely because lawyers will interpret the term literally. Never toss it in carelessly, thinking that it will in itself add a patina of authenticity to the document. *Aforesaid* means you are referring to something mentioned earlier rather than something mentioned afterward. For example, you would say the *aforesaid defendant* only if another defendant is mentioned later and you mean to exclude that other defendant. Do not use *aforesaid defendant* if you have only one defendant or if you mean to include all defendants.

If you observe this rule, you will find that you have few occasions to use *aforesaid*.

AFRICAN AMERICAN OR *AFRICAN-AMERICAN*?

Write it without the hyphen, just as you would write *Swedish American* or *Chinese American*. *African American* is capitalized because it derives from the names of geographic areas. Some people prefer *African American* over *black*; be sensitive to the preferences of your READERS.

AGES

Use the style specified by your reader. In legal writing, generally spell out numbers zero to ninety-nine in text and in footnotes. Ages may be an exception. Newspaper style books differ on this point and use numerals for ages unless the age is the first word in a sentence. These style books also generally use numerals for numbers greater than ten.

Sixty-two-year-olds are eligible for Social Security, but not at the maximum amount.

but

She was 62 when she opted to take Social Security.

Use HYPHENS when the age is expressed as a modifier before a noun.

She was a 6-year-old child.

But do not use hyphens when the age comes after a linking verb.

She was 6 years old.

AGREEMENT, SUBJECTS AND VERBS

Agreement here means using plural verbs with plural subjects and singular verbs with singular subjects. Problems with agreement most frequently occur when the subject and verb are separated by a long phrase and the writer loses track of the subject along the way. As a result, the verb may agree with some intervening noun in the long phrase rather than with the subject. You can usually avoid this problem by keeping the subject and verb close together. This will also improve the readability of your text.

Section 4 of the Export Administration Act has created much controversy. That section gives the President authority to impose foreign policy and national security controls on exports.

rather than

Section 4 of the Export Administration Act giving the President authority to impose foreign policy and national security controls on exports have created much controversy.

For a general discussion of related concerns, see READABILITY, subsection 5; and SENTENCE STRUCTURE.

AGREEMENTS, WRITTEN

See CONTRACTS.

AGREE TO OR *AGREE WITH*?

The choice between *agree to* and *agree with* is based on IDIOM, which means there is a right or wrong choice in most cases. For example, you would always say, *I agree to help you*, but *I agree with your idea.*

In general, use *agree to* when the subject is concurring with something and will act accordingly. For example, *agree to* is frequently used in contracts.

We agree to represent you in this matter.

or

My client agrees to settle out of court with the following provisions.

Use *agree with* when the subject is voicing agreement but not making any actual legal commitments.

I agree with you that large settlements are increasing insurance premiums.

or

The State agrees with the court's concern for the preservation of Fifth Amendment rights, but . . . .

ALL AROUND OR *ALL-ROUND*?

Use *all-round,* because you likely mean *well rounded,* not *circling around.*

ALLITERATION

Alliteration is the repetition of similar consonant sounds, as the *f*s in *fast and furious fighting.* Alliteration can occasionally be useful in legal writing because it can help the reader remember a phrase or can add drama, but it must be used sparingly and with care.

Having been terrified twice by the defendant's previous assaults, the plaintiff hesitated before she fled.

but not

Two times terrified, Theresa tarried before taking off down the turnpike.

When using alliteration, first be sure that the content of the phrase is indeed worth remembering. If it is not, the alliteration will likely be a distraction, no matter how graceful it sounds. Second, make sure that the repeated sound creates an appropriate feeling. For example, a repeated *t* sound can sound harsh, while a repeated *s* can sound soothing.

The attorney was known for her smoothness, simplicity, and style.

Finally, read the passage aloud to make sure it works, because *tongue twisters torture tired readers.* For a discussion of related techniques, see

ASSONANCE and REPETITION, subsection 4. For related information, see ANTONYMS, ASSONANCE, HOMONYMS, and SYNONYMS.

ALL READY OR *ALREADY*?

All ready means a group is *prepared for some sort of action. Already* means *by this or a specified time* or *previously.*

ALL RIGHT OR *ALRIGHT*?

In legal writing, use the space. *Alright* is the informal, less accepted equivalent.

ALL, SINGULAR OR PLURAL?

All is singular when it means *the only thing.*

All that the new law can do is force the courts to resolve the conflict.

All is plural, however, when it means the *whole group.*

All the changes in the contract were made in writing.

ALL TOGETHER OR *ALTOGETHER*?

All together means that a group of people, things, or events are together. *Altogether* means *entirely and with all included,* or *on the whole, with everything considered*; thus *altogether* refers to a whole entity or group.

The plaintiffs were all together as they left the courtroom.

but

Altogether, the medical costs for these victims exceeded $3 million.

ALTERNATIVE

Use *alternative* only when referring to two choices, not more. Commonly *alternative* is used when more than two choices exist; however, readers who enjoy the proper use of language will appreciate your precise use of *alternative.* When discussing more than two choices, use *options, choices,* or another similar term.

ALTHOUGH OR *THOUGH*?

In many situations you can use either word. *Although* is more elegant and therefore more appropriate for briefs, law review articles, and all but informal legal writing.

Use *though* in two situations.

1. Use *though* in such phrases as *even though* or *as though*. Also use *though* when expressing a contrasting thought.

   The judge incorporated some of the ideas expressed in the amicus brief, though she did not refer to it directly.

2. Use *though* at the end of a sentence or at the end of a phrase.

   She promised, though.

   or

   She promised, though, to come to the hearing.

Though at the end of a sentence is correct but rather informal for legal writing, so try substituting the following.

Nevertheless, she promised.

or

She promised, however, to come to the hearing.

ALTOGETHER OR *ALL TOGETHER*?

See *ALL TOGETHER* OR *ALTOGETHER*?

ALWD GUIDE TO LEGAL CITATION

The *ALWD Guide to Legal Citation*, sponsored by the Association of Legal Writing Directors, offers a system of citation forms as an alternative approach to the *BLUEBOOK*. Before you start taking effective NOTES, check with your AUDIENCE and your jurisdiction to see which citation source to use, because your jurisdiction may have its own preferred citation system. Then record your initial citations in the form you will use for the document's final version. For more information on when and how to cite, see CITATIONS; CITATIONS, BASIC FORMATS; CITATIONS, ELECTRONIC; CITATIONS, PARALLEL; CITATIONS, PINPOINT; CITATIONS, STRING; and FOOTNOTES.

A.M.

In all but the most informal email to colleagues, write it *a.m.* and only after an hour. Omitting the periods risks confusing *a.m.* with the verb *am*.

We will meet at 9:00 a.m.

When *a.m.* appears at the end of a sentence, as in the previous example, use only one period.

AMBIGUITY, WAYS TO AVOID

In legal writing, a word or phrase is ambiguous if, in context, it permits more than one meaning. The following four rules should help you avoid ambiguity.

1. Avoid misplaced MODIFIERS.

   Sometimes a phrase, because of its position, could modify any of several words in a sentence, as does *with good reason* in the following example.

   > The defendant refused to service the car belonging to the man who insulted him with good reason.

   Here *with good reason* should modify *refused* instead of *insulted.* To avoid ambiguity, place the modifying phrase next to the word modified.

   > **The defendant refused, with good reason, to service the car belonging to the man who had insulted him.**

   For other problems associated with modifiers, see MODIFIERS, DANGLING; and MODIFIERS, SQUINTING.

2. Avoid ambiguous PRONOUNS.

   Sometimes pronouns cause ambiguity because they can logically refer to either of several nouns. The pronoun most likely to cause ambiguity is *this,* because *this* can refer to any idea or object.

   > You must ultimately make a judgment about the weight of the evidence. This will help you decide what the verdict should be.

   Does *this* refer to *judgment* or *evidence*? To avoid the problem, add the appropriate noun after *this.*

   > **You must ultimately make a judgment about the weight of the evidence. This judgment will help you decide what the verdict should be.**

   The pronoun second most likely to cause ambiguity is *it,* again because *it* can refer to any object or idea. Usually *it* becomes ambiguous when some other noun comes between *it* and the antecedent, which is the noun to which *it* refers.

   > The first will is less ambiguous than the second because it omits the deceased's spouse.

   To solve this problem, you may replace *it* with the noun.

   > **The first will is less ambiguous than the second because the first will omits the decedent's spouse.**

Or you may rephrase the sentence, so that no other noun comes between *it* and its antecedent.

> **The second will created some confusion by referring to the decedent's spouse; as a result, the first will is less ambiguous because it omits the decedent's spouse.**

The third most likely pronoun to cause headaches is *they*. In the past, *they* was always plural, but now it may be the pronoun of choice for a non-binary person. In correspondence with the person, using that person's term of choice is the best option. In documents to other readers, revise to avoid using a pronoun if the person's preferred pronoun may cause ambiguity. For help in this situation, see GENDER IN WRITING.

We is a special problem in legal writing because you may, by using *we*, inadvertently speak for your whole law office or organization. Never use *we* when you really mean *I*; use *we* only when you are speaking officially for the group of which you are a part, as one judge may do when drafting an opinion for the whole bench.

Although *this*, *it*, *they*, and *we* are the most likely offenders, all pronouns should be watched for potential ambiguity. In general, check *he* or *she* whenever the content of your writing involves two people of the same gender. For related information, see ANTECEDENTS and PRONOUNS.

3. Avoid unnecessarily vague word choice.

    (a) Use only one term to identify each key person, thing, or idea.

    > **Even though the defendant admitted while in custody that he had been using drugs, this admission of impropriety is not relevant to the present case.**
    >
    > rather than
    >
    > Even though the defendant commented while in custody that he had been using drugs, this admission of impropriety is not relevant to the present case.

    The latter version leaves the reader guessing but not knowing the exact relationship between *commented* and *admission of impropriety*. Using synonyms is particularly risky with legal readers because they will wonder if you intended to change your meaning, even though you may have only been trying to add variety. For more examples and discussion of this point, see PRECISION, subsection 3; REPETITION, subsections 1 and 3; and SYNONYMS.

(b) Use the most specific word you can.

Often inaccuracies occur because the writer chose an unnecessarily general term and as a result inadvertently broadened the term's reference. For example, do not say *vehicle* when you mean to refer only to *school bus*. For more on this, see PRECISION, subsection 2.

(c) Make the meaning of your words clear in context.

She released him from employment as soon as she was no longer bedridden.

rather than

She let him go as soon as she could get out of bed.

The first version is not as concise or as interesting, but it is accurate.

Although you usually need to be specific in legal writing, you may need to be vague on some occasions. For a discussion of these exceptions, see EMPHASIS, subsection 2; and PASSIVE VOICE.

4. Avoid unnecessary abstraction.

Whenever possible, use concrete nouns and specific verbs rather than ABSTRACT NOUNS and general verbs. This will help focus the reader on your main points.

The defendant moves to dismiss the case under Fed. R. Civ. P. 12(b)(6).

rather than

This concerns the defendant's motion to dismiss.

For related information, see WRITING, PERSUASIVE, subsection 4.

AMENDMENT CAPITALIZED?

Capitalize *Amendment* when you are using it in text to refer to a particular amendment to the U.S. Constitution, but do not capitalize it in citations.

The Fourth Amendment to the United States Constitution prevents warrantless searches except in extraordinary conditions.

but

U.S. Const. amend. IV, 1.

When using the word generally to refer to amendments in other documents, do not capitalize it.

The state legislature ratified four amendments to the environmental impact statute.

AMICUS BRIEFS

See BRIEFS, AMICUS.

AMONG OR *BETWEEN*?

Use *between* when discussing two options and *among* when discussing more than two.

Separate conferences were held between the plaintiff's and the defendant's attorneys, between the plaintiff's attorney and the estate's trustees, and between the defendant's attorney and the estate's trustees.

rather than

Conferences were held between the plaintiff's attorney, the defendant's attorney, and the estate's trustees.

Although the former version is less concise, it leaves no question about who met with whom.

Use *among* to indicate that more than two parties are meeting.

The issue has been discussed among the plaintiff's attorney, the defendant's attorney, and the estate's trustee.

ANALOGICAL REASONING, PRESENTING IT

See REASONING, ANALOGICAL; REASONING, INDUCTIVE; and REASONING, PRESENTING IT.

ANALOGOUS CASES

An analogous case is one that is similar in some way to the situation being analyzed. In traditional U.S. legal reasoning, use analogous cases to support the *stare decisis* rationale that similar situations should be treated similarly. A case may be analogous because of the reasoning, policy, holding, facts, or any other aspect of the case relevant to your client's situation. Be sure to select the case for the aspects that compare most strongly to your situation.

When writing about the analogous case in a memo or brief, communicate the strengths of those analogies in a way that shows the reader how and why the case fits into your overall analysis. Describe the essential details of the analogous case. Which details are essential depends on the point you are making, and may include the rule, rationale, holding, legally significant facts, or dicta of that case. If the case's rationale is similar and sound, use the same rationale in your analysis. If the case's policy principles provide a good foundation for your analysis, use those principles. If the facts are similar, use those.

Make sure to include enough information about the analogous case to allow the reader to compare or distinguish this case from your situation while avoiding unnecessary detail. Above all, focus on explaining your thinking and the support for that reasoning, rather than mechanically filing parts of a case into a paragraph. This should help you avoid a wooden or superficial presentation of your reasoning. For related information, see ARGUMENT SECTION; DISCUSSION SECTION; HOLDINGS; LEGAL ANALYSIS; PARALLEL STRUCTURE, subsection 2; REASONING, PRESENTING IT; and RULES. If you are using artificial intelligence, see ARTIFICIAL INTELLIGENCE AND RESEARCH, ARTIFICIAL INTELLIGENCE AND WRITING, PROMPTS, and RESEARCH STRATEGY GUIDE.

ANALYSIS

See LEGAL ANALYSIS and REASONING, PRESENTING IT.

AND

There are four points to remember about this conjunction. First, although it is not wrong to start a sentence with *and*, doing so draws attention to the word. Therefore, before starting a sentence with *and*, ask yourself if that word is really what you want to emphasize. Often it is not.

Second, use *and* to join sentences only when the sentence logically should be joined with the verbal equivalent of a plus sign.

Third, when using *and* to connect two complete sentences, place a comma before *and*, which means *and* will be followed by a new subject. Do not generally add the comma if the *and* is only adding another verb that shares the same subject. A comma may be added after *and*, however, when needed to avoid confusion. For examples, see COMMA, OXFORD; and COMMAS, subsections 3 and 4.

Finally, avoid overusing *and* to join sentences when it leads to long, lackluster sentences. For related general information, see CONJUNCTIONS.

AND/OR

Avoid this construction because it creates ambiguity.

Either the Company or its agents, or both, may . . . .

rather than

4. **Defendant admits she was driving on Highway 21 on the morning of December 9 but denies driving too fast for conditions.**

2. Beginning or preserving any counteractions.

Think carefully about the decisions you make when answering, for your client's responses begin to shape the course of the litigation. Good legal writing at this point usually requires research and a quick review of all possible substantive and procedural options, including ascertaining the applicable standard of review. By providing such thorough treatment early in the case, you make sure that you do not overlook any claims and thus inadvertently waive any of your client's rights. Answering a complaint requires careful and thorough thought about strategies and issues, which goes beyond the scope of this text.

3. Establishing your theory of the case.

When you answer a complaint, you are framing your theory of the case. What you choose to say or omit initiates your strategy of the case. You may choose to deny everything, suggesting a Motion to Dismiss. Or, knowing the standard of review is *gross abuse of discretion*, you may answer in such a way as to get the case to trial because you are confident you will win there. Make sure you consider all reasonable possibilities before you respond. As with all documents for a court, learn and follow all rules and forms in your jurisdiction. For related information, see COMPLAINTS, PLEADINGS, STANDARD OF REVIEW, and THEORY OF THE CASE.

ANTECEDENTS

An antecedent is the noun to which a pronoun refers.

Ms. Williams' aunt willed her estate to charity.

Here *aunt* is the antecedent of *her*. For problems related to this, see AMBIGUITY, WAYS TO AVOID, subsection 2. For related information, see NOUNS and PRONOUNS.

ANTE- OR *ANTI-*?

Ante- means in *front of* or *before,* as in *antebellum.*

Anti- means *against,* or *opposite,* as in *anti-intellectual* and *antibody.*

ANTONYMS

Antonyms are pairs of words that mean the opposite of each other. For example, *perfect* is an antonym of *defective, support* is an antonym of *abandon,* and *sober* is an antonym of *intoxicated.* Antonyms can be useful research terms. See RESEARCH STRATEGY GUIDE, section 2. Additionally, using accurate antonyms can enhance persuasive writing by emphasizing the opposite alternative. For related information, see HOMONYMS; SYNONYMS; and WRITING, PERSUASIVE.

ANYBODY, SINGULAR OR PLURAL?

Anybody uses a singular verb.

Anybody who believes in justice believes in a fair trial.

Anybody is rather informal, so use *anyone* in formal legal writing, such as briefs or articles.

ANYONE, SINGULAR OR PLURAL?

Anyone uses a singular verb.

Anyone is entitled to a fair trial.

A OR *AN*?

Use *an* before all nouns beginning with a vowel or vowel sound; this includes nouns that begin with *h* where the *h* is not voiced, such as *an hour*. Use *a* before all nouns beginning with a voiced consonant, such as *a hearing*. Use *a* before a voiced consonant even when the actual letter used is a vowel, such as *a Ouachita tribal meeting*. You may see variations on this rule, especially in documents from other countries, such as *an historical document,* but American English still determines the usage by the sound, not the letter following *a* or *an*. For related information, see ARTICLES, GRAMMAR.

APOSTROPHES

Apostrophes, like decimal points, belong in specific places. They have three specific uses:

(1) to create the possessive form of nouns,

(2) to express plurals in some situations, and

(3) to create a contraction.

1. Creating the possessive form of a noun.

   This is needed when the noun modifies another noun. Use *'s* to create the possessive form of a singular or plural noun that does not end in *s*.

   plaintiff's = belonging to one plaintiff, as in *the plaintiff's attorney*.

Dr. Essex's = belonging to Dr. Essex

women's = pertaining to or belonging to women.

Often a singular noun in the possessive form is used in common expressions, such as the following.

at arm's length

out of harm's way

attorney's fees

When a singular or plural noun ends in an *s*, use an apostrophe with no additional *s* in most situations.

plaintiffs' = belonging to more than one plaintiff, as in *the plaintiffs' appeal.*

Pettuses' = belonging to the Pettuses, as in *the Petusses' children.*

With names of companies, published works, and the like, use the form that source uses.

Harpers Ferry

Macy's

Do not add an apostrophe, however, after names of countries or organizations when that name ends in *s*.

Arkansas laws

House of Representatives session

United States dependencies

Also do not add an apostrophe when writing the plural of a spelled-out number or a word being referred to as the word.

fives, twelves

whereases* and *wherefores

When the *BLUEBOOK*'s referenced style manuals differ, as they do on this matter, you have a choice. Ours is to use the apostrophe alone unless the *'s* would actually be spoken.

the Ganges' source or the Ganges's source

Descartes' three dreams or Descartes' s three dreams

Marx's theories or Marx' theories

Dylan Thomas's work or Dylan Thomas' work

When working with a compound noun, which is a group of words that work as one modifying unit, add the apostrophe to the last word in the group.

attorney general's opinion

James Olaniyan, Sr.'s acceptance

Trinidad and Tobago's topography

another company's product

Use separate apostrophes, however, when working with several separate nouns that both modify the same noun.

homeowner's and renter's insurance

Do not use an apostrophe to form the plural of a name ending in *s*. Instead use *es*, as in

the Joneses

For further guidance, see PLURALS OF NAMES.

Do not use an apostrophe to form possessives of PRONOUNS.

its = belonging to it.

yours = belonging to you.

theirs = belonging to them.

whose = belonging to whom.

ours = belonging to us.

hers = belonging to her.

For more explanation, see POSSESSIVES.

2. Expressing plurals in some situations.

Use an apostrophe to create a plural when needed to avoid confusion.

t's rather than ts

A's rather than As

ha's rather than has

*'s rather than *s

Because legal writing is more formal than most other writing, you will often rephrase these terms to avoid that form.

asterisk's

3. Creating a contraction.

Use an apostrophe as a substitution for a letter or letters.

it's = it is

you're = you are

don't = do not

In most legal writing, however, do not use CONTRACTIONS.

APPEAL

Use *appeal* as a term of art only, referring to the appeal of a case. Avoid using *appeal* informally in legal writing.

The appeal will be decided next week.

rather than

The defendant's counsel appealed to the court to deny the motion.

For related information, see TERMS OF ART.

APPELLATE BRIEFS

See BRIEFS, APPELLATE.

APPENDIX

Appendices can be used in any kind of legal writing to assist the reader but not to replace important material that should be included in the text. Legal readers prefer appendices to refer to statutes, cases, excerpts from the record, and similar documents that are not needed in their entirety in the text but are helpful for reference. Therefore, use appendices

- in memos to include applicable statutes, tables, or other technical or supporting data referenced in the Discussion Section;
- in pretrial briefs to include affidavits, any pretrial documents referenced in your brief, and applicable statutes;
- in trial briefs to include any referenced portions of the record and applicable statutes, unless your court prefers them inserted in a section of the brief;
- in appellate briefs to include referenced portions of the pretrial record, trial record, JURY INSTRUCTIONS, and applicable statutes;
- in memos in support of submitted JURY INSTRUCTIONS to include supporting cases or other material; and
- in any document that refers to technical supporting information that the reader might want to see in full.

Label each appendix as Appendix A, B, C, and so forth. Refer to each appendix separately in text by surrounding this phrase with

PARENTHESES: *(See Appendix A)*. In briefs, check your local rules for any specific requirements for appendices. For more information, see BENCH MEMOS; BRIEFS, APPELLATE; BRIEFS, PRETRIAL; BRIEFS, TRIAL; MEMOS; and OPINIONS, LEGAL.

APPLICATION

What most lawyers mean when they say *application* is the reasoning that appears between the presentation of the relevant laws, policies, and philosophies invoked by the legal issues and your conclusion. In an opinion, for example, the application may be a matter of analogizing cases to the parties' situation, weaving ideas together, stating how policies apply to these facts, using hypotheticals, arguing with the dissent, or supporting arguments and countering opposing arguments. In an intraoffice memo, it may be the paragraphs that discuss how the relevant statutes, regulations, and cases you have explained apply to the client's situation.

Your application process actually begins with your research. When you read the law, you analyze the materials and application methods used by courts, opposing counsel, or associates to reach a conclusion. When you write, you use components from those materials and methods as you apply the law to the relevant situation.

This process requires you to select the parts of the precedent and the current situation that are relevant to your analysis and to demonstrate to the reader why these parts are relevant. Application often requires selecting language that reveals this relevance in a different way. For example, an airplane may be described as a *motorized vehicle, a means of public transportation, a source of pollution,* or *a war instrument.* How you characterize that airplane becomes an important part of your application. Rather than tallying up how similar the facts are in two cases, you must explain the relevance of particular similarities, which may be something other than factual similarities. Thus a fact-to-fact comparison, without attention to the reasoning behind that comparison, is likely to go astray.

Some legal writers use the word *application* to refer to most of the analytical process rather than this one part of that process. For guidance on this larger process, see LEGAL ANALYSIS; REASONING, DEDUCTIVE; REASONING, INDUCTIVE; REASONING, MODERN; REASONING, OTHER; REASONING, POSTMODERN; and REASON ING, PRESENTING IT.

You must also use pertinent legal language in your application. For example, if you were arguing that a statute regulating the safety of all motorized vehicles is applicable to airplanes, then you might describe the airplane as a *motorized vehicle* in your application, and you would explain why these aspects of the airplane are relevant here. If, however, you were arguing for the creating of a new, broadly applicable environmental law, then you might use *source of pollution* as the relevant characterization. In any situation, you must present the relevant support in words that demonstrate that relevance, rather than words that do not reflect these considerations. In this way, the reader can better follow your application. For more on precise language, see TERMS OF ART.

To ensure the soundness of your application, compare your explanation of the law and your explanation of its application when REWRITING or early in the REVISING stage. These two components should be congruent in content and wording of key concepts, fitting together like the two halves of a clamshell. Often you may find that revising these two parts to attain this congruency refines and clarifies your analysis as well as its presentation. If you are using artificial intelligence, see ARTIFICIAL INTELLIGENCE AND RESEARCH, ARTIFICIAL INTELLIGENCE AND WRITING, DISCUSSION SECTION, PROMPTS, and RESEARCH STRATEGY GUIDE.

APPOSITIVE

An appositive is a noun or phrase that comes right after a noun and describes that noun.

> **The defendant, Great West Power, settled before the trial began.**

It is useful for inserting extra information into a sentence. It can be particularly useful to clarify a point when some readers might otherwise be confused.

> **Max Avery, who uses *they*, has worked for this company for 12 years. During that time, they have been promoted twice to positions of more responsibility.**
>
> or
>
> **Weatherly, formerly a subsidiary of Solar Supply, is hiring our firm on retainer.**

Keep the appositive short, however, for readability. For related problems, see AGREEMENT, SUBJECTS AND VERBS; and READABILITY, section 5. For a discussion of other uses of appositives, see UNOBTRUSIVE DEFINITIONS, section 1.

ARGUING IN THE ALTERNATIVE

Sometimes when planning your argument you will want to argue alternative theories because you believe you could win under either theory. You can do this, for example, by dividing your Argument into two sections, each with its own major point heading and subheadings. In your

Introduction or Conclusion, you can connect the first and second arguments by wording your transitions appropriately.

> **The evidence should be suppressed not only because the search was unreasonable but also because the evidence was discovered in an area outside the scope of the warrant.**

Arguing in the alternative can become more cumbersome to structure, however, when one argument becomes relevant only if you lose your previous argument. When presenting an alternative you do not want to concede, as in the following example, use the subjunctive mood to indicate that you are not conceding.

> **Even if the Defendant had fired the shot that killed Ms. Jaeger, his action would have been an act of justifiable self-defense, not manslaughter.**
>
> rather than
>
> Even if the Defendant did fire the shot that killed Ms. Jaeger, his action was an act of justifiable self-defense, not manslaughter.

The subjunctive mood is used specifically to communicate something that is not in fact true, and so it keeps that belief in front of the reader, even as you make the alternative argument.

For a different but related point, see COUNTERARGUMENTS, HOW TO HANDLE. For a helpful grammatical tool, see VERBS, MOODS. For context, see ARGUMENT SECTION; BRIEFS; BRIEFS, AMICUS; BRIEFS, APPELLATE; BRIEFS, PRETRIAL; BRIEFS, REPLY; and BRIEFS, TRIAL.

ARGUMENT HEADINGS

See POINT HEADINGS.

ARGUMENT SECTION

The Argument is a section in a pretrial, trial, or appellate brief. This section presents the law and its application from the client's point of view. Specifically, the Argument's goal is to persuade the court by explaining how and why the law supports the decision you advocate. It provides the court with the reasoning it will need when writing an opinion in your client's favor.

Another goal of the Argument is to remind the court why it would be just to apply the law in this way. Yet another is to assist the court in fitting this argument in with past and future situations. While the STATEMENT OF THE CASE should lead the court to want to find for your client, the Argument, done well, persuades the court that your legal reasoning is sound, thus persuading the mind as well as the heart to find in favor of your client.

An effective Argument should incorporate the following elements into a persuasive DESIGN:

(1) the legal standards and standard of review, where applicable;

(2) the theory of the case;

(3) the reasoning that best combines facts, issues, relevant law, and arguments within that theory;

(4) a clear organization of this content; and

(5) a balancing of those arguments to show why your theory should prevail.

All of these components need to be organized to (6) present your arguments persuasively. Your decisions on these elements require some good thinking early in the process. This includes double checking the rules, even if you think you know them, and accurately counting the number of days to the deadline. For example, weekend days or legal holidays may or may not count in your jurisdiction. For more on what to do early, see PREWRITING. If you choose to use artificial intelligence (AI), (7) be strategic and remain vigilant about its accuracy.

1. Determine the legal standards and standard of review, where applicable.

   Set aside adequate time to determine both the legal standard for your client's situation and the STANDARD OF REVIEW. Even if you are writing a pretrial or trial brief, your early decisions and arguments should anticipate an appeal. That appeal will fail if it does not work within the standard of review. If you have a criminal case, for example, the standard may be *de novo*, which will allow you to develop facts and arguments through the appellate process. If you are working on a brief to an agency, the standard may be *arbitrary and capricious*, so you will have very little to appeal if your initial brief does not work. For more help with this component, see RULES and STANDARD OF REVIEW.

2. Select a theory of the case.

   From the various theories and arguments you read when you research, and from your own synthesis of the material, select a theory that you think will win. For example, if you were representing an indigent immigrant, you might want to select a theory that the law must become more tolerant of those in need. If you were representing a client accused of insider trading, you might want to select a theory that the law requires specific, incontrovertible proof. If you are appealing a case, you may select a theory that the trial court *abused its discretion* or was *arbitrary and capricious*. Within your office, different lawyers will feel strongly about one or the other theory. If you are working collaboratively, make sure all the attorneys involved agree on the theory, because your selection of arguments and organization will follow from the theory. For more on this, see THEORY OF THE CASE.

3. Determine the best reasoning.

The structure of the reasoning must reflect the complex combination of legal standard or standard of review with the law, facts, theory of the case, strengths, weaknesses, and context. You may begin determining the structure of your reasoning by focusing your ISSUES and POINT HEADINGS. The law can give you the TERMS OF ART for your legal question, and you can summarize your answers in the reasons given in the headings. Alternatively, you may want to sketch your reasoning first in an OUTLINE that uses the component parts of the law. Then explain the applicable rules, including all that you will use to make your point. Support your assertion that these rules are relevant by explaining enough about the sources so the court will agree with you. Whether you win or lose the case often depends on whether the court applies the law you synthesize.

As you build your reasoning, choose that reasoning in the context of what the court has done and what reasoning may be most persuasive. For example, the court may be persuaded that you have chosen the correct statutory rules because the plain meaning of the law fits the situation, or the legislative purpose behind the law fits the situation. Similarly, the court may be persuaded that you have chosen the correct rules from common law for any or all of the following reasons: they are mandatory authority of the jurisdiction, they were established in cases that solved similar legal problems, they were established in cases with similar facts or outcomes, or they were established in cases with similar policies. For help in sorting and organizing, see AUDIENCE; DESIGN; NOTES; ORGANIZATION FOR THOSE WHO CAN'T OUTLINE; ORGANIZATION, LARGE-SCALE; and OUTLINES. For more ideas on reasoning, see EQUITY; LEGAL ANALYSIS; POLICY; REASONING, ANALOGICAL; REASONING, DEDUCTIVE; REASONING, INDUCTIVE; REASONING; MODERN; REASONING, OTHER; REASONING, POSTMODERN; REASONING, PRESENTING IT; and SYLLOGISMS.

4. Organize your presentation.

Make sure your brief conforms to your local rules on filing briefs. Then, as you refine your presentation, you will be comfortable that the format is correct. After you have checked the rules and clarified your reasoning, you can turn your focus to organizing your presentation of that reasoning.

To unify your organization, consider which reasons are strongest in the court's eyes and, after choosing your reasoning, explain the progression of that reasoning step by step. You usually will not include all of the possible arguments because they will dilute the overall effect. Instead, eliminate those that are unhelpful, weak, or minor, and group together the remaining arguments in select, strong point headings.

Because structure is a critical part of persuasiveness, do not settle for your first try at a sequence of arguments. Test that sequence by creating at least two or three more sequences and sharing them with colleagues, if possible. You can do this in the form of three or so different versions of general point headings. Your colleagues will give you a range of responses that will help you settle on a sequence that best suits the legal situation and your audience. After you settle on the main point headings, include the subheadings, which outline the arguments and give the reasons behind those arguments. For examples, see POINT HEADINGS. For persuasive techniques, see WRITING, PERSUASIVE.

For help with this stage of the WRITING PROCESS, see BRIEFS; ORGANIZATION, LARGE-SCALE; ORGANIZATION, SMALL-SCALE; OUTLINES; REASONING, PRESENTING IT; and REWRITING.

5. Balance the arguments and explaining who should win and why.

Make sure to take into account and respond to the other side's positions, either as you go or in separate point headings. In your enthusiasm to win, or your artificial intelligence's desire to please (see subsection 7 below), you may have a draft that ignores the other side or disparages the opposing attorney. Resist either. Instead, consider their arguments as questions the court might ask. Gently weave your answers into your own arguments; for example, show why these arguments do not conform to the law, are irrelevant or immaterial, or suggest a drastic change in the law's application. For help with this, see COUNTERARGUMENTS, HOW TO HANDLE. If these ideas take too much space in the brief, you can save your longer explanations for a reply brief, but do not ignore them completely. After you have finished these parts of the Argument, you can use your Conclusion to give a salient finish. For more on how best to do this, see BRIEFS, REPLY; and CONCLUSIONS.

6. Present your arguments persuasively.

After you have your content in place, shift your focus to the persuasive aspect of your presentation. In this stage of writing, focus on using your POSITIONS OF EMPHASIS effectively. Make sure your TOPIC SENTENCES convey the point of each paragraph and state your position affirmatively, rather than focusing on the other side's argument first.

Check your paragraph order within sections to make sure that each paragraph is essential to the argument and follows from the previous paragraph. Within paragraphs, check the sentence order and justify the use of each sentence in furthering the argument. Make sure that the POINT OF VIEW has not drifted back toward being too objective, descriptive, or even confusing. Any content cut and pasted during research or writing will retain the point of view of that document, not yours. For help adjusting this, see QUOTATIONS, WHEN TO USE.

Make sure that each sentence argues for your client. Adjust your sentence structure and word choice to emphasize favorable points and deemphasize unfavorable ones. For example, use subject-verb combinations to emphasize the main point of each sentence and to increase conciseness. Relegate background details to subordinate clauses or to lists at the end of a sentence. Use concrete words to emphasize and abstract nouns to deemphasize. For more how-to information, see ABSTRACT NOUNS; CONCISENESS; REVISING; REVISING CHECKLIST; SENTENCE STRUCTURE; SUBJECT-VERB COMBINATIONS; WORD CHOICE; and WRITING, PER SUASIVE.

When you are satisfied with your revisions, remember to remove any errors, for these can undercut your credibility and thus weaken your persuasion. Make sure your words do not deviate in the level of formality and that you have checked for WORDS SPELLCHECKERS MAY NOT CATCH. For more help with this, see FORMALITY, LEVEL OF; POLISHING; and POLISHING CHECKLIST.

7. Be strategic and vigilant about using artificial intelligence (AI).

There are three places in the WRITING PROCESS where AI may be useful in writing an Argument. First, you may want to use AI to get ideas in PREWRITING for possible arguments and sources related to your situation or approaches that may not have occurred to you. For help doing this, see PROMPTS, QUESTIONS PRESENTED, and RESEARCH STRATEGY GUIDE. Second, you may want to use AI in REVISING your draft because it can help you make adjustments, such as minimizing use of PASSIVE VOICE and increasing READABILITY or making it more concise. For help using AI at this stage of the writing process, see REVISING CHECKLIST. Third, you may also find it useful in POLISHING to make sure your document conforms to format requirements or proofreading standards. For things AI may be able to check for you at this stage, see POLISHING CHECKLIST.

AI may be less useful in WRITING because the information it relies on will not include the specific facts of your client's situation. Nor will it be as helpful in REWRITING when you are checking your case's specific law, facts, theory of the case, and sequence of arguments. For a more thorough discussion of AI's possible limitations at these stages, see DISCUSSION SECTION.

Wherever you choose to use AI, make sure you verify its results. For guidelines on this, see ARTIFICIAL INTELLIGENCE AND RESEARCH, ARTIFICIAL INTELLIGENCE AND WRITING, and PROMPTS.

For related information, see BRIEFS; BRIEFS, AMICUS; BRIEFS, APPELLATE; BRIEFS, PRETRIAL; BRIEFS, REPLY; and BRIEFS, TRIAL.

ARTICLES, GRAMMAR

Article is the grammatical term for *a*, *an*, and *the*. For a discussion of their use, see *A* OR *AN*? and *THE*.

ARTICLES, PUBLISHED

See SCHOLARLY WRITING, SCHOLARLY WRITING PROCESS, and SCHOLARLY WRITING PROCESS CHECKLIST. Alternatively, see INFORMATIVE ARTICLES.

ARTIFICIAL INTELLIGENCE AND RESEARCH

Artificial Intelligence (AI) has long been a part of legal research systems, which departed from the strictly Boolean searching that had preceded them. A generative AI system offers a way of researching an enormous knowledge base. AI can help you generate ideas, search with conversational language, explain concepts, summarize information, and create a working draft. It can also help you complete some tasks more quickly.

AI uses Large Language Models (LLMs) to analyze vast amounts of information. Those LLMs "learn" and adapt to new information without human intervention. Be aware that LLMs can generate false information and law, or HALLUCINATIONS, so carefully evaluate results in the context of other research.

Remember that AI is a tool, not a substitute for your own thinking. AI cannot replace your analysis. Consider the following in balancing the woes with the wonders of AI and legal research.

1. Check for any constraints on your use of AI.

   Before you use AI, check if your supervising attorney, firm, court, or professor has a policy about using AI. Also check for any budgetary or confidentiality limits.

2. Choose an AI program appropriate to your legal research purposes.

   Select an AI program that is capable of retrieving the sources you need. First, discern what you can about the material that the LLM captured, including its sources of law. Second, ask AI vendors to see the privacy and confidentiality agreements and then frame your prompt accordingly. Is this program designed to be used by all lawyers for all research? Is it tailored for the use of lawyers in your jurisdiction? In your office? As new research programs are developed, you will likely be able to choose AI programs that are better suited to your needs, but pay attention to the sources used for their training and to any ethical implications.

3. Develop your ability to be specific in your research prompts.

   You will be using language prompts to interact with the system, and language is often ambiguous. In your prompt, be specific about the law, legal question, and legally significant facts. You will also want to include relevant context, point of view, and outcome, among other things. And avoid including anything that will violate confidentiality and privacy. For more suggestions, see PROMPTS FOR LEGAL RESEARCH. If your initial prompt does not produce good results, clarify it or consider entering a new prompt.

4. Be aware of drifting into inaccurate results.

   Begin your conversation with AI as though it is the focused opening question of an interview. Getting your prompt right the first time is safer, because AI does not rewrite and revise as you do. As you get further away from your original prompt, the system can drift away from what you originally asked. Like an overeager assistant who sometimes lies to please you, it may tell you what it thinks you want to hear. If AI does not have enough information to answer your prompt, it may invent it, so be aware of possible HALLUCINATIONS.

5. Evaluate the results in the context of your own knowledge, other research, and common sense.

   Do not accept the results at face value. Compare the findings with your findings using at least two other methods, such as Boolean searches or secondary source commentaries. Your prompt may have been too narrow or broad, and your research in other sources can give you enough context that you can analyze your AI findings accurately. For example, if you submit the same prompt twice, you may not get exactly the same answer, an indication that answers are not immutable.

6. Keep a detailed record of your process.

   Develop an approach for having a research plan and keeping track of your research, such as a system that captures your work automatically. Good NOTES can save you time when using or checking your on-line research and help you track down sources of errors and learn from your mistakes. Your notes can also track your developing analysis. Furthermore, professional responsibility or emerging rules may require you to acknowledge when and where you have used AI to research a document. Finally, always be careful about any confidentiality issues that may arise with client work.

7. Continue to adapt as you become more sophisticated in your use of AI.

   As you become more adept at using AI for research, decide where best to use it in your research strategy. For example, you may want to start with AI, which can point you to other helpful sources. Or if you do not know much about this area of the law, you might use secondary sources to gain context and vocabulary first. If you are an expert in this field, you may want to start with a specifically constructed prompt for a narrow question. If you have limited time, you may want to do a Boolean search and use the results to fashion an effective prompt for AI. Or you may want to use AI at the end of your process to check that you have not missed anything. Always verify your AI results using other research sources.

8. Remember that AI has no ethical responsibility; you do.

   Whatever you decide about when and how to use AI in your research, rely on your ability to verify the results. Never sacrifice your own knowledge of the subject matter, your analysis, your assessment of the results, and your ethics. It is your name and reputation on the line. Carefully consult your ethics rules on competence, communication, client confidentiality, and supervision.

ARTIFICIAL INTELLIGENCE AND WRITING

Generative artificial intelligence (AI) is a broad term identifying a variety of tools that accomplish many writing tasks humans can do, such as generating ideas, analyzing concepts, organizing content, writing grammatical sentences, and editing. Generative AI, if you use it, will change your writing process. It will make some tasks easier and prevent some errors, but it will also create new challenges. Your task is to adapt your process to address these challenges.

Generative AI uses the words in your prompt to draw upon vast knowledge bases. That writing may include documents from the web, social media, books, court cases, statutes, political speeches, law firm documents, and other writing available in electronic form. It uses the knowledge bases on which it was trained to select words and create a response to your prompt. Generative AI creates text by analyzing patterns in large collections of existing writing, then uses algorithms to generate new content that mimics these patterns. It knows how the language's structure works, perhaps better than the average human, but it does not think about the substance or meaning of those words in the same way people do. Extremely quickly, it scans and compares text in its dataset, and makes choices by considering meaning, context, connotation, grammar, readability, and tone, among many other factors. Subsequently, it produces a response to your prompt that generally appears coherent and accurate, but needs to be read with a critical human mind.

To use AI effectively in your writing, consider the following in balancing the promise with the potential problems of AI.

1. Be cognizant of any financial, confidentiality, or other constraints.

   Ascertain any budgetary limits on using AI. AI uses a tremendous amount of energy, which may translate into costs. Do not assume your budget will allow you to use AI if you can otherwise produce results using less expensive means.

   Also observe any confidentiality or policy limits. Judges, supervising attorneys, or others may prohibit certain uses of AI or require you to identify any writing done by AI. A number of publicly available generative AIs will collect the prompts used by users, which means that you could be putting in confidential information about your clients or violating non-disclosure agreements. Some law offices bar use of publicly available generative AIs for that reason. Always read the terms of service.

2. Learn what you can about the scope and nature of the generative AI's knowledge base.

   Ask the appropriate questions to determine the generative AI's scope. For example, is it a general-purpose AI or a specialized AI focused on legal content? Does it include the writing of thousands of writers covering all sorts of general topics, such as some LLMs? Does it include scientific documents that are written in a style and organization that differs from your needs? Or does it include only the legal documents written in your office? Is it focused on government documents in all jurisdictions? The scope of the knowledge base affects the nature of the writing AI generates. AI will create writing that reflects the content it was trained on, and that writing may or may not suit your needs.

While details about AI's training is likely to be proprietary, you may be able to discern something about its possible purpose. Is this program designed to be used by the general public for all sorts of writing? Or is it tailored for the use of lawyers who are writing legal documents? As new programs are developed, you will likely be able to choose AI programs that are better suited to your needs than the programs aimed at very broad use.

3. Develop your ability to be specific in your requests to the generative AI system.

   You will be using language prompts to instruct the system, and language is often ambiguous. In your prompt, be specific about the subject, reader, and format. You may also want to provide other guidance, such as

   - List all the information required for [your topic],
   - Write at a level appropriate to your [specified] reader's education and experience,
   - Include [specified] implications [e.g., economic impact, advantages and disadvantages, viable alternatives], and
   - Use a business-like tone.

   You can add additional prompts to revise the text. For more information, see PROMPTS. Be particularly vigilant in watching for the possibility of HALLUCINATIONS.

4. Rewrite the document according to your own organization and priorities.

   One benefit of generative AI is that it can generate a draft document. However, because AI is so sensitive to the prompt's wording, the draft may need some rewriting. Check the organization and content of an AI draft and rewrite as needed. The organization may not be the one that will be most logical to your reader. There may be some unnecessary or repeated content. Alternatively, there may be some missing steps in the reasoning. There may be some information you want to include that is missing or persuasive. Check the headings to make sure the content and format convey your analysis or argument accurately and readably. Treat the AI draft as you would your own draft, making sure it is correct, complete, and coherent. For related information, see REWRITING, REWRITING CHECKLIST, and WRITING BLOCK.

5. Revise the document so it speaks to your reader in your voice.

   After you have the document's content and organization in place, you can take another pass to revise wording, tone, and sentence structure. This will help you make sure that the document uses your own voice and is readable. Readability becomes even more important when writing to readers dealing with vast amounts of written texts. For example, if a paragraph's main point is not revealed in the first line, the reader will likely miss it. Similarly, if the connections between paragraphs are not readily apparent, the reader may not follow your logic. Excessive use of NOMINALIZATIONS may make the writing harder to process; too much PASSIVE VOICE may also lose readers. In a passage that seems dull, try using a more descriptive verb, IMAGERY, or analogy to add a dollop of interest to an otherwise dry offering.

Finally, polish your document. Remember that AI, including spelling and grammar checkers, is not you, and this document will be under your authorship, your responsibility, and in your voice. For related information, see POLISHING, REVISING and REVISING CHECKLIST.

6. Keep a record of your process.

   Note where and when you used generative AI and what you used it for because your clients and the courts may request this information from you. Also keep notes on your own observations about what worked and what did not. For example, you may also keep track of the prompts that worked well and their corresponding results. Just as good NOTES can save you time when using or checking your online research, good notes when using generative AI for creating can help you track down sources of errors and learn from your mistakes.

7. Continue to be adaptable as you become more sophisticated in your use of AI.

   Adjust over time and remain alert as you use AI. Its effectiveness will evolve, as will your ability to use it. If you are a good editor but dread facing the blank page, you may find it worth your time to have AI generate that first draft. If organizing documents is a challenge, it may be helpful to have AI generate an initial organization. If you enjoy creating a draft but get bored with editing, you may find it helpful to use AI later in your process. But if you already have a good grasp of the content you want to convey, then you may find it more efficient to use speech-to-text technology.

8. Remember that AI has no ethical responsibility; you do.

   Whatever you decide about when and how to use AI, retain your ownership of the document. Never sacrifice your accuracy, your analysis, your voice, or your ethics. It is your name and reputation on the line. Carefully consult your ethics rules on competence, communication, client confidentiality, and supervision.

AS

To avoid ambiguity, avoid using *as* in place of *because*.

The trial was delayed because the plaintiff fell ill.

rather than

The trial was delayed as the plaintiff fell ill.

For related information, see PRECISION and TRANSITIONS.

AS A MATTER OF FACT

You probably do not need this phrase. Try marking it out and revising what is left into a more concise, forceful statement.

It was within her power to do so. She was the supervisor on duty.

rather than

It was within her power to do so. She was, as a matter of fact, the supervisor on duty.

For related information, see CONCISENESS, section 9.

AS IF OR *AS THOUGH*?

Either one means *in the same way that it would be if.* They can be used interchangeably.

AS OR *LIKE*?

In a comparison, use *as* to connect CLAUSES.

She argues as a good lawyer should argue.

rather than

She argues like a good lawyer should.

Use *like* only to introduce a noun phrase.

She argues like Justice Sotomayor.

AS PER

Substitute *under, according to,* or another appropriate term.

Under the terms of this contract, ...

rather than

As per the terms of this contract, ...

or

This number is inaccurate according to the most recent data.

rather than

This number is inaccurate as per the most recent data.

The number of words that substitute for *as per* indicate that the phrase is vague, as well as an example of JARGON.

ASSONANCE

Assonance is repeating vowel sounds within a series of words to create a specific effect. Because it requires a broader discretion in word choice, it is a more useful tool for poets than for legal writers. But it may occasionally be useful in a persuasive Statements of Facts. Use it sparingly, or you may engender unwanted humor. Also avoid sacrificing CLARITY for effect. For example, to create a staccato effect, you might repeat the short *i* sound.

The plaintiff's insistent clicking of her stick against the defendant's chair irritated the situation and provoked the assault.

But repeating an *oo* sound that much would invite readers to giggle, because the repetition is more obvious.

The moonlight soothed the plaintiff's mood, so she was moved to sign the new contract.

For related information, see ALLITERATION, ANTONYMS, HOMONYMS, REPETITION, and SYNONYMS.

ASSURE, *ENSURE*, OR *INSURE*?

Assure, *ensure*, and *insure* can all mean *to make certain of something.* However, only *insure* means to guarantee against loss, and only *assure* has the sense of setting a person's mind at rest. To avoid ambiguity, use the words as follows.

Use *assure* for removing doubt.

The judge assured us that she would give the maximum penalty if the defendant was found guilty.

Use *ensure* for making certain of something.

This signing date ensures that our client can move into the property by January 1.

Use *insure* for guaranteeing against loss.

Our client, State Mutual, insured the plaintiff against hurricane damage.

ASTERISKS

Asterisks (*) are sometimes used for acknowledgments in law review articles or for a single footnote. In typeset print, asterisks are also sometimes used interchangeably with ELLIPSES. In formal legal writing, asterisks are distracting, so use ellipses. In informal writing, asterisks are used to mark a single footnote; in legal writing, this is only likely to happen when adding a small point to an informal memo to a coworker.

For related information, see QUOTATIONS, HOW TO PUNCTUATE.

AS THOUGH OR *AS IF*?

Either one means *in the same way that it would be if.* They can be used interchangeably.

AS TO

As to can be used as a preposition, in which case it takes an object.

As to the adjective: when in doubt strike it out.

—Mark Twain

or

As to jury trials, defendants can waive their rights if they so choose.

Use *as to* rarely and with care to avoid two problems. First, do not use *as to* if it is stuffy in context. For example, in a letter to a client, write the following.

You had requested documentation for . . . .

rather than

As to your request for . . . .

Second, avoid overusing *as to.* If you use it once a page, you are probably overusing it. To find a different but equally accurate connecting phrase, see TRANSITIONS.

AT THE TIME THAT

Use *when* instead. See CONCISENESS.

AT THIS POINT IN TIME

Use *now* or *currently* for CLARITY and CONCISENESS.

ATTORNEY OR *LAWYER*?

Generally, *attorney* is used to refer to the specific person representing a party to a suit, although *lawyer* is also appropriate.

Attorney Schwartz moved for a new trial.

or

The attorney for the defense objected to the question.

The term *lawyer* often refers to the general category of people qualified to practice law, although *attorneys* is also appropriate.

Several hundred lawyers attended last year's ABA convention.

AUDIENCE

To maximize the effectiveness of your writing, understand your audience, which is the aggregate of your various potential readers, before you begin to write. This will help you communicate more effectively. The concept of *audience* or *readers* is one of four principles to keep in mind throughout the WRITING PROCESS. The others are POINT OF VIEW, PURPOSE, and SCOPE. For related information, see *AUDIENCE* OR *READER?*

When you begin a project, identify the potential readers of your document, both (1) your primary reader and (2) all secondary readers. Then (3) adjust your content and presentation to address their expectations.

1. The primary reader.

   The primary reader is the reader to whom you must direct your message, such as your supervising attorney, your client, or the judge. Find out as much as you can about that reader's preferences.

   (a) Is your primary audience a nonlawyer or a lawyer, experienced or inexperienced? Adjust your content, wording, topic sentences, and tone for that reader. For further information, see READABILITY, subsection 3; TONE; TOPIC SENTENCES; and WORD CHOICE.

   (b) What are the reader's objectives regarding this subject? Frame issues that address those objectives and include counterarguments. For further information, see COUNTERARGUMENTS, HOW TO HANDLE; and ISSUES.

   (c) How much detailed support does this reader want? You can gain credibility by providing enough, but not too much, supporting explanation. For further information, see APPLICATION, LEGAL ANALYSIS, READERS, and SCOPE.

(d) Is the reader hostile or open to your position? This will help you know how to structure your argument effectively. For further information, see BAD NEWS, GIVING IT; and WRITING, PERSUASIVE, subsections 1–3.

2. The secondary readers.

Secondary readers are those who read the document for other purposes. Most legal writing is read by more than one person, and those readers each have different levels of expertise, experience, and patience. For example, BRIEFS will be reviewed by judges, the judges' clerks, opposing counsel, clients, and sometimes the press or the public; opinion letters and email may be used in negotiations with other entities or reviewed by supervising attorneys before being sent to clients. Address the concerns of these potential readers without losing focus on the primary reader. This is a challenge for any writer.

To adjust the document for secondary readers, also consider the readers' levels of expertise. If all of the document's readers are lawyers, you may use TERMS OF ART and briefer references to generally held legal assumptions. But if you have some readers who have very little legal experience, avoid unfamiliar words. When terms of art are needed, consider adding definitions or explanations. For help here, see JARGON; LEGALESE; READABILITY, subsection 3; and UNOBTRUSIVE DEFINITIONS. Similarly, you may need to include appendices or summaries. See APPENDIX. If you do not know your readers' level of expertise, it is safest to include the explanatory information needed for the nonlegal reader.

3. Adjusting content and presentation.

When you have examined the range of your readers, try to address their logical needs throughout the PREWRITING and REWRITING stages in your writing process. Make sure each of the primary and secondary readers can continue to understand the questions, the answers, and the reasons supporting those answers. To meet the needs of the primary reader, ask yourself what organization will best track the primary reader's reasoning processes. To meet the needs of the secondary reader, also ask what questions that reader will have beyond those of the primary reader and answer those questions. Use HEADINGS, TOPIC SENTENCES, and graphics to help your audience know at a glance where you are going and how you are getting there.

When you are REVISING, adjust your word choice and sentence structure as appropriate for your readers' preferences. During POLISHING, adjust to your primary reader's preferences if no common ground exists among your readers. When in doubt about whether to include a component, err on the side of including components that will answer, not raise, questions.

For additional information, see COMMUNICATIONS, TONE OF; GRAPHICS, HOW TO USE; ORGANIZE, HOW TO; and TONE. For how-to information, see PROFESSIONAL LANGUAGE AND PRESENTATION.

AUDIENCE OR *READER*?

Both terms are used to identify people to whom writing communicates, and each term contributes to a legal writer's understanding of the task being undertaken. *Audience* invokes the rhetorical significance of communicating with more than one person, each of whom experiences the document through a different set of expectations, references, contexts, and needs. Adjusting writing for this range of readers often requires the writer to make a different series of decisions about design and presentation. *Reader* reflects the fact that writing communicates by being read by individual readers, rather than spoken to a large group. A written document must re-create the writer's thought, with its connotations and nuances, without the benefit of gesture, vocal intonation, pauses, or facial expressions.

Reader also reminds the writer that reading is essentially a private activity. No matter how many people read a given document, each reader is an individual who reconstructs the writer's meaning in that reader's own mind. This is why ambiguity and misunderstanding can occur so readily, especially in quick and casual compositions, such as email. Whether you prefer to use *audience* or *reader*, remember the nuances of both terms and use them to help you make effective decisions about the art of legal writing. For related information, see AUDIENCE; BAD NEWS, GIVING IT; BAD NEWS, SOFTENING IT; CLARITY; EDITING; and READERS.

AUXILIARY VERB

See VERBS, AUXILIARY.

BACKGROUND FACTS

These facts fill in the gaps between legally significant facts. Although they are not essential to the issues, they are essential to the reader's understanding of the general situation. Thus the Statement of Facts contains enough background to complete the context. Background facts should be minimized, however, to avoid making the Statement of Facts too long. For related information, see EMOTIONAL FACTS, LEGALLY SIGNIFICANT FACTS, and STATEMENT OF FACTS.

BAD NEWS, GIVING IT

For any lawyer, being the bearer of bad news is as unavoidable as it is distasteful. Unlike a fortune teller, who can base predictions on the client's desires, the lawyer must base each prediction on sound analysis of law and fact.

A lawyer can, however, use an understanding of readers and of writing to make that bad news more palatable. The following techniques can be helpful for presenting bad news

(1) in a letter,

(2) in an email,

(3) in a memo, or

(4) in a brief.

For related information, see TONE.

1. In a letter.

When you must write a bad-news letter, try organizing the letter into three parts that do the following: (a) set the tone, (b) deliver the bad news, and (c) reestablish the tone. Think of this as a sandwich organization; place your meat between two slices of bread to make it more palatable.

(a) The first slice of bread: set the tone.

In the first paragraph, establish the tone you want to take with the reader. For example, you might want to be kind.

> **Mr. Alexander has asked us to help straighten out some apparent confusion regarding your bill to him for equipment repairs made in June 2024. As I understand it, ...**

Or you might want to be tough.

> **You stated in your letter of March 14 that our client, Mr. Alexander, owes you $1,980 for equipment repairs you made in June 2024. This is incorrect. As Mr. Alexander has explained previously, ...**

You might choose to be warm and personal.

> **Thank you for inviting me to speak at the Society's annual awards banquet. Regrettably, ...**

You might choose to be distant.

> **This letter concerns a bill for $1,980 from Efficient Equipment Repair Service to Alexander**

> **Associates, which states that the charges are for equipment repairs completed in June 2024 . . . .**

If answering a request, you may want to open by restating that request, so that the reader knows you paid attention before saying no.

> **In your letter to Mr. Alexander dated October 14, you asked him to pay $1,980 for "equipment repairs made to three computers in June 2024." You stated that this payment was long overdue and you threatened to bring suit if you did not receive payment by December 1, 2025.**

(b) The meat: deliver the bad news.

At the beginning of the second paragraph, state the bad news plainly so that the reader cannot misinterpret what you are saying.

> **In your letter to Mr. Alexander dated October 14, you asked Mr. Alexander to pay $1,980 for "equipment repairs made to three computers in June 2024." You stated that this payment was long overdue and you threatened to bring suit if you did not receive payment by December 1, 2025.**
>
> **Mr. Alexander, however, does not believe he owes you this money. . . .**

Follow this statement with your explanations, as appropriate. This paragraph will be unemotional and matter of fact, regardless of the tone of the other paragraphs.

> **Mr. Alexander, however, does not believe he owes you this money because he has no record of these repairs being made. Instead, his records show only that Efficient Equipment Repair Service repaired one computer on June 12, 2024. Alexander Associates received a statement charging $940 for this work from the repairman before he left. On July 1, 2024, Alexander Associates mailed a check for $940 to Efficient Equipment Repair Service. . . .**

This section may also extend for several paragraphs if needed.

(c) The other piece of bread: reestablish the tone.

In the final paragraph, reestablish your tone while you state some closing technicalities. It is crucial to echo the same tone used in the first paragraph for credibility and effectiveness. For example, you may suggest that the reader call if any questions remain.

> **If you have any further questions concerning this matter, you may call me at (505) 555–1234.**

If you are being kind, you may wish the reader some sort of relevant good fortune.

> **I enjoyed our conversation at the convention and look forward to reading your article on . . . .**

If you are being tough, you may close with a final declarative statement.

> **I trust that this explains the matter to your satisfaction.**

For related information see BAD NEWS, SOFTENING IT; COMMUNICATIONS, TONE OF; and WRITING TO CLIENTS.

2. In an email.

When presenting bad news in an email, you have only one or two sentences to set the tone before you present your bad news. You need to present the bad news so that it will appear in the initial screen of information or you risk having the reader miss your message. Unlike a letter, in which your reader sees a whole page at once, email presents only a screen of information at a time. Because of this fact, and because readers do not always scroll all the way down to the bottom of a message, you cannot delay the bad news very long.

You can, however, avoid stating the bad news in the subject line or in the first line of the email. To do this, use the subject line to announce the topic of the email but not the outcome. Also be careful about the list of recipients. For help here, see REPLY TO ALL.

3. In a memo.

Sometimes you must tell an assigning attorney that a client does not have a case. When this happens, state your conclusion in specific, matter-of-fact language.

> **Mr. Allen will probably not be able to convince a jury to award damages under the theory of strict liability because he cannot show that . . . .**

Then lay out your reasoning thoroughly. Answer all possible questions your reader will likely ask, one by one.

If possible, offer viable alternatives. Maybe some other theory is possible. Maybe some other approach, such as negotiation, is desirable. These options greatly reduce the sting of a negative answer. Do not, however, commit large amounts of the client's money by researching these issues at length without the client's or your assigning attorney's permission. For related information, see LEGAL ANALYSIS; MEMOS; ORGANIZATION, LARGE-SCALE; and SUBJECT LINES.

4. In a brief.

Sometimes you must deal with precedent, policy, or facts that go against your client's position. For help here, see COUNTERARGUMENTS, HOW TO HANDLE; and WRITING, PERSUASIVE.

For related information, see COMMUNICATIONS, CLOSINGS FOR; COMMUNICATIONS, ELECTRONIC; COMMUNICATIONS, INTERNATIONAL; COMMUNICATIONS, OPENINGS FOR; COMMUNICATIONS, PERSUASIVE; EMAIL; PROFESSIONAL LANGUAGE AND PRESENTATION; SOCIAL MEDIA; WRITING TO ATTORNEYS; and WRITING TO CLIENTS.

BAD NEWS, SOFTENING IT

Soften bad news when you want to keep the reader from reacting to the news in some undesirable way. Be careful about softening bad news so much, however, that the reader misses the point altogether. For example, if in an opinion letter you needed to tell your client that a lawsuit would not prevail, you might state the following.

> **Although you may bring suit, you are unlikely to recover your investment. The company at fault has declared bankruptcy, and thus . . . .**
>
> rather than
>
> Although the results might not be exactly what you desire, you may nevertheless choose to bring suit.

With that caveat in mind, use the following techniques to soften the blow. For related information, see BAD NEWS, GIVING IT; COMMUNICATIONS, TONE OF; TONE; and WRITING TO CLIENTS.

1. Use a dependent clause.

You can put the bad news in a dependent clause (see SENTENCE, PARTS OF) and then put that clause in a sentence based on a more favorable fact.

> **Although he was driving over the speed limit, Mr. Jones was driving no faster than other cars on that road at that time. Indeed he was passed by several cars just a few minutes before the accident.**

This technique is particularly useful in persuasive writing. To determine the most suitable word to use at the beginning of your dependent clause, see TRANSITIONS. For a general discussion of the technique, see SENTENCE STRUCTURE, subsection 3; and WRITING, PERSUASIVE.

2. Use more abstract terms.

A second way to soften bad news is to state it more generally, rather than in specific and concrete terms. This technique is most likely to be useful when you have an unfavorable fact that cannot be logically set in a more favorable context. Thus, if your client hit a parked car, you might refer to the event this way.

> **Both cars were damaged in the collision.**

If, however, the other party hit your client's parked car, you might refer to the same event this way.

> **When the defendant's car smashed into the rear left fender of the plaintiff's car, the impact crumpled the fender and shoved it into the back seat, so that the folded metal came within three inches of the driver's seat.**

The limitations of this method are obvious in this example; even if you offer the court your abstract version, your adversary will probably offer the concrete one. It may be, however, that your adversary will overdo it, or underdo it, and you can take advantage of that mistake.

3. Put the bad news in a less emphatic part of the sentence.

You can use sentence structure to deemphasize one point at the same time you are using it to emphasize another, more favorable point.

> **Although the defendant violated his parole on one occasion three months ago, he has shown exemplary behavior ever since.**

4. Use a less interesting sentence structure.

You can use passive voice, for example, to make a fact stand out a little less. Thus a defendant's Statement of Facts might include the following sentence.

> **Damages caused by the accident included crumpled fenders, broken lights, and other damage to the rear of the plaintiff's car.**

Since less interesting structures are usually harder to read and reduce the appeal of the overall text, use this option sparingly.

For related information, see COMMUNICATIONS, CLOSINGS FOR; COMMUNICATIONS, ELECTRONIC; COMMUNICATIONS, INTERNATIONAL; COMMUNICATIONS, OPENINGS FOR; COMMUNICATIONS, PERSUASIVE; COMMUNICATIONS, TONE OF; EMAIL; PROFESSIONAL LANGUAGE AND PRESENTATION; SOCIAL MEDIA; WRITING TO ATTORNEYS; and WRITING TO CLIENTS.

BAD OR *BADLY*?

Use *bad* when modifying a noun and *badly* when modifying a verb. The main problem writers have here is exemplified in the following sentence.

I feel bad about . . . .

rather than

I feel badly about . . . .

Use *bad* because you are describing your emotions, not your ability to physically feel things. Grammatically, *feel* is a linking verb in the first situation, so the adjective is used. When the verb modified is an action, then the adverb *badly* is used.

He performed badly in the game following the incident.

You will probably find few occasions to use this phrase in legal writing because *bad* is a personal judgment rather than a provable fact. For more information, see ADJECTIVES; ADVERBS; OVERREFINEMENT; and VERBS, LINKING.

BAR GRAPHS

See GRAPHICS, WHICH FORMS TO USE, subsection 2.

BASED ON

Watch this phrase at the beginning of a sentence because it can create a dangling modifier.

Based on the plain meaning of this word, this interpretation of the clause is valid.

rather than

Based on the plain meaning of this word, my client should not have to honor this contract.

The interpretation, not the client, is based on the plain meaning. For related general information, see AMBIGUITY, WAYS TO AVOID, subsection 1; and MODIFIERS, DANGLING.

BASICALLY

This word often has no specific meaning in a sentence; if it does not, omit it. Use *basically* if you are in fact contrasting the basis of something to some other aspect of that same thing.

Basically, this is a good theory, but in practice . . . .

It would be better to state your point more precisely.

This theory is based on precedent, but its application of that precedent is flawed in three ways.

B.C. OR *B.C.E.*?

Use *B.C.E.*, which stands for *before common era*. Use periods after the letters with no spaces between; place it after the date.

3000 B.C.E.

rather than

3000 B.C.

Similarly, use *C.E.*, which stands for *common era*, rather than *A.D.*, punctuating it in the same way and placing it after the date.

99 C.E.

rather than

A.D. 99

B.C.E., like the corresponding *B.C.*, goes after the date, in contrast to *A.D.* Other designations exist in other religions and in some archeology contexts, but *B.C.E.* is the term most likely understood by the broadest audience.

BECAUSE OR *SINCE*?

Use *because* if you mean *because*. *Because* is a precise term with only one meaning; it means that one event or thing is the cause of something else.

The restraining order was issued because the defendant had repeatedly approached the plaintiff, stopping him on the street and even coming to his home.

Use *since* if you mean to show a relationship in time.

Since the restraining order was issued, the defendant has approached the plaintiff four times.

If you are worried about overusing *because*, you can do three things. First, check to see how frequently *because* appears. As a general rule, you need not worry about overusing *because* until it appears once in every paragraph and more than once in many paragraphs. Second, even if you are using *because* frequently, consider whether that use is needed to make your text clear. For example, you may decide that using *because* more frequently is appropriate because you are explaining the reasoning for a particular conclusion. Finally, if you decide you must omit some *because*'s, restructure the sentence to use *as a result, therefore,* or some other accurate transition. For help here, see CONNECTIONS, MAKING THEM; and TRANSITIONS.

BEGINNING

For help beginning the writing process, see GETTING STARTED or WRITING BLOCK. For help with specific kind of documents, see entries for those documents. For ways to use the beginning of a section of writing for emphasis, see EMPHASIS, subsection 1. If you are using artificial intelligence, see ARTIFICIAL INTELLIGENCE AND RESEARCH, ARTIFICIAL INTELLIGENCE AND WRITING, PROMPTS, and RESEARCH STRATEGY GUIDE.

BEING THAT

Avoid this term, especially at the beginning of a sentence. It sounds informal and invites the creation of sentence fragments.

BENCH MEMOS

Bench memos are written by clerks for use by a judge who is preparing to decide a case. Bench memos provide an objective review of both sides of the controversy and evaluate the merits of the arguments made in both briefs. To write an effective bench memo, remember the following three principles:

(1) ask your judge for the preferred approach;

(2) depend on your own legal reasoning, not just the advocates'; and

(3) adjust your writing style to meet the judge's needs.

1. Ask your judge for the preferred approach.

Each judge takes a unique approach to bench memos. Some want an objective memo that summarizes and contrasts the issues and arguments and leaves the decision open to the judge. Others want a memo that analyzes which side is right and why, including a recommendation for the decision and the dispensation. Still others want a draft of the opinion itself. Even if your judge is not asking for the last choice, keep in mind that you are instrumental in shaping that opinion through the analytical, organizational, and technical decisions you are making. See OPINIONS, JUDICIAL.

When organizing the bench memo, do not generally just summarize one side's argument, summarize the other, and then evaluate the case, because this organization is not the most efficient one for the court. The judge has asked you to provide help reaching and drafting the decision. For an alternative and more efficient organization, think about the questions in the judge's mind and then adapt your approach accordingly. An effective structure often includes the following sections.

(a) Procedural Posture: explain how the case arrived in this court and whether there are any procedural issues.

(b) Statement of Facts: organize the facts as one unified summary of the relevant information, noting any points where the two parties differ on the facts.

(c) Summary of the Issues: frame the issues so that the court understands exactly what needs to be decided, and in what order. As you do this, identify where the parties differ on the issues.

(d) Discussion: organize your analysis by explaining the relevant legal standards or STANDARD OF REVIEW and the law the court should use to decide the issue. If there is an issue about what law the court should use, state the choices, discuss each, and then evaluate the choices. If the issue is not about what law applies but how that law applies, then lay out the law and discuss its application, presenting alternative applications where they arise and evaluating the merits of each application.

(e) Conclusion or Recommendation: advise the court what to decide and why.

2. Depend on your own legal research and reasoning, not just the advocates'.

Focus on the best interests of justice and of your reader. Your reader, the judge, usually wants to do what is fair under the law. Your reader also does not want this opinion to be reversed or even criticized by the appellate court. You therefore need to research the law yourself. Then check the sources cited in both briefs to determine whether the attorneys found and interpreted those sources correctly. You can thus determine the appropriate law and how it should be applied to serve its purpose and to conform with precedent, especially with any appellate or supreme court decisions on that issue.

As you complete your own research, you may thus find yourself disagreeing with both of the party's arguments rather than choosing one argument over another. This is normal, because you are reading the law from the wider view of justice and consistency with policy, precedent, or judicial preferences. The attorneys who wrote the briefs were writing in their client's best interests, and often that includes broadening or narrowing the law, giving little context, or taking a short-term view.

To determine your own reasoning, use your own research and frame the issues as the judge will do in the decision. Never trust the attorneys' word alone. Always check their reasoning and measure it against your own objective view as well as against the arguments of the opposing attorney.

For related information, see WRITING, OBJECTIVE. For information on reading and building your Discussion, see CASE BRIEFS; COUNTERARGUMENTS, HOW TO HANDLE; LEGAL ANALYSIS; REASONING, ANALOGICAL; REASONING, DEDUCTIVE; REASONING, INDUCTIVE; REASONING, MODERN; REASONING, OTHER; REASONING, POSTMODERN; REASONING, PRESENTING IT; and SYLLOGISMS.

3. Adjust your writing style to meet the judge's needs.

Judges hire clerks to ease the workload, so make sure that your bench memo meets this objective. As a judge's clerk, you have the luxury of writing for one particular reader, and a reader that you have come to know well. Use this knowledge to organize and write bench briefs that are perfectly suited to that reader. For example, you may like to add a touch of elegance to your writing, but your judge may prefer a straightforward, abrupt style. If this is your situation, then save your elegant touches for other documents. Instead, state the paragraph's point in the first sentence, keep your sentences short and simple, and omit any unneeded information. Or you may have a judge who is particular about specific details, such as citation form or placement of commas. In this situation, proofread your bench memos for these details before you give them to your judge.

If you do not yet know your reader's preferences, you may be able to discover them by studying some of the judge's opinions. For help in making this evaluation, see GHOST WRITING. Often you will learn your reader's preferences through trial and error. Keep a list of those preferences as you discover them, and review the list as part of your normal revision process on every bench memo. This should minimize your errors and help you impress the judge with your writing and your ability to learn.

BENDING THE RULES

This can be done with law, with grammar, or with general writing principles. With the law, you may bend as far as POLICY, EQUITY, canons of construction, custom, and the judges in your jurisdiction allow.

With grammar, bend less. Bending grammatical rules often results in ambiguity, which is costly in legal writing. Further, many legal readers pride themselves on their knowledge of grammatical rules and are easily distracted by any bending. Your goal in legal writing is to have your reader understand your content, not to push the grammatical envelope.

Undaunted, Attorney Jones proceeded with the cross-examination, regardless of the defense's objections.

rather than

Attorney Jones proceeded undauntedly with the cross-examination, irregardless of the defense's objections.

With general writing principles, bend when you have good reason, but only then. Although concrete rules are useful to help any writer make decisions quickly, at some time or another some rules just do not make sense. For example, you may want to use a sentence fragment for emphasis.

Alternatives existed before 2024. Not anymore.

rather than

The court may want to consider the alternatives that existed before 2024, but such choices will not be helpful in this case because they are no longer available.

Here, using the fragment draws the reader's eye to that point and creates a blunt TONE. The safer route, however, is to avoid bending the rule by REVISING.

The alternative may work elsewhere, but not here.

If you cannot revise to avoid the problem, ask yourself, *What will be clear to my reader? What most accurately states my point?* Then, using the answers to these questions and your own common sense, bend the rules if need be. For more detail on this point, see CHOICES IN LEGAL WRITING, COMMON SENSE, and INDEPENDENCE IN LEGAL WRITING. For some related concerns, see ACCURACY; AMBIGUITY, WAYS TO AVOID; GENDER IN WRITING, PRECISION; and READABILITY.

BEST OR *BETTER*?

Better compares two things, *best* three or more.

He was the better of the two lawyers arguing the case; she was the best of the three lawyers in the room.

BETWEEN OR *AMONG*?

See *AMONG* OR *BETWEEN*?

BETWEEN YOU AND ME OR *BETWEEN YOU AND I*?

Use *between you and me*, always; *me*, the objective case, is the object of the preposition *between*.

BILLS, WRITING THEM

See LEGISLATION or REQUESTS FOR PAYMENT.

BLACK

This term is not capitalized. Also see *AFRICAN AMERICAN* OR *AFRICAN-AMERICAN*?

BLUEBOOK

This term refers to *The Bluebook: A Uniform System of Citation*, a recognized authority for citations in the United States. *Bluebook* rules govern citation form for most law review articles and federal courts, although a particular jurisdiction may have its own preferred citation system. Before you start taking effective NOTES, check with your reader's conventions and your jurisdiction to see which citation system to use. Then you can record your initial citations in the form you will use for the document's final version. For more information on when and how to cite, see CITATIONS; CITATIONS, BASIC FORMATS; CITATIONS, ELECTRONIC; CITATIONS, PARALLEL; CITATIONS, PINPOINT; CITATIONS, STRING; and FOOTNOTES. For information about an alternative authority, see *ALWD GUIDE TO LEGAL CITATION*.

BOLDFACE TYPE

Boldface has become a popular substitute for underlining to create emphasis. When used too much within a paragraph, however, boldface text can affect the reader like a sudden increase in the volume of a television: it draws attention, but to the medium rather than the message. For alternative ways to stress a point, see EMPHASIS.

A better use of boldface is for headings or other words that stand apart from the body of the text. The words in bold will stand out on the page, so the reader may scan those words before reading the rest of the text. Therefore, make sure that each boldfaced phrase makes sense. For example, you might use bold for the following.

Do not answer any questions until you have talked to me.

The following version would be less effective.

Do **not** answer any questions until you have talked to me.

As with any graphic device, avoid overusing the technique. For more on the effective use of graphic aids, see GRAPHICS, HOW TO USE, subsection 3.

BOTH

Use *both* when you are joining two people or things logically in a sentence.

Both courts used this reasoning.

but

The cases are similar.

rather than

Both cases are similar.

In the latter example, the writer is not saying that both cases are similar to something else, and therefore the writer should not join the two logically in the sentence.

BOTH . . . AND

Use *both . . . and* to emphasize an upcoming pair of entities or concepts.

Both the mayor and the city council approved this action.

rather than

The mayor as well as the city council approved this action.

Using *both . . . and* adds clarity, especially when each of the two concepts listed requires many words to explain. For related information, see CONJUNCTIONS and TRANSITIONS.

BRACKETS

In general, brackets indicate changes made in a quotation. Use brackets around *sic* to indicate any significant mistakes occurring in an original quotation.

"The court hold [sic] the evidence admissible."

Also use brackets to change a letter from upper case to lower case or vice versa and to substitute words or letters or other material into the text.

> **"[E]xcellence in [administrative] procedures is indispensable to carrying out the statute's intent."**

Brackets have a few other specialized uses, such as marking shortened forms of case names within footnote citations.

For more specific information on how to use brackets in quotations, see QUOTATIONS, HOW TO PUNCTUATE, subsections 7–9. For related information, see *SIC*.

BREAKING THE RULES

See BENDING THE RULES.

BRIEF ANSWERS

In some memo formats, a Brief Answer serves as a substantive executive summary. In this context, the purpose of the Brief Answer is to inform the reader at a glance of the answer to the legal issue and the reasons. This may be the first section the reader reads in a memo, so it should give the answers to the QUESTIONS PRESENTED as definitively as possible, such as *Yes, No,* or *Probably yes,* and then give the specific reason for that answer. This should be done in one concise sentence, if possible. In any case, it should be brief. Avoid simply restating the Question Presented in sentence form or answering in vague terms.

Additionally, a Brief Answer can foreshadow the organization of the coming Discussion Section through its organization and wording. For example, a Brief Answer can consist of two sentences when two major points need to be made to explain the answer. A Brief Answer including a list can be followed by a discussion that uses those listed items as its organizing framework.

Together with the Question Presented, the Brief Answer provides a concise thesis of your memo. For example, if the Question Presented were

> **Under Fed. R. Civ. P. 4(d)(1), Summons: Personal Service, was notice effective when it was delivered to the defendant's wife at her home?**

then the Brief Answer could be as follows.

> **Yes; notice was effective because the home of the defendant's wife is his "usual place of abode," that is, the defendant had lived there within the last year, he had moved back there one week after the summons was delivered, and he had received other mail there.**

After finishing your Discussion, review your Questions Presented and Brief Answers to make sure all parts remain logically and verbally congruent. For more examples, see CONCLUSIONS.

BRIEFS

Briefs are persuasive documents filed with a court to support a client's case. Briefs use persuasive writing to predispose the reader to the client's point of view by informing the reader of the applicable law and persuading the reader to decide the issue in favor of the writer's client. A brief may take the form of a pretrial brief (sometimes called *Memorandum in Support of a Motion* or *in Opposition to a Motion* or MEMORANDUM OF POINTS AND AUTHORITIES), trial brief, post-trial brief, or appellate brief. See BRIEFS, AMICUS; BRIEFS, APPELLATE; BRIEFS, PRETRIAL; BRIEFS, REPLY; and BRIEFS, TRIAL. For general advice, see WRITING, PERSUASIVE. These briefs should not be confused with case briefs, which are a writer's personal research documents. For information on those, see CASE BRIEFS.

The format of briefs varies with jurisdiction, so check your local rules for any variation from the following standard format. The information presented below explains each of the components in the most common form of a brief:

(1) Caption,

(2) Introduction,

(3) Statement of the Case,

(4) Issues,

(5) Argument, and

(6) Conclusion.

Appellate briefs also include additional sections, such as PROCEDURAL HISTORY, TABLE OF AUTHORITIES, and TABLE OF CONTENTS.

1. Caption.

Check your jurisdiction for the formalities of the caption. The caption usually includes (1) the name of the court in which the memorandum is filed; (2) the names of the parties; (3) their status, such as *plaintiff* or *defendant*; (4) the case file number; and (5) the title of the Memorandum of Points and Authorities and a description of the motion the memo supports or opposes. Although the content is formulaic, rigid, and routine, it is crucial to get this information exactly right. The Caption ensures that the document is filed, stored, retrieved, and read in the proper way. For related information, see CAPTIONS.

2. Introduction.

This section usually includes the theory of the case, the desired remedy, and a short synopsis or summary of the argument. This synopsis sets the tone, focuses the reader, and prepares the decision maker for the right disposition of the case. Sometimes the introduction takes the form of an introductory paragraph, rather than a formal introduction section. For more information, see INTRODUCTIONS and THEORY OF THE CASE.

3. Statement of the Case.

The Statement of the Case should contain the relevant procedural history, if this is not set off in a separate section, and the relevant facts. These may be two formal sections or may be combined into one statement. Include those points of procedural history that explain how the case arrived in this court. Omit any extraneous details; include enough to locate the reader in procedure unless your theory is a procedural one. If the theory is procedural, then you may construct the entire Statement of the Case around that procedure.

The Statement of Facts should include the legally significant facts, the background facts, and the significant emotional facts. The facts should be organized logically by topic, by chronology, or by a combination of both. They should tell your client's story in a way that will suggest to your reader a favorable outcome for your client, but they must be scrupulously accurate. For more on how to do this, see ACCURACY; and WRITING, PERSUASIVE. For more discussion of the content, see LEGALLY SIGNIFICANT FACTS, BACKGROUND FACTS, EMOTIONAL FACTS, and STATEMENT OF THE CASE. Facts should be cited to the record or to the pretrial documents as they exist at the time of filing the brief.

For related information on how to present the facts, see NARRATIVE WRITING; ORGANIZATION, CHRONOLOGICAL; ORGANIZATION, TOPICAL; and PARENTHETICALS.

4. Issues.

Issues, or Issue Statements, present the legal questions that, when answered, will determine the outcome of the case. Construct the Issues to show why your client should win both under the law and as a matter of justice. An Issue should include the rule of law applicable in this case, the legal question, and the legally significant facts.

While terminology varies among users, Issues in briefs differ from the Questions Presented in memos by point of view; the Issue is persuasive. It should be worded so that the subject and verb focus the judge on the precise question to be answered, and so the Issue suggests an outcome. For examples and more discussion, see ISSUES and, in rare situations, MULTI-SENTENCE ISSUES.

Many courts like to have the Issues presented first, although some prefer this section to follow the Statement of the Case. Check your jurisdiction's rules early in the writing process, because the placement of the Issue Statement in the document can create a need for changes in its wording. For related information, see QUESTIONS PRESENTED.

5. Argument.

The Argument explains how the law justifies your client's position and why the opposition's arguments should not prevail. Thus, unlike a memo's Discussion, which explores the opposition's arguments and evaluates them, an Argument seeks to shape the law and, by doing so, to preempt the opposition's points. To accomplish this persuasion, organize around your theory of the case. Although you explain why the opposition's points should not prevail, you do so as you argue your point. For more on this, see ARGUING IN THE ALTERNATIVE; ARGUMENT SECTION; COUNTERARGUMENTS, HOW TO HANDLE; LEGAL ANALYSIS, and THEORY OF THE CASE.

Although it has a different point of view, the Argument's content is similar to that of a memo. Like the Discussion in a memo, the Argument presents the general rules of law, any exceptions, and examples of previous applications of that law. The Argument applies that law to this case, often using a form that fuses all raw materials into a coherent whole. The general organization uses point headings and subheadings to outline salient legal points and reasoning. Thus the Argument, like a Discussion, can take organizational cues from the law, but presents the law from the perspective most favorable to the client. For more help here, see APPLICATION; ARGUMENT SECTION; LEGAL ANALYSIS; ORGANIZATION, LARGE-SCALE; ORGANIZATION, SMALL-SCALE; OUTLINES; and SYLLOGISMS. For more suggestions on how to build reasoning, see REASONING, ANALOGICAL; REASONING, INDUCTIVE; REASONING, DEDUCTIVE; REASONING, MODERN; REASONING, OTHER; REASONING, POSTMODERN; and REASONING, PRESENTING IT. For POLISHING details, see CITATIONS and FORMAT.

6. Conclusion.

The Conclusion should summarize briefly the reasoning presented in the Argument, focusing it into a cohesive and eloquent whole. It should also request specific relief. The court should know at a glance what result the writer asks for and why. Avoid the traditional *For the foregoing reasons.* This empty form forces the reader to either review the entire Argument Section or skip the point. Instead, use this last opportunity for a focused summary that delivers the final punch. For related information, see CONCLUSION and POSITIONS OF EMPHASIS.

BRIEFS, AMICUS

An amicus brief is a brief from a friend of the court, that is, someone other than one of the parties in a case. Generally, an amicus brief follows the same approach to persuasion as other briefs and requires the same writing considerations. In these briefs, however, you have more freedom to choose its emphasis because you are not a party. Be sure to check the rules in your jurisdiction for its requirements, because the format and length may be different from other briefs. For guidance, see BRIEFS; BRIEFS, APPELLATE; BRIEFS, REPLY; BRIEFS, TRIAL; and WRITING, PERSUASIVE.

Unlike the briefs from the parties in the case, an amicus brief is not obligatory reading for the court. As a result, you must especially consider ways to entice the judges to read the brief.

Begin preparing this document by focusing on the document's purpose, which is generally to help the court reach what you believe is the right decision. Thus, you can focus on one particular issue from a unique perspective, suggest an innovative approach to a doctrine of law, or clarify a confusing array of issues. For example, an environmental advocacy fund might write a brief to convince the court that a particular decision would benefit or harm the environment. A group of legal scholars might write one to outline potential long-term effects of changing a statute's traditional interpretation. Attorneys for a trade organization might write one to inform the court of standing practices within the trade and the effect a ruling would have on them. A state attorney general might write one to outline how a particular ruling would affect the state. These writers might also write an amicus brief, in part, as a way of strengthening their public profiles. Although any of these reasons may color the approach taken in an amicus brief, the reason must not move the brief outside the bounds of what is appropriate to the situation. The brief should be written to help the court reach its decision, not to provide a soapbox on which to stand.

As you organize and plan your brief, analyze your resources and the existing content. You may have access to the public record below and the parties' briefs, as filed. Note what the parties are covering and emphasizing and what needs clarification, emphasis, or added information. Consider next how to best help that particular court decide the issues, whether by providing additional information, offering a new interpretation, or suggesting specific outcomes.

Design according to the content and purpose you have chosen. For example, if you are emphasizing a particular issue, do not just echo what the parties have stated. Instead present the issue with the clarity of a nonparty perspective. Such an approach may require a different organization, a more elaborate legal foundation, or a reframing of the facts to show how this decision could affect future decisions. You may want to look retrospectively at this doctrine and show the court how this decision best fits with past and current law.

Use your opening paragraphs to seize the court's imagination and attention quickly and write so the Argument holds that attention. A concrete example, vivid image, or stunning statistic may serve your purpose better than a restatement of the parties' positions. But be careful about using such techniques as HUMOR, RHYME, or SARCASM. These techniques only fit a few situations, and they require a particularly deft touch; generally, it is safer to pursue other approaches. Whatever techniques you use, the brief must maintain a professional TONE that avoids sounding petulant, flippant, or intemperate. As always, a concise presentation of solid reasoning, captured in clear topic sentences, can keep the reader reading. For help in these areas, see CONCISENESS; EMPHASIS; IMAGERY; POSITIONS OF EMPHASIS; READABILITY; TOPIC SENTENCES; and WRITING, PERSUASIVE.

BRIEFS, APPELLATE

Writing excellent appellate briefs requires a special focus and consummate writing techniques. For this reason, many law offices have attorneys who specialize in this area. Specifically, these briefs need to be accurate in (1) identifying the standard of review, (2) focusing on the relevant issues, and (3) organizing persuasively. They should also (4) be revised to enhance persuasion, (5) be perfectly formatted, and (6) be submitted on time.

1. Identify the STANDARD OF REVIEW.

   Your first step in preparing the brief is to research the grounds for appellate review. As you do this, you will begin to frame your argument, narrowing it if the standard is strict or broadening it if the standard is more flexible. You will determine when a standard of review or conflicting standards present possible arguments for your client.

   You must organize around those arguments, which will likely differ from the arguments made at trial. This focus on the relevant appellate criteria is often lost, even by experienced legal writers, when faced with the reality of the client's plight. But to win on appeal, you must stay focused on the questions the appellate court will ask, not the desires of a disappointed client. Therefore, use the standard of review to establish your theory of the case. For more information, see ARTIFICIAL INTELLIGENCE AND RESEARCH, PROMPTS, RESEARCH STRATEGY GUIDE, STANDARD OF REVIEW, and THEORY OF THE CASE.

2. Focus the issues.

Unlike trial courts of general jurisdiction, appellate courts have more focused job descriptions. Courts of appeal are error-correcting courts. In each jurisdiction, courts of appeal review claims made by a party (usually the loser) in a previously tried case. State and federal supreme courts have a broader range of issues that they review; nevertheless, they grant petitioners the right to a hearing only for specific reasons.

Your first job in an appellate brief is to convince the court that your case falls into one of those categories. For example, you may claim that some decision of the trial judge was an *abuse of discretion*. You may also be required to show that this error was substantial, or affected the outcome of the case, to get the appellate court to take corrective action. You cannot ask an appellate court to review a case and set aside its result without meeting one of the allowable, specific criteria. For more information, see ISSUES.

3. Organize the argument persuasively.

After you have established your theory of the case and focused your appellate issues, organize your argument to match these. Gather all relevant components: standard of review, issue, facts, law, policy, equity, impact on future cases, and remedy desired. Then review your document's PURPOSE, AUDIENCE, and SCOPE. Experiment with different ways to emphasize your points and different arrangements of the components. Many combinations of these components will be technically correct, but only a few will combine the components to persuade with greatest effect. Your theory will help you select those few organizations that can work. For more on this, see ORGANIZING, HOW TO; OUTLINES; and THEORY OF THE CASE.

You may benefit from sketching out several different possible organizations, rather than settling on the first one that comes to mind. For example, if your theory is that police should not be allowed to get away with this behavior and the standard of review is *de novo*, then you may organize inductively, from the specific incidents to the general points, to demonstrate each police infraction. If your theory is that the trial court did everything well and your standard of review is abuse of discretion, you may organize deductively by first defining the general standard of abuse of discretion and then showing how this specific trial court's decision does not rise to that level. For more ideas on ways to construct your argument, see ARGUING IN THE ALTERNATIVE; ARGUMENT; COUNTERARGUMENTS, HOW TO HANDLE; LEGAL ANALYSIS; REASONING, ANALOGICAL; REASONING, DEDUCTIVE; REASONING, INDUCTIVE; REASONING, MODERN;

REASONING, OTHER; REASONING, POSTMODERN; REASONING, PRESENTING IT; and SYLLOGISMS.

4. Revise to enhance the argument's persuasiveness.

When you find the best arrangement of the components, you may feel a sudden sense of clarity, like the click of a combination lock reaching the final number that opens the lock. You can see the difference, the clarity of the thought, in the version that best fuses the theory and all its parts. At this point, you can turn your focus to the REVISING stage of the WRITING PROCESS. Convey your organization clearly by skillful use of POSITIONS OF EMPHASIS, POINT HEADINGS, and TOPIC SENTENCES. For further help with this, see CONNECTIONS, MAKING THEM; REASONING, PRESENTING IT; TRANSITIONS; and WRITING, PERSUASIVE.

5. Format according to the rules.

Appellate courts have specific rules about the format of appellate briefs. Read your local rules carefully, because most appellate courts will reject briefs that do not conform to their rules. For example, most courts require specific font and font size, margins, and page lengths. Be aware of these rules before you begin writing your appellate brief, so that you know the confines within which you must work. Also check to see whether you are expected to file electronically and confirm those formatting specifications. For help in filing electronically, see METADATA REMOVAL.

Appellate courts also require specific sections in their briefs. Generally, an appellate brief contains

- a TABLE OF CONTENTS that includes the point headings,
- a TABLE OF AUTHORITIES that includes references to specific pages where each authority is used,
- a STATEMENT OF THE CASE with specific references to the record,
- ISSUES,
- an ARGUMENT SECTION with POINT HEADINGS and subheadings, and
- a conclusion (see CONCLUSIONS).

For more information on format, also see BRIEFS.

6. Meet deadlines.

All may be lost if you miss a deadline in the appellate process, so you must plan scrupulously. Check the number of days you have for writing the brief and know how your jurisdiction counts those days.

Pay particular attention to how your jurisdiction counts weekends and holidays. Then mark the deadline on your calendar and count backward to schedule the segments of your WRITING PROCESS. Stay on schedule.

In your schedule, make sure you allow plenty of time at the end for refining the format. Allow enough time so you will be sure to meet your deadline. Do not count on everything going smoothly, because it seldom does. For related information, see DEADLINES, MEETING THEM; and TIME MANAGEMENT.

BRIEFS, BENCH

See BENCH MEMOS.

BRIEFS, CASE

See CASE BRIEFS.

BRIEFS, PRETRIAL

A pretrial brief is any brief written in support of or opposition to a pretrial motion. A pretrial brief uses persuasive writing to inform the reader of the relevant law and to persuade the reader to accept the client's position. It is usually filed with the Notice of Motion and Motion or shortly thereafter. For related information, see MEMORANDUM OF POINTS AND AUTHORITIES, NOTICE OF MOTION, and MOTIONS.

Check your jurisdiction for the particular format requirements. See BRIEFS for a sample format. For persuasive techniques to use, see ARGUING IN THE ALTERNATIVE; ARGUMENT SECTION; COUNTERARGUMENTS, HOW TO HANDLE; REASONING entries; and WRITING, PERSUASIVE. For ways to check the document, see DOCUMENT CHECKLIST.

BRIEFS, REPLY

A reply brief is a short brief filed after both the moving party and the responding party have filed their initial briefs. The responding party may have raised different issues or presented different arguments, so the moving party may file a brief to reply to those new points. Similarly, the responding party may reply to the moving party's reply. Before writing, check the rules in your jurisdiction for the requirements, because the reply brief format and length may differ from other briefs. Generally, a reply brief follows the same approach to persuasion and requires the same writing considerations as any other persuasive document. For guidance, see BRIEFS; BRIEFS, APPELLATE; BRIEFS, TRIAL; and WRITING, PERSUASIVE.

The operative word here is *reply*. A reply brief does not repeat the information or arguments in the initial briefs. The court has those; it does not need to reread that information. Instead, the court wants to see further information or explanation on new points raised by either the parties or the court itself. Thus a reply brief may respond to a new issue with a newly formed argument based on new law, or it may further explain law already cited.

Strategically, you, as the moving party, may wish not to address a particular issue in detail or at all in your initial brief because it is not relevant under your theory of the case. However, the opposing party's theory of the case may emphasize that issue. If so, plan to address that issue in a reply brief and show why it is irrelevant or, in the alternative, nondispositive. See ARGUING IN THE ALTERNATIVE; CONDITIONS, STATING THEM; and COUNTERARGUMENTS, HOW TO HANDLE. For related information, see THEME and THEORY OF THE CASE.

Anticipate writing a reply brief when preparing your initial brief to the court. After you have decided on your theory of the case, decide how you will parcel out your legal arguments. Everything may go into the initial brief, but some things may be better omitted or addressed later and only if they are raised. If you have decided to omit some issues initially, then design the reply brief to include them; do not simply recopy your brief's Argument. For example, if you are responding to a new issue, design the reply brief to refer to your theory and how the other party's argument fits, or does not fit, with your theory. Then address the new issue, perhaps by dismissing it. Alternatively, if you are asked to write more on an issue already covered, remind the court of the basic premises but distill those premises and focus on the new, more detailed explanation of the point.

In summary, use the same persuasive techniques as in any other brief, but concentrate on brevity and clarification. For help in these areas, see CONCISENESS; EMPHASIS; IMAGERY; POSITIONS OF EMPHASIS; READABILITY; TOPIC SENTENCES; and WRITING, PERSUASIVE. Be careful that you do not move into SARCASM by implying an *I already said* attitude. Keep the reply helpful, focused, and consistent with your theory of the case. For ways to check the document, see DOCUMENT CHECKLIST.

BRIEFS, TRIAL

Trial briefs are persuasive documents that attorneys often file with the court before a trial begins. They inform the trial court of counsel's theory of the case by presenting the facts, issues, applicable rules, and arguments in a way that is factually accurate while still conveying a sense that your client's position is just. A trial brief needs to convince the court not only that a fair reading of the law supports your client's position, but also that supporting your client's position is something the court wants to do.

A trial brief should indicate what is to be proved, how it is to be proved, and what the outcome of the case should be. Each side files a trial brief so that the court has an idea of the structure of the trial before it begins. Except under extraordinary circumstances, both sides exchange trial briefs.

As you prepare a trial brief, consider your range of readers; if possible, check with someone who knows the judge. For information about questions to consider on this point, see READERS and AUDIENCE. Also always check your jurisdiction for the specific requirements for format of a trial brief.

Much thought and preparation must go into a trial brief, so the various parts of the trial brief each have their own entries. For details about writing a trial brief, see ARGUMENT SECTION, CONCLUSION, ISSUES, POINT HEADINGS, STATEMENT OF THE CASE, and THEORY OF THE CASE. For ways to handle difficult arguments, see ARGUING IN THE ALTERNATIVE; and COUNTERARGUMENTS, HOW TO HANDLE. Also see the general topics that are especially important in writing trial briefs: AUDIENCE; CITATIONS; FORMAT; READERS; REASONING, ANALOGICAL; REASONING, DEDUCTIVE; REASONING, INDUCTIVE; REASONING, MODERN; REASONING, OTHER; REASONING, POSTMODERN; REASONING, PRESENTING IT; and SYLLOGISMS. For the usual format for a trial brief, see BRIEFS. For ways to check the brief, see DOCUMENT CHECKLIST. If you are using artificial intelligence, see ARTIFICAL INTELLIGENCE AND RESEARCH, ARTIFICIAL INTELLIGENCE AND WRITING, PROMPTS, and RESEARCH STRATEGY GUIDE.

BULLET POINTS

A bullet point, a large, centered dot placed before a line of text, can be useful to mark the division of points when their order and significance are interchangeable.

> **This new will includes the three changes you requested, as we discussed at our last meeting:**
>
> - **a provision for minor grandchildren's college education,**
> - **a designation of alternate personal representatives, and**
> - **a special bequest to Middleton College.**

As with any graphic tool, however, avoid using this solely because it looks nice; use it instead to clarify your meaning without distracting from it. If the sequence of points is significant, use ENUMERATION. If the order moves from most to least important, consider saying so in your introductory sentence. Also avoid overusing this or any particular graphic device. For more on the effective use of graphic aids, see GRAPHICS, HOW TO USE, subsection 3. For related information, see LISTS, STRUCTURE OF.

BUSINESS EMAIL OR LETTERS

See COMMUNICATIONS, CLOSINGS FOR; COMMUNICATIONS, ELECTRONIC; COMMUNICATIONS, INTERNATIONAL; COMMUNICATIONS, OPENINGS FOR; COMMUNICATIONS, PERSUASIVE; COMMUNICATIONS, TONE OF; EMAIL; PROFESSIONAL LANGUAGE AND PRESENTATION; SOCIAL MEDIA; WRITING TO ATTORNEYS; and WRITING TO CLIENTS.

BUT

But is a powerful conjunction that can mean any of the following: (1) *on the contrary*, (2) *however*, (3) *except that*, or (4) *other than*. Use it in legal writing to make a strong distinction between ideas. Because *but* is strong, be careful not to overuse it.

The client has a case for an appeal, but failed to file the notice of appeal on time.

They should have objected, but neither they nor the court noticed the objectionable grounds in time.

But can also be effective to begin a sentence if you want to emphasize the logical connection between two sentences.

No moral right as such exists in America. No state has passed a moral right law. But Congress has made several attempts to add the moral right to Title 17.

For related general information, see CONJUNCTIONS; CONNECTIONS, MAKING THEM; and TRANSITIONS. For the use of *but* to begin a sentence, see POSITIONS OF EMPHASIS.

CAN

Use *can* as an auxiliary word when you want to suggest capacity.

The plaintiff can anticipate such misuses of their product; ample cases of misuse of similar cutting tools exist.

For more information, see *CAN* OR *MAY*? and VERBS, AUXILIARY, subsection 4.

CAN HARDLY OR *CAN'T HARDLY*?

Can hardly is correct. *Can't hardly* is not. In legal writing, it is often better to replace *can hardly* with some other phrase, like *can scarcely* or *can barely*. *Can hardly* is used loosely and frequently in speech, and as a result sounds rather informal.

CANNOT OR *CAN NOT*?

Cannot is the correct form in almost all cases.

I cannot represent you in this case.

Can not appears only when *not* is part of another phrase.

He can not only request a new hearing but also require a change of venue.

CANONS OF CONSTRUCTION

Canons of construction are customs developed in the common law for interpreting statutes. These canons form a backdrop for understanding the reasoning courts may use in construing statutes. The canons are also available to lawyers for suggesting ways to interpret statutes, but no jurisdiction has formally required them. The canons may be most helpful in reading or in prewriting as ways to understand how a statute can work. For example, a common canon suggests that statutes should be construed according to the plain meaning of their texts. Another suggests that the same terms should be construed in the same way throughout the statute. Yet another suggests that grammar and punctuation should be construed according to strict rules. But courts will commonly disregard these canons, stating that such interpretations should be ignored when they reach absurd results or open the statute to several interpretations. Thus, like *STARE DECISIS*, canons of construction describe ways to interpret the law, but they do not substitute for LEGAL ANALYSIS.

CAN OR *COULD*?

See VERBS, AUXILIARY, subsections 2 and 4.

CAN OR *MAY*?

Use *can* when you mean that the subject is able to do something.

The plaintiff can still lift packages weighing up to thirty pounds.

Use *may* when you mean that the subject has permission to do something.

The police may search the glove compartment without first obtaining a search warrant if....

For more information, see *MAY*; and VERBS, AUXILIARY, subsections 4 and 6.

CAPITALIZATION

Capitalization issues arise in five places: (1) with proper adjectives; (2) with titles of officials, courts, and organizations; (3) with the first word after a colon; (4) with common nouns used to refer to specific people or groups; and (5) with subheadings. Over time, capitalization is being used less in newspapers, books, and other printed matter, so you may see examples where capital letters are not used as much as in legal writing.

1. Proper adjectives.

Capitalize most proper adjectives, which are adjectives formed from proper nouns, such as *American banking system, the Atlantic seaboard,* or *Syrian refugees.* Do not capitalize an adjective, however, when it has been used frequently and for a long time in the general language, such as *cesarean operation, india ink, italic type, murphy bed,* or *venetian blinds.* For an extensive list of adjectives derived from proper names, see the most recent edition of the *U.S. Government Printing Office Style Manual.*

When addressing a person by a title that includes an adjective, capitalize the adjective.

Your Honor, Madam Chairman

2. Titles of officials, courts, and organizations.

Capitalize a title, such as *judge* or *justice,* only when it precedes the judge's or justice's name or when it replaces the name.

Only Justice Brennan wrote a concurring opinion.

Thank you, Judge, for your advice.

but

The judge signed the search warrant at 3:00 a.m.

You can also capitalize *court* when you are referring to the judge reading the document or to the U.S. Supreme Court, to show respect. Do not capitalize *court* when you are referring to a different court that decided another case. Different jurisdictions vary, however, so always check for local practice.

This Court has upheld this principle three times.

but

There, the trial court ruled in favor of the defendant.

For related information, see JUDGES, HOW TO ADDRESS.

3. The first word after a colon.

In general, do not capitalize the first word after the colon, because doing so usually makes the sentence self-consciously ornate, like a person wearing a tiara to a picnic.

Only two people will inherit the bulk of the estate: his ex-wife and her son.

Capitalize the first word after the colon only to emphasize that word or phrase.

Plaintiff asks the court to invoke the most severe penalty: Child abuse must be stopped.

For an explanation of when to use colons, see COLONS.

4. Common nouns used to refer to specific people or groups.

Making this distinction takes a little thought. For example, you would capitalize *Elk* in *He was an Elk*, because the word refers to a specific person and organization, rather than to generic elk grazing on the ranges of Montana. Similarly, write *The Representative spoke at length to us,* because the term *Representative* replaces the person's name, and thus refers to a specific person.

This rule is also why you capitalize *Plaintiff* and *Defendant* when they are used in a litigation document in place of the name of the party. In this use, the words are often used without *the.*

Plaintiff objected to Defendant's request for tax records.

But do not capitalize these terms when referring to a plaintiff or defendant in any other case.

A court denied the defendant's request for tax records when the information they contained was irrelevant. <u>Hasbro v. Connoly</u>, 599 N.W.2d 444 (2025). In <u>Hasbro</u>, the plaintiff objected to defendant's request for tax records from 2020–2023 because the alleged fraud occurred well after that time period. <u>Id.</u> at 448.

Capitalize *Constitution* only when naming any constitution in full, as in *Constitution of the State of Iowa*, or when referring to the *United States Constitution.* Also capitalize parts of the U.S. Constitution when referring to them in text.

Fourth Amendment Article I, Section 8 Preamble

But do not capitalize these terms in CITATIONS.

5. Subheadings.

In subheadings, capitalize the initial word and all other substantive words; do not, however, capitalize CONJUNCTIONS or PREPOSITIONS of four or fewer letters. Also do not capitalize *a*, *an*, or *the* unless it is the first word in the heading. One common exception to this is in POINT HEADINGS, where often a specific court will require you to capitalize every word, even conjunctions, prepositions, and articles. See *AMENDMENT* CAPITALIZED?

CAPTIONS

Captions appear at the beginning of intraoffice memos and emails, and all legal documents filed with the court. Captions in court documents identify the parties to the dispute, the type of document, and the purpose of the document. Although the caption may seem to be a troublesome formality, it is a detail that is important for your organization's filing system and to the court record system. Documents with errors in the captions can get misfiled, which can cause all sorts of problems that occasionally defy logic and reason and are therefore hard to fix. Each document has its own specific format and requirements for the caption.

1. Intraoffice memos and emails.

In intraoffice memos, captions should identify to whom the memo is addressed, who wrote the memo, what the subject matter of the memo is, and what the date is. Check the specific requirements of your office for captions because these can vary a good deal. A typical memo caption follows.

MEMO

To: **Fred P. Jones**

From: **Emily Barnett**

Re: **Krugman, file no. 25–6709; possible motion to suppress identification evidence**

Date: **March 27, 2025**

In intraoffice emails, most of this information appears automatically in the email's format. Nevertheless, remember to include sufficient information in the subject line of the message and add any further needed information in the opening sentence of the email itself to orient your reader specifically in this matter. For related information, see COMMUNICATIONS, ELECTRONIC; and MEMOS.

2. Pretrial and trial documents.

The caption for a pretrial or trial document filed with a court usually identifies the court; the parties; the status of the parties, such as *plaintiffs*, *defendants*, *respondents*, or *appellants*; the file number of the case, which will remain the same for every document; and the title of the brief. Always check your jurisdiction for its conventions in doing a pretrial brief caption. For related information, see BRIEFS entries. Many courts will not accept a document for filing if its caption does not conform to that court's rules. A typical caption follows.

IN THE SUPERIOR COURT OF THE STATE OF WASHINGTON FOR KING COUNTY

STATE OF WASHINGTON,	)	
ABRAM AND SARAH GOLD,	)	**NO. 25-3-11658-6**
Plaintiffs,	)	**BRIEF IN SUPPORT OF**
	)	**MOTION**
vs.	)	**TO SUPPRESS**
	)	**IDENTIFICATION**
SIDNEY KRUGMAN,	)	**EVIDENCE**
Defendant.	)	

3. Appellate briefs.

Check your jurisdiction for your specific requirements for the caption of an appellate brief. A typical one follows.

NO. 25-1-01248-5

COURT OF APPEALS, DIVISION II OF THE STATE OF WASHINGTON

STATE OF WASHINGTON,

Appellant,

v.

MITCHELL WAYNE JOHNSON,

Respondent.

APPEAL FROM THE SUPERIOR COURT FOR PIERCE COUNTY

The Honorable Robert H. Peterson, Judge

BRIEF OF APPELLANT STATE OF WASHINGTON

Marilyn F. Corning
Attorney for Respondent
123 Broadway Avenue
Suite 500
Spokane, WA 99201
(505) 555–2222

CASE

To avoid confusion, use *case* only as a term of art when literally referring to a case. For example, instead of *in case of*, use *if*; instead of *in many cases*, use *often*; instead of *that is not the case*, use *that is not the situation*. For related, general information, see TERMS OF ART.

CASE BRIEFS

When briefing cases, consider first the reason for which you are briefing, whether it is for class, for research, or for some other purpose. Then tailor your format to that purpose. Many possibilities exist, ranging from full, formal briefs that find a place for every detail of the case to book briefing, where comments are made in the margins of your casebook. Whatever your system, make sure it works for you.

From the following list and other sources, collect the suggestions that you like to create your own system. Using someone else's system, no matter how comprehensive, will not work unless it makes sense to you.

1. Case briefing for class.

    Brief for classes by focusing on the topic outlined by your professor or referred to in your casebook's table of contents. Then make sure that the issue and HOLDINGS that you articulate in your brief focus on that topic. For example, if the topic is intentional torts, make sure that you frame the issue around some aspect of an intentional tort. Also make sure the holding responds to that issue. If you know that your professor always asks particular questions about the cases in class, add notes for responding to those questions. For related information, see QUESTIONS PRESENTED.

    As you progress through a course and through law school, allow your briefing process to evolve. You will probably see a good deal of change as you gain understanding and build efficiency.

2. Case briefing for research.

Tailor your case brief in research to the project's issues, outlined in Step 3 of the RESEARCH STRATEGY GUIDE. Then brief the case for its purpose in that context and omit information irrelevant to that purpose. For example, if you are researching the question of mistake in formation of the contract, brief the case for what it says about mistake; do not go into the details of any irrelevant procedural questions.

There is one exception to this. You may include some other details, such as reversal based on a procedural issue, when the result of the case being briefed differs from the result you want in your factual situation but you still want to use the case to support your client's position.

3. Format.

Whatever your format, make sure it fulfills your purpose. Consider the following checklist of possible components of your case brief, selecting from it to create a briefing format that works for you.

(a) Citation.

Make sure you put down the complete citation of the case in proper form here; this will save you time later. Use the format you will use in your final document.

(b) Parties.

Include all parties to the suit and their status, such as *plaintiff-respondent-victim* or *defendant-appellant-tortfeasor*.

(c) Prior Proceedings.

Include any relevant procedural history here, such as *trial court found for the defendant; defendant appealed, court of appeals reversed the trial court's decision; and now this appeal is before the supreme court*.

(d) Objectives.

Consider here the objectives of the parties and write them in your own words, such as *getting specific performance: the client wants the goods themselves,* or *getting damages (all $55,000),* or *getting acquitted*.

(e) Theories of the Parties.

Include here the legal doctrine under which the plaintiff or appellant is bringing the case, such as *false imprisonment* or *breach of contract,* and any defenses the defendant might be raising, such as *consent* or *lack of consideration*. This section will usually include at least one TERM OF ART, which may become important in your further research and your writing on the topic.

Try to translate those terms into sentences that represent each party's THEORY OF THE CASE. These one-sentence statements are the thesis statements that combine the doctrine with the party's reason for winning, such as the following.

> **Defendant claims Plaintiff was not falsely imprisoned because she consented to ride in the vehicle.**
>
> or
>
> **Plaintiff claims Defendant breached the contract because of the lack of consideration when Defendant failed to pay for the goods.**

(f) Facts.

List here all LEGALLY SIGNIFICANT FACTS and any BACKGROUND FACTS necessary to your own understanding of the case. Also note any facts that you think will play an important role in differentiating this case from other relevant ones.

(g) Issue.

State the issue in terms of your purpose in reading the brief. Be as specific as you can with respect to that issue. See QUESTIONS PRESENTED and ISSUES.

> **Did defendant Curtis falsely imprison plaintiff Butterworth when he drove around in the car for seven hours without stopping to let her out?**

(h) Holding.

> Answer the issue and give a reason here. See HOLDINGS.
>
> **Yes; Curtis falsely imprisoned Butterworth because he used words and acts intended to confine Butterworth, he actually confined her in the car, and Butterworth was aware that she was confined without her consent.**

(i) Reasoning.

This is probably the most important part of the case brief because it exposes the court's reasons for reaching the holding. By deciphering the reasoning, you can determine how strong or weak the case is, how it can be compared to or distinguished from your case, how outdated or forward-looking the decision is, where it fits in the history of your issue, and so on. This section includes relevant RULES, the APPLICATION of those rules, and the conclusion the court reached. To expose the reasoning, you may want to try stating it in terms of a syllogism: the rule is the major premise, the application is the minor premise, and the conclusion is the logical result. For example, you might first state the entire rule of false imprisonment in your jurisdiction. Then you might show how the court applied that rule to the specific facts of this case; take it step by step so that any holes in the reasoning become clear. Finally, show how the court reached its conclusion. For related information, see REASONING, ANALOGICAL; REASONING, DEDUCTIVE; REASONING, INDUCTIVE; REASONING, MODERN; REASONING, OTHER; REASONING, POSTMODERN; REASONING, PRESENTING IT; and SYLLOGISMS.

(j) Dicta.

In an opinion, *dicta,* which means *words,* is anything a court says that does not have a direct effect on the outcome of the case. Dicta differs from a holding in that dicta is not binding on courts in subsequent opinions. Dicta can be significant, however, in your use of a case in research or in class. Use dicta to predict a trend in the law, to illuminate the reasoning in this case, or to understand future cases. For further discussion, see DICTA.

(k) Comments.

Write here any reaction you have to the case. This may become important when you continue your research or when you are asked in class to give your opinion of the case. Include your gut reaction and any other response you have that synthesizes this case with other cases in the chapter, with other cases in your research project, or with your own understanding of the trend of the law in this particular area. When briefing for class, ask yourself, *Why did the textbook author choose this case? Why is it here?* Answer those questions here.

CASE NAMES, UNDERLINE OR ITALICIZE?

Check first with your primary readers to learn their preferences in presenting case names and then conform to those preferences when deciding what typeface or marking is required. The *BLUEBOOK,* for example, uses italics in scholarly writing and underlining in memos and briefs. When using italics or underlining, include the *v.* and any procedural phrases, such as *in re* and *ex parte,* and include the spaces between the underlined words but not the comma that follows the case name.

***Spann v. Vladeck et al.*, 999 U.S. 101 (2025).**

Spann v. Vladeck et al., 999 U.S. 101 (2025).

Avoid using case names as the subject of a sentence or as an adjective, because the legal reader will expect the case name to begin a citation. Also avoid using full case citations in a sentence. When using just the case name in a sentence, use it in a prepositional phrase and identify the case by using the same script you are using for the full citations, either italics or underlining.

The court in *Spann v. Vladeck* hesitated to go further . . . .

or

While the judge in Spann v. *Vladeck* hesitated to go further . . . .

rather than

The *Spann* court hesitated to go further . . . .

When determining how and when to use abbreviations in the case name, consult the citation guide used in your jurisdiction. These rules are complex, and you may want to tab frequently used references in your manual or keep a separate log of answers that you need to consult frequently. See *ALWD GUIDE TO LEGAL CITATION* and *BLUEBOOK.*

For related information, see CITATIONS entries; FOOTNOTES; ITALICS; and QUOTATIONS, HOW TO PUNCTUATE.

CASUAL LANGUAGE

See COLLOQUIALISM.

C.E. OR *A.D.*?

See *A.D.* OR *C.E.*?

CERTAIN OR *CERTAINLY*?

Use *certain* or *certainly* only if your point is literally certain. Because few points you make in legal writing are indeed certain, beware of frequent use of the word. For a discussion of related concerns, see LITERAL MEANING and MODIFIERS.

CHARTS

Charts can be useful to summarize a mass of detailed data or to communicate its significance. But the points a chart supports should also be stated explicitly in the text; this helps you ensure that your point is communicated to everyone in your AUDIENCE, whether they study graphics or skip them. For more information, see GRAPHICS, WHICH FORM TO USE.

CHOICES IN LEGAL WRITING

You have them. What makes your analysis and writing effective are your intelligent choices among many options as you move through the writing process.

Develop your awareness and use of these choices over your career. Do not be distracted by format. Instead, note the different ways in which writers present what is within each part of the format. Like sonnet writing, legal writing requires you to make creative choices within certain structures. Over time, develop your repertoire of choices.

In PREWRITING, you can select among many relevant sources, forms, theories, arguments, and analytical patterns. For related information, see DESIGN, LEGAL ANALYSIS, RULES, and THEORY OF THE CASE. You can also choose different ways to convey your THEME and logic by choosing from a number of reasoning patterns. For example, see REASONING, ANALOGICAL; REASONING, DEDUCTIVE; REASONING, INDUCTIVE; REASONING, MODERN; REASONING, OTHER; REASONING, POSTMODERN; and REASONING, PRESENTING IT.

In REWRITING, you can rearrange your presentation and add or subtract components. For help with this, see COUNTERARGUMENTS, HOW TO HANDLE; ORGANIZATION, LARGE-SCALE; ORGANIZATION, SMALL-SCALE; PARAGRAPH BLOCKS; and TOPIC SENTENCES.

In REVISING, you can alter paragraphs, sentences, and word choice to create the tone and emphasis you want. See CONNECTIONS, MAKING THEM; SENTENCE STRUCTURE; TONE; and WRITING, PERSUASIVE.

You also have a choice about when and whether to use artificial intelligence as part of your WRITING PROCESS. For help on this, see ARTIFICIAL INTELLIGENCE AND RESEARCH, ARTIFICIAL INTELLIGENCE AND WRITING, and PROMPTS.

CHRONOLOGICAL ORGANIZATION

See ORGANIZATION, CHRONOLOGICAL.

CIRCUMLOCUTION

See CONCISENESS, subsection 2.

CITATIONS

The traditional text for citations is *The Bluebook: A Uniform System of Citation*. Some jurisdictions have adopted the *ALWD Guide to Legal*

Citation. Whatever source they use, most jurisdictions also make some adjustments to these standard citation rules. If your jurisdiction has its own style manual or has otherwise established exceptions to the *Bluebook* or *ALWD* rules, follow those exceptions in all documents filed with courts in that jurisdiction. Whatever rules you follow, be sure to insert citations whenever they are needed and use them properly to assist your reader. For more information, see *ALWD GUIDE TO LEGAL CITATION* and *BLUEBOOK*.

1. When to use citations.

Citations serve two functions: (a) to provide the reader with a specific authority within the text and (b) to replace long explanations of how that authority is used. That use may be, for example, as a quotation, rule, related authority, or an authority that states the contrary of the proposition. Such a specific use is usually signaled at the start of a citation. Correct use of citations and signals both establishes your credibility as a careful analyst and streamlines your legal writing style.

Use citations and signals to make the reader aware of your precise use of authority. For example, using no signal indicates that the cited authority clearly states the proposition, identifies the source of a quotation, or identifies an authority referred to in the text. For further reference, see your specific citation manual and CITATIONS, SIGNALS.

2. How to use citations.

(a) Use citations as separate sentences following a proposition; avoid using a citation at the beginning of a sentence.

A contract can provide some protection for an artist's moral rights. Young v. Taylor, 999, 1003 F.3d 999 (9th Cir. 2025).

rather than

Young v. Taylor, 999 F.3d 999, 1003 (9th Cir. 2025), states that a contract can provide some protection for an artist's moral rights.

A citation stops the reader's eye before the substance of the statement is clear. If it is necessary to cite support for the first proposition in a sentence, you may use a citation as a clause mid-sentence.

While a contract can provide some protection for an artist's moral rights, Young v. Taylor, 999 F.3d 999, 1003 (9th Cir. 2025), no single contract can cover the entire scope of those rights.

This use does not stop the reader as much as placing a citation before the proposition being cited, but it is still less than ideal. For this reason, use this structure only when it would be inaccurate to place the citation at the end. For related information, see INTRUSIVE PHRASES.

(b) Eliminate text that repeats information given in the citation, such as *The court stated that* or *The court went on to say that* or *Another case stated the opposing view*. Such repetitive, descriptive phrases move the important information to a subordinate clause, which deemphasizes the point you are trying to make.

(c) Use short citation forms when citing to immediately preceding authority. If the previous citation is a page or two back, use the full citation, so the reader does not have to backtrack too far.

(d) Give pinpoint citations when referring to any rules, holdings, quotations, specific propositions, or particulars of an authority. See CITATIONS, PINPOINT.

Reason v. Pearson, 999 U.S. 977, 979 (2025).

(e) Observe correct spacing. Put spaces after abbreviations that include both capital and lower-case letters.

33 Wis. 2d 987.

or

222 F. Supp. 3d 346.

Do not insert spaces when the abbreviation is only one or more capital letters. Ordinal numbers (2d, 3d, 4th) are treated as single capital letters.

345 N.W.2d 31.

or

486 P.2d 692.

Check your citation manual and your jurisdiction's rules for its variations on these formats. For related information, see CITATIONS, BASIC FORMATS; CITATIONS, ELECTRONIC; CITATIONS, PARALLEL; CITATIONS, PINPOINT; and CITATIONS, STRING.

CITATIONS, BASIC FORMATS

Check your citation manual for the basic format used by your readers. Some jurisdictions have developed their own variations on the *BLUEBOOK* or *ALWD GUIDE TO LEGAL CITATION*, so be sure to adjust accordingly. What follows are the basic *Bluebook* formats.

Constitution citations include (1) the name of the constitution, (2) the article number, (3) the section number, and (4) the clause number.

U.S. Const. art. I, § 8, cl. 3.

Statute citations generally include (1) the name of the act, if any; (2) the abbreviated name of the code; (3) the numbers that identify the statute; and, in state statutes, (4) the year of the code.

Freedom of Information Act, 5 U.S.C. § 552.

Haw. Rev. Stat. § 567–999 (2025).

Case citations generally include (1) the name of the case; (2) the volume, standard abbreviation for the book, and page number where the case begins in the book; (3) the parallel citation, if required by the jurisdiction's rules; and (4) the year of the decision. The reader should also be able to determine from the citation what court decided the case. Thus, if the name of the court is not evident from the abbreviation of the book, then indicate (5) the court by putting its abbreviation before the date inside the parentheses.

Leraas v. Martin, 999 U.S. 723 (2025).

but

Johnson v. Strus, 999 P.3d 387 (Alaska 2025).

Here, for example, because the Alaska Supreme Court does not have an official reporter, the official reporter for that state's decisions is the Pacific Reporter. Because the Pacific Reporter includes cases from several jurisdictions, the reader would not know what court decided the case unless *Alaska* was put in the parentheses with the date. Similarly, for federal district court decisions and federal circuit court decisions, the court must be indicated inside the parentheses with the date.

Knight v. Skover, 999 F. Supp. 3d 287 (S.D. Iowa 2025).

CITATIONS, ELECTRONIC

You may cite electronic sources when no print source is available or when your reader prefers or expects the electronic citation. Check with your readers to ascertain the expected format.

When citing cases electronically, follow the same general rules used in other citations, giving the (1) case name, (2) docket number, (3) database identifier, (4) court name, and (5) full date of the most recent major disposition of the case. Cite to the case docket number exactly as it appears. If the database contains codes or numbers that uniquely identify the case, include these. Screen or page numbers, if the database assigns them, should be preceded by an asterisk; paragraph numbers, if assigned, should be preceded by a paragraph symbol.

Gau v. Mihalchan, No. 09-6341, 2025 U.S. App. LEXIS 45903, at *21–22 (2d Cir. Oct. 30, 2025).

Arnold v. Metro Dist. Comm'n, No. 9:04CV861(MRK), 2025 U.S. Dist. LEXIS 45297, at *9 n.4 (D. Conn. June 1, 2025).

Demp v. Ash, No. 57628-7, 2025 WA 0365781, ¶ 42 (Wash. Jan. 31, 2025) (VersusLaw).

When citing statutes, follow the same general rules, giving (1) the name of the act, if any; (2) the abbreviated name of the code; (3) the numbers that identify the statute; and (4) the name of the database and information regarding how current the database is, as provided by the database itself. Also, if the code was not published, edited, or compiled by or under the supervision of federal or state officials, give (5) the name of the publisher, editor, or compiler.

18 U.S.C.S. § 1956 (LEXIS through Pub. L. No. 113–108).

Wis. Stat. § 19.43 (Loislaw through 2024–2025 Legis. Sess.).

Wis. Stat. Ann. § 19.43 (West, Westlaw through 2025 Act 26).

CITATIONS, PARALLEL

All United States Supreme Court cases, most state cases, and some federal cases appear in more than one book. Thus a case may have more than one citation, and those are called *parallel citations*.

The United States Supreme Court and most other courts have one official reporter, which is that jurisdiction's authoritative text. For example, the United States Supreme Court's official reporter is abbreviated *U.S.* Your citation manual may require you to cite to that official reporter but not to the parallel citations in the unofficial reporters. For state cases, your citation manual or local rules may require parallel citations to unofficial reporters in certain circumstances. Or you may want to include parallel citations as a courtesy to your reader. When including parallel citations, list the official reporter first.

Fischer v. Doerr, 437 U.S. 893 (2025).

but

Lamb v. Laffon, 145 Ariz. 212, 700 P.3d 1312 (2025).

Check your citation manual or your local rules for specific directions regarding which reporters to cite in parallel citations for each state. When using pinpoint citations, include the specific page number for the parallel citation as well. See CITATIONS, PINPOINT.

CITATIONS, PINPOINT

Pinpoint citations tell the reader exactly where cited information, such as a quotation, holding, or rule, is found in an authority. Depending on the source, pinpoint citations are to the exact page, line, section, or paragraph where the cited information is located. Use pinpoint citations to show your reader the exact source of important points. Pinpoint citations are used more frequently than general citations because most citations refer to quotations, propositions, holdings, or rules. If required to use parallel pinpoint citations, indicate a specific page for both the official reporter and the unofficial reporter or reporters.

In custody disputes, the appellate court will reverse the trial court only where there is an abuse of discretion. In re Marriage of Smith, 99 Wash. 2d 369, 371, 999 P.2d 43, 44 (2025).

and

When there are no exigent circumstances, police must obtain a search warrant before searching the premises. Id. at 486, 999 P.2d at 58.

CITATIONS, SIGNALS

Signals are used before CITATIONS as a substantive shorthand to indicate the citation's relationship to the text. As such, signals replace unnecessary text, such as *the court held that* or *another court also agreed that*. Check your citation manual for the current list of signals and what they mean.

While signals can assist scholars reading scores of footnotes, they can hinder readers of memos and briefs when they become too compact and unreadable. In analytical and persuasive documents, move important information into sentences with TERMS OF ART in the subjects and verbs and use signals sparingly to indicate the significance of the authority from which the concepts are derived, as in the first sample below. When so many signals replace text, as in the second example, the reader may skip the entire paragraph.

Any person who violates any of the rights of the artist as provided in section 106A(a) infringes the rights of the artist. 17 U.S.C. § 5908(a). A person is entitled to obtain all the civil remedies granted under the Copyright Act of 2024 when his rights of attribution and integrity have been infringed. See § 5902(q). For example, an artist was entitled to pursue an award for both an injunction and damages when his painting was attributed to another artist. Martinez, 473 F. Supp. 3d at 922. The remedies for

infringement of an artist's rights of attribution and integrity do include injunctions as well as damages, 17 U.S.C. §§ 5908–5909, costs, and attorneys' fees, id. §§ 5411–5412. But an injunction may be the only practical remedy for artists' rights violations of attribution. 41 Nimmer on Copyright § 224.45 n.9 (2025).

rather than

Any person who violates any of the rights of the artist as provided in section 106A(a) infringes the rights of the artist. 17 U.S.C. § 5908(a). The court held that a person is entitled to obtain all the civil remedies granted under the Copyright Act of 2024 when his rights of attribution and integrity have been infringed. See § 5902(q); see also Martinez, 473 F. Supp. 3d at 922. Remedies for infringement of artist's rights of attribution and integrity include injunctions as well as damages, 17 U.S.C. §§ 5908–5909, costs, and attorneys' fees, id. §§ 5411–5412; contra 41 Nimmer on Copyright § 224.45 n.9 (2025) (stating that "it is arguable that injunction is the only remedy for artists' rights violations of the attribution variety").

See your citation manual for current guidelines on using signals. For related information, see CITATIONS; CITATIONS, STRING; FOOTNOTES; and SCHOLARLY WRITING.

CITATIONS, STRING

String citations include citations to two or more authorities for the same point. Semicolons separate the individual citations in a string citation, and the authorities are cited in order of strength, jurisdiction, or year, depending on the context. Follow each citation within the string with a parenthetical explaining its relevance to the point. For example, the following string citations could be used in a document filed in an Arkansas court.

Arkansas has uniformly applied the rule of awarding children to the parent who can serve their best interests. Lorey v. Jacobi, 99 Ark. 111, 119, 222 S.W.3d 22, 28 (2023) (holding that mother should be awarded custody of 8-year-old son when father cannot support the son); Zuckerman v. Kidwell, 100 Ark. 841, 850, 224 S.W.3d 444, 448 (2024) (holding that mother should be awarded custody of 10-year-old daughter and 3-year-old son when father has been absent for over two years); Arthur v. Christopoulos, 101 Ark. 502, 510, 226 S.W.3d 321, 326 (2025) (holding that father should be awarded custody of 6-year-old twins when mother showed continuous abusive behavior).

String citations can be used to convey the message to the reader that not just one authority stands for a point, but two, three, or four do. If that message is essential to your analysis, then use the string citation. Do not, however, use a string citation just to show that you found more than one authority. If one authority is sufficient to make the point, omit the other citations. For format and order of authorities in string citations, see the citation manual used by your jurisdiction.

String citations were born in law review footnotes and perhaps live better there. Modern readers are not patient with piles of sources; they may skip them altogether. Remember that the doubting legal reader will check each authority, will doubt your credibility if each is not pertinent, and will be annoyed if any are unneeded. A judicial clerk, obligated to check every citation, may also convey that annoyance to the judge deciding your case. You are likely to be more persuasive in memos and briefs by using sentences instead of string citations, as in the following revision.

> **Arkansas has uniformly applied the rule of awarding children to the parent who can serve their best interests. For example, the mother was awarded custody of an 8-year-old son when the father could not support the son. Lorey v. Jacobi, 99 Ark. 111, 119, 222 S.W.3d 22, 28 (2023). The mother was awarded custody of her 10-year-old daughter and 3-year-old son when the father had been absent for over two years. Zuckerman v. Kidwell, 100 Ark. 841, 850, 224 S.W.3d 444, 448 (2024). And the father was awarded custody of 6-year-old twins when the mother showed continuous abusive behavior. Arthur v. Christopoulos, 101 Ark. 502, 510, 226 S.W.3d 321, 326 (2025).**

CITATIONS, VARYING FORMATS

Given the ever-changing nature of citation rules and the various ways in which they are applied, your best source on citation form is your jurisdiction's current citation rules, including the current edition of the citation manual adopted in that jurisdiction.

CLARITY

Clarity means writing so the reader can follow the writing step by step without wondering what a phrase means or what the point of the paper is. When the writing is clear, the reader can forget about the writing itself and focus instead on the merit of the content. The main tools of clarity are (1) matching the document's organization to its message and (2) matching the document's syntax to its substance. Thus a Brief Answer can by its syntax suggest an order for explaining the analysis, and the Discussion can in turn use that same order. For example, the following Brief Answer suggests that a three-part definition of *abode* will be analyzed in a specific order that springs from the fusion of the law and the client's situation.

> **Notice was effective because the home of the defendant's wife is his "usual place of abode": the defendant had lived there within the last year, he had moved back there one week after the summons was delivered, and he had received other mail there.**

A paragraph's structure, rather than following a set formula, can reveal its purpose, such as providing a transition or developing an analogy by giving examples.

> **In contrast, a company's continued use of the plaintiff's signature on its documents after he left the company was not held to be highly offensive to a reasonable person because the use of a signature was by itself not per se offensive, even though it created a false impression before the public. <u>Vang v. Scotioti</u>, 95 N.W.3d 462, 463 (2025). And when a former airline chairman made critical comments about "excesses of power" in the company and resorted to "mere name-calling," the false accusations were not specific enough to be considered highly offensive to a reasonable person. <u>Robinette v. Bethke</u>, 94 N.W.3d 111, 113 (2025).**

Additionally, sentences can be written to use syntactical devices that match the substantive message; for example, parallel structure can be used for parallel ideas and dependent clauses for dependent ideas.

> **Plaintiff admits he was driving without his license, without his lights on, and with an open six-pack of beer in the front seat.**

For more about techniques to increase clarity, see ORGANIZATION, LARGE-SCALE; ORGANIZATION, SMALL-SCALE; PARALLEL STRUCTURE; PRECISION; READABILITY; and SENTENCE STRUCTURE.

CLAUSES

A clause is a group of words that includes a subject and a predicate. Several clauses may be combined to form a compound or complex sentence.

> dependent clause   independent clause
> **Even if the court remands the case, the Plaintiff will not appreciably increase his reward.**

An independent clause can stand alone as a logical sentence.

The plaintiff will not appreciably increase his reward.

A dependent clause cannot stand alone because it begins with a word or phrase that makes the clause depend logically on another point.

Even if the court remands the case

Not knowing the difference between dependent and independent clauses can lead a writer to misuse commas. This occurs most often with the word *however.*

The court remanded the case; however, the plaintiff did not receive an appreciably higher reward.

rather than

The court remanded the case, however, the plaintiff did not receive an appreciably higher reward.

Because *however* joins two independent clauses, those clauses must be separated with a semicolon. For a discussion of clauses in the context of sentences, see SENTENCE STRUCTURE, subsections 3 and 6. For relevant punctuation rules, see COMMAS, subsections 1–3.

CLEANSING ELECTRONIC DOCUMENTS

See METADATA REMOVAL.

CLEARLY

Is the point really clear? If not, omit *clearly*. Similarly, whenever you read the word *clearly* in a text, look for a hole in the writer's logic. In most situations, *clearly* will remind you of the orator who pounds on the podium in the hope that his ardor will obscure his argument's weakness. For a discussion of related concerns, see CONCISENESS, subsection 7; LITERAL MEANING; and MODIFIERS.

CLEAR WRITING

See CLARITY and READABILITY.

CLICHÉ

A cliché is a phrase or idea that has lost its meaning because of overuse, which can create ambiguity. If you find that you have used a cliché, stop and specify what you mean.

That reading is inconsistent not only with the language of DX 2440, but also with the testimony of appellees' own economist.

rather than

That reading is the low-hanging fruit this court should pick immediately.

Clichés often pop into your mind when you are struggling to make a difficult point or when you are trying to create a memorable image. Try to work through your analysis specifically and replace the cliché. If you feel a cliché coming on while you are writing and you do not want to stop, mark it in the text at that time. Return during REWRITING to work through the specific meaning. For more information on using clever language to capture difficult ideas, see FIGURATIVE MEANING; IMAGERY; and WRITING, PERSUASIVE. For related information, see FLOWERY LANGUAGE.

CLIENT CORRESPONDENCE

See WRITING TO CLIENTS.

CLOSINGS FOR LETTERS AND EMAIL

See COMMUNICATIONS, CLOSINGS FOR.

COHERENCE

Coherence in writing means writing so that any reader can see how all the content fits together. Your tools for achieving coherence are organization, consistent and unambiguous wording, and clear and adequate transitions.

For ideas on how to make the whole document cohere, see DESIGN; LEGAL ANAYSIS; ORGANIZE, HOW TO; ORGANIZATION, LARGE-SCALE; OUTLINES; REASONING, PRESENTING IT; and SYLLOGISMS. For detail on how to accomplish this, see AMBIGUITY, WAYS TO AVOID; CONNECTIONS, MAKING THEM; ORGANIZATION, SMALL-SCALE; PARAGRAPHS; PRECISION; REPETITION; and TRANSITIONS.

COLLABORATION

Collaborative writing is wonderful when it works. It improves the product when it builds on individual strengths and compensates for individual weaknesses. It improves the process when it reduces the pressure to be perfect, provides more perspective as the process wears on, and provides someone with whom you can commiserate and celebrate.

Collaboration is not just choosing a coauthor for an independent project. Collaboration occurs within law offices when supervising attorneys assign projects to others. Seen as vertical collaboration that moves a project up and down the hierarchy within the organization, such a process can yield superior results. But without planning, collaboration can foster divisiveness and poor results.

Successful collaboration requires clear-headed planning; the collaborators need to have congruent expectations regarding the project, the process, and each other. The following process is one way to achieve this congruency.

1. Set parameters for the project.

   Meet to decide on the project's purpose and scope. A little time spent determining the goals and limits of the document can help you find common ground and identify any areas where compromise is needed. Then discuss all possible issues, theories, and strategy, and decide which you will pursue. Even at this early stage, begin to develop a sense of your communal voice to the extent you can. For help here, see PREWRITING, PURPOSE, and VOICE.

   Determine concrete constraints such as page length, scope of research, and use of citations. Discuss more abstract but important factors such as the client's priorities, the readers' needs, and the balance you seek between THOROUGHNESS and CONCISENESS. Include other important aspects of the project, such as point of view, level of formality, professionalism, time commitments, and other personal goals regarding this piece of writing. Determine priorities together, identifying what qualities are not just desirable, but essential. This will help you allocate time most effectively and avoid long debates over minor wording or style points as the deadline nears.

   Finally, ascertain what software and technical programs you will be using, including any artificial intelligence (AI). Coordinate your systems so that everyone is on the same page, literally. And be keenly aware of who you are sharing documents with at each stage of the process. For more on this, see REPLY TO ALL.

   For help here, see ARTIFICIAL INTELLIGENCE AND RESEARCH; ARTIFICIAL INTELLIGENCE AND WRITING; AUDIENCE; EDITING; FORMALITY, LEVEL OF; MANAGING WRITERS; PROFESSIONAL LANGUAGE AND PRESENTATION; WRITING AND TECHNOLOGY; and WRITING PROCESS.

2. Establish your technical roles.

   Whenever possible, determine who is in charge of each technical area of writing. For example, choose one person to resolve grammar questions, another to plan persuasive strategy, another to monitor the document's tone, and another to resolve questions of citation and format. Although these questions may not arise until much later, establish your roles early. This division of responsibilities will enable you to avoid time-consuming debates over small points; you can instead refer the question to one collaborator. Additionally, this structure will shift the focus of this part of the collaborative writing process from personal ego to personal responsibility.

3. Establish your procedural structure.

Note the final deadline and set interim deadlines. You will be dependent on each other to finish this document, so be clear on who gets what to the others, and when. When using word processors, check such details as whether you are using compatible software and computer systems and how you will be exchanging texts. Establish a common filing system and procedure for keeping the most recent draft, giving each other feedback and deleting previous drafts. Although this step can seem tedious, it is essential for making sure that all the agreed-upon edits are captured in one master document. This may be easier if one person at a time has control of editing the master document. Be sure to edit the file name, including the date and time, so that you know you are always working on a current draft. For related information, see RESEARCH and WRITING AND TECHNOLOGY. Resolving these questions can avoid costly delays as you near the project's deadline. For further help, see DEADLINES, MEETING THEM; and TIME MANAGEMENT.

4. Clarify tasks throughout the writing process.

Before the end of each meeting, decide together what each collaborator will accomplish before the next meeting. Preferably, write these lists and save them in a shared file so that each collaborator can refer to the same list. These lists encourage helpful communication and reduce the chance for duplication of effort or failure to complete some necessary task.

5. Keep in touch.

Since the main benefits of collaboration flow from an interchange of questions and suggestions, do whatever you can to make it easy for those exchanges to occur. Confer while writing. These conversations need not be long; you may just ask a collaborator a question or share a new idea you plan to bring up at the next meeting. As soon as you finish them, share drafts of essential guiding points, such as issues and point headings, or section headings and subheadings.

Do not wait for several revisions before you share drafts. Long periods of separate work invite writers to become personally invested in their own wording and approaches; that approach makes it harder to listen to suggestions or questions from collaborators. Effective collaboration requires sharing the whole process, not just the responsibility for authorship.

Frequent interchange during writing will also help you develop a consensus of thought that will allow you to fuse the parts into a seamless whole. Without this consensus, no amount of editing can create a cohesive presentation of each message.

6. Focus on the questions that are most important to your stage in the writing process.

During PREWRITING or writing, whenever you have organization roughed out, meet to combine your work and review the overall logic of the organization you have chosen; consider variations on the organization, so you can make sure your choice is the best one. Check your scope to make sure it still fits your purpose and adequately supports your reasoning. Also begin to discuss TONE. Although you will revise for tone later, begin to think about the appropriate tone at this early stage in the process, with your audience in mind. If you wait until revision to address this aspect, you will find it harder to unify the tone.

During WRITING, focus on getting all your thoughts on paper and discerning a possible organization, without getting too attached to the one you use in this initial draft.

During REWRITING, resolve any questions you had about large-scale organization. Ask yourselves if the overall purpose has been sustained, if the theme is consistent, if the law is accurate and complete, and if the organization is coherent to your audience. See LOGICAL FALLACIES; ORGANIZATION, LARGE-SCALE; ORGANIZE, HOW TO; REASONING, PRESENTING IT; RHETORIC; and SYLLOGISMS.

When REVISING, put all collaborators' work together, if you have not done so earlier in the process. Have each collaborator edit the text as a whole, so that individual voices begin to blend into one unified chorus. For qualities to check at this stage, see REVISING CHECKLIST.

When POLISHING, divide the responsibilities between collaborators, so you can be sure to check each aspect of the document. For example, you might check the complete text for consistent use of terms; someone else might check for accurate citations; someone else for conciseness; others for correct spelling, correct use of commas, and so on. For further information on what should be checked, see POLISHING CHECKLIST. Refer questionable passages to the appropriate collaborator whenever possible.

Discuss any remaining debatable points as a group. Move through these questions carefully, but quickly. Avoid the tendency to dwell with great emotion on the placement of a comma or a phrase. You want to get it right, but you must get it written.

7. Celebrate completion.

Congratulate yourselves when you are done. You have all worked hard, and you deserve the euphoria you will likely feel. For related information, see EDITING, GRACE UNDER FIRE, and MANAGING WRITERS.

COLLECTIVE NOUNS

A collective noun represents a collection of persons or things regarded as a unit. A collective noun takes a singular verb and pronoun when it refers to the collection as a whole.

The American Bar Association meets at least once a year.

and

The EPA is determined to press its claim.

rather than

The EPA is determined to press their claim.

A collective noun takes a plural verb, however, when it refers to the collection as separate persons or things.

The Student Bar Association have all gone home.

This structure can often sound wrong, so your best choice may be to rephrase.

The Student Bar Association members have all gone home.

Make sure you do not treat a collective noun as both singular and plural in the same construction. For a general discussion, see NOUNS.

COLLOQUIALISM

Colloquialism refers to an informal or regional phrase, or a word or phrase used in conversation but not in formal writing, such as *ripped off* or *got into*. Rarely will you use colloquialisms in legal writing, not only because they are informal and become dated easily, but also because they are usually not precise. Colloquialisms may appear, however, as a part of a quotation. Never resort to colloquialisms only because you cannot think of another word for the idea. Do not enclose a colloquialism in quotation marks to excuse its use. There is always another word or phrase, so using a colloquialism would be admitting that your vocabulary is inadequate. For related information, see CLICHÉ; FLOWERY LANGUAGE; FORMALITY, LEVEL OF; IMAGERY; LITERAL MEANING; and PROFESSIONAL LANGUAGE AND PRESENTATION.

COLONS

The most common use of a colon in legal writing is to introduce a list.

In justifying the exclusion of expert psychiatric evidence, the court listed three concerns: maintaining the integrity of the bifurcated trial procedure, avoiding allowing the guilty to go free, and preserving the defendant's right against self-incrimination.

or

The Company's liability does not include any of the following:

> **(1) any damage occurring in connection with the use of the equipment in any nuclear facility;**
>
> **(2) any consequential or incidental damages, including but not limited to loss of profit, damage to associated equipment, cost of capital, and cost of substitute products; or**
>
> **(3) any costs beyond the price of the product and service that gives rise to the claim.**

Do not, however, use a colon if each item listed is punctuated as a complete sentence. In that situation, write the introduction to the list as a complete sentence and end it with a period, not a colon.

During the period of this maintenance agreement, if the Company determines that it cannot maintain the equipment in good working order, then the Company must replace the equipment with another unit in good working order. This requirement is subject to the following provisions.

1. **If the Company replaces the equipment within two years of the warranty expiration date, then the replacement unit must be one that is newly manufactured, remanufactured, or reconditioned.**
2. **If the Company replaces the equipment more than two years after the warranty expiration date, then the replacement unit will be one that is refurbished in accordance with the process used to refurbish rental units.**
3. **. . . .**

You may use a colon instead of a period between two sentences if one sentence sets up an expectation in the reader's mind that the next sentence fulfills.

The intent was clear: she pointed the gun directly at the victim's chest.

You may also use a colon, for emphasis, to introduce a phrase that is not a complete sentence.

The plaintiff has only one motive: recovery for his loss.

In general, do not capitalize the first word after the colon, because doing so usually makes the sentence self-consciously ornate. Capitalize the first word after the colon only when it is needed to emphasize that word or concept.

Plaintiff asks the court to invoke the most severe penalty: Child abuse must be stopped.

Follow the colon with one space unless court or other rules require you to use two. Avoid overusing the colon; it creates a dramatic sentence structure that will become too noticeable if overused. For related information, see EMPHASIS.

Finally, colons have other standard uses that generally cause writers no grief. Colons are used at the end of a salutation in a formal business letter.

Dear Dr. Townsend:

To Whom It May Concern:

Colons are used to separate numbers in clock time, ratios, and documents.

12:45 p.m.

The odds were 50:1 that his case would succeed.

John 3:16

They are also used to separate titles from subtitles.

Legal Writing: Getting It Right and Getting It Written

Colons separate the name of a speaker from the words spoken.

Sanchez: Please state your name for the record.

Barber: Charles Gerald Barber.

COMBINING WORDS

There is no easy rule for when to combine words, use a hyphen, or use two separate words. Instead, check the spelling online, consult a dictionary under the particular word, or see the specific word entry in this book. For other general information, see HYPHENS. For an extensive list to guide your decision, see the most recent edition of the *U.S. Government Printing Office Style Manual.*

COMMA BEFORE *AND*?

See COMMA, OXFORD; and LISTS, STRUCTURE OF, subsection 3.

COMMA, OXFORD

This term refers to the comma placed before the last item in a list, as in the following example.

> **In weighing a witness's credibility, you may consider your own observations, the testimony of other witnesses, and any other evidence properly allowed by the court.**

The need for precision in legal writing is paramount, and adding this comma avoids any ambiguity about how many units are included in the list. For example, the comma before *or* in the following sentence makes it clear that the buyer has three options when seeking a refund, rather than two with the second one offering two options.

> **The buyer can receive a refund by returning the item along with a receipt from the store, a canceled check written to the store for the exact amount of the purchase, or a credit card receipt showing payment for the exact amount of the purchase.**

> rather than

> The buyer can receive a refund by returning the item along with a receipt from the store, a cancelled check written to the store for the exact amount of the purchase or a credit card receipt showing payment for the exact amount of the purchase.

In the following example, the question is how much the son-in-law receives. The comma before *and* makes clear that the estate is divided four ways. Without the comma, the sentence could be interpreted to divide the estate into three parts, with the daughter and son-in-law each receiving one-sixth. The comma is necessary before the *and* to remove any ambiguity. The list in the second example below makes the division even clearer.

> **I leave my estate to be divided equally among the following: my wife, my son, my daughter, and my son-in-law.**

> or

> **I leave my estate to be divided equally among the following four parties:**
>
> **(1) my wife,**
>
> **(2) my son,**
>
> **(3) my daughter, and**

(4) my son-in-law.

rather than

I leave my estate to be divided equally among the following: my wife, son, daughter and son-in-law.

COMMAS

One important use of commas is to show how extra information has been inserted into a sentence. The heart of every sentence is composed of the subject, verb, and sometimes an object. Those parts make the sentence complete and grammatical. Usually, however, you want to include more information than that. Commas show the reader how you have added that information.

That extra information may be added

(1) before the subject,

(2) between other parts of the sentence,

(3) after the main sentence, or

(4) after the whole sentence when another sentence has been joined to it.

Commas are also used conventionally to

(5) coordinate dates,

(6) set off quotations,

(7) separate items in a list,

(8) separate parts of a name in some conventional situations, and

(9) indicate the omission of a word.

Do not use a comma to

(10) separate a subject from its verb or

(11) join two sentences without a conjunction.

1. Comma setting off a phrase before the subject.

If you have added extra information before the subject, use a comma to set off that introductory phrase.

In negligence actions, the theory is that the person being sued had a duty to act and failed to fulfill that duty.

If the consumer disagrees with the information in the report, the agency must investigate again.

In contrast, a father who attempted to retain physical possession of his son by the use of a gun was later determined to be a fit parent for custody.

If the introductory phrase is very short and would not be followed by a pause when speaking, you may omit the comma.

Thus the outcome is clear.

2. Comma setting off a phrase between other parts of the sentence.

A pair of commas, placed before and after the extra information, shows that information has been inserted between the subject and verb or between the verb and object.

The case is, however, a sample from that system.

The plaintiff, despite warnings from his friends, jumped off the embankment.

Willard Evans, Louise's father, testified at the hearing on the post-conviction motion.

If the interrupting phrase is longer than seven words, rephrase the sentence. By the time your reader has finished an interrupting phrase that long, the subject will be forgotten.

A pair of commas also marks an insertion within a subordinate clause.

Most economists agree that, in terms of equity, this income should be taxed.

Do not, however, put commas around a restrictive phrase, which comes after the subject but is necessary to describe the subject accurately.

The defendant's belief that the man was reaching for a gun supports instructions about both self-defense and manslaughter.

The standards adopted by the court reflect a prudent lawyer's conduct with clients.

For more explanation of restrictive phrases, see *THAT* OR *WHICH*? For longer interruptions or explanations, consider rephrasing the sentence to avoid the interruption or placing it at the end of the sentence. This is one situation where use of PASSIVE VOICE may be justified. For related information, see PARENTHESES and UNOBTRUSIVE DEFINITIONS.

3. Comma indicating that more information follows after the main sentence.

   A comma can be added after the verb or object to show that extra information has been added at the end of the sentence.

   The holding was poorly reasoned, filled with vague terms and illogical statements.

   This court announced its decision in Sherman v. Freedman, which abolished the locality rule.

   Make sure that phrase is not a complete sentence unto itself. If it is, you need a CONJUNCTION or a SEMICOLON.

4. Comma after the whole sentence when another sentence has been joined to it.

   Use a comma before a conjunction that joins two independent clauses.

   The defendant expressed a desire to change his plea, and his attorney advised him to do this.

   If a conjunction joins two short phrases, you may omit the comma.

   The attorney recommended this action[ ] and the client did not object.

   For related explanations, see CLAUSES.

5. Commas coordinating dates.

   Use a comma between a specific date and the year (*July 4, 2025*). When more text follows after the date in a sentence, also add a comma after the year.

   The contract signed on December 20, 2024, did not take effect until midnight on February 1, 2025.

   Do not place a comma between a month and the year (*July 2025*). Also do not use a comma when the date is written before the name of the month (*4 July 2025*).

6. Commas setting off quotations.

   When the phrase introduces a quotation, use a comma immediately after a phrase preceding the quotation.

   She said, "I killed him."

   Do not use a comma when the quotation is short and is an integral part of the sentence.

   He said "killed" not "stabbed."

When the quotation concludes within the sentence, end it with a comma rather than a period.

She said, "I killed him," before being given her Miranda rights.

Place the comma inside the quotation marks. One exception to this is legislation in some jurisdictions, where the comma goes inside the quotation marks only when it is part of the quotation. Another exception is British English, which also puts commas and periods outside the quotation marks when they are not part of the quotation. For related information, see QUOTATIONS, HOW TO PUNCTUATE, subsections 3 and 4; and LEGISLATION.

7. Commas separating items in a list.

In legal writing, place a comma at the end of each item listed, including the item listed immediately before the *and*.

My estate is to be divided equally among my wife, my son, my daughter, and my son-in-law.

Adding the comma before *and* avoids any possible confusion about how many items are listed. For more detail, see COMMA, OXFORD; and LISTS, STRUCTURE OF, subsection 3.

Also use a comma to separate two modifiers listed before a noun. This comma is the grammatical equivalent of *and* in this situation.

The urgent, persistent messages were ignored by the defendant.

In contrast, if two words work together to state one modifying idea, do not use a comma. In this situation, one of the modifiers is an ADVERB.

The defendant ignored these exceedingly clear messages.

Sometimes, when two nouns work together as one modifier, you may need a hyphen instead.

Age-old traditions do not necessarily create legal precedent.

For related information, see HYPHENS.

8. Use a comma to separate parts of a name in some conventional situations.

Martin Luther King, Jr.

Sergei Ivanov, Esq.

St. Louis, Missouri

Yolanda White, Chair

9. Use a comma to signal the omission of a word or words.

   Before the accident, Ms. Yu had hope. Now, only despair.

10. Do not use a comma to separate a subject from its verb.

    If two verbs share a common subject, do not put a comma before the conjunction between the verbs.

    The driver lost control of his car while moving to the passing lane[ ] and slammed into the rear left fender of the defendant's truck.

    Both the defendant and the plaintiff agree that the defendant had the obligation to post appropriate warnings[ ] and was within her rights when she posted the "no trespassing" signs.

    Similarly, do not use a comma between two subjects that share one verb.

    Both custodial spouses seeking back payments of child support[ ] and divorcing parents seeking an order for child support will benefit from this rule.

    Do not use a comma to separate a long subject from its verb. Instead, reword the sentence so the subject is not so long.

    A bystander does not have a duty to stop and render assistance solely because that bystander passed by soon after an accident occurred.

    rather than

    Any bystander who sees an automobile accident but is in no way responsible for that accident, injured by the accident, or in any other way directly involved other than coming by soon after the accident occurred, does not have a duty to stop and render assistance.

    On the rare occasion where omitting it causes a misreading of a sentence, you may add a comma.

    The defendant did see that an ambulance was called, and notified the proper authorities.

    You may also add a comma if the second verb presents a sharp contrast with the first and functions, in effect, as an INTRUSIVE PHRASE.

    The plaintiff was able to reach, but not grasp, the release lever.

11. Do not use a comma alone to join two independent sentences; add a CONJUNCTION after the comma. Using a comma alone creates a grammar error known as a COMMA SPLICE.

COMMA SPLICE

This is the grammatical term for an error that occurs when a comma alone is used to join two complete sentences, rather than a subordinating conjunction, a semicolon, or a comma and a coordinating conjunction.

The client refused the plea deal offered by the district attorney even though the public defender advised her to accept it.

rather than

The client refused the plea deal offered by the district attorney, the public defender advised her to accept it.

and

The lower court remanded the case; nevertheless, the plaintiff did not receive an appreciably higher reward.

rather than

The lower court remanded the case, nevertheless, the plaintiff did not receive an appreciably higher reward.

and

The statute was repealed, but the court interpreted it as though it were still in effect.

rather than

The statute was repealed, however, the court interpreted it as though it were still in effect.

For more information, see COMMAS, subsection 10; HOWEVER; and SEMICOLONS.

COMMON NOUN

See NOUNS.

COMMON SENSE

You must use common sense in legal writing because few rules are absolute. But proceed cautiously when common sense hints at breaking a rule; do so only if the answer to all of the following questions is yes.

1. Can I break the rule without sacrificing one shred of ACCURACY?
2. Can I break the rule without sacrificing CLARITY?

3. Can I break the rule without sounding cute, trendy, petulant, or overly dramatic?
4. Am I breaking this rule only to meet the requirements of some higher rule?

For example, you might choose a less concise phrase because it is more accurate or more readable. You might break a grammar rule because you must quote the court directly, because the court broke the rule, and because you do not want to call attention to the error with *[sic]*. For related information, see BENDING THE RULES.

COMMUNICATIONS, CLOSINGS FOR

Choose the standard closing that suits your writing style and the tone of your letter or email. In email, closings are often eliminated because the reader knows the sender from the heading. But you may want to create either a friendlier or more formal tone by being less abrupt and including a closing to your email. Think twice, however, before including logos, miniature résumés, and other such items with a closing. These items may instead show up as attachments, which will annoy your readers when they see it contains unneeded information.

If the tone of your letter or email is businesslike yet friendly, try the following.

Sincerely,

or

Sincerely yours,

If your tone is more formal, try the following.

Yours truly,

or

Very truly yours,

Do not worry about seeming insincere; these closings are not taken literally. Using innovative alternatives only creates undesirable responses, rather than underscoring your sincerity. If you were to use something more accurate, like *Don't bother me anymore*, you would only seem unprofessional or petulant. If you omit the closing in a letter, you may create an abrupt, impersonal tone that is usually not appropriate, even in a tough collection letter. For related issues, see COMMUNICATIONS, TONE OF; WRITING TO ATTORNEYS; and WRITING TO CLIENTS.

COMMUNICATIONS, ELECTRONIC

As new technologies emerge, lawyers have new ways to communicate with clients, colleagues, and courts. While these technologies create conveniences and innovations for interpersonal communications, they also create new hazards for legal writers. For help with different forms of electronic communication, see WRITING TO ATTORNEYS and WRITING TO CLIENTS.

Law is a formal profession, and ethical rules apply to all forms of communication. Each can be read as an example of your professionalism. Worse, each may be discoverable. Therefore, treat all electronic postings, personal and professional, as though opposing counsel and members of your local bar association were reading them. Any public posting, even if intended for friends, can affect your general professional standing and even your job searches. For related information, see ELECTRONIC FILINGS and EMAIL OR MEMO? For a discussion of particular communication hazards, see EMOJI, INSTANT MESSAGING, PRIVACY, REPLY TO ALL, SOCIAL MEDIA, and TEXTING UNDER THE TABLE. If you are using artificial intelligence, see ARTIFICIAL INTELLIGENCE AND RESEARCH, ARTIFICIAL INTELLIGENCE AND WRITING, PROMPTS, and RESEARCH STRATEGY GUIDE.

Beware of using these systems casually as a legal writer. While some jurisdictions protect electronic communication as attorney-client privilege, others do not. Even if yours does, speed can be an enemy as much as a friend. You may experience problems if you send offers and other documents back and forth quickly between parties because the lawyers and parties may lack the time needed to consider all the ramifications of the offer. It is also easy for a client or another attorney to become confused about any offer or issue being discussed whenever messages overlap in time.

To avoid the pitfalls that come with every new communication convenience, remember the following points.

1. Write with your professional responsibilities in mind whenever you are writing as a lawyer. Any legal writing can have legal consequences. When you need to vent, do it orally, elsewhere. Do not put your personal emotions into your writing at work.

2. Maintain ACCURACY, even if it requires more words. Remember that HUMOR can go awry easily, especially when it includes double entendres.

3. Be businesslike in TONE. Good intentions do not necessarily lead to good results. When a reader does not know you well or chooses to be upset with you, friendly teasing can be read as caustic jibes, stern reminders as mild advisories, and respectful formality as

condescension. Choose factual terms over emotional ones. Proofread every message as if you were a hostile reader, just to be sure you cannot be misunderstood.

4. Use each communication to build a strong professional image. For help with building and maintaining that image, see ADJUSTING TO A NEW WRITING SITUATION and PROFESSIONAL LANGUAGE AND PRESENTATION.

COMMUNICATIONS, EMAIL

See EMAIL and EMAIL OR MEMO?

COMMUNICATIONS, INTERNATIONAL

If your legal practice reaches across cultures, be sensitive to the cultural differences that require adjusting your communication to make it most effective. As you shape your international exchange, consider your

(1) overall approach to readers,

(2) use of legal authority,

(3) patterns of logic, and

(4) use of English.

1. Overall approach to readers.

   Lawyers in the United States take a direct approach to answering questions and explaining the reasoning by which they reach a conclusion. This approach may seem rude, however, to lawyers from other cultures, who may prefer to be indirect and less obvious. Because the U.S. system of federalism gives equal power to case law, there are also many paths to a conclusion, and U.S. readers expect to see each step along that path. In contrast, lawyers in some cultures may not include all steps in the reasoning because to do so would insult the intelligence of the reader. Additionally, contracts are short in most other countries that rely on code law, but long in the United States because of the common law decisions that have developed contract law and must be accounted for in each contract.

   Research the other culture's approach to the documents you are writing so that you can adjust to your reader's expectations and still retain validity if you are writing about U.S. law. If you are writing about law in the reader's country, write with an awareness of the validity of other approaches to law.

2. Use of legal authority.

   All three branches of law have equal weight in the United States, but cases and executive decisions may be treated differently from statutes in some other cultures. Treatises are primary law in some cultures, but only advisory in the United States. In the United States, many sources are available for analysis: constitutions, statutes, cases, and regulations; U.S. legal history; science, technology, and cultural preferences; and traditions borrowed from English common law, among other things. For example, because of the doctrine of *stare decisis*, traditional legal analysis often includes deference to precedent, which requires careful research into how previous situations have been analyzed. In contrast, referring to cases in other legal cultures may be optional. Thus you may need to explain how the authority works in the United States so that your international readers understand the weight of the authority in your document.

If you are writing to tribunals in other legal cultures, first research how authority is treated in the target legal culture so that you are making accurate decisions about what to search for and use in your analysis. For international tribunals, research what weight they give to treaties, to their own precedents, and to the law of participating nations. Examine how authority is used by your readers and make sure that you have used authority accurately for your and their purposes.

3. Patterns of logic.

Avoid assuming that your U.S. approach to logic is understandable by international readers. It is likely that they have developed a different, equally valid logic. Study the patterns used in the culture with which you are working so that you can develop an approach that honors both cultures and helps you to meet your goals. This may require more explanation of the steps in U.S. logic if you are working within the U.S. system. Conversely, it may require adapting the organization, content, use of honorifics, level of formality, and tone of your writing if your target readers are from other legal cultures. For related information, see FORMALITY, LEVEL OF; and REASONING, PRESENTING IT.

Each legal culture has developed analytical patterns derived from its constitution, history, and practices. These patterns may, for example, begin with the conclusion and then explain it, work through patterns of respect and honorifics before framing the issue, or state only the issue and the conclusion. Some cultures leave the logic entirely to the reader. Few cultures, including other common law nations, use cases and analytical patterns as U.S. lawyers do. So use U.S. patterns when writing to U.S. readers. For more on these patterns, see REASONING, ANALOGICAL; REASONING, DEDUC-

TIVE; REASONING, INDUCTIVE; REASONING, MODERN; REASONING, OTHER; REASONING, POSTMODERN; and REASONING, PRESENTING IT.

4. Use of English.

English in the United States is one of over one hundred varieties of English in the world. It is specific and peculiar, not just to speakers of other languages, but also to clients whose native language is English. Be sensitive to the many variations in English and do not assume that your usage will automatically be understood by others. Others may use more elaborate words or be more formal, indirect, or blunt than you expect. Beware of interpreting these styles of communication as if they were used by U.S. lawyers. Instead, take your time, suspend your judgment and reactions, and listen longer before deciding how to respond.

Global English is an international variety of the language that is accepted in a number of countries. This English is likely to differ from standard U.S. English by dropping some subtler features, such as the difference between *who* and *whom*; the nuance of the subjunctive mood; or the use of articles, prepositions, and some verb tenses. Be patient, open-minded, and cautious in interpreting this use of English, just as you would ask them to be patient with your use of their language. The extra effort this takes will pay dividends in good will and will help you avoid misunderstandings, which can be expensive and problematic, especially in legal situations.

COMMUNICATIONS, OPENINGS FOR

This entry addresses the question of what to write in the first few sentences of your communications. For related information, see SALUTATIONS. In general, open with a sentence or two explaining the point of your communication or why you are writing.

In response to your inquiry, I am enclosing . . . .

or

Last Monday, we met to discuss . . . . This letter formalizes our agreement that I would act as your attorney concerning . . . .

This is usually preferable to starting with a sentence explaining who you are; that opening tempts the reader to say, *Who cares?* You can, however, explain who you are in the second or third sentence, after the reader has some reason to care, or you can add an explanatory reference as part of another sentence.

As your attorney, I want to notify you of some recent changes in the tax law that may require a change in your record-keeping practices.

You may try opening communications with *you* to force yourself to focus immediately on the reader. This will affect your point of view and TONE. But be careful that using *you* does not sound accusatory.

You had asked whether you should create a will or a living trust for your estate.

or

You and I met last week to formalize our agreement that I would act as your attorney.

but not

You did not call me as you promised, so the negotiation is delayed.

In some cases, you may want to be slightly less direct, including a brief explanatory paragraph before your point. See BAD NEWS, GIVING IT; COMMUNICATIONS, PERSUASIVE; and WRITING, PERSUASIVE for ways to handle these situations. For more detail on ways to structure other communications, see other COMMUNICATIONS entries.

Communication in email moves at a quicker pace than in letters. A good general rule is to get to your point within the first two lines of an email because readers of email do not like to scroll down. However, always also remember to consider your tone and add an introductory greeting or other opening if you think the reader will be offended if it is omitted.

For opening routine letters and emails, create your own collection of phrases so that you can communicate in your own voice and still avoid reinventing the wheel. Take care in selecting these stock phrases, because these opening phrases give the reader an impression of your personality, just as your demeanor creates an impression when you meet someone for the first time. In general, avoid stuffy openings, like *Pursuant to your request*, and long-winded ones, like *In regard to the matter of your request,* . . . . When you receive a letter or email that appeals to you, notice the opening. If you like it, modify it as needed and add it to your own collection of stock openings. For related information, see EMAIL, SALUTATIONS, SUBJECT LINES, WRITING TO CLIENTS, and WRITING TO ATTORNEYS.

COMMUNICATIONS, PERSUASIVE

Persuading a reader to do or decide something in your favor is a bit like finding your way through a mine field; you are trying to reach a certain point without setting off any unfortunate reactions. For this reason, persuasive communications will not be as predictably structured as other communications, whether they are written in letters, memos, email, or other forms. For more on this, see EMAIL OR MEMO? In all persuasive communications, however, make at least these four strategic decisions:

(1) choose your message,

(2) choose persuasive reasons,

(3) organize those persuasive reasons, and

(4) keep your tone consistent and appropriate.

The following guidelines should help you make these decisions.

1. Choose your message.

Decide on your message, which can help you to generate the next three steps. For example, the same information can generate a range of messages, all of which are asking the reader to pay half of the bills. Use this one-sentence message to test and decide upon your overall approach, although this sentence may not appear in the actual communication.

Please pay your half of these overdue bills.

Pay up or else.

Do you mind paying half of the bills?

We talked about splitting costs, and here is my proposal.

2. Choose persuasive reasons.

Tailor your persuasive structure and stance carefully to suit your readers. Choose not what persuades you, but what persuades your reader. Whenever possible, look for a goal the reader would like to achieve that can be met by taking the action you want that reader to take.

For example, if you are trying to persuade a party to settle out of court, do not use threats if the party might view those threats as a challenge and submission as a weakness. In general, negative consequences tend to trigger undesirable, unanticipated reactions more than positive incentives. It is usually safer, for example, to explain how an early settlement could bring better results for the party than a costly trial. Similarly, if you think that the reader is motivated by certain values or goals, try to explain how the action you recommend is consistent with those values or goals. For example, you might argue that paying a bill is essentially the same as keeping a promise.

When writing to another attorney, you may choose to focus on what would likely prevail in court or what would be best for the client.

Try to help the reader feel good, or at least not defeated, about taking the action you recommend.

3. Organize those persuasive reasons.

Use the same general organization for any bad news. (See BAD NEWS, GIVING IT.) Start with a paragraph that sets the tone of the letter. The following example establishes a kind tone.

> **Throughout the years, Everly Auto Parts has valued Morgan Auto as a customer. Because Everly hopes to maintain this solid working relationship, Bob Everly has asked me to write to you concerning the outstanding balance in your account.**

Alternatively, you may choose a tough tone, as in the following example.

> **Despite receiving three statements from my client, Everly Auto Parts, your company has not yet paid the balance of $6,015 owed for parts purchased four months ago.**

Or you may choose something in between.

> **My client, Everly Auto Parts, has asked me to write to you concerning the outstanding balance on your company's account.**

Do not go on too long, however, or your reader may become suspicious or cynical about the tone.

By the end of the first paragraph or the beginning of the second, state your point. This sentence must be clear.

> **Please pay the amount due promptly. Everly will not be able to extend further credit to your company until this balance has been paid.**

Then launch into your reasons, stating them factually and neutrally. You need not continue a tough or kind tone within the reasons; here clarity and neutrality in tone should be your main focus. Make one point at a time, rather than rambling back and forth between several points. See PARAGRAPHS.

> **Everly Auto Parts, as a general policy, limits credit to any company to . . . . Additionally, ...**

In the last paragraph close politely, or at least civilly.

> **Everly Auto Parts will appreciate your prompt payment of this outstanding balance and looks forward to your continued patronage.**

4. Keep your tone consistent and appropriate.

   Although you may vary the tone of your opening and closing paragraphs somewhat, use a relatively unemotional, polite tone throughout the body of the communications. When your reader is inclined to disagree with you, the emotions you would arouse would work against you. There are some exceptions to this, such as fund-raising letters to sympathetic constituents or email advising clients to do what they want to do already. Even here, however, you will usually want to present yourself as a logical, reasonable person who, even when impassioned about a cause, is still capable of making a coherent, logical argument. For a discussion of related points, see COMMUNICATIONS, INTERNATIONAL; COMMUNICATIONS, TONE OF; EMAIL; TONE; WRITING, PERSUASIVE; WRITING TO ATTORNEYS; and WRITING TO CLIENTS.

COMMUNICATIONS, REAL-TIME

As an attorney, you must be more careful than the average person about what you put in writing. For that reason, any instant messaging or artificial intelligence (AI) system that allows you to communicate quickly presents three potential hazards: inaccuracies, misunderstandings, and inadvertent leaks. To avoid these, do the following.

1. Proofread.

   Misunderstandings can occur more easily in real-time messages than in other communication forms in part because the brief format forces you to omit details. Therefore, avoid using these brief formats to deal with any content that is unfamiliar to your reader. Misunderstanding can also occur because the speed of the format tempts you not to proofread before you send. To avoid this pitfall, discipline yourself to proofread even the shortest message you send in your role as an attorney. A final source of misunderstanding arises from the likelihood that the message will take on a blunt or gruff tone. Brief messages, like short sentences, tend to sound blunter and tougher. For more on this, see TONE and TOUGH, SOUNDING THAT WAY.

2. Stop.

   Because of inadvertent leaks, jobs have been lost, politicians have been ruined, and evidence has been revealed to opposing parties. Resist the temptation of the quick answer in instant messaging whenever you would regret having the whole legal world know what you have written. You never know when it just might happen.

COMMUNICATIONS, TO ATTORNEYS

See WRITING TO ATTORNEYS.

COMMUNICATIONS, TO CLIENTS

See WRITING TO CLIENTS.

COMMUNICATIONS, TONE OF

Tone is especially important in email, letters, and any other form of person-to-person communication. As the tone of your voice creates an impression in the mind of the listener, so the tone of your communications creates an impression in the mind of the reader. Thus, although your tone may range from friendly to tough, it should always be within the limits of temperate, businesslike communication. A chatty tone will seem slightly unprofessional in all but purely personal email and letters. A tirade will also seem unprofessional, even in the toughest collection letter. A careless tone, even in an email or text message, can send the message that the reader is not important. For more on this, see EMAIL OR MEMO?

Within these limits, however, you must make your own choices, based on what is appropriate to the situation and what suits your personal communication style. To use tone effectively in letters, email, and other person-to-person texts,

(1) choose the appropriate tone,

(2) create that tone through word choice and sentence structure, and

(3) keep the tone consistent.

1. Choose the appropriate tone.

   Before you begin writing, consider your relationship to the reader. For example, if your reader is a judge or your supervisor, you will probably want to use a tone that is both businesslike and respectful. This means that you will state your points as concisely as possible but will not omit appropriate opening and closing sentences, such as the following closing to an email requesting a favor.

   Thank you for your help in this matter.

   If your reader is a client or colleague, you may choose to be polite and businesslike or, if appropriate, you may choose a friendly tone.

   Please call if you have any further questions.

   or even

   I am looking forward to our next tennis match.

If your reader is your client's opponent or a client who has not paid you for three months, you may sometimes choose a tough, businesslike tone.

> **Please pay this bill promptly.**
>
> or
>
> **I trust this settles the matter.**

If you are using an abbreviated form of messaging, avoid using slang or the latest abbreviations for words. In the legal world, misunderstandings can have serious consequences; keep the goals of ACCURACY and CLARITY uppermost in your mind. Even in the smallest messages, remember that you are still at work; be businesslike but not cold. For related concerns, see GENDER IN WRITING, PROFESSIONAL LANGUAGE AND PRESENTATION, and REPLY TO ALL.

2. Create that tone through word choice and sentence structure.

Choosing your words carefully is one effective way to establish your tone. For example, if you want to create an informal and friendly tone, use less formal words, such as *talk* and *meeting*. If you want to create a more formal tone, use more formal words, such as *confer* and *discussion*. Avoid, however, using formal words to the point that your letter becomes hard to read or stuffy.

> **I have conferred about this question with Ms. Jamison's attorney, who explained that . . . .**
>
> rather than
>
> In pursuit of this query, I have held consultations with counsel for Ms. Jamison, who elucidated the point by stating that . . . .

For more help, see FORMALITY, LEVEL OF.

Another way to avoid a stuffy tone is to avoid inappropriately using the third person, such as *this attorney*, when the first person, *I*, is accurate. In general, email and letters are addressed from one person to another, and so the use of *I* is appropriate, or *we* if you are speaking officially for a group of people, such as a whole law office. Avoiding the personal can make it appear that you dislike the reader and want to distance yourself.

You may also establish your tone by using appropriate sentence structure. For example, if you want to create a friendly, informal tone, use longer sentences rather than terse ones.

> **Thank you for your kind invitation to speak at your annual banquet honoring outstanding alumni from the law school.**
>
> rather than
>
> Thank you for the invitation to speak at the law school alumni banquet.

Conversely, if you want to create a tough, no-nonsense tone, use short, rather choppy sentences.

> **My client, Ms. Ambrose, does not intend to pay this bill. She has no reason to pay you. She did not receive any software from your company. She did not order any software from your company. Until receiving your bill, she did not know your company existed.**
>
> rather than
>
> My client, Ms. Ambrose, does not intend to pay this bill because she has no reason to do so. She did not receive or order any software from your company, and in fact did not know your company existed until receiving your bill.

3. Keep the tone consistent.

Inconsistent tone occurs most often when an email or letter includes words that are noticeably more formal or informal than the rest of the email or letter. For example, a writer may use a formal phrase, such as *please be advised that,* in an otherwise informal letter. Or a writer may use a colloquialism, such as *ripped off,* in an otherwise businesslike letter. Uneven tone often reduces CREDIBILITY. For more detailed advice in this area, see PROFESSIONAL LANGUAGE AND PRESENTATION and PRIVACY.

Uneven tone also sometimes occurs when sentence structure changes markedly. For example, a reader might be taken aback by a series of three SHORT SENTENCES near the end of an otherwise friendly email. Similarly, a reader might be put off by a long, complex sentence in an otherwise informal email. Revise your email and letters just for consistent tone.

For more help in choosing the appropriate tone, see the following more specific COMMUNICATIONS entries; FORMALITY, LEVEL OF; REQUESTS FOR PAYMENT; or TOUGH, SOUNDING THAT WAY. For related information, see SENTENCE STRUCTURE and WORD CHOICE.

COMPARE AND CONTRAST

When presenting legal arguments, you will often use comparison and contrast, or analogizing and distinguishing, as part of your reasoning. For example, you may argue that the reasoning used on one case should also be applied to your case because the two cases are similar. And when you contrast facts in two situations, you also need to convince the reader that the difference you have established is indeed relevant to the decision made in the case.

As you do this, remember that one comparison alone does not an analysis make. Only one step in your logical argument is established by convincing a reader that two cases, two lines of reasoning, or any other two components are similar. To complete your argument that the reasoning should be applied, you need many more components, such as an explanation of the significance of the comparison, examples of other cases that are similar or different, or broader policy issues that support the comparison you are making. Fundamentally, you need to convince your reader that analogical reasoning is relevant to the legal decision being made. For help in presenting all the steps of your reasoning when comparing and contrasting, see LEGAL ANALYSIS; LOGICAL FALLACIES; REASONING, ANALOGICAL; REASONING, INDUCTIVE; REASONING, PRESENTING IT; and *STARE DECISIS*.

COMPARE TO OR *COMPARE WITH*?

Use *compare to* when you are introducing a similarity.

> **This harm, losing the ability to continue running competitively, can be compared to losing the ability to continue working.**

Use *compare with* when you are introducing two items you will subsequently compare or contrast.

> **This situation can be compared with the defendant's situation in Wheeler v. Bailey . . . .**

COMPARISON

Three techniques can be used to clarify comparisons: parallel structure, clear transitions, and effective subjects and verbs. Before structuring any comparison, however, make sure that the items are indeed comparable.

1. Use PARALLEL STRUCTURE.

   One of the best ways to write a graceful, effective comparison is to place the items compared in parallel structures. The framework of the parallel structure highlights the similarity or difference in the substance.

> **In Sampson, the landlord had been asked by at least seven tenants to replace burnt-out light bulbs in a stairwell, but had refused to do so. In Smith, the landlord had been asked by a half dozen tenants to repair the security system. And in Ortez, the landlord had been asked by the tenants' organization to schedule roof repairs. In all three cases, the landlord had been asked by tenants to make basic repairs, had failed to act, and was found liable. Similarly, Mr. Tyler has been asked by at least seven tenants to repair the intercom system, but he has refused to do so.**

2. Use clear transitions.

Additionally, you can use TRANSITIONS to let the reader know that a comparison or contrast is coming.

> **In 1919, when the doctrine of the best interest of the child became the controlling consideration in custody disputes, the results of those disputes changed. Until then, custody usually was awarded to fathers. After 1919, however, custody usually was awarded to mothers.**

3. Use effective subjects and verbs.

Another way to make a comparison shine is to make sure that you have placed the items compared in the main parts of the sentence: the subject and verb. For example, the following passage emphasizes the promise. The main parts of the sentences are *the court found that one who promises . . . and then breaks that promise* and *Mr. Derieri promised . . . and broke that promise.* Making these points the main parts of the sentences emphasizes the similarity.

> **In Kwaterski, the court found that one who promises, implicitly or explicitly to satisfy the statute of frauds and then breaks that promise is estopped from using the statute of frauds as a defense. Similarly, Mr. Derieri explicitly promised to make a written agreement and broke that promise. He is therefore estopped from using the statute of frauds as a defense.**

For a general discussion of this technique, see SENTENCE STRUCTURE. For related information, see PREPOSITIONAL PHRASES. For more on analytical comparisons, see REASONING, ANALOGICAL; REASONING, INDUCTIVE; and REASONING, PRESENTING IT.

COMPLAINTS

Generally, a Complaint is the document that starts a lawsuit. Its primary audience is the court and the defendant's attorneys. Its purposes are to inform the defendant and the court about the nature of the action and to withstand any Motions to Dismiss. Another long-term purpose is to succeed on appellate review, so make sure you know the STANDARD OF REVIEW as you begin. Beyond these purposes, a Complaint can be worded strategically either to encourage settlement or to delay informing the defense of your strategy.

A Complaint usually has six parts:

- the caption,
- the commencement,
- the body,
- the demand for judgment,
- the signature, and
- the VERIFICATION.

Although your writing concerns will differ for various parts, your overall priorities will be identifying the content needed, expressing it precisely, and ordering that content effectively.

1. General writing principles for different parts of the complaint.

   Focus on observing all pertinent court rules and avoiding unnecessary legalese when drafting the caption, signature, and verification. You may find it helpful to look at samples of other Complaints before writing your first one; see CAPTIONS and FORM BOOKS for ways to do this effectively. For related information, see POLISHING.

   When writing the body and demand for judgment, focus on identifying all the needed content while omitting extraneous information. The Complaint must be precise enough to provide adequate notice to your opponent and to survive a Motion to Dismiss, yet flexible enough to allow you to include information you may want to introduce at trial.

2. Process for identifying the content.

   To identify your content effectively, you need to research thoroughly so you can develop your theory and practical goals for the case, including avoiding any appeals. To make certain that you do not miss any needed points, try working backward.

   - Identify the relief you want, including alternatives the trial court might provide.

- Identify the causes of action that support the request and the relevant law.
- Identify the elements of each cause of action and choose the facts that are sufficient to show those elements are met.
- Anticipate possible appeal issues and any content you need to include to prepare to prevail on these issues, including the STANDARD OF REVIEW for each issue.

This should provide the content you need for your Complaint.

3. Organizing the content.

You may find it most effective to organize the Complaint inductively, alleging the specific facts going to this particular element, then the element those facts show, and finally the legal conclusion supported by the facts and elements alleged.

Here is an example of one common organization. Usually, the first paragraphs identify the parties. The next paragraphs lay out the evidence establishing that the first element of the first charge is met. After this evidence is stated, the following paragraph asserts that the evidence shows the ultimate fact, or the logical conclusion stating that an element of the cause of action has been met.

1. [identity of plaintiff]

2. [identity of defendant]

3. [identity of additional defendant]

4–5. [evidence of standard sanitization practice used at hospital]

6–7. [evidence of actual practice used on a particular day when injury occurred]

8. [ultimate fact that hospital staff failed to exercise due care]

9–20. [other evidence, followed by ultimate facts establishing other elements of negligence]

21. [assertion that defendant's actions constituted negligence]

22. [allegation of damages plaintiff suffered as a result of the negligence]

WHEREFORE [demand for judgment, including all legally allowable forms of relief]

As in all court documents, observe your jurisdiction's format and customs; for example, many jurisdictions divide the content into numbered paragraphs, as illustrated above.

For ways to check your document, see DOCUMENT CHECKLIST.

COMPLETELY

If it is not literally complete, do not use *completely*. Also see LITERAL MEANING and MODIFIERS.

COMPLEMENT OR *COMPLIMENT*?

Use *complement* when referring to something that completes, balances, or adds useful information. Thinking of the word *complete* may help here.

The city attorney's research complements that done by the historic preservation board on the feasibility of moving historic buildings.

Use *compliment* for a statement that expresses esteem, admiration, respect, or some other positive attribute.

The mayor complimented the district attorney on her transparent prosecution process.

COMPLEX SENTENCES

A complex sentence has two or more CLAUSES, or groups of words that each have their own subject and verb; however, unlike a compound sentence, a complex sentence contains a dependent clause, as in the following example.

Although John was in the room while his father was reading and discussing the will with the attorneys, John sat on the opposite side of the room and did not participate in the discussion.

A dependent clause cannot stand on its own as a sentence because it is attached to the other clause with a subordinating conjunction.

although John was in the room

while his father was reading and discussing the will with the attorneys

Complex sentences are useful for downplaying information because the reader views the independent clause as more important than the dependent clause. But use this structure with discretion; if too many clauses are added to one sentence, the text becomes hard to read.

If you wanted to read about complicated sentences, rather than about the grammatical category of complex sentences, see READABILITY, subsections 1 and 5; or SENTENCE STRUCTURE, subsection 6.

COMPOUND SENTENCES

A compound sentence has two or more independent clauses that are joined by a conjunction. An independent clause has a subject and verb and could stand on its own as a complete sentence. Although compound sentences are not as frequently useful in legal writing as complex sentences, they can be helpful for combining two points that are both logically and structurally parallel.

> independent clause
> **Other doctors in similar situations do disclose some risks to their patients,**
>
> conjunction
> **and**
>
> independent clause
> **thus you may argue that Dr. Walker did not meet the standard of disclosure set by his profession for cases such as yours.**

Occasionally compound sentences can also be helpful for avoiding undue emphasis of a minor point. Short sentences are emphatic, so putting a minor point in a short sentence confuses the reader by overemphasizing that point.

> **The supervisor told Mr. Sykes to remove the cartons from the loading dock before the end of the day, and Mr. Sykes did so.**
>
> rather than
>
> The supervisor told Mr. Sykes to remove the cartons from the loading dock before the end of the day. Mr. Sykes did so.

For related information and definitions, see CLAUSES, COMPLEX SENTENCES; CONJUNCTIONS; and SENTENCE STRUCTURE, subsection 3.

COMPOUND WORDS, WHEN TO HYPHENATE

See HYPHENS.

CONCISENESS

Conciseness is highly valued in legal writing. Achieve it whenever possible, although never at the expense of accuracy, thoroughness, or readability. Attaining conciseness is best approached as a revision task, after you have determined what content is needed and how that content is most effectively organized. For an explanation of the larger process, see WRITING PROCESS and REVISING.

After you have reshaped your document's overall structure in the rewriting process, revise for conciseness by doing the following.

1. Eliminate facts or law that do not bear on this particular analysis.

   Concentrate on the scope of this problem, so the reader can concentrate on that too. For example, if the only legal issue being discussed in a memorandum is *whether or not there has been an intentional tort*, do not include facts or law in the analysis that do not bear on that issue. For related information, see STATEMENT OF THE CASE or STATEMENT OF FACTS.

2. Make sure that each paragraph advances one of the points in your reasoning.

   This should help you avoid circumlocution, or discussing again a point already established. Similarly, present only one main point in a paragraph. This will help you make sure you support and explain that point adequately, which will lessen the chance that you will repeat the point later to bring in further support. For related information, see ORGANIZATION, SMALL-SCALE; and PARAGRAPHS.

3. Move important material to the beginning of paragraphs and sections.

   Moving this information to the beginning will eliminate long explanations that reach a result. Instead, give the result and explain it. For more detail and related information, see POSITIONS OF EMPHASIS.

4. Use the key words in a sentence for your subjects and verbs.

   Exigent circumstances justify the police's failure to obtain a warrant.

   rather than

   The crucial fact here is that exigent circumstances existed, justifying the police's failure to obtain a warrant.

5. Make citations speak for themselves.

   Begin the sentence with your content, rather than using *the court held* or *the court went on to say*.

   The doctrine of moral right is not expressly recognized in New York. Hesler v. Alley Book Division, 999 N.Y.S.2d 552, 555, 999 Misc. 2d 104, 105 (2025).

rather than

The New York Court in Hesler v. Alley Book Division, 999 N.Y.S.2d 552, 555, 999 Misc. 2d 104, 105 (2025), has stated that the doctrine of moral right is not expressly recognized in New York.

For more information, see CITATIONS.

6. Use active voice.

Whenever possible, use active voice, rather than passive, because passive voice often requires more words.

The defendant argued that the court should suppress the evidence.

rather than

It was argued by the defendant that the evidence should be suppressed by the court.

For more information, see ACTIVE VOICE; and VOICE, ACTIVE OR PASSIVE?

7. Omit unneeded adjectives and adverbs.

Let the facts speak for themselves, rather than adding your opinion about those facts.

The court in Thomas does not specifically define "major question."

rather than

Obviously, the court in Thomas appears to fail to definitively establish an unambiguous and undebatable determining standard for when a piece of legislation raises a "major question."

8. Omit duplicate terms.

For example, use the following

The donation's purpose was to provide assistance to the community's AIDS victims, not to expand the program's administration.

rather than

The donation's thrust and purpose was to provide aid and assistance to the community's AIDS sufferers or victims, not to augment or expand the program's administration and overhead.

9. Delete unneeded prepositional phrases.

For example, substitute *legally* for *on a legal basis* and *defendant's* for *of the defendant*.

> **The defendant's obligation may have existed morally, but not legally.**
>
> rather than
>
> The obligation of the defendant may have existed in a moral sense but not on a legal basis.

10. When possible delete *that* constructions.

These constructions usually make sentences longer and more complicated. Examples of these constructions are *there are . . . that*, *there is . . . that*, and *it is . . . that*. When possible, revise the sentence so the construction is unneeded.

> **You must go through this process to identify any opinion's key facts.**
>
> rather than
>
> This is the process that you must go through to identify any opinion's key facts.

11. Delete empty phrases.

These phrases are groups of words that may sound good when rolling off the tongue but actually add no meaning. If sentences were twenty-mule teams, these phrases would be weak mules dragging down the rest of the team. For example, remove *it is clear that*, and just state your point. Remove *it is important to state at the outset that* and just say *first*.

CONCLUSIONS

The Conclusion brings together an analysis and demonstrates the culmination of reasoning. Use the Conclusion to finalize your proof, whether in the final paragraphs of an opinion letter, the formal Conclusion of a memo or a brief, or the less formal oral presentation.

Rather than merely repeating what has gone before, the Conclusion has a *therefore* quality. It synthesizes your findings. Situated at the end of the document, the Conclusion is the second most important position of emphasis, so avoid skipping the Conclusion or using *For the foregoing reasons* to conclude a brief. Using that phrase would force the reader either to remember the Discussion or Argument or skip the culminating moment completely. Instead, use the Conclusion to deliver a final message, soften the bad news, or lead to practical advice.

In its simplest form, a Conclusion is the final section of a syllogism, the part that shows that the middle term is shared by the major premise and the minor premise. In the following example, *derivative work* is the middle term.

Major premise: **All derivative works are copyrightable only for their original aspects.**

Minor premise: **"Four Beyoncés" is a derivative work.**

Conclusion: **Therefore, "Four Beyoncés" is copyrightable only for its original aspects.**

rather than

Major premise: All derivative works are copyrightable only for their original aspects.

Minor premise: "Four Beyoncés" is a derivative work.

Conclusion: Derivative works are copyrightable in part and "Four Meryls" is one of them.

In a memo, distinguish the Conclusion from the Brief Answer, which gives the ultimate good news or bad news, the remedy, or the desired result. The Brief Answer usually appears at the beginning of the document, the analytical conclusion at the end. While they have features in common, the Conclusion should have the quality of unifying the analysis, not summarizing it. Your Brief Answer in a memo may be the following.

Probably yes. "Four Beyoncés" is largely reminiscent of Warhol's "Four Marilyns" because both are paintings, both have quadrants, and both show the identical faces of a famous actress. While "Four Beyoncés" uses more natural colors and shows a profile of the musical star, those elements are not enough to make it an original work. Laffon can copyright only those two original aspects of his work.

The Conclusion in the same memo might be the following.

"Four Beyoncés" is a derivative work because it is so distinctly reminiscent of the Warhol piece. The name, the quadrants, the identical profiles, and the musical star all recall Warhol's work. Such similarities make the work derivative, not original. To be original, the work would have had to be substantially different, such as using a different medium as in *Scallon*, posing the subject in different postures, as in *Laurel*, or creating a different effect on the audience, as in *White*. We should advise Mr. Laffon that his work is derivative and that only the colors and profiles are copyrightable as original.

The Conclusion encapsulates the memo's reasoning but accounts for more details than the Answer and heads in the direction of advice or recommendation. In a memo or opinion letter, the Conclusion encapsulates the reasoning that led to the shorter Brief Answer and may also add a recommendation based on that analytical Conclusion. In a brief, the Conclusion brings the reasoning to a head and often ties that legal reasoning to the desired remedy.

In your writing process, write your Conclusion when it is most helpful to do so. For example, if you are having trouble seeing how all your points fit together, you may find it helpful to write the Conclusion before finishing the rest of your draft. Conversely, you may find it more helpful to write the Conclusion only after you have written the rest of your draft and your reasoning is clarified. For related information, see EXECUTIVE SUMMARY.

CONCLUSORY

This term refers to a presentation of legal analysis that jumps from the general principle or rule to the conclusion. A conclusory presentation omits the reasons for reaching the conclusion as well as the logical connections between the steps in the reasoning. In a syllogism, conclusory analysis jumps from the major premise to the conclusion, omitting the minor premise.

Major premise: All dogs have four legs.

Conclusory conclusion: Clearly, then, Spot has four legs.

Make sure your analysis is complete so no reader will apply the term *conclusory* to your writing. For more related information, see SYLLOGISMS. For how-to information, see LEGAL ANALYSIS and REASONING, PRESENTING IT.

CONCRETE NOUNS

See ABSTRACT NOUNS.

CONDITIONS, STATING THEM

The cleanest way to do this is to use one of the following phrases.

if, when, only if, only when, but only if, but only when

Often the most logical way to include a condition is to state it at the beginning of the sentence so that the reader can decide immediately whether the condition applies.

If you choose to employ our services in this matter, please sign the enclosed contract.

rather than

Please sign the enclosed contract if you choose to employ our services in this matter

Choose the term that most precisely states when the condition applies. For example, you might write the following:

The seller agrees to replace any defective widgets, but only if the buyer notifies the seller of the defect within forty-eight hours of delivery.

rather than either

The seller agrees to replace any defective widgets on the condition that the buyer notifies the seller of the defect within forty-eight hours of delivery.

or

The seller agrees to replace any defective widgets with the condition that the buyer notifies the seller of the defect within forty-eight hours of delivery.

On the condition that and *with the condition that* are best avoided because they are wordy and not as precise as other choices.

CONFORM TO, *CONFORM WITH*, OR *CONFORM IN*?

Conform to.

CONJUNCTIONS

Conjunctions join phrases, words, or sentences. Three questions arise with conjunctions:

(1) how to classify them,

(2) how to use them effectively, and

(3) how to avoid problems with them.

1. How to classify conjunctions.

Conjunctions can be classified as *coordinating*, such as *and*, *but*, *or*, or *for*. Conjunctions are *correlating* when they include two words working together, such as *both . . . and* or *either . . . or*. Finally, they are *subordinating* when they introduce dependent clauses, such as *although*, *because*, *unless*, *despite*, or *until*.

2. How to use conjunctions effectively.

Conjunctions serve as clear and effective transitions only when used accurately, so choose the conjunction that most accurately communicates the logical connection between the two sentences.

> **Although the project was not finished by the date scheduled for completion, the contract was not breached because the delay was due to a hailstorm.**
>
> rather than
>
> The project was not finished by the date scheduled for completion and the contract was not breached because the delay was due to a hailstorm.

For help in finding the most accurate conjunction, see TRANSITIONS. For related information, see CONNECTIONS, MAKING THEM.

3. How to avoid problems with conjunctions.

Two problems to watch for when using conjunctions are (1) overusing one conjunction, such as *and*, and (2) using a conjunction to join two things not logically and grammatically parallel.

> **Therefore, without a working alternative, the agency may be forced to continue using the current, antiquated system. This situation will decrease efficiency and increase cost, so finding an alternative form of electronic filing must be a priority.**
>
> rather than
>
> So, without a working alternative, the agency may be forced to continue using the current system that is so antiquated and time-consuming. This situation will decrease efficiency and increase cost, so finding an alternative form of electronic filing must be a priority.
>
> and
>
> **Her duties included organizing and maintaining electronic files, keeping records of all communications, and maintaining the record-keeping system.**
>
> rather than
>
> Her duties included organizing and maintaining electronic files, responsibility for record keeping of all communications, and maintenance of the record-keeping system.

For more information, see PARALLEL STRUCTURE. For advice on the use of specific conjunctions, see *AND*, *AND/OR*, *BOTH . . .*

AND, BUT, NOT ONLY . . . BUT ALSO, NOT SO MUCH . . . AS, and *OR*. For related information, see *HOWEVER* and SENTENCE STRUCTURE, subsection 2.

CONNECTING WORDS

See TRANSITIONS.

CONNECTIONS, MAKING THEM

Making the connection clear between phrases or sentences is like using your car's turn signals correctly when leading a convoy. By letting your readers know where you are going, you increase the chance that they will be able to follow your logical route. Consider the following techniques in constructing strong connections.

1. Use parallel structure.

   This structure can immediately underscore both similarities and differences. For example, you can compare two items like this.

   > **In Sampson, the landlord had been asked by at least seven tenants to replace burnt-out light bulbs in a stairwell, but he had refused to do so. In Smith, the landlord had been asked by a half dozen tenants to repair the security system. And in Ortez, the landlord had been asked by the tenants' organization to schedule roof repairs. In all three cases, the landlord had been asked by tenants to make basic repairs, had failed to act, and was found liable. Similarly, Mr. Tyler has been asked by at least seven tenants to repair the intercom system, but he has refused to do so.**

   For more about this technique, see PARALLEL STRUCTURE, subsection 2.

2. Repeat key terms.

   Use repetition of key terms to show how a sentence picks up the previous content and moves to the next step in your logical progression. Often this combines with *this* or *these*, as in the following example of a thesis sentence that could follow the previous sample paragraph.

   > **These seven requests provided sufficient notice of the hazard that . . . .**

   For more on this technique, see REPETITION, subsection 3; and CONNECTIONS, MAKING THEM. For related information, see ACCURACY, subsection 1; and TOPIC SENTENCES.

3. Use a transition.

A transition, such as *furthermore, because, although,* or *even if* can add clarity quickly. Keep in mind, however, that this connection is only as good as the accuracy of the transition word.

The Act did not successfully treat the broader problem of marital status discrimination. Instead, it shifted inequitable tax burdens between taxpaying groups.

rather than

The Act did not successfully treat the broader problem of marital status discrimination; however, it shifted inequitable tax burdens between taxpaying groups.

Because using an inaccurate transition is more confusing than using none, never throw in a transition carelessly. For help with this choice, see TRANSITIONS. For related information, see CONTEXT, CLARIFYING.

CONNECTORS

See CONNECTIONS, MAKING THEM; and TRANSITIONS.

CONNOTATION

Connotation refers to the meaning implied by a word that goes beyond that word's literal meaning. For example, a person holding the same position could be described as *stalwart, resolute, determined, unwavering, headstrong, stubborn, mulish,* or *pigheaded.* These words do not differ so much in literal meaning as they do in connotation.

As you can see from these examples, words do not just have a positive or negative connotation but fall on a continuum stretching from extremely positive to extremely negative. The extremes of the continuum are effective only if the reader or listener already agrees with you. In legal writing, because you are not addressing such an audience, avoid the extremes on either end of the continuum. For a discussion of this and related concerns, see AUDIENCE; WORD CHOICE; and WRITING, PERSUASIVE, subsection 4(i). For a related explanation, see LITERAL MEANING.

CONTACT

Contact as a verb is rather vague; before you use the word, make sure you want to be that vague. For example, *contact* is not as specific as *telephone, write,* or *meet with.* For related concerns, see PRECISION.

CONTEND

Courts do not *contend,* only counsel does. Generally, avoid using *contend* in arguments because it creates a defensive tone and adds unnecessary words. For alternatives to this wording, see COUNTERARGUMENTS, HOW TO HANDLE. For related general techniques, see SUBJECT-VERB COMBINATIONS.

CONTEXT, CLARIFYING

To keep your readers engaged, remind them often of the context in which you are explaining, comparing, arguing, or illustrating your specific content. Avoid the pitfall that engulfs many legal writers, who lose their readers by racing into an idea without connecting it logically to the previous section or paragraph. Remind your reader of your topic, answer, analysis, or direction in the following ways.

1. In memos.

   Create clear Questions Presented that focus the reader on the precise question being resolved. In Brief Answers, use details that orient the reader and a structure that foreshadows the structure of the discussion section. For related information, see MEMOS.

2. In briefs.

   Explain in the introduction specifically why the case is before the court. Use the point headings to remind the reader of the context throughout the document. For more details, see BRIEFS.

3. In communications.

   In your opening sentence, remind the reader of the reason why you are writing. When writing to other lawyers or anyone receiving the communications at work, refer to the specific project in a way that allows the reader to pull up the relevant information quickly. Remember that these readers are dealing with many different projects at any one time, so they will appreciate help in getting oriented quickly.

   When writing to clients, clarify where you are in the process of serving them. Also attend to your tone, thus reminding them that this correspondence is written in the spirit of helping them solve their problems. Because most individuals do not have many legal matters in play at one time, this reassurance that you are in their corner is probably the more important context. For more information, see TONE.

4. In private legislation, such as CONTRACTS or Memoranda of Understanding.

   Maintain the positive context of the parties agreeing on action by placing their mutual agreements early in the document before listing all the protective measures that deal with things that can go wrong. Avoid focusing so much on protecting the party you represent that the document loses its focus on making the relationship work. For more information, see the entry under the kind of document you are writing.

5. In all documents.

   Use headings, in sentence form, to explain your message and to guide the reader through the document. To make sure that these headings present a complete and unified synopsis of your message, read them in order without the intervening text. For examples, see POINT HEADINGS.

   When writing in paragraph form, use the topic sentences as the first sentences of paragraphs. These sentences can sometimes relate to the previous paragraph or to the overall message as well as introduce the idea of this paragraph. In opinion letters, the topic sentences often relate how the content applies to the reader's situation. To check the logical flow of your presentation, read through all your topic sentences without the supporting text. To clarify the logical flow, use techniques explained in CONNECTIONS, MAKING THEM.

   Four other techniques can add substantial clarity. You can use sentence structure that reflects the logical structure of the content. For how-to information, see PARALLEL STRUCTURE and SENTENCE STRUCTURE, subsection 6. You can also use repetition of key words to show how central concepts recur throughout the text. For how-to information, see REPETITION, subsection 3. You can also chain ideas together from sentence to sentence. For example, the idea at the end of one sentence often reappears early in the next.

   The judge omitted the jury instruction on strict liability. Because of this omission, ...

   Finally, finish your reasoning. Follow it step by step until you reach the answer to the reader's question. Do not leave the reader wondering, *So what is the answer to my question?*

CONTEXT-INDEPENDENT WRITING

Most legal writing should be self-sufficient; that is, it should include all the information needed to understand the full meaning. Many legal documents have long lives and potentially broad audiences, so include enough information or cross-references to enable a new reader to understand the document without further research. Making the document context independent will build your credibility, ease the reader's burden, and keep the document resilient through its potentially many uses. For related information, see CREDIBILITY.

In a memo, for example, include all the legally significant facts and any other facts needed to understand the memo without having to go to the pleadings, correspondence, or previous memos. This inclusion is needed because a memo written to a supervising attorney in June may be used in December by a new lawyer assigned to the case. Include enough about the cases for the reader to understand your reasoning without having to read the cases themselves. Similarly, cite to the record in a brief and include essential excerpts in an APPENDIX. These additions will avoid requiring the judge to leave the brief and search the record to understand the Argument. When writing to clients or other attorneys, include enough information in the heading or first sentence to remind the reader of your communication's context. This may be as simple as referring to the date and medium of your last communication, summarizing the client's request, or restating the issue you are negotiating on your client's behalf. For related information, see the entry for the kind of document you are writing.

CONTINUAL OR *CONTINUOUS*?

Continual means *intermittent* or *repeated at intervals,* such as *continual requests for advice. Repeated* may be a clearer alternative.

Continuous means *uninterrupted* or *unbroken,* such as *continuous vigil* or *continuous preoccupation with the law.*

CONTRACTIONS

Generally, do not use contractions such as *don't* or *isn't* in legal writing. They are too informal for almost all legal situations.

> **The plaintiff does not want to proceed because she cannot afford an attorney.**
>
> rather than
>
> The plaintiff doesn't want to proceed because she can't afford an attorney.

The only exception may be in writing to a familiar individual when you want to sound casual. For example, in an email, you might write the following.

> **I can't meet on Tuesday because I'm in court all day.**

CONTRACTS

When writing contracts, your dominant concerns must be thoroughness, accuracy, and consistency. To achieve these, keep the following ideas in mind throughout the drafting process.

1. When negotiating or determining the terms.

   Listen to your client carefully. Understand what the parties in fact want and what they can afford. Precisely because this is an obvious point, it is often overlooked. Remember that the goal of this document is to reach an agreement between both parties; avoid pushing for a contract so favorable to your client that the other party will walk away. Your goal is to create an agreement that works.

2. When PREWRITING.

   Make sure you are clear about what parts the contract must include and what situations the contract must cover. Try outlining the contract to make sure that all the needed pieces are included and are organized logically. Avoid, however, worrying so much about covering every contingency that you allow the contract to grow beyond a workable size or expense. You need to find a balance. Remember your client's budget and include what the client most needs without creating an overwhelmingly detailed contract. For ways to accomplish this, see ORGANIZATION FOR THOSE WHO CAN'T OUTLINE, OUTLINES, and THOROUGHNESS.

   Also make sure you are clear about local practices and conditions. Contract drafting can be more traditional than other legal writing, and you may be bound to follow what has preceded you. Be careful about incorporating clauses mindlessly, though. Make sure you understand each sentence in any contract you are transcribing. For related information, see FORMS and FORM CONTRACTS.

3. When WRITING.

   Reconcile yourself to writing many drafts of the contract to get it right. If you try to get all the details right in the first draft, you are likely to miss some important larger points. For example, you may initially focus on including the period of time covered by the agreement, the consideration, all the duties, and the way you will handle problems that may arise. On a second pass, add definitions as needed and contingency clauses. On a third pass, add the technical clauses needed to make the contract work legally and to close any unintended loopholes. Make a separate pass over the document to make sure that you have kept your handling of each situation consistent, that all parts of the document match, and that there are no extraneous sections. For help in organizing your drafts, see WRITING PROCESS.

4. When REWRITING.

Make each clause do one thing, not more. If you have used any clauses from forms, check to see if these clauses need to be divided because they cover multiple points. OUTLINES can help you here by breaking down the whole contract into a series of small points. This separation of points also helps keep the contract workable even if one clause is found invalid by a court. For help stating conditions clearly, see CONDITIONS, STATING THEM.

5. When REVISING.

Use clear, simple, businesslike language. Much progress has been made in this area, particularly in the areas of insurance and finance. Be on guard, however, for slipping back into the mire of LEGALESE. Use only the technical terms you need and define them if necessary. If technical terms are used from the business the contract addresses, be sure to use them in their common meaning within that field. If many definitions are needed throughout the contract, you may include a definition section to define all your key terms. For alternative ways to include definitions, see UNOBTRUSIVE DEFINITIONS.

Check for ambiguities. The most effective way to accomplish this to make multiple passes through the document, finding each use of a word to make sure its meaning is consistent. For example, check your use of key terms in two different ways.

(a) Check to make sure that you have used only one term for each item or person. Referring to the same person, item, or concept by two different terms creates an ambiguity that invites misunderstandings later. This check is more important than it may seem, because many unwanted ambiguities in contracts have been caused by use of synonyms instead of one consistent term, and these ambiguities can engender expensive litigation.

(b) Checking the text from another point of view, make sure that you have not used one term for several different items or persons. To complete this check, look at each use of every key term throughout the contract, focusing on one term at each pass. This requires many passes through the contract, but each pass is relatively quick, and this focus on one term at a time makes the checks less stressful and much more thorough. For discussion of related ideas, see AMBIGUITY, WAYS TO AVOID; KEY TERMS; LISTS, STRUCTURE OF; PUNCTUATING LISTS; and SYNONYMS.

After you have checked your use of terms, check for structural ambiguities. Check each list to make sure it is logically and grammatically parallel. Make sure that the wording indicates whether each list is conjunctive (*including all of the following*) or disjunctive (*including any of the following*). Even the smallest grammatical or punctuation errors can cause confusion in a contract.

At some point, consult with others. No one person can imagine all the pitfalls that the parties to any contract are hoping to avoid. No one person can imagine all the ways some reader can misconstrue a point.

6. When POLISHING.

   Proofread each clause in the contract and then reread the document as a whole, looking for larger contradictions between parts of the contract, rather than wording problems within one clause. In your concern for the details, you may have overlooked some larger ambiguities.

CONTRAST

The writing techniques useful in presenting a contrast are the same as those needed for a comparison. For specific information, see COMPARISON.

CORPORATE DOCUMENTS

Corporate documents cover a wide range of needs, from CONTRACTS to charts to detailed exchanges within the corporation. When you find yourself facing one of these new writing challenges, follow these basic steps.

1. Assess your time.

   Expect this document to take twice as much time as other documents of similar length. Any new task requires extra research and thought. You may end up spending more time on the document than you can bill; if so, view the extra time as an investment in future, similar projects. Console yourself with the knowledge that this investment is at least cheaper than law school.

2. Compare.

   Find similar documents from form books, colleagues, and sources online that provide examples and checklists. Look for elements that all samples include and develop a beginning list of components you need in your document. Avoid relying on only one source, however; seek out an array of examples to develop your understanding of what is possible, what is common, and what is unusual. For more on this, see FORMS.

3. Research relevant law and custom.

   Now that you have a beginning idea of what your document may look like and include, research the topic to become familiar with the legal requirements and the things that have gone wrong and led to litigation. The relevant case law is more likely to tell you what to avoid than what to do, but you can learn from other attorneys' mistakes.

4. Think.

Rather than rushing to copy the best of what you have found, think about the purpose of the document. What does your client need the document to accomplish? Identify the elements needed to complete your document, omitting any unneeded elements found in the forms but inappropriate to your document. Carefully review each phrase you incorporate from other models to make sure it contributes to your task. Do not include something you do not understand; persist with your research until you do understand it. Avoid the embarrassment of having your client ask you to explain a clause you cannot.

5. Organize the components you have collected into a cohesive whole.

Start with the statement of purpose, move to the explanation of essential points, and then move the specialized caveats and contingencies toward the end of the document. This beginning organization follows a logical progression that works for most documents, moving from the general overview to the explanation of covered content to the technicalities that are necessary but not central to the purpose of the document. This general organization also tends to create a positive tone, rather than a punitive or defensive one, and that tone makes it more likely that the parties will see the document as a constructive instrument.

6. Repair.

Fix all the little inconsistencies and errors. Reform the content as needed until you have a cohesive whole. Check for logical inconsistencies: use the same word for the same idea and avoid having two sentences or sections cover the same point, because these will create AMBIGUITY. Revise for consistent TONE. For help with this, see PROFESSIONAL LANGUAGE AND PRESENTATION.

7. Edit.

Check the whole document for CONCISENESS and READABILITY. Many forms, especially from FORM BOOKS, have unneeded LEGALESE, FLOWERY LANGUAGE, obtuse SENTENCE STRUCTURE, and unnecessary words. See REVISING CHECKLIST and POLISHING CHECKLIST.

8. Seek review from a trusted colleague.

Consider the advice you get carefully. All the effort you have invested in this document may have left you with some blind spots. While you are waiting for the colleague's feedback, work on other projects. Letting this document rest for a while helps you look at it afresh when you return to make your final changes. For information on documents that may be related, see CONTRACTS, FORMS, INFORMATIVE ARTICLES, NOTICE OF MOTION, ORDERS, WILLS, WRITING TO ATTORNEYS, and WRITING TO CLIENTS.

CORPORATIONS, *THEY* OR *IT*?

The corporation is *it* because it functions as a single entity. For related information, see COLLECTIVE NOUNS.

CORRELATING CONJUNCTIONS

See CONJUNCTIONS and READABILITY, subsection 7.

CORRESPONDENCE

For help with specific parts of correspondence, see COMMUNICATIONS, CLOSINGS FOR or COMMUNICATIONS, OPENINGS FOR. For help with specific readers, see WRITING TO ATTORNEYS or WRITING TO CLIENTS. For help with specific situations, see COMMUNICATIONS, ELECTRONIC; COMMUNICATIONS, INTERNATIONAL; COMMUNICATIONS, PERSUASIVE; COMMUNICATIONS, TONE OF; EMAIL; PROFESSIONAL LANGUAGE AND PRESENTATION; or SOCIAL MEDIA.

CORRESPOND TO OR *CORRESPOND WITH*?

Use *correspond with* if you mean that you and another party are writing to each other. Use *correspond to* if you mean that one point is analogous to another.

COULD

Use *could* to suggest a capacity that has not been used.

The defendant could have prevented the misunderstanding simply by answering the plaintiff's question about the backhoe's maintenance requirements.

Thus *could* is useful to add a negative shading to an action by suggesting that it was possible for something else to have happened. For related general information, see VERBS, AUXILIARY.

COULD CARE LESS OR *COULDN'T CARE LESS*?

Use neither in legal writing.

COULD OR *CAN*?

Could implies a capability that was not used. *Can* implies a capability that will be used. For examples and more detail, see *CAN* OR *MAY*? and VERBS, AUXILIARY.

COUNSEL

Counsel is used to refer to the attorney representing a particular person or organization.

> **Mr. Yang has retained counsel to represent him in these negotiations.**

Do not confuse *counsel* with *council*, which refers to an organized group that works on particular issues.

> **Mr. Yang presented the plan to the City Council.**

COUNSELING CLIENTS

You are a counselor to your clients, which incorporates giving a wide range of legal advice. In our legal culture, the client is the decision maker, so your job is to provide enough information to enable your client to agree or disagree with your advice. You are providing information, synthesizing the law, and showing how the law works and can lead to different conclusions. You are often in the position of protecting your client or preventing bad decisions, so before proceeding make sure that your client understands the case's legal context, background, chance of success, and any obstacles.

If you decide to proceed with the matter, keep your client updated and aware of your legal research and analysis. You may send them formal memos on the law, executive summaries with memos attached, or even copies of the statutes and cases. You may want to set up a system for answering questions as you proceed so that both of your expectations are met throughout the case. Your client may want to depend on your advice without hearing all it is based upon, but be sure that you give your position's strengths and weaknesses so that the client is aware of any risks going forward.

Unless you are also a trained psychiatrist or psychologist, do not let your counseling spill into the realm of therapy. Know when to recommend other professionals and have a list ready so that your client can make that decision. Also be aware of any other ethical responsibilities, such as reporting the furtherance or concealment of a crime. For related information, see BACKGROUND FACTS; EMOTIONAL FACTS; INTERVIEWING CLIENTS; LEGALLY SIGNIFICANT FACTS; OPINIONS, LEGAL; RECOMMENDATIONS, LEGAL; RESEARCH

STRATEGY GUIDE; TIME MANAGEMENT, and WRITING TO CLIENTS.

COUNTERARGUMENTS, HOW TO HANDLE

When defending against a counterargument, do so without losing the focus of your own argument. To do this, use the POSITIONS OF EMPHASIS to advance your position. Begin your PARAGRAPH BLOCKS, PARAGRAPHS, and sections with your affirmative position.

> **The proper standard here is the strict level of scrutiny; the category of persons suffering the discrimination is clearly defined.**

Then, after you have established your reasoning in the reader's mind, address the alternative position, usually later in the paragraph. As you do this, you may refer to the opponent's reasoning, but do so briefly, as an introduction to your counterargument. Rather than spending a sentence referring to the opposing position, merely imply that position as you state your own. As in the following example, relegate the opponent's position to a dependent clause, such as *when this court has allowed a lower standard;* keep your SUBJECT-VERB COMBINATIONS focused on your own assertions, such as *the category of persons being discriminated against was not clearly defined.*

> **When this court has allowed a lower standard, the category of persons being discriminated against was not clearly defined. In contrast, here the category is unquestionably women in their fifties and sixties.**

> or

> **Although the defendant quoted reasoning from several cases that applied a lower standard of scrutiny, those cases did not address the precise issue of the age of the persons who were discriminated against. They dealt with factors such as personality traits and personal behavior. But the category in this case is women of a certain age. Thus . . . .**

> rather than

> The defense argues that a lower standard of scrutiny should be applied to this case because the plaintiff is not part of a clearly defined group, as would be the case if discrimination were claimed to be based on race or gender. The defendant cites many cases to support this proposition. These cases include arguments of discrimination based on personality traits not directly related to the person's job or on the plaintiff's behavior in personal life. Those cases did not address the precise issue of this case, which is the combination of the gender and age of the plaintiff.

By putting your argument first and subordinating your opponent's position, you clarify the surrounding reasons for your discussion while still maintaining your own position. It helps you avoid allocating too much space in your brief to your opponent's arguments and prevents the opponent's brief from dictating your organization.

When phrasing your counterargument, avoid wording that focuses on the opposition, such as *the opponent contends*. Similarly, avoid inserting personal attacks, such as *opposing counsel's claims are unreasonable and unwarranted* or *opposing counsel did not research*; these phrases detract from your CREDIBILITY and add no substance to your argument.

For ways to word alternative arguments, see VERBS, MOODS, subsection 2. For a different but related issue, see ARGUING IN THE ALTERNATIVE. For more on context, see BRIEFS; BRIEFS, AMICUS; BRIEFS, APPELLATE; BRIEFS, PRETRIAL; BRIEFS, REPLY; and BRIEFS, TRIAL.

COURTS, HOW TO ADDRESS

See JUDGES, HOW TO ADDRESS.

COURTS, *THEY* OR *IT*?

Even though several judges together make up the court, refer to the court as *it* when discussing the legal entity.

> **The court made its reasoning clear when it stated that it would not grant a new trial.**

Use *they* only in two situations: when you are referring to the individual judges serving within one court or when the judge uses the pronoun *they*.

> **When preparing to hear oral arguments, the appellate court may ask their individual clerks to prepare bench briefs. They may also specifically ask their clerks to review the record when the briefs present disparate accounts of the facts.**

In the first situation, however, it would probably be clearer to use *judges* or *justices* instead of *court*.

CRAC

This, like IRAC, is a mnemonic device used by some to address one aspect of legal reasoning. See FORMALISM; ORGANIZATION, LARGE-SCALE; and ORGANIZATION, SMALL-SCALE. For help with the process of organizing, see ORGANIZE, HOW TO. For more ideas about analytical choices, see LEGAL ANALYSIS; REASONING, ANALOGICAL; REASONING, DEDUCTIVE; REASONING, INDUCTIVE; REASONING,

MODERN; REASONING, OTHER; REASONING, POSTMODERN; and REASONING, PRESENTING IT.

CREDIBILITY

Your credibility as an attorney and a person is affected by your writing. To make sure that the effect is positive, do the following.

1. Be accurate.

   Misstating facts, citing incorrect sources, and misrepresenting the situation would be remembered not only through this legal situation, but also in future dealings with this reader. For more how-to information, see ACCURACY.

2. Keep to the point.

   Make sure your documents do not stray from the problem you are trying to solve. A clear focus will save your reader time and will help you earn a reputation as an incisive and clear-headed writer who takes time to understand thoroughly the problem being addressed. For related information, see COUNTERARGUMENTS, HOW TO HANDLE; and ORGANIZATION, LARGE-SCALE.

3. Avoid unnecessary modifiers.

   Most of them are not legally significant, and they crowd your analysis. Check particularly for labels that substitute for logic, such as CLEARLY and OBVIOUSLY.

4. Maintain consistent TONE.

   If your tone vacillates from friendly to tough, or from formal to casual, the reader will be left uneasy and wondering about your command of the content and your attitude toward the reader. For how to manage this, see PROFESSIONAL LANGUAGE AND PRESENTATION.

5. Hold your temper.

   No matter how irate you are, avoid resorting to name calling. For alternatives, see BAD NEWS, GIVING IT; BAD NEWS, SOFTENING IT; and TOUGH, SOUNDING THAT WAY.

6. Check your citations.

   Make sure that each is impeccably presented, both in content and form. These are the proof that you have carefully researched the subject and that you are both familiar with the law and certain about its precise use for this case. Check statute numbers, case names, pinpoint citations, and signals. For related information, see CITATIONS.

7. Proofread.

   See that all documents leaving your office are proofread for correct spelling of names, correct dates and times, and correct spelling, punctuation, and grammar. For more help, see POLISHING CHECKLIST.

8. Meet your deadlines.

   This alone shows that you are in command of the case. If you know that you cannot meet the deadline, such as when it conflicts with other court dates, identify the problem at the outset and seek an extension immediately. Asking for extensions at the last minute would impair your credibility. See DEADLINES, MEETING THEM; and TIME MANAGEMENT.

For related information, see GRACE UNDER FIRE. If you are using artificial intelligence, see ARTIFICIAL INTELLIGENCE AND RESEARCH, ARTIFICIAL INTELLIGENCE AND WRITING, PROMPTS, and RESEARCH STRATEGY GUIDE.

CUTTING CORNERS

Generally, this is unwise in legal practice. Instead, create systems that allow you to be both efficient and thorough. For help in doing so, see CREDIBIILTY; DEADLINES, MEETING THEM, subsection (2)g; DOCUMENT CHECKLIST; MULTI-TASKING; NOTES; PRIORITIES WITHIN ONE PROJECT; RESEARCH STRATEGY GUIDE; TIME MANAGEMENT; and TRIAGE.

CYBERSECURITY

A major issue in the practice of law, cybersecurity is essential to protecting confidentiality. While most cybersecurity systems will be set in place by your employers, you can at the very least make sure you remove any compromising information before others see your work. See METADATA REMOVAL.

DANGLING MODIFIERS

See MODIFIERS, DANGLING.

DASHES

The dash, the gigolo of the punctuation world, has its uses and its dangers. It intrigues the writer with its drama and its convenient ambiguity. Like a gigolo, however, its effectiveness is determined by the user's *savoir faire* and restraint. If you overuse the dash in legal writing, you run the risk of looking desperate.

1. Danger of the dash.

Beware the ambiguity of the dash. It can replace a colon, a pair of commas, a transition, or parentheses, so you might use it without thinking too much. As a result, the reader has to do the extra work of determining how the dash is functioning in this particular context. The reader may not appreciate doing this, may decide not to bother, or may come to the wrong conclusion.

> **Ms. Willard has decided not to pursue the action further because litigation would be too expensive.**
>
> rather than
>
> Ms. Willard has decided not to pursue the action further—litigation would be too expensive.

2. Uses of the dash.

(a) Use an em dash, which is the equivalent of two hyphens, to make a phrase stand out on the page. If you use dashes for drama, make sure the content within the dashes is indeed dramatic and important. There are no spaces before or after the dash.

> **The defendant's action in this case—both understandable and humane—cannot be rightly condemned.**

COMMAS would be more formal here, but not as dramatic. When in doubt about whether dashes are deserved, use commas.

(b) Use an em dash to show a sudden turn of thought with an undercurrent of humor. This is a pleasing and deft touch, but one for which legal writing provides few opportunities.

> **Mrs. Smith thought the intruder might be a burglar—or her husband.**

Again, you must be very sure that the content can sustain the drama and wry humor the dash promises.

(c) Use a pair of em dashes to set off a mid-sentence phrase when commas would confuse the reader and parentheses would trivialize the content of the interruption.

> **Julia was also on a large and complex daily regimen of drugs. Daily she took three kinds of barbiturates—Tuinal, Fiornal, and Fiornal with Codeine—one of which included an opium derivative.**

Here you are using it out of rude necessity, and you may prefer to revise the sentence.

> **Julia was also on a large and complex daily regimen of drugs. Daily she took three kinds of barbiturates, one of which included an opium derivative. These barbiturates included Tuinal, Fiornal, and Fiornal with Codeine.**

For alternative punctuation marks, see COMMAS, subsection 2; COLONS; and PARENTHESES. For related information and techniques, see EMPHASIS.

(d) Use an en dash, which is essentially a HYPHEN, to separate numerals and letters in situations where it is needed for clarity and accuracy. It is also used after a birth year when the person is still living and between numbers or words to identify a range.

> **C-SPAN**
>
> **4-H Club**
>
> **Roosevelt's 1932–36 term**
>
> **1991–**
>
> **Steps 1–9**

3. Length of the dash.

Printing terms describe three different dash lengths: the em dash, the en dash, and the 3-em dash. The em dash, which is the most common dash, is the equivalent of two hyphens. It is used to set off phrases, as in (a) through (c) above. The en dash is the equivalent of the hyphen and has equivalent uses, such as to separate components within one term, as in (d). A 3-em dash, the equivalent of three hyphens, is used in some bibliography styles to indicate repetition. For related information, see HYPHENS.

DATA

Data means *information* and is now commonly used in both the singular and the plural, as in *these data are fascinating* or *this data is inconclusive.* When your AUDIENCE includes scientists or mathematicians, always treat *data* as plural.

DATES, ABBREVIATIONS OF

See ABBREVIATING DATES, NAMES, STATES, AND TITLES.

DEADLINES, MEETING THEM

Meeting deadlines is a skill you must develop to succeed as a legal writer, because failure to meet them can be malpractice. The secret to meeting deadlines successfully is becoming familiar with your overall writing process and adjusting it, so that you do not get behind at any stage in the process. For more on this, see WRITING PROCESS. After you have developed your own process, break that process into subsections and set interim deadlines. Mark those deadlines on your calendar, moving backwards from the deadline date, and work to meet each of those interim deadlines.

1. Common problems and possible solutions.

If you have trouble getting started, sometimes it helps to tie the deadline to a person, such as a person who will do a readthrough of the document. The potential embarrassment of publicly missing the interim deadline may motivate you. If you have trouble getting started because you feel overwhelmed, make a list of tasks on your mind, distinguish the essential from the others, and begin working on one of the essential tasks. For more help, see GETTING STARTED.

If you find yourself falling behind, examine your list of tasks and focus on only the essential tasks. For example, you may not have updated your cases and instead you are spending time reading law review articles. Or you may be spending too much time revising and leaving no time for POLISHING or for absorbing unforeseen disasters. Force yourself to shift to completing the critical tasks before you spend time on nice-but-nonessential tasks. For more help here and with related broader issues, see TIME MANAGEMENT and TRIAGE.

If you feel uncomfortable or bogged down, pinpoint which part of the process is uncomfortable. Overcoming this discomfort can help you meet deadlines. For example, you may feel uncomfortable in

- PREWRITING, when you are doing research, collecting facts, taking notes, reading the law, and organizing;
- WRITING, when you are actually translating ideas to paper;
- REWRITING, when you are checking large-scale organization and making sure that all parts of your analysis are present and in a logical order;
- REVISING, when you are checking small-scale organization to unify paragraphs, increase readability, and unify tone;
- POLISHING, when you are checking CITATIONS, spelling, and punctuation; or
- allocating time for each stage of the writing process.

One way to overcome this discomfort is to divide that uncomfortable stage into subparts and attack those subparts individually. Look under specific entries for each subpart for more information in this area, or see WRITING BLOCKS.

2. Meeting deadlines throughout the writing process.

One secret to meeting a final deadline is to set interim deadlines and be as disciplined about meeting them as you are about meeting the final, overall deadline. Be concrete and realistic in planning your schedule. Do not plan the timing assuming everything will go well. Instead, allow extra time in your schedule to accommodate problems, such as having to reorganize, being out sick for a day, or being delayed by someone's failure to get needed information to you. Laying out a schedule early in the writing process will help you focus and divide the task into manageable pieces.

Sample Interim Deadline Schedule for an Appellate Brief

4/16 File Notice of Appeal	4/17 Read record for error	4/18 Finish record	4/19 Confer with reader	4/20 Draft issues, research strategy
4/23 Research Issue I	4/24 Research	4/25 Research Issue II	4/26 Research	4/27 Research Issue III
4/30 Research	5/1 Research	5/2 Finish preliminary research	5/3 Arguments selected	5/4 Outline & draft point headings
5/7 Fill in holes by more research	5/8 Write (dictate) first draft	5/9 Finish first draft	5/10 Issue I to reader	5/11 Issue II to reader
5/14 Issue III and Conclusion to reader	5/15 Review reader feedback	5/16 Rewrite Issue I	5/17 Rewrite Issue II	5/18 Rewrite Issue III
5/21 Pull Table of Cases, Contents	5/22 Revise Issue I	5/23 Revise Issue II	5/24 Revise Issue III	5/25 Polish point headings
5/28 Polish text, Conclusion	5/29 Polish cites and tables	5/30	5/31 Brief Due	

Sometimes writers delay starting or stopping some parts of the writing process. The following suggestions should help you avoid this pitfall. By focusing on specific goals at each stage of the writing process and by meeting your interim deadlines, you can successfully meet your final deadline. For related concerns, see WHEN TO STOP.

(a) In PREWRITING.

If you are uncomfortable in prewriting, give yourself a time limit for finishing this stage of the writing process. Then divide your prewriting tasks by doing background research, briefing, and outlining separately. This can help you focus on each task so you do it more efficiently. Set a time to translate that prewriting to writing and force yourself to meet that deadline. Forcing yourself to meet these interim deadlines will help you avoid unnecessary procrastination and will allow adequate time to fix any problems you find throughout the subsequent stages of writing.

You may also find it helpful to spend a few minutes writing out the document's PURPOSE and SCOPE. Try to capture these points in just a sentence or two and let those sentences guide you as you make choices throughout the writing process.

If you are using artificial intelligence (AI) to help generate ideas or possible structures, be sure to build in time to verify the results. For more help, see ARTIFICIAL INTELLIGENCE AND RESEARCH and PROMPTS.

Sometimes in prewriting you can let PROCRASTINATION work for you by putting down one project and picking up another. A short detour to another project may refresh your mind. But do not let your procrastination slide into avoidance. As you delay writing, keep a notebook handy for any new ideas that can occur any time. Develop a system of taking NOTES that allows you to incubate your ideas, even if you are not actually at your desk or in the library. Thus procrastination becomes creative incubation. For related concerns, see GETTING STARTED.

(b) In WRITING.

If you are uncomfortable about writing the first draft, remember that the goal here is not to get it right, but to get it written. Do not revise as you write. It takes too much time, is too painful, and distracts you from your main task at this stage, which is to get all your ideas down on paper. Let the ideas flow, no matter how strange they seem. Just get your ideas into words somehow and finish the draft within the time period you set. Then do something else. Let the draft sit. For related concerns, see WRITING BLOCK.

If you use artificial intelligence (AI) to generate a draft, be aware that it may take more time to verify the results than to generate your own draft. For help on this, see ARTIFICIAL INTELLIGENCE AND RESEARCH, ARTIFICIAL INTELLIGENCE AND WRITING, DISCUSSION SECTION, and PROMPTS.

(c) In REWRITING.

Rewriting is often ignored or subsumed within other writing stages, and this causes problems with meeting deadlines. Give rewriting its own time, again by clearing the calendar and setting aside one large block of time or several small blocks only for that. If you have used artificial intelligence (AI) at any previous stage in the process, build in time here to make sure the organization is optimal for this document. For help here, use the REWRITING CHECKLIST.

At this stage, do any major shifting of large sections. Check large-scale organization and make sure all the ideas you wish to include have been stated and are placed in a logical order. Delete unfruitful digressions and unnecessary content. Draft preliminary HEADINGS to help you see your larger organization. Move each paragraph's thesis sentence to the beginning of a paragraph and read those alone to see if your logic flows clearly and to see that no logical steps are omitted. See also ORGANIZATION, LARGE-SCALE.

(d) In REVISING.

After rewriting, shift to the revising stage. This is the stage where you can focus on paragraphs and sentences now that the content is in place. To help you attend to all the details this stage involves, see ORGANIZATION, SMALL-SCALE; PARAGRAPHS; READABILITY; SENTENCE STRUCTURE; TONE; TOPIC SENTENCES; TRANSITIONS; and WORD CHOICE. Give particular attention to your ISSUES or QUESTIONS PRESENTED and CONCLUSIONS. You may find it helpful at this stage to use artificial intelligence (AI) tools that check grammar and usage.

(e) In POLISHING.

Allow at least one day to proofread large documents. Check citations, punctuation, spelling, grammar, wrong words, and any problems peculiar to your writing. See POLISHING, PROOFREADING, and WORDS SPELLCHECKERS MAY NOT CATCH.

(f) When time is short.

If time is so short that you need an emergency plan, see TRIAGE.

DEEM

Deem is LEGALESE for *is* or *hold*. The court may deem something to be a conclusion, but this word is an imprecise assessment of the court's action.

> **The court held that the GSA Administrator has the authority to enter into a lease on behalf of the government for up to twenty years.**
>
> rather than
>
> The court deemed the GSA Administrator has the authority to enter into a lease on behalf of the government for up to twenty years.

Identify the action as a HOLDING or as DICTA, but avoid *deem*, which is ambiguous and archaic.

DEFINITELY

Definitely means *for certain* or *assuredly*, and therefore should be avoided in legal writing unless the point is literally definite. For related information, see LITERAL MEANING.

DEFINITIONS, WHEN AND HOW TO INCLUDE

Add a definition when you are using any technical term, legal or otherwise, that may be unfamiliar to your reader and that is central to your point. If you are worried about insulting the reader by defining a term or wondering how best to include your definitions, see UNOBTRUSIVE DEFINITIONS. For related information, see CONTEXT-INDEPENDENT WRITING.

DEGREES AFTER NAMES

See ABBREVIATING DATES, NAMES, STATES, AND TITLES.

DEMAND FOR PAYMENT

See REQUESTS FOR PAYMENT.

DEPENDENT CLAUSES

A clause is a PHRASE that includes a subject and a verb; a dependent clause is a clause that is inserted into another sentence and cannot stand alone as a sentence. A dependent clause begins with a subordinating conjunction, such as *when*. For example, in the following sentence, *when it refused to submit a jury instruction on manslaughter* is a dependent clause.

> **The court abused its discretion when it refused to submit a jury instruction on manslaughter.**

For more on how these dependent clauses work in sentences, see SENTENCES, PARTS OF, subsection 8; and SENTENCE STRUCTURE, subsection 3. For related definitions, see CLAUSES.

DESIGN

Just as an architect designs a building, so you can design a legal document. You can consider what kind of document it is, how long it is supposed to last, how big it is, how many sections will be needed, what the relationships are among those sections, and where the document is generally situated, such as in a public or private setting.

You are not building your dream house. Rather, as a designer, you are creating a document to be used by others to help them accomplish or prevent a particular result. In doing so, you are asking questions and making decisions about your design. You can begin by asking general questions about how the document is situated.

- What are the document's purposes? Which PURPOSE is most important and why?
- Who are the document's READERS, which together are its AUDIENCE? Who is most important and why?
- What is the document's SCOPE? How big will it be and why?
- What is the document's stance or POINT OF VIEW? From what angle do you want others to view it?

You will return to these questions throughout the design process, reviewing your choices and priorities. In a sense, these four questions are at the center of a circle that represents both your personal writing process and the product itself. That product can be thought of as involving questions about design elements, such as these.

- What is your document's message or THEME? Can you summarize it in one sentence?
- What materials are you using and why? What is essential and what do you leave out? What arguments, policies, facts, laws, and so on must be included?

- What structure or form are you designing? What goes first and why? What goes second, third, and so on? How are the parts related to each other? How do you demonstrate the interrelationships? How does the form flow from the document's purposes? How does the form address the document's audiences? How many entrances does the document have, that is, does the reader have to move from the beginning to the end, or can the reader enter the document at various, well-marked places? Is the overall form dictated primarily by a doctrinal structure (such as elements of a statute), your arguments (such as strongest to weakest), your facts (such as unfavorable ones buried), or a complex combination of all of them?
- Do the proportions reflect the relative weight of each section to the theme? Are more important sections longer? Are unimportant sections shorter?
- What does the interior design look like? Are sentences, word choice, transitions, and syntactical structures traditional or modern? Are long sentences and elaborate words intertwined with modifiers to suggest a stuffed nineteenth century interior? Or are they short and minimalist?
- What is the document's finish like? Is it clean, free of typos and format inconsistencies? Is every detail accounted for? Is the overall effect consistent?

These questions require revisiting throughout the writing process. Keep returning to your drafting board to make adjustments as you answer the questions.

Also be willing to try several different designs before settling on your final choice. Quite often, your first design choice is writer-based; it makes sense to you but not to your readers. Try to move from this first choice to create a design that is reader-based. There are always several possible designs that work; the key is selecting the one that best fits with your answers to the questions above. For related information on structure, see COHERENCE; ORGANIZATION, LARGE-SCALE; ORGANIZATION, SMALL-SCALE; ORGANIZATION FOR THOSE WHO CAN'T OUTLINE; ORGANIZE, HOW TO; and OUTLINES. For ways to open your document, see EXECUTIVE SUMMARY. For more ideas about analytical choices, see LEGAL ANALYSIS; REASONING, ANALOGICAL; REASONING, DEDUCTIVE; REASONING, INDUCTIVE; REASONING, MODERN; REASONING, OTHER; REASONING, POSTMODERN; and REASONING, PRESENTING IT.

DESPERATION

See HELP.

DICTA

In an opinion, *dicta*, which means *words*, includes anything a court says that does not have a significant effect on the outcome of the case. Dicta differs from a holding, which is the case's outcome, and a rule, which is a more general statement of the legal foundation for the holding, both of which are binding on courts in that jurisdiction in subsequent opinions. Dicta is not binding on courts in subsequent opinions. Dicta can be significant, however, in your use of a case in research or in class. Use dicta to predict a trend in the law, to illuminate the reasoning in a case, to develop a new theory, or to understand future cases. For context and contrast, see CASE BRIEFS, HOLDING, and RULES.

DICTATION

Dictation software allows you to speak while your device types. This frees you to use the voice as your medium. Many lawyers who use voice-to-text software also do so because it saves time and because it makes them better speakers with clients, in conferences, and in the courtroom. Speaking has its own strengths, including fluidity, spontaneity, and energy. Writing on a computer may sometimes become too formal.

When you initialize your system, you will need to allow time to dictate the sentences required by the program, which memorizes your voice. As you dictate the first time, allow enough time to get used to the quirks of the program you are using, and then use the guidelines below.

If you have never dictated, begin with a small text, such as an email or notes from a meeting. Before dictating

- make some notes for your reference, perhaps by hand to focus your thoughts;
- have your large-scale organization written out and dictate accordingly;
- use numbers and parallel structure to help keep your dictated text organized; and
- remind yourself that you will revise and correct after the first draft is completed, not now.

If you are uncomfortable dictating, begin by dictating some short notes for your own reference, at least a paragraph or two. Speak normally so the device learns your natural voice. Speak as though the AUDIENCE is in the room facing you.

Do not correct the document as it appears on the device, for this will interrupt your train of thought and greatly slow down the process. Keep going, using the energy of your speech to move the document along. Look away from the device's screen as you dictate to avoid the temptation to edit before you have dictated a complete draft.

When you are finished, read the draft and delete or revise any passages that are too conversational or otherwise inappropriate. In particular, check for wordiness and incorrect translation, both common problems in dictated texts. For help here, see CONCISENESS. Also check for clear, coherent organization. For help here, see ORGANIZATION, LARGE-SCALE; ORGANIZATION, SMALL-SCALE; ORGANIZE, HOW TO; and TRANSITIONS. As you discover what your dictation habits are, you can work gradually to eliminate the bad habits, so that less rewriting will be necessary.

Eventually, with concentration, you can use dictation to close the gap between speaking, which can be too colloquial and wordy, and writing, which can be too stiff. As you revise works you have dictated, work to bring a readable quality to the text; note the changes and try to integrate them into your dictation so that you develop a versatile VOICE.

For related information, see DEADLINES, MEETING THEM; PROFESSIONAL LANGUAGE AND PRESENTATION; and TIME MANAGEMENT.

DICTION

Diction includes your choice of words and vocabulary in speaking and writing. To keep your diction precise, consider the following guidelines.

1. Avoid jargon and legalese; use plain English instead. For how-to information, see READABILITY, subsections 3 and 4.
2. Use one sentence per legal point, and in that sentence use words that frame your meaning precisely. For help here, see SUBJECT-VERB COMBINATIONS.
3. Avoid unnecessary modifiers, which may muddle, rather than clarify, your meaning. Modifiers may also raise questions of subjectivity. Your reader may doubt your assessments and be unnecessarily lured away from your precise meaning. For how-to information, see MODIFIERS.
4. When polishing your writing, take time to check for the grammar problems that you know are most likely to occur in your writing. Especially check SUBJECT-VERB AGREEMENT in complex sentences. For how-to information, see POLISHING.

For related information, see ORAL PRESENTATIONS and PROFESSIONAL LANGUAGE AND PRESENTATION.

DIFFERENT FROM OR *DIFFERENT THAN*?

Different from is always correct. *Different than* is allowable sometimes, according to some sources, but the rule is unsettled here. Use *different from* to be safe.

DIGRESSION

Digression, or straying from the main point, usually occurs when you are not sure of the main line of the analysis, when you have lost track of the document's main purpose, or when you want to say something even though it is not needed in the situation. For example, if you feel yourself digressing when writing a memo, stop and reread your QUESTIONS PRESENTED or ISSUES and the rules you are applying. Think about them. Then reanalyze your organization and decide whether the point is essential to the analysis. For help, see LEGAL ANALYSIS and RULES.

If you are still uncertain, leave the point and move to your Brief Answer or Conclusion. Try to see the larger picture and the result, both of which may illuminate the point's relevance. Alternatively, move to another part of the analysis and then come back. If you can sense that a point is digressing, fight the temptation to elaborate on it, or you will have to eliminate a great deal of your text when REWRITING.

Digression is especially troublesome in email. Because readers want to finish reading emails quickly, and because emails tend to be more informal, take particular care when writing them. Get to your point as quickly as possible and retain the same focus that you would in a more formal document; make sure nothing strays too far from your topic, stated in the subject line. For more help, see COMMUNICATIONS, ELECTRONIC. In longer letters, check your TOPIC SENTENCES and subheadings to make sure they create a coherent whole. If you find you are straying, resist the temptation to use a footnote to solve the problem. Instead, organize around your theme and either find an appropriate home for the stray thought or delete it.

When you are researching, stay with the mandatory authority that addresses the questions your client's situation has raised. It is easy to be drawn to other jurisdictions, unrelated issues, or just some interesting facts. These digressions are costly in time and money, so stay focused on your QUESTIONS PRESENTED, allowing the research itself to guide your decisions. If the research answers the question, amends it, or advances your analytical thinking for a better result, then it is useful. If it does not, do not pursue that line of research further.

For related writing problems, see CONCISENESS. See also BRIEF ANSWERS; CONCLUSIONS; CONTEXT-INDEPENDENT WRITING; ORGANIZE, HOW TO; and SUBJECT-VERB COMBINATIONS.

DIRECTING OTHERS' WORK

See EDITING; INSTRUCTIONS, GIVING THEM; and MANAGING WRITERS.

DIRECTIONS, GIVING THEM

See EDITING; INSTRUCTIONS, GIVING THEM; and MANAGING WRITERS.

DIRECT OBJECTS

See SENTENCE, PARTS OF, subsection 4.

DISCUSSION SECTION

The Discussion is the section in a memo or analytical email that presents and analyzes the law. As such, it explains to the reader how the law applies to the facts under analysis and predicts the possible outcome of the problem. The Discussion should use an objective style and should consider the specific requests of the audience. For help here, see WRITING, OBJECTIVE. For related information, see AUDIENCE.

A conventional Discussion should incorporate the following elements into a logical, unified whole:

- the rules relevant to the analysis;
- holdings from cases that define the rule;
- descriptions of cases that are analogous to the facts, issues, and reasoning being analyzed;
- an application of this law to the current situation, which includes both sides' arguments about how the law applies to the facts being analyzed;
- policy and equity arguments, which are woven into both sides' arguments;
- a balancing of those arguments and an analysis of who wins and why; and
- a balancing of both sides' arguments that explores the approaches that might be strongest for your client and justifies a prediction of an outcome.

For help with these components, see ANALOGOUS CASES; APPLICATION; DESIGN; EQUITY; HOLDINGS; MEMOS; ORGANIZE, HOW TO; ORGANIZATION, LARGE-SCALE; REASONING, PRESENTING IT; RULES; and WRITING, OBJECTIVE.

When deciding how to organize the Discussion, let your theme, the logical organization of the law, and its legal setting dictate your organization, rather than the history or sources of that law. For example, if discussing a tort with three elements, you might organize by discussing the elements in the order presented in a statute or in the order that most favors your client. Do not, however, organize by grouping the cases according to chronology or whether the plaintiff won or lost, without regard for the reasons.

Move from the rule to be applied through the application to the specific outcome. Avoid writing as if the law, application, and outcome are discrete subsections. For example, if you have a simple rule you might state the rule, give an example of it, apply it to your facts, and then reach a conclusion. If, however, you have a complicated rule with several subparts that are logically independent, you might state the point of law for each subpart and apply it to your facts before explaining the next subpart. For broader context, see REASONING, ANALOGOUS; REASONING, DEDUCTIVE; REASONING, INDUCTIVE; REASONING, MODERN; REASONING, OTHER; REASONING, POSTMODERN; REASONING, PRESENTING IT; and SYLLOGISMS.

Artificial intelligence (AI) may be useful in writing a Discussion at three points in the WRITING PROCESS. First, you might want to use AI in PREWRITING both to jump start your research and to discover potential approaches to your analysis. For help doing this, see PROMPTS, QUESTIONS PRESENTED, and RESEARCH STRATEGY GUIDE. Second, you may want to use AI in REVISING to help with specific edits, such as minimizing use of PASSIVE VOICE, increasing READABILITY, or achieving CONCISENESS. For help using AI at this stage of the writing process, see REVISING CHECKLIST. Third, you may also find AI useful in POLISHING to proofread or check for format consistency. For help here, see POLISHING CHECKLIST.

As tempting as it may be to have AI generate your draft, however, it may be less useful in WRITING. In this stage, you must be vigilant about your client's specific information. Before you enter that information, check all pertinent confidentiality and privacy requirements as well as whether the AI system you are using retains and publishes this information. In WRITING, AI may also be too indiscriminate about legal content. For example, AI may not discern between MANDATORY AUTHORITY and PERSUASIVE AUTHORITY and may not focus on the analytical patterns most appropriate to your case. For help in analyzing the strength of a draft generated by AI, see COHERENCE; ORGANIZATION, LARGE-SCALE; ORGANIZATION, SMALL-SCALE; ORGANIZATION FOR THOSE WHO CAN'T OUTLINE; ORGANIZE, HOW TO; and OUTLINES. For more about analytical choices, see LEGAL ANALYSIS; REASONING, ANALOGICAL; REASONING, DEDUCTIVE; REASONING,

INDUCTIVE; REASONING, MODERN; REASONING, OTHER; REASONING, POSTMODERN; and REASONING, PRESENTING IT.

In REWRITING, AI may be less helpful because you are checking your case's specific law, facts, potential theories, threshold issues, and possible sequences of arguments. If you did use AI to generate a draft, use the REWRITING CHECKLIST yourself to ensure the document is specific to your client's needs and reflective of your own thinking.

Wherever you choose to use AI, make sure you verify its results. For guidelines on this, see ARTIFICIAL INTELLIGENCE AND RESEARCH, ARTIFICIAL INTELLIGENCE AND WRITING, and PROMPTS.

DISINFORMATION

Disinformation is false information intended to obscure the truth and mislead. As you research and read the work of others, be alert to the use of disinformation. Intentionally misstating the facts directly violates the Model Rules of Professional Responsibility, which forbid lawyers from engaging in conduct involving dishonesty, fraud, deceit, or misrepresentation. Even if it seems persuasive to use disinformation, it endangers your reputation and your client's case. For related information, see ACCURACY, MISINFORMATION, PROFESSIONAL LANGUAGE AND PRESENTATION; and QUOTATIONS, WHEN TO USE.

DISINTERESTED OR *UNINTERESTED*?

Use *disinterested* if you mean that the person is neutral on the point. Use *uninterested* if you mean that the person does not care about the point.

DO

As an auxiliary verb, *do* adds emphasis, especially when answering a question affirmatively when the reader is expecting a negative answer.

> **Our client does expect to have the building ready for occupancy by the agreed-upon date.**

For related information, see VERBS, AUXILIARY, subsection 9.

DOCUMENT CHECKLIST

The following checklist is designed to give you a point of departure for checking analytical documents. This list can be applied, for example, to an advisory email, memo, brief, or agency decision. You can edit this list according to your readers' preferences, your writing concerns, and your project's purpose. For guidance on other types of documents, see COMPLAINTS, CONTRACTS, CORPORATE DOCUMENTS,

INFORMATIVE ARTICLES, INTERVIEWING CLIENTS, LEGISLATION, ORDERS, PLEADINGS, and WILLS.

You might also use some of these questions as a guideline for discovering the expectations of an assigning attorney. If you manage writers, you may use this to guide your directions and responses.

1. PURPOSE.

(a) Is the document's main theme or message clear?

(b) Is it stated within the first two paragraphs or in the issue and answer?

(c) If an issue is required, are its subject and verb focused on important terms?

(d) If an answer is required, is it stated with reasons specific to this situation?

2. CONTENT.

(a) Is the law itself quoted or accurately paraphrased?

(b) Is each legal element clearly delineated and consistent with the law?

(c) Are the principles of statutory interpretation accounted for?

- Context?
- Plain meaning?
- Internal consistency?
- Previous interpretations?
- Legislative intent?
- Purpose?
- Policy?

(d) Are TERMS OF ART used accurately?

(e) Is any non-legal, technical material accurate?

(f) Are your client's arguments included?

(g) Are the other side's arguments addressed as needed?

(h) Are the arguments compared to each other so that the reader understands why one prevails over the other?

(i) Is each section or element of the presentation adequately resolved before moving to the next point?

(j) Are sections and elements connected to each other, where appropriate?

(k) Are all conclusions on individual sections and elements synthesized in the last paragraph?

(l) Are recommendations made?

3. Organization.

(a) Is the organization consistent with the law and appropriate to these readers and this purpose?

(b) Does the organization lead logically to the recommendation?

(c) Can any legal reader not misunderstand the scheme?

(d) Do the first sentences of the paragraphs guide the reader through the document?

For help here, see ORGANIZE, HOW TO.

4. READABILITY and CLARITY.

(a) Are the SUBJECT-VERB COMBINATIONS effective?

(b) Are subjects and verbs close together?

(c) Are TRANSITIONS accurate and adequate?

(d) Are sentences generally less than four lines in length?

(e) Is the tone appropriate to this audience? Are terms of address appropriate?

(f) Does the document use only terms the reader will understand or add definitions for required, unfamiliar terms?

(g) Is ACTIVE VOICE used whenever possible?

5. Finishing touches.

(a) Have techniques for CONCISENESS been applied?

(b) Is the SENTENCE LENGTH varied?

(c) Are POSITIONS OF EMPHASIS used effectively?

(d) Are SUBORDINATE CLAUSES used effectively?

6. MECHANICS.

(a) Are all required conventions followed?

(b) Are the citations accurate in form and substance?

(c) Are grammar errors removed by using a grammar checker and a careful reading?

(d) Has the spellchecker been run?

(e) Are there any wrong WORDS THAT SPELLCHECKERS WON'T CATCH?

(f) Are all typographical mistakes corrected?

For more detailed questions to ask at each stage in the writing process, see PREWRITING CHECKLIST, REWRITING CHECKLIST, REVISING CHECKLIST, POLISHING CHECKLIST, WRITING PROCESS, and WRITING PROCESS CHECKLIST. If you are using artificial intelligence, see ARTIFICIAL INTELLIGENCE AND RESEARCH, ARTIFICIAL INTELLIGENCE AND WRITING, DISCUSSION SECTION, PROMPTS, and RESEARCH STRATEGY GUIDE. For more ideas on responding to writing, see EDITING and MANAGING WRITERS.

DOVETAILING

See CONNECTIONS, MAKING THEM.

DRAFTING

Drafting as used in legal writing refers to creating documents that themselves have legal consequences similar to statutes and ordinances. Because they have legal consequences, they are written with a special focus on accuracy, precision, and scope. See the entry for the specific kind of drafting you are doing, such as BRIEFS, COMPLAINTS, CONTRACTS, CORPORATE DOCUMENTS, LEGISLATION, NOTICE OF MOTION, MOTIONS, or WILLS. For general writing concerns particularly important in drafting, see ACCURACY; AMBIGUITY, WAYS TO AVOID; LISTS, STRUCTURE OF; ORGANIZATION, LARGE-SCALE; and PRECISION. For general relevant topics, see ORGANIZE, HOW TO; and WORD CHOICE.

DRAFTS

Plan for enough time to write more than one draft of any document. Let the first draft be creative, thorough, and imperfect. Include everything you think necessary to the piece and all things that you think might be useful. Your goal at this point may be to get it written, rather than getting it right, with yourself as the primary reader.

Then use subsequent drafts for getting it right, considering all READERS. For help here, see REWRITING, REVISING, and POLISHING. For related information, see WRITING, and PERFECTIONISM.

DUE TO

Use *due to* only after a linking verb, such as *is* or *seemed*, and only where the phrase following *due to* modifies the subject of the sentence.

This omission was due to negligence, not unforeseeable circumstances.

Here *due to* modifies *omission* and *was* is a linking verb. See VERBS, LINKING.

In all other situations, use *because of.*

This omission occurred because of negligence, not unforeseeable circumstances.

Here *because of* modifies *occurred,* and *occurred* is a transitive verb. Using *due to* to modify a verb may become universally acceptable someday, but for now it is safer to avoid it. For related information, see TRANSITIONS.

DUNNING LETTERS

See REQUESTS FOR PAYMENT.

DURING THE TIME THAT

Try substituting *while,* for CONCISENESS.

EACH

Each means one of two or more persons, objects, or things considered individually. As such, *each* takes a singular verb when used as a pronoun.

Each lawyer has a preferred approach to presenting an opening argument.

Fourteen exhibits were presented at the trial; each is important to the outcome of the case.

EDITING

Whether you are editing your own writing or someone else's, you will find that editing involves adopting a role distinct from that of the writer. If your job is editing another's work, then make only the adjustments that are necessary for accuracy, grammar, and readability. If your job is to supervise this writer, you do not want to take an editing approach. For help with that role, see MANAGING WRITERS.

To adjust quickly and comfortably to this editing role, consider the following general principles, specific techniques, and overall process.

1. General principles.

   (a) Focus on the task.

   Edit the document to fulfill its purpose and communicate to each of the readers in its audience. Editing a document does not involve questions of personal style, nor does it involve evaluating the writing or the writer. Unlike teaching, editing focuses on the document itself and how it will affect the reader. For related information, see AUDIENCE, PURPOSE, and READERS.

(b) Focus on particular aspects of writing.

As you edit, focus on only a few aspects at a time. Avoid reading from beginning to end and looking for everything at once. Most texts need attention on several levels, from the overall structure to the polished details. Therefore looking for everything at once creates fatigue and inefficiency. Instead, create a system of TRIAGE for checking important content points first. When those are in place, turn your focus to coherent organization. Then move to issues of READABILITY. Finally, use a separate pass through the document to correct smaller errors in grammar, citations, and spelling. For some ideas on what to check on each pass, see ORGANIZE, HOW TO; REWRITING CHECKLIST; REVISING CHECKLIST; and POLISHING CHECKLIST.

(c) Review the document in different sequences.

Adjust your editing plan so that each part of the document receives a careful edit. Editing is hard work, and attention tends to lag after a few hours. If you always begin your editing at the same place, such as the beginning of the document, you are likely to have a document that is flawless at the beginning, adequate in the middle, and weak at the end. The techniques listed in the previous paragraph should help you avoid this problem. Additionally, when you reread the whole text, begin at different points in the document as you edit for particular aspects of writing. This approach increases the likelihood that you will catch any errors you missed on your previous editing pass.

2. Specific techniques.

(a) Avoid personal references in comments.

When making comments to the writer, speak in terms of the reader and the document, not the writer and editor.

> **Reader may need a definition or paraphrase to follow this point.**
>
> rather than
>
> You didn't define this.

This helps reduce the sting of having one's work criticized. It also creates a broader sense of audience expectation, which the writer can apply to the next project.

(b) Avoid absolute judgments.

Instead of stating judgments about the overall writing quality, describe the problem or revision within this specific context.

The logical link between these two paragraphs could be clearer—add a transition phrase? Repeat a key word?

rather than

unclear logic

Although this focused editing may require more words, it will save you time in the long run, because the clearer comment helps the writer revise successfully and willingly not only in this draft but also in the next draft; you will avoid volleying comments and building tension.

(c) Comment on strengths as well as weaknesses.

Add a few comments on strong passages as well as weak ones. This will help the writer see your goals more clearly, besides avoiding the purely negative context most writers have come to expect and dread. Resist the urge to omit compliments, even when you are pressed for time. The good will that comes from those compliments will ultimately save time because writers tend to remember positive comments and apply them to future documents.

3. Overall process.

Even when time is limited, try the following three-step triage approach to editing. This approach helps you avoid the frustration of writing detailed comments that become moot later in the process.

(a) Scan the document once as the reader.

Read through the document quickly from a reader's point of view. Ask yourself, *What does this reader want to know from this document? How will the reader use the document?* Without stopping, flag any places where you were confused or had unanswered questions.

When you have finished this first reading, pause to consider whether REWRITING is needed. If so, focus on those areas only. Save the REVISING details for another pass. For example, note any of the following problems:

- content problems, such as
  - missing or unclear overall thesis or THEME,

  - overly general ISSUES,
  - missing or vague TOPIC SENTENCES,
  - problems with ACCURACY,
  - missing support,
  - missing logical links,
  - inaccurate or incomplete CITATIONS,
  - unaddressed counterarguments,
  - unnecessary content, and
  - distracting or unhelpful tangents; and
- organization problems, such as
  - missing logical steps,
  - two steps blurred together,
  - one step split unnecessarily,
  - steps out of logical order, and
  - missing connections or TRANSITIONS.

When any of these problems is significant, note the areas where the problems occur, note possible causes of the problem, and return the document to the writer. Because the content and organizational changes often fundamentally change the document, you are saving time by not editing text that will ultimately be deleted or totally reworked.

If your suggestions for REWRITING are minor, move on to REVISING concerns.

(b) Check the document for READABILITY and lack of AMBIGUITY.

Reread the text and mark any passages that force you to slow down or backtrack. Specifically, check the text for the following problems:

- words unfamiliar to the reader,
- inconsistent terms,
- vague phrases,
- double entendres,
- poorly worded transitions,
- inaccurate or inadequate signals of structure,
- long introductory phrases,
- long sentences,

- choppy sentences, and
- confusing lists.

If the document needs substantial work, divide this review into multiple passes, scanning for just one or two problems at each pass. Dividing the tasks is also helpful when you are fatigued, because you are more likely to be reliable when checking for only a few variables at one time.

When improvements occur to you readily, note them. When you see a problem, but a solution does not readily come to mind, describe the problem in your role as reader.

If the changes here are so significant that you cannot see how the text will look after they are made, return the document to the writer. If not, proceed to the next stage of editing.

(c) Review for smoothness and professional polish.

As you begin this set of passes over the document, focus on POLISHING. Check for the following:

- inconsistent TONE,
- awkward WORD CHOICE,
- distracting REPETITION,
- unneeded PASSIVE VOICE,
- inappropriate or inconsistent level of formality,
- incorrect format,
- PUNCTUATION inaccuracies,
- GRAMMAR inaccuracies,
- typographical errors, and
- anomalies caused by previous changes.

If you see repeated PATTERNS of problems, note this objectively, so the writer can begin to check future documents for these problems.

For related information, see ADJUSTING TO A NEW WRITING SITUATION, DOCUMENT CHECKLIST, GRACE UNDER FIRE, and PRINCIPLES OF GOOD LEGAL WRITING.

EDITING QUOTATIONS

Although some editing of quotations is desirable for effective focus and READABILITY, too much can make the reader suspicious, as in the following example.

> The court stated its reasoning explicitly when it said, "[W]e cannot ignore the plaintiff's complaint . . . . [because] [i]n this case, the issue of mutuality . . . requires . . . examin[ing] . . . the parol evidence. . . ."

When faced with this situation, paraphrase or summarize the quotation rather than overediting. Be sure to add pinpoint citations after the paraphrase. For specific ways to handle quotations, see PARAPHRASE and QUOTATIONS, HOW TO PUNCTUATE, subsections 7–9.

EFFECT OR *AFFECT*?

See *AFFECT* OR *EFFECT*?

E.G.

See SIGNALS.

ELECTRONIC ETIQUETTE

Law is a formal profession, with ethical rules that apply, no matter what the form of communication. Email and other electronic communications can be fast, informal, and convenient. They can also be read as examples of your professional posture. Worse, they may be discoverable. Therefore, treat all electronic postings, personal and professional, as though members of your local bench and bar association were reading them.

Any public postings, even if intended for friends, can affect your job searches and your general professional standing. Avoid using any electronic communications for negative or very informal comments, for serious problem solving, or for confidential material. As in any written communication, be aware of TONE and ACCURACY. For related information, see ELECTRONIC COMMUNICATIONS, ELECTRONIC MESSAGING, EMOJIS, PRIVACY, PROFESSIONAL LANGUAGE AND PRESENTATION, SOCIAL MEDIA, and TEXTING UNDER THE TABLE.

ELECTRONIC FILINGS

Most courts and agencies accept or require electronic filings of documents. When you begin your project, check the rules and dates for filing those documents. Similarly, check with your reader to discover whether an electronic version of a document is preferred, whether it should be attached to or incorporated in an email, or even whether the preferred method is physical delivery of paper copies.

One major concern with electronic filings is the potential problem of including information you did not mean to reveal. For help with this issue, see METADATA REMOVAL. If you do not read electronic versions accurately, plan enough time to review a printed copy because seeing a document in a different medium often helps you see errors.

For related information, see DEADLINES, MEETING THEM; TIME MANAGEMENT; and WRITING AND TECHNOLOGY.

ELECTRONIC MESSAGING

As new technologies emerge, lawyers find new ways to communicate with clients, colleagues, and courts. These technologies create conveniences and innovations for interpersonal correspondence, such as speed, immediacy, and a way to take care of non-substantive matters efficiently. These technologies also create new challenges and hazards for legal writers, such as sending messages prematurely or not being able to adequately evaluate communications done on your phone. To choose your best means of communicating, remember the following points.

1. Write on your phone for only non-substantive matters. This simple practice will keep you safe from premature or overly informal communications. It will also help you keep a clear record of your communications because your phone is not a part of your office's record-keeping system.
2. Write with your professional responsibilities in mind whenever you are writing as a lawyer. Word your communication as if it might be read aloud in court, even if you think otherwise; it could be discoverable or violate client confidentiality. Any legal writing can have legal consequences, so substantive matters may be best left to carefully constructed EMAIL. Additionally, develop the habit of pausing before you hit REPLY TO ALL.
3. Be businesslike in TONE and maintain ACCURACY in content, even if it requires more words. Choose factual terms over emotional ones because emotional words can create ambiguity. Good intentions do not necessarily lead to good results. For example, when a reader does not know you well or chooses to be upset with you, friendly teasing can be read as caustic jibes, stern reminders as mild advisories, and respectful formality as condescension. Remember that HUMOR, for example, can go awry easily, especially when it includes double entendres.
4. Proofread every message as if you were a hostile reader, just to be sure you cannot be misunderstood. This step will help you to catch any errors in TONE or CONTENT. The time invested now will save future time clearing up any misunderstandings.
5. Use each work message to build an appropriate professional image. For help using those messages to maintain that image, see

ADJUSTING TO A NEW WRITING SITUATION and PROFESSIONAL LANGUAGE AND PRESENTATION. For related information, see EMOJIS, SOCIAL MEDIA, and TEXTING UNDER THE TABLE.

ELECTRONIC RESEARCH

See RESEARCH STRATEGY GUIDE.

ELEGANT VARIATION

Elegant variation means using different words for the same idea, solely for variety. Do not use this technique in legal writing, especially when using terms of art or key legal terms.

This contract supersedes all previous contracts.

rather than

This document supersedes all previous contracts.

In the latter version, the reader cannot determine whether the *document* is a contract or something else. For more examples and discussions of related general points, see REPETITION, subsections 1 and 2. For related general information, see WORD CHOICE.

ELLIPSES

An ellipsis is a series of four spaces alternated with three periods **(. . .)** used to show omissions in quotations. Although some text-producing programs provide a single character of three unspaced periods as an ellipses (…), the *Chicago Manual of Style* and *U.S. Government Printing Office Style Manual* both require spaced periods. In government documents, asterisks often replace the periods, but the spacing rules remain the same.

An ellipsis is never needed at the beginning of a quotation; instead, this change is signaled by placing brackets around the beginning letter of the quotation, which has been changed from either upper or lower case to fit into the sentences around it grammatically. An ellipsis does not replace the original punctuation of the sentence. For example, if words are omitted at the end of a sentence, the period ending the sentence follows the ellipsis.

He argued in the alternative, explaining that the motion would be premature even if it were justified factually.

becomes

He argued in the alternative . . . .

But if a sentence is complete before the omitted text, the period comes before the ellipses.

He argued in the alternative, explaining that the motion would be premature even if it were justified factually. His arguments were extensive and detailed. These arguments convinced the court.

becomes

He argued in the alternative, explaining that the motion would be premature even if it were justified factually. . . . These arguments convinced the court.

Finally, an ellipsis must be kept together on one line of text. For details of its use, see QUOTATIONS, HOW TO PUNCTUATE, subsection 8.

EM OR EN DASH?

See HYPHENS and DASHES.

EMAIL

Email serves a variety of purposes, ranging from rendering a formal legal opinion to answering a brief logistical question. Each email can affect credibility and professional reputation just as much as any other legal writing. Therefore, treat all email as significant, using a writing process that includes safety and quality checks. By using the following guidelines, you can ensure that your email is received as you intended.

1. Determine the READERS.

   Think of all possible readers for the email. You may think that you are writing a quick note to a supervising attorney, but that attorney may forward it as an opinion to a nervous client. Decide to whom you will address it and who might receive courtesy copies. Your writing decisions will depend on your readers' knowledge of the email's content and context. If you are writing something that will eventually reach the client, see WRITING TO CLIENTS for more guidance. To avoid problems with including the wrong people, see REPLY TO ALL.

2. Determine the purposes.

   Have a clear idea of why you are writing the email. In legal practice, the purpose of writing an email often falls into one of five categories:

   (a) answering quick questions,

   (b) making requests,

   (c) giving formal legal opinions,

   (d) negotiating, and

   (e) keeping a record.

You may also be writing the email for less official purposes, such as building business, stopping an annoying discussion, or encouraging a different approach to a case.

(a) Answering quick questions.

You may answer a quick question with one email and the subject will be closed. This is rare. Often in practice, discussions you thought finished will later revive. So you may want to keep files of any email that address a particular case, useful source, or common issue. To be safe, include the sender's message with the reply. You can keep the quick question in context by continuing to reply to the current email and keeping the trail of correspondence within each email. This approach also facilitates record keeping because you have the whole conversation saved in one email.

(b) Making requests.

State the request in a sentence or two, explaining the context in which you are making the request. If you have multiple requests, make that clear to the reader, whether by enumeration, separate paragraphs, or some other means. Some readers like to respond within the message, and dividing the request clearly facilitates that kind of response. As with any request, your goal is to communicate that the request is in the reader's interest and then make it as easy as possible for the reader to respond.

(c) Giving formal legal opinions.

Treat the analysis formally and thoroughly. Use an effective introduction or EXECUTIVE SUMMARY that includes your conclusion. Make sure you include all steps in the reasoning and add an explanation of all needed legal caveats. Show that you understand the reader's situation and have taken it into account.

If your purpose is to communicate something long and complex, you may want to consider putting it in a readable attachment that your reader can easily download. When you think the reader may not bother to open the attachment, make sure your brief email explains why the document is necessary. Because these documents are complicated and critical, see OPINIONS, LEGAL and WRITING TO CLIENTS.

(d) Negotiating.

As you approach these emails, consider your reader's positions on various points at each stage of the negotiation process. Look for common ground, because that is a good place to find solutions. You may want to begin the email by recognizing that common ground or incorporate those points as you offer alternatives. This will show that you have considered and understood the reader's positions and that you are willing to negotiate.

Because emails can so easily be misread, work especially hard on TONE and fill in contextual points. Email can be too cold or one-way for careful discussion of sensitive issues and can also elicit quick *no* responses, so you may choose to call or meet with the recipient when your physical presence will have a greater effect than your electronic one. For more tips, see BAD NEWS, GIVING IT; BAD NEWS, SOFTENING IT; and WRITING, PERSUASIVE.

(e) Keeping a record.

To help your readers use and file emails appropriately, create a system for subject line, client, and general topic. If you are attaching a file like others being submitted to the reader, put your name on the file, e.g., *Smith comments on Russell brief.* If you are suggesting a direction a case might take, label your suggestion, e.g., *Russell brief-economics theory on issue #2.* You may also want to label the priority of your email or color code it if your system allows you to do so.

Use an effective SUBJECT LINE that meshes with your record-keeping system. Readers use the subject line to determine how to treat and file the email, so address only one topic in an email. Use the case number or the client's name and the subject of the email, such as *Russell case—deposition with Dr. Windemere.* If you anticipate creating a series of emails on the same subject, you can even number them: *Russell #1—deposition information, Russell #8—confirmation of pretrial hearing date.* Be as specific as you can.

Re: Canceled meeting on Russell defense

rather than

Meeting canceled

Within the body of the email, write context-independent texts that include pertinent information to remind your reader of the email's overall context. Just a phrase or two will orient the reader, such as, *As you recall, we need to call Dr. Windemere as an expert on product safety. He will be deposed on January 22, 2025, at 11:10 a.m. in our conference room 10A.* For related information, see CONTEXT-INDEPENDENT WRITING and RECORDS, KEEPING THEM.

3. Determine the SCOPE.

Decide what information and analysis is essential to the email's subject. Focus on that content and give enough reminders and context so that the readers can make sense of this email. When organizing this information, try to communicate the main message in the first line so that they know why they should continue reading. You also can help limit the length of the email by focusing each email on one point only. Including multiple concerns in one email makes filing and storage much more difficult and increases the chance that some information may get forwarded inappropriately.

4. Determine the appropriate TONE and FORMAT.

If you are writing to a reader for the first time, use a tone that is respectful and businesslike. The reader's reaction to your tone will outlast the message, so decide what STANCE is appropriate for the email's audience and purpose. If you are responding to an email, note the tone and format of the incoming email. You may want to respond in a similar format and reflect the tone, if it is appropriate. This attention to detail shows that you are reading carefully and picking up on the writer's approach. If you respond in a different format, your email may seem either abrupt or too formal. For related information, see COMMUNICATIONS, TONE OF and TONE.

5. Use the first paragraph as an executive summary.

If you cannot summarize the content in the subject line, state your point and a summary of the content immediately. This allows the reader to prepare for anything more detailed. Although you do not want to be too abrupt, state the major points early. Get your message across in one screen. For handling difficult situations, see BAD NEWS, GIVING IT and BAD NEWS, SOFTENING IT.

6. Identify subpoints within the text.

If you have several points or questions, numbering them will help your reader respond easily. Additionally, you may want to use HEADINGS to identify your points and clarify the organization. For related information, see LISTS, STRUCTURE OF.

7. Check for ACCURACY and CLARITY.

Reread the email to make sure the content is correct. Make sure that the subject line, executive summary, and points are all accurate. Set up your email's spellchecker to check each email when it is queued. Check for terms the reader may not understand or steps omitted in the logic. Too often, email remains writer-based, clear to the writer but not the immediate reader nor anyone to whom the email will be forwarded.

8. Beware of crossing emails.

   When correspondence reaches a fast pace, your emails can cross each other and create confusion. For example, in the heat of negotiations or settlements, your emails can cross with your opposing attorneys', which can result in ambiguous references to what is agreed upon. Pause. Avoid writing multiple responses to a single email before you have received a response from your reader.

9. Assume the email will be forwarded.

   Email can be forwarded easily and even accidentally, so compose the email as though anyone might read it. This means that content, tone, and style should be appropriate to the message and conform to standards accepted by the public. Avoid personal references, opinions you do not want public, or any random or casual thoughts.

For related information, see PROFESSIONAL LANGUAGE AND PRESENTATION.

EMAIL, HOW TO MANAGE

Reading your email may make or ruin your day, depending on how you do it. If you always read all your email first, no matter how much you have, you may find the job expanding to take your whole morning. If you read every email whenever it comes in, you may find it difficult to focus on any other tasks. In contrast, if you read email at designated times throughout your day, you can preserve time for your other work tasks, such as researching, writing, and meeting with people. The following techniques can help you keep email under control.

1. Set aside specific times to read your email.

   You may want to do this on the hour, as a break from composing, or at a given time morning and afternoon. Make an appointment with yourself to read email and concentrate completely on that task. Otherwise, turn off the email signal and the screen pop-ups and allow yourself to be free of interruptions as you do your other work.

2. Create a system of triage.

   When time is short and email messages are numerous, you may need to perform TRIAGE. To do this, scan the names of people sending you email and read essential ones first, such as messages from clients or your supervisor. Then scan the SUBJECT LINE of any remaining email and read those that may need immediate attention, such as queries about current projects or meetings scheduled for the same day. Save other topics, such as ongoing discussions on listservs, to read at a later time when you are not so rushed.

If possible, dispose of each email once you read it. Delete, respond, or file. If you defer an email to another time, give it an electronic home or a marking that will set it up to be responded to later.

3. Time how long it takes you to read.

   Look at the clock when you begin and note the number of email messages to be read. Look at the clock when you finish and note how many minutes you average per email. Do this a dozen times to determine your average; this will help you determine how much time you need to set aside for reading and responding.

4. Create an electronic filing system.

   (a) Create folders to house groups of email.

   Move your email on the same case or topic to one folder on your hard drive. Use subfolders to file them according to particular subcategories of the case, just as you would organize paper folders. Create a system that allows not only you to retrieve the documents quickly but also anyone working with you on the case.

   (b) Back up your hard drive.

   Especially when electronic files replace the hard copies, make sure that you have a separate backup system. Do this regularly and keep it in a separate place to be safe. For current files, you may want to preserve the electronic folder on a separate device or a flash drive that is properly protected and secured.

   (c) Print only essential documents.

   Decide what selected documents to print, if any. These might be documents you need while you are in court or while you are negotiating a deal.

For more tips on efficiency, see NOTES; PRIORITIES; RECORDS, KEEPING THEM; and TIME MANAGEMENT. For hazards to avoid, see REPLY TO ALL.

EMAIL OR MEMO?

As you begin writing an answer to a research request or a client's question, decide which form the document will take.

You may use email if all of the following three factors are true: (1) your answer to a question is three paragraphs or fewer, (2) your response will be used within your law office for a short-term purpose, and (3) you are responding to a thread of discussion begun in email. Start the email with a paragraph that states the question, answer, and a reason, because many readers will not read more or read an attachment. Make sure the email is properly formatted and professional.

Use a memo if your document addresses a complicated issue that requires a longer answer, that might be used for purposes broader than answering the immediate question, or that must be scrutinized thoroughly for its analytical accuracy and depth by a broader audience. When the content covers issues that may apply to several clients, the memo format will be more easily accessible to future readers. Memos are also more appropriate for complicated analyses, alternative solutions, bad news, or sophisticated explanations. Memos are more formal than emails, and that formality may be appreciated by your clients and colleagues when dealing with challenging circumstances. Finally, many supervising attorneys prefer a memo's detailed analysis, on which they can base their advice and from which they may distill a concise email to send to a client.

You may send a memo by attaching it to a short cover email. Because readers have low tolerance for long emails, use the cover email to give an EXECUTIVE SUMMARY of the memo's content but also invite the reader to look at the memo's full analysis. For related information, see BRIEF ANSWERS; EMAIL; CONCLUSIONS; MEMOS; and QUESTIONS PRESENTED.

EMINENT OR *IMMINENT*?

Use *eminent* when you mean standing out above the others, as in eminent domain. Use *imminent* when you mean about to happen.

> **Justice Holmes was an eminent figure in American case law.**
>
> but
>
> **The case will probably not go to the jury because a settlement is imminent.**

EMOJIS

These nonverbal forms of communication, like their ancestors pictographs and hand gestures, communicate various emotions or attitudes in social media. But they are still too undefined to use in legal writing. While emojis use computer pictures, such as little yellow smiling faces, and emoticons use combinations of punctuation marks, both forms try to get beyond the limitations of words, usually to communicate a feeling.

Law depends on words to define and control meaning, so emojis are dangerous territory for legal writers. A legal writer using a nonverbal symbol cannot contain that symbol's meaning, so using it releases the text from the writer's control.

Accurate communication also requires some ability to predict a reader's response, and nonverbal symbols are not yet able to provide that predictability. One reason is that these symbols are not used consistently worldwide. While words are defined within their given languages and cultures, nonverbal symbols can cross these barriers, and their definitions usually change as they do. Another reason is that an emoji's interpretation depends largely on context. A final reason is that they communicate emotions, which are by nature wild things. One smiley face may signal an apology while another signals sympathy. A picture is worth a thousand words, and that is the problem.

For related information, see COMMUNICATIONS, INTERNATIONAL; ELECTRONIC MESSAGING, ENGLISH AS A SECOND LANGUAGE, SOCIAL MEDIA, SYMBOLS IN EMAIL, and TEXTING UNDER THE TABLE.

EMOTIONAL FACTS

As used in persuasive writing, these facts are carefully chosen and included in a statement of the case when they are needed to subtly persuade the reader. They have no bearing on the legal reasoning, unlike LEGALLY SIGNIFICANT FACTS. Nor are they the chronological or informational facts necessary to complete a legal analysis, like BACKGROUND FACTS. Rather, they play on the reader's emotions. For example, if Malcolm assaulted Alice one Saturday night with an unloaded gun, the writer may tell the reader that they had a sexual relationship in the past. This is an emotionally significant fact that has no bearing on the legal definition of assault. Because these facts are not legally significant, avoid inserting them carelessly, too often, or too obviously. Too much use of emotional facts can impair your CREDIBILITY. For related information, see WRITING, PERSUASIVE.

When writing objectively, you may occasionally find that you need to inform a colleague of emotional facts that might affect decisions about actions to take on behalf of the client. Before including these emotional facts in a written document, consider carefully whether that document could be discoverable in any context. Sometimes you may find that these facts should be communicated orally, rather than put in writing.

EMOTIONAL LANGUAGE

Emotional language is appropriate only in persuasive writing, and then only if used sparingly. Use emotional language to describe significant emotional facts, emotional arguments, or possibly POLICY arguments. Use emotional language only if it is necessary to convey the point and if it does not impair your TONE. Emotional language can also impair credibility if used inappropriately, personally, or excessively.

Admitting this evidence would rob the defendant of his due process rights.

rather than

The plaintiff's counsel foolishly suggests the court admit the evidence; such a move would be silly, unjust, and just plain wrong.

For related problems, see CONNOTATION and CREDIBILITY. For related information, see EMOTIONAL FACTS; STATEMENT OF THE CASE; and WRITING, PERSUASIVE, subsection 4(i).

EMPHASIS

When emphasizing a point, you want to emphasize the content, not the writing. For this reason, avoid heavy-handed use of any emphasizing techniques. With that caveat in mind, try using one or more of the following techniques to emphasize your point:

(1) put the point in a position of emphasis;

(2) state the point in concrete, specific terms;

(3) put the point in a short sentence;

(4) put the point in a one-sentence paragraph;

(5) use strong subject-verb combinations; or

(6) put the point to be emphasized in an inverted sentence structure.

1. Put the point to be emphasized in a position of emphasis.

To emphasize a point, place it at the beginning or end of a sentence or a paragraph. Conversely, bury phrases you want to deemphasize in the middle of paragraphs or sections where they will get less attention than the beginning or end. One way to do this is to use citations at the ends of sentences, not as introductions to a sentence.

Only under exigent circumstances may police enter a person's home without a warrant or consent. Dayton v. New York, 945 U.S. 573, 590 (2025).

rather than

Dayton v. New York, 945 U.S. 573, 590 (2025), states that only under exigent circumstances may police enter a person's home without a warrant or consent.

In legal writing, the beginning gets more attention than the end because the legal reader does not always finish reading. Therefore, get your main points in early. This technique is particularly useful for introducing key terms and terms of art that will reappear throughout the text, because the terms can both gain emphasis and serve as transitions. See POSITIONS OF EMPHASIS, TERMS OF ART, and PARAGRAPHS.

2. State the point in concrete, specific terms.

This increased specificity adds emphasis to a point. Conversely, use abstract or more general terms to deemphasize a point. When a point is stated in concrete or specific terms, the reader creates a mental picture of the point; this picture makes the point easier to remember. In contrast, something stated abstractly or generally does not leave a picture in the reader's mind and is harder to remember.

When asked where he had been at 10:00 p.m. on the night of the assault, the alleged assailant looked away and mumbled, "Nowhere."

rather than

When asked where he had been, he seemed uneasy.

When stating the point more generally, avoid becoming CONCLUSORY. For related information, see ABSTRACT NOUNS.

3. Put the point to be emphasized in a short sentence.

Because short sentences are relatively rare in legal writing, they are particularly effective for emphasis. A short sentence will make a stronger statement and will also be easier to read; both work together to make the point easier to remember.

The defendant then fired three shots.

Be aware, however, of using several short sentences in a row because this can create an impatient, slightly angry tone. For occasions when you want to create this tone, see TOUGH, SOUNDING THAT WAY. For related information, see SENTENCE STRUCTURE, subsection 1.

4. Put the point to be emphasized in a one-sentence paragraph.

Use this technique only when you have a sentence that can stand on its own logically. When you can use a one-sentence paragraph, however, it can make the point stand out from other paragraphs, just as a short sentence stands out from other longer sentences. For more information, see ONE-SENTENCE PARAGRAPHS.

5. Use strong subject-verb combinations.

The reader of English must identify the subject and verb in every sentence to understand and process the content of that sentence. Therefore strong, clear words used as subjects and verbs will emphasize the terms central to your point. These subjects and verbs may often include terms of art or other words you want to emphasize.

The Family Car Doctrine holds parents liable for their children's accidents.

rather than

Under the Family Car Doctrine, liability exists for parents whose children have accidents.

Or use the following when representing the plaintiff.

Panicking, the defendant accelerated and struck the plaintiff's stalled vehicle at 40 miles per hour.

rather than

Seeing the plaintiff's stalled vehicle in the road, the defendant panicked, stepping on the wrong pedal and accelerating to 40 miles per hour.

Conversely, deemphasize points by putting them in dependent clauses. For example, the following sentence deemphasizes *the defendant had not come to a full stop* by placing it after *although.*

Although the defendant had not come to a full stop at the official stop sign, he had slowed to less than five miles per hour and was not accelerating at the time of the accident.

For related information, see KEY TERMS, SUBJECT-VERB COMBINATIONS, and TERMS OF ART.

6. Put the point to be emphasized in an inverted sentence structure.

In general, something unusual gets more attention just because it is unusual.

Imprudent it was, but not illegal.

Beware of overusing this technique. Inverted sentence structure draws attention to the writing itself as much as to the content; if you use it frequently, the reader will start to think about your writing style and may be distracted from your content.

For information on creating large-scale emphasis, see ARGUMENT SECTION; BRIEFS; COHERENCE; DESIGN; LEGAL ANALYSIS; ORGANIZATION, LARGE-SCALE; ORGANIZATION, SMALL-SCALE; REASONING, PRESENTING IT; and WRITING, PERSUASIVE.

EMPHASIS ADDED

See QUOTATIONS, HOW TO PUNCTUATE, subsection 6.

END RESULT

Result is adequate unless you are discussing complicated math formulas with both interim results and end results.

ENGLISH AS A SECOND LANGUAGE

If English is your second language, you will need to remember cultural and linguistic differences throughout the writing process, beginning in prewriting. For example, consider the following questions.

1. In PREWRITING.

   Begin by asking yourself, *What are the expectations of this audience?* The U.S. legal audience often expects detailed analysis that reveals every step in the reasoning process. Because the U.S. system is historically based on *stare decisis*, your briefs and memos need to include more information about cases than would be expected in a civil code context. Although this may seem unnecessary to non-U.S. readers, it is a necessary component because U.S. readers use this information to determine how the law should be applied in subsequent cases. For more on how to do this, see SUPPORT, *STARE DECISIS*, and AUDIENCE. You also might want to begin a project by studying several examples of the type of writing you are doing, such as briefs, memos, letters, or pleadings. For help with these documents, see entries under the document names.

2. In both PREWRITING and REWRITING.

   Ask yourself, *Does the organization reflect the logic of the content?* Organization may be the place where contrasts are strongest between your legal culture and ours. The hybrid system of statutory and common law yields dozens of organizational approaches, many of which may work, one of which is best for your document. You can derive examples from the cases you read for class and for research. You will see that no single pattern appears; rather, U.S. legal writers choose a combination of approaches that best suits the doctrine and the document. As you decide how to organize your document, keep in mind some basic principles of traditional U.S. legal reasoning.

   Traditional U.S. legal reasoning often moves from the general to the specific, using a deductive structure. For example, you may choose to state a statute and then apply it to reach a conclusion, which is a deductive approach. Or with a common law doctrine, you may choose to state the common law rule, which is a synthesis of the holdings that have developed that common law, then apply that rule to reach a conclusion. That overall approach may seem very similar to what you do in your legal culture.

Within that overall deductive structure, however, U.S. lawyers use cases as illustrations and analogies, and explaining these entails using inductive structures that move from specific to general. You can use cases inductively in at least two ways: to define the statute's terms and to give examples of how that statute has been applied previously. In the first, use case holdings to define the statute's terms. You can include the holdings after you state the general statute or as you introduce each statutory term. These illustrations are inductive because they use specific examples to illustrate what the statutory terms mean. The second way is to use cases to give parameters of what courts have held. For example, you can group together case holdings that show particular outcomes as examples of when courts have applied the statute to reach certain results. You can group together other holdings that show opposite results. These groups are inductive because they demonstrate several examples that together explain the range of results under the statute.

As you proceed through a traditional U.S. analysis, you are expected to compare your situation to previous ones to show how your situation fits or does not fit with precedent. The many components you can compare offer several different variations and combinations, from which you must select one. For example, you may compare holdings, rules, policies, facts, DICTA, or equities. When making your choice, select the combination that best suits your audience and choose one that favors the result you want in a persuasive document. After you have developed your analogy, you can explain the reasoning that leads to your conclusion.

For more information, see CASE BRIEFS; HOLDING; LEGAL ANALYSIS; REASONING, ANALOGICAL; REASONING, DEDUCTIVE; REASONING, INDUCTIVE; REASONING, MODERN; REASONING, OTHER; REASONING, POSTMODERN; REASONING, PRESENTING IT; RULES; and SYLLOGISMS.

3. In REVISING.

As you review your text, ask yourself, *What writing conventions are appropriate for U.S. legal writing?* Generally, U.S. legal readers expect the writer to state the point directly and to guide the reader through every step in the analysis. To meet this expectation, state the main point at the outset of the document, and use the first sentence of each paragraph to introduce the main idea in that paragraph. Again, this may seem rude, but is simply considered straightforward by U.S. legal readers. Then use transitions to explain how each part of your analysis is related to the next part. Generally, confine each sentence to one legal point, each paragraph to one idea. Concentrate on specific subjects, verbs, and objects; omit unnecessary modifiers and vague terms. Also omit lengthy introductions to the main point, such as *it is my considered opinion that.* Finally, whenever possible, use the ACTIVE VOICE rather than passive voice. For how-to information, see CLARITY; CONCISENESS; CONNECTIONS, MAKING THEM; TOPIC SENTENCES; and TRANSITIONS.

When wording topic sentences and support, U.S. legal readers prefer straightforward wording and shorter sentences over either erudite or emotional wording. The desire for efficiency in the U.S. legal culture means that readers often get impatient with wording that is longer or more obscure than is necessary to convey the points. Additionally, while obviously emotional wording connotes sincerity in some cultures, it tends to suggest a loss of reasonableness in the U.S. legal culture. For more on this, see READABILITY.

4. In POLISHING.

As you finalize, ask yourself, *Do the language and citations conform to legal conventions and U.S. English usage?* Because U.S. legal decisions are influenced directly by written documents and are themselves issued in writing, U.S. lawyers rely on precise, correct expression. To bring your written English closer to that standard and to sound more idiomatic, evaluate the patterns in your writing. For example, you may discover that you omit articles or use several clauses in one sentence. Or you may have a problem with comma usage. Short form citations may give you trouble. Whatever pattern you find, check exclusively for it. Then check for the next pattern, and so on.

When crossing over to English from another language, you may bring writing patterns that are closer either to your language or to British English. With the help of a native speaker, identify successful and unsuccessful patterns in format, content, and style. After you have identified any patterns that are not used in U.S. English, read through your paper, checking exclusively for these non-native patterns. For example, if your native language uses complex sentence structure separated by commas, adjust throughout for the shorter and more direct English structure; separate the thoughts into complete sentences. If your language does not use articles, read your final product specifically for those and insert them. Check also for proper use of prepositions. For help here, see WRITING PROCESS CHECKLIST and specific entries for the grammar areas that concern you.

For more details on each of these topics, see the current edition of Jill J. Ramsfield, *Culture to Culture: A Guide to U.S. Legal Writing* (Carolina Academic Press). For more information about approaches, see COMMUNICATIONS, INTERNATIONAL.

ENGLISH IN INTERNATIONAL SITUATIONS

See COMMUNICATIONS, INTERNATIONAL; and ENGLISH AS A SECOND LANGUAGE.

ENSURE, INSURE, OR *ASSURE*?

See *ASSURE, ENSURE,* OR *INSURE*?

ENUMERATION

Enumeration, or inserting numbers into a list, can clarify a potentially overwhelming amount of information. Generally, enumeration is an option when each item in the list is more than a few words long or when the list includes more than four items. Alternatively, you may want to choose bullets for some lists and reserve enumeration for the lists that imply an actual sequence. For more detail on how and when enumeration is useful, see LISTS, STRUCTURE OF.

If enumeration is used too much in a document, however, it becomes distracting rather than helpful. Scan the pages of your documents to see if the frequency of enumeration draws the eye from the content. For related information, see BULLET POINTS; GRAPHICS, WHEN TO USE; and LISTS, PUNCTUATION OF.

EQUITY

Equity refers to justice and fairness. If, for example, legal procedures and existing laws give inadequate or no redress for a grievance, then *equity* would require creating some redress. It is a TERM OF ART, so use it in legal writing only within that legal meaning.

Equity has several shades of meaning, which are beyond the scope of this book, but be sure to consider equity in making a complete analysis in your discussion section, argument section, or explanation in an opinion letter. For related information, see POLICY.

ETC.

Use *etc.* only in informal writing, because it looks rather informal and can be vague in some circumstances. Instead, use *and so forth, and others,* or another appropriate phrase. Better yet, complete the phrase with specific terms.

EVERYBODY

Everybody is rather informal; consider substituting *everyone.* If you do use it, use a singular verb.

Everybody has the right to a fair trial.

EVERYONE

Everyone takes a singular verb.

Everyone is writing an outline for the course.

Do not confuse *everyone* with *every one*; *every one* refers to each person or thing of a specific group, and is usually followed by *of*.

Every one of the defendants is at fault.

EVIDENCE

Evidence takes a singular verb.

The evidence points to this conclusion.

This is true even if there are many bits of evidence, because *evidence* is a collective noun. If you want to use a plural verb, you will need to make some other word the subject.

All the pieces of evidence point to this conclusion.

For related information, see COLLECTIVE NOUNS.

EX-

There are two situations when *ex* should be separated from the rest of a word:

- as a prefix to a noun or proper noun, use *ex* with a hyphen

  ex-wife, ex-Governor Smith

- as a part of a Latin phrase, write it as a separate word

  ex post facto, ex officio

In other situations, write it as part of the word.

excoriate, excommunicate, extend

EXACTNESS

See WORD CHOICE.

EXCLAMATION

Exclamations are used in legal writing only as part of a quotation. For related information, see INTERJECTIONS.

EXECUTIVE SUMMARY

An executive summary condenses your message and analysis into one page or less. In legal documents, it is usually placed at the beginning. Most legal readers expect you to have done the analysis for them, and they want the analysis' essence at the beginning of your document; the executive summary provides this. To write an effective executive summary, finish writing your analysis first. After you have rewritten and revised the document, you will find it easier to write an accurate and concise summary. You may be able to use your Conclusion or Brief Answer as the executive summary if no further context is needed.

Use the topic sentence to add context that orients the reader. For example, you can rephrase the memo's Question Presented by beginning with, *You asked whether* . . . . Follow this by stating the bottom line of each part of the document, knitting them together so the readers sees how all parts are related to the overall question. You can also add a final sentence that gives the reader practical advice, legal advice, or a suggestion about the next steps that need to be taken. For specific advice, see EXPLANATIONS, WHEN AND HOW MUCH? For related information, see BRIEF ANSWER, CONCLUSION, POWER POINTS, and QUESTIONS PRESENTED.

EXCLAMATION POINTS

An exclamation point is rather like shouting and thus is not used in legal writing, except as part of a quotation. Let someone else do the shouting. For better ways to emphasize a point, see EMPHASIS and POSITIONS OF EMPHASIS.

EXPLANATIONS, WHEN AND HOW MUCH?

Explanations, like good motor oil, can reduce friction and increase efficiency. But also like oil, too much can create a sticky situation.

Explain a point when it is your professional responsibility to do so. For example, explain why you recommend a specific way of structuring a bequest in a client's will, even if the client is inclined to trust you and does not seem to require the explanation. Similarly, explain your reasoning in an opinion letter so the client has enough information to determine whether or not to follow your advice.

Explain the reason for an action or a request whenever your reader would want an explanation. Different readers require different levels of explanation. Also explain when it is the reader's right or business to know the explanation. So, for example, explain to a client why you are requesting a piece of information whenever that reason is not readily apparent.

In persuasive writing, explain the reason for a request or action when you think that the explanation will increase the likelihood of a favorable response. Thus you might explain to an opposing attorney why you think a negotiation meeting between your two clients would be beneficial.

In contrast, do not explain reflexively, solely out of habit. Sometimes silence is wiser. It might be inappropriate or unwise to explain the motivations behind your client's request for a negotiation meeting. It would also be ineffective to explain to your superior why the memo you are submitting is longer than expected; in that situation, the context needs to communicate your reason.

For related information, see CONTEXT-INDEPENDENT WRITING; DEFINITIONS, WHEN AND HOW TO INCLUDE; EXECUTIVE SUMMARY; POSITIONS OF EMPHASIS; UNOBTRUSIVE DEFINITIONS; and WRITING, PERSUASIVE.

EXPLANATORY PHRASES

If you want to explain a term that some readers may not understand, you may choose to add a short phrase within the sentence stating your point.

The gaffer, or stage electrician, was responsible for setting up the band's equipment.

For other ways to include definitions gracefully, see UNOBTRUSIVE DEFINITIONS. For related information, see APPOSITIVE, CONTEXT-INDEPENDENT WRITING; DEFINITIONS, WHEN AND HOW TO INCLUDE; EMPHASIS; POSITIONS OF EMPHASIS; and WRITING, PERSUASIVE.

EXPOSITORY WRITING

Traditionally, the primary function of expository writing is to inform a reader, rather than to narrate or convince. Much legal writing is expository writing. Expository writing explains factual information, supports a subject, or presents an idea. You often do all three when writing a memo, opinion letter, substantive email, or scholarly article: you describe the legal foundation of the analysis, support your reasoning, or present a new theory of law.

In legal writing, you are concerned with effectiveness rather than pure literary form. So, if it is effective to do so, combine expository writing with narration or persuasion. For example, in a memo's DISCUSSION SECTION, you may narrate the facts of a case that is dramatically similar to yours and then use the expository device of comparison to show how the court is likely to rule in your client's favor because of the similarity.

Whatever your choices, make them carefully and deliberately so that the document's reasoning fulfills its purpose.

As a reference, you can consider the seven traditional devices for expository writing listed here. They may help you to formulate components of your own reasoning. Remember, however, that there are dangers in following any prescription too rigidly. See FORMALISM.

1. Enumeration.

   Enumeration explains a topic by identifying its divisions. For example, a memo might be structured by listing a statute's elements, the subissues that might be raised when considering a larger issue, or a series of provisions in a contract.

2. Definition.

   Definition explains a topic by setting the limits of the topic or locating the topic within a larger structure or explanation. For example, an article might define a legal issue by placing it within a larger legal context or by classifying the issue and then distinguishing it from other issues within that class. This technique is useful for isolating and distinguishing an issue from related issues or for defining subissues.

3. Process.

   Process explains a topic by listing the steps that lead to the completion of an action. This device is often used to address a topic, event, or idea that involves some sort of change or development; the device identifies the steps in that change and their order. For example, you might use process to identify the steps in filing a suit, in completing a settlement negotiation, or in gathering information for a will.

4. Analysis.

   In the expository sense, analysis explains a topic by describing its separate components. This may be accomplished by division, classification, or a combination of the two. Analysis by division is used when a subject is analyzed as a singular item and its component parts are used to explain it. In contrast to enumeration, which simply lists the parts in the whole, division analyzes how the parts together create the whole. For example, several causes of action may make up an entire case, several errors by the trial court may constitute an abuse of discretion, and paralegals, associates, and partners may make up a law firm.

   Analysis by classification is used when a subject is viewed as a set of items bearing common characteristics. This method focuses on the whole more than the parts; the whole is then analyzed in relation to a larger subject, rather than the parts of the topic in relation to itself, as in division. In a memo, for example, the law applicable to your client's case may be divided into statutes, cases, and regulations; all of these are then applied to your client's factual situation. In a scholarly article, several cases may have developed a trend in a legal doctrine; that doctrine is then used to create a new legal theory.

5. Cause and effect.

This device explains why an event occurred. It is used to develop reasoning, to create proof, or to establish an explanation. For example, if a defendant watched a violent movie and then subsequently committed a similar crime, the defendant's attorney might argue that the crime was caused by the first event.

To determine a cause-and-effect relationship, first sift through facts, law, practical circumstances, and your own point of view; then determine the premise, the causal relationship, and the conclusion. Beware of several traps, including hasty generalization, *non sequitur*, and the *post hoc* fallacy. In a hasty generalization, only one reason is used to create a cause-and-effect generalization when in fact many other reasons could contribute. In a *non sequitur*, there is no connection between the first and the second events, so there can be no cause and effect. In a *post hoc* fallacy, there is a false assumption that where there is a time relationship between two events, there is also a cause-and-effect relationship between them.

6. Comparison and contrast.

This device explains the subject by measuring it against something else. This is often used in traditional legal writing when analogizing and distinguishing cases. To predict an outcome in a MEMO, for example, you may analyze your client's case by noting the similarities and differences between it and previous cases.

7. Illustration.

Illustration explains a topic by using an example or analogy to give concrete meaning to abstract ideas, to clarify or refine definitions, or to provide precise instances and meanings for generalizations. An example illustrates a point by giving a concrete illustration; an analogy compares the situation to something that is more familiar to the reader.

For related information, see WRITING, OBJECTIVE.

EXTENDED QUOTATIONS

Resist the urge, please, to use quotations that extend for whole pages. No matter how good the quotation is, many readers will skip over it, so use quotations of more than a few sentences only when neither paraphrasing nor editing quotations is a viable alternative. If you must quote an extended passage, such as the full text of a statute, do so, but make sure the explanation surrounding it is adequate to make the reader see that essential use. If possible, append the full text and then refer to that appendix, unless referring frequently to the appendix will distract the reader. See also APPENDIX; PARAPHRASE; and QUOTATIONS, HOW TO PUNCTUATE.

FACT OF THE MATTER, THE

This phrase can almost always be omitted with no loss of meaning.

The plaintiff did not raise this claim until she learned of the defendant's affluence.

rather than

The fact of the matter is that the plaintiff did not raise this claim until she learned of the defendant's affluence.

For further discussion, see SUBJECT-VERB COMBINATIONS.

FACTS

There are at least four types of facts in legal writing. LEGALLY SIGNIFICANT FACTS are the facts that, if changed, would change the outcome of the analysis or case. BACKGROUND FACTS are the contextual facts that readers need to make sense out of the legally significant facts. EMOTIONAL FACTS are facts that are not legally significant but may evoke an appropriate reader response to a difficult or unusual situation. Finally, extraneous facts are true but not relevant to the legal subject you are addressing. Most legal documents require all legally significant and some background facts, while some persuasive documents require a few emotional facts. Almost no legal documents, however, require extraneous facts.

Choose carefully what to use. One way to do so is to write, rewrite, and revise your legal analysis or argument first. Then highlight the facts you use to reach your conclusions. Those are the facts needed at the opening of the document, whether in a fact statement or summary. They should always be included, appropriately shaped to foreshadow your analysis.

On rare occasions, some information should not be put in writing, perhaps because the information may be discoverable in some future context. In these situations, consider whether the fact must be communicated; if you find yourself in that situation, find another way to do so, such as orally or at a different time. Some facts are not legally significant and thus may not need to be communicated at all.

If you need to communicate facts to your reader that are particularly sensitive, use POSITIONS OF EMPHASIS and choose your TONE wisely. Always remember the context in which a document will be used. Balance ACCURACY with PURPOSE.

FACT SHEETS

Fact sheets are one-page summaries of information used to inform or update readers about specific situations. They often include tables, graphs, or other visual aids to communicate supporting information concisely. For help writing these, see INFORMATIONAL ARTICLES; GRAPHICS, WHEN TO USE THEM; and GRAPHICS, WHICH ONES TO USE.

FACT THAT, THE

Avoid this phrase. Usually it adds extra words without adding extra meaning.

This failure was caused by the machine's inadequate design.

rather than

This failure was caused by the fact that the machine was inadequately designed.

For related information, see CONCISENESS.

FALLACIES

See LOGICAL FALLACIES.

FARTHER OR *FURTHER*?

Farther refers to literal distance.

She moved farther away from me than I wanted.

Further refers to all other senses, such as additional degree, time, or quantity.

The attorney stretched the argument further than anyone could have imagined.

Further also denotes figurative distance.

That line of reasoning is further from the truth than would be acceptable.

FAXING

A fax, short for *facsimile,* is an image of a document that is made by electronic scanning and transmitted via telephone. It is therefore safer than email for communicating sensitive or confidential information quickly because it bypasses the internet. Faxes use either a printer with faxing capability or an app. You can use fax to send forms, signatures, and handwritten documents.

As with email and instant messaging, the speed of faxing can create pitfalls for legal practice. Whenever possible, set a document aside for a few hours or overnight and review it again before faxing it; the mental distance afforded by this pause can often prevent expensive errors. For related information, see ELECTRONIC MESSAGING.

FEEL

Use this word when you mean to talk about emotions, rather than thoughts or beliefs. Often in legal writing *think* or *believe* is the more accurate choice.

The defendant felt remorseful about her actions.

but not

The defendant felt that she did the wrong thing.

FEWER OR *LESS*?

Fewer refers to things that are being viewed as individual units and that would be counted as such. It takes a plural verb.

Fewer students are enrolling than the university had projected.

Less refers to things that cannot be counted.

Plaintiffs believed there was less likelihood of success if they waited too long to file.

We need less talk, more action.

Less also refers to things that could be counted but are being referred to as a group rather than as individual units. Examples of this include periods of time, sums of money, measures of distance, and weights.

Plaintiff must file in less than sixty days.

The prayer for relief asked for less than one million dollars.

While the plaintiff weighed almost 200 pounds, the defendant weighed less than 130 pounds.

When used as a subject, *less* takes a singular verb.

Less is more.

FIGURATIVE MEANING

When you write in figurative language, you create an image that is not literally accurate; instead it creates an image that creates your meaning in a non-literal way. In legal writing, do not use a word figuratively, rather than literally, if there is any chance that the legal reader could take you literally.

When he tried to drive his car out of the marsh, he instead drove it deeper into the mud.

rather than

When he tried to drive his car out of the marsh, he foundered in a swamp he himself created.

You may use a word figuratively when (1) the word cannot be misunderstood as literal and (2) the figurative term is commonly used by the reader.

The plaintiff's own word bars his suit.

In this example, nothing is *barred* in the sense of *barred from entering the room,* but any legal reader will know what you mean.

You may also use figurative meaning, with restraint, for EMPHASIS in persuasive or scholarly writing. For examples, see IMAGERY. For related concerns, see AMBIGUITY, WAYS TO AVOID; LITERAL MEANING; JARGON; and SYNONYMS.

FIND

In legal writing, use this term of art precisely. Courts *find*; counsel does not. See also *FIND, HOLD,* OR *REASON*?

FIND, *HOLD*, OR *REASON*?

Technically, *hold* refers to a specific legal outcome in a given case.

The court held that the defendant's actions were willful because he consciously chose between two alternatives.

Find refers to an outcome, usually a more general one.

The court found the defendant guilty.

It also may be used in the phrase *fact finding* or *finding of fact,* as distinguished from the determination of the answer to a legal question.

Reason refers to the more complicated series of analytical steps that the court used to reach its decision. Avoid depending on *reason* as a verb. Instead, explain your reasoning fully.

> **The court compared Defendant's decision to turn the respirator off to a truck driver's decision to take a back road, a housewife's choice to bake chicken instead of ham, and an athlete's decision to turn and run up field, all of which were willful actions.**
>
> rather than
>
> The court reasoned that the defendant's actions were willful.

FLOWERY LANGUAGE

Avoid flowery language, or the use of unnecessarily ornate words in legal writing. Usually the ideas in legal writing are so complicated that flowery language will only serve to make them more complicated. The only time that flowery language might be appropriate would be if requested by a reader, such as a client requesting it in a will. Be forewarned, however, that clients probably want flowery language much less than lawyers think they do.

In law review articles you may bend this rule a little; a few arcane words are allowable if they do not hide crucial meaning. Do not, however, *surfeit your reader with a multifarious array of sententious phrases.* Too quickly that becomes obnoxious and loses the reader. See also ELEGANT VARIATION, JARGON, and LEGALESE.

FOCUS

Being able to maintain focus is an essential skill for a legal writer. If you can focus on the essentials before nonessentials in your writing process, you can avoid wasting time and energy. When researching and choosing content, remember to stay within the SCOPE of the document. When organizing, focus on your primary reader's point of view. When writing, focus on simply getting all your ideas into written form rather than getting them all polished into final form. When REWRITING, focus on ACCURACY, THOROUGHNESS, and organization. Focus on READABILITY, TRANSITIONS, and other related concerns in a subsequent REVISING pass through the text. When setting up your schedule of deadlines, focus on the parts of the process that are most difficult or uncomfortable for you and give those parts more time.

Focusing on the factors essential to the final product avoids wasting the reader's time on unnecessary tangents. For example, when writing a brief, focus on the precise questions the court must answer to resolve each issue; this focus will help you resolve such varied questions about the final product as what research to include, what argumentation to use, and what TONE to create. Similarly, when writing a memo, focus on the questions the supervising attorney wants answered. When writing to a client, focus on what information the client needs to make a decision or take action, and let that focus dictate which points you emphasize.

Your focus on the audience, purpose, and scope, together with your understanding of the process, will keep your product useful and your process efficient. For related information, see AUDIENCE, COLLABORATION, PURPOSE, TIME MANAGEMENT, WRITING PROCESS, and WRITING PROCESS CHECKLIST.

FONT CHOICES

Check with your AUDIENCE to determine the appropriate font for your documents. Courts often make specific requirements about font, so always check their rules early in the writing process. Follow any rules exactly, because filings that do not comply will be returned. Similarly, attorneys in your firm may favor certain fonts in their communications with clients. Therefore, check to see if your office has any rules or procedures for particular attorneys or particular documents.

Font preferences do change over time, and sometimes exist for unusual reasons. For example, Times New Roman has been popular for a long time in writing memos because it has been used in general publications. Arial is often the default font in tables and email simply because it is the default in the computer programs that create those documents. Century Gothic is sometimes preferred because it saves ink.

If there are no preferences or regulations, choose your font and type size based on READABILITY first, then on overall appearance. Fonts may be generally easier to read in print if they use serifs, which are the short, horizontal lines that appear at the ends of the strokes in a letter. For this reason, newspapers, dictionaries, and books usually use serif types for the body of the text. *Sans serif* typefaces, which omit these strokes, have a more modern look but are somewhat less quickly read in print. For that reason, *sans serif* styles are best used in headings or in documents only read online, rather than in the body of a printed text.

Font choices can create different looks and thus can be a way to express yourself, but legal readers are generally not impressed by extravagant or unusual choices. Remember that the content should be the reader's focus, not the typeface in which the content is presented. To give your document a clean-looking, professional polish, avoid using many different font styles within one document.

For related information, see FONT SIZE and TYPEFACE.

FONT SIZE

Choose your font size according to the court's requirements or your reader's preference. Follow a court's rules exactly or you risk having your document rejected. Resist the urge to use 10-point type to squeeze more words onto a page; the reader will know. For related information see FONT CHOICES.

FOOTNOTES

Use footnotes in scholarly articles and treatises, but avoid them in LETTERS, MEMOS, pretrial documents, OPINIONS, or BRIEFS. Also avoid using them as a substitute for making hard decisions about content.

1. Use in scholarly articles and treatises.

   In scholarly writing, where legal footnotes were born, footnotes are appropriate. In this situation, footnotes assist readers who are using the article for different purposes, whether they are reading it for its general information or as part of their own research in a related topic. Specifically, you may want to think of footnotes for scholarly writing as falling into three categories: citing directly to authority, giving attribution to the ideas of others, and adding text to elaborate on a particular point. For example, a footnote in an article might give the text of a statute or case that is better read on that page than appended to the main text. A footnote can also substantiate points or provide valuable historical or background information. It can include references valuable to future researchers.

   Avoid using footnotes just for appearance; instead make sure they are sensible, useful to the reader, and appropriate within the publishing context. For additional information, see SCHOLARLY WRITING, SCHOLARLY WRITING PROCESS, and SCHOLARLY WRITING PROCESS CHECKLIST.

2. Avoid using in letters, memos, pretrial documents, opinions, and briefs.

   In legal documents other than scholarly writing, citations appear in text immediately after the relevant content and are used to establish authority and credibility. Legal readers of these documents are often impatient with footnotes, so using them can detract from your overall purpose of informing or persuading. Footnotes require readers to decide whether to stop reading the text to find the footnote or to skip checking the reference. This process disrupts the flow of your logic; readers then must create their own coherence, and you may lose them. One common exception in practice is to use footnotes strictly for citations, no text. While some readers accept this use, many do not, so check with your readers for their preferences.

3. Avoid using as a shortcut for indecision.

Footnotes sometimes appear because the writer has something to use but cannot find a good place for it; down to the basement it goes, rather than out to the curb. Make the hard choice and omit the footnote. If the information is needed, include it in a way that increases READABILITY. For example, if the footnote would include the full text of a statute, put it in a separate section, an appendix, or a well-stated paragraph. If the point seems tangential, make the difficult decision to exclude it. If you think a point should be included, rewrite the paragraph or section so that its inclusion is easily understood by the reader, such as putting it at the middle or end of the paragraph, breaking it up into smaller points, or condensing the information into a series within a sentence. As you do this, avoid cluttering the text with too many PARENTHESES, which can also reduce readability.

FOR

Sometimes *for* is used as a subordinating conjunction.

She had no patience with imprecise language, for she had a background in legal drafting.

Although this use of *for* is not grammatically wrong, it suggests a rather fuzzy logical relationship. *For* is not as precise as *because*. If you mean to show a causal connection, use *because*.

The operator cannot be considered negligent because she was not told that it was her job to check the hoses before starting the motor.

If you mean something less precise, try to revise to state exactly what you mean. For related information, see CONJUNCTIONS and TRANSITIONS.

FOR ALL INTENTS AND PURPOSES

Find a shorter way to say this idea or omit the phrase. If the sentence needs something more, try to find one word that makes your point.

Therefore my client is innocent.

rather than

For all intents and purposes, my client is innocent.

FORCEFUL WRITING

See EMPHASIS and POSITIONS OF EMPHASIS.

FOREGO OR *FORGO*?

Both words are verbs, but with very different meanings. *Forego* means *to go before.* This is an archaic verb, which is now generally used only as an adjective in the phrase *a foregone conclusion.*

Use *forgo* to mean *do without,* which is the word you will occasionally use as a verb, as in *The defendant's attorney decided to forgo other pretrial motions and instead focus on the Motion to Dismiss.*

FORMALISM

Formalism refers to strict adherence to rules, norms, forms, structures, or practices. Such strict usage can help in starting projects. For example, you may find forms useful as guidelines for starting to draft a contract or will. You may like to use mnemonics like CRAC to help you remember principles of law or models for deduction. Or you may create your own forms to start your research, such as using a three-part Question Presented or using a research database's system for brainstorming search terms. Similarly, you may have a case briefing method that offers a list of useful aspects of cases. And you can use syllogisms to deconstruct the logic of cases or compare structures of reasoning.

But beware of formalism when it elevates form over substance. Good legal writing requires a healthy suspicion of forms and formats. These forms or practices may have been invented as reference points or helpful guides to understanding, but they can quickly obscure or omit crucial content that does not fit tidily within them. Because laws and methods of analysis are dynamic, formalism can lure you away from analyzing, inventing, or adapting to specific problems and solutions. Formalism can oversimplify legal analysis and writing, which are as complex as architectural design or surgery.

Instead of depending solely on rules, forms, and the like, keep developing your repertoire of approaches; focus on making sure your document design fits its purpose and suits its audience. For related information, see DESIGN; FORMS, USE OF; LEGAL ANALYSIS; ORGANIZATION, LARGE-SCALE; ORGANIZE, HOW TO; OUTLINES; REASONING, INDUCTIVE; REASONING, DEDUCTIVE; REASONING, MODERN; REASONING, POSTMODERN; REASONING, PRESENTING IT; RESEARCH STRATEGY GUIDE; and SYLLOGISMS.

FORMALITY, LEVEL OF

The level of formality used in communication greatly affects tone in writing. That tone, in turn, greatly affects the reader's attitude about the writer. Just as you choose the appropriate degree of formality or informality when you dress for an event, you should choose the appropriate level of formality when writing legal documents. To extend the analogy, using overly formal language in a letter to a client is like wearing a tuxedo to a business meeting.

> Our firm is most appreciative that you have entrusted this establishment with the provision of representation in your legal affairs, and will endeavor to justify this placement of your confidence with alacrity and perseverant diligence.

Overly formal language tends to be multi-syllabic, Latin or Greek in origin, filled with NOMINALIZATIONS, and used in speeches but not normal business conversation.

Overly informal language, on the other hand, is like wearing a sleeveless T-shirt and shorts to a meeting with a new client.

> Thanks again for hiring me—see ya!

Informal words are generally shorter, have more emotional overtones, are more colorful, often change in different social groups, and are common in conversation but not in formal debates. Informal phrases are often verbs followed by prepositions.

> Let's have a sit down and think over the issues.

Aim for a safer middle ground that sounds more businesslike. Whether it is a three-piece suit or a collared shirt, it is not so likely to make the client regret hiring you.

> **We appreciate your trust in us and hope to justify that trust with diligent service.**
>
> or
>
> **Thank you for choosing me as your attorney. I will be in touch within two weeks to update you on my progress.**

Whatever level of formality you choose within the safe middle range, take care to maintain that level consistently. To help you develop an ear for these different levels of formality, review the following table, which illustrates synonyms that communicate different levels of formality. You may want to add your own arrays of synonyms to the list. You will also notice that many words do not fall neatly into one of the four categories listed below. Instead, most words fall on a continuum, requiring your judgment and sense of the overall tone of the document.

Levels of Formality

Tuxedo	Three-Piece Suit	Dress Shirt	T-shirt
inebriated	*intoxicated*	*drunk*	*plastered*
deluded	*deceived*	*tricked* *misled*	*hoodwinked* *duped*
ruminate *cogitate*	*weigh* *review*	*consider*	*think about* *chew on*
conclude	*determine*	*decide*	*opt for*
in a pique	*irritated*	*angered*	*p.o.'ed*
remunerate	*reimburse*	*pay*	*shell out*
acceded to	*consented to*	*agreed to*	*gave in to*
elect	*select*	*choose*	*pick*
make an attempt to	*attempt*	*try*	*take a shot at*
lacks the capacity to	*is incapable of*	*cannot*	*can't*
came to naught	*was ineffective*	*failed to*	*didn't cut it*
brought to a conclusion	*concluded*	*ended*	*over with*

For general help in choosing and controlling your level of formality, see PROFESSIONAL LANGUAGE AND PRESENTATION and TONE. For information related to overly formal writing, see FLOWERY LANGUAGE and LEGALESE. For information related to informal writing, see SLANG. For context, see ORAL PRESENTATIONS.

FORMAT

Legal readers are particular about format because they want the structure to be transparent enough to make the substance visible. For example, know and follow the requirements of the format peculiar to your jurisdiction when writing briefs. Similarly, know and follow also the demands of your employer for format in email, memos, opinion letters, or other documents. For specific formats, see MEMOS; BRIEFS; COMPLAINTS; and OPINIONS, LEGAL.

FORMS

Referring to forms can save time and avoid the problem of missing a needed element in a routine task. Using forms, however, can also cause problems, such as including contradictory clauses in a contract or nonsensical phrases in a letter. Therefore, do not use forms as a substitute for your own thinking.

With this caveat in mind, when you do refer to forms, you can make good use of them if you remember to do the following three things.

1. Compare.

   Compare different forms before you settle on one to follow. Comparing different forms, whether from form books, online samples, or samples you have collected, helps you see which content and formats are common and which are unique to certain forms. This comparison in turn helps you get a clearer sense of the options you have and of the standard content and format used for this kind of legal document.

2. Prepare.

   Prepare by identifying all the elements needed to complete your document, omitting any unneeded elements found in the forms but inappropriate to your document and checking for logical inconsistencies between these elements. Check carefully for those logical inconsistencies, so that your document is not the next in the line of cases that outlines the problems of ambiguous and inconsistent clauses. Resist the temptation to include even one word you do not understand.

3. Repair.

   Finally, repair the elements you have chosen from various forms. Draft original sections as needed to cover all aspects of your situation. Then organize all sections and check for completeness and consistency. When all content is in place, edit the whole document. Many forms, especially from form books, have unneeded LEGALESE, FLOWERY LANGUAGE, obtuse SENTENCE STRUCTURE, and unnecessary words. You have used the forms to get a sense of content, structure, and format; you can retain those elements and still revise to gain increased READABILITY. For help in omitting unnecessary words, see CONCISENESS. For related information, see CONTRACTS, WILLS, NOTICE OF MOTION, and ORDERS.

FORM CONTRACTS

Form contracts can be useful as long as they are used as a resource rather than a substitute for your own thinking about the agreement. To use forms effectively, follow the three steps listed under FORMS. For a checklist for drafting contracts, see CONTRACTS.

FORMER

Former refers to the first of two things mentioned; *latter* refers to the second. This elegant pairing can be effective in fixing two thoughts in the reader's mind. If the reference of *former* is more than a few words back, however, repeat the word to which you are referring rather than using *former*. To understand what *former* means, the reader must remember the items listed, remember which was first, and then insert that information into the sentence. As a result, *former* can inconvenience the reader, which should not happen just for the writer's convenience.

Also remember that *former* and *latter* can be ambiguous when they refer to a list of more than two items.

FOR THE PERIOD OF

For CONCISENESS, use *for*.

FURTHER OR *FARTHER*?

See *FARTHER* OR *FURTHER*?

FUTURE PERFECT TENSE

See VERBS, TENSES, subsection 9.

FUTURE PROGRESSIVE TENSE

See VERBS, TENSES, subsection 8.

FUTURE TENSES

See VERBS, TENSES, subsections 7–9.

GENDER IN WRITING

Gender refers to a person's identity, rather than *sex*, which refers to traditionally male and female characteristics. As the range of terms used to describe gender expands, use the terms that most accurately capture the legal meaning for your reader. Your client may use *they* and *their* as singular pronouns, and using these pronouns may work. But sometimes these pronouns may not work because your reader may be confused if *they* suggests a plural entity. Also, in drafting documents that have legal consequences, such as wills, research your jurisdiction's requirements to make sure that using the client's term will not cause ambiguity. See the subsections below for ways to do this.

1. Shift the relevant nouns to plural.

   With this approach, you can use plural pronouns without any ambiguity.

   Attorneys whose membership fees are up to date will have their fees waived for this event.

   rather than

   Any attorney whose membership fees are up to date will have their fees waived for this event.

2. Replace the pronoun with a noun.

   This approach is a quick fix that works as long as the result does not create awkward repetition. Simply repeat the relevant noun instead of using a pronoun.

   When we met with Helen and Vee Germain, Helen agreed to the approach we discussed, but Vee did not.

   rather than

   When we met with Helen and Vee Germain, she agreed to the approach we discussed but they did not.

   or

   The Germains do not both agree to the approach we discussed with them yesterday.

   Any client who requests copies of all relevant court documents may have them as long as that client agrees to pay the cost of copying those documents.

   rather than

   Any client who requests copies of all relevant court documents may have them as long as he or she or they agrees to pay the cost of copying those documents.

3. In documents that will have multiple readers, use an APPOSITIVE to avoid confusion.

   Max Avery, who uses *they*, has worked for this company for twelve years. During that time, they have been promoted twice to positions of more responsibility.

   rather than

   Max Avery has worked for this company for twelve years. During that time, they have been promoted twice to positions of more responsibility.

4. Use an article (*a*, *an*, or *the*) to replace the pronoun.

Sometimes you can replace the pronoun with *a*, *an*, or *the* with no loss of meaning.

Vee Germain's will is not valid without a signature.

rather than

Vee Germain's will is not valid without their signature.

5. Use PASSIVE VOICE to avoid needing the pronoun.

Although using too much passive voice makes text less readable, here it provides a useful alternative.

Professional responsibility requires the attorney to advise the client of the downsides of the approach that was chosen.

rather than

Professional responsibility requires the attorney to advise the client of the downsides of the approach that he or she has chosen.

6. Use a noun with a MODIFIER to omit a reference to the actor.

This approach takes a little more thought but can often trigger you to think of more apt phrasing.

Professional responsibility requires the attorney to advise the client of the downsides of the chosen approach.

rather than

Professional responsibility requires the attorney to advise the client of the downsides of the approach that they have chosen.

7. Use a different SUBJECT-VERB COMBINATION for the second part of the sentence.

Closely related to the previous technique, this approach allows you to focus on a term that can provide an opportunity for useful emphasis.

Professional responsibility requires the attorney to advise the client whenever a particular approach has potential downsides.

rather than

Professional responsibility requires the attorney to advise the client of the downsides of the approach that they have chosen.

8. Avoid using gendered phrases whenever possible.

 People often prefer raising children with the help of their immediate family.

 rather than

 Men and women often prefer raising boys and girls with the help of their immediate family.

 For related information, see SEXIST LANGUAGE, WAYS TO AVOID.

GENERAL CORRESPONDENCE LETTERS AND EMAIL

See COMMUNICATIONS; CLOSINGS FOR; COMMUNICATIONS ELECTRONIC; COMMUNICATIONS, INTERNATIONAL; COMMUNICATIONS, OPENINGS FOR; COMMUNICATIONS, PERSUASIVE; COMMUNICATIONS, REAL-TIME; EMAIL; WRITING TO ATTORNEYS; and WRITING TO CLIENTS.

GENERALLY

Generally is an adverb that means *for the most part* or *usually*. Be careful to use it in its exact meaning, rather than as a meaningless introduction.

Generally, "private sector" means private individuals and enterprises that are run by private individuals or groups.

but not

Generally, the private sector is different from the public sector.

GERUNDS

Gerunds are NOUNS formed from the *-ing* form of a verb.

Seeing is believing.

Using gerunds can often make a sentence more concise.

Imagining alone does not constitute intent.

rather than

The act of imagination alone does not constitute intent.

Gerunds, however, sometimes create subjects that are too long. Remember to keep the subject and verb within seven words of each other, for readability.

Any attorney finds it difficult to master both persuasive and objective writing.

rather than

Becoming a writer equally skilled in both persuasive and objective legal writing is difficult for any attorney.

GETTING ORGANIZED

For help here, choose the entry most closely related to your concern: GETTING STARTED; NOTES; ORGANIZATION FOR THOSE WHO CAN'T OUTLINE; ORGANIZE, HOW TO; OUTLINES; PAPERLESS PRACTICE; PREWRITING; RESEARCH STRATEGY GUIDE; WRITING BLOCK; WRITING PROCESS; or the entry about the specific document you are writing.

GETTING STARTED

You may have trouble getting started for any of multiple reasons. You may dread the job because it is boring, difficult, or crucial to your career. You may not know where to start. Or you may just be stuck at some stage of the writing process. Do not despair; all of these problems are fixable. To solve these problems, however, you may have to change your approach to the problem. For related information, see HABITS, WRITING; and WRITING BLOCKS.

1. When you dread the job.

   Try listing what needs to be done and then dividing the tasks on the list into subtasks. Keep dividing them until you get down to tasks that are small enough to feel manageable. Even if the list seems very long, just start completing the tasks one by one. If time is short, review the list and distinguish those tasks essential to the job, such as clear organization and mandatory authority, from those desirable but not necessary, such as emphatic sentence structure. Then work on the essential tasks first. For help determining these tasks, see TRIAGE. For more ideas, see DEADLINES, MEETING THEM.

   Sometimes you may dread the job because it is important to you and you fear failure. If this is the case, do not hesitate to begin the job. You will not feel any better if you procrastinate, and your chance of success will be lessened. Instead, proceed quickly to divide the writing into subtasks, as described in the previous paragraph. Additionally, divide your goal of sufficient quality into subtasks. You need to get it written before you can get it right. For example, focus first on getting some ideas on paper. As a second step, focus on getting all the supporting sources listed. Later focus on explaining each point clearly and then, separately, explaining how those points fit together, like a syllogism, to make your point. Save concerns about conciseness, clarity, grammar, and other qualities for the revision process. When the job is important, you especially need to divide and conquer, and you need to do it early in the writing process.

2. When you do not know where to start.

   Start anywhere. Many people think that they have to start with an outline, but in reality, you can start in any of several places. For example, you might start drafting one subpoint of the Discussion of a memo because you understand that particular point best. Or you might start by trying to get your QUESTIONS PRESENTED exactly right. In a law review article, you might start with one sentence that sums up the point of your whole article, not worrying about whether that sentence will appear in the final draft. Then you could list the points needed to back up that statement and develop that list into an OUTLINE. For more ideas, see PREWRITING.

3. When you are stuck.

   Sometimes shifting your writing medium may help. For example, leave the computer and walk to a colleague's office to talk about the topic. After a few minutes, you may be able to return with a clearer idea of what you want to say. Or shift to a program that translates speech into text and dictate. You might even write on paper by hand for a bit. Often just looking away from the text you have written and talking to yourself can help you find the words you need.

   Alternatively, try starting at a different point in the document. For example, if you cannot get the QUESTIONS PRESENTED right, try writing the DISCUSSION SECTION or the CONCLUSION. If the Argument is rambling, try revising your Issues or writing your STATEMENT OF THE CASE. You may discover that starting with any one of these always helps you get the job done more efficiently. The best starting place for one person is not the best for another, so experiment to discover what works for you. Remember, good writing does not depend on whether you start in the right place; it depends on whether you do all you need to before you stop.

   You may also find generative artificial intelligence (AI) helpful at this point because it can provide a very rough draft to get you started. Be sure to rewrite and revise it until it becomes your own, however. AI-generated text, while it may sound reasonable, can be rather general in its statements, and HALLUCINATIONS remain a risk. If you are using AI, see ARTIFICIAL INTELLIGENCE AND RESEARCH, ARTIFICIAL INTELLIGENCE AND WRITING, DISCUSSION SECTION, PROMPTS, and RESEARCH STRATEGY GUIDE.

GHOST WRITING

As a legal writer, you may be called upon to become a ghost writer, that is, to write documents for another author in that author's style. For example, you might be asked to write a letter or email from a supervising attorney, signed by that attorney, not you, that speaks in that attorney's voice. To do this well, you need to study the attorney's writing characteristics. Some authors use short sentences and words to create a blunt, businesslike effect. Others avoid formality, using contractions, informal language, and short paragraphs. Yet others are consistently formal, never splitting infinitives and often employing the subjunctive mood.

You may consider the writing good, bad, or otherwise; ghost writing requires you to set aside that judgment to imitate the other author's work. Such imitation helps you learn more about writing by reverse engineering another's work.

This book's entries offer categories for studying an author's writing characteristics, such as FLOWERY LANGUAGE, JARGON, TOPIC SENTENCES, HEADINGS, SENTENCE LENGTH, SENTENCE STRUCTURE, TONE, VOICE, and WORD CHOICE. As you reverse engineer another author's writing, consider the following, in addition to the entries listed above.

1. Ask about the author's preferences.

   Ask your author about particular writing characteristics that the writer values. Some authors will give specific directions on being terse, elegant, or no nonsense. Study samples of the author's writing and translate these qualities into the appropriate writing choices, as described below. If you are using generative artificial intelligence (AI), you can use this information in your PROMPTS.

2. Consider other variables.

   Note the document's setting and audience. If it is a letter to a familiar client, you may be imitating an informal, friendly approach; if it is the third pretrial brief in tiresome litigation, you may be imitating an impatient, curt approach.

3. Collect and review samples.

   Ask your author to provide some samples, or research to find samples of the author's work. Try to get at least three samples of the kind of writing you are imitating, such as a letter, formal email, brief, contract, or opinion. If you have an in-house generative AI program, these samples may already exist in the knowledge base. As you review samples of the author's other writing, note the author's writing patterns in this particular kind of document.

(a) Consider how the author presents the subject of the document. For example, the author may use any of the following:

- a sentence near the beginning or the document,
- a formal Issue,
- a paragraph at the end of the introductory section,
- a preamble, or
- a separate section later in the document.

(b) Consider the document's structure. For example, the author may use any of the following structural devices:

- headings,
- strong topic sentences,
- a paragraph describing the document's structure, or
- an outline format.

Also consider the logical flow that your author prefers. For example, the author may develop points in any of the following ways:

- from general point to specific support, or deductive;
- from specific example to general point, or inductive;
- from illustrative example to general point to specific support;
- from familiar to new information;
- from the reader's preferences to contrary views;
- in the order traditionally used when discussing these points; or
- by the major policies behind the points.

For other possible patterns, see ORGANIZATION, LARGE-SCALE; and OUTLINES.

(c) Consider how your author tends to group information. Some authors work with larger groups of information, others prefer smaller groups. For example, you may notice any of the following in your author's writing:

- frequent paragraphs running one-half a page,
- frequent short or one-sentence paragraphs,
- frequent sentences running more than four lines,
- frequent sentences running one line or less,

- frequent use of several long sentences followed by a short one that acts as a punch line,
- headings or subheadings appearing on every page,
- headings or subheadings appearing on every fourth page,
- lists,
- relatively long and detailed headings, or
- relatively short and spare headings.

(d) Consider the writer's word choice. Just as some attorneys choose to dress more formally than others, some writers choose different levels of formality in their words. For example, your writer may frequently use any of the following:

- formal or scholarly words;
- down-to-earth or familiar words;
- strong SUBJECT-VERB COMBINATIONS;
- intransitive subject-verb combinations, such as *there are* or *it is*;
- short words;
- multisyllabic words;
- NOMINALIZATIONS;
- INTRUSIVE PHRASES;
- long introductory phrases;
- specific and detailed descriptions;
- general, broader descriptions; or
- rhetorical questions.

(e) Consider how strictly the author honors conventions. For example, determine which of the following conventions are important to this author:

- *BLUEBOOK* or *ALWD* or local citation conventions,
- comma usage,
- editing of quotations,
- use of parenthesis, or
- use of underlining or boldface for emphasis.

4. Try to hear the author speaking.

Look for patterns in tone and voice. By being a good ghost writer, you create a document ready-made for the author. By analyzing the author's writing, you add to your own repertoire of writing techniques. Even if you would not choose to use the same patterns, your awareness of the author's patterns makes you more selective of your own. When you have this imitative writing opportunity, enjoy it as a way of building your writing repertoire.

GIVEN THAT

See BEING THAT.

GLOBAL ENGLISH

See COMMUNICATIONS, INTERNATIONAL.

GOOD OR *WELL*?

Use *good* to modify a noun.

She had good reason to doubt his word.

Use *well* to modify a verb or an adjective.

She could hear well enough to understand the general topic of the defendants' conversation.

Use *good* after *feel*, because *good* here modifies the subject, not the verb.

I feel good about this decision.

Well would be correct only if you were talking about your ability to feel physically, which almost never comes up in writing. For related information, see BAD OR BADLY?

GRACE UNDER FIRE

This compliment is given to people who stand up under criticism without either folding or firing back. If you can achieve this, even as a new attorney, you will gain self-confidence as well as the respect of others.

When your writing is criticized, and it will be criticized someday by someone, view it as valuable reader feedback. Listen to the comments without defending or even explaining your words, at least initially. Your silence does not mean that you are accepting the criticism as correct; you are simply reserving judgment and focusing on understanding the substance of the criticism. Ask questions in an honest, inquiring tone. Resist any anger or dismay. Try to feel curious rather than attacked. Tell yourself that you are only collecting information at this point; you will decide on the validity of that information later.

This response buys you time and space to determine how you will approach the revision. It also presents you to others as someone who is not defensive or closedminded, even in difficult circumstances. Thus later, you will look flexible and receptive as you make changes. If you find the suggestions lead to incorrect information or reasoning, you can explain your position calmly, with your reasoning in place.

Finally, remember to choose your battles. After you have had time to consider the criticism, determine whether being right matters in the situation at hand. Arguing with a superior about comma placement may not be worth the cost, even if you are right.

For related information, see ADJUSTING TO A NEW WRITING SITUATION; DEADLINES, MEETING THEM; MANAGING WRITERS; PRINCIPLES OF GOOD LEGAL WRITING; PRIORITIES WITHIN ONE PROJECT; PROFESSIONAL LANGUAGE AND PRESENTATION; and TIME MANAGEMENT.

GRAMMAR

Grammar refers to the rules for constructing communications in a language. In contrast, *usage* refers to how words are used by native speakers, and *style* is a more amorphous concept that usually implies a set of additional conventions adopted by a particular set of writers, such as journalists, scientists, or scholars. Differing from the reader's expectations in any of these areas may make the meaning awkward, ambiguous, or hard to understand, but grammar errors make it incorrect.

As in other kinds of professional writing, grammar counts in legal writing. An error in grammar usually makes the communication inaccurate or unclear. Grammatical mistakes are potholes in the superhighway of a presentation. Therefore, use grammar carefully to convey your legal ideas clearly, and revise specifically for its proper use. For help in this area, see POLISHING.

For specific grammar information, see MODIFIERS; PARALLEL STRUCTURE; PARTS OF SPEECH; PUNCTUATION; SENTENCE STRUCTURE; SUBJECT-VERB AGREEMENT; and VERBS, TENSES.

GRAPHICS AND SYMBOLS IN EMAIL

See SYMBOLS IN EMAIL.

GRAPHICS, HOW TO USE

The audience's familiarity with graphics has reached the point where graphics may communicate your point more clearly than the written word, but only when used effectively. In all situations, the graphic aid should support and clarify the information in the document's text; you must be sure it will enhance the reader's understanding rather than detract (for more on this, see GRAPHICS, WHEN TO USE).

Graphics aids may be as elaborate as flow charts and three-dimensional graphs, or as simple as subheadings and tabulation. No matter what tool you are using, follow these guidelines to make sure your graphics enhance understanding.

1. Keep the content of the graphic aids as simple as possible.

   The reader sees a graphic presentation as a whole first; then the eye scans around the graphic for details. To make the most of that first impression, omit any information that distracts from the main point. For example, if you wanted to communicate that the chance of a drowning occurring increases as the depth of a pool approaches 15 feet, and that this correlation is more significant than other factors, you might first present a graph establishing the correlation with depth.

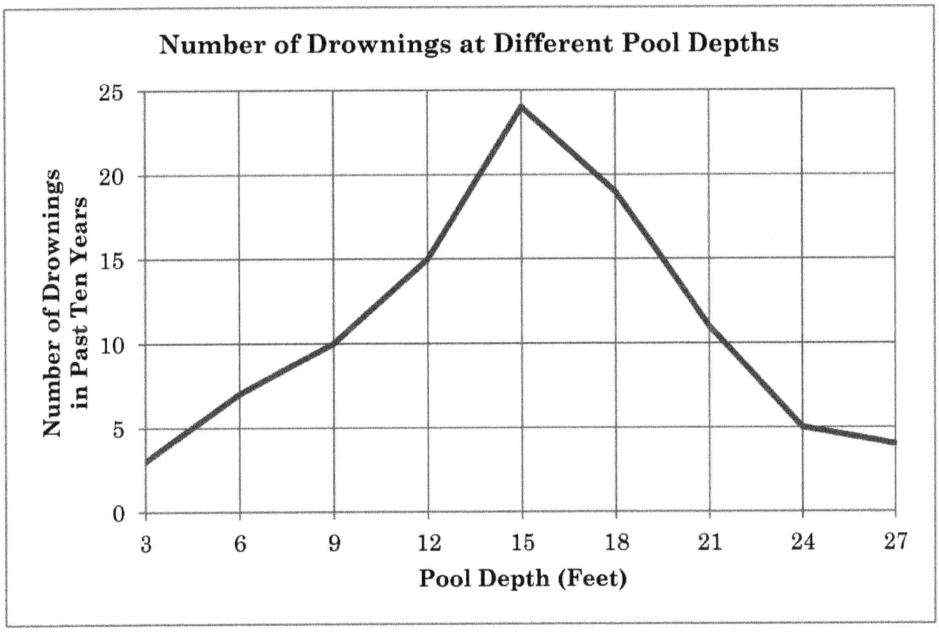

Then you could explain that this correlation was stronger than other factors, perhaps representing each other factor in a separate graph, like the one below, that could be compared with the first.

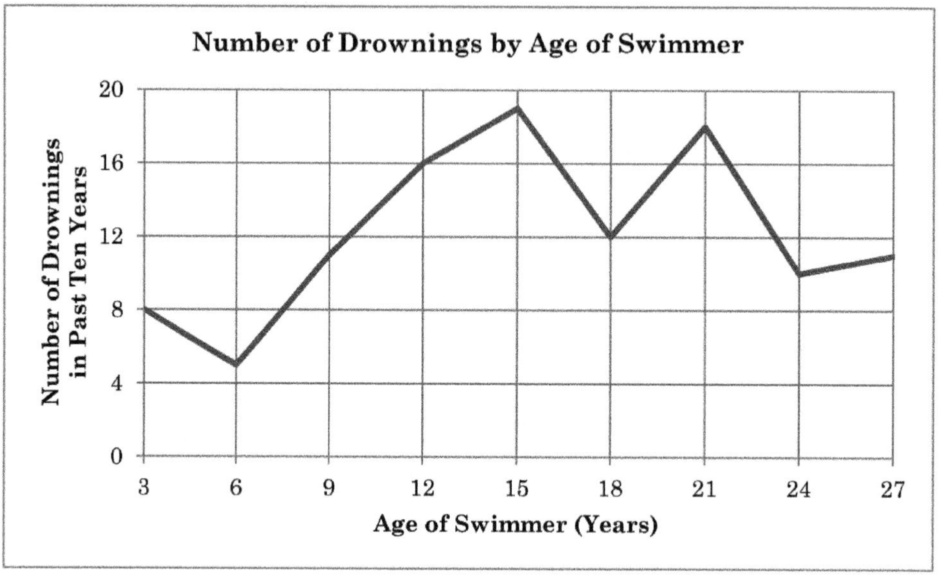

Avoid trying to present all the information in one graph; so much information together is likely to confuse the point rather than underscore it.

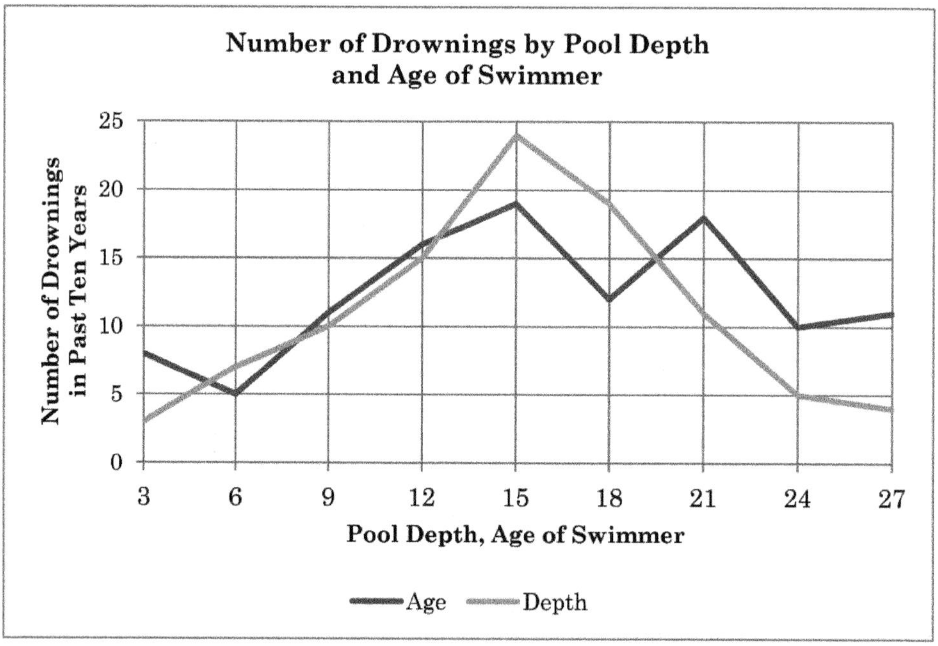

Separating the information makes each point clearer.

2. Make sure that both the graphic aid and the text communicate the message.

 Some readers will skip the text and go directly to the graphics. For that reason, word the titles and legends of inserted graphics to communicate the same message as your text. Other readers will skip the graphics, so summarize in the text any message illustrated in the graphics.

 For example, the following map communicates the story of what happened in an accident.

Map of Accident

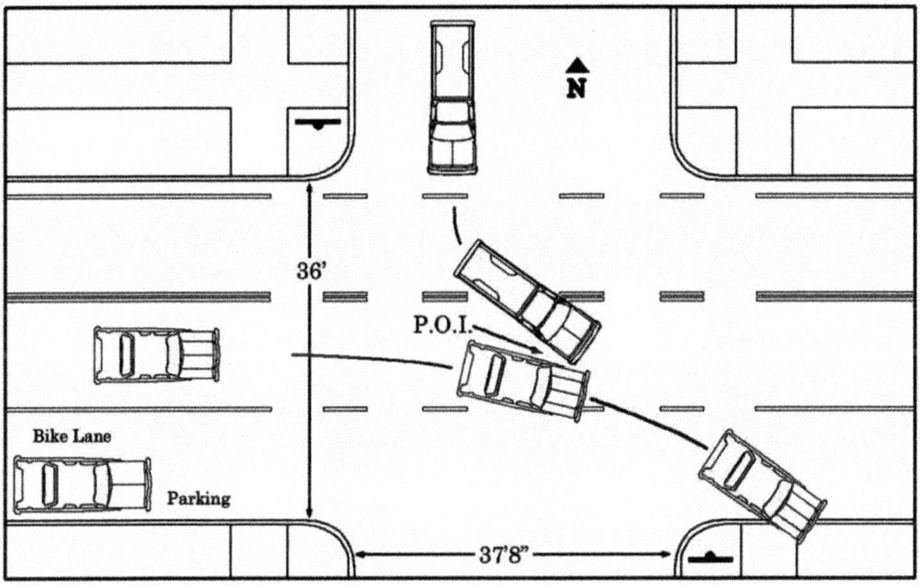

3. Use, but avoid overusing, smaller graphic tools within the text.

 Smaller graphic devices, such as tabulation or bullet points, can help a reader negotiate a formidable list of necessary details. But do not overuse graphic aids to the point that readers notice the graphics more than the content. You want your reader to remain focused on the content, rather than consciously noticing all the graphic aids. For help deciding when bullets or tabulation can help, see LISTS, HOW TO STRUCTURE.

4. Use graphics to summarize appended material.

 The purposes of graphic aids vary depending on whether the aid will be used within the text or added as an appendix. For auxiliary or supporting information that does not need to be inserted into the text, consider the following guidelines when deciding whether to use a graphic aid. Use a graphic form when that form does any of the following.

- The graphic form makes a better reference because it allows the reader to retrieve a particular piece of information more easily.
- The graphic form creates a more efficient document because it allows the writer to present the information more concisely while maintaining clarity.
- The graphic form creates a more pleasing document because it makes the information either more visually pleasing or less overwhelming.

If you answer any of these questions affirmatively, create the graph and append it to the document, with references to it inserted in text.

5. Make sure the visual impression of a graphic reflects your point.

Graphics, whatever their form, communicate a feeling subconsciously before the reader even gets to the content. For example, the first graph under this entry illustrates that there is a distinct peak in the information, communicating that this point is critical to determining other factors. When that initial impression is congruent with the point you want to make, this subconscious effect works to underscore the point. If, however, you did not want to communicate a particular turning point, that same graph would undercut your message. For more on how to develop graphic aids that reinforce your meaning, see GRAPHICS, WHEN TO USE; and GRAPHICS, WHICH FORM TO USE.

GRAPHICS, WHEN TO USE

When deciding whether to use graphics within the text, consider using graphics only when all of the following are true:

- the information you are communicating in graphic form is central to your overall message,
- the graphic form communicates your information more clearly than words, and
- at least some of your readers will understand the information more readily in graphic form than in words.

If you have answered all of these questions affirmatively, then create the graphic aid and insert it immediately after the written explanation.

When using graphics in appendices, your reasons for including them differ. For help doing this, see GRAPHICS, HOW TO USE, subsection 4; and GRAPHICS, WHICH FORM TO USE.

GRAPHICS, WHICH FORM TO USE

The form of a graphic aid communicates immediately, before the reader studies the content it includes. As a result, you must use the graphic form that accurately conveys your meaning. Some common graphics and their uses are outlined below.

1. Pie charts.

   Pie charts show how a whole unit is apportioned between subcategories. For example, they can show how much of your workday is devoted to various legal tasks or what portions of a company's income come from different sources.

Jayco Revenue Sources (by subsidiary)

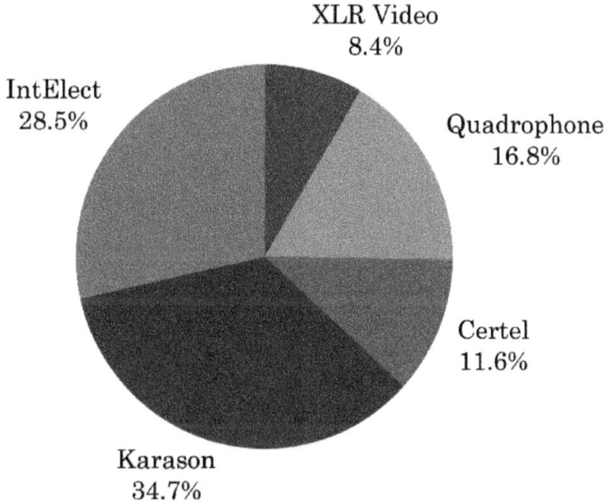

   Pie charts are the natural choice for showing how a whole is divided, especially because most readers are familiar with this use. But avoid using them for other purposes, because most would be confused by that nonstandard use.

2. Bar graphs.

   These graphs usually show how the quantity of something changes across the items compared. They suggest a pile of something, such as money, and so are particularly useful for this kind of information. For example, they can show how many complaints a company received over time regarding an item it continued to produce or how much income a company generated in different quarters or years.

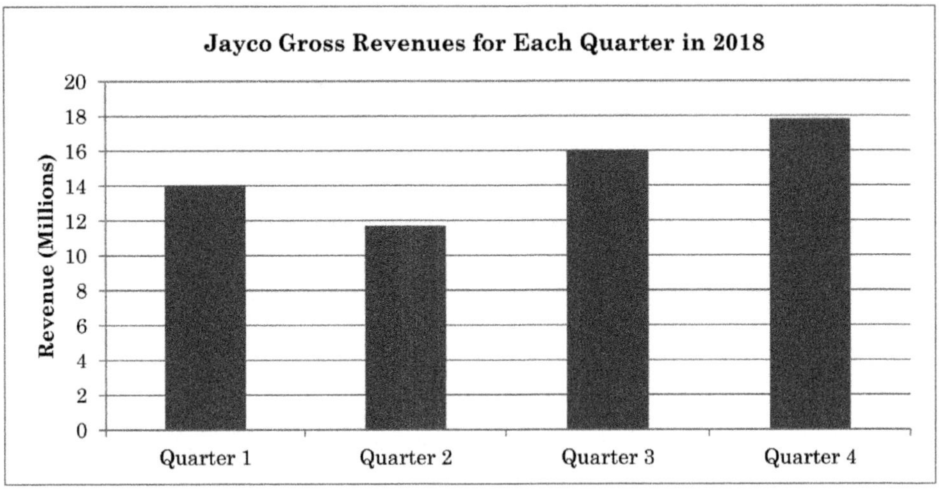

Watch the arrangement of bar graphs to make sure that you do not communicate an upward or downward trend if you do not intend to do so. For example, the following graph suggests bad news where none was intended, solely because of the order in which the categories are placed.

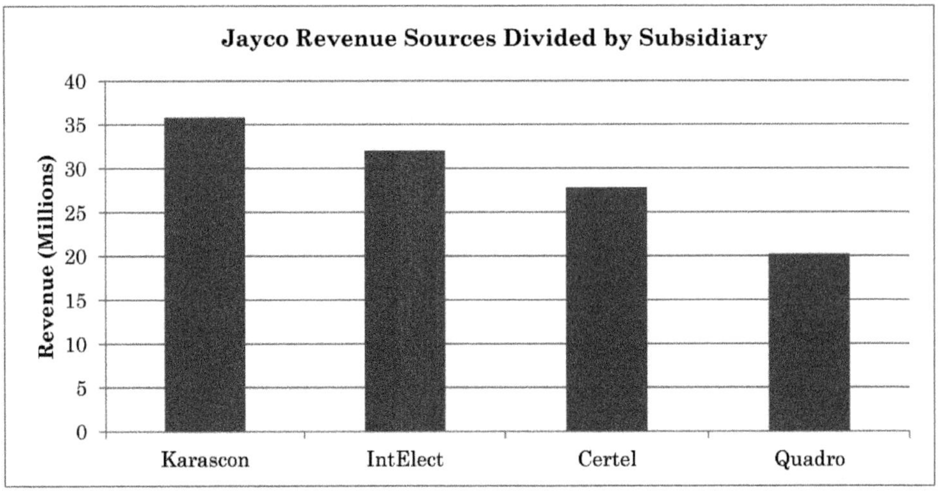

3. Stacked bar graphs or side-by-side bar graphs.

These formats enable bar graphs to compare two quantities with each other while also showing how both change across the items compared. For example, a side-by-side bar graph could show how one neighborhood's real estate taxes have risen in comparison to the taxes of the larger community.

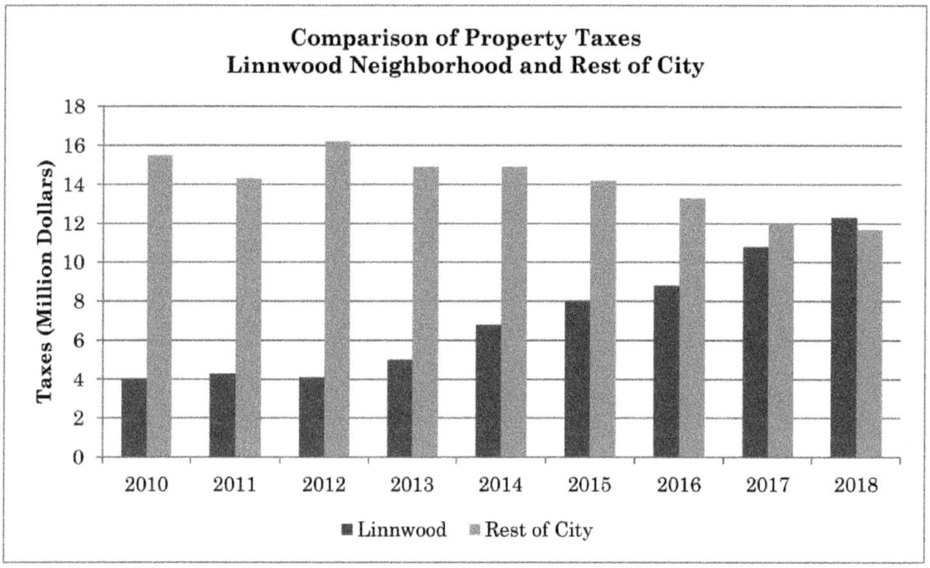

Similarly, a stacked bar graph can show how the neighborhood's taxes have risen even while the overall community's tax rate remained relatively unchanged.

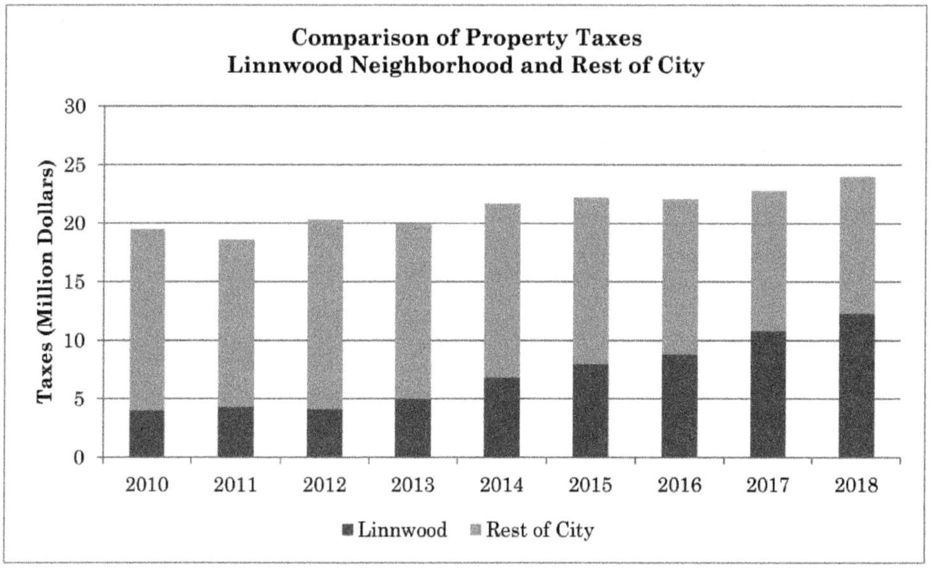

4. Line graphs.

Line graphs often show change across time or compare two variables that interact. These graphs suggest numbers and change, more than the discrete quantities that bar graphs suggest. For example, line graphs can illustrate the variability in a fire station's response time or the rise in accident rates at a particular intersection over several years. They communicate a trend, either upward or down, so avoid using them if you do not want to communicate such a trend.

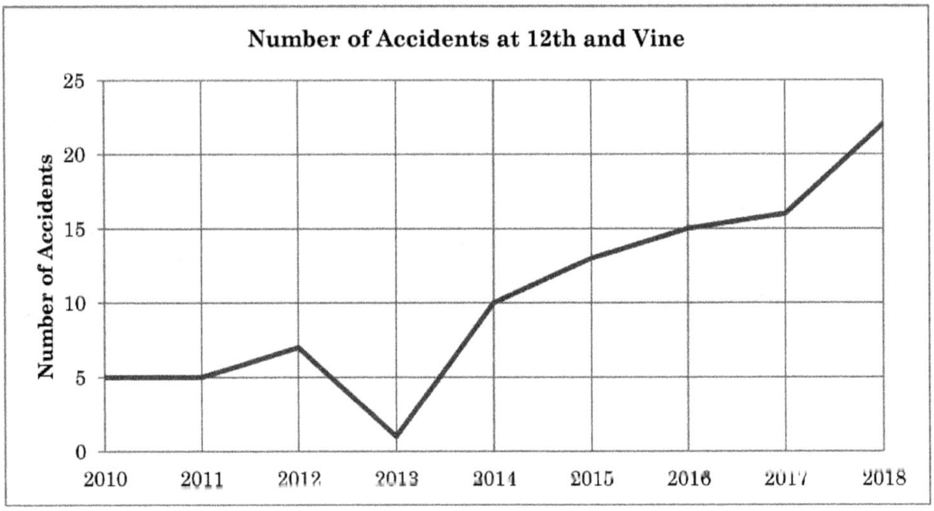

5. Tables.

These divide data into discrete categories and coordinate those categories so any reader in your audience can find a particular category quickly. A table also organizes and unifies data, so the detail does not overwhelm any reader. For example, a table could chart how many clients came to a firm with each particular legal problem a firm handles, how many problems were subsequently settled out of court, and how many went to trial.

Summary of 2025 Cases by Problem and Settlement Level

Cases		Level at Which Settled					
Client	**Problem**	**Prelim. Corres.**	**Pre-Trial**	**Trial**	**Pre-Appeal**	**Post-Appeal**	**Total**
Family	Custody	2	3	2	40	23	70
	Child Support	3	3	21	45	9	81
	Maintenance	5	9	12	23	9	58
	Other	15	20	4	3	0	42
Business	Contract Litig.	2	7	2	0	1	12
	Debtor	36	35	15	5	0	91
	Other	8	8	14	0	0	30
Injury	Worker's Comp.	0	2	13	0	2	17
	Tort	10	36	34	4	2	86
	Other	3	15	7	2	0	27
	Total	84	138	124	122	46	514

To design useful tables, you need to determine what information your audience needs and what kind of category is most likely to be meaningful to that audience. Then divide the information about those categories into groups that answer questions the audience will have. This step is important, because often the categories that are meaningful to the audience differ from those that occur first to the writer. For example, when categorizing patients receiving cancer treatments, you might first think of grouping them by the kind of cancer they had. Your reader, however, might be more concerned about the nature of the treatment provided, the effectiveness of the treatment, or the cost of providing that treatment. As always, be governed by what will be convenient and effective for the reader, rather than for the writer. For related information, see GRAPHICS, WHEN TO USE; and GRAPHICS, HOW TO USE.

HABITS, WRITING

Habits form in writing just as they do everywhere else. Good writing habits can make work more effective, efficient, and pleasant. In contrast, keeping bad writing habits can cost both you and your client, especially because legal writing often requires high productivity in short periods of time. Habits are not inevitable, however. You can transform your approach to writing over time; as a result, you can look back over your career and say that you have had twenty years of writing experience, rather than one year of writing experience twenty times. This change takes work.

Therefore, in moving from the PREWRITING stage through WRITING, REWRITING, REVISING, and POLISHING, consider which habits work for you and which habits do not. Then start with the most troublesome habit and eradicate it by replacing it with a better habit. For example, if you habitually try to revise each sentence as you write, you will probably find that the writing process has become very time consuming and agonizing. Instead, try giving yourself a time limit and forcing yourself to write without any revision until you finish your first draft. Then go back and rewrite. Similarly, if you spend too much time doing research, you may not have enough time for the actual writing. Instead, pause periodically in your research and reevaluate your document's PURPOSE and SCOPE. Streamline your research strategies accordingly. Determine how much time you need to write and allocate time accordingly.

For suggestions for breaking habits in each stage of the WRITING PROCESS, see the entry for that stage. For help in facing the writing process itself, see DEADLINES, MEETING THEM; GETTING STARTED; NOTES; ORGANIZATION FOR THOSE WHO CAN'T OUTLINE; OUTLINES; PERFECTIONISM; PRIORITIES WITHIN ONE PROJECT; PROCRASTINATION; RESEARCH STRATEGY GUIDE; TIME MANAGEMENT; TRIAGE; WHEN TO STOP; and WRITING BLOCK. For help using artificial intelligence, see ARTIFICIAL INTELLIGENCE AND RESEARCH, ARTIFICIAL INTELLIGENCE AND WRITING, DISCUSSION SECTION, PROMPTS, and RESEARCH STRATEGY GUIDE.

HALLUCINATIONS

Hallucinations are the inaccurate statements that occur when artificial intelligence (AI) generates something that is not factually or legally true. These hallucinations occur when inaccurate assumptions are used to train the AI model, when the mass of information that the AI model studies includes biased or faulty examples, when the AI itself makes wrong guesses about what word should follow the previous one, or when the AI makes a conclusion that is incorrect, among other possible sources of error. Hallucinations are especially dangerous in legal writing, where a factual error or a citation to a fictious case in a brief can ruin a lawyer's credibility or lead to malpractice. If you use artificial intelligence to aid you in your research or writing, be vigilant for hallucinations and verify your results. See ARTIFICIAL INTELLIGENCE AND RESEARCH, ARTIFICIAL INTELLIGENCE AND WRITING, and PROMPTS.

HANGED OR *HUNG*?

If you are talking about a person being *hanged by the neck until dead,* use *hanged.* If you are talking about *hung* in any other sense, such as a thing *hung on the wall,* use *hung.* Informally, you may refer to a *hung jury.*

HARDLY

Hardly is more informal than its synonyms *scarcely* or *nearly,* so avoid it in formal writing, such as MEMOS and BRIEFS. See also *CAN HARDLY* OR *CAN'T HARDLY*? and SYNONYMS.

HEADINGS

In most legal writing, headings identify the subsections of a memo, email, brief, letter, or article. Headings should reveal the large-scale organization and overall themes of the document. Thus they ease the eye and the mind of the reader by making the legal analysis easier to follow. In briefs, headings take the specific form of point headings, subheadings, and sub-subheadings, which outline the specific legal points of the argument and the reasoning behind those points. These headings should be sufficient to communicate the basic legal argument even when read without the text. In memos, headings distinguish each part of the memo, such as Questions Presented, Brief Answers, Discussion, and Conclusion. Subheadings may be used to divide the Discussion, so that the reader can see at a glance which legal issues are being discussed where. Usually these subheadings take the form of a label, such as

False Imprisonment

or

Jurisdiction

although a sentence can be even more helpful.

This District Court Has Jurisdiction.

In long opinion letters, subheadings similarly subdivide the explanation. The same is true with articles.

In your headings and subheadings, try to convey a definite message to the reader. When it will help your reader, use complete sentences in your headings and perhaps subheadings as well, rather than single words or abstract phrases. When appropriate, use parallel structure to convey your theme from one heading to the next. For help doing this, see CONNECTIONS, MAKING THEM. Include law, facts, and other information specific to your analysis, so the reader can understand the overall logic and content just by reading the headings. For related information, see POINT HEADINGS and SCHOLARLY WRITING.

HEADNOTES

Headnotes are numbered paragraphs in legal reporters that summarize the legal points of a court's opinion. These summaries are written by the editors of the reporter in which the case appears, and they appear before the actual text of the case begins.

Headnotes are designed as research tools to aid the reader in using the case. For example, if you are researching intentional torts and a case contains, among others, a procedural headnote on jurisdiction and a substantive headnote on intentional torts, then you can use the headnote number to find the section of the case discussing intentional torts where that number reappears. Using that headnote, you can update just that section of the case on intentional torts. See UPDATING THE LAW.

Because headnotes are research tools and are not written by judges, never cite to a headnote. Also, never depend on the headnote to supply your understanding of the case. Read the text and check whether you believe the case indeed covers this point.

HELP

If you have turned to this, you are probably in the midst of your writing process and under pressure. You can get the job done one step at a time. Divide the tasks and conquer. Consult the most relevant of the following entries: DEADLINES, MEETING THEM; GETTING STARTED; ORGANIZATION FOR THOSE WHO CAN'T OUTLINE; ORGANIZE, HOW TO; OUTLINES; PERFECTIONISM; PROCRASTINATION; TIME MANAGEMENT; TRIAGE; WHEN TO STOP; WRITING BLOCK; or WRITING PROCESS. Also look for an entry under the particular kind of writing that concerns you, such as BRIEFS, CASE BRIEFS, CONTRACTS, COMMUNICATIONS entries, LEGISLATION, MEMOS, OPINIONS, PLEADINGS, WILLS, and so forth. If none of these entries seems right, consult the master list of entries in the front of the book.

HELPING VERBS

See VERBS, AUXILIARY; and VERBS, TENSES.

HE OR SHE?

Avoid resorting to the outmoded phrase *he or she*. When the gender of the person referred to is unknown, rewrite the text to avoid any reference to gender.

The judge has the authority to select the jury instructions and revise them as needed.

rather than

The judge exercises his or her authority to select the jury instructions and revise them as he or she sees fit.

For multiple ways to avoid using gendered pronouns, and a general discussion of this question, see GENDER IN WRITING and SEXIST LANGUAGE, WAYS TO AVOID.

HEREBY

Avoid using this term unless absolutely needed. See LEGALESE.

HE/SHE, WHEN TO USE

This option is fading from use. Replace it with the appropriate noun or use another approach to avoid needing a gendered pronoun. For how to do this, see GENDER IN WRITING and SEXIST LANGUAGE, WAYS TO AVOID.

More broadly, use a slash construction only in a form document when the signer is meant to strike out the inappropriate choice.

HOLD

Courts *hold*; counsel does not.

For related information, see *FIND*, *HOLD*, OR *REASON*? and TERMS OF ART.

HOLDING

The holding is the decision a court reaches in a case. A holding thus disposes of an issue raised in the case, whether procedural or substantive. As such, it theoretically binds that court and those under it to follow that decision in making subsequent holdings in similar legal situations. Therefore, holdings often provide a focal point for research, constructing arguments and measuring the strength of a client's case. Consider the following in using case holdings.

1. In CASE BRIEFS.

   Use the holding to state the answer to the issue and give a reason for that answer.

   > **Yes; Curtis falsely imprisoned Butterworth because he used words or acts that intended to confine Butterworth, he actually confined her in the car, and Butterworth was aware that she was confined.**

For related information, see ISSUES, DICTA, and CASE BRIEFS.

2. In a MEMO.

Use holdings to explain rules.

Hospitalization for alcohol abuse does not preclude being awarded custody of a child. Nagle v. Nagle, 999 P.3d 1, 3 (Utah 2025). But long-term institutionalization because of drug dependency does preclude an award of custody. James v. James, 999 P.3d 433 (Utah 2024).

Use holdings to describe analogous cases.

In Nagle, the mother was awarded custody of the daughter despite her previous hospitalization for alcohol abuse. Nagle, at 3. And in Carter, the mother was awarded custody when she showed successful completion of an Alcoholics Anonymous program. Carter, at 767.

For related information, see RULES and ANALOGOUS CASES.

3. In BRIEFS.

Use a holding to argue.

Even a mother who has been hospitalized for alcohol abuse can win custody of her daughter. Nagle v. Nagle, 999 P.3d 1, 3 (2025).

4. In PARENTHETICALS.

State the holding as it relates to the use of the cases.

Artists must look outside the moral rights doctrine for protection. *See* Peabody v. Percival, 999 F.3d 17 (9th Cir. 2025) (holding that moral right is limited in the United States, so breach of contract can be used to compensate artists whose work is mutilated).

HOLDING OR *RULE*?

A holding is the outcome in a specific case, such as the following.

The Court awarded custody to the father because he was able to spend more time with and provide a safer environment for two children, ages 10 and 12.

Although you may accurately use *the court held* to introduce a holding, this phrase usually is unnecessary.

A rule is the law that was used to reach the holding, such as the following.

In this jurisdiction, the court awards custody to the parent who can better serve the child's best interests.

Use the rule to establish the foundation of your analysis or argument. Use the holdings to define and illustrate how the law works, and to demonstrate the parameters of the law as applied previously.

HOMONYMS

A *homonym* is a word that sounds or is spelled the same as another word but has a different meaning, such as *their* and *there*, or *rose* and *rows*. Homonyms can be treacherous in legal writing if not caught when they create not just an obvious error, but an imprecision. Additionally, they may become a problem when you use voice-to-text technology. Be aware of those used often in legal writing, such as the following.

accept (to include)	*except* (other than)
compliment (to give praise)	*complement* (to work well with each other)
counsel (to advise)	*council* (group meeting)
halve (to cut in two)	*have* (to possess)
lead (metal)	*led* (past tense of *to lead*)
least (minimum)	*leased* (past tense of *to lease*)
principal (most important)	*principle* (belief)
warn (to caution)	*worn* (used)

For related information, see ANTONYMS, SYNONYMS, and WORDS THAT SPELL CHECKERS MAY NOT CATCH.

HOPEFULLY

When you need to refer to *hope*, use the verb, such as *I hope* or *our client hopes*. Use the adverb *hopefully* only when you mean that something was done in a hopeful way.

The Pilgrims sailed hopefully for America.

It is rare that you will mean this. While *hopefully* is used widely in speaking to mean *it is hoped*, that is not its literal meaning; therefore, it is usually not precise enough to be used in legal writing.

HOWEVER

However has two different uses: as a transition and as an adverb. Each use can cause problems for the legal writer.

1. As a transition.

However is a concise way of saying something roughly equivalent to *on the other hand*; it signals a shift to the other side or a contrasting subpoint. One way this may be done is to place *however* right after a semicolon joining two sentences.

> **The defendant has testified that she was not present at the scene of the crime; however, two witnesses have contradicted this.**

When using *however* this way, do not use it with only a comma. You must put a semicolon before *however* and a comma after. The semicolon is necessary because *however* is not a conjunction, like *and* or *but*.

> **The court remanded the case; however, the plaintiff did not receive an appreciably higher reward.**
>
> rather than
>
> The court remanded the case, however, the plaintiff did not receive an appreciably higher reward.

Another way *however* may be used as a transition is to place it a few words into a sentence.

> **The defendant has testified that she was not present at the scene of the crime. Two witnesses, however, have contradicted this.**

2. As an adverb.

As an adverb, *however* modifies a part of the sentence rather than serving as a transition between sentences.

> **However it happened, the defendant has lost the use of his arm as a result of this accident.**

Often this use of *however* sounds awkward in formal writing. In this situation, you may substitute another phrase.

> **No matter how it happened, ...**
>
> or
>
> **Regardless of the cause of the accident, ...**

Avoid overusing the word. If, for example, you see *however* appearing in every paragraph you write, you are probably overusing it. To correct the problem, first check your organization: Are you trying to cover two points that would be better presented in two separate paragraphs? Are you wavering between two views, avoiding taking a stand when it is your job to take a stand? If so, see ORGANIZE, HOW TO; and PARAGRAPHS for possible solutions. Second, check the accuracy of your word choice: Are you using *however* when you really mean *nevertheless*, *additionally*, or something else? See TRANSITIONS for a list of transition words that may communicate your point more accurately. Usually the answers to these questions will show you how you must revise. If not, consider using synonyms for *however* to avoid overusing it.

HUMOR

Effective humor is a deft and welcome stroke in legal writing, but it requires a precise choice of location and time. Some judges may find humor a welcome relief when working on a case that has at most minor consequences, so it may be effective to file a complaint in the form of poetry or to make light of a small point in a brief. Be particularly sensitive, however, to your overall AUDIENCE; the client or opposing party is not likely to be amused. Also do not use humor with a serious topic, as with any behavior causing serious harm to someone. When legal writing is reaching an audience not so immediately involved in the topic, such as in scholarly writing, you may use humor to underscore your point or perk up interest. Do not, however, insert humor that does not assist in your purpose. For related information, see VOICE and PURPOSE.

HUNG OR *HANGED*?

See *HANGED* OR *HUNG*?

HYPERBOLE

Hyperbole is an excessive exaggeration used as a figure of speech; avoid it generally, because its excesses often reduce the writer's credibility, as in the following examples.

Defendant was dying to get out of the courtroom.

The judge hung the defendant out to dry.

HYPHENS

Hyphens have three main uses in legal writing: (1) joining MODIFIERS that work together, (2) connecting some prefixes to words, and (3) separating words or letters.

1. Joining modifiers that work together.

Use a hyphen to signal that the words hyphenated work together to modify a subsequent noun.

bone-jarring blow

high-pitched voice

work-related expenses

owner-occupied housing

3- to 5-year sentence

There are two exceptions to this rule. Proper names are not hyphenated: *Southeast Asian conflict, Supreme Court opinion, West Coast phenomenon.* Also, modifying words are not hyphenated when they follow a linking verb, rather than preceding the word they modify.

The blow was bone jarring.

rather than

The blow was bone-jarring.

When following this rule, you may sometimes find the text awash in hyphens. If this happens, revise some sentences or reword descriptions to reduce the number of hyphens.

Euphoric after winning a close football game, the 16-year-old driver was laughing with his friends and waving to teammates in another car when he ran a stop sign and hit a heavily loaded dump truck crossing the intersection. The collision resulted in life-threatening injuries to his passengers, who were not wearing seat belts. The airbags and his seat belt, however, prevented serious injury to him. The fear-stricken youth was filled with guilt, to the point that he could not move from the street.

rather than

Punch-drunk with euphoria after winning the close-fought football game, the 16-year-old was laughing with his friends and waving to glee-filled teammates in another car when he ran a stop sign and hit the dirt-filled dump truck in the intersection. The T-bone collision resulted in blunt-force-caused injuries to his passengers, who were not wearing seat belts. Although the airbags deployed and prevented serious injury to him, some of his passengers faced life-threatening injuries. The fear-stricken, guilt-ridden youth could not move from the street.

2. Connecting some prefixes to words.

Use a hyphen to connect some prefixes.

(a) You may use a hyphen when adding a prefix to a proper name.

un-American,

pre-Columbian

(b) Use a hyphen when the prefix ends with the same vowel that begins the main word unless the word is commonly used without the hyphen.

semi-independent

re-examine or **reexamine**

In words that have become familiar through common use, however, the hyphen is usually omitted, such as *subissue*, *looseleafs*, and *email*.

(c) Use a hyphen with *self-* as a prefix to another noun.

self-employed

self-sufficient

For more examples, see *SELF-* OR *SELF*?

(d) Use a hyphen with *ex-* when it means former.

ex-wife

ex-President Obama

Do not use a hyphen when *ex* is part of the word: *exonerate*. Use *ex* as a separate word when it is used as such in part of a Latin phrase. When in doubt, look up the spelling.

ex post facto

deus ex machina

(e) Use a hyphen whenever omitting it will confuse readers.

He wanted to re-lease the apartment.

Or reword the sentence to avoid the problem.

He wanted to lease the apartment again.

3. Dividing and separating words or letters.

Use a hyphen to divide a long word coming at the end of a line in the rare situation where you do not have proportional spacing. Check the dictionary if you are not sure where the hyphen should go. Do not add a hyphen to a hyperlink. Do not hyphenate proper names and avoid hyphenating at the end of a page, as a favor to your reader.

Use a hyphen to separate letters when indicating the spelling of a word and to replace illegible letters in a quoted document.

His name should have been spelled as "H-y-r-a-m" rather than "H-i-r-a-m."

An em dash, rather than a hyphen, is added to replace missing or illegible words.

The handwritten letter left her estate to "my th— husband," leaving open the question of whether she intended her "then" husband or her "third" husband to inherit.

I

Use this pronoun when referring to yourself doing your job. Thus in a letter to a client, write the following, rather than resorting to passive voice.

I have forwarded the forms to the IRS.

But do not use *I* in other circumstances. Keep the focus on the content, not the writer. So in a brief, you might conclude as follows:

The defendant was fairly treated.

But you would not write this sentence because your point of view is implied, and the court will do the concluding.

I therefore conclude that the defendant was fairly treated.

For a general discussion of the reasons behind this use of *I*, see TONE, subsection 1(b).

IDIOM

Many idioms are informal, and thus should be avoided in documents such as briefs to the court, contracts, and other public documents. An *idiom* is an expression or phrase that is acceptable English even though it cannot be understood by interpreting the literal meaning of its elements. For students of English as a second language, mastering an understanding of American idioms is a major accomplishment.

We gave up on that project.

or

How do you do?

Idioms are often metaphors that have become so common that the original metaphorical image is lost: *to catch a cold* or *to strike a bargain.* Although some idioms are acceptable in standard English, avoid idioms that are ambiguous in context or that sound too informal.

He dropped off the package.

She was reeling from the bad decision below.

The judge caught the drift of his argument.

As these examples show, many idioms consist of a verb with a preposition following it, creating a meaning that is different than either of the two words suggest separately. Idioms are often the cause of sentences that end with a preposition, a situation that is not wrong but often sounds informal.

I.E.

The abbreviation *i.e.* stands for *id est*, or *that is*. As an abbreviation, you may use *i.e.* in place of those two words in legal writing, particularly in the context of further explanation, as in an explanatory footnote.

The 12(b)(6) motion succeeded, i.e., the case was dismissed.

Avoid using *i.e.* in any text where it could create ambiguity or be unfamiliar to any of your readers. For example, you might use *that is* in a letter to a client, where *i.e.* might sound stuffy. You might also avoid *i.e.* in a contract if it can create ambiguity. Use *that is* or another appropriate phrase instead.

He agreed to the condition when he signed the waiver.

rather than

He agreed to the condition, i.e., he signed the waiver.

Avoid confusing *i.e.* with *e.g.*; *i.e.* introduces a phrase that explains in other words, but *e.g.* introduces an example.

IF

If is useful in legal writing because *if* has only one meaning and therefore provides a precise transition between clauses. Because *if* is precise and because you will often be writing about points that logically are *if . . . then* situations, do not worry too much about overusing *if*. Worry only when several sentences in a paragraph contain *if* and when those *if*s are not logically parallel. For related information, see SENTENCE STRUCTURE, subsection 3; and TRANSITIONS.

If the *if* phrase is quite long, use a *then* after the comma at the end of the *if* phrase.

If the court extends this reasoning to include all victims of industrial accidents, then Harris can establish a cause of action.

IF AND WHEN

Usually you can delete the *and when*; *if* says it all. You only need both terms if you need to specify both *if something happens* and *at the time something happens*. In that situation, *if or when* would be more accurate. In most situations, however, *if* covers the meaning adequately because the time at which something happens is not relevant to the consequence being outlined.

IF OR *WHEN*?

Use *if* to suggest that something may or may not happen.

If the bill is not paid within 60 days, the refrigerator will be repossessed.

Use *when* to discuss something that will happen.

When the electricians complete their work, the inspector will arrange an appointment to see the house.

Thus, on some occasions, you may choose between *if* and *when* to suggest pessimism or optimism about the likelihood of something happening.

When our candidate is elected, the convention center will be built.

or

If the campaign were to fail, the convention center would remain on the drafting board.

When using *if* to suggest that something will not happen, also shift the verb to the subjunctive mood. For more explanation, see VERBS, MOODS. It is unlikely that you will need to write *if and when* because the consequences and the different connotations suggested by the two words will not be compatible with one outcome.

When I have a better job, I will buy a new car.

rather than

If and when I have a better job, I will buy a new car.

IMAGERY

Imagery has as much power in legal writing as it does anywhere else. Giving a reader an image that captures a legal situation can be more persuasive than pages of traditional legal proof. Imagery can also be memorable for its misuse and can suggest other arguments or responses that detract from the main issues. Use imagery sparingly, then, to capture what cannot be done in a better way.

Defendant's actions conform to every element of the statute.

rather than

Defendant went out in a blaze of glory.

but

Defendant landscaped his tax garden with a variety of perennial loopholes.

rather than

Defendant violated many tax laws.

When using imagery, focus your fire. Develop one image that can remain in the reader's memory. If your creative juices are flowing and you create many wonderful images, resist the urge to include them all. Choose the one best image and save the others for another day. For related information, see CLICHÉ; FLOWERY LANGUAGE; and GRAPHICS, WHEN TO INCLUDE.

IMMINENT OR *EMINENT*?

See *EMINENT* OR *IMMINENT*?

IMPACT

Use *impact* as a noun.

The impact caused extensive damage to defendant's vehicle.

The impact of such a decision would be far reaching.

Although *impact* is sometimes used as a verb, as in *to impact a decision*, its meaning is vague and its use in this way is not yet acceptable in all quarters. For some readers, *impact* should refer only to such things as teeth.

His wisdom tooth was impacted.

IMPERATIVE MOOD

See VERBS, MOODS, subsection 3.

IMPLY OR *INFER*?

These words are not interchangeable. *Imply* means to *suggest* or to *express indirectly*. *Infer* means to *surmise* or to *derive a conclusion from the information*. As a result, use *imply* when the subject is a piece of writing, a thing, a speaker, or a writer.

This reasoning implies that . . . .

Use *infer* when the subject is a reader or a listener.

The court inferred from this phrase that . . . .

IN ADVANCE OF

Use *before* for a cleaner, more concise sentence. For a discussion of the general principles behind this, see CONCISENESS, subsection 9.

INCLUDING, BUT NOT LIMITED TO

Including is usually sufficient in general legal writing because it indicates, by definition, that something is a component part of a whole. In modern usage, *including* is sometimes replacing the more traditionally explicit phrase *including, but not limited to* when introducing lists in drafting. Nevertheless, many lawyers prefer the latter because it may protect the meaning of the sentence, particularly in a contract. Before you depend on this phrase to protect the meaning of a contract's clause, however, research the issue in your jurisdiction. Try to word your clause to say unambiguously what you mean, rather than relying on this phrase alone to do the job.

INDENTED QUOTATIONS OR QUOTATION MARKS?

Use quotation marks around direct quotations of forty-nine or fewer words and around titles of articles. When a direct quotation is longer than forty-nine words, indent it, single-space it, and omit quotation marks. The only time you will use quotation marks in an indented, single-spaced quotation is when there is another quotation within the indented quotation. For related information, see QUOTATIONS, HOW TO PUNCTUATE.

INDENTING

See QUOTATIONS, HOW TO PUNCTUATE.

INDEPENDENCE IN LEGAL WRITING

You have it; the question is when and how to exercise it. Because legal writing is so dependent on readers' needs and preferences, you must ascertain what will best meet those concerns lest you exercise your independence at the wrong time or place. As a good architect learns about a client's lifestyle before designing a home, you must learn as much as you can about who will use your document, how often, and how long the document is expected to last, and then build accordingly. You are not building your own dream house with each document, so you cannot exercise total independence. Rather, you are building something for others to use, so your creativity and independence are exercised in the way you design the document and make it work for your readers.

Those readers include your colleagues, who may be reviewing the document as it develops. They, too, will have strong ideas about how to approach the document, from research to proofreading. Be sensitive to their independent thoughts, and use the readers' needs to find common ground.

For example, if you are writing a quick email response to a colleague, you can be quite independent because your ideas are sought exclusively in that context. But you have less independence if you are drafting a contract for two businesses, when the contract must last much longer than the current negotiation and must include the results of that negotiation. Similarly, if you are part of a team drafting an appellate brief, your independence is less important than your teamwork. As part of a good team, you will need to negotiate everything from the theory to the word choice to agree on the best way to meet the readers' needs. For related ideas, see CHOICES IN LEGAL WRITING, EDITING, MANAGING WRITERS, TIME MANAGEMENT, and STYLE.

INDEPENDENT CLAUSE

See CLAUSES or SENTENCE, PARTS OF, subsection 8.

INDICATIVE MOOD

See VERBS, MOODS, subsection 1.

INDIRECT OBJECTS

See SENTENCE, PARTS OF, subsection 5.

INFER OR *IMPLY*?

See *IMPLY* OR *INFER*?

INFINITIVE VERBS

See VERBS, TENSES, subsection 10.

INFORMAL LANGUAGE

See COLLOQUIALISM.

INFORMATIVE ARTICLES

As part of their service to the public, many organizations occasionally ask their attorneys to write fact sheets, white papers, newsletters, or other informative brochures. These documents inform or update readers on specific situations. They may be fact sheets provided by government agencies to advise citizens about a particular matter, newsletters mailed out by not-for-profit enterprises to provide useful information for their clients or donors, or informative letters sent by law firms to update their clients on recent changes in the law. Often these documents also fulfill a public relations function and may be used to attract new clients. Because they present the organization's face to the public, these documents must be accurate, user-friendly, and focused on the user's point of view.

Creating any of these documents requires you to shift your writing priorities to those of a journalist, but without losing accuracy. Besides presenting the relevant who, what, where, why, and how on the topic, these documents must catch the reader's interest. Although they are meant to provide the reader with relevant information, the reader is often interested in the topic but not in immediate, urgent need of the information. You are therefore writing a document that the reader is not required to read, so you need to begin your document with information that will engage that reader, just as a journalist needs a good lead for a news article.

To create an interesting lead to your document, review the content you need to convey to find what is most relevant to your audience. For example, you might begin with an anecdote that illustrates the problem you are addressing or a statistic that readily conveys the relevance of the content. You might begin with a question that the reader will want to see answered or an interesting and relevant quotation. As a process matter, a good lead may occur to you only after you have written the body of the document; in the rewriting process, after reviewing all your content, you can select the point that will catch a reader's eye. See AUDIENCE and REWRITING.

When organizing your content, remember to organize from the point of view of your audience, which will often differ from the perspective of your employer. As you enter the rewriting stage of your writing process, consider several possible organizations rather than settling on the first organization that occurred to you. Divide your information into paragraphs that run no more than a quarter-page, and consider using graphics where appropriate. For related information, see GRAPHICS, HOW TO USE; POINT OF VIEW; and WRITING PROCESS.

As you are revising the document, check to make sure that every term used is understandable to everyone in your audience. Include legal or technical terms only when necessary and define them whenever needed. For ways to include these definitions gracefully, see UNOBTRUSIVE DEFINITIONS. Be scrupulous in citing sources for your information, so you are not accused of plagiarism. For related information, see REVISING.

Remember to polish your fact sheets, just as you would a more formal legal document. These documents can have long lives and wide circulation so, as always, you want to protect your professional reputation by making sure all information is accurate and errors are removed. For help, see POLISHING CHECKLIST and WORDS SPELLCHECKERS MAY NOT CATCH.

For related information, see INSTRUCTIONS, WRITING THEM; SCHOLARLY WRITING; and WRITING, OBJECTIVE. For ideas on how to use artificial intelligence, see ARTIFICIAL INTELLIGENCE AND

RESEARCH, ARTIFICIAL INTELLIGENCE AND WRITING, DISCUSSION SECTION, PROMPTS, and RESEARCH STRATEGY GUIDE.

-ING WORDS

See GERUNDS.

IN, *INTO*, OR *IN TO*?

In means *inside of*, *during*, *as part of the act or process of*, or *among other things.*

He is in the room.

Into means *to the inside of* or *to the action or occupation of.*

She will go into law.

In to is used when an infinitive verb is used in a prepositional phrase.

My supervisor came in to introduce me to a new client.

The idiom *into* is too informal for legal writing.

My friend is into body building.

For related information, see PREPOSITIONS.

INITIALS

When initials are used in a person's name, put a period after the initial.

Helen C. Walrich

When several initials are used in place of a person's first name, use periods after each initial, with no spaces between initials.

D.H. Lawrence

When initials are used in place of a name, use periods with no spaces between initials.

J.F.K.

The name United States is abbreviated when it precedes the word *Government* or when it precedes the name of a government organization. Use periods after the letters, but no spaces.

U.S. Navy

Initials are often used when they are more familiar to the readers than the full written title. When initials are used in place of the full name of a company, organization, or government agency, use no periods and no spaces between the initials.

NLRB

MIT

NAACP

TVA

But remember the audience. If some of your readers cannot readily decipher the initials, avoid using them, or place the written name in parentheses after the first use of the initials.

IN ORDER TO OR *TO*?

In legal documents, you can use *to* alone. The first two words do not add to the meaning.

> **Counsel shifted her reasoning to ask for a different remedy.**
>
> rather than
>
> Counsel shifted her reasoning in order to ask for a different remedy.

IN QUESTION

This phrase is often used to describe issues under consideration in the present legal analysis or discussion. It is legal jargon. If used frequently, this phrase robs the text of CONCISENESS. Therefore, when possible, avoid this phrase by using *these* or *this*: *these facts*, rather than *the facts in question*; *these parties* rather than *the parties in question*, or *this issue* rather than *the issue in question*.

INSERTED PHRASES

See INTRUSIVE PHRASES.

INSTANT MESSAGING

See ELECTRONIC MESSAGING and SOCIAL MEDIA.

INSTRUCTIONS TO THE JURY

See JURY INSTRUCTIONS.

INSTRUCTIONS, WRITING THEM

As an attorney, you may write instructions in many forms, usually in the context of other tasks. For example, you may request information in communications with clients, recommend specific actions in a written opinion or research memo, or define procedures in legislation. A little extra time spent creating instructions will pay great dividends in response time and accuracy. This includes writing instructions for completing assignments within a law office. The time you take writing careful instructions designed for the user may save you hours redoing the tasks you thought you had delegated. Consider the following suggestions for creating effective instructions and making the process of writing them more efficient.

1. Provide an overview before launching into any detailed steps.

   Readers are more likely to understand specific instructions if they know the larger context of each step. They are therefore less likely to follow instructions incorrectly. In the long run, this will save both the reader and the writer time and energy spent clearing up confusion. This overview can often be created by adding only a single phrase.

   > **To determine the options you have for settling this matter, I will need to review several more documents. These include . . . .**
   >
   > rather than
   >
   > Please send me the following documents at your earliest convenience: . . .

   This addition also often improves the TONE of the communication.

2. Include the benefit to the reader for added motivation.

   > **To reduce the cost of preparing your will, please send me the answers to the attached questionnaire so I can be sure the will fulfills your intentions. Your answers will give me the specific information about your assets and your preferences for how those are to be distributed among your heirs. Using those answers, I can write a detailed draft, which I will send you before we meet.**

   When including this motivation, try to word it so that it underscores the ultimate benefit to the reader, rather than focusing on how it saves you time or effort. For example, the following version, by failing to make this adjustment, would be less effective.

   > As part of the process of preparing a new will for you, I will need to obtain some more specific information about your assets and your preferences for how those are to be distributed among your heirs. To that end, I have attached a questionnaire for you to complete. Although the questionnaire will require a good bit of effort to complete, the

information it provides will reduce the time I need to spend preparing the will.

3. List the steps in the order that will be most convenient for the reader.

Often the order in which instructions occur to you, the writer, will differ from the order most useful to the reader. Take a moment to reflect on this point and adjust your list accordingly. Imagine your reader holding your instructions in hand and move through the process of filling the requests from that POINT OF VIEW.

> **When assembling the information requested, please do the following.**
>
> **(1) Assemble all correspondence related to the disputed payment, including**
>
> - **copies of all mail you received from Chalmer's Repair,**
> - **copies of all mail you sent them,**
> - **copies of all emails you received from Chalmer's,**
> - **copies of all emails you sent them,**
> - **transcripts or substantive notes of all phone messages you received from Chalmer's,**
> - **transcripts or substantive notes of all phone calls you made to Chalmer's, and**
> - **notes about any other contact you may have had with Chalmer's during the time of the dispute, even if it was unrelated to the dispute.**
>
> **(2) In each document, highlight**
>
> - **the date of the document**
> - **the author of the document,**
> - **. . . .**
>
> **(3) Organize these documents chronologically.**
>
> **(4) Deliver them to my office personally or send via . . . .**

rather than

> When assembling the information requested, please highlight the date and author on all documents related to your communication with Chalmer's Repair, including any mail you received or sent, any email correspondence, notes on any phone conversations and their dates, and any other information you have about any communication with

Chalmer's in whatever form, from the time you requested their services until now, even if that communication did not have to do with the repair in question. It might also be helpful to highlight the date of the document and who wrote it . . . .

4. Enumerate or tabulate the list.

When instructions involve lists of more than three items, consider placing the instructions in an enumerated or tabulated list. As the previous examples show, a list is much less confusing than complicated sentences, even though the sentences are more concise. The list has the additional advantage of providing a useful checklist for the reader, and that fact alone may increase the chance that you will get exactly the information you need in response to your first request, which will save you writing subsequent explanations and requests. For related information, see ENUMERATION; LISTS, WHEN TO USE; and LISTS, STRUCTURE OF.

For further ideas, see INFORMATIVE ARTICLES, WRITING TO ATTORNEYS, and WRITING TO CLIENTS.

INSURE OR *ENSURE*?

See *ASSURE, ENSURE,* OR *INSURE*?

INTERJECTIONS

Interjections are just that, interjections of exclamation.

Outstanding!

Because they are emotional and informal, do not use them in legal writing, except as part of a quotation.

IN TERMS OF

Reword to avoid this phrase, because it often invites imprecision.

This court has previously addressed the issue of when adult invitees are responsible for their actions, but not whether minor invitees have equivalent responsibility.

rather than

The issue is resolved in terms of the responsibilities of adult invitees for their actions, but not of minors for theirs.

INTERVIEWING CLIENTS

When you are preparing to interview a prospective client, use an interviewing document to structure the interview. In your practice, you may create a variety of interviewing documents to address different situations. Make these documents comprehensive but not onerous. Because clients can omit significant information, the requests in your document will help you capture what is significant and avoid later calls to ascertain more information.

Your interviewing document may include the following:

- Goals: what the client hopes to achieve.
- Legally significant facts: who, what, where, why, and how the situation has occurred.
- Emotionally significant facts: how the client is reacting and why.
- Key background facts: how the client's situation arose.
- Legal issues: what substantive questions arise as you are interviewing the client.
- Legal context: where the situation fits into the law, possible legal theories.
- Omissions: what the client may have left out.
- Practical limitations: any obstacles that may affect the case.
- Reality check: how resolvable the case seems at first impression, to be adjusted after research.
- Rights and obligations: what both you and the client must provide and communicate as the case continues.
- Budget: what resources the case will require and how affordable it will be for the client.

For related information, see COUNSELING CLIENTS. For ways to request information in writing, see WRITING TO CLIENTS.

INTERNATIONAL LEGAL WRITING

See COMMUNICATIONS, INTERNATIONAL.

INTRODUCTIONS

Great introductions, like great photographs, are well framed and focused. An introduction should set up the reader's expectations for the document's content and organization without repeating the work of other sections.

You are most likely to need an introduction

(1) when your document is long,

(2) when your reader prefers an executive summary,

(3) when the issues or facts are so complex that the reader needs special preparation, and

(4) when you need to engage the reader in the content.

Introductions also are often useful

(5) to answer questions in letters and email and

(6) to communicate the essence of your argument in briefs.

1. Use an introduction when the document is long.

Use an introduction to capture the document's THEME and PURPOSE in memos with multiple issues, such as long reports, deposition summaries, longer bench memos, and motion briefs. For example, consider adding an introduction whenever your reader is likely to feel confused or overwhelmed after reading the first two pages. The introduction focuses the AUDIENCE's attention on the message the document conveys and prepares the reader for what is to come.

2. Use an introduction when your reader needs or prefers an EXECUTIVE SUMMARY.

Some readers, like businesspeople, want a salient summary that presents the content in a quick overview. This gives the essence to a busy reader and also serves as a reference during a phone call or meeting. Be careful not to oversimplify the contents in these introductions. Give the main message, such as whether action needs to be taken, whether the news is good or bad, or whether the negotiations hinge on a particular point. Then explain why or how that message was reached, outlining reasoning in the same organization used in the document.

3. Use an introduction when the materials are complex.

In complex documents, use an introduction to prepare the reader for the document's SCOPE, stating what it will cover and why. Because of the document's complexity, the reader needs more guidance, a framework that helps the reader mentally store the document's information. The introduction can explain what the document is, where it fits in the context of a case or client relationship, how it is useful, and what it contains. This introduction, in sequence and wording, foreshadows the organization of the document. It may also provide background information essential to understanding the document's content. This kind of introduction can act as a helpful guide to the document.

4. Use an introduction when needed to engage the reader in the content.

Sometimes a reader may need an introduction as a reminder of the purpose of a large and complex document, particularly if the reader will be deciding whether to read the rest of the document. The introduction may motivate the reader by communicating the importance or relevance of the content. In this situation, the introduction is more likely to include an example, a quick vignette of a key fact, or a telling statistic. Like the introduction to a law review article or a longer journalistic piece, it provides a hook that pulls the reader into the content of the larger document.

5. Use an introduction to answer questions.

In general correspondence and email, use the first paragraph both to remind the reader of the question and to give the answer. Unless it creates an accusatory tone, beginning with *you* often introduces the issue or purpose of the letter, and the remainder of the paragraph can introduce the letter's contents by giving the theme or answering the question. See WRITING TO CLIENTS and WRITING TO ATTORNEYS.

> **You had asked whether your product, BUG-RID, could be exempted from FDA review. This letter confirms our January 12th conversation, in which I explained to you both the FDA's (Food and Drug Administration's) position regarding your product and our desire to settle this case with a Consent Decree. As we discussed, the FDA maintains its stated position: "BUG-RID" Cat Cleanser, produced by your client Cuddle Laboratories, does not fall within the protection of the Grandfather Clause of the 2025 amendments to the Food Drug and Cosmetic Act, and BUG-RID is therefore not exempt from review as a new animal drug.**

6. Use the introduction to communicate the essence of your argument.

In briefs, use the introduction to tell the court what you are asking it to do and why. Because the opening sentence is the most important of the POSITIONS OF EMPHASIS, use it to be practical and persuasive. If possible, set a theme and frame a point of view that will guide the court through the analysis.

> **This case should be dismissed for lack of ripeness because the Compliance Policy Guides (Guides) serve only to guide Food and Drug Administration (FDA) personnel; they do not declare all compounding by**

pharmacies illegal. The policy is familiar, the practices not new.

The Guides outline circumstances in which compounding by pharmacies may amount to manufacturing and thus may be subject to regulatory action by the FDA under the adulteration, misbranding, and new drug provisions of the Federal Food, Drug, and Cosmetic Act (Act). See CPG 7132.16 at 6. They do not proscribe all compounding. Such guidelines are in keeping with past practices and policies.

The Guides do not interfere with the traditional practice of pharmacy. See CPG 7132.16. The Guides do not affect the compounding of drugs in reasonable quantities upon receipt of a prescription for an individually identified patient from a physician or other licensed practitioner. See CPG 7132.16 at 1. Nor do the Guides require that pharmacies submit a new drug application for all medications they compound, as plaintiff asserts. See id. The issue, as plaintiff describes it, is not grounded in the Guides, is therefore not ripe, and should be dismissed.

7. Do not include introductions when they are unneeded.

Do not use an introduction when it would be redundant. For example, the memo uses the QUESTIONS PRESENTED and BRIEF ANSWERS to introduce the document's structure and content; the brief uses the ISSUE and POINT HEADINGS; the contract uses a preamble; and legislation uses a purpose statement. Similarly, do not use an introduction when you have a formal Summary of the Argument.

For related information, see MEMOS; and OPINIONS, LEGAL, section 2.

INTRUSIVE PHRASES

Intrusive phrases are phrases inserted into a sentence in a way that interrupts the sentence's ordinary flow.

Anorexics, by failing to eat, passively expose themselves to harm.

You may use short intrusive phrases to emphasize a point, because the reader will naturally pause to understand and integrate the point in the intrusion.

> **These facts, which are not common knowledge, illustrate the kind of information expert witnesses can provide.**
>
> **These issues, controversial and crucial, must nevertheless be resolved.**
>
> **Dr. Janssen, the defendant's physician in the emergency room, testified that her injuries were caused by the faulty design of the steering wheel.**

Do not use phrases longer than approximately seven words, however, because phrases that long will cause the reader to lose track of the point the rest of the sentence was making.

> **Without realizing she would be punished by this court for her action, the defendant committed perjury.**
>
> or
>
> **The defendant committed perjury without realizing she would be punished by this court for her actions.**
>
> rather than
>
> The defendant, without realizing she would be punished by this court for her actions, committed perjury.

If the information is essential, you can often move the intrusive phrase to the beginning or the end of a sentence, as in the previous example.

Avoid using intrusive phrases if you do not want the reader to stop. Also avoid overusing intrusive phrases because they can make your style too cumbersome. For the larger context, see SENTENCE STRUCTURE.

INVERTED ORDER

See SENTENCE STRUCTURE, subsection 4.

IRAC

This, like CRAC, is a mnemonic device used by some to address one aspect of legal reasoning. See FORMALISM; ORGANIZATION, LARGE-SCALE; and ORGANIZATION, SMALL-SCALE. For help with the process of organizing, see ORGANIZE, HOW TO. For more ideas about analytical choices, see LEGAL ANALYSIS; REASONING, ANALOGICAL; REASONING, DEDUCTIVE; REASONING, INDUCTIVE; REASONING, MODERN; REASONING, OTHER; REASONING, POSTMODERN; and REASONING, PRESENTING IT.

IRREGARDLESS OR *REGARDLESS*?

Use *regardless*, always.

ISSUES

An Issue is part of a brief to a court. It frames the question to be decided in a legal argument. Its answer determines the outcome of the case. In complicated cases including several issues, the synthesis of those answers determines the outcome. The Issue is the lens of the legal analyst's camera, so focusing it is of utmost importance. For this reason, you may want to include an Issue even when the rules do not require it, because courts read specifically to identify what issues are raised and must be resolved. For information on framing issues for objective documents, see QUESTIONS PRESENTED.

The Issue focuses on the essence of the reasons why your party should prevail. So frame the Issue as early as you can to aid you in your research process. To begin this focusing process, first identify the three parts of each Issue. Fuse these three parts into a single statement, which provides a preliminary Issue. Then, as you develop your document, refine this Issue to reveal how these parts together form the essential question to be resolved, according to your THEORY OF THE CASE. For more on this, see PROMPTS and RESEARCH STRATEGY GUIDE.

1. Identifying the parts of the Issue.

   Any Issue can contain three parts:

   - a reference to the law under which the question is being asked;
   - the legal question, which combines the key terms in the law with the legally relevant facts of this case; and
   - the facts that gave rise to this question and affect its outcome, which are the LEGALLY SIGNIFICANT FACTS.

The following preliminary draft of an Issue illustrates these three component parts.

reference to the law

Under Sec. 102.03(1)(f), Stats. Worker's Compensation,

legal question

was the plaintiff "going to and from employment to perform a service" or "deviating for a private purpose"

legally significant facts

when (1) he was a produce buyer for a market, (2) he went to the public library to research current crop conditions, and (3) he was injured while on his way from the library to the market?

2. Drafting the Issue.

When first drafting the Issue, you may begin by drafting each part separately. This separation in the preliminary stages reveals each significant segment of the legal analysis. Then unify the three parts to assemble your complete sentence.

(a) Make sure the law is coherently framed. You may identify the law by naming the statute, describing the relevant area the statute covers, identifying the area of case law, or summarizing the rule being applied.

(b) Phrase the legal question using terms that are central to your analysis, which often means you will use TERMS OF ART or descriptions of a key concept or fact.

was the plaintiff going to and from employment

was an employee deviating for a private purpose

To aid readability, try to keep your subject and verb close together. This usually means that the legal question forms the subject and verb of the Issue. (For reasons why this is best, see INTRUSIVE PHRASES.)

(c) Group the facts together in the preliminary statement, rather than commingling the law and facts. This separation allows you to sort legal points more easily at the beginning of your process and keep the Issue readable at the end.

(d) As you assemble these three parts into one sentence, place the longest of the three parts at the end of the preliminary Issue, after the subject and verb. Because the facts are often the longest part, these can go at the end of the draft Issue. That leaves one component to be placed in the sentence, the reference to the law. Try writing this as an introductory phrase coming before the subject and verb.

This order of law, question, and facts is not required. It is, however, a good place to start when drafting your Issue, because it is generally readable and clear for the purposes of checking it against your research, theme, and purpose. You can then revise the order later as needed for strategic or other reasons. For help with this, see READABILITY; and LISTS, STRUCTURE OF. In the extremely rare situation where you cannot use this structure, see MULTI-SENTENCE ISSUES.

Under Wis. Stat. § 102.03(1)(c), which allows compensation for workers injured while going to and from employment to perform a service, was a produce buyer "performing a service" when, after researching

current crop conditions at a library, he was injured while traveling to the Market that employs him?

or, for the opposition

Under the Workers Compensation Statute, which excludes compensation to employees injured while engaged in a deviation for a personal purpose, was an employee "deviating for a private purpose" when he stopped at a local bar before going from the library to the warehouse?

3. Refining the Issue.

As you research and develop your theory of the case and your legal document, you will be able to focus your Issue more precisely. For example, your research into the law may zero in on a particular area, such as your state's *Workers Compensation Statute.* Your legal terms may become more explicit and move your core question beyond *is the defendant liable* to *was a produce buyer performing a service.* Your facts may be rephrased to clarify the legally relevant aspect of that fact, *when he stopped for lunch at a local bar before going from the library to the warehouse.* Move back and forth as needed between drafting the Issue and other parts of your writing process. Do not expect the Issue to be completed as one unified step in isolation from the rest of your writing process.

Furthermore, allow for the possibility that your Issue's sentence structure may change. If the phrasing describing the law becomes lengthy, you may move that component to the end of the sentence. If the law becomes brief, it may merge with the legal question. Similarly, a key fact may move into the legal question, becoming the subject of the sentence. This kind of development is natural and desirable. The form of the sentence stating the Issue must reflect the organization of the content, rather than being imposed arbitrarily. Thus the initial three-part structure here offers a beginning point, but not a required format for the final structure of the Issue. For example, the following sample Issues, filed in a case before the U.S. Supreme Court, do not follow standard form yet are still effective.

Petitioner's Issue

Is a large law firm exempt from Title VII of the Civil Rights Act of 1964, and therefore free (1) to discriminate on the basis of sex, race, or religion and (2) to discharge those associates whom they did not admit to partnership based on reasons of sex, race, or religion, merely because the firm is organized as a partnership and has an established "up-or-out" policy?

Respondent's Issues

I. Are law partners organized for advocacy entitled to constitutionally protected freedom of association?

II. Through Title VII of the Civil Rights Act of 1964, did Congress intend to give the Equal Employment Opportunity Commission, a politically appointed advocacy agency engaged in litigation, jurisdiction over invitations to join law firm partnerships?

4. The Issue's role in various documents.

Issues are part of pretrial briefs, trial briefs, appellate briefs, amicus briefs, reply briefs, and other persuasive documents. The Issue is often the first part the reader consults to focus on the law, the facts, and the question their combination raises. Thus courts usually require Issues in briefs to be placed before the Argument section to provide a focus for reading that argument.

In contrast, objective issues, called Questions Presented, focus the reader without persuading.

Under Iowa Code Section 99.99.99, Custody of children, is it in two children's best interests to award their mother custody when she has been their main care provider and has never been known to physically punish them, but when she has a history of alcohol abuse and has been overheard shouting at other adults?

In persuasive writing, the Issue must not only focus but also persuade the reader. This persuasion is usually achieved by framing the law to reveal its favorable aspects, by making subtle changes in the wording of relevant facts, and by using sentence structure techniques to put structural emphasis on favorable and significant aspects of the facts. In sum, creating a persuasive Issue involves making subtle changes to the objective base issue, not wholesale changes in substance.

Under Iowa Code Section 99.99.99, which establishes "best interests of the children" as the basis for custody decisions, is it in two children's best interests to award their mother custody when she has a history of alcohol abuse, has shown no signs of abstention from alcohol, and is given to frequent oral outbursts?

For related information, see ARGUMENT SECTION; BRIEFS; BRIEFS, APPELLATE; BRIEFS, AMICUS; BRIEFS, REPLY; BRIEFS, PRETRIAL; BRIEFS, TRIAL; MEMORANDUM OF POINTS AND AUTHORITIES; QUESTIONS PRESENTED; WORD CHOICE; and WRITING, PERSUASIVE. If you are using artificial intelligence, see ARTIFICIAL INTELLIGENCE AND RESEARCH, ARTIFICIAL INTELLIGENCE AND WRITING, DISCUSSION SECTION, PROMPTS, and RESEARCH STRATEGY GUIDE.

IT

Minimize the use of this pronoun as a sentence's subject because too often its antecedent is unclear. See AMBIGUITY, WAYS TO AVOID, section 2. For related definitions, see ANTECEDENTS and PRONOUNS.

ITALICS

The italic forms of typeface provide a graphic aid for the reader by identifying specific kinds of words in text. To avoid confusion, italics should not be used to add emphasis in the general text of formal legal writing. Instead they should be used only for these specific reasons:

(1) to add emphasis to terms or phrases in quotations;

(2) to highlight some words in some legal documents, and;

(3) to mark words from a foreign language, like *savoir faire*.

(4) Avoid using italics to add emphasis within ordinary text.

In law review footnotes, use italics for case names and article titles. You may also use italics for case names in briefs. For related information, see BOLDFACE TYPE and UNDERLINING.

1. Adding emphasis to terms and phrases in quotations.

Italics add emphasis to important terms in quotations, such as in a rule or holding. When you use italics as part of a quotation, add (*emphasis added*) after the citation following the quotation.

> **As this court itself has stated, "[T]he court must intervene because the issue of mutuality, not to mention that of duress, requires that the court examine *the parol evidence surrounding the signing* of the contract." Holmes v. Cardozo, 945 F. Supp. 3d 641 (D.D.C. 2025) (emphasis added).**

Similarly, use italics to add emphasis to the key phrase in a quotation that is long enough to be indented and single-spaced in the text. Using italics may encourage the legal reader to read the quotation by making the single spacing more palatable. When you use italics, add (*emphasis added*) after the citation on the first line of text following the indented quotation, not within the indented quotation itself. Placing the phrase (*emphasis added*) within a quotation would signal that the phrase was emphasized in the original quotation.

> **The court in this case addressed the issue of mutuality.**
>
> > **Despite the defendant's emotional plea regarding the centrality of upholding contracts to the free working of a democracy, we cannot ignore the plaintiff's complaint. In this case, the court must intervene because *the issue of mutuality*, not to mention that of duress, *requires that the court examine both the contract's wording and the parol evidence* surrounding the signing of that contract.**
>
> **Holmes v. Cardozo, 945 F. Supp. 3d 641 (D.D.C. 2025) (emphasis added).**

2. Highlighting some words in some legal documents.

In some specific legal documents, a word or phrase is placed in italics to indicate the beginning of a key part of the document, such as *resolved* in a bill and *ordered* in a court order. In contracts, italics are often used to indicate defined terms. In some briefs or memos, italics are used in place of underlining for case names and citation signals, such as *id.* or *accord.* When MATHEMATICAL SYMBOLS are used, they are also written in italics: $A+B = C$.

3. Identifying foreign words or phrases.

Italicize words and phrases from other languages if they are not commonly incorporated into English. Often, however, the phrase you use will have been incorporated, such as Latin phrases that are TERMS OF ART.

> **The court appointed a guardian ad litem.**
>
> but
>
> **In France, this right is known as the *droit moral*.**

4. Avoiding italics for the emphasis of speech.

Do not italicize text in an attempt to create the emphasis you would give a word when speaking. This use of italics is acceptable in casual writing, such as in an email to a friend or an informal memo to a coworker, but it is less effective in briefs, articles, or research memos for several reasons. First, the use of italics can confuse a legal reader, whose first reaction is to assume you are highlighting a quotation or indicating one of the other specific uses of italics in legal writing.

Second, legal readers may think you are resorting to the obvious, which can make you seem less in control of the text. To avoid this problem, use positions of emphasis and sentence structure techniques instead of italics. For ways to do this, see EMPHASIS and POSITIONS OF EMPHASIS. For related information, see CITATIONS; and QUOTATIONS, HOW TO PUNCTUATE.

IT IS SAID THAT, IT WOULD SEEM THAT, IT MIGHT BE SAID THAT

If you have reservations about the point you are making, state them. Do not rely on these phrases, because they make you seem uncertain without indicating the sound reasons for your lack of certainty.

IT IS . . . THAT

Often this phrase can be omitted for a stronger, more concise sentence.

The attorney must prepare a thorough and accurate statement of fact.

rather than

It is important that the attorney prepare a thorough and accurate statement of fact.

For related information, see CONCISENESS, subsection 10.

IT OR *THEY*?

For COLLECTIVE NOUNS, which treat a group as one functional entity, use *it*.

As the crowd grew in size, it inched toward the cordoned-off area.

For a group of many individuals, use *they*.

As people crowded into the area, they moved closer to the cordoned-off area.

For related, specific questions, see COURTS, *IT* OR *THEY*? and COLLECTIVE NOUNS.

ITS OR *IT'S*?

It's = it is.

Its = belonging to it.

Legal readers are annoyed if one is confused with the other.

JARGON

Jargon is a pejorative term for technical language that the reader does not understand, such as *price/cost elasticity,* although the writer and others in the writer's field of expertise would understand it. *Legalese* is jargon used by lawyers. Legalese includes both specialized words unfamiliar to nonlegal readers, such as *estopped,* and flowery words that (1) are unfamiliar to the reader, such as *abovementioned* and *heretofore,* and (2) could be avoided by using a more familiar word, such as *this* or *previously.*

Because you as a writer are trying to communicate to the reader, you want to avoid using jargon. Remember that nonlawyers are not the only ones who will resent jargon; judges are just as likely to resent an unfamiliar or unnecessary technical term.

Therefore, if you must use a technical word that is unfamiliar to your reader to make your point, add a definition in text so the reader does not have to look it up elsewhere. See UNOBTRUSIVE DEFINITIONS for ways to do this. For related information, see LEGALESE.

J.D. OR *JD*?

J.D. See ABBREVIATING DATES, NAMES, STATES, AND TITLES, section 1; and JUDGES, HOW TO ADDRESS.

JUDGES, HOW TO ADDRESS

Use *Your Honor* when speaking to a judge. When writing or speaking about a judge, use *the honorable Judge [Name]* for lower court judges and *the honorable Justice [Name]* for higher court justices. Always precede the judge's name with *Judge* or *Justice.* This is what the *J.* preceding a judge's name in an opinion represents.

JUDGMENT

A judgment is a court's final determination of the parties' rights in a legal controversy. In the United States, judgment has only one *e*:

judgment

rather than

judgement

JUDICIAL OPINIONS

See OPINIONS, JUDICIAL; and OPINIONS, READING THEM.

JUDICIAL OR *JUDICIOUS*?

Use *judicial* when you want to refer to the courts; use *judicious* when you mean using sound judgment.

Determining the length of the sentence was properly left to judicial discretion.

but

The court appreciates a more judicious use of objections during a trial.

JUMP CITATIONS

See CITATIONS, PINPOINT.

JURISDICTION

Paying attention to jurisdiction early in a case reaps benefits and avoids costly and embarrassing errors. *Jurisdiction* describes what judicial entity has authority in any given legal matter. When a court has jurisdiction over a given matter, that court has the authority to decide the outcome of a dispute in that matter. Jurisdiction can be limited by geography or the law covering the dispute. For example, Virginia state courts have jurisdiction over legal issues within the geographical boundaries of the state of Virginia and within the legal boundaries of state questions. But the federal district courts in Virginia, the Fourth Circuit Court of Appeals, and the U.S. Supreme Court have jurisdiction over federal questions that arise within the state of Virginia.

When researching a legal problem, ascertain what court has jurisdiction so you know you are evaluating the mandatory law. When you are drafting a COMPLAINT, establish the court's jurisdiction as part of your pleadings. When writing persuasively, use the proper jurisdiction to define the law and support your arguments. For example, you may be able to get a case dismissed because you can argue that the court does not have jurisdiction in the matter. You may be able to limit the scope of a court's authority by arguing that a court has only limited jurisdiction in the matter. Or you may be able to write new law by arguing that a specific entity has jurisdiction over a matter not yet decided. In any case, make sure you are aware of all jurisdictional boundaries for any legal issue you are analyzing. For related information, see MANDATORY AUTHORITY; PERSUASIVE AUTHORITY; and RESEARCH STRATEGY GUIDE, subsection 4.

JURY INSTRUCTIONS

Jury instructions are read aloud by the judge to the jury to explain how the jury should view the evidence and reach a decision. Sometimes the jurisdiction has form instructions that cover each point the judge needs to explain; when no form instruction exists, the judge prepares the needed instruction. In many jurisdictions, attorneys for both parties draft jury instructions and submit them to the court; by doing so, each side is asking the court to use their instructions during the trial. The court chooses which set to use, a choice that can be reviewed on appeal. If your instructions are chosen by the judge to be read, you have gained a great deal, because the law will be explained in a way that is congruent with the case you have prepared.

To write effective jury instructions that the court will accept, you need to understand not only the general legal issues but also the ways in which those issues can be framed to be accurate yet persuasive. To accomplish that, you can use a checklist of specific techniques to make your instructions clearer.

1. General issues when drafting jury instructions.

When drafting jury instructions, you must reconcile conflicting matters in two areas. First, you must strike a workable balance between two readers. Jury instructions explain the law to jurors, yet they must be accepted by the judge. As a result, you need to use some legal terms but also explain them in everyday language.

Second, you must conform patterned jury instructions to the specifics of your case. Most states provide patterned jury instructions that are general statements of the established law. Check your jurisdiction for any specific requirements. Although the model instructions provide a good starting point, they usually need editing to be relevant to the facts involved in your case. For example, you may have to delete statements addressing issues settled before trial or you may have to combine several instructions to address the multiple issues in your case. Check your jurisdiction's requirements; some states do not allow any modification of model jury instructions, but others encourage it.

2. Drafting checklist.

The following checklist can help you balance these factors when writing jury instructions.

(a) Use elements of the standard jury instructions.

For example, you might keep the wording of the standard instruction but break it into several shorter sentences to make it more readable. Similarly, you might retain the legal terminology in the instructions but increase understandability by adding definitions if you think they are needed. For help here, see READABILITY, subsection 1; and UNOBTRUSIVE DEFINITIONS.

(b) When appropriate, include support.

Providing citations or explanations with your submitted instructions can let the judge know there are legitimate reasons for your changes.

(c) List all the legal questions the jury must resolve to decide in your client's favor.

When choosing the instructions you will use, you need to lay out the specific law the jury will need to resolve all the legal questions in your case. This thorough preparation can help you avoid gaps and present a logical overall package.

(d) Revise the instructions for clarity.

In some jurisdictions, the jury may hear the instructions but not receive a written copy. As a result, you must reorder your priorities to meet the needs of the listener: you must worry more about CLARITY and less about conciseness. The following techniques can help you.

(e) Use understandable words.

- Use words that will be familiar to the jury. For example, use *automobile* rather than *motorized vehicle.*

- Use verbs instead of nouns whenever possible.

  You should consider all the evidence as a whole.

  rather than

  You should give consideration to all the evidence as a whole.

- Avoid using several negative words in one sentence.

  Mr. Allen should have come to a complete stop at the crosswalk.

  rather than

  Mr. Allen must not have failed to come to a complete stop at the crosswalk.

- Use transitions or phrases that precisely communicate the logical relationship between two points.

Even if Mr. Allen did stop at the crosswalk, he should have also stopped again at a point where his view was not obstructed.

rather than

Mr. Allen should have also stopped at a point where his view was not obstructed.

For more information, see CONNECTIONS, MAKING THEM; and TRANSITIONS.

(f) Use understandable sentence structure.

- Keep sentences simple by making only one legal point per sentence.

  You may decide that the testimony of one witness is entitled to greater weight than that of another witness, or even of several witnesses. In weighing the evidence, you may consider your own knowledge, observations, and life experiences.

  rather than

  In weighing the evidence, you may consider the testimony of one witness as entitled to greater weight than that of another or several others, your own knowledge, what you have observed, and the experiences you have had in life.

- Use only one word for one idea. For example, use *capable* rather than *capable and able.*

- Place lists at the end of a sentence.

  In weighing the evidence, you may consider your own knowledge, observations, and life experiences.

  rather than

  You may consider your own knowledge, observations, and life experiences in weighing the evidence.

  For more information, see CONDITIONS, STATING THEM.

(g) Personalize the instructions if permissible in your jurisdiction. You can still remain objective by using only objective, factual terms.

If Mr. Ellis had a gun concealed . . . .

rather than

If the defendant had a weapon concealed . . . .

3. Drafting jury instructions when no model exists.

   Sometimes you will need an instruction for which your state has no model. When that happens, simply draft an explanation of the law, making sure you are stating the law accurately. Then revise that draft using the techniques listed in subsection 2.

4. Making jury instructions part of your advocacy.

   To help make your instructions an extension of your advocacy, consider framing the instructions early in the litigation process, when you are drafting your brief, or at least before the start of the trial. Then you can word your arguments so that they lead to the conclusions you want to reach, based on the law laid out in the instructions.

5. Using jury instructions as a research tool.

   If your jurisdiction has published jury instructions, you may find them an effective starting place for your research. They may cite the most recent statutes and cases, which gives you a quick jumping off point for mandatory authority. Update that authority and be sure to add research that gives you the issue's complete context.

JURY, PLURAL OR SINGULAR?

Use a singular verb with *jury* when it is a collective noun, which it usually is.

The jury receives instructions at the end of the trial.

Use a plural verb only when you refer to the jury as a collection of individuals.

The jury appear nervous.

Better yet, avoid this awkward-sounding phrase by using *members of the jury* or another similar phrase.

The members of the jury appear nervous.

or

Each jury member appears nervous.

KEYCITE

See UPDATING THE LAW.

KEY TERMS

Key terms are words describing concepts or facts crucial to an issue. As such, key terms work in tandem with TERMS OF ART to define and discuss legal issues. As terms of art are derived from the law, key terms are derived from LEGAL ANALYSIS, POLICY, BACKGROUND FACTS, EMOTIONAL FACTS, and LEGALLY SIGNIFICANT FACTS. Thus, key terms may be definitions, facts, or descriptions of desired results, among other things.

For example, in a custody dispute where *best interests of the children* is a term of art from the statute, the key terms in the Discussion or Argument might be *custody dispute, father-son relationship,* or *son's wishes.* For related information, see ISSUES or QUESTIONS PRESENTED.

LARGE-SCALE ORGANIZATION

See ORGANIZATION, LARGE-SCALE.

LATIN PHRASES

In general, limit your use of Latin to those phrases that enjoy widespread usage. Some of these phrases are more concise and are easily understood by lawyers, but not by nonlawyers. For example, you may need to use *res ipsa loquitur, habeas corpus, prima facie, stare decisis, res judicata,* and *sui generis.* But in almost all other cases, rewrite using the English equivalent; Latin phrases are jarring to the modern reader, even when that reader is a lawyer.

The defendant pleaded no contest.

rather than

The defendant pleaded *nolo contendere.*

No one would be impressed by this use of Latin; it would risk losing nonlawyer readers and irritating legal ones. For more information, see WRITING TO ATTORNEYS. For specific questions, see *AD HOC, I.E.,* DICTA, *PER, VIZ.,* and *ETC.*

LATTER

See FORMER.

LAW REVIEW ARTICLES

See SCHOLARLY WRITING, SCHOLARLY WRITING PROCESS, and SCHOLARLY WRITING PROCESS CHECKLIST.

LAWYER OR *ATTORNEY*?

See *ATTORNEY* OR *LAWYER*?

LAY OR *LIE*?

Lay means *to place or set down* or *to deposit*, among other things. It is a transitive verb that always takes a direct object.

Today I am laying out my strategy for the trial.

The attorney laid the exhibit carefully on the bench before the bailiff.

She had laid her briefs down on the desk before she left the office.

Lie means to *recline* or to *remain in a specific condition*, among other things. It is an intransitive verb that never takes a direct object.

The site of the crime lies between Fargo and Grand Forks.

When I lay down yesterday, the phone rang.

The gun had lain in the snow for months before it was discovered.

LEAD OR *LED*?

Lead is the present tense of the verb *to lead.*

You lead the efforts to get this verdict overturned, and I can lead the team preparing the appellate brief.

Led is the past tense, not to be confused with the noun referring to the element *lead.*

When he appeared before the Supreme Court, he led with an argument to ignore current law, but he was not successful.

LEGAL ANALYSIS

Literally, *analysis* means understanding something by studying its parts. *Legal analysis* has a slightly different meaning. Functionally, legal analysis means studying the parts of a legal problem and combining them into a coherent explanation of how the law in a specific area addresses or solves that problem. The more component parts there are, the more possibilities exist for permutations and combinations of those parts. In each legal culture, traditions and practices have developed about how to combine those parts into a cogent legal analysis.

In the United States, those parts include constitutions, statutes, cases, and regulations; U.S. legal history; science, technology, and cultural preferences; and traditions borrowed from English common law, among other things. For example, because of the doctrine of *stare decisis,* traditional legal analysis often includes deference to precedent, which requires careful research into how courts have analyzed previous situations. But lawyers and judges also face unanticipated situations and must develop approaches to legal analysis that fit accordingly. U.S. legal analysis thus requires legal writers not only to follow past patterns but also to improvise. Sometimes improvisation can overtake tradition, and the law and precedent may be modified or replaced to suit the current situation.

With so much research to gather, the possibilities for legal analysis are many and varied. Traditional legal analysis thus requires mastery of the following, not necessarily in this order:

(1) selecting relevant legal materials,

(2) dividing those materials into their component parts,

(3) determining which components are relevant to the analysis,

(4) applying relevant components to correlating components in the problem to be solved,

(5) recombining components to reveal the reasoning,

(6) accounting for both strengths and weaknesses, and

(7) demonstrating how the combination leads to a particular conclusion.

1. Selecting relevant legal materials.

Your selection of the materials for your legal analysis depends on your client's situation, the legal issues it raises, and the relevant jurisdiction. To clarify this focus, frame your preliminary legal questions first. Also remember your client's budget and your audience. When you begin researching, you can select materials according to the issues and situation. For example, you may need only the relevant Illinois cases to answer a short question on Illinois tort law directed to a partner. You may need statutes, cases, rules, and regulations for a tax appeal to an IRS agent on behalf of your client. Or you may need cases, previous office memos, and several sample contracts for a transactional document designed for a corporate client. Avoid shopping for sources; instead frame your search carefully. For possible methods, see RESEARCH AS WRITING and RESEARCH STRATEGY GUIDE. Your preliminary sense of legal issues, PURPOSE, and AUDIENCE will also assist you in selecting while you read.

2. Dividing materials into component parts.

You divide a source into components by identifying its legal subparts. You can use the legal doctrine itself to identify the categories, such as when you divide a tort or criminal statute into its elements. You can impose categories that help you sift through the material, such as when you brief a case by facts, procedural history, issues, holdings, and so on, or by characterizing the specific facts in slightly more general terms. You can also use components emerging from your situation, such as when you identify legal questions from your notes about your client's issue, or when you research parts of a contract by identifying your client's goals. Most law students learn some categories for components in the early months of law school. Throughout law school and subsequent work experience, an attorney's knowledge of the law and its corresponding categories increases.

3. Determining which components are relevant to the analysis.

After you have listed the components parts, determine which parts are central to the outcome of the analysis by comparing them to your situation. A statute may list the elements for a cause of action, but, in your situation, the third element is not disputable. So, for example, in a negligence question, when no one disputes that there was a *duty*, no lengthy discussion of duty is necessary. The essential components that define, identify, and establish the duty are enough. If the *breach* of that duty is disputed, then more components from other sources may be necessary to define what a *breach* is, is not, or may be. The history of this doctrine and its current legal context may also be significant. Thus your issue and your facts help you determine what RULES, HOLDINGS, policies, arguments, counterarguments, and equities to pull from other sources.

4. Applying relevant components to correlating components.

When you have determined what the relevant components are, you can select sources with similar components and correlate those components with your situation. Details will be needed about the relevant components, although the detail that is needed from precedent cases or other sources will vary depending on which components of the source you are using. Those details may include the rule, the rationale, the holding, the legally significant facts, or dicta central to understanding the case's significance. When writing your analysis, describe those essential details sufficiently. Whenever the comparison is essential to the analysis, make sure that you include enough material to allow the reader to apply the law to the relevant details of your client's situation.

As you apply the legal components, avoid including unnecessary detail. If the doctrine requires you to analyze three elements, you can determine what needs to be discussed under each element in your situation, rather than including everything under each element. A component's legal significance is what triggers the correlation: do not dwell on whether a *vehicle* was a *private vehicle* unless you have determined that this particular difference is legally significant; do not describe the history of a tax regulation unless that history affects the analytical outcome. As you choose what to include, remember that your application goes beyond the facts; you may be using or comparing equities, policies, outcomes, parties' goals, statutory construction methods, and so on.

5. Recombining components to reveal the reasoning.

As you decide which components are most important, you will begin to determine how to recombine those important components in the presentation of your reasoning. Sometimes you will follow the order used repeatedly by all courts when analyzing these issues because that order will be familiar to your readers. Sometimes, especially in persuasive writing, you may want to put the most favorable components first. If you are presenting a new legal theory, you may recombine components to show the relevance of the theory you are advocating.

Often you will apply the law according to its own structure. If your rule evokes a balancing test, you may apply the rule to the facts by showing one part of the test, then the other part, and finally how they balance against each other. If the doctrine requires analysis of three elements, you may apply each element to your situation before presenting the next. Or if the theory of the case requires a threshold issue to be discussed, you may cover that component first. For greater organizational clarity, order components by their legal relationship, rather than the outcome of the comparison. Thus you will seldom first compare all the similar components and then contrast all the differing ones.

You may impose or invent a structure that best supports your point of view or fits the components together. You may use induction to synthesize the rules, then analogy to show how your situation fits within current case law. You may use the doctrine of legal realism that puts the law in the context of social conditions and include an examination of the purpose and policy behind the law. Or you may base your argument in a larger theoretical context, such as law and economics or due process.

After you have decided on your overall approach to reasoning, you may find it useful to use expository writing devices, such as definition, cause and effect, or enumeration. If you want to show that your client did not violate a restrictive covenant, for example, you can first show the rules on restrictive covenants and then define violations of that covenant by showing what actions the courts have held to be violations in previous cases. Then you can compare or contrast your client's situation with those of the previous cases. For some ideas for presenting reasoning, see ARGUMENT SECTION; ORGANIZE, HOW TO; REASONING, PRESENTING IT; RULES; and SYLLOGISMS.

Also see REASONING, ANALOGICAL; REASONING, DEDUCTIVE; REASONING, INDUCTIVE; REASONING, MODERN; REASONING, OTHER; and REASONING, POSTMODERN.

6. Accounting for both strengths and weaknesses.

Examine both the strengths and weaknesses of your client's case and balance them against each other. The reader should know how the rules, policy, equities, economics, or practicalities can be used to build or challenge your arguments. Then the reader should know how and why these factors tip the balance in one direction. For example, if you are arguing that your client's actions did not violate a restrictive covenant, you must address similar actions by others who violated the covenant and distinguish your client's actions.

When examining the strengths and weaknesses, do not limit your analysis to an explanatory list. Instead, weave these strengths and weaknesses together as they relate to the law and facts themselves. Create an organized analysis of the situation, rather than a mechanical listing. Provide this analysis to give your readers the confidence that you have included all relevant components, examined all arguments thoroughly, and constructed a coherent presentation of your reasoning. For related information, see APPLICATIONS, ARGUMENT SECTION, DISCUSSION SECTION, and RULES.

In briefs, present your strong arguments by structuring the brief around them. Address the other side's arguments within that structure as necessary. Omit arguments that are irrelevant to your theory. In some cases, you may wait to address the other side's arguments in a reply brief. In negotiations, anticipate the various positions each party can take and decide how you will present, address, or avoid those positions in the negotiation process. Remember that there are always more than two approaches to issues and that a strong legal analysis not only accounts for all approaches but also presents them in a way that demonstrates their relation to each other and to the document's theme. See BRIEFS, REPLY; COUNTERARGUMENTS, HOW TO HANDLE; and WRITING, PERSUASIVE.

7. Demonstrating how the combination leads to a particular conclusion.

However you recombine the components, you need to explain to your reader why each step in your reasoning is valid. Do not jump to any conclusions. Instead, explain your reasoning for each step and explain how each component is connected to the others. Leave no assumptions to the reader. For example, if you do not need to develop one element of a doctrine, explain why it is not needed. Rearrange it or give it shorter treatment, but do not eliminate it without explanation. If you are comparing your client's situation to others, use previous holdings to define a doctrine's elements and then show where your client's situation fits into this definition. One comparison usually does not make an analysis.

Often you will need to characterize the components of your client's situation more specifically to reveal your reasoning fully. To do this, describe the component using words that are narrower than those used in the rule of law but broader than the actual specific details. This characterization forms the bridge that spans the gap in your reasoning. The following two examples illustrate diverse ways components can be characterized to reveal different lines of reasoning. Note how the shaded phrases characterize the components differently and suggest the different combinations.

Rule

Commercial drivers are held to a higher standard of care.

Fact

Our client offered to drive his friend to the airport for $20 on two separate occasions.

Characterization

Our client, like a commercial driver, offered to provide a service for payment.

Conclusion

Our client will probably be held to the higher standard.

For a different conclusion,

Characterization

The client, unlike a commercial driver, was not offering services to the public for payment.

Conclusion

The client will probably not be held to the higher standard.

This characterization and combination of components is the essence of your legal analysis. It also is the place where many legal debates have their center. Therefore, be flexible when considering all the reasonable possibilities; do not overlook the best argument because you settled for the superficial one. Also be rigorous in your thinking, so you do not follow a line of reasoning that will not stand under a court's or other legal reader's scrutiny.

If you are using artificial intelligence, see ARTIFICIAL INTELLIGENCE AND RESEARCH, ARTIFICIAL INTELLIGENCE AND WRITING, DISCUSSION SECTION, PROMPTS, and RESEARCH STRATEGY GUIDE.

LEGALESE

Legalese is a pejorative term for technical legal words or phrases, and it implies that the legal words are unneeded. To avoid the problem, avoid legal terms whenever common language can convey the meaning.

> **The testator, William James (James) then signed the will, which was witnessed by Ellen Brady, Katrina Birchler, and Mella White.**
>
> rather than
>
> The said testator, one William James, (hereinafter referred to as James) then duly signed the aforementioned said will, in witness whereof were Ellen Brady, Katrina Birchler, and Mella White.

Similarly, although you will find that you do need to use many technical legal terms, you do not need to overuse them. You will be able to keep your writing style more direct and concise if you do the following.

Replace this phrase	**with this version.**
as per your request	**at your request**
defendant pleaded nolo contendere	**defendant pleaded no contest**
(hereinafter referred to as Plaintiff)	**(Plaintiff)**
i.e.	**that is**
in re	**regarding**
in the event that	**if**
now comes the Plaintiff	**the Plaintiff**
per diem	**daily, per day**
pro forma	**a formality**
provides	**states**
supra	**previous**
the above Client	**the Client**
the aforementioned statement	**this statement**
the client decided *sua sponte*	**the client decided**
the court deemed that	**the court held that**

Replace this phrase	**with this version.**
the duly designated person	**the designated person**
the said Plaintiff	**the Plaintiff**
the signers whereof	**the signers**
viz.	**namely**
whereas the owner has	**because the owner has**

If you must use a technical term and you are not sure the reader will know the meaning, add a definition.

The tortfeasor, who is the person committing the tort, ...

For ways to do this, see UNOBTRUSIVE DEFINITIONS. For a discussion of a related problem, see JARGON.

LEGALLY SIGNIFICANT FACTS

Legally significant facts are facts that, if changed or deleted, would affect the outcome of the case. Although you may have initial ideas about what facts are legally significant, you need to read the law to verify those ideas. As you compare the law to your situation, certain facts will emerge as significant, just as white emerges under a black light.

For example, a case may state that waving a loaded gun in someone's face is an assault, and in your facts your client might have waved a gun that was not loaded. As part of your analysis, you would have to decide whether the fact that it was unloaded was legally significant because that difference might mean your client was not guilty of assault. In another situation, you might read that an accountant cannot exercise an accountant-client privilege, but your client might be both an accountant and a tax attorney. This fact would be legally significant because it might mean that your client could exercise the privilege.

In a memo, legally significant facts can appear in the Statement of Facts, in the Question Presented, in the Brief Answer, and in the application part of the Discussion. Any legally significant facts used in the application should appear in the Statement of Facts first, in detail. No surprises. Similarly, in briefs, legally significant facts should appear in the Statement of the Case, the Issues, the point headings, the application in the Argument, and in abbreviated form in the Conclusion. In an opinion letter, include legally significant facts in the separate section on facts, in the application during the explanation, and in the recommendation.

If you are using artificial intelligence in PREWRITING, be careful about using your client's facts in a prompt because you may be violating client confidentiality and privacy requirements. For help with this, see

ARTIFICIAL INTELLIGENCE AND RESEARCH, ARTIFICIAL INTELLIGENCE AND WRITING, DISCUSSION SECTION, PROMPTS, and RESEARCH STRATEGY GUIDE.

For an explanation of other kinds of facts, see BACKGROUND FACTS and EMOTIONAL FACTS. For related information, see BRIEF ANSWERS, ISSUES, LEGAL ANALYSIS, QUESTIONS PRESENTED, and STATEMENT OF FACTS.

LEGAL OPINIONS

See OPINIONS, LEGAL.

LEGAL WRITING CHECKLIST

See DOCUMENT CHECKLIST or PRINCIPLES OF GOOD LEGAL WRITING.

LEGISLATION

Drafting legislation requires particular skill, for legislation must bear up under long-term and detailed scrutiny, often from readers who want to find loopholes. This drafting also requires patience and persistence, for the writing process necessarily involves many people with various agendas. Although you must consider all these factors, avoid considering them all at once. Trying to plug all the loopholes and accommodate all interests in one first draft results in unclear structure and convoluted, unreadable sentences. The following guidelines can help you create workable legislation without losing all hope of writing clearly.

1. If you are writing at the request of legislators or others, interview those people to determine their purpose. Try to get beyond their suggestions for specific wording to the substance of what they are trying to accomplish. This approach helps minimize misunderstanding and frees you to find the wording that is more likely to accomplish what they want. Keep adequate notes on your thoughts and research at this and all subsequent stages, because you are likely to return to it as you answer questions or make later revisions.

2. Research existing law in the area, noting terms that are common or defined. Also identify the tools that will be used by judges or agencies to interpret the legislation. When a term is ambiguous, research the ways it is interpreted. Assume that at some point your legislation will end up needing judicial interpretation and prepare for that stage.

   This step is particularly important because drafted legislation often includes some controlled ambiguity. Controlled ambiguity involves using a term that the drafter knows will need to be interpreted by a court or agency later. Sometimes this is needed as a compromise to get legislation passed; sometimes it is used because the legislators want to leave that problem to others.

3. When you have a sense of the legal context in which this legislation will operate, draft the original idea you have in mind as clearly as you can, in your own words. Take your time at this point and review each important term in your initial draft, including the following steps.

   (a) Select the most relevant word to describe the thing being regulated. For example, you might have initially used *alternative energy source* or *solar power* when you really wanted to include *all non-carbon-based forms of energy*. Selecting the right noun or phrase early on can head off the need for a patchwork of limiting phrases later in the process. Allow yourself to think outside the box of usual phrases, but think thoroughly and carefully. For related information, see PRECISION.

   (b) Check each term you have used to see if it is defined anywhere within the applicable legislation. If it is and the definition does not fit your meaning, choose another term or, if that is not possible, draft the definition you want to apply.

   (c) Check the verbs you have used to make sure they state the consequences you want to include and propose consequences that are constitutional and legal within the context of other relevant law.

4. Revise your draft for READABILITY and then check to make sure that your revisions have not created any ACCURACY problems. You now have a draft you can submit to others for review.

5. Before sending your draft to several different readers, consider whether you know of any questions they may ask. If so, you may want to include some brief notes explaining why you made the choices you did. Above all, prepare yourself mentally and emotionally to accept criticism, questions, and suggestions about your draft. Avoid expecting your AUDIENCE to be aware of or appreciate all your previous effort. Reconcile yourself to making explanations and answering questions. This is why you kept good notes throughout the earlier stages of the process.

6. After receiving feedback on your draft, begin the long process of adjusting the language to resolve any problems that have emerged, either in the writing or in political concerns. This stage is likely to involve more frequent passes back and forth between you and your various readers.

7. Adjust the language to accommodate any ancillary problems created in the process of revising the legislation.

(a) Keep subjects and verbs close together. Avoid including a definition as the subject of a sentence. Although this approach is common in legislation, it inevitably makes a sentence hard to read. When this happens, state the definition in a separate sentence.

(b) Avoid extra phrases that raise, rather than answer, problems. For related information, see ACCURACY, subsections 1 and 2.

(c) Use PLAIN ENGLISH.

(d) Use clear, familiar words. See LEGALESE.

(e) Replace or define all terms that might lead to ambiguity. For help here, see AMBIGUITY, WAYS TO AVOID; and UNOBTRUSIVE DEFINITIONS.

8. Unify style when the legislation has been drafted by more than one person. For ways to do this, see REVISING CHECKLIST.

9. Check the placement of quotation marks as part of the POLISHING process. When using quotation marks in legislation, put other punctuation marks, such as periods or semicolons, outside the quotation marks unless that punctuation mark is part of the quotation.

   "Dwelling", when used in this section, means . . . .

   This differs from the use of quotation marks in general writing, where commas and periods always are placed inside the quotation marks.

Because there are so many readers to please and so many things to consider in drafting legislation, do your best under the circumstances to create the clearest results. Your understanding of context, language, intentions, and possible interpretations will help you to draft resilient and useful legislation. Effective legislative language is like a well-built lighthouse; its careful construction enables it to withstand the challenges it must face over time.

LENGTHY QUOTATIONS

See EXTENDED QUOTATIONS.

LESS OR *FEWER*?

See *FEWER* OR *LESS*?

LETTERS

Letters are written to a specific person, and as such they create a special form of communication. In letters, your information is not the only thing you communicate to the reader. Just as the clothes you wear to an interview communicate something about your general personality, the way you put together a letter communicates your attitude toward the reader and the content.

This overall impression of an attitude can easily have a greater impact on the reader than the actual content. Fortunately, you can use three basic writing tools to establish the appropriate impression by establishing the appropriate tone: WORD CHOICE, SENTENCE STRUCTURE, and overall structure. For details about how to construct your letters, see BAD NEWS, GIVING IT; BAD NEWS, SOFTENING IT; COMMUNICATIONS, CLOSINGS FOR; COMMUNICATIONS, ELECTRONIC; COMMUNICATIONS, INTERNATIONAL; COMMUNICATIONS, OPENINGS FOR; COMMUNICATIONS, PERSUASIVE; COMMUNICATIONS, TONE OF; EMAIL; PROFESSIONAL LANGUAGE AND PRESENTATION; SOCIAL MEDIA; WRITING TO ATTORNEYS; and WRITING TO CLIENTS.

LIE OR *LAY*?

See *LAY* OR *LIE*?

LIKE OR *AS*?

See *AS* OR *LIKE*?

LIMITS OF PROOFREADING

See PROOFREADING and WORDS SPELLCHECKERS MAY NOT CATCH.

LINKING VERBS

See VERBS, LINKING.

LINK ROT

Link rot, or *site rot,* refers to the phenomenon that occurs when a website, document link, or other electronic location changes over time until it becomes a source of quite different information or no longer exists. When you refer to a website in a document and that site has changed substantially, your reference becomes unhelpful at best, and malpractice at worst. Whenever possible, cite to a recognized archive source. In any event, include the date in your citation so the reader will at least be aware of the potential for change if the website appears irrelevant or no longer supports your statements. For related information, see CITATIONS, ELECTRONIC. Also see ARTIFICIAL INTELLIGENCE AND RESEARCH and ARTIFICIAL INTELLIGENCE AND WRITING.

LISTS, STRUCTURE OF

Lists are as common in legal writing as menus in restaurants. You cannot avoid them; this entry is intended to make it easy for you to manage them effectively and correctly. By reading the first sentence after each number in this entry, you should be able to decide quickly how to structure and punctuate each list. This structure should, in turn, save you time making decisions about how to make your lists more readable.

1. Make sure the items in the list are both logically and grammatically parallel.

   You may decide that the testimony of one witness is entitled to greater weight than that of another witness, or even of several witnesses. In weighing the evidence, you may consider your own knowledge, observations, and life experiences.

   rather than

   In weighing the evidence, you may consider the testimony of one witness as entitled to greater weight than that of another witness or several others, your own knowledge, what you have observed, and the experiences you have had in life.

   In the first example, two ideas (*weighing evidence* and *using personal experience to weigh the evidence*) are divided into two sentences. Additionally, the list of kinds of personal experience in the second sentence is revised to be grammatically parallel. For related information, see PARALLEL STRUCTURE.

2. Avoid having more than one list in a sentence.

   As the previous bad example shows, having more than one list within one sentence substantially decreases the readability of a sentence. For that reason, divide a sentence that includes multiple lists as a wiser alternative.

   The prosecution offered three reasons for setting a high bail: a chance of fleeing, a diagnosis of mental illness, and a danger to the community. That danger included a series of threats, two recent batteries, and one suspected arson.

   rather than

   The prosecution offered three reasons for setting the bail very high, namely, danger to the community, which included a series of threats, two recent batteries, and one suspected arson, a chance of fleeing, and an expert's assessment that he is mentally ill.

3. Use commas to separate items in the list.

    The defendant moved his car into the left lane to pass, lost control on the snow-packed pavement, slid back into the right lane, and collided with the plaintiff's truck.

    When writing a list in legal writing, it is best to put a comma before the *and* or *or* that introduces the final item in the list. Even though some sources omit the comma, including it precludes any confusion about how many units are listed. For example, in the following sentence, the comma before the *and* makes it clear that there are four shares, not three.

    My estate is to be divided equally among my wife, my son, my daughter, and my son-in-law.

    For more information, see COMMA, OXFORD.

4. Do not use semicolons just because the list is set off from the text. Instead keep the same punctuation that you would use if the list were not tabulated.

    "Remanufacturing equipment" includes the following processes:

    (1) disassembly to a predetermined standard established by the manufacturer for each model,
    (2) cleaning,
    (3) refinishing,
    (4) inspecting and testing to new machine test standards,
    (5) installation of all retrofits, and
    (6) operational testing.

    rather than

    "Remanufacturing equipment" includes the following processes:

    (1) disassembly to a predetermined standard established by the manufacturer for each model;
    (2) cleaning;
    (3) refinishing;
    (4) inspecting and testing to new machine test standards;
    (5) installation of all retrofits; and
    (6) operational testing.

    If the sequence of the items is not critical, and your document's format allows, you may use bullets instead of enumeration.

"Remanufactured equipment" includes the following components:

- **motors,**
- **transmissions or gear assemblies,**
- **linkages,**
- **switches and levers,**
- **thermostats,**
- **chassis, and**
- **exterior frames.**

5. Use semicolons only if there is a comma within one of the listed items.

When there are no commas within individual items, there is no need to use semicolons, no matter how long each item in the list is. See subsection 4 for an example of the correct use of commas. The following examples show the correct use of semicolons with commas.

The Company warrants for one year that its compressors (1) are free from defects in material and workmanship; (2) have the capacities and rating set forth in the Company's catalogs, provided that no warranty is made against corrosion, erosion, or deterioration; and (3) meet all relevant federal safety standards.

and

The Company is not liable for any delay in performance because of any of the following:

(1) any act of God, including but not limited to floods, epidemics, fires, storms, or earthquakes;
(2) any acts of others beyond the reasonable control of the Company, including but not limited to strikes or other labor disturbances, riots, wars, acts of civil or military authority, or acts of the Customer; and
(3) any cause beyond its reasonable control, including but not limited to delays in transportation, inability to obtain necessary materials or components, or labor shortages.

6. Whenever possible, put the list at the end of the sentence.

Lists are easier to read at the end of a sentence, after the reader has the main framework of your idea in mind. With that framework clarified, the reader can then attach all the details included in a list.

In justifying the exclusion of expert psychiatric evidence, the court listed three concerns: maintaining the integrity of the bifurcated trial procedure, avoiding allowing the guilty to go free, and preserving the defendant's right against self-incrimination.

rather than

The concerns of maintaining the integrity of the bifurcated trial procedure, avoiding allowing the guilty to go free, and preserving the defendant's right against self-incrimination justify the exclusion of expert psychiatric evidence.

7. Choose the format for your list by considering the complexity of the list.

In general, as items become more complex or the list becomes longer, you need to use more graphic aids to help the reader. Use your common sense and consider the following guidelines.

(a) Run the list in text if each item is one to three words long and there are two to five items in the list.

The plaintiff paid the defendant $2,550 in installments of $510, $700, $850, and $490.

(b) As this sentence illustrates, run the list in text and insert parenthetical numbers before each item if (1) each item in the list is several words long and (2) the list includes three or fewer items. This can be useful in those rare situations when accuracy necessitates including a list within a list.

The defendant agreed to (1) provide the roofing materials needed and (2) construct the new roof or subcontract the job to a bonded roofer.

(c) Introduce the list with a colon and insert parenthetical numbers if the list does not occur in highly formal writing, and if either most items are more than three words long or you have more than five items.

Before drafting this warning letter, I will need the following information: (1) copies of all previous written correspondence you have had with Mr. Jones regarding this matter, (2) any information you may have forgotten during our interview regarding your conversations with Mr. Jones, and (3) copies of the relevant pages of your bookkeeper's records on accounts receivable.

(d) Introduce each item on the list with the same word (1) if you want to remain more formal, (2) if the items on the list are more than three words long, or (3) if the repeated word contains an idea you want to emphasize.

> **A doctor may forgo disclosure to his adult patient if any of the following situations occur: if the patient is unconscious, incompetent, or otherwise incapable of understanding the information; if in the doctor's opinion the information would have a disproportionately adverse reaction on the patient's ability to make a rational decision; or if an emergency exists which allows no time to safely consult with the patient.**

(e) Use a colon and parenthetical numbers and also tabulate the list if (1) most of the items on the list are more than ten words long, (2) the items are phrases but not complete sentences, and (3) there are more than three items in the list.

> **The Company's liability does not include any of the following:**
>
> **(1) any damage occurring in connection with the use of the equipment in any nuclear facility;**
> **(2) any consequential or incidental damages, including but not limited to loss of profit, damage to associated equipment, cost of capital, and cost of substitute products;**
> **(3) any costs beyond the price of the product and service that gives rise to the claim; or**
> **(4) any claims arising from advice or assistance given by the Company without separate compensation for that advice.**

(f) Set off complete sentences in a list, each introduced with a number, when the list format is needed but the sentences in the list are themselves complex. This is likely to happen when each sentence in the list runs for more than ten words and when the list includes more than two sentences. If the format of your document allows, you may set off those sentences as in the following example.

> **During the period of this maintenance agreement, if the Company determines that it cannot maintain the equipment in good working order, then the Company must replace the equipment with another unit in good working order. This requirement is subject to the following provisions.**

> **1. If the Company replaces the equipment within two years of the warranty expiration date, then the replacement unit must be one that is newly manufactured, remanufactured, or reconditioned.**
>
> **2. If the Company replaces the equipment more than two years after the warranty expiration date, then the replacement unit will be one that is refurbished in accordance with the process used to refurbish rental units.**
>
> **3. If the Company cannot replace the equipment with another unit of the same model, then the replacement unit will be substantially similar or will have greater capabilities.**
>
> **4. . . . .**

8. When your format makes the tabulated list look cluttered or too informal, you can keep the listed items in separate sentences in the text, using *first*, *second*, and so on to introduce those sentences. If you use *first*, be sure that there is at least a *second*, or your reader will be lost looking for the rest of the list.

> **The appellate process has two major objectives, both critical to success. First, the appellate process must give litigants a fair opportunity to have legitimate claims resolved by a court of law. Second, the appellate process must provide a framework within which the common law can develop in an orderly manner.**

Separate sentences are more likely to be your best choice for the list's structure when the items in the list introduce points that will be discussed at length. For related information, see LISTS, WHEN TO USE; and PARALLEL STRUCTURE.

LISTS, WHEN TO USE

Use a list whenever you have three or more items that are logically parallel. Also use a list when you have a lot of information that the reader needs to remember, because grouping items into a list makes both reading and remembering easier. For help doing this, see LISTS, STRUCTURE OF. Two problems with lists are handling multiple lists and long lists.

1. Handling multiple lists.

Avoid using too many lists at once. For example, avoid using more than one list in a sentence. If you need to include several lists, try to put each lengthy list in a separate sentence. Also try to separate clearly any small lists of two or three items, so the reader can process each list separately as part of its own sentence.

> **Seller is to comply with all requirements of laws and regulations, whether federal, state, or local. For example, these requirements include but are not limited to compliance with laws and regulations relating to labor, worker's compensation, wages and hours, unemployment compensation or insurance, old age benefits, other social security and welfare laws, and payment of payroll taxes.**
>
> rather than
>
> Seller is to comply with all requirements of federal, state, and local laws and regulations, including, for example, but not limited to, compliance with laws and regulations relating to labor, worker's compensation, wages and hours, unemployment compensation or insurance, old age benefits, any other social security and welfare laws, and all requirements concerning the payment of payroll taxes.

2. Handling long lists.

If you can reduce the number of items listed, do so, because lists are hard to read if they run long, such as more than five items. The reader has difficulty remembering that many items at once. But, because often you cannot shorten the list in legal writing, you may have to try some other techniques. Try grouping the listed items into logical subgroups. For example, four lists of four items each is much easier to read than one list of sixteen items. If subdividing is not possible, use graphic devices to make the list easier to follow. For samples of these see LISTS, STRUCTURE OF.

LITERAL LANGUAGE

Literal language is used almost exclusively in legal writing because it is precise and accurately defines things. For a definition, see LITERAL MEANING. For uses of figurative language, rather than literal, see FIGURATIVE MEANING.

LITERALLY

Literally in a strict sense means *really* or *actually*. *Literally* is often misused to mean *figuratively*. The following sentence uses *literally* correctly.

> **There were literally three hundred people in the courtroom.**

This means that there were actually three hundred people there. The following example uses *literally* incorrectly.

I am literally dying of boredom.

I am dying of boredom is sufficient to communicate the hyperbole; boredom does not literally cause death. For related information, see HYPERBOLE and LITERAL MEANING.

LITERAL MEANING

A word's literal meaning is its actual or exact meaning. Its meaning is not generally debatable. Literal meaning avoids exaggeration, metaphor, or embellishment; it therefore conveys the explicit meaning of the word or words.

Four witnesses gave statements after the accident.

rather than

A handful of witnesses painted a vivid picture of the tragedy.

Legal writers expect literal language in drafting and objective writing. Save FIGURATIVE MEANING for persuasive or scholarly style.

LOGICAL FALLACIES

Logical fallacies are those patterns of thinking labeled in classical western thought as improper methods of reaching conclusions. These patterns reach invalid conclusions. For related information, see LEGAL ANALYSIS; REASONING, PRESENTING IT; and SYLLOGISMS.

LOGICAL LINKS

Logical links are those clues that show the reader how your sentences and paragraphs fit together logically. As such, they are an important part of your small-scale organization, aiding READABILITY. For ways to show the logical links in your argument, see CONNECTIONS, MAKING THEM; PARAGRAPHS; and TRANSITIONS.

LONG QUOTATIONS

See EXTENDED QUOTATIONS.

LUCIDITY

See ACCURACY and READABILITY.

-LY OR NOT?

The suffix *-ly* is used to make adverbs out of adjectives, such as *carefully* from *careful* or *generously* from *generous*. When using *-ly*, make sure that the word is being used as an adverb, that is, it modifies a verb, an adjective, or another adverb.

Taxpayers must file directly with the IRS on these matters, rather than through another service.

The Code is carefully constructed to be readable to users.

If the word is modifying a noun or pronoun, there should be no *-ly*.

The statute's careful construction makes it immediately understandable.

For related information, see ADJECTIVES and ADVERBS.

MAIN SENTENCES

See TOPIC SENTENCES.

MANAGING WRITERS

Good management creates active, engaged, continually improving writers; bad management creates passive, hostile, unresponsive ones. To get writers you want, comment in a way that engenders a thoughtful response from the writer. To do this, you must get to the *why* behind the need for a revision so that the writer sees how the change matters in this context and how to make similar changes in the future. If you only edit the paper, you doom yourself to editing every future paper from that writer. If you instead teach that person to edit, you create an independent writer.

Managing writers effectively requires clear initial directions, precise and timely feedback, attention to writers' needs, and a focus on the long-term goal. If this focus and attention are not communicated, writers may be unable either to meet your needs or to improve over time. Most writers are mystified by unexplained changes or cuts and cannot improve when they see nothing beyond excessive red lining that obliterates their work and does not relate to clearly defined goals.

1. Give written directions.

   These directions are particularly useful at the start of the project. Most writers respond well to clear directions, so give the writer a clear idea of the document's parameters and possible results. Having the instructions in writing allows the writer to refer to those directions throughout the WRITING PROCESS. For help on this, see AUDIENCE; INSTRUCTIONS, GIVING THEM; ISSUES; PRINCIPLES OF GOOD LEGAL WRITING; and PURPOSE.

2. Set realistic deadlines together.

As you set deadlines, include interim deadlines to check issues, organization, and overall structure so neither you nor the writer find yourself panicking as the final deadline nears.

3. Meet for clarification.

After the writer's initial research has clarified the issues, have the writer return them in written form for your review. Make sure that the issue's focus is specific enough yet not too narrow and that it is substantively accurate. Use these written issues to ascertain whether the writer is following directions and remaining within the scope of the project. The time this takes will save both of you more time later. If you have new ideas since you gave directions, use the issues to help the writer incorporate those ideas. As you comment on the issues, and in all your later comments, remember to teach rather than to tell. Explain the how and why behind your changes, so the writer can learn to make these changes in the future. This approach also teaches you over time because you gradually understand why you do what you do, and you will come to realize what is necessary for ACCURACY and READABILITY. You will also realize what are your personal preferences and therefore not required in documents from other writers.

4. Meet to plan the overall document.

After this initial research, meet periodically to discuss approaches to planning the overall document, especially if it is a big one. Together, choose the best approach or organizational scheme. This helps keep the writer invested in the project and helps the writer understand your reasons for suggesting specific structural approaches. To unify the organization and help the writer build the structure, tie your suggestions to the overall purpose and audience.

5. Focus on helping the writer rewrite before revising.

When you receive the first draft, assist the writer by addressing REWRITING concerns rather than REVISING ones. Look at the writing with a wide-angle lens, not a microscope. Evaluate the structure and content against the original parameters and objective. Suggest changes in large-scale organization, paragraphing, and content of headings. Note places where supporting content needs to be added or moved and mark content that can be omitted. Avoid making changes in sentences unless they are needed to avoid ambiguity. For example, avoid editing for tone, wordiness, or other small-scale concerns, which lead you to appropriate the text and alienate the writer. Editing extensively at this stage would be inefficient, in any event, because some of the sentences you edit will disappear in later drafts.

This focused approach is particularly important with weaker writers. When facing a draft that needs extensive changes, both you and the writer can become overwhelmed and exasperated. Focusing on just the content and organization first can limit the time you must spend reviewing and commenting on the document, can provide a more manageable set of changes for the writer to face, and can often help the writer clarify understanding of the content while reorganizing, which may lead the writer to correct some smaller errors along the way.

Help the writer see what rewrites are necessary, rather than doing the rewrites yourself. Give comments that foster continued progress, encourage excellent analysis, and increase the product's usefulness. Thus your comments will focus on substantive changes and their reasons. For specifics, see REWRITING CHECKLIST.

6. Give reasons for your edits.

   Include your reasons for making changes. These can be brief, just *to clarify* or *for conciseness*. Reasons are important; writers respond better if they know why you have changed something.

7. Identify patterns when moving to revision.

   After the writer has completed the rewriting you requested, review the document again, this time with a focus on REVISING. Comment on the clarity of TOPIC SENTENCES and overall READABILITY. In this review, you are likely to focus first on patterns of error, as the next point explains. For help with this stage, see CONNECTIONS, MAKING THEM; and REVISING CHECKLIST.

   Avoid, however, commenting on every single error in the whole document. If you need to edit in detail, edit only one page or paragraph. Then identify the PATTERNS in the writer's work. For example, you may notice unusually long sentences, legalese, or weak topic sentences; identify these and ask the writer to edit the document throughout for similar examples.

8. Set an example of timeliness.

   Return the drafts on time so your writers get a strong sense of the importance of meeting deadlines.

9. Teach the writer to polish the document.

   In later drafts, move from revising to polishing concerns. For guidance here, see POLISHING CHECKLIST. Give unambiguous, consistent comments that help the writer move swiftly to the desired results. Continue to comment on patterns rather than making all the corrections yourself. Also continue to tie comments to the document's purpose and audience, not your personal preferences. Avoid changing words just to change them; if the writer has captured the concept so that any reader would find it unambiguous, leave it. Try to be as precise, organized, and specific as you expect the writer to be. If particular tools, such as grammar or spellcheckers and other artificial intelligence (AI) tools are helpful to you, you may suggest them to the writer. For specific commenting techniques, see EDITING. For further information, see ARTIFICIAL INTELLIGENCE AND WRITING and PROFESSIONAL LANGUAGE AND PRESENTATION.

10. Take a long-term view.

    To create long-term improvement, help your writers determine their respective strengths and weaknesses overall. You might want to discuss those at the start of their tenure with you by having each writer self-evaluate. Then, together, you can design a long-range program that develops their writing and evens out their abilities. As each project closes, or at the end of a group of projects, relate each writer's development to the long-range plan.

    Similarly, determine your strengths and weaknesses as a manager. Periodically, you may want to ask for feedback on your management techniques so that you can increase your effectiveness. Receiving feedback openly and implementing good ideas will give a strong message to your writers that you can help each other.

For related information, see DOCUMENT CHECKLIST, EDITING; GRACE UNDER FIRE; FORMALITY, LEVEL OF; ORAL PRESENTATIONS; PRINCIPLES OF GOOD LEGAL WRITING; and REPLY TO ALL.

MANDATORY AUTHORITY

Mandatory authority is the primary source of law for a specific legal question in a specific jurisdiction. Mandatory authority includes the statutes, constitution, regulations, and cases that have been created in the specific jurisdiction in which your client's legal issue arises. This authority is *mandatory* because it must be followed in that jurisdiction. That jurisdiction is determined by the location of relevant events and parties and the type of issue raised. For example, state law is mandatory authority when this issue is in tort law. If the relevant events and parties were in Illinois, the mandatory authority includes the statutes passed by the Illinois legislature, the Illinois cases construing those statutes, and any regulations promulgated under the statute. It also includes the Illinois state constitution because all statutes must be constitutional.

For federal issues, only federal law is mandatory, and only within the federal jurisdiction within which the question arises. For example, mandatory authority for a federal income tax dispute in California will be the IRS Code, the regulations promulgated under that code, the decisions of the IRS, the case law in the federal district court where the suit is brought in California, the case law in the Ninth Circuit, case law in the U.S. Tax Court, and any decisions made by the U.S. Supreme Court on the matter. Finally, the U.S. Constitution is mandatory because all laws must be constitutional.

Some issues involve both state and federal law. For example, mandatory authority for an environmental issue in New Mexico includes federal law, environmental statutes passed by Congress, regulations under those statutes, federal cases in the New Mexico district court and the Tenth Circuit Court of Appeals, and regulations in that jurisdiction because most environmental issues are considered federal; the law must also be constitutional. There may also be state laws that fill in gaps left by the federal law on the issue. In that situation, New Mexico's environmental statutes, cases, and regulations are also mandatory authority, and they must be constitutional within both the state and federal constitutions.

Lawyers are ethically required to find, analyze, sort, and use all pertinent mandatory authority. Check your local jurisdictions because some have rules that affect what is mandatory and persuasive, particularly among appellate court divisions. For related information, see PERSUASIVE AUTHORITY and RESEARCH STRATEGY GUIDE.

MATHEMATICAL SYMBOLS

In the relatively rare circumstance where you need to write out a mathematical formula in a legal document, place the math process symbol (+, –, x, ±, ÷, etc.) immediately next to the unit in the equation. Italicize the formula.

3–2 = 1

A+B = C

rather than

3 – 2 = 1

A + B = C

However, if the symbol is between words, place a space between the symbol and the word. This is likely to occur only if you are writing about a hybrid in biology or botany, as in *The new tulip, Snow White x Sunlight, produced a bloom with a stable variation in color.*

If your legal writing involves more complicated use of symbols, such as complex mathematical formulas, consult any rules provided by the relevant legal agency or the most recent version of the U.S. Government Printing Office Style Manual.

MATTER OF FACT, AS A

See *AS A MATTER OF FACT.*

MAY

Use *may* to communicate permission from an authority.

Under this statute, the corporation may defer payment of income taxes for one year if three criteria have been met.

You can also use *may* to communicate possibility.

The outcome of the trial may depend on the credibility of the two attorneys.

In contrast, *can* suggests capacity or ability.

The corporation can file its return on either of two dates.

Because it has two possible meanings, watch for potential ambiguities when using *may* in drafting. Sometimes, but not always, the meaning of *may* will be clear in context. When ambiguity is possible, use *might* for possibility and add some phrase like *if the client chooses* for permission.

For related information, see MIGHT and VERBS, AUXILIARY.

MAY OR *CAN*?

See *CAN* OR *MAY*?

MAY OR *MIGHT*?

Used as an auxiliary verb, *might* expresses possibility or permission, with the connotation that the action will not happen.

Although he never has done so before, Defendant might enter a guilty plea.

May, in contrast, expresses possibility or permission with the connotation that the action may indeed occur.

Because it will reduce his sentence, Defendant may enter a guilty plea.

Might thus indicates less probability than *may*. When you want to suggest that something is not probable, use *might*; when probable, use *may*.

MEANING OF WORDS

For topics in this area, see CONNOTATION; FIGURATIVE MEANING; LITERAL MEANING; PRECISION, subsection 2; and WORD CHOICE.

MEMORANDUM OF POINTS AND AUTHORITIES

A Memorandum of Points and Authorities outlines the legal arguments to be made on a narrow legal issue. In some jurisdictions, this terminology is used because the format requires the writer to make each legal point separately and give authority for it. Check your jurisdiction for the appropriate terminology and format. For an example of one kind of format, see BRIEFS. For related information on formulating arguments, see WRITING, PERSUASIVE.

MEMOS

Memos are intraoffice communications that convey information from researchers to decision makers before, during, and after litigation and negotiations. Memos usually (1) inform the reader, who is often the decision maker, how the law measures the strengths and weaknesses of the client's position; (2) predict the court's decision or the negotiation's outcome; and (3) advise the reader on a decision that reader must make.

Because the memo is commonly a vehicle for making in-house decisions, the reader's professional reputation is on the line. In effect, the reader must trust the writer with the reader's reputation because the reader will use the memo to decide about the situation and in turn communicate advice to a client, draft a brief, or begin a negotiation. Thus the memo is not a test of the writer by an informed reader but rather a way for the writer to communicate to the reader the law, analysis, objectives, alternatives, and possible results. The writer's reputation is on the line, too, because it is often through memos that the writer demonstrates research prowess, analytical ability, intellectual flexibility, and creative problem-solving techniques. Therefore, if you use artificial intelligence to generate any part of this document, verify all results and notify your readers. For related information, see ARTIFICIAL INTELLIGENCE AND RESEARCH, ARTIFICIAL INTELLIGENCE AND WRITING, EMAIL, PROMPTS, and WRITING, OBJECTIVE. If relevant to your task, see BENCH MEMOS.

Often your law office or the memo's primary reader may have a preferred organization. If so, use that format. Some readers prefer including an Introduction to remind the reader of the assignment and to summarize the memo's purpose and scope. Others may want an EXECUTIVE SUMMARY. If included, it should be a short paragraph of just a few sentences. Some readers even use the Introduction to replace the Statement of Facts, Questions Presented, and Brief Answers. In this variation, the Introduction will be longer and will include the information that is otherwise included in the three sections below. This longer Introduction also includes a transition to the Discussion.

A common format for a memo follows.

MEMO

The caption contains information that gets the memo filed accurately and makes it useful for future reference. For more information see CAPTIONS.

To:
From:
Date:
Re:

STATEMENT OF FACTS

The Statement of Facts explains the situation that led to this legal problem. In doing this, it summarizes the procedural facts, legally significant facts, and needed background facts. If the memo is written in the context of a dispute, it might explain the facts in dispute and the claims made by each side. The Statement may also note what information must still be obtained. The Statement of Facts may precede or follow the Questions Presented and Brief Answers, so check with your reader to determine the order. For more detail, see STATEMENT OF FACTS. For related information, see BACKGROUND FACTS, EMOTIONAL FACTS, LEGALLY SIGNIFICANT FACTS, and NARRATIVE WRITING.

QUESTIONS PRESENTED

The Question Presented section tells the reader the legal question that, when answered, will determine how this problem is resolved. Because this is the analytical focal point of the document, the Question Presented should distill the legal question into a form that allows the reader to prepare for the analysis that follows. To do so, it should contain some version of the following three elements: the general law governing the situation, the specific legal question being answered, and the legally significant facts on which the situation turns. These three aspects of the legal analysis give the reader the general legal context for the situation, the specific question that arises from this situation, and the specific facts on which the reader should focus. To arrive at this final Question Presented, begin with the preliminary Question Presented as it was formulated in Step 3 of the RESEARCH STRATEGY GUIDE.

Under [general rule of law],

did (or was) [legal question]

when [legally significant facts of this case]?

Under Wyoming law on false imprisonment, did Orth falsely imprison Leitner when she drove him around in her car without letting him out?

Then refine the question as your research develops.

Under Wyoming Stats. 432.17, did Orth falsely imprison Leitner when she forced him into the car, drove him around for seven hours without stopping, and refused his request to be let out of the car?

Check with your reader to see if the Question Presented should be worded generally or focused on the client's situation. Your reader may prefer that the facts be stated in general terms so that the memo is easier to use as a reference in future cases, such as in the following example. Note that this form can take the present tense.

Under Wyoming Stats. 432.17, does the driver of a car falsely imprison a passenger when she forces him into the car, drives him around for seven hours without stopping, and refuses his request to be let out of the car?

Some readers may prefer a question beginning with *whether*, but this is generally a less readable format. For examples and more discussion, see QUESTIONS PRESENTED. Generally, keep this question to one sentence. For the rare occasion when one sentence doesn't work, see MULTI-SENTENCE ISSUES. To see how to format the question, see section 3 in RESEARCH STRATEGY GUIDE and ISSUES. To put the question in analytical perspective, see LEGAL ANALYSIS.

BRIEF ANSWER

The Brief Answer gives the writer's prediction of how a court would answer the question and encapsulates the reasons for this answer.

Yes. Orth falsely imprisoned Leitner because she intended to confine him in the car, because Leitner was actually confined in the car, and because Leitner was aware of his confinement.

The Brief Answer can also foreshadow the organization of the upcoming Discussion by using language that communicates the legal criteria required in this area of law and by listing those criteria in the order in which they will be discussed. Here, the Discussion should have three parts, each discussing an element of false imprisonment: intention, actual confinement, and awareness. The Brief Answer can serve as an executive summary of the document, the place where the reader will find the reasons for the writer's legal conclusions. For examples and more discussion, see BRIEF ANSWERS.

DISCUSSION

To write an effective Discussion, you need to be clear about its purpose and its organization.

The purpose of the Discussion is to explain the legal reasoning that supports the writer's answer, allowing the reader to be assured that the answer is based on reliable reasoning. This section is generally substantially longer than the other parts of the memo, with good reason. Its content is crucial to the usability of the entire document. The reader will be using the memo to advise a client about how to proceed, draft a brief in the midst of a case, or establish an approach to negotiations.

A good Discussion explains, concisely and precisely, how the law supports the answer. When the Discussion is well written, the reader knows that the legal conclusion is valid, barring a substantial misstatement of the law. The reader can understand the logic behind the answer, which helps the reader in turn explain the answer to the client.

A good Discussion also eases the writer's nerves. As a new employee on the lower rungs of the career ladder, you may find it difficult to commit yourself to a specific and useful answer to a legal question. As you lay out your reasoning in the Discussion, however, you are able to justify your recommendations. If your Discussion lays out the full analysis, misses no logical steps, considers viable alternatives, fully explains reasoning, and predicts possible and practical results, then your memo is likely to be useful to the reader. Be sure that the Discussion fulfills the PURPOSE discussed in the initial assignment.

The organization of the Discussion in large part depends on two factors: the structure of the law you are using and the interests of your reader. Often these two factors converge to create the Discussion's organization. Your reader most often is an attorney who understands that the first step in predicting how a court will resolve an issue is determining what legal standards the court will use. Thus the legal reader's first question naturally is *What is the governing law on this?* You can begin by addressing that question.

For example, to organize the Discussion explaining the previous sample Brief Answer, you could look first at Wyoming law on false imprisonment. If that law established a three-factor test, then you could begin the Discussion by presenting those three factors.

> **When determining whether false imprisonment exists, the court considers three factors. . . .**
>
> or
>
> **To establish false imprisonment in Wyoming, the plaintiff needs to establish that (1) the defendant . . . , (2) . . . , and (3) . . . .**

The opening paragraph of this traditional approach could then explain the components of the law, or the RULES, that resolve this issue and how those rules fit together. This overview prepares the reader to follow the organization of the rest of the Discussion.

But this overview alone does not provide the reader with enough information to determine whether that overview is correct or whether the law implies anything specific. The following paragraphs will address those details. As you explain the law, you need to explain what each element or component of the law means and how it is actually used. That may involve enacted law, case law, or both. If a statute or administrative rule establishes a legal rule, begin by explaining that law. When you do this, focus on PRECISION and ACCURACY. Thus you usually do not just cut and paste the statute into your Discussion because that would leave to the reader the task of sorting out the precise, relevant language. Neither do you go to the other extreme, paraphrasing the law so broadly that the TERMS OF ART and accuracy are lost. Find a workable balance by identifying the key phrases you need, often including terms of art, and paraphrasing the background parts of the rule. For help doing this, see QUOTATIONS, WHEN TO USE. Also focus on the law that is relevant to the particular component at hand. This will help you avoid presenting unreadably long passages of law.

In a traditional approach, you also need to place the components in a logical order. Sometimes the components logically require a given sequence. For example, depending on how Wyoming law was structured, you might need to discuss first whether Leitner was actually confined before discussing whether Leitner was aware of the confinement. If no confinement existed, the question of awareness would be moot. If, however, the factors did not logically require a particular sequence, you could choose the sequence that made more sense given your facts. For example, if the actuality of Leitner's confinement were not debatable but Orth's intent and Leitner's awareness were both less clear, you might address the actuality of confinement first, covering it quickly and then moving to the more debatable components. If, however, both the actuality of confinement and Leitner's awareness were not debatable, you might cover intent first, resolving that issue before addressing the two straightforward points.

For each component, the Discussion often begins with the general rules of law and amplifies the meaning of the rules through analogous cases. That rule usually begins with the governing statutes. When including case law in this traditional approach, be mindful of your jurisdiction. Use cases from your jurisdiction when they exist, going to persuasive authority only after you are sure your jurisdiction has not resolved the issue. Also be mindful of using only that portion of the statutory and case law that addresses the component you are discussing. Your reader wants to know how mandatory, relevant law addresses that component, not to read a book report on the whole case. Therefore include only the detail needed from the relevant case to explain the component, whether it is facts, reasoning, policy, or any other aspect. Rather than just reporting details from the precedent case, explain their significance. For more detail, see REASONING, PRESENTING IT; RULES; and SYLLOGISM. For related information and other forms of presentation, see LEGAL ANALYSIS; REASONING, ANALOGICAL; REASONING, DEDUCTIVE; REASONING, INDUCTIVE; REASONING, MODERN; REASONING, OTHER; and REASONING, POSTMODERN.

After you have explained the rule of law in this traditional approach, you need to explain how you believe that law will be applied to your situation. To do this, do not simply compare your facts to those of precedent cases. The factual comparisons may or may not be significant. Instead, just as you explained how the precedent case's components were significant, now you explain how any similarity, difference, or quality in any of the components is significant enough under the law you are applying to affect the analytical outcome. For related information, see APPLICATION.

Finally, you need to decide how to present the law and its application. If each element can be applied independently, then you may apply the law after each element. If, however, the law really must be applied as a unit, you may need to present all the law on an issue before applying it. Thus you will not necessarily have all the law in one place and all the application in another, but rather for each point of the analysis, you might state the law and then apply it. For related information, see LEGAL ANALYSIS and PRINCIPLES OF GOOD LEGAL WRITING. For more help, see ORGANIZATION, LARGE-SCALE; and ORGANIZATION, SMALL-SCALE.

After you have drafted your explanation of the law and its application to the facts, compare the two sections to make sure that they are congruent. If your application of the law included a more thorough discussion of a particular aspect of the facts, make sure that this aspect is indeed what was treated as significant in the explanation of the law. If these two parts are not congruent, review your analysis looking for the mental error that caused the incongruence.

Given all the specificity of reasoning and content needed in this section, this is where you are most likely to demonstrate your analytical prowess. So if you use artificial intelligence (AI) to generate a draft, verify and review the results carefully, using the analytical parameters described here. See REWRITING CHECKLIST. For more, see ARTIFICIAL INTELLIGENCE AND RESEARCH and ARTIFICIAL INTELLIGENCE AND WRITING.

CONCLUSION

This section summarizes the main points made in the Discussion, giving a capsule of the reasoning that led to the Brief Answer. Just as the introductory paragraph provided an overview of the law, the conclusion can provide an overview of the application of that law. The reader is thus reminded of how the previous components do indeed, when taken together, answer the question. And just as the explanation of law and its application should include congruent parts, the Introduction and Conclusion should also be congruent.

Sometimes the Conclusion may also contain recommendations to the reader. It does not, however, include any information or reasoning not covered in the Discussion. For related information, see CONCLUSIONS.

MERELY

Avoid this word, especially in persuasive writing. Most legal matters would not be *mere* or you would not be writing about them. Additionally, this word is often substituted for LEGAL ANALYSIS: rather than proving the proposition, the writer relies on a label. Avoid this shortcut and make your point directly.

Defendant was not at the scene of the crime.

rather than

Plaintiff merely guesses where defendant was at the time of the crime.

METADATA REMOVAL

Remove any hidden and potentially problematic information from an electronic document as part of your POLISHING process. Embedded in electronic documents is metadata, such as deleted words, time stamps, edits, editing dates, and authors' and reviewers' identity and comments.

You may want to remove that metadata before returning the document to another reader inside the office; you certainly want to remove it before sending the document outside the office. Some courts require you to do so. Use the method provided by the program you are using. Here are some general suggestions for removing this metadata.

1. Be aware of the information included in the electronic form you are using.

   For example, an email message contains a significant amount of contextual information when sent. It may include details such as the date and time the message was sent, the application used to send the message, and information about the device or computer which sent the message. Remember that the receiver can view this information. Whenever the document has been reviewed by multiple people, those comments or suggested edits may remain. These may be hidden by *track changes* or a similar function.

2. Remove any undesired hidden information.

   Remove any background information, such as specific author names or dates when the changes were made in the document. Remove any unwanted text from the document. Simply covering the unwanted text with a black background will not make that text disappear.

3. Use removal programs.

   Use trusted professional services or programs to help you ensure that important documents are thoroughly cleansed. Set up a system to keep abreast of the protection needed and of relevant changes in the technology of document transmission. Remain alert to new hazards in the ever-changing world of electronic communication.

4. If needed, send the document in a form that does not allow changes to be made.

   You must also protect your document from subsequent changes unless these are requested. At this stage, know the form you are using and make sure it does not allow inclusion of any information you do not want sent. It is better to check a document twice than to accidentally send information you should not have. Remember that paper transmission may still be an option.

   For related information, see COMMUNICATIONS, ELECTRONIC; PRIVACY, and REPLY TO ALL.

MIGHT

Might is used to suggest the possibility of the action occurring, often if a condition is met.

If we drop this third cause of action, the court might grant a summary judgment on the first two.

It is also sometimes used with suggestions to help create a tone of deference.

When deciding whether to accept this settlement, you might want to consider the legal cost you will incur by proceeding with the lawsuit.

For related information, see VERBS, AUXILIARY.

MIGHT OR *MAY*?

See *MAY* OR *MIGHT*?

MISINFORMATION

Misinformation is false, inaccurate, or misleading information, and it includes getting the facts wrong or leaving them incomplete. It differs from disinformation, which is created and used to deliberately mislead. To avoid misinforming, always make sure you are being scrupulously accurate. When the source of your facts is only one person's statement, make that clear. When stating the facts, use objective language to avoid inserting your opinion into the statement. When writing a STATEMENT OF THE CASE for a court, include all LEGALLY SIGNIFICANT FACTS. While the court may not be obliged to consider all BACKGROUND FACTS and EMOTIONALLY SIGNIFICANT FACTS, include those that make your case coherent, and properly set it in context. When writing a STATEMENT OF FACTS for a memo, include all the facts that may affect the reader's decisions. Above all, never resort to DISINFORMATION. Particularly be aware of any misinformation generated by artificial intelligence. For related information, see ARTIFICIAL INTELLIGENCE AND RESEARCH, ARTIFICIAL INTELLIGENCE AND WRITING, HALLUCINATIONS, and PROMPTS.

MISSPELLINGS, HOW TO AVOID

You cannot avoid misspellings just by running a spellchecking program. Sorry. While spellcheckers have improved and do reduce the number of misspellings that appear in most documents, they usually do not catch homonyms or cousins to your selected word, like *trail courts* or *witch all due respect.* You must pay attention and proofread meticulously. For help with this process, see POLISHING and WORDS SPELLCHECKERS MAY NOT CATCH.

If you want to improve your spelling, you can use several relatively painless measures.

1. Record your problems.

   Write on a sticky note three words you need to use frequently but have trouble spelling, such as *defendant* or *conceive*, and highlight the part that gives you trouble. Then put the note somewhere where you will see it frequently, such as on your bathroom mirror or inside your computer case. Do nothing more for two or three weeks. By that time, you will probably find that you can close your eyes and see the note in your mind, thus seeing how to spell the problem words. As you gain confidence with these three words, substitute new ones on the list.

2. Make a list.

   Make an alphabetized list of words that commonly give you trouble, but keep the list to one page. Then carry this list with you, perhaps in your phone, and look up the problem word any time you need to write it. With this technique, you are not trying to learn to spell the words; you are finding a way around the problem, which is a practical alternative.

MODELS

See FORMS.

MODIFIERS

A modifier adds information about a noun or verb; this modifier can be either a single word or a group of words. Avoid using too many modifiers because they weaken the sentence. Particularly avoid using modifiers that include two words meaning the same thing, such as *first and foremost* or *separate and apart*. Also avoid modifiers that have little substantive meaning, such as *in this manner*, *very*, or *obviously*.

> **These are the specific words of Minnesota lawmakers; consequently, the words must be given special significance.**
>
> rather than
>
> Clearly these are the specific and precise words of Minnesota lawmakers regarding the issue; consequently, the words must be given special significance and appropriate attention.
>
> and
>
> **Higgins does not establish a standard for a "reasonable rate of speed" other than the general use of "reasonable."**

rather than

Obviously, the court in Higgins appears to fail to definitively establish an unambiguous and undebatable determining standard for "reasonable rate of speed."

If you find yourself needing to add several modifiers for accuracy, consider whether you need to change the original noun or verb. Sometimes adding modifiers turns out to be an attempt to fix an error in the original subject-verb combination, like painting over a crack in the wall.

For more general information on modifiers, see ADJECTIVES, ADVERBS, and PREPOSITIONAL PHRASES. For more on problems associated with the use of modifiers, see MODIFIERS, DANGLING; MODIFIERS, MISPLACED; MODIFIERS, SQUINTING; and SUBJECT-VERB COMBINATIONS.

MODIFIERS, DANGLING

A dangling modifier is a modifying phrase that does not modify any word in the sentence. This situation invites ambiguity. Usually these dangling modifiers occur at the beginning of a sentence.

To argue contributory negligence, all elements of negligence must be shown.

It is not clear here who will be doing the arguing. In contrast, see the following revision.

To argue contributory negligence, the defense must show all elements of negligence.

You can avoid this problem by doing the following: when you start a sentence with an introductory phrase beginning with a verb, such as *to argue* or *arguing*, make sure that the subject of that verb is also the subject of the sentence following the introductory phrase. For related information, see AMBIGUITY, WAYS TO AVOID, subsection 1; MODIFIERS, MISPLACED; and MODIFIERS, SQUINTING.

MODIFIERS, MISPLACED

Sometimes a modifying phrase, because of its position, modifies the wrong phrase in a sentence.

The defendant refused to service the car belonging to the man who insulted him with good reason.

Here *with good reason* should modify *refused* rather than *insulted*. To avoid ambiguity, place the modifying phrase right next to the word modified, such as *refused* in this example.

The defendant refused with good reason to service the car belonging to the man who had insulted him.

For other problems associated with modifiers, see MODIFIERS, DANGLING; and MODIFIERS, SQUINTING.

MODIFIERS, SQUINTING

Squinting modifiers create ambiguity because they can modify terms either before or after the modifier. The term *squinting* is a metaphor describing the fact that you cannot tell whether the modifier is looking toward a word that follows, *only suggested* in the following example, or back to a previous word, *only Ms. Sparks.*

Ms. Sparks only suggested filing a suit for adverse possession.

To correct this problem, either move the modifier to an unambiguous location in the sentence or reorganize the sentence.

Only Ms. Sparks suggested filing a suit for adverse possession.

or

Ms. Sparks suggested but did not recommend filing a suit for adverse possession.

For a discussion of related problems, see MODIFIERS, DANGLING; MODIFIERS, MISPLACED; and ONLY.

MOODS

See VERBS, MOODS.

MOST IMPORTANTLY

Avoid it. This phrase both gratuitously points a finger at this part of the document and diminishes the importance of the rest of the document. Instead, use POSITIONS OF EMPHASIS, WORD CHOICE, and TERMS OF ART to show your point's inherent importance. If you must, use *most important.*

MOTIONS

A motion is a request to a court to rule or issue an order in the moving party's favor. Motions may be made orally, as an objection during trial, or may be written, as a motion to dismiss a claim. In most jurisdictions, the written motion must be filed with the court as a separate document. In some jurisdictions, it is combined with a Notice of Motion, which tells the opposition when the court will hear the motion. Check your jurisdiction for specific format and filing requirements. The motion is usually just one or two pages long. It includes a CAPTION, references to the statute or common law supporting the motion, the reason the motion is justified, and the specific request for relief. Motions are read primarily by judges, lawyers, and other legal professionals, so traditions of LEGALESE may persist. Nevertheless, PRECISION and CONCISENESS are important, as is THOROUGHNESS.

Often you will file a brief in support of the motion. This brief is designed to persuade the court to rule in your client's favor. When the opposition responds to the motion, it will usually file a brief in opposition to the motion. For a basic format, see BRIEFS. For related information, see BRIEFS, PRETRIAL; BRIEFS, REPLY; MEMORANDUM OF POINTS AND AUTHORITIES; NOTICE OF MOTION; and WRITING, PERSUASIVE.

MS., *MRS.*, OR *MISS*?

If possible, find out from the person addressed what that person prefers. If you are unsure of the gender reference the person uses, try to ascertain this information. Failing that, see GENDER IN WRITING; SALUTATIONS; and SEXIST LANGUAGE, WAYS TO AVOID.

MULTI-SENTENCE ISSUES

Effective ISSUES need to be as focused as possible, so reading one, carefully worded question is favored by most legal readers. Beware of allowing your desire for thoroughness or your hesitation to edit to overtake that focus. Remove all facts and legal terms that are not essential to that focus or that do not add to your persuasiveness.

> **Under N.M. Stat. 999.20, <u>Right of Way for Military Convoys</u>, is a ten-vehicle, private convoy a "military convoy" when it similarly impedes traffic by carrying supplies and church volunteers to a building site?**
>
> or
>
> **New Mexico courts have consistently included funeral processions under Statute 999.20, Right of Way Military Convoys because both similarly impede traffic. Does a convoy similarly impede traffic, thus qualifying it as a military convoy, when it consists of ten private vehicles carrying supplies and church volunteers to a building site in a neighboring community?**
>
> rather than
>
> New Mexico courts have consistently held that Statute 999.20, the right of way statute for military convoys, applies to funeral

> processions because both create similar challenges for surrounding traffic. Under this reasoning, does the statute also apply to ten private vehicles that were carrying building supplies and church volunteers to a building site in a neighboring community?

As you edit, do not use overly general or generic terms, such as *apply* or *regarding*, which postpone the specific questions.

If you cannot create a readable one-sentence Issue or if your AUDIENCE prefers these longer Issues, here are some guidelines for dividing your Issue into several sentences.

1. Check your court's rules to make sure your court allows multi-sentence issues.
2. Determine whether the description of the law or of the facts is the longest part of your Issue and separate that into one sentence. Write this as the preliminary background for your Issue.
3. Place the SUBJECT-VERB COMBINATION of your Issue and the other portion, either facts or law, in the second sentence. Make sure your core question is as focused as possible.
4. Pay attention to the link between the two sentences; make sure the logic flows smoothly between the sentences (See TRANSITIONS for ways to do this.)
5. Edit the Issue once more for CONCISENESS and READABILITY.

MULTI-TASKING

Be wary of the alleged benefits of multi-tasking. While you may be able to wash dishes while watching television, you are likely to make embarrassing mistakes if you try to organize a brief while participating in an office meeting. Relatively few lawyerly tasks are automatic enough to allow multi-tasking. Give each task the attention it deserves, as if the client paying for your work were sitting in front of you. Change tasks when you find yourself slowing down or losing focus, but avoid shifting back and forth so quickly that the tasks blur together. In the long run, focused time will be more efficient.

When communicating with others, avoid multi-tasking. People notice the lag in response time and know they do not have your full attention. For related information, see DEADLINES, MEETING THEM; NOTES; RESEARCH STRATEGY GUIDE; SOCIAL MEDIA; TEXTING UNDER THE TABLE; and TIME MANAGEMENT.

MUST

Must communicates a requirement.

Whenever a pedestrian is in a school crosswalk, all drivers approaching that crosswalk must stop. . . .

Must is a clearer indication of requirement than *should*, which in general speech can mean either must or ought. *Shall* is sometimes used instead of *must* in legislation, but is not more precise grammatically. For related information, see LEGISLATION; and VERBS, AUXILIARY.

MUST OR *SHOULD*?

Use *must* to indicate requirement, inevitability, or legal obligation. *Must* has a more absolute connotation than *should*. Use *should* to indicate moral or ethical obligation, probable occurrence, or uncertainty about a future event.

You must register before you can vote.

but

You should vote in the coming election.

NAMES

In general, use the same form the entity does, punctuating it as the entity does. For example, when writing a proper noun or name that includes a possessive term, use the same form used by that entity, which may or may not use an apostrophe.

Harpers Ferry

Young Women's Christian Association

Macy's

Johns Hopkins University

When making a name plural, add an *s*.

There are three Marys in the firm.

When the name ends in *s*, add *es*.

The Joneses are tenants in common.

In names that have a particle, such as *den* or *van*, capitalize the particle when it begins the name you are using, but do not capitalize it when it comes between a first name and surname.

Von Braun but **Dr. Wernher von Braun**

If, however, the person has a different individual usage, use that capitalization.

Resist any urge to create any other variation by analogy from other common nouns.

The Zimmermans have both reviewed the will.

The Olympuses are joint tenants.

The Chanticleers all have equal shares in their company.

The wording of the will is ambiguous because the family includes two Jameses.

rather than

The Zimmermen have both reviewed the will.

The Olympi are joint tenants.

The Chanticleer all have equal shares in their company.

The wording of the will is ambiguous because the family includes two James's.

For related information, see GENDER IN WRITING.

NAMES, ABBREVIATIONS OF

See ABBREVIATING DATES, NAMES, STATES, AND TITLES.

NAMES OR GENERIC DESCRIPTION?

There are two schools of thought on whether to use clients' names in legal writing. The first school holds that names are appropriate because they focus the reader on the specific outcome of the case being analyzed. The second school prefers using more general terms because the reader can get a concept of the legal question being analyzed, which in a memo will also be of use in similar, future cases. Consider your AUDIENCE and PURPOSE, and write accordingly.

Under Washington law on false imprisonment, did Orth falsely imprison Leitner when she drove Leitner around in the car for seven hours without letting him out?

or

Under Washington Law on false imprisonment, does the driver of a car falsely imprison a passenger when she drives the passenger around for seven hours without stopping and letting him out of the car?

Whichever format you use, remain consistent throughout any piece of legal writing. If you choose to use names in objective writing, use them in each subsection of the memo or opinion letter. Choose the form of name most appropriate to the setting, such as *Mr. Jones*, *Theodore Jones*, or *Ted*, depending upon your familiarity with the party and the formality of the document you are writing. Similarly, if you choose to use names in persuasive writing, use them in each part of the brief or opinion letter.

Choose the form of name most favorable to your client. For example, use *Mr., Ms., Miss*, or *Mrs. Smith* if you wish to dignify the party by using a formal tone. In briefs, use first names only if needed for clarity or if referring to a juvenile. For example, if two brothers were contesting a will, you might use first and last names, such as *Allen Anderson* and *Andrew Anderson*, to distinguish the two. If one party was an eight-year-old girl, you might use the first name only, such as *Betty*, to underscore the sympathy the court might feel for the child.

Avoid using names of anyone other than the parties, such as the names of opposing counsel. Such references detract from the purpose of your argument. For potential hazards related to using names when using generative artificial intelligence (AI), see ARTIFICIAL INTELLIGENCE AND RESEARCH and ARTIFICIAL INTELLIGENCE AND WRITING. For related information, see PERSONAL REFERENCES; PROFESSIONAL LANGUAGE AND PRESENTATION; TITLES, ABBREVIATIONS OF; and TONE.

NAMES WITH TITLES

See ABBREVIATING DATES, NAMES, STATES, AND TITLES.

NARRATIVE WRITING

In contrast to expository writing, narrative writing tells a story. When well-constructed, it can also support an argument. In legal writing, narratives appear in Statements of Facts, illustrative anecdotes, and longer hypothetical examples. As a form of argumentation or scholarship, narrative writing seeks to convince the reader or listener that the story itself is compelling enough to suggest a certain legal result or mode of thinking. It is not, however, free of the obligation to remain accurate at all times.

Although chronological organization may be used in narration, narrative writing is not equivalent to chronological organization. For example, a Statement of Facts might start with the first event of significance to the issues rather than the first chronological event. Thus in a divorce case, the Statement of Facts might begin as follows.

> **After thirty years of marriage, Edgar Plantagenet has decided he wants to divorce his wife.**
>
> rather than
>
> Edgar and Mary Plantagenet were married on June 6, 1988.

Often an organization other than a strict chronology is more effective for emphasis or clarity in the narration. For example, you might begin with a statement of the problem so that the audience will read the subsequent details in light of the legal question involved.

> **This case arises from an arrest of Defendant after the warrantless search of her house.**

This is particularly useful when you need to minimize the effect of some facts that occur early in the chronology but are not sympathetic to your client. If the narration will be extensive or complex, you may begin with a summary of the situation.

> **Veldmar, Inc. and Thanco Corporation both agreed to a merger plan in July 2025. Since that time, however, a complex series of events has made this merger economically impossible for Veldmar.**

This overview provides a framework so that readers understand why they are reading the subsequent details.

For persuasion, you may begin with a fact that deserves emphasis and that can make sense to the reader even out of the larger context of the other facts. Then move into your chronological narration after that dramatic statement.

> **Alexander Oliaka, who used to run three miles each morning, will never run again. He will spend the rest of his life in a wheelchair as a result of spinal injuries he suffered in an automobile collision. The collision occurred on August 17, 2025.**

This opening allows the reader to focus fully on one dramatic, sympathetic fact. The impression is made, then the rest of the narration adds the other facts needed to fill in the rest of the picture. For ways to emphasize key facts through word choice or sentence structure within a narration, see EMPHASIS. For related information, see EXPOSITORY WRITING; ORGANIZATION, CHRONOLOGICAL; ORGANIZATION, TOPICAL; STATEMENT OF FACTS; STATEMENT OF THE CASE; WRITING, OBJECTIVE; and WRITING, PERSUASIVE.

NEGATIVES

Negative statements are harder to understand than positive ones, so state things positively whenever possible.

> **Come to the meeting at 3:00 p.m. or later.**
>
> rather than
>
> Do not come to the meeting before 3:00 p.m.

The negative statements that are hardest to read are those including *unless, neglect to, not unlike, hardly, scarcely,* and other such words. These negative words can be easily misread and so should be avoided when possible. Multiple negatives are also hard to read, so avoid them.

Come to the meeting only if you are required to do so.

rather than

Do not come to the meeting unless you are told not to neglect to come.

NEITHER

Use *neither* only when listing two items. Like *either*, *neither* is a helpful signal for the reader when it is followed by two listed items; it is much less helpful when it is followed by a list of more than two items, because *neither* leads the reader to expect only two. Therefore, if you are introducing a list of more than two items, try using *none of the following*, which will prepare the reader for a longer list.

Further, make sure that the terms after *neither* and *nor* are logically and grammatically parallel.

Neither the defendant's own testimony nor her written records supports this assertion.

rather than

Neither the testimony offered by the defendant nor the defendant's own written records support this assertion.

For related information, see PARALLEL STRUCTURE.

NEWSLETTERS

Occasionally you may be asked to write an article for an organization's newsletter or for your own firm. This kind of article requires you to adjust your writing style to a new AUDIENCE and new writing situation. For help writing newsletter articles, see INFORMATIVE ARTICLES.

NOBODY

Nobody takes a singular verb.

Nobody has arrived for the hearing yet.

Nobody knows the trouble I've seen.

Nobody sounds slightly informal, so you may prefer *no one* in most legal writing.

NOMINALIZATION

Nominalizations are nouns derived from adjectives, adverbs, and verbs. Those nouns are grammatically correct, but their overuse can make the writing sound bureaucratic and stodgy. They also make a document harder to read because actions are hidden in the noun form. When possible and appropriate, replace a nominalization with the verb, adjective, or adverb form.

Use the following phrases	rather than these.
stated	made the statement that
coin-operated machines	machines operated by means of insertion of a coin
Counsel objected to the expert's testimony.	Counsel made an objection to the expert's testimony.
He was devoted to his father.	He showed great devotion to his father.

But use nominalizations where they make more sense, such as when the noun forms are terms of art.

He is accused of alienation of affection.

rather than

He alienated her affections toward her husband.

NONE, SINGULAR OR PLURAL?

None means *no one of*, and so is singular.

None of the reasons given is valid.

NO ONE

No one takes a singular verb; related personal pronouns and adjectives must also be singular.

No one has testified that the plaintiff was innocent.

and

No one has all of the pretrial discovery ready.

rather than

No one has all of their pretrial discovery ready.

For related information, see *THEY* AS GENDER NEUTRAL and *THEY* OR *HE OR SHE*?

NON OR *NON-*?

Attach the prefix *non* without a hyphen when it is part of the word.

nonentity, nonnegotiable, nonprofit

Use a hyphen when it modifies the original word but is not really part of the word.

non-Russian, non-Euclidean

Use *non* followed by the space when it is used as a Latin term as part of a phrase.

non prosequitur, non pro tunc, non troppo

NONRESTRICTIVE PHRASES

Nonrestrictive phrases describe, but do not limit, the words preceding them. They are surrounded by commas, which act as a kind of parentheses, because even if the nonrestrictive phrases were taken out of the sentence that sentence would still be accurate. Nonrestrictive phrases often begin with *which* or *who.*

The defendant, who thinks he is innocent, looks terrified.

The Fourth Amendment, which protects citizens against unlawful searches and seizures, provides the foundation for this suit.

For related information, see *THAT* OR *WHICH*?

NONVERBAL SYMBOLS

See EMOJIS, MATHEMATICAL SYMBOLS, or GRAPHICS.

NOR

Nor is a conjunction that continues the negative force of *neither, never,* or *not,* and therefore can be used effectively in persuasive writing.

The defendant was never read his rights, nor was he allowed to make a phone call, nor was he allowed to talk with an attorney within the first twenty-four hours of his internment.

and

The respondent objected neither to cross-examination nor to introduction of the evidence at trial.

and

> **The statute has never been construed to have such a result, nor is such a result possible under the Constitution.**

When using *nor*, as with any conjunction, make sure the parts you are coordinating are grammatically and logically parallel. For related information, see *NEITHER* and PARALLEL STRUCTURE.

NOT

Not is a small word that changes the meaning of a whole sentence. Therefore, proofread your text to make sure *not* is placed accurately. Additionally, whenever possible, try to write so the point will not be lost if the reader overlooks the *not*.

NOTES

Develop an effective system of note taking so that PREWRITING is comfortable for you. Your system is personal, of course, but taking effective notes throughout research and prewriting will make writing and rewriting go much faster. In developing your own system, consider the following.

1. Play to your strengths.

   Whatever note-taking system you use, make the most use of that approach. Find note-taking software that works for you and allows you to take detailed notes and see the big picture. Organize your files so notes can be easily located and retrieved. You may wish to make separate files for each source, naming them so that they will be alphabetically organized within a subdirectory. Or you may wish to separate notes by substantive issue, then subdivide according to sources, your own notes, your emerging outline on that issue, and your questions. Sometimes you may have to collect your notes for a while before you can determine how best to file your work, but try to discover your filing system soon, before you become lost in the details.

   Confusion often occurs when material can be organized in several separate ways. If you begin to feel lost in the forest of information, consider changing the way you see the information. Try grouping your materials in different ways, which can reveal alternatives and help you understand what was confusing you. Label each group with a descriptive phrase. Summarizing groups this way can help you distinguish the larger patterns in the materials. Then focusing just on the summaries, see which grouping makes sense. For more help here, see ORGANIZATION FOR THOSE WHO CAN'T OUTLINE; ORGANIZATION, LARGE-SCALE; ORGANIZE, HOW TO; and OUTLINES, section 2.

   If you are stuck or bored, you could try working with physical materials. Use note cards, legal size paper, sticky notes, or even cut-

and-pasted printed text. If you work with printed text, print on only one side of the paper so that information can be physically moved easily.

2. Save the citation.

If an authority looks at all usable, record the entire correct citation right at the beginning. This will save you time when you use that authority later; you can transfer the correct citation directly into your document rather than return to researching the citation.

When using quotations, rules, propositions, reasoning, or holdings from any case, note the exact page number so you can incorporate pinpoint citations in the final draft without returning to the original source. Consider either printing out hard copies of any quotations you plan to use or saving the original excerpt in a separate file. You may then paste the quotation into your document where needed and use the original version to verify the details of punctuation and wording.

3. Organize a system.

Try to develop a system that organizes notes by topic, such as one using headings, colors, or tabs, so the notes can be easily organized according to issue. In a complicated project, keep a record of your research path, listing all the sources checked, even if they are not fruitful, so you do not retrace your steps.

4. Think.

Take command of your analysis by noting why you selected your sources and how you may be able to use them. Write down your reasons as you work so that you can track your analytical development. Mindlessly cutting and pasting excerpts from resources is a form of PROCRASTINATION that will make WRITING much harder. Instead, think while you research, constantly returning to your issues to analyze, amend, and develop them according to the materials you are reading. Thus your note taking will become your draft as you see patterns of analysis emerging to shape the answers to your issues.

5. Be understandable.

Whether you type, dictate, or handwrite your notes, make them sufficiently legible and thorough so that you will not waste time later trying to decipher them.

6. Avoid distracting sidelines.

Focus on the legal issue or theme that you are researching by translating your notes into relevant TERMS OF ART. After you have formulated the Question Presented or theme as described in Step 3 of the RESEARCH STRATEGY GUIDE, begin reading your sources with that issue or theme in mind; record holdings, propositions, rules, and concepts by translating them into the terms of art important to that issue. For example, if you are researching whether your client committed an intentional tort, use *intend* as your main verb when stating the holding.

> **A 5-year-old boy could not intend to injure an elderly woman because 5-year-old children are not capable of forming intent.**
>
> rather than
>
> Child not held responsible for elderly woman's fall.

7. Record your ideas.

   Add your own notes as you continue thinking about the problem. Those notes may include either cross-references or your own thoughts as the research and writing process progresses. As needed, record these ideas in a way that makes it easy to distinguish these thoughts from the original sources. For example, you may allocate a column on the right of your notes for these thoughts, you may highlight them, or you may use a different color for this text.

8. Discover the big picture.

   Your own synthesis of the information and ideas will help you begin to organize and understand the significance of your research and will help you build your case, explain your answer, or suggest your advice. Accordingly, integrate your notes and your own thoughts into whatever you are writing.

   As you move from information gathering to problem solving, you are shifting your focus from developing your own understanding to explaining that understanding to the reader. From the various possible ways to present this explanation, choose the one that best communicates to your reader, even if it is not the pattern most appealing to you personally. For more help on seeing the patterns, see REASONING, ANALOGICAL; REASONING, DEDUCTIVE; REASONING, INDUCTIVE; REASONING, MODERN; REASONING, OTHER; and REASONING, POSTMODERN.

   Above all, remain flexible. Remember not to become wedded to ideas too early, but to remain open to several analytical possibilities as your thinking matures on the topic. As your legal practice matures, you can develop a range of note-taking systems adapted for a variety of projects.

For additional help, see RECORDS, KEEPING THEM and WRITING AND TECHNOLOGY.

NOTICE OF MOTION

A Notice of Motion accompanies a Motion, which is a document submitted to a court to obtain a specific result. The Notice's purpose is to notify the other party of the time and place the Motion will be heard. Often a Brief in Support of the Motion also accompanies the Motion and Notice.

In some jurisdictions, you may incorporate the Notice into the Motion's preamble, as shown in the following example. Combining the two, however, may create an awkwardly long sentence. When deciding which form to use, base your decision on your court's preferences, rather than your own. For related information, see MOTIONS and BRIEFS.

STATE OF WISCONSIN
DANE COUNTY BRANCH IX
CIRCUIT COURT

OLAF PETERSON,	)	
HENRY PETERSON and	)	
DOROTHY PETERSON,	)	
	)	
Plaintiffs,	)	**NOTICE OF MOTION AND**
vs.	)	
	)	**MOTIONS AFTER VERDICT**
BUDGET INSURANCE	)	
COMPANY, et al.,	)	**Case No: 000999**
	)	
Defendants.	)	

TO: Attorney David A. Salverson
Salverson & Johnson, S.C.
Suite 6032
9101 West Wisconsin Avenue
Milwaukee, Wisconsin 53203

PLEASE TAKE NOTICE that on September 29, 2025, at 10:30 a.m., at the Courthouse in the City of Madison, Circuit Court, Branch IX, the Honorable Albert Purdy, presiding, the Defendants, by their attorneys, will move the Court on Motions After Verdict as follows:

1. For judgment notwithstanding the verdict, dismissing the Complaint of the Plaintiffs, for reasons evident in the record and stated in these Motions;

2. In the alternative, to change the answers to Questions No. 1 and 2 from "Yes" to "No," dismissing the Complaint of the Plaintiffs on the ground of insufficiency of the evidence to sustain the answers;

. . . .

8. In the alternative, to set the judgment aside and order judgment in favor of the Defendants, dismissing the Plaintiffs' Complaint on the ground that the Plaintiff's negligence was a superseding cause of his injuries.

Dated August 15, 2025.

POTTERS, PEARSON, PEEPLES & PRINCE

BY: ____________________________

JOSEPH E. POTTERS,

Attorney for Defendants,

Budget Insurance Company

and Far Horizons Foundation, Inc.

P.O. Box 6666

Madison, Wisconsin 53701

NOT . . . BUT

These two words can be partners as conjunctions. In persuasive writing, use the pair to emphasize the contrasts between two points.

> **Not one, but three times Mr. Perry has denied that he made an offer on the property.**

In objective writing, use the pair to make a point about the specific relationship between two points.

> **Borders are significant in immigration patterns not for their literal placement, but for their figurative power to prevent potential immigrants from attempting to cross them.**

In using this pair of conjunctions, remember to use *but* after *not*. Do not confuse *not . . . but* with *not only . . . but also* because *not . . . but* means almost the opposite of *not only . . . but also*.

> **The defendant abused not only the privileges offered him, but also the procedure designed to protect him.**

rather than

The defendant abused not the privileges offered him, but the procedure designed to protect him.

For related information, see *NOT ONLY . . . BUT ALSO.*

NOT ONLY . . . BUT ALSO

These two phrases belong in partnership as conjunctions. In persuasive writing, use the pair to foreshadow and emphasize the logical parallels of two arguments.

Not only has the plaintiff failed to show that the father gave the son implied consent, but the plaintiff has also failed to show that the father provided the car for the son's use.

In objective writing, use the pair to connect legal concepts clearly.

The plaintiff must show not only that the father gave implied consent, but also that the father provided the car to the son.

In using this pair of conjunctions, remember to use *but also* after *not only*. Do not use *not only . . . but*. The mismatched *not only . . . but* is particularly confusing to readers because *not . . . but* means almost the opposite of *not only . . . but also.*

Also make sure that the term following *not only* is structurally and logically parallel to the term following *but also.*

The defendant abused not only the privileges offered him, but also the procedure designed to protect him.

For related information, see *NEITHER . . . NOR, NOT . . . BUT, NOT SO MUCH . . . AS,* and PARALLEL STRUCTURE.

NOT SO MUCH . . . AS

Like *not only . . . but also,* these words work together as conjunctions and should be used together. This conjunction suggests a comparison based on degree, rather than category. Thus it is useful when suggesting one factor outweighs the other.

The key is not so much the existence of central authority as the frequency with which that authority is exercised.

rather than

The key is not so much the existence of central authority but the frequency with which that authority is exercised.

NOUNS

To lawyers, nouns are probably second only to verbs as the most important part of speech. Nouns name clients, theories, causes, damages, results, and rights. Thus legal writers must choose nouns carefully and precisely. To do so, (1) understand the uses of the various noun classifications and (2) avoid the common problems associated with the use of nouns in legal writing.

1. Classifications of nouns and their uses.

(a) Proper nouns name specific persons, places, or things, and are capitalized.

San Francisco, Sandstrom, Bill of Rights

(b) Common nouns do not refer to specific persons, places, or things, and thus are not capitalized.

lawyer, courtroom, trial, verdict

(c) Abstract nouns name concepts or ideas, rather than tangible things.

fairness, right, protection, justice

Abstract nouns are necessary and useful in legal writing, but if misused or overused they make the content less memorable for the reader. Therefore they need to be used with precision.

The jury awarded damages to reimburse the plaintiff for his loss.

rather than

Fairness dictates that plaintiff's rights should be protected.

(d) Concrete nouns, in contrast, name tangible things.

lawyer, courtroom, Doberman, knife

Concrete nouns create a specific picture in the reader's mind and thus provide more information. Therefore, use concrete nouns whenever they add clarity. Because they are more memorable, also use them in persuasive writing to emphasize a point.

Four witnesses testified that Mr. Noble was mentally incompetent, and he should therefore be spared the death penalty.

rather than

Fairness dictates that my client's mental state should absolve him of guilt.

(e) Vague nouns include so many possible items that the reader gets no clear picture of any one item. A noun can be concrete, but still vague.

money, building, person

For more examples, see EMPHASIS, subsection 2.

In legal writing, vague nouns can cause ambiguity when they force the reader to break them down and supply a surmised meaning to the various items to which the vague noun might refer. Be specific as to which item you are referring.

Plaintiff should have filed the motion by the deadline.

rather than

Plaintiff should have followed the procedure.

(f) Collective nouns name groups that are to be treated logically and grammatically as a single unit.

The Supreme Court holds . . . .

With collective nouns, use the singular form of the verb, such as *holds*, even though the noun refers to a group, such as a court made up of several justices. For more information, see COLLECTIVE NOUNS.

(g) GERUNDS are nouns formed from the *-ing* form of a verb. As such, they communicate the idea of taking an action, which is somewhat more abstract than a statement that someone is completing the action. Gerunds can be useful to focus the reader on an action as an idea rather than a particular event.

Speaking of violence is not the same as acting violently.

Additionally, using gerunds is often helpful because it makes a sentence more concise.

Imagining is not intending.

rather than

The act of imagination alone does not constitute intent.

(h) Many nouns refer to a broad, general category of concrete items. These words are not necessarily termed abstract nouns, but often have the same effect.

plants, animal, person, vehicle

Use these general nouns with restraint because they can make your meaning vague and less memorable. Often your better choice will be a more specific term.

shrubbery, squirrel, toddler, motorcycle

2. Common problems with nouns in legal writing.

Three common problems occur with nouns in legal writing: they are used imprecisely, inconsistently, and in clusters. First, choose the noun that most precisely states your meaning. As someone once said, "The difference between the right word and the almost right word is the difference between *internment* and *interment*." Second, do not change a noun solely for variety. The legal reader will assume a different noun represents a different idea. For more explanation and examples, see WORD CHOICE and PRECISION. Third, avoid stacking too many nouns against each other. This makes a sentence much harder to read. For more about that problem, see NOUN STRING.

NOUN STRING

This phrase describes three or more nouns placed together without any connecting words between them to signal their interrelationship. Noun strings are concise but often hard to understand.

Operations Reduction Contingency Plan Agreement

The difficulty occurs because the reader has to fill in the connecting words to understand the meaning. When the noun string is unfamiliar to even one of your readers, fill in at least some of the prepositions and other helpful structural signals.

Agreement to a Contingency Plan for a Reduction in Operations

or

They agreed to use a contingency plan to reduce operations.

Noun strings are often a form of jargon, and as such may be familiar to some readers. They are also common in bureaucratic language. Use these noun strings only when they will be easily understood by all your readers, as when all the words in the string are familiar, as in

unemployment benefits claim

or when the string is a term of art.

work product privilege

Confrontation Clause issue

Do not use noun strings out of habit, but rather when they are the most readable way to present the idea. For related information, see JARGON.

NUMBERS

See NUMERALS.

NUMERALS

The common question here is whether a number should be spelled out in words or written as a numeral.

1. Spell out a number that begins a sentence.

   One hundred twenty-five pieces of evidence were admitted at trial.

   The one exception to this rule is years.

   1984 was not what we expected.

2. Spell out zero to ninety-nine in text and footnotes in law review articles. This is the current *Bluebook* rule.

   The court requested that twenty-seven exhibits be referred to the jury.

   Different sources list different upper limits on spelling out numbers. Check your court rules or citation manual. According to the most recent *U.S. Government Printing Office Style Manual,* units of measurement are an exception. See subsection 9 below.

3. Spell out *million, billion,* and so on, rather than using zeroes, because this form is easier to read.

   127 million

   Also spell out numbers in indefinite expressions.

   The plaintiff is in her seventies.

   Similarly, spell out round numbers larger than ninety-nine, if you choose, as long as you are consistent throughout the text.

4. Add parenthetical numbers only in drafting.

   Spell out numbers and then insert numerals in parentheses only in legal drafting, and then only when the duplication is needed to avoid the possibility of a critical inaccuracy caused by a mistyped numeral.

   In consideration for these agreements, Howard Industries agrees to pay Liveson Construction the sum of fourteen thousand dollars ($14,000).

5. Use numerals for numbers larger than ninety-nine.

   The prosecution introduced 173 separate documents to support this claim.

6. Use numerals if, in one series, you have numbers both over ninety-nine and ninety-nine or under.

   The numbers of computers taken in these four robberies were 7, 25, 102, and 130.

7. Use numerals for a section of a document when that section itself is identified by a numeral.

   This exception is covered in contract subsection 5.

8. Use numerals for fractions and decimals.

   The total purchase price was $10.4 million.

   The production cost is now 2½ times greater than it was when the contract was signed.

9. Use numerals for units of measurement, such as for age, weight, money, and time.

   6 years old, 95 pounds, 2700 yen, 4:30 p.m., 1.3 liters

Be sure to proofread all numerals to make sure they are accurate and equivalent to the spelled-out version, if any.

OBJECT

See SENTENCE, PARTS OF, subsections 4 and 5.

OBJECTIVE WRITING

See WRITING, OBJECTIVE.

OBJECTIVITY

Objectivity is essential to all forms of legal writing at some stage. You must remain particularly objective when assessing your client's situation so that you can correctly anticipate all possible arguments on all sides of the issues. Equally important, you must remain objective in any oral presentations designed to inform the court or another attorney of the law, such as in pretrial or intraoffice conferences.

Objectivity is paramount in preparing for negotiations and in pretrial work because, to advise your client, you must accurately assess the relative strength of the arguments and be detached about the outcome. This objectivity paves the way for accurate use of law, facts, practical circumstances, economics, social concerns, and POLICY to persuade the court in briefs and oral arguments or to help your client to negotiate satisfactory results. Therefore, in intraoffice documents, such as memos, present information objectively. For related information, see POINT OF VIEW, OBJECTIVE TO PERSUASIVE; and WRITING, OBJECTIVE.

OBJECT OF A PREPOSITION

See PREPOSITIONS and SENTENCE, PARTS OF, subsection 6.

OBLIVIOUS OF OR *OBLIVIOUS TO*?

If you mean *unaware,* use *oblivious of.* If you mean *forgetful,* use *oblivious to.* Of the two, *oblivious of* is the narrower meaning. To avoid confusion, consider using another word, such as *unaware* or *unmindful.*

The defendant was unaware of the significance of this waiver.

rather than

The defendant was oblivious of the significance of this waiver.

The defendant was unmindful of her duty to see that all the children's seat belts were properly fastened.

rather than

The defendant was oblivious to her duty to see that all the children's seat belts were properly fastened.

OBVIOUSLY

Use *obviously* only when the point is indeed obvious. Use *obviously* sparingly in legal writing, because you seldom state an obvious point, and even when you do state it, you seldom want to underscore its obviousness. If the point is not obvious, labeling it as such insults your reader and impairs your credibility. For related concerns, see LITERAL MEANING.

OF COURSE

This phrase is best avoided in legal writing; *of course* implies that the point is obvious, but the legal reader may not see your point as being this clear cut. Do not use *of course* to gloss over assumptions that need to be supported. For related problems, see *IT IS SAID THAT*, MODIFIERS, and *OBVIOUSLY*.

OK, *O.K.*, OR *OKAY*?

None of the above is common in formal writing, so avoid using them. If you need to use one of the three, *OK* is the most widely used form.

OMITTING WORDS FROM QUOTATIONS

For when and how to omit words from QUOTATIONS, see QUOTATIONS, HOW TO PUNCTUATE, subsections 7, 8, and 9. Also see EDITING QUOTATIONS.

ONE

One as a pronoun indicates a single person, a single unit, or a single thing. It takes a singular verb.

> **One of the defendants is moving to have the case dismissed.**
>
> **One of the problems with teaching legal analysis is that not all professors agree on the best way to teach it.**

Avoid using *one* in an attempt to sound formal or to avoid personal references, because it almost always sounds stilted, and it is often unclear whether or not the writer is addressing the reader personally.

> **Testators usually name several alternate personal representatives in their wills.**
>
> rather than
>
> One usually names several alternate personal representatives in one's wills.

ONE-SENTENCE PARAGRAPHS

Use one-sentence paragraphs for EMPHASIS or transition, but only occasionally. If you have several in a short brief or memo, you are probably overusing them. The following one-sentence paragraph, coming after a detailed explanation of a Congressional policy statement, effectively emphasizes a point and leads into the next discussion.

> **While this Congressional policy does not directly affect commerce regulations, it may be so strong that future policymakers will think twice about restricting scientific transnational communications.**

For problems one-sentence paragraphs may signal, see PARAGRAPH LENGTH, subsection 2. For related information, see ORGANIZATION, SMALL-SCALE; and PARAGRAPHS.

ON LINE, *ONLINE*, OR *ON-LINE*?

Use *online*. The steady use of these two words together is so common now that the hyphen has disappeared. For related information, see HYPHENS.

ONLY, WHERE TO PLACE

Each time you use *only*, check its placement; in general, place it immediately before the word it modifies. A misplaced *only* can create ambiguity, and often in legal writing that ambiguity is serious. For example, the following sentence is not clear.

> Shares are sold to the public only by the parent corporation.

Are shares sold *only to the public*, or *only by the parent corporation*? Although the reader might be able to reason out the meaning in context, the sentence should be written so the meaning is unmistakable. Often ambiguity occurs because *only* comes too early in the sentence.

> You should only introduce this evidence if the defendant chooses to testify.

The writer did not mean to say that the reader should *only introduce* this evidence and do nothing else with it. To avoid this ambiguity, try placing *only* as late in the sentence as possible without creating an inaccuracy.

> **You should introduce this evidence only if the defendant chooses to testify.**

For related information, see also ACCURACY, subsection 2; AMBIGUITY, WAYS TO AVOID, subsection 1; and MODIFIERS, SQUINTING.

ON THE CONDITION THAT OR *WITH THE CONDITION THAT*?

The most likely option here is a shorter, clearer phrase that avoids the question. Try replacing the phrase with the most accurate choice from the list in CONDITIONS, STATING THEM. For related information, see *IF* OR *WHEN*?

OPENINGS FOR LETTERS

In general, open with a sentence or two explaining the point of your letter or why you are writing.

> **In response to your inquiry, I am enclosing . . . .**
>
> or
>
> **Last Monday, we met to discuss . . . . This letter formalizes our agreement that I would act as your attorney concerning . . . .**

This is usually preferable to starting with a sentence explaining who you are; that opening tempts the reader to say, *Who cares?* You can, however, explain who you are in the second or third sentence, after the reader has some reason to care, or you can add an explanatory reference as part of another sentence.

As your attorney, I want to notify you of some recent changes in the tax law that may require a change in your record-keeping practices.

In some cases, you may want to be slightly less direct, including a brief explanatory paragraph before your point. See BAD NEWS, GIVING IT and LEGAL OPINIONS for ways to handle these situations. For related information and details on ways to structure other letters and emails, see COMMUNICATIONS, CLOSINGS; COMMUNICATIONS, ELECTRONIC; COMMUNICATIONS, OPENINGS; COMMUNICATIONS, PERSUASIVE; EMAIL; WRITING TO ATTORNEYS; and WRITING TO CLIENTS.

For opening routine letters, have stock phrases so that you avoid reinventing the wheel. But take care in selecting these stock phrases, because these opening phrases give the reader an impression of your personality, just as your demeanor creates an impression when you meet someone for the first time. In general, avoid stuffy openings, like *Pursuant to your request*, and long-winded ones, like *In regard to the matter of your request* . . . . When you receive a letter that appeals to you, notice the opening. If you like it, modify it as needed and add it to your own collection of stock openings. For related information, see SALUTATIONS.

OPINION LETTERS AND EMAIL

See OPINIONS, LEGAL. For more on how to compose these, see COMMUNICATIONS, CLOSINGS; COMMUNICATIONS, ELECTRONIC; COMMUNICATIONS, PERSUASIVE; EMAIL; WRITING TO ATTORNEYS; and WRITING TO CLIENTS.

OPINION OR ADVICE?

When writing an opinion letter or conferring with a client, an attorney may give a client a legal opinion on a matter as long as that opinion is based on the law and the reasonable boundaries of the law. An attorney may also advise a client to pursue a certain legal course. Be careful, however, of personal, as opposed to legal, advice that could cross the line from professional opinion to coercion. Such advice could violate the *Model Code of Professional Responsibility*, a question beyond the scope of this book. For related information, see OPINIONS, LEGAL.

OPINIONS, JUDICIAL

A judicial opinion is written to several different primary audiences and many potential secondary ones. As a result, its organization differs from the more straight-to-the-point form of many legal documents. When writing a judicial opinion, consider the steps listed below to increase your effectiveness and efficiency.

1. AUDIENCE.

Opinions are written in part to explain the court's decision to the people who brought their problem to the court for resolution. Usually, the judge wants both parties to see the fairness of its resolution. For the winning party, this task is not so difficult; the winner, after all, believed the law favored that side's position. The winner is not likely to scrutinize the opinion for every error. The losing party, however, will scrutinize that opinion and will not be inclined to accept the court's reasoned opinion, so the reasoning must be presented carefully and thoroughly.

Opinions must also be written to withstand judicial review if the case is appealed. As a result, the writer must include all the information needed to meet the relevant criteria of that potential review. The writer must also remember the relevant standard of review and select all content needed to meet that standard because no judge wants to have an opinion reversed.

Finally, judicial opinions may be read by the press, the public, legal scholars, and future law students. In high-profile situations, these concerns may mean that the writer needs to expend extra effort to choose content and words carefully.

2. Priorities for content and TONE.

For courts of first impression, one priority is always convincing the losing party of the fairness of the court's decision. This usually means that the writer needs to include enough information about the losing party's argument to show that its positions were considered and explain why those positions did not prevail.

To stand up under the scrutiny of an appellate review, the court of first impression must include findings of fact on all elements of a charge, claim, or any other required points and must state those findings clearly enough to avoid questions of ambiguity. The court must also include all relevant law and explain how and why the specific application of that law results in this conclusion. Relevant context is also necessary, which might include the development of that law, current issues, reasons for changes through this opinion, technology and science, and so on.

Generally, the tone should be neutral, avoiding any hint of impatience toward or contempt for the losing party, although opinions may not be quite so kind to the losing party's lawyers. Although judges may vent their personal frustrations in opinions, doing so may create complications with a judicial review, with local attorneys, and with reelection when that is an issue.

3. Overall organization.

If you are a clerk creating a preliminary draft for a judge, use the organization preferred by that judge. If you are writing your own opinion, you may want to start with the most common organization used by other judges and then modify it as you develop your reasoning. One common organization is the following:

- the procedural history, which reminds the reader where the case is in the judicial process;
- a summary of the relevant facts and facts to be discussed, which often means including facts that the losing party thought were important but that will not ultimately factor into the outcome;
- a discussion of the issues that the parties raised in the case and whether they are determinative;
- other issues that the court sees as relevant;
- the legal standard for each issue;
- the reasoning that moves the analysis from the standard to the conclusion; and
- any other information relevant to the court's reasoning and the conclusion.

If you vary this organization, make sure you retain all these necessary components. For related information on structuring arguments, see ORGANIZATION, LARGE-SCALE; REASONING, DEDUCTIVE; REASONING, INDUCTIVE; REASONING, MODERN; REASONING, OTHER; REASONING, POSTMODERN; REASONING, PRESENTING IT; SYLLOGISMS; and WRITING, PERSUASIVE.

4. Appellate opinions.

If you are drafting an appellate opinion, include the STANDARD OF REVIEW appropriate to this issue. Appellate courts generally have narrower, specific requirements for reviewing cases, and these govern the opinion's content, reasoning, and outcome. For related information, see BENCH MEMOS.

OPINIONS, LEGAL

When drafting opinion letters and emails, pay attention to both the general context and the overall organization.

1. General considerations.

Opinion emails or letters serve the client in two ways: (1) they inform the reader of the writer's legal analysis of the situation and any updating information and (2) they predict a possible outcome or recommend a certain path. Whether addressing complex or simple questions, these documents must also clarify the necessary legal limitations of the opinion and fulfill the lawyer's professional responsibility to the client. Whatever the medium, the message is important. Do not mistake opinion emails for chatty news; they are legal documents that may be forwarded to others and that can have legal consequences.

Treat these legal communications carefully by considering your point of view, context, tone, and readers. If you are not advising the client to take a particular action, focus on informing the client of the situation and the client's options. If you are advising the client that a particular option would be best, such as settling out of court, then not only inform the client of all of the options but also explain why one option is preferable. For more information on writing choices, see STYLE and WRITING, OBJECTIVE; for more information on handling bad news, see BAD NEWS, GIVING IT; and BAD NEWS, SOFTENING IT.

Choose the tone appropriate for your audience. If you know the reader well and it seems appropriate, use a friendly-but-businesslike tone; if you do not know the reader well, be more formal but not stuffy. Choose a style that considers the reader's needs and experience in law. For examples and techniques, see COMMUNICATIONS, TONE OF and FORMALITY, LEVEL OF.

Finally, be sure to address the needs of your audience. Because your reader has asked a specific legal question, do make sure you answer the question in language your reader can understand. Do not write an abstract essay or a law review article on the general topic. Instead answer the question as specifically as you can. Write in clear and understandable language, defining legal terms as needed and avoiding legalese. For related information, see AUDIENCE, LEGALESE, and CLARITY.

2. Organization.

An opinion email or letter should contain any or all of the following, depending upon the status of the legal situation.

(a) A heading, including the date. Make sure the email subject line is specific so that the reader can read, file, and remember it accordingly.

RE: Merits of Pursuing Negligence Claim against Poole

rather than

RE: Merits of Claim

(b) A salutation. Because this is a more formal communication, a salutation may be appropriate even in email.

Dear Dr. Brand:

For more information, see SALUTATIONS and SUBJECT LINE.

(c) An opening or introduction.

In the opening paragraph, state the question the letter will answer and refer to the request you received. This information is important because (1) the question clarifies the SCOPE of the answer and limits its application to that particular question and (2) the client will be billed for the opinion, so you need to clarify that this opinion was specifically requested. As you write this information, however, word it to communicate your desire for clarity and reliability, rather than creating a tone that focuses on protecting you from liability.

When we met on Wednesday, June 14, you asked for my written legal opinion about the possible success of a negligence suit against Amblore Trucking for the injuries you suffered in a collision caused by one of their trucks, which ran a red light and hit your SUV as you were making a left turn. Specifically, your question was whether Amblore Trucking could be found legally responsible for the truck driver's negligence when the driver was violating Amblore's written policy, which forbids its drivers from texting while driving.

rather than

When we met on Wednesday, June 14, you asked whether you could sue Amblore Trucking for your injuries caused by one of their truck drivers. Answering this question required me to research several issues and write this legal opinion for you.

If the news is good and the answer clear cut, you may include the conclusion and recommendation to the client here. Even if the news is bad, your reader often wants to know your answer, so you may delay the conclusion somewhat but not too much. Either way, be sure to maintain accuracy; avoid oversimplifying an answer even as you try to answer as clearly and specifically as possible.

(d) An explanation of all needed legal caveats.

Opinion emails or letters are necessarily limited in several ways; these caveats must be stated explicitly. The challenge you face here is to explain these limitations without making the opinion letter seem useless or making you seem more interested in protecting yourself than in helping the client. This challenge can be difficult, so when you find a structure that accomplishes the task, save it to use as a guide in future letters. Some common limitations for opinions include the following: (1) the answer applies only in a given jurisdiction and under the law in effect at a given time, (2) the answer is reliable only if the facts as stated are accurate and therefore the client must alert you to any errors in the facts, and (3) the answer cannot be relied upon by other people whose facts will necessarily differ. You may include all these caveats in one separate paragraph if this does not create a defensive tone. Alternatively, you can place them in different places as they apply. For example, you could add the following sentences to the end of the example paragraph above.

> **In answering this question, I have researched the relevant law in Arizona, where your accident occurred. Therefore my opinion is necessarily limited to that jurisdiction and to the law currently in effect. My answer also relies on the specific facts as stated below and will not apply to any other situation. For that reason, please read the following summary of facts carefully and notify me immediately of any inaccuracies or omissions you find. No matter how small those changes in facts may be, they could change my answer to your question.**

This organization can provide a useful transition to the summary of facts and can motivate the reader to review those facts carefully, rather than skipping that section because it is familiar information.

(e) A summary of the facts.

Include the legally significant facts, the background facts, and any other facts the client and other potential readers should know that could affect the case. If you are writing a long letter, set this section off with a subheading, such as the following.

> **FACTS OF THE CASE**
>
> or
>
> **RELEVANT FACTS**

or just

FACTS

Clients may omit facts unfavorable to their position, so before writing you may want to probe to get those unfavorable facts that might influence your opinion. If appropriate, you may even draft the facts section and get the client to review it for accuracy before drafting the opinion itself. Ask the client to advise you of any additions or corrections because your analysis depends on the accuracy of these facts. For related information, see LEGALLY SIGNIFICANT FACTS.

(f) Your conclusion, if this was not included earlier.

Make sure you answer the client's question. If the conclusion is long, you may set it off by using another subheading. See CONCLUSIONS.

(g) An explanation of your conclusion.

With your explanation, include a summary of the law and explain how the law applies to the client's facts. This section can be challenging to write clearly, especially if your client is unfamiliar with legal terms, which is likely. If you are using subheadings, include one for this section.

(h) Clear signals of your organization.

In the explanation section, lay out your reasoning step by step (see ORGANIZATION, LARGE-SCALE). Also take care to avoid using unneeded legal terms (see LEGALESE) and to define those legal terms that are needed (see UNOBTRUSIVE DEFINITIONS). Whether and when you include CITATIONS is a matter of judgment, depending on the sophistication of your reader, the extent to which your opinion rests on the case cited, and the possibility of the client misunderstanding the significance of the citation. Including citations, however, does not greatly affect readability; readers can skip over citations easily if they so choose.

(i) If relevant, a prediction or recommendation.

You may include a prediction of the outcome of the case based on the overall balance of the strengths against the weaknesses in the application of the law to the facts.

When making a recommendation, you will be balancing your professional responsibility to inform the client fully and your need to protect yourself against potential malpractice problems. Do cover yourself, but do it by explaining the specific caveats and reasons behind your opinion, not by using spineless, general phrases that only create ambiguities. Avoid phrases like *in effect*, *it is said that*, and *of course*. For example, the following paragraph hedges by explaining the writer's position rather than by inserting spineless phrases.

> **Thus litigation would not be economically worthwhile, so you may want to settle this claim. Current New York law favors Mr. Poole's position in all but one of the most recent cases. By arguing that your situation is similar to that case, we might be able to reach a satisfactory arrangement. At trial, however, you would be running a substantial risk of losing this claim even after investing the substantial amount required to litigate the case.**

Sometimes you will have to say that clients cannot do what they want. When possible, make this bad news more palatable by offering alternatives that lead to the same objective or to similar ones. For example, you may have to state that a lawsuit would probably be financially unfeasible, but you may be able to add that negotiation might bring about some of the desired result. When your answer is no, also include in your conclusion a brief outline of your strong reasons for the no, in case an unhappy or angry client skips reading the reasons section. For related information, see BAD NEWS, SOFTENING IT.

(j) A specific directive to the client to call or come in to discuss the matter further.

Your client needs to be clear on the next step, whether it is just to contact you if there are further questions or to let you know what the client decides to do. Unless the letter is meant to do so, add a sentence explaining to your reader that your letter does not create any legal rights. For related information, see OPINION OR ADVICE?

(k) A closing.

Sincerely yours,

or

Yours truly,

For related information, see COMMUNICATIONS, CLOSINGS.

For a discussion of letters in general, see WRITING TO CLIENTS. For related information, see COMMUNICATIONS, TONE OF. For advice when using technology, see ARTIFICIAL INTELLIGENCE AND

RESEARCH, ARTIFICIAL INTELLIGENCE AND WRITING, PROMPTS, and WRITING AND TECHNOLOGY.

OPINIONS, READING THEM

When reading a judicial opinion, consider the steps listed below to increase both your effectiveness and your efficiency.

1. General considerations.

Keep in mind the purpose for which you are using that opinion. For example, if you are reading an opinion to learn about a particular subject for class, such as *personal jurisdiction*, read the opinion for what it offers to enhance the definition and analysis of that concept. If you are reading the opinion for research, read with the thesis or issue of your memo, brief, or paper in mind.

Also understand the purpose for which the opinion was written, which differs from your purpose as you read the opinion now. Opinions are written, first, to explain the court's decision to the people who brought their problem to the court for resolution. The judge wants both parties to see the fairness of its resolution. For the winning party, this task is not so difficult; the winner, after all, believed the law favored that side's position. The winner is less likely to scrutinize the opinion for every error. The losing party, however, will scrutinize that opinion and will not be inclined to accept the court's reasoning.

The judge understands the loser's position and often writes the opinion with that position in mind. For example, after explaining the facts of the case, the judge often presents the losing party's arguments and explains the flaws in those arguments. Then, after explaining the arguments that did not prevail, the judge presents the reasoning upon which the court relied. Thus the court often does not start with its winning argument, even though in other legal writing the strongest argument usually goes first.

When writing an opinion, the judge also has the appellate court in mind, writing so that the opinion will stand up under appellate review. Therefore the opinion carefully details the procedure followed by the court and often includes rather lengthy explanations of why certain facts were not relevant and certain arguments made by either attorney did not prevail. Much of this information may be irrelevant to your purposes, but it may become useful if it suggests arguments that might work in a different situation. Develop your analytical peripheral vision so that you do not overlook parts of the opinion; make sure that you understand these parts well enough to include or omit them from your notes with confidence.

2. Specific techniques.

Because you are looking for something more specific, your purpose differs from that of the opinion writer. Therefore, you may want to read through the opinion once to get the gist of it, without marking the text or taking extensive notes. This aids your understanding by helping you see the overall framework of the case before you begin dealing with the details. Note who won the case and why. You may even want to begin by reading the end of the opinion to see the results; then go back to get an overview of how the court reached that result.

Then read more specifically for your purpose. Focus on the holding, the result of the case, and relate that holding to your topic or issue. For example, if a new trial was granted because evidence was not properly suppressed, then study the case to extract a definition of when evidence should be suppressed.

Next reread the case, briefing it according to your preference. Note how the court uses the law, facts, trends, reasoning patterns, and social context to reach its result. Determine, or brief, the following:

- the procedural posture, or where the case is in the judicial process;
- the holding, or what result the court reached and why;
- the legal rule, or how the court established the fundamental legal basis for the opinion;
- the court's reasoning, including
  - how it proceeded from its basis to its conclusion,
  - how it put the arguments in context and accounted for practical circumstances,
  - how it addressed specific arguments and relevant policy arguments,
  - how it adopted other specific types of arguments (such as law and economics, critical race theory, judicial economy, and statutory construction),
- how it eliminated or omitted other possible results; and
- which facts were critical to the outcome.

For suggestions on how to do this, see CASE BRIEFS.

3. Appellate briefs.

If you are working on an appellate brief, also note the standard of review, because this may affect your use of the case.

For related information, see CASE BRIEFS, NOTES, and STANDARD OF REVIEW.

OPTIMAL OR *OPTIMUM*?

Optimal is the adjective form, while *optimum* is the noun form, although *optimum* is also used as an adjective.

The parties concurred that this was the optimum of the available solutions.

For PRECISION, do not use it to mean best in an absolute sense.

The parties agreed that this decision was the optimum.

Optimal is more frequently used as an adjective in modern use, while *optimum* is the older form; either is correct.

This is the optimal situation for the plaintiff, who would prefer to settle rather than file suit.

or

This is the optimum situation for the plaintiff because we settled for more than she had asked.

Optimum refers to the best condition, amount, or degree for a particular situation.

OR

Or is a conjunction that signals to the reader that you mean *any one of the listed items*, rather than *all of them*. Thus *or* is disjunctive. In legal writing, misuse of *or* can create ambiguity in two situations.

1. *Or* alone is not always enough to communicate your meaning.

   Often you must clarify by adding other explanatory phrases, such as

   by any of the following means

   or

   any of the following subsections.

2. *Or* alone is usually not enough to signal clearly that a long list is disjunctive.

   When you rely solely on *or* to show the structure of the list, the reader must read through most of the list before finding out whether this is an *and* or an *or* situation. Therefore, if your list is very long, let the reader know before the list that this is an *or* situation.

Either party may notify the other of a delay by any of the following means: telephoning the other party, sending an agent with a written message, sending an agent with an oral message, sending a telegram addressed to the other party personally, sending a certified letter, or meeting with the other party in person.

rather than

Either party may notify the other of a delay by telephoning the other party, sending an agent with the message, sending a telegram, sending a certified letter, or any combination of these.

For related information, see *AND/OR*; CONJUNCTIONS; and LISTS, STRUCTURE OF.

ORAL OR *VERBAL*?

Verbal refers to any communication using words, whether spoken or written; *nonverbal* refers to gestures, actions, and other unspoken communication.

A successful lawyer is usually a master of verbal communication.

Oral refers to any communication that is spoken, rather than written. Do not use *verbal* when you mean *oral.*

The contract was based on an oral agreement made July 6, 2025.

rather than

The contract was based on a verbal agreement made July 6, 2025.

ORAL PRESENTATIONS

Oral presentations must convey the essence of written presentations, but more simply. Whether it is an objective presentation to an assigning attorney or a persuasive argument before a court, the presentation should focus on the issue to be resolved, the answer, and a clear explanation.

Oral presentation adds the advantages of voice, volume, gesture, pace, and eye contact—all qualities that are much harder to convey in writing. Make the most of these tools to be effective and to build your professional image over time. The general speaking techniques listed below can help you present this content effectively. Above all, attend to your listener. If the listener seems restless, confused, or in any way uneasy, adjust your presentation. If necessary, ask the listener, *Does this make sense?*

Consider the following when preparing objective or persuasive presentations and when developing your overall speaking techniques.

1. In an objective oral presentation.

   (a) State the issue to which the listener wants an answer. Incorporate the same three parts used in Issues: the general law under which the question is being asked, the legal question, and the legally significant facts pertinent to that question. Do not do this mechanically, but use these aspects of the Issue and appropriate background to orient your listener appropriately. For examples, see ISSUES and QUESTIONS PRESENTED.

   (b) Give the answer. Do not make the listener wait for this. For examples, see BRIEF ANSWER and CONCLUSION.

   (c) Make sure your listener is familiar with the facts of the case; if you are not sure, ask the listener. If more facts are needed, give a succinct presentation of the legally significant facts, the background facts, and any significant emotional facts, if they relate to the issue and answer and are necessary to make your point. Keep this summary as short as possible.

   (d) Explain your analysis as succinctly as possible. Make sure extraneous detail is omitted and remaining details are clearly connected to each other and to your conclusion. The listener wants to hear an explanation that justifies your main message and the sound reasoning that supports your position. The listener also wants to know that accepting your position will not precipitate any negative ramifications. These goals exist in any kind of oral presentation, whether to a supervising attorney, to a client, or to a colleague.

   (e) Be extremely flexible in answering questions. It is likely that you will get interrupted by any listener, so use the questions to explain to the listener what the answer is and to move gracefully through the pre-planned parts of your presentation. For example, if you are asked a question about the third issue you wanted to discuss while you are discussing the first, answer the question about the third issue and move gracefully back into the first. You can do this by saying something like *which is why we are arguing under the first issue that . . . .*

2. In persuasive oral presentations.

   (a) State the issue to be resolved and your answer to that issue. State it first, so you can get this information out before you are interrupted.

(b) Explain the plan of your argument to defer questions about later issues.

(c) Make sure the listener knows the facts. If you are the moving party, present the listener with the facts of the case unless the listeners waive that presentation.

(d) State the conclusions the court should reach, including a brief statement explaining that a decision in your client's favor is consistent with principles of law and fair under these facts.

(e) Know the record and the law thoroughly. There is no substitute for this. If you are comfortable with the record and the law, there will be no hesitation or weakness in your argument. Your confidence should then come automatically.

(f) Address the case's impact on the law in general, especially if addressing an appellate court. The listener wants to know how the decision in this case will affect subsequent cases.

(g) Be candid and flexible; deal with weak points directly and welcome questions as an opportunity to explain the answers to the listener.

(h) Be respectful: show good manners and good humor and keep personalities out of the argument.

3. General speaking techniques.

(a) Use your natural speaking voice. Do not try to move to a different voice, or you risk sounding strained or nervous. Be careful of using vocal fry, or speaking well below your natural range, because it can both distract your listener and permanently damage your vocal cords.

(b) Avoid developing distracting vocal habits. Watch out for vocal sounds inserted during pauses, such as *uh*, and habitual use of certain words to begin a statement, such as *clearly*, *but*, or *however*. Also avoid distracting signals of your mood, such as shifting to a higher pitch, a nasal tone, or a faster pace when you are feeling defensive, angry, or nervous. Become comfortable with silent pauses, rather than feeling as though you must fill every moment with sound.

(c) Improve aspects of your speaking voice over time. Tape yourself, listen, and keep the qualities you like. Work on changing bad habits. For example, you may realize that you tend to speak in a monotone. If so, try moving your voice up and down, varying the pitch for emphasis. Or you may speak too quickly. If so, try changing the pace of your presentation, adding pauses to vary the rhythm, and pausing to breathe at appropriate times. Study good speakers, in law and other professions, and mimic their approaches. Some may work, and others may not, but keep imitating to increase your range and effect.

(d) Measure the effect of your voice on listeners. If you are asked to repeat yourself often, you may be mumbling or speaking too fast. If you are asked to speak up, you may be speaking too softly. If your listeners are looking down or elsewhere, seek advice or get training to improve your presentation skills. Use these audience responses to keep improving your voice; ask for feedback from trusted observers, consider it carefully, and as appropriate use it to guide your efforts to improve.

(e) Adjust your natural gesturing habits to become more effective. If you naturally gesture freely when you speak, consider whether you need to reduce the gestures when speaking to avoid distracting the audience. Particularly watch for small, quick movements that can convey nervousness. As the size of the room and the audience increases, the breadth of your gestures can increase. For example, when sitting with your audience around a table, your gestures may include movement of the hands and lower arm, but spreading your arms to full width would be too much. In contrast, spreading arms to full width might be more effective than small gestures when speaking from a podium to hundreds of listeners.

If you tend to cling to the podium or conference table, try to add some gestures to emphasize points and keep your audience visually engaged, using the guidance listed above to choose appropriate gestures.

Also consider your posture when speaking. Stand up straight; avoid slouching over the podium or leaning on the table when you are speaking. You may, however, lean forward slightly to communicate your engagement with the audience. When speaking to a small audience around a conference table, consider remaining seated or, if standing, avoid standing so close to the table that your audience feels you are dominating them.

When appropriate in the context, moving away from the podium can help keep the audience engaged, for people naturally follow movement. This may come naturally if you are using visual aids, but it can also be used in other situations. If you are using a white board, avoid talking while your back is turned to the audience, for this can make it much harder for people to hear you.

(f) Maintain appropriate eye contact with your main audience. While you want to avoid staring at any one person too long, you do want to look at them frequently, moving your eyes from one member of the AUDIENCE to another as you speak. While it may be uncomfortable for those who are naturally shy, this is one of the most important skills you need to develop to be an effective speaker.

For related information, see INTERVIEWING CLIENTS, POWERPOINT, PROFESSIONAL LANGUAGE AND PRESENTATION and TONE.

ORDERS

Orders are brief documents issued by the court that state a decision on a motion and any action that the court is ordering as a result of that decision. For the court's convenience, attorneys are often expected to draft the orders they want the court to sign if their sides prevail. Your main goals when writing orders are to include all needed information precisely and to avoid unneeded verbiage and legalese. As with all court documents, be sure to check and follow any rules in your jurisdiction.

1. Including all the parts of an order.

   An order includes the caption, the body, and the signatures. The caption follows the same form as the caption on the complaint, motions, and other documents in the case. The word *order* simply goes in the location where the names of the other documents were. For examples, see CAPTIONS.

   The body of the order often begins with a reference to the procedure, to show that proper procedure has been followed.

   > **The defendant filed a Motion to Dismiss the complaint on the ground that it failed to state a claim upon which relief can be granted. After hearing oral arguments and receiving briefs, the court rendered its ruling to dismiss the complaint on January 9, 2025, which is incorporated here by reference.**

   It then includes the details of the order itself.

   > **IT IS HEREBY ORDERED that Plaintiffs' complaint and all causes of action arising under it are dismissed against Defendant on the merits, with cost.**

   If the order involves several items, they can be tabulated to make the content easier to read. The signature line should then follow the form in your jurisdiction, leaving a line for the judge to sign.

2. Avoiding unneeded legalese.

   Use terms of art when needed, but avoid legalese. For examples of both, see LEGALESE and TERMS OF ART.

ORDINANCES

See LEGISLATION.

ORGANIZATION, CHRONOLOGICAL

Chronological organization means organizing events in the order in which they happened. Use chronological organization in a Statement of Facts or Statement of the Case when the order of occurrence is legally significant.

As tempting as this form of logic is, it can be bland, long, and even confusing when the nature of events, not their chronology, is your subject matter. So avoid using this scheme when another form of organization matches your analysis. Sometimes combining chronological organization with topical or another form works best; in a Statement of Facts, for example, you might separate the facts into substantive and procedural categories, group facts under each heading, and then organize each group in chronological order.

Rather than being wedded to one form of organization, shape your presentation according to the document's purpose. For example, if you are trying to persuade a court, you may want to use an organization of the facts that best suits your desired remedy or theory. For related information, see NARRATIVE WRITING; ORGANIZE, HOW TO; ORGANIZATION, LARGE-SCALE; ORGANIZATION, TOPICAL; STATEMENT OF THE CASE; and STATEMENT OF FACTS.

ORGANIZATION FOR THOSE WHO CAN'T OUTLINE

Achieving your desired purpose in legal writing depends a great deal on presenting your content in a clear and coherent organization. Sometimes, however, arriving at that organization can seem overwhelming, especially when the content does not lend itself to an organizational pattern that you have commonly encountered. This is most likely to happen in a complicated brief, a law review article exploring an innovative area, or a contract covering an unusual business relationship.

When you encounter a situation where organization is eluding you, you may need an alternative approach to achieving an outline. The following steps can help you organize successfully, even if you are not able to master outlining in the usual way. If you use artificial intelligence to generate an outline, you can also use the following steps to tailor the results to your project.

1. Brainstorm.

   Try listing all the points you want to make or might want to make, or just list everything that you can think of about the topic. Do not worry about order, quality, or anything else at this stage except coming up with ideas. This stage could take the form of free writing, which is drafting without stopping to look at notes or revise spelling. Or it could take the form of note taking, jotting down all sorts of ideas in a list or on cards. The form does not matter here so much as the result. Do not stop to delete or revise any ideas; editing at this point can distract you from the primary task of generating ideas. You want to seek out many options, so that you have more to choose from later.

2. Group your ideas.

   Read through all your drafting or all your listed points and see if they fall into any logical groups. See if some major ideas emerge from the list. Try grouping the points several different ways before you settle on one way that makes the most sense to you. Often the organization that occurs to you first will be adequate, but not optimal. Alternatively, if your list of points includes six or fewer items, you may already have your logical groups. If so, fill in more supporting points on those items and then check to see if you are still satisfied with those groups.

3. Organize the groups.

   Look at each group and decide which points are the major ones and which are subordinate, or supporting, points. At this stage you may still find some errors in your grouping, but you can revise those groups as needed. You may also find that you have stated the same thing in two different ways, so that you can strike out redundant points. You may also delete points that are clearly irrelevant.

4. Subdivide further, if needed.

   Divide your arguments and divide the subpoints made in those arguments. Check each item to make sure that it should not be subdivided further. Remember that you need to make only one point at a time. Even though all your points are inextricably interrelated, you must divide them into manageable portions for the reader. For related information, see PARAGRAPHS.

5. Order the groups, points, and subpoints.

   After the points are divided, decide how to order them. To determine this order, think about what will be logical to your reader, rather than what seems important to you. To help determine what is logical to the reader, ask yourself the following three questions.

(a) Is there some threshold point that comes first? For example, if your case involved a jurisdiction question, that question would logically come first because the court will not look to any other issues until they have determined that it is the court's job to decide those issues.

(b) Is one point more significant than the others? For example, if your case involves clear-cut violations of freedom of speech and also involves some technical violations of proper notice, you may want to start with the violation of the freedom of speech. This point may convince your reader that justice favors your side and will probably make more compelling reading. The technical point may then provide a convenient peg upon which to hang the hat of justice.

(c) Is one point stronger than the others? For example, if your case involves a clear-cut violation of proper notice but also involves a potential-but-debatable violation of freedom of speech, you may start with the violation of proper notice. This way you can establish some justification for your client's position before you present more questionable justifications.

6. Write.

At this point you will have all the information provided by a traditional outline, and you can rewrite it in outline format, if you wish, or go directly to writing your rough draft. If you had started trying to outline by writing a roman numeral at the top of the page, you would have been expecting yourself to do all of these previous steps in your head, which is why trying to write a traditional outline is not a good starting point for many people.

7. Check the organization.

Once you have written your full draft, recheck your organization. In fact, some successful writers write a rough draft first and then outline or go through the organization steps listed above. One way to check your organization is to read the first sentence of each paragraph throughout the document. This should give you a summary of the points of the paper, although it will not document the proof of those points.

For other information on organizing, see ORGANIZATION, LARGE-SCALE; ORGANIZE, HOW TO; PREWRITING; and WRITING PROCESS. For related information, see GETTING STARTED; ORGANIZATION, SMALL-SCALE; and PARAGRAPHS.

8. Verify AI results.

   If you are using artificial intelligence, verify the results. Be particularly alert to protecting client confidentiality as you move through each step. For help with this, see ARTIFICIAL INTELLIGENCE AND RESEARCH, ARTIFICIAL INTELLIGENCE AND WRITING, DISCUSSION SECTION, PROMPTS, and RESEARCH STRATEGY GUIDE.

ORGANIZATION, LARGE-SCALE

Large-scale organization conveys the overall coherence of any piece of writing. Large-scale organization is communicated throughout the document in its tables of content, summaries of argument, executive summaries, headings, introductions, and topic sentences that incorporate accurate transitions. The logic of this organization should flow from a careful balancing of many factors, including (1) content and legal analytical patterns, (2) purpose, (3) audience, and (4) local traditions. After you have addressed organization initially in your outline and first draft, begin your REWRITING by focusing on (5) communicating this organization clearly.

1. Content and legal analytical patterns.

   Content affects your organization when the law is strongly and consistently discussed in particular patterns. A statute may have four elements, all of which courts consistently discuss in the same order. Rather than disrupt that scheme, you may choose to present your document by following it. Or when particular arguments appear consistently in a string of cases, you may choose to group your analysis of those arguments similarly. If a trend is emerging in a series of cases, you may want to pick up that trend in your analysis. Alternatively, if the content of a transaction is suggesting its own unique scheme, you may fashion the contract accordingly and reject more traditional structures. The law usually offers several possible structures for a document. It is up to you to decide how much that law will actually inform your document's structure. The facts and context may also suggest a particular structure, such as in a case involving a long-standing feud or in a case where many briefs have already been written. Then judicial economy may be the legal theme, within which the substantive issues are analyzed.

   Broader legal analytical patterns also influence your organization, and these may be the richest and most subtle adjustments you make. From your general legal reading, you will discern common analytical patterns used in U.S. legal practice. Those patterns range from traditional deductive patterns, such as general-to-specific and rule-to-conclusion, to inductive patterns such as examples-to-generalities. You will also note other patterns, such as the balancing tests used in constitutional issues or in law and economics arguments. In some judicial decisions, you will see a postmodern array of opinions, concurrences, and dissents, out of which you must extract the law. All of these patterns and more are available to you, too. You may see several that will work. When several patterns are possible, choose the pattern that best allows you to convey your message to your audience. For more on analytical patterns, see REASONING, ANALOGICAL; REASONING, DEDUCTIVE; REASONING, INDUCTIVE; REASONING, MODERN; REASONING, OTHER; REASONING, POSTMODERN; and REASONING, PRESENTING IT.

If you are using artificial intelligence to discover analytical patterns, see ARTIFICIAL INTELLIGENCE AND RESEARCH, ARTIFICIAL INTELLIGENCE AND WRITING, DISCUSSION SECTION, PROMPTS, and RESEARCH STRATEGY GUIDE.

2. PURPOSE.

Adjust the organization to fit the document's purpose. If you are organizing a memo that exposes weaknesses in your client's case and you want to discourage the client from proceeding, you may begin with those weaknesses. But if the client wishes to proceed, you will organize the brief differently, probably beginning with the client's strongest arguments because your purpose then will be to win. Similarly, you may organize the duties enumerated in a contract chronologically if the sequence of actions outlined is central to the agreement. But you may organize the duties in a contract topically if the working relationship includes several different areas of responsibility. Because your purpose is usually to encourage the non-represented party to sign, you would place affirmative statements of duties before descriptions of penalties incurred by breach.

3. AUDIENCE.

Adjust the large-scale organization as needed to fit the way your reader may think of the content or the way you would like your audience to think of the content. When writing briefs to a court, always check the procedural posture and the procedural rules, which will help you understand how the court will approach the issues in your case. For example, when organizing a brief for a court, consider what question will be first in the court's mind and try to begin with that, such as whether this court has jurisdiction over the issue. That procedural issue would probably be discussed first; if the answer is no, the substantive questions will not matter. When organizing an opinion letter, you may need to begin with the client's question because the client is expecting an answer to that, even if it is not the main legal question.

If you believe that any of your primary readers would think about the content in a different way, compensate by adjusting your organization to address that approach. For example, you may need to adjust the traditional organization of a law review article when discussing some innovative ideas of an unusual case; if you can reorganize the content for the reader without violating your thinking, do so. If you cannot, then inform the reader early and clearly of your organization, so the reader can adjust to follow the document. For help choosing the organization, see LEGAL ANALYSIS, MEMOS, *PROCEDURAL* OR *SUBSTANTIVE*? and SCHOLARLY WRITING.

4. Local Traditions.

Local traditions may also affect your organization. Your local court, or your firm, may organize certain documents or doctrines, such as summary judgment or international arbitration, in prescribed ways to which all local readers are accustomed. Research those traditions as you make your final organizational decisions.

5. Communicating your organization.

Always communicate your document's overall large-scale organization in your HEADINGS, INTRODUCTIONS, CONCLUSIONS, TOPIC SENTENCES and QUESTIONS PRESENTED or ISSUES so that your choice of organization communicates to the reader how each subpart fits in the whole. For example, if there is a question of governmental immunity in your memo and two subissues must be raised to answer the larger issue of immunity, organize both the Question Presented and the discussion section so that the reader sees how the subissues fit into the larger question of immunity. For how-to techniques to communicate the organization, also see CONNECTIONS, MAKING THEM.

Work on large-scale organization as early in the writing process as you can and keep working on it until it is clear to you. Most issues can be organized in several ways, and your paper must be organized in a way that makes sense to your readers. Consider your possible large-scale organization as you gather research in prewriting, as you outline, and as you rewrite. If the large-scale organization is not working at any of these three points, try rearranging. Avoid getting stuck on one way to organize; if this organization arose early in your process, it may be more writer- than reader-based. If you wait until revising or polishing to adjust the structure for your readers, it may be too late and too frustrating to change. For related information, see ORGANIZATION FOR THOSE WHO CAN'T OUTLINE; ORGANIZE, HOW TO; OUTLINES; REWRITING; and WRITING PROCESS. For help organizing particular documents, see BENCH MEMOS; BRIEFS, AMICUS; BRIEFS, APPELLATE; BRIEFS, PRETRIAL; BRIEFS,

REPLY; BRIEFS, TRIAL; COMPLAINTS; CONTRACTS; MEMORANDUM OF POINTS AND AUTHORITIES; SCHOLARLY WRITING; or WILLS.

ORGANIZATION, SMALL-SCALE

Small-scale organization guides the reader smoothly through a document from phrase to phrase, sentence to sentence, and paragraph to paragraph, connecting all these parts and remaining congruent with the large-scale organization. It conveys the organization between and within paragraphs and sentences; it communicates the logical links between those paragraphs and sentences through transitions and clear thesis sentences. When the small-scale organization is effective, the reader can group and coordinate words into meaningful units more quickly, which speeds the reading process. It also aids understanding by organizing smaller pieces of information into one unit, so that the reader can remember the information as one item and have more short-term memory free for remembering how all the content fits together.

In contrast, large-scale organization communicates the coherent flow and logical interrelationships between paragraphs and larger segments of a piece of writing. This flow and interrelationship is communicated in the headings, topic sentences, grouping and sequencing of content, and organization of the analysis. It conveys the larger purpose of the writing as the reader scans the text. As the reader studies the text in detail, it reminds that reader of the larger purpose and how the specific content relates to that purpose.

Small-scale organization involves six aspects of writing, each of which is explained in detail in a separate entry.

- For creating unified, focused paragraphs, see PARAGRAPH ORGANIZATION.
- For opening paragraphs to unify ideas, see TOPIC SENTENCES.
- For putting sentences in logical order, see SYLLOGISMS.
- For clarifying logical connections between sentences and paragraphs, see CONNECTIONS, MAKING THEM; and TRANSITIONS.
- For choosing the most effective sentence structure, see SENTENCE STRUCTURE.
- For making lists readable, see LISTS, STRUCTURE OF.

The revision for small-scale organization should take place after writing and rewriting, so that you are not struggling with fundamental ideas at the same time you are straightening out the expression of those process will help you identify your major issues. After you have identified those, follow a similar process for each issue, listing subissues, needed sources, supporting examples or facts, and other supporting details. From these you can see what must be included in the organization.

To complete your organization, connect these points coherently, checking to see if your organization is the best by considering alternative possible organizations. For help doing this, see LEGAL ANALYSIS; and ORGANIZATION, LARGE-SCALE.

(b) You may find that the middle level of organization occurs first to you: you know what analogies you want to make, what cases and statutes you want to use, or what examples are needed. If so, begin by listing these points and then asking yourself why those points are needed, or what point they prove. The answer to that question can help you determine what your theme or message is and what broader context your points fit into. Thus you have begun with the *A.* level of organization and used that to help you determine the roman numeral level.

To organize this way, you can list all the points that you think you need to include in your document and then group each individual point with others that seem related. Experiment with different groupings until you find the pattern that seems logical and provides a place for each point you have listed. When you have settled on a grouping, ask yourself why those groups make sense, or how you would label those groups. The answer to that question gives you your roman numeral level of organization. When you have determined these points, you can decide which of the points you have listed are subordinate to others and what order is most effective for presenting those points. This step should help you determine the logical connections among the various points you will be including and identify any holes in your reasoning that you can fill. Thus you knit your points together in ways that help you to choose the best organization for the readers.

(c) If you prefer to start at the micro-level, you can begin by gathering all the information you need on paper, electronically, or both. Then, when your content is captured on paper, start to look for ways to group that content coherently. You can begin by grouping items you know belong in a list. Look at each piece of content to find logical links to other pieces of content. Write down labels for the groups as they occur to you, thinking of these labels as the beginnings of thesis sentences or subheadings for groups of paragraphs. Move from grouping individual pieces and labeling them to coordinating the groups into still larger groups, labeling those by asking yourself why that group of support is needed or what it proves. This step should help you find your larger issues or headings: the roman numeral level of your outline. Thus you have moved from the *(i)* level of your outline up to the *A.* level and on to the roman numerals that mark your major headings or issues.

See what approach to organization works best for you and your readers and then adapt the process as you become more comfortable. For further help, see HABITS, WRITING; and WRITING PROCESS. For various ways to organize, see DESIGN, GETTING STARTED, ORGANIZATION FOR THOSE WHO CAN'T OUTLINE, OUTLINES, PREWRITING, and SYLLOGISMS.

3. How to choose the best organization for your AUDIENCE.

Make sure you have an organization that makes sense to your readers, not just to you. If needed, experiment again with different major steps or a different order of presentation. There are usually several coherent ways to organize, each of which can still conform to your purpose. Sketch many versions, at least three, even if one of them seems unlikely. By comparing them all, you will get a stronger sense of which one is best. Consult with your colleagues about possible approaches, if possible. Then choose the organization that best fits your purpose and your readers. For related information, see ORGANIZATION, LARGE-SCALE.

4. How to present your organization to your audience.

After you have completed a draft of your content, check to make sure your organization is conveyed clearly to your readers. In legal writing, worry more about making your organization clear to each reader, less about being too obvious. For example, you may use enumeration, such as *first, second, third,* or *(1), (2), (3)* for parallel points. Use transitions, such as *additionally* or *in contrast.* Use repetition of key terms as needed in headings and subheadings. For help here, see CONNECTIONS, MAKING THEM; HEADINGS; and TRANSITIONS.

Use focused paragraphs that include topic sentences, usually at the beginning of the paragraphs, and include support for the topic sentences in the paragraph that follows. Those topic sentences can relate to the overall theme, to the previous paragraph, to the current paragraph, or to all three. See PARAGRAPHS and TOPIC SENTENCES. Remember that the reader needs guidance, reminders, and a sense of the whole, so present your analysis or argument in a way that will keep the audience engaged throughout the document.

For more information, see ORGANIZATION, CHRONOLOGICAL; ORGANIZATION, SMALL-SCALE; and ORGANIZATION, TOPICAL. If you are using artificial intelligence, see ARTIFICIAL INTELLIGENCE AND RESEARCH, ARTIFICIAL INTELLIGENCE AND WRITING, and DISCUSSION SECTION.

ORNATE LANGUAGE

See FLOWERY LANGUAGE.

OTHERWISE

Otherwise means in another way or apart from that.

We cannot locate our expert witness, but otherwise the case is in good shape.

It can sound rather informal, so use it sparingly. Also avoid overusing *otherwise* or using it loosely.

If they accept this offer, we will settle. If they refuse, we will sue.

rather than

If they accept this offer, we will settle. Otherwise, we will sue.

OUTLINES

Outlines can help writers before or after writing a draft. Outlines can take any form: lists, barely legible scratching, flow charts, webs, Venn diagrams, or traditional outlines. Whatever the form, outlines help the writer make sure any reader can understand the document's organization. This entry illustrates three ways to reach your goal of having a workable outline, including (1) a classic approach, (2) an approach for those who start with a few big ideas, and (3) an approach for people who start by thinking of all the details they need to include. All three approaches, while beginning at different points, can achieve the same end of a cogent, focused outline that includes the needed content. With any of these approaches, (4) try to remain flexible, looking at different possible organizations before you settle on one.

1. Classic approach.

   Make an outline, either before or after writing your initial draft, by sketching a general portrait of the large-scale ideas, such as the following.

   Custody disputes

   Was "tender years"

not any more

ERA contributed

changed in 1973

Now statutory—five factors + 1 = “best interests”

Apply here—probably mother

Conclusion

Then fill in the details as you reread authority and rethink your ideas.

Custody disputes

Was “tender years”

“best interests of child” paramount then Jones at 48, 50

Mother used to be thought best Id.

ERA, general social changes say father or mother can “mother” Smith at 97

Led to partial codification, some changes in 1993

Statute R.C.W. 29.09.999 (quote)

Court must show they looked at factors Smith at 85, all five + anything else relevant

Broad discretion, but must be more structured now Id.

Apply here

Factor 1—wishes of parents

both want, but both will give visitation rights

Factor 2—wishes of child

nothing expressed

Factor 3—Interrelationship of children w/parents

mother drinks (Johnson mom drank too—distinguish)

father strict (Pines—father got son—same?)

mother stable? (see Schwartz—not as crazy as this woman: distinguish)

Factor 4—Child’s adjustment to home & community

with mom now, no adjustment

father will live in same city, but move required

Factor 5—Mental and physical health

mother stable? (see <u>Schwartz</u>; distinguish this mother, not that crazy)

father unemotional

Other factors—adultery, moral character

father having an affair, missed meeting with kids

cf. <u>Hildebrand</u>—doesn't mean he can't "mother"

Conclusion

Mom probably gets them because she is more responsive to their needs, has them now, hasn't missed any time with them

Keep filling in and refining your outline, as detailed in 4 below.

2. Approach from a few big picture points.

When this large-scale organization is not readily apparent to you, step back and begin by just listing all the points you know you need to cover. If your list is very short, try this approach. If your list is long, try approach #3.

Custody disputes

Governed by statute

mother more likely here

When your list is short, your best next step is to fill in supporting details for these main points.

Custody disputes

Changed from "tender years" to "make parent rights equal"

Now statute lists factors to consider

Governed by statute

changed in 1973

five factors + 1 = "best interests"

Mom more likely here

mom responsive to needs

has had continual contact

has custody now, so not disruptive to kids

Keep filling in supporting points you need to include, allowing yourself to rearrange points when you realize that one item is subordinate to another. Be especially watchful for this issue because often one of the initial points you list will logically fit under another, and often you will have missed one of your major headings in that initial list. Gradually, as you move information around, you will develop your full outline. Be sure to check that you have included adequate support, because your initial short list suggests that you naturally focus on the big picture, rather than the supporting details.

3. Approach when you have many points you want to cover.

If your initial list was rather long, as in the following example, you may benefit from taking a different approach to outlining.

Custody disputes was "tender years"—custody went to mother

"best interests of child" paramount then Jones at 48, 50

ERA, general social changes say father or mother can "mother" Smith at 97

Led to partial codification, some changes in 1973

Statute R.C.W. 29.09.999 (quote)

Court must show they looked at factors Smith at 85, all five + anything else relevant

cf. Hildebrand—a father can still "mother"

father strict but can get kids still (Pines)

Broad discretion still there, but more structured now Id.

Factor 1—wishes of parents

Factor 2—wishes of child

Factor 3—Interrelationship of children w/parents

Factor 4—Child's adjustment to home & community

Factor 5—Mental and physical health

mother drinks (Johnson mom drank too—distinguish)

mother stable? (see Schwartz—not as crazy as this woman: distinguish)

with mom now, no adjustment

father will live in same city, but move required

mother stable? (see Schwartz; distinguish this mother, not that crazy)

father unemotional

father having an affair, missed meeting with kids

both want, but both will give visitation rights

Mom is more responsive to their needs

Mom has them now

Mom hasn't missed any time with them

The length of your list reveals that you already sense a number of the details you need to include. When this is the case, your next step is to group listed items as you see relationships. You will often see several possible groupings, and this may be part of the reason that the organization is more difficult in this document. When you see several possibilities, try listing them. As you begin to see which of your points are logically subordinate to others, move them over into subcategories.

Law

- **Custody disputes was "tender years" custody went to mother**
- **"best interests of child" paramount then Jones at 48, 50**
- **ERA, general social changes say father or mother can "mother" Smith at 97**
- **Led to partial codification, some changes in 1973**
- **Statute R.C.W. 29.09.999 (quote)**
- **Court must show they looked at factors Smith at 85, all five + anything else relevant**
- **cf. Hildebrand—a father can still "mother"**
- **father strict but can get kids still (Pines)**

Facts

- **mother drinks (Johnson mom drank too—distinguish)**
- **mother stable? (see Schwartz—not as crazy as this woman: distinguish)**
- **with mom now, no adjustment**
- **father will live in same city, but move required**

mother stable? (see Schwartz; distinguish this mother, not that crazy)

father unemotional

father having an affair, missed meeting with kids

both want, but both will give visitation rights

Mom is more responsive to their needs

Mom has them now

Mom hasn't missed any time with them

Conclusion

Mom probably best choice

Then you can refine the outline further, developing subpoints that help you define the organization more clearly.

Law

Previous law

Custody disputes was "tender years" custody went to mother

"best interests of child" paramount then Jones at 48, 50

ERA, general social changes say father or mother can "mother" Smith at 97

Led to partial codification, some changes in 1973

Current law

Statute R.C.W. 29.09.999 (quote)

Five factors: Court must show they looked at factors Smith at 85, all five + anything else relevant

Factor 1—wishes of parents

Factor 2—wishes of child

Factor 3—Interrelationship of children w/parents

Cf. Johnson case—mother drank too much

mother drinks but not too much as Johnson

father having an affair, missed meeting with kids

cf. Pines—father strict but can get kids still

father here unemotional

Factor 4—Child's adjustment to home & community

Factor 5—Mental and physical health

Application to facts

Factor 1—wishes of parents—both want custody

Factor 2—wishes of child—unknown

Factor 3—Interrelationship of children w/parents

cf. Hildebrand—a father can still "mother"

father strict but can get kids still (Pines)

mom more responsive to kids

Factor 4—Child's adjustment to home & community

Kids now with mom—no adjustment needed

Father will live in same city

Factor 5—Mental and physical health

cf. Schwartz—unstable mother

mother stable? (see Schwartz—not as crazy as this woman: distinguish)

cf. Hildebrand—a father can still "mother"

father unemotional

Conclusion

Mother better choice

4. Completion of the outline process.

Whatever way you begin your outline, discipline yourself to sketch out several different organizations. Use these sketches to make sure you come to understand your major points. As you develop your outline from these sketches, remember your document's purpose, audience, and scope. For example, the first outline listed above takes its major cue from the statute itself, following the elements in order. But it may be too long and may not have enough persuasive impact. You can experiment by writing point headings that group the components differently, such as putting together all the factors that are not in dispute.

I. THE TRIAL COURT SHOULD AWARD CUSTODY TO MRS. DAVIS BECAUSE IT IS IN THE CHILDREN'S BEST INTERESTS TO STAY IN THEIR FAMILY HOME.

Factors not in dispute

A. Interrelationship strong

B. No adjustment needed

C. Mental and physical health optimal

II. THE TRIAL COURT SHOULD NOT AWARD CUSTODY TO MR. DAVIS BECAUSE HE CANNOT DEVOTE ENOUGH TIME TO THE CHILDREN.

A. Interrelationship weak

B. Adjustment too hard

C. Mental and physical health will be impaired

D. Affair will be devastating

Do several different versions to clarify your understanding of how all the ingredients combine, affect one another, and interrelate. If you can, test the versions by showing them to another reader or two. Ask which one makes the most sense in this context. From that input, recombine the ingredients as needed to arrive at the strongest organization. This process will help you avoid falling in love with your first outline, which is often writer-based: the first outline may make sense to you, but not necessarily to anyone else. Experimenting will broaden your thinking and your analytical approach enough to transform it to be more reader-based. If you reach a decision on the outline before writing the first draft, then at the writing stage you can just fill in the blanks left in the outline. Make lots of notes in the margin to remember details about each point; this will make writing easier.

If you outline after writing, you can use the outline to check logic and details. Any reader should be able to write your outline after reading your writing, so you can make sure your writing is clear by outlining it yourself. To do this, print out the draft and highlight the initial sentence of each paragraph. Then read those sentences aloud, checking for logical flow. Read critically, making sure each step of your presentation is congruent with the overall logic. A problem with this approach, as with any other, is that it can remain writer-based, making sense to only you. Try reading the draft in bad faith, as many of your audiences will. Criticize its structure and ask what would make it clearer. Or ask another reader or two to outline it from the draft. From their responses, clean up the outline and move parts accordingly.

If organization is a problem for you, outlining may offer a solution. If outlining does not work for you, see ORGANIZATION FOR THOSE WHO CAN'T OUTLINE; or ORGANIZE, HOW TO. For other aids to organization and related problems, see ORGANIZATION, LARGE-SCALE; WRITING BLOCK; and WRITING PROCESS.

OVERDONE

See FLOWERY LANGUAGE, MODIFIERS, and EMOTIONAL LANGUAGE.

OVERREFINEMENT

This term refers to the kind of errors writers commit when they are trying hard to be correct but do not quite understand the rules. For example, a writer might use *I feel badly* even though *I feel bad* is correct. For other common overrefinement problems, see *BETWEEN YOU AND ME* OR *BETWEEN YOU AND I*?, *CAN* OR *MAY*?, *GOOD* OR *WELL*?, *PRIOR TO, IN ADVANCE OF*, and *WHO* OR *WHOM*?

In a broader sense, *overrefinement* refers to the tendency some writers have to revise their writing too much. For example, a writer might remove important transitions in the name of conciseness, or create figurative language when literal language conveys the point better. Fight the temptation to overrefine, which can rob your STYLE of its spontaneity and READABILITY. Overrefinement can also add unnecessary time to your schedule. For help with this problem, see DEADLINES, MEETING THEM. For ways to refine effectively, see REVISING and POLISHING.

OXFORD COMMA

See COMMA, OXFORD; and COMMAS, subsection 7.

PADDING

In legal writing, avoid padding, or adding content not because it is needed but solely to increase length. Legal readers prize CONCISENESS; padding will not impress them.

PAPERLESS PRACTICE

You may be overwhelmed by paper, or you may just want to reduce it. If so, you can remove clutter and recreate your filing system if you are willing to work electronically. Consider the following steps in creating a paperless practice.

1. Assess what must be done in paper form.

   Be exacting in discovering what is required to be in paper form. Your jurisdiction may require you to save some paper copies or file documents in paper form, so you may need to keep using paper to meet these requirements. Make notes of these requirements and then list what other types of papers are on your desk. You may also want to save paper copies of items to protect against hacking or system failure. List the other types of papers that you can deal with electronically.

2. Decide what to change first.

   You may want to list these matters from easiest to hardest, or vice versa. If you work with someone who helps you file or organize, decide together what paper to eliminate first. If you are working alone, you may want to start with the paper that bothers you the most, such as old files, junk mail, or untouched reading materials.

3. Establish a filing system that works for you.

   Electronic storage will benefit you when you are able to retrieve documents easily. Although you will necessarily adapt your filing system over time, you need to start with a workable basis.

4. Change one thing at a time.

   Concentrate initially on one set of materials. If you are able to eliminate, store, or scan large files, you may want to start there to have the greatest impact. If that is complicated or overwhelming, you may want to start with your desk. Clear all the paper from it and then sort what is essential to your legal work from things that distract you. Find an electronic home for the latter or simply eliminate it.

5. Set a realistic timetable.

   Be realistic about how long it will take for the paper to disappear. It may take a year to convert to this approach. Your brain may need to make some adjustments if you are used to working on paper to review your documents, for example, so allow time to try this on several projects until you can read well on the screen.

6. Find a balance.

   You may get fatigued if you work only electronically. Printing the difficult part of a draft may allow you to see more clearly what adjustments need to be made. Using paper to sketch an organizational scheme or take notes in a client meeting may be more effective than working electronically. Many systems allow you to save your handwritten document electronically later. For more on this, see PAPER, USING IT.

For more help in being efficient, see DEADLINES, MEETING THEM; MULTI-TASKING; NOTES; PRIORITIES WITHIN ONE PROJECT; RESEARCH STRATEGY GUIDE; TIME MANAGEMENT; and TRIAGE.

PAPER, USING IT

Using paper may be faster or more effective at times than using a keyboard or drawing on the computer screen. You may capture your research more clearly if you work tactilely, such as making charts by hand on paper or writing out themes that connect sources. You may prefer to draw the outline or schema of your brief first before dictating or typing it. You may even prefer to draft by hand on paper because that pace follows the articulation of your thinking more appropriately than typing. The feedback loop among hand, eye, and mind enhances memory and may help you capture your thoughts more securely. Using paper in prewriting may help you to arrange details so that you have less rewriting and revising to do. And, of course, paper can be safer than electronic files others may be able to access. In any event, technology will allow you to save those handwritten notes electronically if needed. For related information, see METADATA REMOVAL. For more help in being efficient, see DEADLINES, MEETING THEM; MULTI-TASKING; NOTES; PRIORITIES WITHIN ONE PROJECT; RESEARCH STRATEGY GUIDE; TIME MANAGEMENT; and TRIAGE.

PARAGRAPH BLOCKS

A paragraph block is a group of paragraphs that fit together as a visual and substantive unit, just as sentences fit into the unit of a single paragraph. It is created by adding an extra space before the first and after the last paragraph in the block.

1. When to use.

   Paragraph blocks are most likely to be useful when your analysis requires a sub-subsection of explanation in the text; in this situation, you often will not want to add another level of heading because you already have headings and subheadings, and a third level might fragment the organization too much. The visual separation of a paragraph block is not as strong as that created by a subheading, and thus it is useful without distracting from the headings already in place. The paragraph block is most likely to be useful in longer documents. In shorter documents, headings, subheadings, and paragraphs should provide sufficient organizational tools. For related information, see HEADINGS, PARAGRAPHS, POINT HEADINGS, and TRANSITIONS.

2. How to use.

   To create a paragraph block visually, put an extra blank line between the previous text and the first paragraph of the block. At the end of the paragraph block, again add an extra blank line. Paragraph blocks work best if they are limited to three to six paragraphs; if the blocks are longer, the reader forgets about the paragraph block and its organizing value is lost. If the block consists of only two paragraphs, the reader may think that the blank lines are typographical errors.

   Remember that substance dictates the form of your writing. Therefore, avoid creating a paragraph block solely for looks. Create one only when your analysis requires the sub-subsection.

PARAGRAPH LENGTH

In a brief, memo, or longer opinion letter, you should average two or three paragraph breaks per page. In business letters or email, you will have more paragraphs per page. In any document, however, you should divide paragraphs logically rather than periodically. Therefore, first divide paragraphs logically; then in revision change this paragraph division, if needed, using the following guidelines.

1. Long Paragraphs.

   If you find one paragraph that runs about half a page, leave it undivided if it is logically one unit. If you have one paragraph that runs for more than two-thirds of a page, try to divide it, because the reader needs a visual break. Look for a logical subdivision in the paragraphs content and add a new TOPIC SENTENCE that reveals the connection between the two subdivisions. If you have many paragraphs that run two-thirds of a page, check for general organization problems. You may be focusing on the connections between points but ignoring subtler distinctions, which will make the overall organization muddy.

2. Short Paragraphs.

   If you have written a one-sentence paragraph or many short paragraphs, check to see if you have supported your points adequately. Also check for paragraphs that present fragments of a full development; these paragraphs may need to be unified for logical flow. Revise your topic sentences as needed to reflect this unity.

   A one-sentence paragraph can be used for emphasis or for a transition between major points, but not often. It should be rare enough to be deliberately eye-catching. For more on this, see ONE-SENTENCE PARAGRAPHS. For related writing problems, see PARAGRAPHS and SENTENCE LENGTH.

PARAGRAPHS

In legal writing, each paragraph should focus on only one point or logical conclusion, and each should also have a topic sentence that states that point, usually at the beginning of the paragraph. In other disciplines, such as literary criticism, this more obvious form of logical organization is often disfavored. Obvious organization, however, is rarely criticized in legal writing. Instead, your reader will be grateful to you for making it easy to see the main point each paragraph advances or supports.

For example, in the following paragraphs, the points are much clearer when two paragraphs are used, one for each point made, and when each point is stated in a topic sentence at the first of the paragraph.

> **To complain about the illegality of a search, the defendant must, as the State correctly asserts, have an expectation of privacy in the place searched. United States v. Park, 990 U.S. 314, 316 (2024). The State implies that solely because the defendant's office, desk, and files were within a public building, he knowingly exposed them to the public. This is incorrect. The uncontroverted testimony in this case established that the defendant did expect his office, desk, and files to be private because he exercised exclusive use and control over those areas and in things present in those areas. (R. 207–209).**
>
> **This expectation of privacy, however, must be justified under the law. In this case, the defendant was justified in expecting privacy in his private office. There was no free public access to these areas. The sole fact that a private office is located in a public building does not satisfy the "plain view" doctrine as restated in United States v. Peabody, 999 U.S. 22, 26 (2025). The trial court in this case thus found that defendant had rights guaranteed by the Fourth Amendment of the United States Constitution and by article I, section 2 of the Constitution of the State of Iowa, and that these rights were violated.**

rather than

> The trial court in this case found that defendant had rights guaranteed by the Fourth Amendment of the United States Constitution and by article I, section 2 of the Constitution of the State of Iowa, which were violated. To complain about the illegality of a search, the defendant must, as the State correctly asserts, have an expectation of privacy in the place searched. United States v. Park, 990 U.S. 314, 316 (2024). The State implies that because the defendant's office, desk, and files were within a

public building, he knowingly exposed them to the public. This is simply not the fact in this case. The uncontroverted testimony indicates the defendant did expect his office, desk, and files to be private and that he exercised exclusive use and control in these areas (R. 207–209). There was no free public access to these areas. The location of a private office in a public building does not satisfy the plain view doctrine as restated in United States v. Peabody, 999 U.S. 22, 26 (2025). Further, the defendant's expectation of privacy in his private office is justified under the law.

For related information, see ONE-SENTENCE PARAGRAPHS, PARAGRAPH LENGTH, and TOPIC SENTENCES.

PARALLEL CITATIONS

See CITATIONS, PARALLEL.

PARALLELISM

See EMPHASIS; LISTS, STRUCTURE OF; and PARALLEL STRUCTURE.

PARALLEL STRUCTURE

Parallel structure means using the same grammatical structure in two or more places. It is best used for things that are logically parallel because it reinforces the meaning. For example, parallel adjectives can describe parallel qualities.

Defendant was hostile, abusive, and violent.

rather than

Defendant was hostile, abused the officer, and had violent behavior.

Parallel prepositional phrases can also describe parallel qualities.

Plaintiff admits he was driving without his license, without his lights on, and with an open six-pack of beer in the front seat.

Parallel structure creates a grammatically transparent framework that allows substantive points to shine through in clear relation to each other. This structure is useful in legal writing because it simplifies syntax and focuses on substance. Therefore, four common places to use parallel structure are

(1) in lists,

(2) in comparisons or contrasts of cases,

(3) in persuasive writing to add emphasis, and

(4) in headings to remind the reader of the larger organization.

1. Use parallel structure in lists.

> **The plaintiff parked his car, turned the wheels toward the curb, and set the handbrake.**

and

> **This point was established in the testimony of the defendant, of the police officer investigating the accident, and of a passerby who observed the accident.**

Parallel structure is useful for emphasizing the logical parallels between the items in a list, such as in the following list of facts. See EMPHASIS.

> **The trial court found that Cox Realty displayed the Realax logo at its office, signs, and forms; that Cox's employees each wear a blue blazer with the Realax logo on it; and that Cox Realty benefits from nationwide advertising identifying Realax franchises as "local professionals."**

2. Use parallel structure to compare or contrast cases.

One place where parallel structure is particularly desirable is in the analogy of two similar cases, as shown by the following example taken from the middle of a paragraph. (Citations are omitted.)

> **In <u>Rickaby</u>, the plaintiff's reputation in the community was not impaired even though the employer disclosed his reasons for discharging the employee in a judicial proceeding. Similarly, in this case Elmore's reputation in the community has not been impaired merely because the employer disclosed her reasons for discharging Elmore in conferences with union officials.**

As this example shows, using accurate transitions, such as *similarly*, can also enhance the point of the parallel.

Parallel structure can also underscore a contrast. By making similarities obvious, parallel structure allows the differences to stand out.

> **In <u>Rickaby</u>, plaintiff's reputation in the community was not impaired even though the employer disclosed his reasons for discharging the employee in a judicial proceeding. In contrast, Elmore's reputation was impaired because his employer not only disclosed her**

> **reasons for discharging Elmore in conferences with union officials but also disclosed those reasons at an office party and in a reference letter written to Elmore's prospective employers.**

For more information on this technique, see COMPARISON.

3. Use parallel structure to add emphasis.

   In the following example, two points support the implied point that the defendant deserves no sympathy. The parallel structure of *failed to schedule*, *failed to have*, and *failed to warn* thus reflects the logical parallels of the content and also allows the writer to use repetition to emphasize a point.

   > **The defendant company failed to schedule routine maintenance for the press, failed to have a technician check the press when operators complained of its malfunction, and failed to warn the plaintiff about those malfunctions.**

   For related information, see REPETITION, subsections 2–4.

4. Use parallel structure to add clarity to headings in larger documents.

   > **The District Court Clearly Erred When It Determined That Wilma Had PTSD.**
   >
   > and
   >
   > **The District Court Clearly Erred When It Concluded That Ansdell's Supervisor Allowed Co-Workers To Make Discriminatory Comments.**

   Avoid overdoing the repetition needed for parallel structure, however; use just enough to signal the larger structure.

PARAPHRASE

Paraphrasing is restating someone else's ideas in your own words. Paraphrasing is legitimate if you give credit when you have used a specific source and if you avoid misstating the original point. Paraphrasing is more useful than quoting when the original language is hard to understand, is lengthy, or incorporates irrelevant information that could confuse your reader.

> **The court stated that it must intervene in this case to resolve the issue of mutuality despite the emotional pleas for freedom of contract.**

changed from the original

> Despite the defendant's emotional plea regarding the centrality of upholding contracts to the free working of a democracy, we cannot ignore the plaintiff's complaint. In this case, the court must intervene; the issue of mutuality, not to mention that of duress, requires that the court examine both the contract's wording and the parol evidence surrounding the signing of that contract.

In this example, the full quotation would be too long and would include too many distractions, and an edited quotation would need so many deletions and changes that it would make the reader question its accuracy.

As a general rule, quote only when the exact language is needed, as when discussing the interpretation of a phrase in a statute, or when you could not say it better yourself, as with an apt and relevant phrase in an opinion.

In writing memos or briefs, it is sometimes permissible to quote a rule that is worded the same way in multiple cases without quotation marks, but be sure to use a pinpoint citation. Often this is true for short phrases that are TERMS OF ART. Occasionally, however, it may apply to a complete sentence. You will be able to identify these phrases when you discover that many sources use exactly the same phrase.

> **Use of a criminal defendant's silence for impeachment purposes violates the defendant's due process rights. Boyle v. Kentucky, 999 U.S. 810, 817 (2025).**

For more information, see QUOTATIONS, WHEN TO USE. For related information, see CITATIONS, PINPOINT. For related general information, see BRIEFS and MEMOS.

PARENTHESES

Use parentheses in legal writing only in the situations listed below. If the matter is important enough to be in the text, it should be stated outside the shadow of parentheses. Additionally, avoid overuse of parentheses because it can create the impression that the writer is disorganized. For related information, see PARENTHETICALS.

1. When to use parentheses.

   (a) Use parentheses to enclose information useful to the reader if that information is not an integral part of the text itself. For example, use parentheses to refer to the transcript.

   > **The defendant testified that he had never seen the plaintiff (Tr. 349).**
   >
   > **The defendant testified that he had never seen the plaintiff (See Appendix A).**

(b) Use parentheses to introduce abbreviations. For example, if one of the parties in your brief is *Leitner Systems, Inc.*, and you want to use *LSI* in the text, write out the complete name the first time you use it and then put the abbreviation in parentheses afterwards.

Leitner Systems, Inc. (LSI).

Do not state *hereinafter referred to as* before the abbreviation. See LEGALESE.

The best practice is to use the term most familiar to the reader in text and place the less familiar information within the parentheses.

Previously he was employed by OSHA (Occupational Safety and Health Administration).

(c) Use parentheses in drafting contracts to enclose NUMERALS repeating a number spelled out.

For the sum of five hundred dollars ($500). . . .

(d) You may use parentheses instead of commas to enclose examples when the examples are necessary but do not require a separate definition. See UNOBTRUSIVE DEFINITIONS.

Crimes against property (such as trespass and encroachment) are usually considered less serious than crimes against persons.

(e) Use parentheses to enclose numbers or letters inserted in text to mark units of a list. For examples and specific details, see LISTS, STRUCTURE OF, subsection 7.

2. How to punctuate within and around parentheses.

If they are written inside another sentence (*this is an example of a parenthetical sentence inside another sentence*), parenthetical sentences do not begin with capital letters or end with periods; but when other punctuation marks are appropriate, they are used (*do you understand this rule?*). If they are written outside other sentences, parenthetical sentences begin with capital letters and end with periods inside the parentheses.

Defendant's car was parked in the north lot. (The lots have since been reassigned numbers and this is now lot #3.)

3. When to avoid using parentheses.

Avoid using parentheses to insert a long phrase within another sentence, because doing so interrupts your line of reasoning. It is also informal. Instead, restructure the text so that each thought stands on its own and connects logically in the sequence of sentences. For related information, see INTRUSIVE PHRASES.

PARENTHETICALS

Parentheticals appear in specific places in legal writing to give the reader information about authority. Proper use of parentheticals saves time and text. Improper use or overuse of parentheticals disrupts the flow of the text and irritates most readers. Parentheticals were invented to supplement citations in scholarly footnotes, not to abbreviate legal analyses or argumentation. Keep that original purpose in mind as you use parentheticals. When you use them, check your citation manual for guidelines. The most helpful uses of parentheticals include the following.

1. Use parentheticals in statute citations to convey the following information.

   (a) Use them to show the code location of statutes cited to session laws or secondary sources.

   > **Popular Names Act of 2004, Pub. L. No. 102–113, 999 Stat. 111 (codified at 99 U.S.C. §§ 2222 to 2232).**

   (b) Use them to give the unofficial section when an unofficial code is numbered differently from an official code and when the section does not yet appear in the official code.

   > **Mich. Comp. Laws 999.09 (2025) (Mich. Stat. Ann. § 111.01 (Callaghan 2025)).**

   (c) Use them to identify useful dates, such as the effective date of a statute.

   > **Alaska Stat. § 99.09.090 (2025) (effective July 1, 2025).**

   (d) Use them to indicate the repeal, amendment, or prior history of a statute.

   > **99 U.S.C. § 999(b) (2020) (repealed 2025).**

   (e) Use them to give any other relevant information about a statute.

   > **99 U.S.C. § 999(b) (requiring IRS agents to give proper notice of auditing procedures to those being audited).**

2. Use parentheticals in case citations to convey the following information.

   (a) Use them to indicate the weight of the authority, such as memorandum decisions, opinions written by notable judges, or language that is not the single, clear, holding of a majority of the court.

California v. Blunt, 999 U.S. 99, 140 (2025) (5–4 decision) (Sharma dissenting).

(b) Use explanatory parentheticals to provide any information about the case that may be helpful to the reader. This use predominates in scholarly footnotes; in emails, memos, and briefs, place the information in a sentence that precedes the citation, thus omitting the need for a parenthetical.

Arnold v. Butters, 999 F. Supp. 3d 111, 128 (W.D. Wis. 2025) (holding that moral right is not a cause of action for an artist whose painting was separated into four pieces).

3. Use multiple parentheticals in a citation to provide all needed information about that authority. For example, the following case citation includes a weight of authority parenthetical and an explanatory parenthetical. Consult your citation manual for rules about all types of parentheticals and their preferred order.

California v. Blunt, 999 U.S. 99, 130 (2025) (per curiam) (holding that an "indicium of reliability" is necessary for an informer's information to support a search warrant).

PARTICIPLES

See VERBS, PARTICIPLES.

PARTS OF A SENTENCE

See SENTENCE, PARTS OF.

PARTS OF SPEECH

Parts of speech is the grammatical term that summarizes the eight categories into which all English words are divided: NOUNS, VERBS, ADJECTIVES, ADVERBS, PREPOSITIONS, PRONOUNS, CONJUNCTIONS, and INTERJECTIONS.

PARTY

Use *party* when needed for precision, but avoid using it unless it is really needed. Overuse of *party* is one example of LEGALESE.

PASSIVE OR ACTIVE VOICE?

See PASSIVE VOICE and VOICE, ACTIVE OR PASSIVE?

PASSIVE VERBS

See PASSIVE VOICE.

PASSIVE VOICE

Use active voice rather than passive in both objective and persuasive writing to promote clarity and precision. In passive voice, the subject receives the action; in active voice, the subject does the action. And remember that not all uses of the verb *to be* are passive. For help identifying what is and is not passive voice, see VERBS, LINKING and VOICE, ACTIVE OR PASSIVE?

Use passive voice strategically but avoid using it habitually. The following subsections explain how passive voice creates problems and when use of passive voice is warranted.

1. Difficulty caused by using passive voice.

Passive voice makes the reader stop at the end of the sentence and think back through the sentence to sort out who did what. This mental act happens quickly, but nevertheless slows down the reading process and, over time, tires the reader. This happens because the subject of the sentence receives the action, rather than causing the action. In contrast, active voice keeps the reader moving forward and clarifies both the subject and the action.

The plaintiff was hit by the defendant. [passive voice]

but

The defendant hit the plaintiff. [active voice]

A decision was made by the court. [passive voice]

but

The court made a decision. [active voice]

or

The court decided. [active voice]

Passive verbs also sometimes further reduce clarity when they leave the actor out of the picture.

The plaintiff was hit.

A decision was made.

This use of passive voice often creates ambiguity. For example, the following regulation would be inadequate if it did not specify who has the responsibility for the clean-up.

> **Any manufacturer who generates toxic waste must dispose of that waste by one of the following means.**
>
> rather than
>
> Toxic waste must be disposed of by one of the following means.

2. Uses of passive voice.

Passive voice is useful in four specific situations. In legal writing, use it consciously and for these reasons only; otherwise eliminate it.

(a) Use passive voice to deemphasize unfavorable facts or law. For example, the attorney for the defense might want to write the following.

> **The plaintiff was assaulted by the defendant.**

The attorney for the prosecution, however, might write the following.

> **The defendant assaulted the plaintiff.**

(b) Use passive voice to hide the identity of the actor.

> **A decision was made to cut your salary.**
>
> rather than
>
> We have decided to cut your salary.

Here passive voice avoids telling who made the decision.

(c) Use passive voice when the subject is very long. In this situation, using passive voice creates a more readable sentence because the active voice would put the subject and verb so far apart that the sentence would be too hard to read.

> **This action is required by statutory law, by the common law principle of due care, and by a general sense of justice.**
>
> rather than
>
> Statutory law, the common law principle of due care, and a general sense of justice require this action.

(d) Finally, use passive voice when the subject is much less important than the object.

> **Freedom of speech cannot be encumbered by concerns of propriety.**

rather than

Concerns of propriety cannot encumber freedom of speech.

For related information, see ACTIVE VOICE and CONCISENESS, subsection 6.

PAST PARTICIPLES

Past participles are the *-ed* form of regular verbs, such as *decided, moved, assaulted.* Irregular verbs form past participles differently, such as *held, gone,* and *been.* See VERBS, IRREGULAR and VERBS, PARTICIPLES.

PAST PERFECT TENSE

See VERBS, TENSES.

PAST PROGRESSIVE TENSE

See VERBS, TENSES.

PAST TENSE

See VERBS, TENSES.

PATTERNS

Patterns appear in writing as repeated use of favorite phrases, syntaxes, words, or structures. These patterns are the evidence of the writer's habitual writing choices, and they combine to form a significant portion of a writer's style. As you refine and develop your legal writing style, develop patterns that do not sacrifice readability. Instead, develop healthy patterns that enhance readability while expressing your own professional personality.

1. Patterns that enhance readability.

As you read writing that you admire, note the patterns used by other writers that make the text more readable. Then, as you write, be aware of your own patterns, keeping those that promote readability and avoiding those that do not. The following patterns, for example, can increase your readability.

Use this readable pattern	to replace this pattern.
Subjects and verbs close to each other	Subjects and verbs separated by long phrases
Parallel structure	Lack of parallel structure
Substantive topic sentences	Vague or no topic sentences
Clear transitions	Inaccurate transitions or no transitions
Precise terms of art	Vague language
Focused, concise quotations or paraphrase	Large blocks of quoted material
Active voice	Passive voice
Active verbs	Linking verbs with nominalizations
Important content within the main text	Important content in footnotes or parentheticals

For related information, see PRINCIPLES OF GOOD LEGAL WRITING, READABILITY, and TRANSITIONS.

2. Patterns in personal professional style.

To develop a personal legal writing style, also note the patterns and variations used by other writers whose writing you admire. Just as music is pleasant to hear because of the interplay of predictability and variation, writing is pleasant to read when it employs a similar interplay of routine and variety. As you write, use some variations in your routine, readable patterns to enhance an important point and to enrich your professional style. The more conscious you are of the patterns, the more versatile you will be in using them to move your reader.

Some variations you can incorporate into your personal style include the following:

- variation in sentence length, using occasional short sentences for EMPHASIS;
- occasional sentences with INTRUSIVE PHRASES to emphasize the content in the interruption;
- occasional sentence with long introductory phrase and short main clause to create some suspense and emphasize the short concluding phrase;
- REPETITION of key word or unusual vocabulary to emphasize that term;

- ALLITERATION or ASSONANCE to create a staccato or flowing sound;
- IMAGERY or metaphor to make a concept more memorable;
- slightly more formal or informal vocabulary to add emotional punch to a concept;
- rhythm to create a particular mood or pace to the text; and
- short quotations to emphasize and reinforce a point.

For related information, see CHOICES IN LEGAL WRITING, PERSUASION, STYLE, and TONE.

PEOPLE OR *PERSONS*?

Use *people* to refer a group of individuals collectively. Use *persons* when referring to a small and specific number.

All people of this country have constitutional rights.

but

Defendant has assaulted nine persons in the last month.

PER

Per means *for each* and is useful when talking about ratios.

The defendant company promised different rates of pay to different sales personnel, ranging from the $5 per call paid to secretaries who worked in the company headquarters, to $1 per call paid to employees who made the calls from their homes.

Per should not be used in other contexts because it often creates a stilted TONE.

Regarding our previous request for payment, ...

rather than

As per our previous request, ...

PERCENT, *%*, OR *PER CENT*?

Percent means *out of one hundred parts of the whole.* When using words, spell out *percent.*

Within our office, forty percent of the lawyers prefer using traditional electronic research tools, while the rest rely on both AI and traditional electronic search engines.

When using numerals rather than words, use the percent sign, with no space between the numeral and the sign.

> **Our statistics show that 56% of our clients report being completely satisfied with our firm's efforts, while 38% are generally satisfied.**

The rarer version, *per cent,* is not considered correct in some manuals, so your safer choice is to avoid this form. If you use it, be aware that *per cent* means either *in a hundred items* or *of a hundred items.* These two meanings differ substantially, so make sure the correct meaning is clear in context. For example, use the following sentence.

> **In the past year, sixty per cent of our clients have been female.**
>
> rather than
>
> In the past year, our clients have been sixty per cent female.

The latter version could be read as clients being partially, but not completely, female. For related information, see NUMERALS.

PERFECTIONISM

Perfectionism can be the enemy of creative thought. Relegate your perfectionism to REWRITING, REVISING, and POLISHING in the WRITING PROCESS. In PREWRITING, contain your perfectionist tendencies by balancing time constraints against scholarship and by concentrating on substantive ideas rather than the methodology of note taking, outlining, and other prewriting tasks.

When researching, focus first on getting the relevant law in your governing jurisdiction. Avoid spending lots of time looking for the perfect precedent from some other jurisdiction. For more on this, see MANDATORY AUTHORITY and PERSUASIVE AUTHORITY.

When WRITING, do not allow your perfectionist editing voice to restrict your creative writing voice. Try not to perfect each sentence as you go, but rather try to write the entire paper without revising. This will allow your ideas to flow as you focus on content, not form. Then go back to perfect your paper in the later stages, when you can let your perfectionism work within your time constraints.

For further help, see WHEN TO STOP. For a discussion of related problems, see DEADLINES, MEETING THEM; GETTING STARTED; GRACE UNDER FIRE; HABITS, WRITING; MULTI-TASKING; NOTES; PROCRASTINATION; TIME MANAGEMENT; and WRITING BLOCK.

PERFECT TENSES

See VERBS, TENSES.

PERIOD OR QUESTION MARK?

See QUESTION MARKS.

PERIODS

Periods have four common uses in legal writing, and some places where they should not be used.

1. Periods ending sentences.

   Use a period after full sentences in text. If your sentences routinely run for more than four lines of text, use more periods. See SENTENCE LENGTH and READABILITY. Use a period when a heading is a complete sentence unless your reader requires otherwise.

   Witness A testified that the police did not fire first.

   and

   THE TRIAL COURT ABUSED ITS DISCRETION WHEN IT AWARDED CUSTODY TO AN ALCOHOLIC MOTHER.

2. Periods ending abbreviations.

   When an abbreviation comes at the end of a sentence, use just one period.

   The meeting is scheduled for 9:00 p.m.

3. Periods in parentheticals.

   If they are written inside another sentence (*this is an example of a parenthetical sentence inside another sentence*), parenthetical sentences do not begin with capital letters or end with periods; but when other punctuation marks are appropriate (*do you understand this rule?*), they are used. If they are written outside other sentences, parenthetical sentences begin with capital letters and end with periods inside the parentheses.

   Defendant's car was parked facing north. (R.P. 31.)

   or

   Defendant's car was parked facing north (R.P. 31).

4. Periods with quotation marks.

   In the United States, a period goes inside quotation marks, even if the period is not part of the quotation.

The term on which we must focus is "intent."

This rule is the same for both double quotation marks ("—") and single ones ('—'). The rule is not meant to reflect logical concerns, but rather historic ones. In early U.S. presses, the periods and commas kept breaking off. Statutory drafting is one exception to this rule, where periods are treated like all other punctuation marks. For more, see LEGISLATION, subsection 9.

5. Places where periods are not needed.

You may use periods after headings and titles or after letters used as generic replacements for names, though that use is disappearing.

Section 6

Brand X

Title IX Claims

Do not add a second period to end a sentence when the sentence ends with a period used for another purpose.

Ms. Cho stated at that point, "I want an attorney."

PERSONALITY IN LEGAL WRITING

Personality can come through in any kind of legal writing. It is the human voice behind the analysis, settlement, brief, or email exchange. It can carry concern, respect, appreciation, humor, or dignity. Most important, it may be what helps your reader remember what you are writing.

The key to incorporating your individual writing personality in your professional writing is balancing that personality with the reader's practical needs and the requirements of the specific legal task. If your preferred way of explaining the content gets in the way of the reader's understanding, then you need to modify the writing to accommodate the reader's needs. In contrast, your way of explaining the problem, perhaps through IMAGERY or GRAPHICS, may help the reader understand the content. In that situation, your personality works as a professional asset. Therefore allow your professional writing personality to emerge when it can serve the reader and the writing task. But do be careful of allowing your personality free reign, such as when you write in haste. For example, in electronic media, where a pressured or frustrated tone may come through too easily, you may write something you regret later.

Generally, legal readers are less interested in your specific personality than in your reliability, sincerity, and earnestness. Legal writing is functional writing, which means that your readers are interested in a practical result, not in your opinion of the situation. Clients, however, are often interested in the way in which they sense that you are taking care of them and the situation. So develop your personality through a careful, conscious use of writing techniques that resonate with you and work for your readers. For ways to do this, see CHOICES IN LEGAL WRITING; COMMUNICATIONS, TONE OF; INDEPENDENCE IN LEGAL WRITING; PROFESSIONAL LANGUAGE AND PRESENTATION; STYLE; and VOICE.

PERSONAL REFERENCES

Personal references are appropriate in legal writing only if the reader and writer are familiar with each other and if appropriate given the document's purpose. Avoid them otherwise; they impair both credibility and meaning.

> **Although the plaintiff argues that there is a dispute as to the material facts, the affidavits show otherwise.**
>
> or
>
> **The affidavits show there is no dispute as to the material facts.**
>
> rather than
>
> Attorney Cromwell on page sixteen of his brief argues incorrectly again that there is a dispute as to material facts.

For related information, see COMMUNICATIONS, TONE OF; *I*; and TONE.

PERSON: FIRST, SECOND, OR THIRD?

First person is *I* or *we*, second person is *you*, and third person is *he*, *she*, *it*, or *they*. Because person identifies the reader and writer, your relationship to the READERS determines which to use. In any given piece of legal writing, choose one person and use it consistently throughout.

1. First person.

   Use first person singular, *I*, when giving a personal opinion. Use first person plural, *we*, when including the reader in the scope of the discussion or when representing the collective opinion of several specific people, as in a letter that speaks for a law office.

   > **I suggest we try to settle this out of court.**
   >
   > or
   >
   > **We can argue that this issue is moot, but the defense will likely appeal.**

Avoid the editorial or royal *we* because it can be ambiguous. Instead, use *I* or avoid referring to any persons.

> **I understand your dilemma.**
>
> rather than
>
> We recognize your dilemma.
>
> and
>
> **The second element of first degree murder is intent.**
>
> rather than
>
> We must next consider the second element of first degree murder.

For an explanation of the particular dangers of using the first person plural incorrectly, see *WE*.

2. Second person.

Use the second person, *you*, to address the reader directly, when appropriate. For example, an email may include *you* because it may require a more personal TONE.

> **You asked that I write to you about the legal consequences of your accident.**

Avoid using second person when addressing a court.

> **Granting this motion is appropriate for three reasons.**
>
> rather than
>
> You ought to grant this motion for three reasons.

3. Third person.

Use third person most often in BRIEFS, MEMOS, MOTIONS, and most formal legal documents. Identify parties in the third person, your clients as well as their opponents.

> **Defendant pled not guilty; he denies all charges.**
>
> and
>
> **The law favors the plaintiffs in this class action, so they will likely move for a summary judgment.**

PERSONS OR *PEOPLE*?

See *PEOPLE* OR *PERSONS*?

PERSUASIVE AUTHORITY

Persuasive authority is a primary source of law from another jurisdiction. It is not mandatory authority because it is not a primary source of law from the jurisdiction in which the case is being adjudicated. For example, a case decided by the Arizona state supreme court might be persuasive to a New Mexico judge deciding a similar issue, but it is not mandatory that the judge follow the Arizona case. Persuasive authority should not be quoted, stated, or analyzed as part of the law on which the decision maker bases an opinion, but it can be used to advise the decision maker about how to proceed.

Use persuasive authority when the mandatory authority in a jurisdiction is incomplete or in some way inadequate to address the issue. For example, you might use persuasive authority when a newly enacted statute has no cases construing it, but another jurisdiction's court has construed a similar statute. Although this authority is not binding on the current decision maker, it can be persuasive when other lawmakers have addressed the issue in similar circumstances.

The value of persuasive authority varies depending on its origin. For example, many states look to New York and California on issues of intellectual property because these states house most U.S. entertainers and therefore have developed more law on this topic. But many states ignore those jurisdictions on local issues, such as tort law, education, or property. Those local issues are more dependent on local demographics, so a state is likely to turn to a neighboring state: Wisconsin might look to Minnesota or Iowa law, and West Virginia might look to Ohio or Kentucky law. The same is true at the federal level. Federal district and circuit courts are not binding on each other. They will look for persuasive authority in distant jurisdictions for some issues, nearby jurisdictions for others. To discover persuasive authority favored by your decision maker, you might note the jurisdictions used in the authority you find during your research to know what sources of persuasive authority have been cited most frequently in your jurisdiction.

PERSUASIVE CORRESPONDENCE

See COMMUNICATIONS, PERSUASIVE; and WRITING, PERSUASIVE.

PERSUASIVE WRITING

See WRITING, PERSUASIVE.

PHENOMENA OR *PHENOMENONS*?

Most dictionaries list either as the acceptable plural of phenomenon, but *phenomena* is preferred.

PHRASES

A phrase is a group of words working together, such as prepositional phrases, *in this case*; noun phrases, *the experienced supervising attorney*; and verb phrases, *had been reviewing*. In contrast, a clause is a phrase that includes both a subject and verb.

subject verb

The supervising attorney had been reviewing the case.

For an explanation of the use of phrases, see SENTENCE STRUCTURE and SENTENCE, PARTS OF, subsections 6 and 7. For related information, see CLAUSES.

PIE CHARTS

See GRAPHICS, WHICH FORM TO USE, subsection 1.

PINPOINT CITATIONS

See CITATIONS, PINPOINT.

PLAGIARISM

Using someone else's phrases, sentences, paragraphs, or point headings while claiming that it is your own writing is plagiarism. In legal writing, this is unacceptable. If you use generative artificial intelligence (AI), you may be required to reveal when and where you used it in your research and writing process. To avoid plagiarism, you must verify both the accuracy and source of any statements that are not yours, whether from AI or any other source.

To maintain accuracy in your documents, cite every source specifically each time you use it, including a pinpoint citation to the particular page where the cited language appears. It is permissible to paraphrase someone else's words, that is, to put their ideas into your own words, but only when you specifically acknowledge the source of that idea. Thus you may paraphrase and then cite to the authority for any holding, proposition, rule, quotation, or point of law. You may also quote passages from law review articles verbatim, but they must be marked as quotations and cited.

For related information, see ARTIFICIAL INTELLIGENCE AND RESEARCH; ARTIFICIAL INTELLIGENCE AND WRITING;

CITATIONS, PINPOINT; PARAPHRASE; PROMPTS; QUOTATIONS, HOW TO PUNCTUATE; and QUOTATIONS, WHEN TO USE.

PLAIN ENGLISH

The term *plain English* became popular in the 1970s, and it remains a useful concept for lawyers to remember and embrace. In legal writing, plain English is English that is simple, clear, and readable. Many states require plain English in any consumer document, and some offices have style guides requiring plain English. Check your jurisdiction for its specific laws on plain English, but in general free your writing of jargon, legalese, and any undefined terms that will send a reader scurrying to a dictionary. For ways to revise for plain English, see READABILITY, subsections 3 and 4. See also ELEGANT VARIATION, PLAIN MEANING, SIMPLICITY, and UNOBTRUSIVE DEFINITIONS.

PLAIN MEANING

Plain meaning is a method of construing statutes that interprets each term by its dictionary meaning. This is a literal interpretation and is often the point of departure for interpreting a statute. For example, when a court is interpreting a statute for the very first time and there is little or no legislative history, the court may resort to the dictionary meaning of each word in the statute to apply the statute to the facts before the court. Therefore, as it relates to legal writing, plain meaning becomes important in drafting legislation and government documents. It also is often important in consumer contracts, which may be required by law to be written in plain English. Be sure that each term you use in drafting stands up under the dictionary's scrutiny. See LEGISLATION and CONTRACTS.

PLEADINGS

Legal pleadings, which ask the court to take an action, come in various forms and serve varied purposes. Common pleadings include complaints, answers, and cross complaints. For example, a complaint may start the litigation process, frame a dispute, encourage the opponent to negotiate, stop the running of the relevant statute of limitations, or perform a combination of these purposes. An answer may help the parties see what facts are at issue, what facts are not debated by either party, and what strategy the other party is developing. A cross-complaint may introduce a new party to the action or put the original plaintiff on the defensive.

Whatever purpose your pleading serves, following these steps will help you produce an effective document.

When PREWRITING, do each of the following.

1. Record deadlines on your calendar and schedule enough time to consider thoroughly the substance and strategy of the case. For more on this, see TIME MANAGEMENT.
2. Clarify your goals and strategy early in the writing process, so you include all needed information in your pleading while omitting unnecessary details. Determine whether you want to include only the information necessary for the pleading's success or include more information to communicate the strength of your case to encourage settlement.
3. Research your facts and law thoroughly to avoid costly errors. Allocate enough time for this because you need to think through the case to the appeal level before you draft the pleadings. For more on this, see RESEARCH STRATEGY GUIDE, STANDARD OF REVIEW, and THEORY OF THE CASE.

Be sure to consider the following at some time during your writing process, although it may be in prewriting, writing, or rewriting. See WRITING PROCESS.

4. Include enough information to withstand adverse motions.
5. Include all information needed, so that no likely arguments are waived.

When REWRITING, check that you have done the following.

6. Make only one point per paragraph.
7. Organize inductively, so that paragraphs asserting the evidence to support an element precede the paragraph stating that the element has been established. For examples, see COMPLAINTS and ANSWERS.

When REVISING, check the following.

8. Word each paragraph specifically enough to withstand adverse motions, yet generally enough to maintain some flexibility later in the legal process.
9. Make sure all assertions are free of ambiguity so that they forestall unclear answers.

When POLISHING, do the following.

10. Check caption, signatures, and all other parts to make sure all court-required forms and conventions are followed.
11. Check all dates, numbers, names, addresses, and other particulars accurate.
12. Check spelling, punctuation, and other grammatical and mechanical concerns.

PLEAD, *PLEADED*, OR *PLED*?

Plead is the present tense of the verb, *pled* is the past tense. Use accordingly.

She wants to plead guilty, but she is afraid of the consequences.

and

He pled not guilty last week but wants to change his plea this week.

Although *pleaded* is also a correct past tense form of *plead* and is used more often in everyday speech, *pled* is more commonly used when referring to the legal action.

PLURALS OF NAMES

When making a name plural, add an *s*.

There are three Marys in the firm.

When writing initials that are commonly written in all capital letters, add a lower case *s*.

Many NGOs use this approach.

When the name ends in *s*, add *es*.

The Joneses are tenants in common.

Resist any urge to create any other variation by analogy from other common nouns.

The Zimmermans have both reviewed the will.

The Olympuses are joint tenants.

The Chanticleers all have equal shares in their company.

The wording of the will is ambiguous because the family includes two Jameses.

rather than

The Zimmermen have both reviewed the will.

The Olympi are joint tenants.

The Chanticleer all have equal shares in their company.

The wording of the will is ambiguous because the family includes two James's.

P.M.

It is written *p.m.* and in business writing is used only after a number, as in *7:15 p.m.* When it appears at the end of a sentence, only one period is used, as in the previous sentence.

POINT HEADINGS

Point headings, also known as argument headings, are conventions in argumentative writing designed both to tell the audience the legal point made in a section of the Argument and to outline the reasons supporting that legal point. Point headings also appear in the tables of contents of appellate briefs. The point headings, when read together, should give the reader an outline of the writer's argument.

1. Content and format for point headings.

Main point headings correspond to the Issues. They provide the answer to the legal question asked in each Issue, and so there should be a point heading for every Issue. Compose your main point headings as complete sentences. Use capital letters, single space, and use a roman numeral. Include the legal point and the reason if there are no subheadings or multiple reasons; include only the legal point if subheadings will indicate the reasons.

I. THE TRIAL COURT ABUSED ITS DISCRETION WHEN IT AWARDED CUSTODY TO AN ALCOHOLIC MOTHER.

or

I. MR. SMITH HAS NO RELEVANT EXPERIENCE THAT QUALIFIES HIM TO RENDER AN EXPERT OPINION IN THIS CASE.

Include enough legally significant facts to make your Argument specific to this case but avoid cluttering the point heading with so many facts that it becomes too long. For related information, see ISSUES and LEGALLY SIGNIFICANT FACTS.

Subheadings are used to give more specific reasons for the main legal point. Usually a paragraph or two of summarizing text follows a main heading, and then the first subheading follows that text. Subheadings are also written as complete sentences. In subheadings, you may indent and capitalize the first letter of each main word; add underlining or bold face if it is customary in your jurisdiction. Or you may use some other graphic device that distinguishes it from major headings, sub-subheadings, and the rest of the text.

A. Mrs. Davis' History of Alcohol Abuse Demonstrates She Cannot Act in the Best Interests of the Children.

Sub-subheadings give particulars of the Argument under the subheading and appear most often in appellate briefs. Use sub-subheadings to highlight important points in your Argument, but limit them to six at the most. Overusing them may make the brief look more like an outline than a cohesive argument. Sub-subheadings are often, but not always, complete sentences. Always check your court rules and compose all headings to conform to those rules.

Indent the sub-subheading and capitalize only the first word. Precede it with an Arabic numeral.

1. Mrs. Davis has been arrested repeatedly for drunken driving.

2. Techniques for writing point headings.

(a) Make one legal point in each heading.

(b) Use a strong, accurate connecting word, such as *because*. See TRANSITIONS.

(c) Include a summary of the reason for the main legal point.

I. The Beach Renourishment Project Is Not Exempt Because It is No Longer Emergency Work Under 44 C.F.R. § 306.22(c).

(d) Use persuasive writing, concentrating on strong SUBJECT-VERB COMBINATIONS and eliminating unneeded modifiers. For more detail, see WRITING, PERSUASIVE, subsection 4(a).

(e) Make the point heading no longer than three single-spaced lines, if possible.

(f) Use parallel structure in all main headings and in all subheadings.

For related information, see HEADINGS.

POINT OF VIEW, OBJECTIVE TO PERSUASIVE

Point of view in legal writing travels along the spectrum from objective to persuasive. The writer's point of view leans toward the objective in memos, opinion letters, communications that give information, and law review articles that synthesize or summarize information. Using a more objective point of view allows the writer to remain detached from the decision while informing the reader of the law and predicting any outcome or change in trends.

The point of view tends toward the persuasive in memoranda of points and authorities, pretrial briefs, trial briefs, appellate briefs, some law review articles, and some email or letters. The purpose of using the persuasive point of view is to persuade the audience to accept the writer's argument.

After you have chosen the appropriate point of view, remain consistent throughout any given piece of writing. For advice on ways to establish these points of view, see BRIEFS; MEMOS; WRITING, OBJECTIVE; and WRITING, PERSUASIVE. For related information, see AUDIENCE and PURPOSE.

POLICY

Policy refers to the goals and reasons behind the law. These goals and reasons are rooted in the values of the general culture, the reasons we have laws in the first place. Policy precedes the law, gives rise to the law, and helps readers to interpret the law. It thus goes beyond a literal reading of the law. Policy may include factors such as social change, economic conditions, or unjust results from a literal interpretation of the law. Policy is often used to help interpret the meaning of the law. For example, if a state introduced laws for uninsured motorists but in the process created a gap in protection against under-insured motorists, attorneys might argue to the court that, as a policy matter, consumers should be protected from all improperly insured motorists and not just a subgroup. Often policy questions arise in Arguments when one party desires that the law be reinterpreted in response to changing social or economic values. For a broader context, see APPLICATION; DISCUSSION SECTION; LEGAL ANALYSIS; and REASONING, PRESENTING IT. For related information, see EQUITY.

POLISHING

Polishing, the last step in the WRITING PROCESS, includes checking for errors rather than making any major changes in your document. For example, when polishing, you will check for citation, grammar, usage, and typographic errors. This process requires a different mindset and attention to detail. As grammar checkers and other artificial intelligence (AI) tools improve, you may find them increasingly useful at this stage.

Always polish your documents. The legal reader is concerned with detail, so failure to polish the presentation can undermine your credibility and can erode the document's meaning.

Develop your own system for polishing, but make sure each aspect gets enough time, especially if you tend to skip it. For example, you might try the following process.

1. Read the document sentence by sentence from front to back, checking for any word usage or grammatical problems.
2. Read each citation from the back to the front of the document for correct citation form.
3. Read just for spelling and errors that a spellchecker will not catch, such as incorrect or missing words. In particular, watch for missing negatives, such as *not*. For related information, see MISSPELLINGS, HOW TO AVOID; and WORDS SPELLCHECKERS MAY NOT CATCH.
4. Check any text that has been cut and pasted for changes in font size, spacing, and other such details.
5. Reread for any problem peculiar to your own writing, such as dangling modifiers, overuse of *however*, or improper use of semicolons.

Develop your own techniques for keeping polishing effective while making it more efficient. The following suggestions may help you with this process.

6. Read with a ruler or a magnifying ruler, or enlarge the view on your screen. This will force you to read every word.
7. Read aloud. You may be able to hear what you cannot see.
8. Read in small out-of-order pieces. This will force you to focus on small bits and not skip over text because you are moving too quickly and supplying the information that is not actually on the page.
9. Create your own way to read carefully so you will concentrate on every word to ensure its correctness.
10. You may also find artificial intelligence tools useful for parts of this process, such as spellcheckers or grammar checkers. But do not abdicate all responsibility to these mechanical tools, which may miss important details. For help here, see POLISHING CHECKLIST.

POLISHING CHECKLIST

As you polish, which is the last step in your WRITING PROCESS, you are removing errors rather than rethinking the choices you have made in earlier stages. This process requires a different mindset and attention to detail. To ensure time for polishing, work backward from the deadline and give yourself a reasonable amount of time to polish smaller details. Depending on the size of the document, you may need four minutes to four hours; be assured it will take longer than you think.

The following list can help you identify the ways you need to check for these errors. You may want to adapt this list to include even smaller steps, which often makes the polishing process more effective and less overwhelming. It also helps you keep track of what you have done when you are interrupted or when you take breaks. Divide longer documents so you can polish individual parts rather than reviewing the whole document at one time. This usually helps you stay alert and be more effective at catching errors.

1. Do all citations conform to the *BLUEBOOK* or other required source for citation form?
   (a) Are CITATIONS complete, accurately ordered, and accurately punctuated?
   (b) Are pinpoint citations used for specific propositions, rules, holdings, quotations? See CITATIONS, PINPOINT.
   (c) Are case names spelled accurately?
   (d) Are page numbers and years accurate?
2. Does the document conform to all required formats, if any exist? Is the format consistent throughout the document? Check especially for changes in font size, spacing, and other such details that can occur when text has been pasted in from other documents or cut and pasted from another part of this document.
3. Are all quotations letter perfect? See QUOTATIONS, HOW TO PUNCTUATE.
4. Are all key details correct?
   (a) Are numbers accurate, including such details as numbers in citations and dollar amounts?
   (b) Are all names spelled properly?
5. Is spelling and word usage correct?
   (a) Are all words flagged by any electronic spellchecker correct?
   (b) Are all names spelled correctly? Is the status of each party stated correctly?
   (c) Are there any wrong words in the text, caused by spelling correctors choosing the wrong word? For help with this, see WORDS SPELLCHECKERS MAY NOT CATCH.
   (d) Are any words omitted? Particularly check for the word *not*.
   (e) Are all words written in all capitals spelled correctly, if your spellchecker does not check these words?
   (f) Is all punctuation and spacing correct? In documents to the court, are all spacing uses correct?

6. Are headings and subheadings correct?
   (a) Are they consistent in format?
   (b) Are they complete enough to communicate the overall points of the document?
7. Are the introduction and conclusion congruent and clear?
   (a) Are they consistent in word choice and tone?
   (b) Do they adequately communicate the main points of the document?
8. Is the overall document structure correctly presented?
   (a) Is the caption accurate in form and content?
   (b) Are page numbers consistent in form?
   (c) Are any footnotes or end notes in proper form and correctly coordinated with the text?
   (d) Are all lists, tables, and similar components consistent in format and grammatical structure?

After you have completed this checklist, check the overall document one last time, perhaps reading aloud, for missed words, incomplete sentences, or any other errors that may have appeared during the final stages of revising and polishing. Over time, refine your checklist to include errors that repeatedly occur in your own writing so that you can strengthen any weaknesses.

POSITIONS OF EMPHASIS

Positions of emphasis are locations in a written text that get more attention than the text in general. They include the beginnings and ends of sentences, paragraphs, sections, and entire works. Use these positions of emphasis to convey major legal points and arguments. All the points you want to emphasize should be in positions of emphasis, with less important or unfavorable information placed in between.

> **The best interests of children are of paramount concern to courts in custody disputes.**
>
> rather than
>
> Most courts consider the best interests of children in custody disputes to be of paramount concern.
>
> and
>
> **Although the trespassers caused much physical damage, their purpose was not to cause mental anguish.**
>
> rather than

The trespassers caused much physical damage, but causing mental anguish was not their purpose.

For related information, see PARAGRAPHS and SUBJECT-VERB COMBINATIONS. For ways to adjust your verbs to be more persuasive, see VERBS, AUXILIARY.

POSSESSIVES

In the law, possessives become important to PRECISION, such as *daughter's half or daughters' half* of an estate, so make sure you follow these rules.

1. When a noun does not end with an *s*, add an apostrophe and an *s* to make the noun possessive; this applies whether the noun is singular or plural.

   John's = belonging to John.

   plaintiff's = belonging to a plaintiff.

   statute's = belonging to a statute, as in *statute's language.*

   someone's = belonging to someone.

   women's = belonging to women.

   children's = belonging to children

2. When a noun ends with an *s*, add an apostrophe without an additional *s* to make it possessive. This also applies whether the noun is singular or plural.

   Jones' = belonging to one Jones.

   Joneses' = belonging to all the Joneses.

   plaintiffs' = belonging to all the plaintiffs.

   witness' = belonging to one witness

3. Add only an *s* to a pronoun to make it possessive.

   its = belonging to it. It's = it is. *Its'* is never correct.

   yours = belonging to you.

   hers = belonging to her.

   For related information, see APOSTROPHES.

4. In general, when a name includes a possessive word, use the same form used by that entity, which may or may not use an apostrophe.

   Harpers Ferry

   Macy's

   Johns Hopkins University

When the entity does not have a preferred form, you have a choice because the *BLUEBOOK*'s referenced style manuals differ on this matter. Our preference is to use the apostrophe alone unless the *'s* would actually be spoken.

the Ganges' source or the Ganges's source

Tacitus' *Histories* or Tacitus's *Histories*

Marx's theories or Marx' theories

5. When working with a compound noun, which is a group of words that work as one modifying unit, add the apostrophe to the last word in the group.

attorney general's opinion

James Olaniyan, Sr.'s acceptance

Trinidad and Tobago's topography

Use separate apostrophes, however, when working with several separate nouns that both modify the same noun.

homeowner's and renter's insurance

Use an apostrophe with an *s* to form the possessive of initials, abbreviations, or symbols.

JFK's writings

2024's campaign

But form the plural of letters, figures, or symbols by adding *s* without an apostrophe whenever this is possible without confusion.

1960s

URLs

***s**

Because legal writing is more formal than most other writing, you will often rephrase these terms when workable to avoid that form.

emcees

asterisks

POWERPOINTS

PowerPoint or a similar software program can be useful for presenting complex information to clients or others. These programs offer a format for using graphics to organize, illustrate, or explain information. Organized for persuasion, the presentations may also serve that purpose. Used ineffectively, they can numb the viewers' minds. As you design your presentation to be successful, balance many factors, including (1) audience and purpose, (2) message, (3) scope of content, and (4) organization.

1. Focus on your audience and purpose.

   You may have a range of viewers, from experts to novices, or you may have a room of experts only. Focus on who will be there and what you want to accomplish. You may want to update them on the law or simplify complex issues. You may want to convince them to hire you or to avoid making a bad decision. Write down the range of people who will view the presentation and why you are designing this series of slides.

   Think, too, about how the presentation will be used. If the purpose is to create talking points to generate discussion, limit your screens to three or fewer points. To prompt active participation, invite the audience to respond within the first ten minutes of the presentation. If you speak for longer than ten minutes, they may become much less likely to respond to your prompts. If the purpose is to show the audience all the information they will take from the presentation, then label the main point at the top of each portion of the more detailed presentation.

2. Decide on your message.

   When you can picture who will be viewing your presentation and why, consider what message you want to convey. Write this down before you begin designing your slides so that you are not distracted by the medium itself. It may be a message to clients, such as *You will have to pay the tax unless you can adjust your holdings before this date*, or *Recent decisions in drug laws require more stringent reporting*, or *You want to use our firm because we have been successful in numerous cases similar to yours*. As you create the slides, you can then connect and unify them to convey this message.

3. Decide on the scope of your content.

   Viewers can absorb only so much. Start with the number of minutes you think will be appropriate to cover this material—from the viewer's perspective. Fifteen to twenty minutes is usually the maximum attention span for this kind of presentation. You may want to start with a number of slides, such as twenty, and adjust the content accordingly. Think about this before you make the first slide so that you do not get caught in a writer-based whirl of demonstrating how much you know. Decide on the appropriate level of detail, the content, and the approach.

4. Make the medium serve your content.

   As you build your presentation, do not allow the medium itself to overtake your message. For example, keep the proportion of the slides congruent with the importance of your points. Avoid distracting your audience with too many special effects. Choose only two or three special techniques so that the eye-catching techniques do not distract from your content.

   Finally, as part of your polishing, check to make sure your format is consistent, including font size, outlining format, use of sentences or phrases, and color choices.

5. Communicate your organization.

   After you follow the directions for using this software program, consider more than one organization. You may want the slides to pose questions and then answer them; give a history and then show the consequences; or give a general overview and then present detail on the significant questions. Fit the presentation to your THEME and PURPOSE, repeatedly reflecting on how each specific slide supports the overall theme. Make sure the slides connect so that the viewer can follow your logic. When the content is in place, you can adjust your graphics to connect ideas, such as using the same color for a subtheme or the same type of graph to compare statistics. For related information, see FORMALITY, LEVEL OF; GRAPHICS, HOW TO USE; GRAPHICS, WHEN TO USE; GRAPHICS, WHICH FORM TO USE; ORAL PRESENTATIONS; and PROFESSIONAL LANGUAGE AND PRESENTATION.

PRECISION

While accuracy means the reader can understand your meaning, precision means your reader must understand it. Law is a matter of controlling actions through words, so controlling meaning—precision—is central. Precision involves taking care in five aspects of writing: (1) planning, (2) word choice, (3) consistency, (4) sentence structure, and (5) presentation.

1. Precision in planning.

   Include only needed content. This will help you control the meaning in your document. Select carefully the materials and reasoning you will use in your document. The temptation is great to include everything you find in your research, every section from all the form contracts you read, every fact that seems sympathetic to your client. But resist. Instead, carve your materials precisely by asking what each piece of content contributes to the document's goal, its message, or with the analysis itself. Use your understanding of varied purposes and readers to decide what is needed. Resist the urge to *throw something in just in case.* Include everything that is needed; nothing more and nothing less.

2. Precision in word choice.

Overly broad legal terms are also a common source of imprecision, so use words that are no broader in meaning than you intend. For example, use *automobile* rather than *motorized vehicle* if you did not mean to include motorcycles. Make sure your topic sentences, headings, issues, and other key sentences are focused precisely. Similarly, focus each part of your Question Presented or Issue.

> **Under Missouri's assault law, which requires a showing of intent, was a child capable of intending assault when the child was only 5 years old and the child's act consisted of pulling a chair out from under a woman as she was sitting down?**
>
> rather than
>
> Under tort law, did an assault occur when a 5-year-old pulled a chair out from under an elderly woman?

In the more precise Issue, the law is focused on assault rather than all of tort law and identifies the relevant jurisdiction. The question, by using *capable of intending,* refers to the specific legal question being asked. The facts include all the information needed to understand both why intent may not be present (the age of the child and the indirectness of the act) and why it may be assault (the fact that the woman was just sitting down when the child pulled out the chair).

Similarly, use appropriate terms of art and avoid vague words in point headings.

> **IN FAILING TO SUPPRESS THE EVIDENCE, THE TRIAL COURT ABUSED ITS DISCRETION BECAUSE THE GUN WAS PRODUCED AS THE RESULT OF AN ILLEGAL SEARCH.**
>
> rather than
>
> THE TRIAL COURT ERRED BECAUSE THE SEARCH WAS IMPROPER.

In general, use concrete and specific words rather than abstract or general ones.

> **The defendant said that he had a gun as he grabbed Ms. Delaney's arm and poked her in the back.**

rather than

The defendant said he was armed as he accosted the victim.

Use the latter version only if you mean to obscure the facts. For related information, see ABSTRACT NOUNS; EMPHASIS; and WRITING, PERSUASIVE.

Also avoid ambiguous wording. While overly broad terms include more meaning than is intended, ambiguous terms include two or more different meanings. For example, avoid using *promised* in a contract when the readers could debate whether this term created a contractual obligation or was a non-contractual statement of existing fact. For related information, see ANTONYMS and SYNONYMS. Finally, check numbers and cross references, where a mistake can be both difficult to see and expensive to miss.

3. Precision through consistency.

When you have identified the precise content and words needed in a document, check your document carefully for their consistent use. This polishing detail, which is desirable in legal writing generally, becomes essential in drafted documents where a misstatement can have substantial ramifications. Whether you are drafting complaints, contracts, or briefs, use TERMS OF ART that unify the document and appear wherever appropriate throughout the document. Particularly if you are using excerpts from past samples, inconsistencies are likely to appear.

4. Precision through sentence structure.

Avoid ambiguous sentence structures. For example, your topic sentences should include a subject and verb that are focused on your main point and subordinate phrases that add the detail relevant to that particular point.

The issue that the appellant raises on this appeal is whether the trial court erred in applying the statute when it summarized its findings in only one sentence.

Trial court erred in applying the statute refers to the error raised on appeal, and the statement *in only one sentence* highlights a legally significant fact in this case. For more help, see SUBJECT-VERB COMBINATIONS and ISSUES.

5. Precision in presentation.

In the midst of making many large decisions, you may forget the small ones. You may use inconsistent formats for headings or fail to conform to local format requirements. These small imprecisions can undercut your credibility as well as your effectiveness. These matters deserve attention. If you are following a form within your jurisdiction, check for conformity as to page length, spacing, and other details. If you are putting dates in the document, doublecheck that the dates are accurate. Use pinpoint citations for any rule, holding, proposition, quotation, or specific reference.

An implied duty exists not to make changes in the work that would render the work a false attribution. Williams v. ABC, 938 F.3d 14, 16 (2d Cir. 2025).

Just as all parts of your presentation should unite to send one overt and consistent message, your precision in presentation sends the more subtle message that you have taken meticulous care in preparing the document.

PREDICATE

See SENTENCE, PARTS OF.

PREFIXES, WHEN TO HYPHENATE

See HYPHENS, *EX-*, and *SELF-* OR *SELF?*

PREPOSITIONAL PHRASES

A prepositional phrase is a group of words that work together to show the relationship of a noun or pronoun to the rest of the sentence. This noun or pronoun is called the object of the preposition. A preposition, which is always the first word in a prepositional phrase, shows how the rest of that phrase is logically related to the sentence. Examples of prepositions are *of*, *to*, *on*, *off*, *between*, *through*, *in*, *at*, *without*, *over*, and *under*. The following examples of prepositional phrases illustrate the variety of information they can convey.

He built the house with his own hands.

All nonresidents living in Illinois for more than three months of a calendar year must complete the following section.

The contract will have been signed by that date.

The settlement among the three parties was reasonable.

For more information and a list of prepositions, see PREPOSITIONS. For potential problems caused by prepositional phrases, see CONCISENESS, subsection 9.

PREPOSITION, ENDING A SENTENCE WITH

Style books allow ending a sentence with a preposition. The rule against it originated in the 18th century, perhaps because of the popularity of Latin at that time. Now the rule is archaic, even in the law. Ending with a preposition may sound too informal for some legal situations, but it is not technically incorrect. So revise the sentence when ending with a preposition creates inappropriate informality or awkward phrasing or when it will distract your AUDIENCE.

The witness was absolutely sure of these facts.

rather than

The witness stated that these were the facts he was absolutely sure of.

Do not, however, revise the sentence if the revision is more awkward than the original. Such fussiness is called *hypercorrection*.

This is a rule I will not put up with.

rather than

This is a rule up with which I will not put.

PREPOSITIONS

Prepositions go before nouns, pronouns, or phrases working as nouns (that is the *pre-*), and show the relationship of that noun, pronoun, or phrase to the rest of the sentence (that is the *position*). Prepositional phrases thus begin with a preposition and end with a noun or pronoun.

in the car

beyond the cost

of this litigation

without his testimony

English has approximately 150 prepositions, but the following list contains the most common words that can be used as prepositions. Some of these words can also serve as other PARTS OF SPEECH, depending on the structure in which they are used. For example, the first sentence that follows uses *over* as a preposition; the second uses *over* as an adverb.

She was upset over the residue chemicals near her yard.

but also

Over twenty chemicals have been discovered in the ground near the plant.

Spatial	Temporal	Directional	Relational
in	before	to	with
on	after	from	for
at	during	toward	of
under	throughout	up	but
over	since	down	including
beside	ago	into	except
below	until	out of	despite
above	for (duration)	past	by
by	on (with dates)	across	for
between	at (with time)	along	about
around	following	beyond	amid
outside	about	near	beside
inside	around	outside	like
through	between	around	without
near	from	behind	unlike

The noun or pronoun at the end of the phrase is called the object of the preposition. Prepositional phrases are useful and necessary but watch for four problems when using them.

1. Too many prepositional phrases in a row.

   Prepositional phrases have a rhythm something like that of a slow waltz, and many of them in a row can waltz your reader right off to sleep.

   The department is required to submit a written explanation if its income deviates substantially from predictions for the past year.

   rather than

   The department is required to submit a written explanation in the case of deviations of substantial size from the predictions of income for the calendar year of 2024.

2. A prepositional phrase when a shorter grammatical phrase is as precise.

   If the hearing is delayed, ...

   rather than

   In the event of the occurrence of a delay of the hearing, ...

For related concerns, see CONCISENESS, subsection 9; and NOMINALIZATIONS.

3. A nominative pronoun following a preposition.

   Use the objective case (such as *me, us, him, her*, or *them*) of a pronoun that ends a prepositional phrase.

   This written contract between you and me should help us avoid any confusion in the future.

   rather than

   This written contract between you and I should help us avoid any confusion in the future.

4. Awkward phrasing created by a preposition.

   Sometimes you may need to reword a sentence to avoid the awkward phrasing that a preposition can create. You are most likely to sense this problem when you find yourself ending a sentence with a preposition; this structure is not grammatically incorrect, but some readers may think it is. More likely the problem will be that the sentence will sound inelegant to your ear.

   The final version of the advertisement was nothing like the mockup.

   After being awakened by his neighbor's barking dog four nights in a row, he could no longer put up with it.

   At this point, the defendant gave up.

   The secret to avoiding this problem is to change the word that requires the preposition.

   The final version of the advertisement was nothing like the original.

   After being awakened by his neighbor's barking dog four nights in a row, he decided he could no longer tolerate it.

   At this point, the defendant stopped resisting.

PRESENT PARTICIPLES

See VERBS, PARTICIPLES; and VERBS, TENSES, subsections 5 and 8.

PRESENT PERFECT TENSE

See VERBS, TENSES, subsection 3.

PRESENT PROGRESSIVE TENSE

See VERBS, TENSES, subsection 2.

PRESENT TENSE

See VERBS, TENSES, subsections 1–3.

PRETRIAL BRIEFS

See BRIEFS, PRETRIAL.

PREVIOUS TO

Usually you can substitute *before* for greater readability and conciseness.

PREWRITING

Prewriting includes all work done before writing the first substantial draft of a document. According to many successful legal writers, clear thought and focused effort at the prewriting stage will save hours of time later in the other stages of writing: WRITING, REWRITING, REVISING, and POLISHING. Prewriting includes organizing your research strategy, taking notes on the research found, interviewing clients, looking up forms where needed, and thinking about your organization. When no further research is needed, prewriting includes thinking clearly about the purpose of the document and the organization that best fulfills that purpose. Planning that organization can include thinking and outlining or some other means of organization. See ORGANIZE, HOW TO; PREWRITING CHECKLIST; PROCRASTINATION; and WRITING PROCESS. Also see the entry for the particular kind of legal document you are writing.

Organizing your thinking is the key to successful prewriting. Many writers are so eager to jump into researching or drafting that they forget to think first. This can be even easier to do if they are using artificial intelligence (AI) to get started. As a result, they quickly find themselves drowning in materials, ideas, and concepts. Instead, as soon as possible, categorize the sections and subsections of your problem so that the work can be done in compartments. For example, if you are writing a three-issue appellate brief, you might organize your prewriting by those three issues and work on only one issue at a time. Some writers prefer to begin the writing process by writing a very rough preliminary draft as soon as possible, rather than beginning with other prewriting activities. If you are one of these writers, you may apply the techniques below after your preliminary draft.

If you are comfortable with prewriting activities, be careful not to stay in this stage so long that the later stages of writing, rewriting, revising, and polishing are short-changed. The following techniques can help make your prewriting stage successful.

1. In all your preliminary meetings with your assigning attorney, client, or supervisor, take thorough notes and ask questions as needed to clarify so that you have a clear understanding of the document's PURPOSE, AUDIENCE, SCOPE, and POINT OF VIEW, and any time or budgetary limitations.
2. Think before you begin your research. In particular, do some version of the first six steps of the RESEARCH STRATEGY GUIDE, writing down your plan so you can stay focused and avoid delays when moving from task to task. If you are using artificial intelligence to assist in this step, see ARTIFICIAL INTELLIGENCE AND RESEARCH and PROMPTS. If you are writing a will, or contract or complaint, gather at least three forms or models that you can compare.
3. Plan your research the way you might plan a trip to the grocery store or a day of running errands. Before you begin, verify your jurisdiction so that mandatory authority has priority. Then list the sources you want to use and order the list. Include in-house resources, such as document libraries and experts who have worked on similar cases.
4. Have your system of note-taking ready to go before you begin. See NOTES and READING.
5. Coordinate dates and duties with collaborators, and schedule interim and final deadlines.
6. As soon as you can, draft preliminary statements of the issues that you are researching or that arise in the context of producing the document. Return to these throughout your research, revising them as they become clearer to you.
7. Try to list or outline the important points that you want to make under each part of the document. Even though this list may be flawed, it will help you focus your research. If listing does not work for you, try writing out an explanation of the important points as if you are explaining it to a colleague. Although this is not a rough draft of your document, it can help you find words you need and discover the organization that will work best. See OUTLINES and ORGANIZATION FOR THOSE WHO CAN'T OUTLINE.
8. Allow yourself to think about the problem even when you are not taking notes; if a good idea comes to mind, record it so that you can easily file it with its issue. As you are researching, also allow yourself to make your own comments and commentary as you take notes, to help you pull the pieces together in your own mind.

9. Pull all the pieces together by letting the law and THEORY OF THE CASE dictate the organization of a memo or brief; resist using a preprogrammed organizational scheme, but instead respond to the organization of the law. For example, you might discover several elements to a rule and use them as subdivisions. Or you might have only one test to be applied to the facts in one unit. In a will or contract, consider traditions in your jurisdiction and specific factors in your client's situation. For more on specific documents, see the entry for that document. For help knowing when to move from prewriting to writing, see WHEN TO STOP, subsection 1.

For related information about decisions to make in prewriting, see REASONING, ANALOGICAL; REASONING, DEDUCTIVE; REASONING, INDUCTIVE; REASONING, MODERN; REASONING, OTHER; REASONING, POSTMODERN; and REASONING, PRESENTING IT. For help if you are using artificial intelligence, see ARTIFICIAL INTELLIGENCE AND RESEARCH, ARTIFICIAL INTELLIGENCE AND WRITING, and PROMPTS.

PREWRITING CHECKLIST

When beginning a writing project, as you are researching and preparing to create your first substantial draft, you want to be certain you follow steps that will help you proceed smoothly. If you have difficulty knowing where to start, the hesitation can cost you valuable time and energy. To get a quick start on the project and to avoid any uncertainty, use the following list of questions to provide clarity and refine the first steps in your writing process, modifying it to suit your individual needs. To understand the elements involved in this stage of writing, see PREWRITING and WRITING PROCESS.

1. Have I taken effective notes from the assigning attorney, supervisor, client, or other AUDIENCE? If not, what questions do I need to ask to get the clarity I need?
2. Do I have a clear understanding of the document's PURPOSE?
3. Have I considered the document's SCOPE?
4. Do I have a sense of the document's POINT OF VIEW?
5. Do I have a clear sense of the client's needs? Do I have a sense of how much time I should allocate overall to this document?
6. Have I checked for in-house resources, such as similar documents produced in the past or people with experience in the area?
7. Have I written down a research strategy that is designed specifically for this project, my experience level, my client's budget, and my research resources? See RESEARCH STRATEGY GUIDE.

8. Do I have my note-taking system organized and ready to use as I research? For more help, see NOTES.
9. Have I coordinated dates and duties with any collaborators?
10. Have I scheduled and recorded interim and final deadlines?

As you immerse yourself in the process, periodically remind yourself of the overall concerns in developing your analysis or approach. For example, ask yourself the following questions.

11. Have I planned and written down the issues or thesis statement? Do I return to these periodically to keep my FOCUS and PURPOSE clear?
12. Have I allowed myself to think about the problem as I research? Have I written down those thoughts in my notes?
13. Have I allowed the issues, research, and organization to evolve as the analysis emerges?
14. Am I trying several approaches to the problem, so as to best explain it to the readers, rather than staying with my first thoughts?
15. Have I allowed the law and my THEORY OF THE CASE to drive the organization rather than following a pre-programmed organizational scheme?

PRINCIPAL OR *PRINCIPLE*?

Use *principal* when referring to people, things, and matters of primary importance. A *principal* is your *pal* in the school office; it is also the person bearing the main liability in a case. Additionally, *principal* is a capital sum placed at interest or the main body of an estate. It is also a way of marking the main matter under discussion.

Our principal concern is custody of the children.

and

The principal amount of the debt is $456,873.

Use *principle* when referring to an underlying truth, axiom, or rule of behavior.

Defendant has no clear set of principles that prevent him from stealing again.

PRINCIPLES OF GOOD LEGAL WRITING

Writing is complicated and nonsequential; it is easy to feel lost among the details. The following broader principles, however, can help you remember the forest as well as the trees. They fall into three main areas: priorities, process, and product.

1. Priorities.

Good legal writing must always communicate your meaning accurately and be sufficiently thorough to meet the readers' needs. Most of the time, except under extreme time pressure or in unusual circumstances, it should always be easy to read. Whenever possible, it should also be appealing to the reader, a pleasure to read. These three qualities—accuracy, ease of use, and appeal—form a ready guideline to help the legal writer assess the importance of various writing tasks.

Relative importance cannot reliably be assigned to such qualities as complete research, good organization, precise wording, elegant sentence structure, or correct spelling. Rather, their importance depends on the effect on the content or the reader. For example, word choice errors may be minor but can have serious consequences; using some overly formal wording would be less than ideal, but it would not be as serious as using an incorrect legal term to identify a central issue. Using a sentence structure that must be read twice to be understood affects readability, which is a concern worth fixing. But that would not be as serious as wording a sentence in a statute so badly that it is interpreted by the courts in a way that counters the legislature's intent. Similarly, the organization problem of repeating information unnecessarily in a brief can annoy a judge, but omitting adequate legal support for an argument can lose the case. Even the small omission of a punctuation mark can be critical, as in the situation where *ten foot-long rods* was written in a purchase order instead of the correct *ten-foot-long rods*. The order was for uranium rods, and the cost of the error ran into the millions. Sometimes a mediocre-but-serviceable organization in a contract is not such a serious error as the omission of a critical clause.

Therefore the legal writer needs to measure the importance of various writing qualities by the effects they have. Evaluate the importance of writing tasks based on their effect on accuracy and thoroughness, ease of use, and appeal. Always check large and small aspects of writing for accuracy and thoroughness, no matter how rushed you are. Review all documents whenever possible for all aspects of writing that affect READABILITY.

2. Process.

A healthy writing process involves a rhythmic alternation between two contradictory subprocesses: creation and critique. As in a breath, a heartbeat, or a footstep, both subprocesses are needed to complete the task, but those subprocesses cannot be undertaken simultaneously. A breath requires both expansion, which takes in needed oxygen, and contraction, which expels carbon dioxide. Similarly, writing requires the expansive act of creation—considering and laying out various possibilities—and the contracting act of critiquing, which eliminates possibilities that are not workable. Many writers have problems writing because they are either trying to complete these contradictory tasks simultaneously or they are alternating too frequently between the two tasks, which adds stress to the writing process.

These two aspects of the writing process must alternate efficiently, at a pace that is optimal for the individual writer. Some writers will perform better when they write a complete rough draft of a section before stopping to revise any details within the section. Other writers will perform better by stopping to revise after a few paragraphs or sentences. A few writers will even be comfortable alternating quickly between creating and critiquing, editing as they write. Whatever the rate of alternation, any writer will benefit from understanding the process and adjusting it as needed to enhance the overall writing process. The following list provides an overview and starting point for refining your own process. For related information, see DOCUMENT CHECKLIST and WRITING PROCESS.

(a) PREWRITING.

At this stage, focus on framing your issues, gathering your materials, and deciding how to design something appropriate for your AUDIENCE. Develop the document's PURPOSE, decide on the appropriate SCOPE, and choose a STANCE. Once you have gathered the materials, think about several possible ways to assemble them to meet your purpose. Reflect long enough to clarify both your thinking about the content and the organization that will appeal to your reader. Your final organization should be based more on the reader than on your own inclinations. Remember that good writing is good thinking, so make sure you have done enough of the second before you start the first. See also ORGANIZATION FOR THOSE WHO CAN'T OUTLINE, OUTLINES, and PREWRITING CHECKLIST. If you use artificial intelligence (AI) in PREWRITING either to jump start your research or to discover potential approaches to your analysis, see PROMPTS, QUESTIONS PRESENTED, and RESEARCH STRATEGY GUIDE.

(b) WRITING.

At this stage, focus on getting it written, not getting it right. Let your thinking flow onto the page in the first draft, without stopping to edit too frequently. When in doubt about the need for any supporting content, err on the side of inclusion at this stage. You can omit any content that is unneeded during the next stage of the process, but you might not remember to add it later if needed.

If you are considering using artificial intelligence (AI) to generate your draft, be aware of its limitations at this stage in your process. For example, be vigilant about entering your client's specific information in the PROMPTS. Before you enter that information, check all pertinent confidentiality and privacy requirements as well as whether the AI system you are using retains and publishes this information. Also be alert to its handling of legal content, such as whether it has discerned the difference between MANDATORY AUTHORITY and PERSUASIVE AUTHORITY and whether it focuses on the analytical patterns most appropriate to your situation.

(c) REWRITING.

After you have gotten your thoughts written out, allow yourself to rework main ideas and large-scale organization as needed to get it right. Add content if necessary. Mercilessly delete interesting-but-unneeded tangents. Assume you will need to rework something. Consider more than one possible organization. Few writers hit it right the first time, and no writers accomplish that every time. For related information, see ORGANIZATION, LARGE-SCALE; ORGANIZATION, SMALL-SCALE; PARAGRAPHS; REWRITING CHECKLIST; and TOPIC SENTENCES.

Using AI to do the actual rewriting may be less useful because this is the stage where you get the analysis right. If you did use AI to generate a draft, use the REWRITING CHECKLIST yourself to ensure the document is specific to your client's needs and reflective of your own thinking. Make sure you are checking your case's specific law, facts, potential theories, threshold issues, and possible sequences of arguments.

(d) REVISING.

Reconcile yourself to the fact that it will take multiple passes to get the text right. If you focus on specific aspects of writing in each pass, however, this will not be onerous. For example, you can work through the document once revising just for ACCURACY. Then, you can work through the document multiple times, focusing in turn on READABILITY, CONCISENESS, TONE, and EMPHASIS. In particular, revise POINT HEADINGS, ISSUES, TOPIC SENTENCES, and CONCLUSIONS because your reader will pay special attention to these parts of any legal document. For help breaking revision into smaller tasks, see REVISING CHECKLIST or the checklist for the specific document you are writing. You may want to use AI in REVISING to help with specific edits, such as minimizing use of PASSIVE VOICE, increasing READABILITY, or achieving CONCISENESS. For help using AI at this stage of the writing process, see REVISING CHECKLIST; see also ARTIFICIAL INTELLIGENCE AND WRITING.

(e) POLISHING.

At this stage, you stop making judgment calls and focus instead on correcting any remaining errors, such as wrong words, punctuation errors, and format errors. Use whatever technique works for you: moving from back to front, reading through separately for each kind of revision needed, reading aloud, or working section by section. Your credibility is linked to your attention to detail. You may also find AI tools useful in POLISHING as you proofread or check format for consistency. For help completing this task, see POLISHING CHECKLIST and WORDS SPELLCHECKERS MAY NOT CATCH.

3. Product.

While concerns about the WRITING PROCESS focused on how you get a document written and then right, concerns about the product itself, the final document, deserve their own focus. Your written documents will build your legal reputation to a large extent and, after you have developed a comfortable personal writing process, the product itself can be your main focus. You can work consistently to maintain accuracy and ease of use on every document you write, adding appeal to the extent that time allows. Doing this can help you lift any document from mediocrity to excellence.

Before you release your document to your audience, look at it as a whole product. Look at it through your readers' eyes and see if the message is clear and unified, if the needed materials are included to support that message, and if the structure matches and reinforces that message. Move from being the writer to the reader by asking yourself the following questions.

(a) Is the document tailored to your audience and purpose?

Make sure that you have made the best decisions about purposes and readers, and that you have understood the practical constraints involved, the document's context, its historical setting, and its scope. Here you can also check your stance or point of view to make sure it is consistent throughout. For related information, see AUDIENCE, PURPOSE, and PROFESSIONAL LANGUAGE AND PRESENTATION.

Because there are so many possible permutations and combinations of the components of legal analysis, the choices are many. Here reasonable minds often differ about how best to present the components. When choosing between competing approaches, choose the structure that will appeal to most of your readers. For example, while the structure may make sense to you because it follows the elements of a statute, your readers may be unpersuaded by such a dry presentation, even though you think it is inherently logical. Perhaps the elements should be rearranged to put the most persuasive ones first or to reflect a policy shift.

(b) Is the document unified by one message?

Whether the document is answering one legal question, advancing one theory, or building one transaction, it has a message to which every part must contribute. Check the main message to make sure its language is precise; then check for consistency and support throughout the document, probably using the same terms.

(c) Does the document contain appropriate materials?

The materials needed in the document may include law, facts, arguments, counterarguments, contract provisions, policy statements, tables of data, definitions, or other supporting information. Cull from those possibilities the materials essential to the document's purpose and audience. Include legally significant facts but not the entire background; use mandatory law first, going to persuasive only when necessary; and use only contract provisions that apply to this transaction. Your materials are the key to the document's structure.

(d) Does the document use a coherent analysis and structure?

To make your document coherent, you can use your message to unify it, making sure the order flows from that message. Include all steps in your reasoning without digressing on tangents. If you are using headings, make sure that, together, they convey the analysis or argument in a step-by-step manner. Your choice of analytical pattern should be apparent to any reader and flow easily from one point to the next. To keep that flow, place your important points in POSITIONS OF EMPHASIS, such as headings, topic sentences, and conclusions.

Know how each point relates to what preceded and follows it and why; make sure you have connected these in ways your readers can follow. Account for weaknesses in your analysis and other arguments made by an array of interested parties. Include all relevant information without confusing or distracting the reader, and try to do so without footnotes unless you are writing scholarly articles. Keep working at the structure until any legal reader cannot misunderstand it. For help, see COUNTERARGUMENTS, HOW TO PRESENT; LEGAL ANALYSIS; ORGANIZATION, LARGE-SCALE; PRECISION; REASONING, PRESENTING IT; and REWRITING CHECKLIST.

(e) Does the document use appropriate proportions for each section?

Part of the document's message lies in the amount of text devoted to each section. Usually, the longer the text, the more important the reader assumes it is. Similarly, if there is heavy citation, the reader assumes the section is important. What confuses the reader is when much text is devoted to a small point or when an important point goes by too quickly. The proportions should reflect the relative importance of the components.

(f) Do substance and sentence structure match?

Readers also look for messages not just from words but also from the sentence structure, or syntax, within which those words reside. Use cohesive devices that reinforce the meaning, such as TRANSITIONS, REPETITION of a word or structure, and other verbal connections between sentences and within a paragraph. (For relevant techniques, see COHERENCE; CONNECTIONS, MAKING THEM; and PARAGRAPHS.) Finally, match substance and syntax by using dependent clauses for dependent ideas, PARALLEL STRUCTURE for parallel ideas, and main clauses for main ideas. Use semicolons to show two ideas are more closely related than if a period separates them. For related information, see PARAGRAPHS, REVISING CHECKLIST, and SENTENCE STRUCTURE.

(g) Is the document polished?

Your credibility is linked to your attention to detail. Readers often believe that, if there is a typographical mistake, there is probably a research mistake, too. Even those jurisdictions that purport to relax about citation form or those supervising attorneys who say *Just give me what you've got,* do not tolerate typographical errors, substantive citation mistakes, misspellings, and grammar miscues. Build credibility by polishing the document to the last dot. For help with this final, important stage, see POLISHING CHECKLIST.

PRIORITIES COORDINATING MULTIPLE PROJECTS

See TIME MANAGEMENT.

PRIORITIES WITHIN ONE PROJECT

As a good legal writer, you will strive for high quality, but you will rarely reach perfection. It is in the nature of writing that we aim for the best we can do in the time we have. Without limitations, any project will expand to fill the space in your time schedule. The key to quality is to make sure that which is essential to the task is always achieved, whether or not you impress the reader with your brilliance. Having a clear set of priorities at each stage of the WRITING PROCESS can help with this. In general, ACCURACY must always be a priority; even when time is extremely short, you must be sure to be accurate. Second, you must include sufficient information to support or explain your point. Whenever possible, take time to make sure that your writing will be understandable to your AUDIENCE. Then, as time allows and as the importance of the document increases, spend more time revising the writing so that it reads smoothly, is concise, and has an even TONE.

To accomplish these priorities, you must apply the right priority at each stage of writing. The following list can help you do this.

1. When PREWRITING, make sure you are clear on what the legal question is in the situation to avoid researching ancillary-but-unnecessary questions. Research until you find the same sources reappearing and you have checked to make sure the law on which you rely is current. Be sure you have all the relevant facts in hand.
2. When WRITING, focus on what you want to say or your answer to the legal question. Avoid worrying about the details of a polished presentation; instead focus on including all the information you need in the document and finding the organization that makes the most sense. For help, see ORGANIZE, HOW TO and THOROUGHNESS.
3. When REWRITING, consider whether you need to reorganize any of the content to clarify the presentation. Add more information where needed for CLARITY. Delete any unneeded and distracting information. Also see ACCURACY; ORGANIZATION, LARGE-SCALE; TOPIC SENTENCES; and HEADINGS.
4. When REVISING, shift your focus to sentences and paragraphs, first checking to be sure that all your content is accurately stated. Then focus on READABILITY to make it easy for your reader to understand the content and TONE to reassure the reader of your professionalism.
5. When POLISHING, remove any errors that remain, focusing first on those that might affect the reader's understanding of the content. Especially check all names, numbers, and quotations for any errors. Then remove other errors that are, in effect, bumps and potholes along the path that presents your legal thought.

Even when time is extremely short, check for accuracy and tone. You must always be accurate, and a bad tone can create distracting problems in the communication process. If you get bogged down at any stage of the process, see the relevant sections of WHEN TO STOP and TIME MANAGEMENT. For related information, see DEADLINES, MEETING THEM; MULTI-TASKING; NOTES; RESEARCH STRATEGY GUIDE; and TRIAGE.

PRIOR TO

Prior to sounds a bit stuffy and can be ungrammatical. To avoid *prior to*, use *before.*

Before the accident, she ran three miles each morning.

rather than

Prior to the accident, she ran three miles each morning.

Or use *to.*

To receive this summary of past complaints, the consumer must file . . . .

rather than

Prior to receiving this summary of past complaints, the consumer must file . . . .

PRIVACY

As an attorney, you have a heightened duty to protect the privacy of many communications within your profession. In particular, you want to protect the privacy of clients, colleagues, work product, and workplace concerns. Use of artificial intelligence (AI) introduces particular privacy concerns and liabilities. Before you enter any information specific to your client, check all pertinent confidentiality and privacy requirements as well as whether the AI system you are using retains and publishes this information.

Additionally, the speed of law practice and the tenuousness of security systems may cause your communication to inadvertently reach an AUDIENCE wider than you intended. Therefore, be circumspect when at work and even in your own life. Remember, for example, that your social media postings may eventually be read by your employers, your clients, or your legal opponents. For good or ill, an attorney must be more restrained and professional in communication than the average citizen. For related information, see CREDIBILITY, METADATA REMOVAL, PROFESSIONAL LANGUAGE AND PRESENTATION, REPLY TO ALL, and SOCIAL MEDIA.

PROCEDURAL OR *SUBSTANTIVE*?

Use these terms precisely because the distinction between them is critical in legal writing. *Procedural* refers to legal process, or the legal machinery for carrying on a suit. This machinery includes pleading, evidence, process, and similar practical matters. For example, the question of whether a court has jurisdiction over a particular suit is a procedural question; the question of whether post-verdict motions were filed on time is also procedural.

Substantive refers to the law itself, which regulates and defines the rights and duties of parties to the suit. For example, a defendant's right to be represented by counsel is a substantive right; a party's right to bring an action for wrongful death is also a substantive right.

Often substantive rights are referred to as the merits of a case. For example, to say *The judge is ready to make a decision on the merits* is to say that all the procedural matters have been settled so that the court may judge the remaining issues on the basis of the parties' duties and rights. Following this philosophy, often procedural issues must come early in the organization of briefs and memos, before substantive issues.

PROCESS AND PRODUCT COMPARED

The writing product is the document itself, which is subject to scrutiny and evaluation by your AUDIENCE and those who evaluate your performance, whether supervisors, clients, judges, or professors. To assist and even impress them, your product must exhibit ACCURACY and CLARITY, regardless of the constraints imposed on you by less-than-ideal conditions.

In contrast, your writing process is your personal way of getting the job done. It includes every aspect of your work, such as your time allocations for different tasks, your order for doing these tasks, and your style of interacting with others involved in the project. It is affected by your habitual ways of completing all the tasks involved in your writing process, such as ordering your research strategy, writing by dictating or typing, and proofreading. It is also affected by external factors that vary with the situation, such as your client's demands, your supervisor's agenda, and your energy level on the day you write.

Although your process is not generally scrutinized by others, it deserves your personal scrutiny because it can dramatically affect the product. Refining your legal writing process, particularly noting how it may differ from nonlegal writing processes, also has personal benefits; it can make you more effective, efficient, and confident. For ways to make this evaluation, see WRITING PROCESS.

PROCRASTINATION

Procrastination works if it is incubation, fails if it is postponement. If it is postponement for you, see WRITING BLOCK for ways to address the problem. To make procrastination work for you, do the following.

1. Start early.

   Do short PREWRITING tasks early and then think. For example, write a preliminary version of the Questions Presented as soon as you begin working on a memo and then think about them. Alternatively, gather the research, read it, and then think about it. For example, if you are working on a contract, gather samples of previous contracts and study them to help you determine what components your contract needs to include.

2. Keep the project on your personal radar.

   Complete your research, draft some of the more standard contract sections, or take whatever notes work for you. Try to do something each day to keep the project alive. While you work on other projects during the day, this project can breathe, turn over, and move about in your mind. Keep it alive by jotting down ideas as they come to you. See CASE BRIEFS; NOTES; OPINIONS, READING THEM; and RESEARCH STRATEGY GUIDE.

3. Create a design or plan.

   Set a time for completing the research and writing an outline. However cursory this outline may be, this step will usually force the procrastinating to end and the organizing to begin. This is the hardest step to take, but you must take it; skipping it can ruin worthwhile incubating. See OUTLINES or ORGANIZATION FOR THOSE WHO CAN'T OUTLINE.

4. Use the calendar.

   Similarly, set a time to have each early draft completed, even if you are the only one who knows the deadline. By putting interim deadlines on your calendar and tying them to another person or task, you force yourself to avoid further procrastination by sheer embarrassment. If you key in your own draft, try to find someone who will be a listener or a reader for your paper at a specific time, again so you have a deadline tied to another person. See DICTATION.

5. Use interim deadlines.

   Finally, schedule small interim deadlines instead of just one final deadline and stick to your schedule. This will break down your temptation to postpone.

6. Try something different.

   Vary your approach. You may want to start writing at the end of the document, not at the beginning. You might try voice-to-text technology for taking NOTES or generating your draft. You may need to take a walk or talk to someone about the project. You may want to use artificial intelligence (AI) to generate ideas in PREWRITING. For more help here, see ARTIFICIAL INTELLIGENCE AND RESEARCH, ARTIFICIAL INTELLIGENCE AND WRITING, and PROMPTS.

For related information, see DEADLINES, MEETING THEM; DICTATION; GETTING STARTED; MULTI-TASKING; NOTES; ORGANIZATION FOR THOSE WHO CAN'T OUTLINE; PERFECTIONISM; RESEARCH STRATEGY GUIDE; TIME MANAGEMENT; WHEN TO STOP; and WRITING BLOCK.

PROFESSIONAL LANGUAGE AND PRESENTATION

Through your written documents, your language communicates your professional image and your role in each given legal situation. Making a good impression on your readers helps you to achieve your purposes and avoids distraction. That good impression relies on your professional responsibility, use of legal conventions, and choice and consistency of TONE. Finally, you want to develop over time your personal professional style so the reader remembers you, your message, and your good work.

1. Professional responsibility.

   Your professional responsibility varies as the particular situation and legal document vary, so take time to ascertain your responsibilities in each situation; then make sure you meet them. For example, in an opinion email, you have a duty to remind the client that the choice is finally up to that client, even though you recommend one particular course of action. To meet that duty, take care to explain with equal clarity both the reasoning behind your advice and the limits of your role as advisor. Explain clearly and completely so your reader can make an informed decision either way. Similarly, when you write a brief, you have a duty in most jurisdictions to acknowledge a precedent that seems unfavorable to your case. To meet that duty, cite the case but also argue that it is distinguishable based on different facts or reasoning.

2. Use of legal conventions.

   Use conventional grammar, word choice, and style. Legal writing is one of the last genres of language to change its habits or conventions. Logic supports this conservative bent because legal writing needs to avoid the AMBIGUITY that new terms and usages create. While electronic communications embrace many abbreviations, incomplete sentence structures, and nonverbal symbols to add emotional overtones and speed the process of writing, legal writing is not yet ready to do so. Resist the urge to use these shortcuts in any communication to clients, courts, and colleagues who are older than you.

> **Are you planning to bring the most recent contract draft to our meeting this afternoon? Please let me know as soon as possible.**
>
> rather than
>
> R U bringing K draft PM mtg—need asap ans.

As always, consider your reader when you write.

3. Consistent and appropriate TONE.

Keep the formality of your language consistent rather than mixing formal and informal language in the same document.

> **Please send us the information requested in the enclosed questionnaire as soon as possible.**
>
> rather than
>
> Please send us the information requested per the attached questionnaire pronto.
>
> or
>
> The attached questionnaire asks for some info we need so please complete it with all due haste.

The first example uses consistently plain language to preserve a collegial tone. In the second and third examples, the overall tone shifts from phrase to phrase, leaving the reader uneasy about the writer's attitude toward the subject and the reader. This shift in formality may suggest that the writer does not control the vocabulary and therefore may not understand the content, an unfair leap that may nevertheless undercut the reader's confidence. The change in level of formality also signals a shift in the relationship between the writer and the reader as the tone shifts between reserved and formal to casual and informal. This shifting relationship can leave the reader feeling uneasy, although the reader will seldom be aware of the cause. This uneven level of formality is often the cause for comments that the writing does not "sound professional."

To remedy this problem, replace any words that seem a little more formal or informal than the rest of the text. Move the tone of the text toward the safe middle ground that is most common in business communications. Sounding professional means creating a consistent, professional tone through your word choice; it does not mean using fancier language.

Avoid using so much formal language that you create a stuffy tone. To confident readers, this will seem like the writer is trying too hard to impress them. To less confident readers, it will seem condescending.

> **Are you planning to bring the most recent contract draft to our meeting this afternoon? Please let me know as soon as possible.**
>
> rather than
>
> At your earliest convenience, please advise me as to whether or not you will provide a current contract draft for this afternoon's meeting.

For help avoiding this problem, see FLOWERY LANGUAGE, PLAIN ENGLISH, and TONE. Too many uses of CONTRACTIONS or a COLLOQUIALISM can have a similarly negative effect. Strive to be consistent in keeping with the document's purpose and your personal style.

4. Personal style.

Besides meeting your professional responsibility, you may want to communicate and develop a personal style. For example, compared to other attorneys, you may be more formal or informal, more personal or impersonal, more impassioned or unemotional. Your presentation can make the difference between remembering or forgetting your message, so be conscious and conscientious about what style will come across best to your audience. Find a style that suits you and develop it, even though you will probably adjust this style somewhat in each document you write, just as you adjust your manner of speaking when talking to different people. As you develop your personal legal style, you want to remain within the range of possibilities that your readers consider appropriate for an attorney in your position. After you settle on your personal style, inspire confidence in your professional ability by being consistent in levels of formality, tone, and writing structures. For more on this, see AUDIENCE; BAD NEWS, GIVING IT; BAD NEWS, SOFTENING IT; FORMALITY, LEVEL OF; ORGANIZE, HOW TO; and POINT OF VIEW, OBJECTIVE TO PERSUASIVE.

For related information, see DICTATION, GENDER IN WRITING, ORAL PRESENTATIONS, and POWERPOINTS.

PROFESSIONAL POSTURE

See PROFESSIONAL LANGUAGE AND PRESENTATION.

PROFESSIONAL TONE

See PROFESSIONAL LANGUAGE AND PRESENTATION and TONE.

PROGRESSIVE TENSES

See VERBS, TENSES.

PROMPTS

A *prompt* is a written question or request submitted to a generative artificial intelligence (AI) system that instructs the model to produce a written response. That response is generated based on the training data used in the model's design, which may or may not be reliable for your purposes. Prompts should be designed to optimize the results obtained from Large Language Models (LLMs). The better the prompt, the better the results. As with all research, think before crafting any prompt you submit to an LLM.

Approach this conversation with AI as if you are talking to a knowledgeable person who takes everything literally. How you craft the prompt depends on the AI's knowledge base. For example, if you are using an AI program designed for law, it will understand specific legal terms and context better than a general AI program. Depending on your access to AI models, you may divide the process of developing prompts into several stages, using different prompts at different stages.

Before you draft your prompt, keep in mind the following.

1. Protect confidentiality.

   Unless you are using a generative AI system protected within your organization's secure environment, be careful. Always review and understand the LLM's privacy standards. Remember that all information that goes into the system may stay there and be shared, even your prompts. Remove any names or details that will reveal confidential or private information.

2. Observe any financial or other constraints.

   Ascertain any policy or budgetary limits on using AI. Judges, supervising attorneys, or others may prohibit certain uses of AI. Budgetary constraints may significantly change how and when you use AI. For example, you may want to do preliminary research elsewhere to orient yourself to pertinent laws and TERMS OF ART.

3. Decide how you are going to use AI.

   This powerful tool can be used in many ways. LLMs excel at explaining concepts and idea generation, both of which are useful at the beginning of a project. But unlike secondary book sources, LLMs can craft an explanation specifically tailored to your legal issue. For example, you may prompt an LLM to explain a specific area of law new to you. You may prompt it to answer a narrow question. You can prompt it to identify all available arguments. Or you can prompt it to draft a BRIEF ANSWER. Whatever use you choose, craft a prompt specific to your purpose.

Draft your prompt with the following in mind.

4. Be as specific as you can about the law, legal question, and facts.

The more specifically you can locate the law in your AI program, the more likely you are to get accurate results. For the legal question, use verbs drawn from the TERMS OF ART in that statute, regulation, or case. Precise subjects, verbs, and SUBJECT-VERB COMBINATIONS in your prompt will generate more precise results. If you do not know the specific terms, using AI may help you locate those terms.

Determine the LEGALLY SIGNIFICANT FACTS and KEY BACKGROUND FACTS and incorporate those into your prompt so that you can find information similar to those facts. In a separate prompt, one option may be to use ANTONYMS to find the situations that your opponents will find. As noted in #1, review and understand the LLM's privacy settings before entering any facts that might be confidential.

You may develop the prompt similarly to writing an effective QUESTION PRESENTED. For example, you might write the following prompt rather than using the short phrases that follow.

> **Write a discussion of the following legal question, discussing both sides of whether, under Federal Rule of Civil Procedure 4(d)(1), a notice is effective when it is delivered to defendant's wife or spouse and the defendant does not reside at that address.**
>
> rather than
>
> Explain Federal Rule of Civil Procedure 4(d)(1)
>
> or
>
> When is a notice effective under the Federal Rules of Civil Procedure?

You may find a general prompt more useful when you do not have all of this specific information.

5. Include information about the legal context.

   Keeping the LLM's privacy and security standards in mind, decide what to include about the situation. This might include procedural posture and timing, possible outcome, or STANDARD OF REVIEW.

6. Specify the point of view.

   If this is useful to your research, you may want to suggest a point of view, such as to represent your client, to offer arguments in your opponent's favor, or to generate a specific TONE. You may, however, want to remain objective in your initial prompt so that you see a range of arguments, not just one side's.

7. Identify the desired product.

   If you are creating a product to be read by others, say what output you want from AI, such as consequences, opposing arguments, history of cases, or financial implications.

8. Evaluate and verify the results.

   Use your own expertise, common sense, and knowledge to verify the accuracy and precision of your results. Determine whether something seems amiss. While a legal LLM's knowledge will be more vast and impressive than a general AI's, the selection of that knowledge may be incomplete or may rise to the level of MISINFORMATION.

   Verification of your results is not optional. You may verify with your own knowledge, do independent research, or ask an expert. If you have done preliminary research, then you can see if the results fit into what you have found thus far. If you are not sure about the results, do more research elsewhere.

For related information, see ARTIFICIAL INTELLIGENCE AND RESEARCH, ARTIFICIAL INTELLIGENCE AND WRITING, subsection 3; ISSUES; KEY BACKGROUND FACTS; LEGALLY SIGNIFICANT FACTS; QUESTIONS PRESENTED; and RESEARCH STRATEGY GUIDE.

PRONOUN REFERENCE

See AMBIGUITY, WAYS TO AVOID, subsection 2.

PRONOUNS

Pronouns take the place of nouns, and they have many uses.

He is the officer who gave me a ticket.

Without it, they have no case.

The plaintiff must take the responsibility upon himself.

Each of you should write to your senator.

That may not be the most effective support for her position.

Five common questions arise about using pronouns:

(1) when to use commas with relative pronouns, especially *that* or *which*;

(2) when to use *who* or *whom*;

(3) when to use *he*, *she*, or *they*;

(4) when to use *we*; and

(5) how to create possessive pronouns.

1. When to use commas with relative pronouns.

Relative pronouns, one subcategory of pronouns, deserve special attention because they are used frequently in legal writing and their proper use is often crucial to ACCURACY. Relative pronouns include *who, whose, that, which, whoever, whichever*, and *whatever*. These relative pronouns introduce subordinate clauses, or groups of words that include a subject and verb but cannot stand by themselves as sentences.

Your car, which was still in the lot at midnight, was towed.

This issue was resolved by the court in Barker v. Holmes, which stated . . . .

Any nonresident who has lived in the state for more than three months must fill out this portion of the form.

All cars that remain in the lot after 10:00 p.m. will be towed.

All operators whose licenses expire this month must show the supervisor their renewed licenses.

Sometimes a subordinate clause adds extra information to the sentence but is not essential to the accuracy of the sentence. To punctuate this clause correctly, place commas before and after the subordinate clause and use *which* rather than *that*.

Your car, which was still in the lot at midnight, was towed.

Sometimes, however, a subordinating clause is essential to the meaning of the sentence because the clause narrows the subject, or restricts the meaning of the subject. In this situation, removing the subordinate clause would make the sentence inaccurate. To punctuate this kind of subordinate clause correctly, do not put commas before or after the clause and use *that* rather than *which.*

All cars[ ] that remain in the lot after 10:00 p.m.[ ] will be towed.

Any nonresident[ ] who has lived in the state for more than three months[ ] must fill out this portion of the form.

All operators[ ] whose licenses expire this month[ ] must show the supervisor their renewed license.

For more examples and related information, see *THAT* OR *WHICH*?

2. When to use *who* or *whom.*

The distinction between *who* and *whom* may be fading in English, but it is not gone yet. Use *who* as a subject, *whom* as an OBJECT. For example, use *whom* as the object of a preposition.

To whom did you present the question about the gun?

Also use *whom* as the object of a verb.

Whom did you see on the night of the incident?

This use also applies to clauses that are inserted within another sentence, as in the following example.

The defendant is the person whom the plaintiff saw on the night of the crime.

Whom is needed here because it is the object of the verb *saw* in the clause explaining *person.*

Use *who* as a subject of a sentence or of a clause.

Who took my shoes?

He is the person who called me yesterday.

For an explanation of related terms, see PREPOSITIONS; and SENTENCE, PARTS OF, subsections 3–6.

3. When to use *he, she,* or *they.*

For precision in writing, you will have to balance the desires of the individual against the need for accuracy. Use *they* when referring to more than one person. When referring to a single person, use the term that person prefers whenever it will not create ambiguity. Use a noun when you are referring to one person but do not know the gender of the person. Although *they* is often used in speech to replace *he or she,* using a plural term for a singular entity is still literally inaccurate and therefore can create ambiguity in some legal documents. For more on this topic and six techniques to avoid using pronouns, see GENDER IN WRITING. For related information, see SEXIST LANGUAGE, WAYS TO AVOID.

4. When to use *we*.

   We is a special problem in legal writing because you may, by using *we*, inadvertently speak for your whole law office or organization, possibly creating legal obligations. Never use *we* when you really mean *I*; use *we* when you are speaking officially for the organization of which you are a part, as one judge may do when drafting an opinion for the whole bench.

5. How to create possessive pronouns.

   Add an *s*. Do not use an apostrophe.

   its = belonging to it.

   yours = belonging to you.

   theirs = belonging to them.

   whose = belonging to whom.

   ours = belonging to us.

   hers = belonging to her.

   For more explanation, see POSSESSIVES.

PROOFREADING

Yes, you still need to do it, even with all the computerized aids available. In part you need to do it because no spellchecker yet invented is foolproof. In part you need to do it because a wrong word can have embarrassing and sometimes legally significant consequences. Finally, you need to proofread because your legal skill and professionalism will be judged by details such as spelling errors and wrong words.

If you have trouble proofreading, try the following.

- Read in small doses, concentrating on one page at a time.
- Read randomly, doing page six, then one, then eight, and so on.
- Read aloud, slowly.
- Read backward from the end of the document, one sentence at a time.
- Print up the document in larger typeface or enlarge the document on your screen and use that for proofreading.

For related information, see DEADLINES, MEETING THEM; MISSPELLINGS, HOW TO AVOID; PERFECTIONISM; POLISHING; POLISHING CHECKLIST; TIME MANAGEMENT; and WORDS SPELLCHECKERS MAY NOT CATCH.

PROPER NOUNS

Proper nouns are names of specific persons, organizations, publications, and other such entities. *Franklin Delano Roosevelt, American Bar Association, Texas Law Review*. Capitalize them.

PROVIDED THAT

Replace this phrase with *if* for greater CONCISENESS and CLARITY.

Our client has the contractual right to reject any shipment if she notifies Norcross of her decision within forty-eight hours of receiving that shipment.

rather than

Our client has the contractual right to reject any shipment, provided that she notifies Norcross of her decision within forty-eight hours of receiving that shipment.

Sometimes *provided that* may have been used to introduce something that will most likely happen; then you may replace it with *when*.

The transfer of ownership will occur at closing, when the seller provides the title, and the buyer pays the full purchase price.

rather than

The transfer of ownership will occur at closing, provided that the seller provides the title, and the buyer pays the full purchase price.

PUNCTUATING LISTS

See LISTS, STRUCTURE OF.

PUNCTUATION

Punctuation is critical to accuracy, and ACCURACY is critical in legal writing. Punctuation marks tell the reader how words should be grouped, whether in phrases or sentences, so their meaning can be understood more readily. Punctuation can also serve as a signal of structural problems in writing. For example, if a sentence requires a great deal of punctuation to be understood, that is a signal that the sentence needs restructuring. The trend to minimize punctuation is sound if it is combined with this awareness of the need to structure sentences so that less punctuation is needed. Simply omitting punctuation without fixing the sentence structure, however, adds confusion rather than CLARITY. For ways to punctuate sentences, see EXCLAMATION POINTS, PERIODS, and QUESTION MARKS. For ways to punctuate phrases within a sentence, see COMMAS, DASHES, SEMICOLONS, and COLONS. For ways to punctuate lists, see LISTS, STRUCTURE OF. For ways to punctuate quotations, see QUOTATIONS, HOW TO PUNCTUATE. For punctuation marks used within words, see APOSTROPHES, BRACKETS, and HYPHENS.

PURPOSE

Establish your document's overall purpose before you get too far along in the writing process. Although you may brainstorm a first draft or some notes, take time to think about why you are writing as well as what you want to say and to whom you will say it. Take time to be honest with yourself about your purposes: there may be many. For example, you may be writing to impress a new boss as well as to advise on a decision. This honesty often does not mean you state these purposes explicitly in the document, but it will nevertheless make your writing more effective and more efficient. You may want to write out your primary and secondary purposes. Then you can focus on meeting those purposes throughout writing, rewriting, and revising.

Your READER will help you to determine your purpose. A supervising attorney may want a quick, direct answer; a worried client may want a long, gentle explanation. Thus your purpose is also linked to SCOPE; once you decide on your purpose, you will have a more definite idea of how long your document should be.

Discern the range of possible purposes for your document. For example, your purpose may be to complete a transaction, untangle two or more related issues, create a paper trail, change a reader's mind, or present a new legal theory.

Writing out your purpose is also helpful because it can help you eliminate ancillary goals that may otherwise unconsciously affect your writing. For example, your professional goal will not be to insult your reader, to frighten someone, or to impress your reader with your superior knowledge, even though those are frequent human desires. Realizing this at the start of the writing process can help you focus on the task and delegate the venting of your feelings to a conversation with a trusted colleague, a private journal entry, or a vigorous workout.

For more information on how to frame, develop, and present your purpose, see AUDIENCE; GETTING STARTED; ORGANIZE, HOW TO; ORGANIZATION FOR THOSE WHO CAN'T OUTLINE; and OUTLINES.

PURSUANT TO

Avoid this phrase when you can, because it is usually less clear than the alternative. Also avoid it because it is legalese.

In preparation for our meeting on estate planning, I am enclosing a questionnaire to help you collect the relevant information.

rather than

Pursuant to our meeting regarding estate planning, I am enclosing a questionnaire to help you collect the relevant information.

and

To conform to this new regulation, we are revising our administrative procedures.

rather than

Pursuant to this new regulation, we are revising our administrative procedures.

QUALITY AS A MODIFIER

In formal legal usage, *quality* is still a noun, not an adjective. Technically, you can use *quality* as an adjective to mean *excellent*, but avoid doing so if it creates ambiguity.

He did an excellent job arguing in front of the jury.

rather than

He did a quality job in front of the jury.

Quality needs a modifier, such as *high*, *poor*, or *questionable*. Standing alone, it does not automatically mean *high* quality. So write

The product is of high quality.

rather than

This is a quality product.

QUESTION MARK OR PERIOD?

See QUESTION MARKS.

QUESTION MARKS

You know to use question marks with questions. The problems occur with sentences like the ones that follow.

The question is whether federal taxes on this investment must be paid through January 15 of this year.

Here a period, not a question mark, is used because the main subject and verb, *the question is,* makes a statement. But in the following sentences, use a question mark.

The court asked defendant's attorney, "Are you saying that federal taxes on this investment must be paid through January 15 of this year?"

and

The boy, when confronted by the clerk, said only, "Who, me?"

When a question mark comes at the end of a sentence, no period is used after the question mark. A question mark can be used mid-sentence, after the question, but then a period is still used at the end of the sentence.

Can taxes on this investment be deferred? is the question.

This structure is rare and thus looks odd to most readers; try rewording the sentence whenever you can to avoid putting a question mark in the middle, even if it is grammatically correct to do so.

The question is, "Can taxes on this investment be deferred?"

On rare occasions, you may choose either a question mark or a period.

May we hear from you within one week.

Here the choice between a period and a question mark is a tactical one. When you are asking a question but implying a demand, you may use a period. This is not particularly advisable, however, because of the tone it creates. For handling question marks and quotation marks together, see QUOTATIONS, HOW TO PUNCTUATE, subsection 4.

In legal writing, it is unwise to use a question mark within parentheses to suggest doubt, because this form does not precisely state what the doubt is.

The victim described his attacker as over six feet tall, but he may be inaccurate because the victim himself is only five feet tall.

rather than

The victim described his attacker as over six feet tall (?) and weighing about 260 pounds.

QUESTIONS PRESENTED

The lens of the legal analyst's camera, the Question Presented focuses on the specific question to be answered in a legal memo. This term is used by many attorneys to differentiate it from the Issue in a persuasive piece of writing, though the latter is sometimes also called a Question Presented. In its objective form, the Question Presented can outline the memo because it can have three parts: (1) the general rule of law governing the question, (2) the legal question to be answered in this situation, and (3) the legally significant facts necessary for the analysis.

reference to the law
Under Fed. R. Civ. P. 4(d)(1), Summons: Personal Service,

legal question
was a notice effective

legally significant facts
when it was delivered to defendant's wife and defendant did not reside at his wife's address?

These three parts are combined and written in either question form or *whether* form. The *whether* form enjoys common use among established lawyers, but it is grammatically incorrect because it is an incomplete sentence. The *whether* form also implies a statement rather than a question and can add extra words.

In either form, keep subject and verb close together to increase readability.

Under Fed. R. Civ. P. 4(d)(1), Summons: Personal Service, was a notice effective when it was delivered to defendant's wife and when defendant did not reside at his wife's address at the time of delivery?

or

Whether notice was effective under Fed. R. Civ. P. 4(d)(1), Summons: Personal Service, when it was delivered to defendant's wife and defendant did not reside at his wife's address.

The *whether* form is often less readable when *whether* is followed by a detailed description of the facts or a long description of the law.

Whether a notice that was delivered to defendant's wife when defendant did not reside at his wife's address was effective under Fed. R. Civ. P. 4(d)(1), Summons: Personal Service.

To avoid this problem, put the longest component of the question last. Usually, you can put the legally significant facts at the end of the Question Presented so that the reader is focused by moving from general to specific.

Placing the legally significant facts at the end also helps keep the question readable because it places the list at the end of the sentence. For related information, see LISTS, STRUCTURE OF. In the rare situation where you are unable to use this structure, see MULTI-SENTENCE ISSUE.

Finally, check with your reader to see if the particular facts of your case should be included in the Questions Presented, which will focus the questions on the client's situation. Pay attention to the wording of the facts because PRECISION here increases CLARITY. For related information, see ANOTONYMS and SYNONYMS. Additionally, your reader may prefer that the facts be stated in general terms so the memo is easier to use as a reference in future cases. For related information, see AUDIENCE, ISSUES, and READERS.

Be particularly careful if you are using artificial intelligence (AI) here. Before you enter your client's specific information, check all pertinent confidentiality and privacy requirements as well as whether the AI system you are using retains and publishes this information. For help doing this, see ARTIFICIAL INTELLIGENCE AND RESEARCH, ARTIFICIAL RESEARCH AND WRITING, PROMPTS, and RESEARCH STRATEGY GUIDE.

QUOTATION MARKS

Common concerns about quotation marks include (1) when to use them, (2) when not to use them, (3) whether to place other punctuation before or after the quotation marks, and (4) when to use single quotation marks.

1. When to use them.

Use quotation marks for quotations of forty-nine words or fewer.

One eye witness described his behavior as "out of control, like a crazy person."

Use quotation marks to indicate titles of works smaller than books or journals that need to be cited within the text, rather than in a citation sentence or clause.

He was rising to sing "The Star-Spangled Banner" when he lost his balance and fell forward onto the person seated in front of him.

Also use quotation marks to indicate that you are referring to a word itself, rather than the thing the words stand for, as in the following example.

"Hearsay" refers to a statement, other than one made by the declarant while testifying, offered in evidence to prove the truth of the matter asserted.

2. When not to use quotation marks.

For quotations longer than forty-nine words, indent the text on the left and right and omit the quotation marks.

In legal writing, do not use quotation marks around words to indicate a sarcastic tone or to, in effect, apologize for using an informal term. Find another way to communicate your meaning, because quotation marks used in these ways usually create ambiguity and introduce emotion into the text without clarifying the writer's exact meaning.

3. Whether to place other punctuation before or after the quotation mark at the end of a quotation.

Place periods and commas within the quotation marks, even if the punctuation is not part of the quotation, unless you are quoting statutory language. For more on this, see QUOTATIONS, HOW TO PUNCTUATE.

4. When to use single quotation marks.

When it is necessary to use quotation marks again within a larger quotation, use single quotation marks.

His promise "to grant reproduction rights of 'Redundancy' " was limited to the duration of the contract.

Because Great Britain's rules differ on this point, you may occasionally see single quotation marks used for the original quotation and double quotation marks used for the internal quotation. The U.S. custom for using double quotation marks as the primary marking for quotations may change some day in the future, but do not hold your breath.

QUOTATION MARKS IN LEGISLATION

See LEGISLATION.

QUOTATION MARKS OR INDENTED QUOTATIONS?

See QUOTATIONS, HOW TO PUNCTUATE, subsections 1 and 2.

QUOTATION MARKS, SINGLE

Although writers in some other countries conventionally use single marks ('___') instead of double marks ("___"), lawyers in the United States use double marks. Single quotation marks are used only for a quotation within a quotation. For related information, see QUOTATIONS, HOW TO PUNCTUATE.

QUOTATIONS, HOW TO PUNCTUATE

These rules are picky and extensive but worth observing. It is important to be accurate in legal writing, and particularly important to be accurate when quoting. These rules include

(1) when to use quotation marks,

(2) when to indent a quotation,

(3) when to use a comma before or after a quotation,

(4) how to use other punctuation marks with quotation marks,

(5) when to use single quotation marks,

(6) when and how to underline parts of a quotation,

(7) how to mark changes in a quotation,

(8) how to mark omissions from a quotation, and

(9) how to maintain credibility when editing a quotation.

1. When to use quotation marks.

Use quotation marks to mark any direct quotation that runs for forty-nine words or fewer.

The court reasoned that "any error must in this situation be material."

Also use quotation marks to indicate that a word is being used to refer to the word itself, rather than to the meaning of the word. Thus, put quotation marks around a word when you could insert *the term* or *the word* before that word.

The court focused on "reasonable" when interpreting the meaning of this clause in the contract.

Avoid using quotation marks to indicate slang, sarcasm, irony, or anything other than direct quotations or words used as words. The precision of legal writing requires the precise use of punctuation, including quotation marks. If you feel uncomfortable using a word because it is informal or ambiguous, change the word rather than putting it in quotation marks.

The attorney's complaint about the assistant's typographical errors cannot be considered slander.

rather than

The attorney's complaint about the assistant's "typos" cannot be considered slander.

2. When to indent a quotation.

When the quotation is longer than forty-nine words, indent both the right and left margins, use single spacing, and omit quotation marks. Put the citation on the first line of text following the quotation, rather than within the indented quotation itself.

In this case, mutuality required the court's closer scrutiny.

> **Despite the defendant's emotional plea regarding the centrality of upholding contracts to the free working of a democracy, we cannot ignore the plaintiff's complaint. In this case, the court must intervene because the issue of mutuality, not to mention that of duress, requires that the court examine both the contract's wording and the parol evidence surrounding the signing of that contract.**

<u>Hartman v. Legler</u>, 986 F. Supp. 3d 192, 198 (S.D. Ind. 2025). Mutuality emerged from the contract's wording because . . . .

3. When to use a comma before or after a quotation.

Use a comma if the phrase before the quotation introduces it.

She said, "I killed him."

If the quotation is an integral part of the larger sentence, do not use a comma.

He said "killed," not "stabbed."

When the quotation concludes within the sentence, end it with a comma rather than a period.

She said, "I killed him," before being given her Miranda rights.

4. How to use other punctuation marks with quotation marks.

In the U.S., quotation marks go outside commas and periods, even if the comma or period is not part of the quotation.

The term on which we must focus is "mutuality."

This rule is the same for both double quotation marks ("—") and single ones ('—'). The rule is not meant to reflect logical concerns, but rather historical ones. Periods and commas on early U.S. presses kept breaking, so they moved them inside the quotations. One exception to this rule is legislation, where periods and commas are generally treated like all other punctuation marks. As always, check and follow your jurisdiction's rules. Another exception is British English, which also puts commas and periods outside the quotation marks when they are not part of the quotation.

All other punctuation marks go inside the quotation marks if they are part of the quotation, outside if they are not.

> **Common law recognized a defense to a privacy action where "the incident was a public concern and record"; however, the statutory policy had in effect eliminated this defense.**

The semicolon is not part of the quotation, so it goes outside the marks.

> **Smith reports "a majority of the jurors thought 'infer' meant 'assume'!"**

The exclamation point is part of the quotation, so it goes inside the quotation marks. *Infer* and *assume* refer to the words as words, rather than the concepts the words describe, and so are put in quotation marks. Single marks are used because the words are within another quotation. For related information, see EXCLAMATION POINTS.

5. When to use single quotation marks.

In the United States, use single quotation marks only when quotation marks are needed within other quotations.

> **The defendant said, "He told me to 'get lost.' "**

6. When and how to underline or italicize parts of a quotation.

Underline or use italics to add emphasis to the key phrase in quotations long enough to be indented and single-spaced in the text. Underlining or italics may encourage the legal reader to read the long quotation by making it more visually pleasing. When you underline or italicize, add *(emphasis added)* after the citation.

> **As this court itself has stated,**
>
> > **[T]he court must intervene because the issue of mutuality, not to mention that of duress, requires that the court examine the parol evidence surrounding the signing of the contract. Such an intervention often illuminates the intentions of the parties, the nature of the contract, and the level of commitment to the agreement.**

Durant v. Colt, 945 F. Supp. 3d 641, 655 (D.D.C. 2025) (emphasis added).

or

As this court itself has stated,

> **[T]he court must intervene because the issue of mutuality, not to mention that of duress, requires that the court examine *the parol evidence surrounding the signing* of the contract. Such an intervention often illuminates the intentions of the parties, the nature of the contract, and the level of commitment to the agreement.**

***Durant v. Colt,* 945 F. Supp. 3d 641, 655 (D.D.C. 2025) (emphasis added).**

When the quotation is indented, put the citation and *(emphasis added)* on the first line of text following the citation for the indented quotation, not within the indented quotation itself. For limits to this technique, see EXTENDED QUOTATIONS.

7. How to mark changes in a quotation.

In general, use brackets to mark any changes you make in the wording of a quotation.

(a) If you are changing or adding a word to a quotation to make it fit grammatically into your sentence, put brackets ([ ]) around that word.

> **As the court explained, "Despite the defendant's emotional plea regarding the centrality of upholding contracts to the free working of a democracy, [the court] cannot ignore the plaintiff's complaint."**
>
> changed from the original
>
> Despite the defendant's emotional plea regarding the centrality of upholding contracts to the free working of a democracy, we cannot ignore the plaintiff's complaint.

(b) If you are adding or changing a letter within a word, put brackets around the part of the word changed. Even if all you do is change a letter from lower case (*a*) to upper case (*A*), you must put brackets around the change.

> **The court made this explicit when it said, "[W]e cannot ignore the plaintiff's complaint."**
>
> changed from the original

Despite the defendant's emotional plea regarding the centrality of upholding contracts to the free working of a democracy, we cannot ignore the plaintiff's complaint.

(c) If you are adding *sic*, put it in brackets. Add *sic* when you want to inform the reader that the error in the text was in the original, rather than being an error you made when copying the quotation.

"In this cause [sic], Ms. Hofner did not realize she was waiving this right."

Always consider whether correcting the error would be a better tactical choice. For more on this, see *SIC*.

8. How to mark omissions from a quotation.

In general, use ellipses to mark any omissions you make in a quotation. An ellipsis is a series of four spaces alternated with three periods (. . .) used to show omissions in quotations. To be accurate, you must not only use ellipses to mark any omissions; you must also be accurate in your placement of any punctuation before or after the ellipses, as the following rules explain. These rules are intricate, but important and useful to the careful reader. If ellipses are used accurately, the reader can tell exactly what changes you made in the original without having to look up the source. And if the reader checks your work, you will gain enormous credibility from having marked the quotation accurately.

(a) If you are omitting a word or words within one sentence, use the ellipses with its four spaces and three periods.

"The issue of mutuality . . . requires that the court examine both the contract's wording and the parol evidence surrounding the signing of the contract."

changed from the original

The issue of mutuality, not to mention that of duress, requires that the court examine both the contract's wording and the parol evidence surrounding the signing of the contract.

(b) If you are omitting the rest of an entire sentence, put a period after the ellipsis. This fourth period represents the period at the end of the original sentence.

"There can be no negligence without duty . . . ."

changed from the original

There can be no negligence without duty, and in this case there is no duty.

(c) If the sentence being quoted ended with a question mark or exclamation mark, use that mark rather than a period after the ellipsis.

> **"The jury thought 'imply' meant 'assume' . . . !"**
>
> changed from the original
>
> The jury thought "imply" meant "assume" in this situation!
>
> and
>
> **"Did the defendant take all reasonable precautions . . . ?"**
>
> changed from the original
>
> Did the defendant take all reasonable precautions before starting up the mower?

(d) Similarly, if you are omitting the rest of one sentence and then continuing the quotation at the start of the next sentence, put a space before the ellipsis, and a space and period after the ellipsis. After the fourth period, add one space and then begin the next sentence, just as you would after the period at the end of any other sentence.

> **"The court cannot base its decision on sympathy. . . . There can be no negligence without duty . . . ."**
>
> changed from the original
>
> The court cannot base its decision on sympathy. To do otherwise would subvert the law. There can be no negligence without duty, and in this case there is no duty.

Again, if the sentence you are editing ended with a question mark or exclamation point, repeat that mark instead of the fourth period.

(e) If you are quoting the end of a sentence, omitting one or more sentences, and then continuing the quotation with a later sentence, do the following. First, put a period, question mark, or exclamation point immediately after the last word of the quoted sentence right before the ellipsis, just as you would have done if you were not omitting sentences. Second, put in the ellipsis. Third, space once and then begin the next quoted sentence.

> **In this case, the court must intervene. . . . The issue of mutuality, not to mention that of duress,**

requires that the court examine both the contract's wording and the parol evidence surrounding the signing of that contract.

changed from the original

In this case, the court must intervene. Despite the defendant's emotional plea regarding the centrality of upholding contracts to the free working of a democracy, it cannot ignore the plaintiff's complaint. The issue of mutuality, not to mention that of duress, requires that the court examine both the contract's wording and the parol evidence surrounding the signing of that contract.

(f) If you are quoting the end of a sentence, omitting one or more sentences, and then continuing the quotation mid-sentence, follow the same procedure explained in subsection (e), but also put brackets around the first letter of the first word after the ellipsis if you are changing that letter from lower case to upper case.

In this case, the court must intervene. . . . [M]utuality requires that the court examine both the contract's wording and the parol evidence surrounding the signing of that contract.

changed from the original

In this case, the court must intervene. Despite the defendant's emotional plea regarding the centrality of upholding contracts to the free working of a democracy, it cannot ignore the plaintiff's complaint. The issue of mutuality requires that the court examine both the contract's wording and the parol evidence surrounding the signing of that contract.

(g) Never use an ellipsis at the beginning of a quotation, even if you have omitted the first word or words of the quoted passage. The ellipsis is unneeded because the fact that the first word of the quotation was not originally capitalized is sufficient to indicate that words have been omitted.

[T]here can be no negligence without duty.

rather than

. . . there can be no negligence without duty.

changed from the original

As the defense so aptly argued, there can be no negligence without duty.

9. How to maintain credibility when editing a quotation.

Avoid extensive editing of a quotation, even when you can do it accurately. If you use ellipses and brackets too much, the reader will find the quotation awkward to read and will probably suspect that you are misrepresenting the original idea. The solution in this situation is not to omit ellipses and thus sacrifice ACCURACY; it is to PARAPHRASE or to find another quotation that fits the situation without needing such extensive surgery.

The court stated that it must intervene in this case to resolve the issue of mutuality despite the emotional pleas for freedom of contract.

rather than the extensively edited version

Despite the . . . emotional plea regarding . . . upholding contracts to the free working of a democracy, [the court] cannot ignore the plaintiff's complaint. . . . [T]he court must intervene; the issue of mutuality . . . requires that the court examine both the contract's wording and the parol evidence . . . .

changed from the original

Despite the defendant's emotional plea regarding the centrality of upholding contracts to the free working of a democracy, we cannot ignore the plaintiff's complaint. In this case, the court must intervene; the issue of mutuality, not to mention that of duress, requires that the court examine both the contract's wording and the parol evidence surrounding the signing of that contract.

QUOTATIONS, LONG

See EXTENDED QUOTATIONS.

QUOTATIONS, WHEN TO USE

Use quotations if the particular phrasing is central to your issue, such as phrases including TERMS OF ART or key passages from the applicable statute. Otherwise use quotations only if the answer to each of the following questions is *yes*.

1. Does the quotation contain information directly pertinent to the point?
2. Is the quotation no longer than one long paragraph, unless content requires all of it?

3. Does the quotation communicate the information more clearly than you could by using a PARAPHRASE? Alternatively, does this quotation communicate the information more eloquently than you could in a paraphrase?
4. Are you sure the quotation is accurate?
5. Have you verified the quotation source?

Particularly beware of quotations you collected from sources other than legal cases or statutes or sources that use generative artificial intelligence. Do not depend on the accuracy of a second-hand reference to a quotation. For help on this, see ACCURACY, ARTIFICIAL INTELLIGENCE AND RESEARCH, ARTIFICIAL INTELLIGENCE AND WRITING, NOTES, PROMPTS, RESEARCH STRATEGY GUIDE, and UPDATING THE LAW.

On rare occasions, you may have a supervising attorney who wants you to cut and paste extensive quotations into your documents. Although this will not create a readable or attractive document, remember your practical situation, and do the best you can. See also QUOTATIONS, HOW TO PUNCTUATE; and EXTENDED QUOTATIONS.

QUOTATION WITHIN A QUOTATION

See QUOTATIONS, HOW TO PUNCTUATE, subsection 5.

RAMBLING

To avoid this problem, see ORGANIZE, HOW TO and PARAGRAPHS.

RE

You may use *re* in SUBJECT LINES for letters or memos, but do not use it in the text of the letter or memo. Instead use *regarding.*

READABILITY

Many factors work together to enhance the readability of a document. Here is a checklist of some of the most useful ones.

1. Use shorter sentences.

   Check to make sure that your sentences do not habitually run more than three-and-one-half lines. One easy way to do this is to put a slash after each period in the draft. You can do this without actually reading the text; just skim for the periods. Then, looking at where the slashes fall, check for places where there are several long sentences in a row. Divide at least some of these into shorter sentences.

You may decide that the testimony of one witness is entitled to greater weight than that of another witness, or even of several witnesses. In weighing the evidence, you may consider your own knowledge, observations, and life experiences.

rather than

In weighing the evidence, you may consider the testimony of one witness as entitled to greater weight than that of another witness or several others, your own knowledge, what you have observed, and the experiences you have had in life.

Even though the revision is just as long as the original, it will be read more quickly by the reader. Therefore the text will not seem wordier or longer. If a sentence contains a list at the end, it may not need to be divided. For ways to handle the list, see the next subsection.

2. Use clear and logical lists.

Careful structuring of lists greatly increases readability. First, always make sure that the elements of your list are both logically and grammatically parallel.

The defendant moved his car into the left lane to pass, lost control on the snow-packed pavement, slid back into the right lane, and collided with the plaintiff's truck.

rather than

The defendant moved his car into the left lane to pass, was losing control, slid back into the right lane, and caused injury to the plaintiff when he hit her truck.

Then structure your sentence so that the list comes at its end. Additionally, when the list is long or complex, use signals, such as parenthetical numbers or tabulation, to help the reader see immediately the structure of the list.

To justify the exclusion of expert psychiatric evidence, the court discussed (1) maintaining the integrity of the bifurcated trial procedure, (2) avoiding allowing the guilty to go free, and (3) preserving the defendant's right against self-incrimination.

rather than

The court discussed maintaining the integrity of the bifurcated trial procedure, avoiding allowing the guilty to go free, and preserving the defendant's right against self-incrimination to justify the exclusion of expert psychiatric evidence.

For more detail about ways to do this, see LISTS, STRUCTURE OF.

3. Use familiar words.

Use words that your reader will understand without having to resort to a dictionary.

Counsel, by using apt wording and artful presentation, minimized this weak point in her argument.

rather than

Counsel, by applying her verbal acumen and felicitous propensity for oratory, accomplished a feat of legerdemain regarding this conceptual proposition.

Unusual words, even if the reader does know what they mean, force the reader to stop and think. Busy legal readers usually will not stop mid-thought to ponder the nuances of an individual word, and so your meaning may be lost. For more information, see FLOWERY LANGUAGE and JARGON.

4. Use consistent wording.

Use the same term for the same concept throughout the document; do not change it just for VARIETY.

The defendant argues that his repair of the water heater was adequate. This argument, however, ...

rather than

The defendant argues that his repair of the water heater was adequate. This suggestion, however, ...

Using consistent terms aids readability by helping the reader know immediately that you mean the same thing. For more on this point, see CONNECTIONS, MAKING THEM; or REPETITION.

5. Keep the subject and verb undivided and focused on your point.

Keep the subject within seven words of the verb and make sure the subject and verb state the main point of the sentence.

If this case were retried, the result would be different because of the combination of the numerous defects in the proceedings below and the newly discovered evidence.

rather than

The total effect of the numerous defects in the proceedings below, which in combination with the newly discovered evidence referred to above creates a miscarriage of justice, would if this case were to be retried under optimum circumstances produce a different result.

In the second example, the subject (*effect*) is divided from the verb (*would produce*) by twenty-four words, and the two words of the verb (*would* and *produce*) are divided by ten words. By the time readers finally find the verb, they will have forgotten the subject and have to reread the sentence several times to find it. For more ways to restructure sentences, see SENTENCE STRUCTURE.

Additionally, precision is lost when the subject and verb do not clearly state the writer's point. In the previous example, *effect would produce* does not state the reader's main point. Moving the subject and verb together would have exposed this problem to the writer, who could then revise it to *the result would be different*. For more on this see SUBJECT-VERB COMBINATIONS.

6. Use precise transitions.

Use transitions that convey exact connections. For example, use *nevertheless* only when *nevertheless* is the logical connection between the two thoughts.

The litigation may cost more than the amount our client could recover if she wins the suit. Nevertheless, she has chosen to pursue her claim.

rather than

The litigation may cost more than the amount our client could recover if she wins the suit, although she has chosen to pursue her claim.

In the second example, using the wrong transition confuses the reader. For more on this and for a list of transitions, see TRANSITIONS.

7. Use consistent word signals.

If you use *second*, make sure that you used *first* earlier. Similarly, if you used *not only*, use *but also* later. Without these parallel signals, the skilled reader is left frustrated, like the waiting listener who hears one shoe drop but never hears the second. For related information, see CONNECTIONS, MAKING THEM.

8. Use accurate and adequate punctuation.

Punctuation marks are the road signs of legal writing, and inaccurate punctuation can lead to wrong turns. Whenever time allows, revise once just for accurate punctuation. For more information on punctuation needed but often omitted, see COMMAS and SEMICOLONS. For ways to spot these problems, see REVISING.

READERS

While writing creates a communication that lasts over time and beyond the moment of writing, reading happens within a particular time and specific context. Your writing, therefore, will be more effective as you better understand how your readers process your text. Research on this topic has uncovered some basics that can help you as a writer.

1. Organize your document to allow entry from several places.

   Readers do not necessarily read a text from top to bottom, left to write. For example, some begin by reading headings throughout the document, some skim the text quickly, and some read the conclusion section first. This means that your document must communicate your meaning not only in its wording, but also in its headings, paragraphing, and all other aspects of organization. To make sure you communicate your point to readers no matter how they approach the text, check the following aspects of your document.

   (a) Read your HEADINGS separately, without intervening text, to make sure they communicate your overall message and structure, use wording consistent with that of the text itself, and are parallel in structure and format.

   (b) Read the first sentence of each paragraph throughout the text, making sure that your main points are stated in these sentences and logically flow from one to the next. Attend to TRANSITIONS between these opening sentences. Ascertain whether a key term appears in the first half of the first line of each paragraph, so that the reader sees the content quickly.

   (c) Read your introduction and conclusion without the intervening text to make sure these sections are consistent in focus and phrasing of key ideas. These two sections should encapsulate the content by conceptually bracketing the body of the document.

2. Trim information.

   Readers, rather like computers, have only a limited amount of space in their short-term, working memories. A reader can hold only five to nine items in mind at a time. With more information than that, the reader has to move to long-term memory, which takes a much greater commitment of effort. Avoid asking your readers to do this extra work by doing the following.

   (a) Limit interruptions in sentences to eight words or less. For help here, see INTRUSIVE PHRASES. Place longer units of words, such as lists, at the end of your sentence.

   (b) Avoid creating lists of more than seven items whenever ACCURACY allows. In longer lists, consider whether grouping the items into several sublists is logically possible. This approach does the grouping for the reader, making it easier to retain all the information.

3. Make the document context-independent.

Reading is affected by external factors. Because you cannot control the context in which your reader encounters your text, you must avoid factors that trigger that context to the extent you can.

(a) When writing documents such as law review articles that will be read months or years in the future, avoid using terms that will become obsolete. For example, avoid referring specifically to the latest social media format because it is likely to become obsolete or dated by the time some readers encounter them. Similarly, avoid using current informal expressions; imagine describing an event as *groovy* or *a ripsnorter* and you will understand the problem.

(b) Review any analogies you use to consider whether they will hold up over time. For example, an analogy to a current news event, book, or movie is somewhat risky because you cannot predict what its future associations will include. A reference to an older example, however, may be more effective because its associations are already well established. Thus you might refer to *Watergate, Moby Dick*, or *Casablanca* with greater assurance that your reference will be understood as you intended.

4. Omit distractions.

Readers do not necessarily focus their attention where you want them to focus. Some readers are easily distracted by details, while others tend to overlook those same details. Yet other readers are particularly sensitive to the emotional undertones of text, which can affect their reaction to the content. To cope with these differences, do not skip the following steps when POLISHING your text.

(a) Review headings and other large-scale organizing signals, as listed in the previous section, to make sure that they include enough information to communicate your important points.

(b) Review your document to make sure it maintains a professional tone and avoids unnecessary emotional words. For help with this see TONE and PROFESSIONAL LANGUAGE AND PRESENTATION.

(c) Proofread to remove small errors, which can distract readers from your important content. See PROOFREADING.

(d) Whenever there is a risk of revealing proprietary or confidential information, take the additional step of METADATA REMOVAL.

For a discussion of the issues involved in dealing with multiple readers, see AUDIENCE. For a comparison of these two terms, see *AUDIENCE* OR *READER*?

READING LEGAL SOURCES EFFICIENTLY

This entry focuses on ways to enhance your reading techniques; for information about how others read your writing, see READERS and PROFESSIONAL LANGUAGE AND PRESENTATION.

Your writing is affected by your own critical reading of others' writing. Also, because reading is a large part of what you do as a lawyer, you want to gain the most benefit from that reading. The following ideas can help you accomplish this.

1. Establish your purpose before reading.

   Consider your purpose and then read accordingly. You may be reading for background information because you are new to the subject, for procedural information regardless of the substantive issue, for support for an argument, or for a thorough treatment of every current case in the jurisdiction. If you are reading to collect information for a memo, you will read more thoroughly than if you are skimming cases to see if there are any decisions at all on the topic. If you have several purposes, as you often do, prioritize them.

2. Take notes according to your purposes.

   Take notes on information related to your priority of purposes and move more quickly over the rest of the material. If you are collecting all current law on a narrow topic, you may need to create a subfolder for each source. If you are taking notes on cases for three legal issues, you may need to create a folder for each issue. Cross-index sources by creating a spreadsheet or table. Or you may be able to organize background information by drawing a web.

3. Decide what relationship the source has to your issue.

   If you are reading for research, decide how the source answers your question or redefines it. If you are reading for class, decide why the case is in that section of the book. Note also where it falls in the syllabus and connect it accordingly to the cases around it. Connect your source to the issue substantively by seeing what theme or subtheme it suggests. Note, for example, how a holding can define a term from a statute. Distinguish dicta from those holdings to refine the definitions.

4. Be aware of the source's context.

   Nothing is written in a vacuum. Make a note of the source's year, its legal or policy context, its reaction to previous authorities, or its innovative elements. This context can offer tools for interpreting the source's subsequent impact. If a statute is codifying case law, it validates earlier cases, which means that they are still good law. If a case is reacting to legislation, it may be invalidating the legislation or reshaping it for policy purposes. If a treatise is summarizing law from several states, it may be restating it too generally for application in your particular jurisdiction. Read the source not only for its literal, legal statements, but also for its context so that you glean information accurately.

5. Note the source's internal elements.

   A statute will have various sections; decide what they are, why they are there, and how they interrelate. A case may ramble or be divided into sharply defined sections; use a case brief template to analyze what each part says. An article may be structured to have a certain impact. Step back, note the structure, and analyze it. By noting not just the substantive nuggets, but also the structure itself, you can read thoroughly and safely. For related information, see OPINIONS, JUDICIAL.

6. Relate those elements to similar elements in other sources.

   As you read, note any patterns you see among sources, any themes emerging, any fallacies in argumentation being repeated, and any contract sections that occur in every example. Analyze why those elements exist by comparing and contrasting them. Doing so allows you to, in turn, explain these patterns to your reader, who wants to know how sources relate to each other.

7. Read for use of TERMS OF ART.

   Note how the source uses the terms of art you have defined in your question. Are they the same or different? Does use of the term vary within the document or among various sources? Your reader will want consistent definitions, so you need to harmonize usage of terms of art.

8. Note the source's construction.

   As you read for content, also notice the writing itself. You may want to determine whether it is coherent and readable, whether the reasoning is logically based, or whether the writer has manipulated the reasoning to arrive at particular results. Such a critical reading of the source's own integrity heightens both your ability to use the source accurately and your ability to integrate your document and write well for another reader.

9. Verify any results gained from using artificial intelligence (AI).

   Because of the risk of HALLUCINATIONS and other potential inaccuracies, be particularly vigilant if you have used AI for research, generating outlines, writing drafts, or any other results. For help here, see ARTIFICIAL INTELLIGENCE AND RESEARCH, ARTIFICIAL INTELLIGENCE AND WRITING, PROMPTS, and RESEARCH STRATEGY GUIDE. You may particularly want to use the REWRITING CHECKLIST, REVISING CHECKLIST, and POLISHING CHECKLIST.

For related information, see CASE BRIEFS; NOTES; REASONING, PRESENTING IT; RESEARCH AS WRITING; and RESEARCH STRATEGY GUIDE.

READING OPINIONS

See CASE BRIEFS; NOTES; OPINIONS, JUDICIAL; READING LEGAL SOURCES EFFICIENTLY; and RESEARCH STRATEGY GUIDE.

REALLY

Really means *in reality* or *indeed.* It is overused, so avoid it unless it accurately conveys your meaning. Because *really* is used frequently and loosely in informal speech, it is probably best to replace the word with *in reality* in formal legal writing.

REASONED

See *FIND*, *HOLD*, OR *REASON*?

REASONING, ANALOGICAL

Analogical reasoning is a form of inductive reasoning that compares one source to another and suggests that they should be treated in like manner. In the U.S. common law system, writers use analogical reasoning to compare past cases to a current case to suggest that the latter is similar enough to be treated similarly. The same process is used to contrast past cases with a current case to suggest that it should be treated differently. These comparisons and contrasts can focus on any of the elements of the case, including facts, reasoning, holdings, and dicta. For related information see CASE BRIEFS.

Because any two cases are never exactly the same, there is an inherent weakness in this reasoning; this weakness offers room for argument and weakens the conclusion. For this reason, analogical reasoning is considered one of the weakest forms of inductive reasoning in classical rhetoric. If you are using this form of reasoning, be precise about the comparisons and contrasts, and give enough detail to lead your reader through your comparison without having to jump to any conclusions. Do not rely on a superficial similarity or difference to make the case; instead explain why that similarity or difference is legally significant. For information about reasoning in general and some of its other forms, see REASONING, DEDUCTIVE; REASONING, INDUCTIVE; REASONING, MODERN; REASONING, OTHER; REASONING, POSTMODERN; and REASONING, PRESENTING IT.

REASONING, DEDUCTIVE

Deductive reasoning is a form of reasoning that moves from general to specific by stating a general principle and showing how a specific situation fits within that general principle to reach a specific conclusion.

All dogs have four legs.

Spot is a dog.

Spot has four legs.

If the general principle or premise *All dogs have four legs* is accepted as true, then fitting in the specific situation that *Spot is a dog* leads to the conclusion that *Spot has four legs.* Legal writers use deductive reasoning in analyses and arguments to move the reader from a general rule of law through a specific situation that invokes that law to a legal conclusion about that situation. Many cases and analyses use this pattern, which is essentially a SYLLOGISM.

There are intricate variations on deductive reasoning because of the complicated nature of ever-changing law and ambiguous fact situations. When a statute is being applied to a factual situation, a simple deductive process may work: give the terms of the statute as the rule or major premise; analyze the facts using the terms of the statute as the minor premise; and conclude by showing how the rule applied to those facts reaches a specific conclusion.

In a more complicated analysis, the overall organization may move from general to specific and thus be deductive. But inductive reasoning may be used to establish both the major and minor premises that are subsequently used in the deductive syllogism. For example, establishing the general, or major, premise may require an inductive process of synthesizing the appropriate statute with a series of holdings from the cases construing that statute. Establishing the minor premise may also require an inductive process of comparing the current case with the cases construing the statute to reach the principle of how this case fits into precedent. Once those premises are reached, then the specific conclusion for this situation under this statute can be drawn.

This general-to-specific form of reasoning is popular because it allows fewer questions about each step in the logic. If you are using this form of reasoning, be precise about the language used to present the major premise and use that language to state the minor premise and conclusion. For information about reasoning in general and some of its other forms, see REASONING, ANALOGICAL; REASONING, INDUCTIVE; REASONING, MODERN; REASONING, OTHER; REASONING, POSTMODERN; and REASONING, PRESENTING IT.

REASONING, INDUCTIVE

Inductive reasoning is a form of reasoning that moves from specific to general by extrapolating general principles from several examples. For example, an observer might see that a yellow dog has four legs, a spotted dog has four legs, a black dog has four legs, an injured dog has three legs, a small dog sometimes does tricks while on two hind legs, and a brown dog has four legs. From these examples, the observer may reach the general principle that *All dogs have four legs.* While there are some variations and exceptions, the general principle seems to hold.

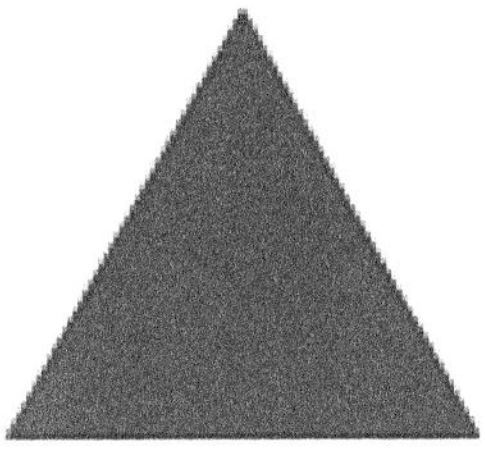

Fido has four legs.

Loki has four legs. Milo has four legs.

Rocky and Coco and Bear each have four legs.

Peaches has three legs, but she was in an accident.

THUS: ALL DOGS HAVE FOUR LEGS.

Legal researchers use inductive reasoning when they gather sources from a variety of cases to glean a current rule of law. A researcher using a common law rule or statute will gather holdings that have been used since the rule or statute was established; from those original statements and holdings, the researcher will extrapolate the current rule and its exceptions. In predicting a judge's ruling, an attorney may study how the judge has handled similar cases in the past and extrapolate from that a likely ruling in a current case. This inductive process requires a leap from the specific examples to the general principle. That leap allows space for argument, depending on how many examples are used and how current those examples are.

One form of inductive reasoning is analogical reasoning, where a current case is compared or contrasted to previous cases to argue that the former is similar enough to the latter to be treated similarly, or different enough that it should be treated differently. These comparisons and contrasts can focus on any of the elements of the case, including facts, reasoning, holdings, and dicta. For related information see CASE BRIEFS.

Because of the leaps from specific to general and because a current case is never exactly the same as previous cases, there is usually room for argument, which can weaken the conclusion. If you are using this form of reasoning, be precise about the specific examples and the comparisons and contrasts, and give enough detail so that your reader follows your inductive process without having to jump to any unsupported conclusions. If your opponent is using this kind of reasoning, look for room to make arguments. For information about reasoning in general and some of its other forms, see REASONING, ANALOGICAL; REASONING, DEDUCTIVE; REASONING, MODERN; REASONING, OTHER; REASONING, POSTMODERN; and REASONING, PRESENTING IT.

REASONING, MODERN

Modern reasoning is a form of reasoning that imposes on a legal situation an analysis from another field of study, such as economics, psychology, or sociology. Modernism reacts against traditional forms of logic. Modernism grew out of the Legal Realist movement in U.S. legal history. The Realists argued that the traditional forms of reasoning (induction and deduction) did not reach the best results, often omitting such important matters as context, economics, process, and public policy.

This form of reasoning takes a broader view of the law and uses different forms of logic. For example, the Legal Process movement that grew out of the rewriting of the Rules of Federal Procedure suggested that legal analysis should examine whether all steps in the process were met, essentially making a chronological examination of how the case was treated according to those rules, before looking at the substantive merits of the case. The Law and Economics movement suggested that a general cost-benefit analysis should be used, rather than a deductive application of a rule. The Law and Society movement suggested that sociological factors should frame legal analysis, such as the economic standing of both plaintiffs and defendants. And the Narrative or Voices approach suggested that narratives or personal stories should compel specific results.

These movements introduced new forms of logic to legal analysis and greatly expanded the possibilities for a THEORY OF THE CASE. For information about reasoning in general and some of its other forms, see REASONING, ANALOGICAL; REASONING, DEDUCTIVE; REASONING, INDUCTIVE; REASONING, OTHER; REASONING, POSTMODERN; and REASONING, PRESENTING IT.

REASONING, OTHER

Every legal culture offers varied forms of logic, and each form is available to consider using in an analysis. For example, writers in code law countries may use a form that begins with the relevant language from a statute and argues deductively from that statute's language. Writers in common law countries may use a form that begins with an inductive synthesis of relevant primary, mandatory cases to form the rule and then proceeds deductively to the conclusion. Within the U.S., judges may vary in their choices of reasoning to reach a conclusion, even though the legal issues are the same. For example, in analyzing the validity of an executive order, one federal circuit court may use a chronological explanation of the history of the limits of executive power, while another circuit may use an inductive explanation of where this action fits within the definition of intent. Thus the federal circuits may become split on their views of the same issues. Similarly, judicial opinions contain an array of reasoning patterns. If you watch for them, you can discern these patterns. All these forms of reasoning are available to you, and they continue to evolve as the law itself evolves. Enrich your approach to legal problem-solving by remaining aware of the broad range of approaches to reasoning and by choosing what best fits your situation, audience, and purposes. Thus it is that two briefs to the same court may each frame the ISSUES differently, each choose a different THEORY OF THE CASE, and each use a different organization. For more help, see ORGANIZE, HOW TO. For information about reasoning in general and some of its other forms, see REASONING, ANALOGICAL; REASONING, DEDUCTIVE; REASONING, INDUCTIVE; REASONING, MODERN; REASONING, POSTMODERN; and REASONING, PRESENTING IT.

REASONING, POSTMODERN

Postmodern reasoning is a form of reasoning that reacts against modern reasoning and its perceived oversimplification of legal problems. It introduces analysis based on a range of perspectives, such as feminism, race, or poverty. Postmodernism, which takes its name from the architectural movement, rejects the simple lines of modernist reasoning and introduces more eclecticism, complexity, and personal perspective. This reasoning, which envelops an ever-greater range of structures than modernism, suggests that no neutral system of thinking can be imposed on a legal problem. Instead, results depend on highly subjective matters, such as who is asking the question, what social situation the problem solvers come from, and how society prefers certain outcomes.

By definition, there is no one approach in this movement, but a range of approaches. The structure of this reasoning ranges from personal viewpoints to examples to narrative, anecdote, and rejection of other forms of reasoning. For example, U.S. Supreme Court decisions, which used to have one majority opinion and one dissent, may now have nine opinions, each taking a different approach to the outcome. All of these approaches are available as structures for a legal analysis. For information about reasoning in general and some of its other forms, see REASONING,

ANALOGICAL; REASONING, DEDUCTIVE; REASONING, INDUCTIVE; REASONING, MODERN; REASONING, OTHER; and REASONING, PRESENTING IT.

REASONING, PRESENTING IT

Reasoning is the analytical process that moves a reader from an original idea or premise to a conclusion. In the U.S. legal community, reasoning takes many forms. Common law fosters a form of analogical reasoning; statutory, or code, law often lends itself to deductive reasoning; legal process theories suggest a sequence of points; and legal realism theories replace literal interpretations of the law with sociology and empiricism. All these forms of reasoning arose from our culture's history, traditions, and sense of logic and fairness, and they are just a few of the choices you have in reasoning.

The U.S. legal reader is particularly interested in seeing each step of the reasoning process, whichever form you choose. The unique relationship among U.S. constitutional, statutory, and common law generates many possible interpretations and forks in the analytical road. Therefore, nothing can be assumed: several legitimate interpretations and logical choices occur at each step in the reasoning. For that reason, explain each step in your reasoning. Although obvious steps may be covered concisely, they should not be omitted. For guidance in how to analyze the facts and law to determine your reasoning, see LEGAL ANALYSIS.

In a more complicated analysis, the overall organization may move from general to specific and thus be deductive. But inductive reasoning may be used to establish both the major and minor premises of the larger syllogism. For example, establishing the general, or major, premise may require an inductive process of synthesizing the appropriate statute with a series of holdings from the cases construing that statute. Establishing the minor premise may also require an inductive process of comparing the current case with the cases construing the statute to reach the principle that reveals how this case fits into precedent. After those premises are reached, then the specific conclusion for this situation under this statute can be drawn. For descriptions of these two kinds of reasoning, see REASONING, DEDUCTIVE and REASONING, INDUCTIVE.

CONVENTIONAL REASONING

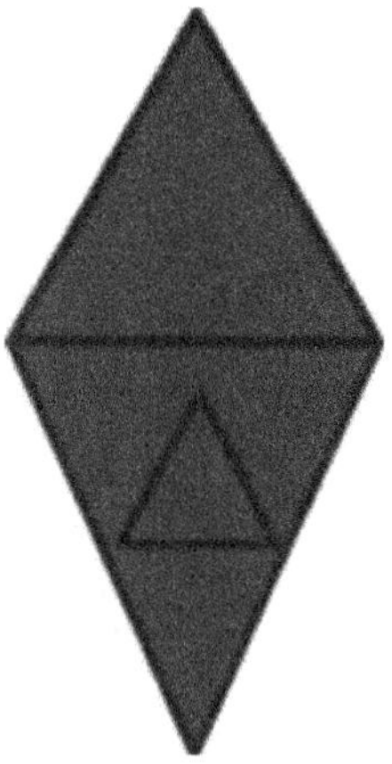

Induction is used to determine the rule, or major premise

Deduction is used to move from the general rule to the specific conclusion

Induction is used again to determine the minor premise, e.g., using analogy to determine where these facts fit within the parameters of previous cases

Conclusion

As you explain the strengths of your thesis or THEORY OF THE CASE, also address the potential weaknesses in your position. To make your reasoning complete, anticipate the barriers in your readers' way. To be fully informed, your readers need to know all aspects of your situation. If they are not aware of the counterarguments, bad news, or other scholarly positions until your opponent presents them, they are less likely to believe your position is sound. Such omissions in turn affect your credibility. For help presenting this in persuasive writing, see COUNTERARGUMENTS, HOW TO HANDLE.

Select the form of your reasoning and organization that best matches your purpose, your research, and your readers' preferences to accomplish your purpose. Then lay out that reasoning step by step.

For example, if you choose a conventional approach to reasoning, which includes elements of deduction and induction, you must (1) frame your legal questions, (2) organize carefully and consciously, (3) establish a basis in legal rules, (4) apply those rules to your situation by demonstrating how your situation is similar to or different from legal precedent in some relevant aspect, and (5) prove your conclusion by showing why your situation falls closer to one type of precedent than to another. In creating this traditional reasoning, consider the following concepts. While they offer a rudimentary starting point, they cannot offer a formula for every situation because reasoning is a complex process, unique to each problem.

1. Frame your legal questions.

   Focus your reader by stating what legal questions are raised in this situation. Be as precise as you can by including the specific law, the TERMS OF ART used to define this question, and the facts pertinent to this question. You can foreshadow your reasoning by using the same order in the issues. If you are moving from general to specific in your analysis, then state the law, legal question, and facts in that order in your issue. If you are using an inductive form of reasoning in your analysis, move from specific to general in your issue by stating the facts, legal question, and law in that order. After you have refined your reasoning, refine the issues' focus so that they connect accurately with your reasoning pattern. For more information on framing questions, see ISSUES and QUESTIONS PRESENTED.

2. Establish a basis in the legal rules.

Provide a thorough-yet-concise presentation of the rules needed for this analysis. For example, if an entire section of a statute is necessary for analysis, include that section at the beginning of the reasoning process, but if only a few sections of the statute are necessary, include those portions only. If several cases must be synthesized to present one general rule, include them all; if only one or two cases are sufficient, limit the section to those two. If there are any relevant exceptions to the rule, include those. Resist the temptation to include any authority just because you found it. Select carefully according to your document's purpose, your readers' needs, and your issue's scope. For more information on presenting the law, see LEGAL ANALYSIS and RULES.

Explain the rules precisely, with an eye toward your ultimate application. Focus on the particular phrases and TERMS OF ART that express the legal terms and concepts you will be using later in your application. Select the essential key terms to present; these terms are often most effective if they appear in the subjects and verbs of your sentences. Explain the relevant reasoning behind the rule enough to convince your reader of its merit. Avoid, however, including more language than needed because it will diffuse the focus of your analysis. Synthesize the terms that are relevant to your issue, rather than reporting on all the details discussed in the statutory or case law you are using.

If, for example, your message is

A tank may be put in a park as a memorial,

you will need to present the language of the statute,

All vehicles that are capable of moving faster than 40 m.p.h. are prohibited from entering the parks in the City,

and show how it applies to this situation. You will need to define the statutory terms, such as *all*, *entering* and *capable*; the history and context of that statute, such as its purpose of providing safe recreation; and perhaps the context for the statute itself, such as its location within the statutes on public safety or military honorifics. While the outcome may seem obvious at first, the rule can be interpreted to reach the opposite outcome. So, as shown below, you will use this rule to develop the arguments for and against your position, such as *it is unsafe* or *it is not going to be moving.* You will also present a logical order that accounts for all parts of the rule and all relevant arguments. You will then demonstrate which arguments under this rule are better and why, thus proving your conclusion that the tank as a fixed monument is, or is not, allowed to *enter the park.*

When using a case as a source of your rule, focus not just on the general language of the rule, but also on the holding. The HOLDING gives the legally significant facts and the reason, which then becomes a part of this rule of law. The holding's language may explain the relevant reasoning used by courts in applying that rule. Stating the rule and a few relevant facts from the case is not always sufficient because the reader needs to know why the court saw those facts as relevant. For example, if the court emphasized the term *unequal bargaining power* in a previous case and that term is relevant to your client's situation, use that term. Beyond just stating the term, though, identify the facts that made it significant to the outcome of the case, that is, what was unequal. Because you will be defining the rule in the context of your client's situation, define its terms so that the reader understands the relevant meaning of that law.

If, for example, you have cases construing the statute, use their holdings to define what has or has not been allowed in the park. One holding may be the following.

> **Defendant violated the statute because his three-wheeled "offroad recreational dirt bike" is a "vehicle capable of reaching a speed of 40 m.p.h." under the statute.**

But another holding may be the following.

> **A wagon is a toy to be enjoyed by children and neither a "vehicle" nor a safety hazard.**

Explain the legally significant components of the source being analyzed. For example, the components of a case include the facts, reasoning, policy, or other elements of the case that, if changed, would change the outcome. This may not include all the components that were significant in the original case, so edit according to your issues. As you explain these components, show how they fit under the rules.

3. Organize carefully and consciously.

What you include in your presentation depends on what contributes to your reasoning. For example, you may want to emphasize any one of the following: the policy, the procedural posture, the holdings, the facts, or the equities. What you select depends on your overall message, the strengths and weaknesses of your situation, and the match between your situation and your sources. Thus the message runs like a bright thread through the fabric of your analysis, guiding the reader along your line of reasoning. The selection of your content is not driven exclusively by a prescribed format, but rather by your understanding of the law, the facts, and the logical thread that runs through all this information.

That logic must be organized in a way that matches your overall purpose. When organizing your reasoning, remember that where you include information also depends on the relationships among your sources and your situation. Therefore, sometimes the decisions of *what* and *where* are interrelated. Allow for several good organizational possibilities; then you can select the best. For example, when you see elements that suggest an element-by-element approach, you may want to follow them as the statute presents them. Do not, however, make that decision automatically. If it turns out that the first two elements are unfavorable as compared with your situation, you may want to begin with element three, which is more favorable. Perhaps you have holdings in five previous cases to go with element three, four of which are favorable and one of which is unfavorable. You can decide, then, to rearrange the elements to begin with element three and synthesize the four favorable holdings to set up a favorable comparison with your case. You are selecting a reasoning pattern based on putting the most favorable dispositions first. You could also group together two neutral elements and put them at the beginning to get past them. Or you may decide that your audience will be confused by any departure from the statute's order, so you distinguish the first two elements strongly under one heading.

If, for example, you want to show that the tank is an exception to the statute, you may want to give the statutory language and examples of what have been considered *vehicles* in previous cases, and then show that this is not a *vehicle* as defined by the statute. Or you may want to begin with a history of the statute and show that it is about preventing speeding in the parks and that the statute thus does not apply to a *vehicle* used as a memorial. Or you may want to show that the tank is not *capable of moving faster than 40 m.p.h.*, and thus the statute does not apply. All these choices are available from the statutory language.

4. Apply the rules to your situation.

Because statutes are the law, you can often use a statute's structure or sequence as cues for your own analysis. You can use the statute's terms of art in turn to define what is relevant and what arguments can be made for each pertinent element of the statute. You may use holdings from previous cases to define the statutory terms and the parameters of previous applications of the statute. Then you can demonstrate where your situation fits within those parameters and what outcome is likely or preferred.

For example, in traditional analogical reasoning, your decisions are driven by similarity between many aspects of your client's situation and your sources. When the law you are citing applies because the holdings are favorable, your reasoning will synthesize those holdings. When you find a case that has legally significant facts very similar to yours, your reasoning will present those facts, probably in more detail than when you are using only a rule or a holding. When, however, the reason you are using this case is because the policy is relevant, then you will emphasize the court's discussion of policy. Your choices of emphasis and order are then essential parts of the reasoning.

Application, however, involves more than a simple comparison of fact to fact or holding to holding. You must also convince the reader that the similarity you present is legally significant. To do this, explicitly explain how the component is relevant to the reasoning, purpose, or other relevant legal concept. This is easier to do when your rule has been set up properly, because you will have already presented this connection in your presentation of the rule when you explained the way the rule was applied in the precedent case. In your application, you will now echo that earlier reasoning, reapplying it to your client's case. Thus, to be most effective, the explanation of the rule and the application of that rule must be carefully coordinated and unified. As you use similar wording and even sentence structures when you now apply rules you presented earlier, you can create this coordination, unifying the whole analysis around your theme.

If, for example, you are showing that the tank is not a vehicle, you can use the statutory terms and case holdings to define it and prove the exception.

> **A "vehicle" is "motorized, has two to four wheels, and includes, but is not limited to, cars, trucks, and motorcycles." City Code Ann. § 100–2(b) (2023). The common use of the term "vehicle" would normally not include a large, heavy, vehicle with no wheels that operates on two belts. <u>Compare</u> <u>Webster's Ninth New Collegiate Dictionary</u> 775 (2025) (defining "vehicle" as "a two- to four-wheeled automotive vehicle having an engine, doors, and a chassis") <u>with</u> <u>id.</u> at 1205 (defining "tank" as "an enclosed heavily armed and armored combat machine that moves on two endless metal**

belts"). Similarly, a three-wheeled "off road recreation dirt bike" is a "vehicle capable of reaching a speed of 40 m.p.h." under the statute. Alton at 21. But a wagon is a toy to be enjoyed by children and neither a "vehicle" nor a safety hazard. Smith at 33. Unlike the off-road recreational vehicle, the tank is not capable of moving over 40 m.p.h., and, like the wagon, it cannot go at that speed and is instead intended to be enjoyed by park-goers as a monument.

As you explain the strengths of your argument, also address the potential weaknesses in your position. To be fully informed, your readers need to know all aspects of your situation. If they are not aware of the counterarguments, bad news, or other scholarly positions, they are less likely to believe your position is sound. Such omissions in turn affect your credibility. For help in how to lay this out, see COUNTERARGUMENTS, HOW TO HANDLE.

Explain how the relevant information is of use in your case. Use your research to define the rules and strengths and weaknesses of your client's situation. Consider several legitimate ways in which you can reason to your conclusion. Then select both your content and your order accordingly, both what to include and where to put it, so your readers can follow each step to your conclusion.

If, for example, your message is that the tank should be allowed in the park, account for the other sides' arguments.

Here, as in Alson, the tank does not create a danger to park users or mar the park's beauty. Immobile, it will not pose a danger to children. Although Representative Jones stated that ten people were injured in accidents in City Parks in 2024, no injury involved playground equipment or a memorial. As in Smith, the tank will not require the destruction of any trees for its placement. Thus, without posing a danger to either children or the environment, the tank should be allowed in the park.

For related information on constructing legal analysis, see ARGUMENT SECTION, DISCUSSION SECTION, and LEGAL ANALYSIS. For other approaches to reasoning, see REASONING, ANALOGICAL; REASONING, DEDUCTIVE; REASONING, INDUCTIVE; REASONING, MODERN; REASONING, OTHER; REASONING, POSTMODERN; and SYLLOGISMS.

5. Prove your conclusion.

   Complete your reasoning by explicitly connecting to your client's situation those concepts that emerged as important. This part of your reasoning may seem obvious to you and, if you have done a good job, you may think it will be obvious to your reader. Nevertheless, you must say it specifically in most settings. To do this, you often refer to the key concept or the term of art that is the focus of your rule, such as *unequal bargaining power,* and tie this concept to one of your client's legally significant facts, such as *high school dropout* and *certified public accountant.* The cord that binds the facts to the key legal concept is another phrase that is narrower than this concept but broader than the facts themselves, such as *greater education and financial experience.* Often you will not find this phrase verbatim in either your facts or the law itself. The concept will instead be implied through the pattern of application and through the facts the courts choose to emphasize in precedent cases. You must craft this phrase yourself, and crafting it correctly is the heart of the legal reasoning process.

   If you have gone through all elements of the statute, your conclusion can bring the analysis together, using the language of your message.

   The tank may be placed in the park because it is not a "vehicle capable of reaching speeds of 40 m.p.h." and it will not create a safety hazard if properly installed.

   When you do complete your reasoning, your reader will be grateful to be led away from the trees and reminded of the forest. This completion justifies your journey by reminding both you and the reader why you engaged in this reasoning in the first place.

   For related information, see CONCLUSIONS.

RECOMMENDATIONS, JOB-RELATED

When asking someone to recommend you to a potential employer, allow that person ample time to complete the process. Ask and confirm in person, if possible, and never take a recommender for granted. Asking in person also allows you to recognize any signs of reluctance. If you receive permission, make the process as comfortable as possible by providing the following:

- your résumé or C.V. (*curriculum vitae*);
- your cover letter or personal statement, which reveals why you are interested in the position;
- a website or brief description of the job for which you are applying;
- qualities the employer is looking for;

- the person to whom the recommendation should be sent;
- how the recommendation should be delivered (if needed, provide a pre-addressed, stamped envelope); and
- the due date.

This package not only makes it easier for the person to say *yes,* but it also shows the person that you are organized, considerate, and serious about the job. All this provides material that may be mentioned in the recommendation itself.

When you are asked to write a recommendation for someone, ask for all the information listed above. As you write the recommendation, include information pertinent to the job description. Specifically address all important relevant qualities that you can because an omission may be read as a weakness on the part of the candidate. When you have specific examples, include them. Specific compliments are more believable than vague generalizations. Also offer to talk directly to the potential employer if you are willing. Oral recommendations are often more useful and effective because the employer can ask about any particular concerns and you can answer more directly, often, than you could in writing. For related information, see PROFESSIONAL LANGUAGE AND PRESENTATION.

RECOMMENDATIONS, LEGAL

Recommendations are appropriate in a memo's conclusion when the memo's purpose is to analyze the law and to predict the outcome in the context of pretrial discovery. Often the reader, another person in the same office, has assigned the writer the job of analyzing the law so that the reader can make a decision about a particular pretrial or pre-negotiation activity. For example, a supervising attorney might assign an associate to write a memo on whether to move for summary judgment in a case. The associate should make the recommendation as specific as possible, after explaining the reasons in the Discussion.

Similarly, an attorney might recommend certain action in an opinion letter. This recommendation may be located wherever it is most logical: in the opening paragraph or the closing one, or under a separate subheading. Wherever it appears, the recommendation should be within the realm of professional, not personal, advice. Always be aware of your professional responsibility when making a recommendation. For related information, see CONCLUSIONS; MEMOS; OPINIONS, LEGAL; and OPINION OR ADVICE?

RECORD, CITING TO IT

Cite to the record in the Statement of the Case in a pretrial, trial, or appellate brief. As you cite, be scrupulous about using pinpoint references so the reader can quickly locate exact passages. For the reader's convenience, also refer to the record in the Argument if the reader might need to verify sources as an integral part of the argument.

Check your jurisdiction for the appropriate format for these citations to the record. Some prefer parentheses, *(Tr. 38)*, some use none, *CP 19*, and others use periods, *R. 76*. For related information, see CITATIONS and CITATIONS, PINPOINT.

RECORDS, KEEPING THEM

As a lawyer, you need to keep track of what you are doing and when and why you are doing it. Some of your recordkeeping involves your own substantive, problem-solving NOTES. In addition, you need keep clear and useable records in at least the following categories:

(1) using your law office's system,

(2) keeping client information confidential,

(3) filing emails, and

(4) preserving and accessing precedents.

1. Using your law office's system.

   Your office will have invented a system for filing documents and keeping records. Learn it as quickly and thoroughly as possible so that you are fitting your work into that system immediately. Do not rely on others to do it for you because you may inadvertently omit important information or include inappropriate information. For example, if you are filing a brief, you want to make sure that it is filed internally in your law office's system as well as properly with the court. And if you are taking notes during a meeting, you will want to find out how best to preserve those notes for referral by all relevant people within the firm. Your office may also be using artificial intelligence (AI) to capture documents, so you will want to know the parameters of preserving confidentiality within that system. For related information, see WRITING AND TECHNOLOGY.

2. Keeping client information confidential.

   Whether you are taking notes during a meeting, sending an email, or writing a memo, make sure you create a system that flags confidential information. Be sure that your recordkeeping system protects that confidential information and does not mix it with your more general research so that nothing leaks outside the firm. Also be particularly careful that you have preserved client confidentiality when you frame prompts for legal research or use AI, because some AI systems capture and keep prompts and other confidential information. For more on this see ARTIFICIAL INTELLIGENCE AND

RESEARCH, ARTIFICIAL INTELLIGENCE AND RESEARCH, and PROMPTS.

3. Filing email.

For email, create a system for subject line, client, and general topic so that you can easily refer to and find relevant emails. You may want to use subdirectories to keep track of separate issues. Use an effective SUBJECT LINE that meshes with your record-keeping system. Use the case number or the client's name and the subject of the email, such as *Russell case—deposition with Dr. Windemere.* If you anticipate creating a series of emails on the same subject, you can even number them: *Russell #1—deposition information, Russell #8—confirmation of pretrial hearing date.* Be as specific as you can.

Re: Canceled meeting on Russell defense

rather than

Meeting canceled

Within the body of the email, write context-independent texts that include pertinent information to remind your reader of the email's overall context. Just a phrase or two to orient the reader is helpful, such as, *In the Russell case, we need to call Dr. Windemere as an expert on product safety. He will be deposed on January 22, 2025, at 11:10 a.m. in our conference room 10A.*

Consider how your readers will file your correspondence. For email, readers use the subject line to determine how to treat and file the email, so address only one topic in an email, if possible. For example, if you are attaching a file that is similar to files the reader might be receiving from other senders, put your name on the file, e.g., *Smith comments on Russell brief.* If you are suggesting a direction a case might take, label your suggestion, e.g., *Russell brief-economics theory on issue #2.* You may also want to label the priority of your email or color code it if your system allows you to do so.

Finally, remember that any email may be forwarded, so mark the email "confidential" if necessary, and double check that the email's context can be discerned easily by the readers and whoever reads the forwarded email.

4. Preserving and accessing precedent documents.

Your law office may want to capture your writing as precedent for others who may be drafting a memo, contract, or other document on a similar subject. Learn how that precedent system works, how to access it appropriately, and how to add your documents to the library. Be sure to remove confidential information before releasing your document to the system.

RECUR OR *REOCCUR*?

The difference in meaning between these two words is slight, but in some contexts it is important. *Recur* implies that the event happens repeatedly; *reoccur* implies that the event is repeated only once.

REDUNDANCY

See CONCISENESS. For related information, see REPETITION.

REFERENCES

See CITATIONS; FOOTNOTES; and RECORD, CITING TO IT.

REFERENTS

See ANTECEDENTS.

REGARDLESS OR *IRREGARDLESS*?

Regardless, always.

REGULATIONS, DRAFTING

See LEGISLATION.

REJECTION LETTERS

See BAD NEWS, SOFTENING IT and BAD NEWS, GIVING IT.

REPETITION

Repetition by careful design works in legal writing. Rather than avoiding repetition absolutely, avoid it when it does not have one of the following uses.

1. Use repetition when it is needed for accuracy.

   If you mean *contract*, do not shift to *document* or *agreement*. Changing terms confuses legal readers, who will think that you must mean something else if you changed terms. For more help, see ACCURACY, subsection 1. For related information, see SYNONYMS.

2. Use repetition when it is needed for readability.

   For example, repeating the same first word at the beginning of each item in a list can be very helpful to the reader when each item in the list is long.

   Any proposed method for reducing marital status discrimination must reflect the statutory complexity

creating discrimination, must avoid reproducing the undesirable effects of the current taxation structure, and must show awareness that compromising one or more important policy goals is necessary in any tax scenario.

For more on this technique and others, see LISTS, STRUCTURE OF, subsection 7; and READABILITY, subsection 4.

3. Use repetition as a transition to connect, or dovetail, two sentences or paragraphs.

Environmental Impact Studies could be handled similarly without delaying the hearing. Even if there were some delay, ...

Repeating a key word from a previous sentence or paragraph shows how the idea that word represents fits in with the idea of the new sentence of paragraph.

4. Use repetition to create emphasis.

Sometimes the very fact that a repeated word gains attention can be an advantage. For example, you may repeat a word or structure that states a dramatic or important point.

The defendant stated this intention to his girlfriend. He stated it to his coworkers. He stated it to the cabdriver who took him to the airport.

For a broader context, see EMPHASIS.

5. Use repetition when it is required by format or convention.

It is appropriate to repeat content from the main text in some circumstances. For example, when you write conclusions and introductions, which summarize the body of a text, you must by definition repeat key terms and major themes. Similarly, you will necessarily need to repeat some information when you write captions for appendices, graphs, or tables.

6. Use repetition of a singular noun when needed to avoid resorting to the outdated *he or she* or using *they* as a singular pronoun.

Each applicant must sign the affidavit using the applicant's full legal name.

For more on this issue, see GENDER AND WRITING.

REPETITION OF SOUNDS

See ALLITERATION and ASSONANCE.

REPLY BRIEFS

See BRIEFS, REPLY.

REPLY TO ALL

When writing any electronic communication, draft it before putting any recipients' names in the *To* or *cc* or *bc* lines. Then review it. That delay allows you to reflect before sending. It should also prevent you from inadvertently sending it before it is finished.

When you are ready to send it, decide if you want to send it to each reader on the list. The minute it takes to do this carefully may save you hours of remorse and explanation, particularly if someone has inadvertently added to the list a person with whom confidentiality is not protected. Verify, always. For more information about avoiding email hazards, see ACCURACY; BAD NEWS, GIVING IT; COMMUNICATIONS, TONE OF; EMAIL; SUBJECT LINE; and TONE.

REQUESTS FOR PAYMENT

There are four do's here.

1. Do consciously decide what you want.

   If you want money, focus on that and set aside your moral outrage at the way your client has been treated. In contrast, if you really want to express your moral outrage, do so in temperate language. Realize, however, that this expression may not do much to help you get any money for your client or yourself.

2. Do consider your reader's motivations.

   It is always useful to remember the possible motivations your reader may have and try to employ those motivations to get what you want. Choose not what persuades you, but what will persuade your reader. For example, if you are trying to persuade a party to pay an outstanding bill, do not use threats when you think the party would view that threat as a challenge and submission as a weakness. In that situation, you might instead explain that the cost of appearing in court because of nonpayment would exceed the cost of settling the account.

   Similarly, if you think that the reader is someone motivated by certain values, try to explain how the action you recommend is consistent with those values. For example, you might argue that paying a bill is essentially the same as keeping a promise. In short, try to explain how the action you recommend is consistent with some goal the reader has. Try to help the reader feel good, or at least not defeated, about taking the action you recommend.

3. Do consider tone.

Consciously decide what tone you want to create. For example, do you want to be nice, giving the reader the benefit of the doubt, or do you want to be tough? If you want to be nice, you may use kind opening and closing paragraphs. For more on this, see BAD NEWS, SOFTENING IT. If you want to be tough, you may use shorter sentences and impersonal language. For more on this, see TOUGH, SOUNDING THAT WAY. For related information, see COMMUNICATIONS, TONE OF.

4. Do retain accuracy.

Make sure what you say is literally correct. Satiric comments or broad hints can be misread easily and can lead to further delays in getting the results you want. Do not resort to diatribe, even if your anger is completely justifiable. Lay out in objective language the facts, the options, and the results. Similarly, do not make empty threats; if your reader knows or finds out that one threat is empty, that reader may assume that later ones are empty, too. See EMOTIONAL LANGUAGE.

RESEARCH

See ARTIFICIAL INTELLIGENCE AND RESEARCH; MANDATORY AUTHORITY; NOTES; PERSUASIVE AUTHORITY; PROMPTS; RECORDS, KEEPING THEM; RESEARCH AS WRITING; RESEARCH STRATEGY GUIDE; STANDARD OF REVIEW; UPDATING THE LAW; WHEN TO STOP; and WRITING AND TECHNOLOGY.

RESEARCH AS WRITING

Legal research is more than just gathering materials. It is part of the analytical process itself. As you gather, read, sort, and assess your content, you also begin to design your document. If you write out your thoughts, you reap multiple benefits from your research, in effect writing at the same time.

1. Research to refine issues.

Whether or not you have a precise idea of your issue when you begin your research, each source you find may help define or redefine the issue. Ask, *How does this source answer, amend, or advance the issue?* and take notes accordingly. Note how the source addresses your issue, namely, how it uses particular verb phrases to respond to the issue, uses specific language that refines your issue, or uses reasoning that expands or advances the issue. Decide how the material supports, undercuts, or distracts from your analysis.

Although you focus on your issue and your client's desired outcome as you gather the materials, you must also account for analytical obstacles. Your goal is to discover any obstacles yourself early in the process, so you can prepare to address them. You want to do this as you research, minimizing your research of unessential sources you will subsequently discard.

Use your research time to cull and sort. Research actively, not passively. Gather your sources intentionally. Rather than researching like the hungry impulse shopper, research like the chef who knows what courses must be served and whose guests arrive within a few hours. Make a list, as suggested in the RESEARCH STRATEGY GUIDE, and research accordingly.

2. Research to analyze.

Each source is connected in some way to another. As you read, you are deciding (a) what those connections are and (b) whether those connections are pertinent to your analysis. As you take notes, sort the information into categories and decide how the sources connect in relation to your issues. You may not be able to sort and identify all the connections as you read the first time, but you will start to see patterns develop. Your sorting decisions will not be final, but they reveal possible ways of explaining what you are reading.

Review your document's purposes and your audience's needs to make final decisions on sources. If you are informing, you need to include all relevant and mandatory authority. If you are delivering bad news, you need enough accurate information to explain the results. If you are completing a contract, you need enough research to make sure the desired contract provision stands. If you are unsure about where a source may fit into your analysis, you may want to include it until you make your final design decisions.

3. Research to design.

As you see the analytical connections among your sources, your facts, and your document's purposes or audiences, your design choices emerge. Those possibilities come from the variety of ways in which you can connect the analytical components. Those connections come from the component's relationship to your theme.

When you read a source, you often know whether or not it will be significant in answering your question and delivering your message. You may want to number your sources accordingly, from 1–10. If you know it is essential and will appear often, it gets a *1*. If it is related, will probably be important, perhaps it gets a *3*. If not related at all, it gets a *10*, and so on. You may add a sentence or two at the top of the source that shows its relationship to the issue and to any other sources. You may change your mind as you complete the cycle of reading, so allow for that. This system, or one like it, allows you to go back and do so.

If you are a visual learner and you see patterns emerging, you may want to draw a web that connects the ideas, or use Venn diagrams or boxes within boxes. If you are a linear learner, you may see an outline emerging. If you are an auditory learner, you may be able to dictate the overall contours of the analysis.

Make sure you allow for several possible designs. As Steven Spielberg says, "Always allow for the second idea, which may be better." Or the third or fourth. Often your first design is writer-based, a report on your research. This design explains what you have found—to yourself. If you need to do such a plan, do not consider it a draft of the final project. Instead, consider it as preliminary notes that you can later reshape to suit your purposes and audiences. Your best design, analysis, and writing springs from original research, carefully followed as your mind wraps itself around the problem. With attention on your issue, your sources' connections to one another, and your design possibilities, you will gain the most from your time researching.

For related information see ARTIFICIAL INTELLIGENCE AND RESEARCH; DEADLINES, MEETING THEM; DESIGN; LEGAL ANALYSIS; NOTES; ORGANIZE, HOW TO; PRIORITIES WITHIN A PROJECT; PROMPTS; QUESTIONS PRESENTED; REASONING, PRESENTING IT; SECONDARY SOURCES; TIME MANAGEMENT; and UPDATING THE LAW.

RESEARCH PROCESS CHECKLIST

Legal research can go on indefinitely, so circumscribe it by assessing your available resources, your experience level on the topic, and the project's cost, time, and scope. Use the following checklist both to plan your approach and to evaluate when to stop researching. This is not a rigid list of requirements, so adapt it to your project and research preferences. For related information, see ARTIFICIAL INTELLIGENCE AND RESEARCH, PROMPTS, RESEARCH STRATEGY GUIDE, and WHEN TO STOP.

1. Have I researched effectively?
   - (a) Developed a flexible strategy?
   - (b) Adapted my strategy when the sources dictate a change?
   - (c) Allocated time appropriately for each step and each source?
   - (d) Avoided tangential research?

2. Have I taken effective notes?
   (a) Recorded the date of the source and of my notes?
   (b) Routinely written down the full citation, in whatever form required in the final version of this document?
   (c) Related my source's information to my issues?
   (d) Kept track of all the sources I checked, even if they were unfruitful, so I will not repeat any research?
   (e) Updated all of my sources?
   (f) Stopped to reflect on my sources to synthesize an overall understanding of the relevant law?
3. Have I organized effectively for the readers?
   (a) Found a way to organize my materials for ready access?
   (b) Taken NOTES on how my research connects with my outline, with cross-references or other indicators?
   (c) Considered other organizational approaches, so I know I chose the best approach?
   (d) Begun translating my research into an outline?
   (e) Checked with my supervising attorney about the overall organization, where appropriate?

RESEARCH STRATEGY GUIDE

Research can be fast and effective or slow and miserable. If you do not have a system that works for you, or if you fall into the same habits regardless of the project, research can also be expensive in money and time. Research is a product of multiple factors: your experience on the topic, available sources, time, the client's budget, the supervising attorney's suggestions, and so on. Your efficiency depends on your ability to take these factors into account.

Your credibility depends on your ability to find exactly what is needed. To achieve this credibility, develop a research ethic of seeking the mandatory authority quickly. As part of this ethic, use your projects to familiarize yourself with all possible legal research sources, not just the comfortable ones. The following guidelines can help you maximize your research efficiency and effectiveness.

Any research strategy begins before you access your sources, so stop: go through the first six steps listed below before you begin to research. By taking these steps, you can decide what sources you should go to first, second, third, and so on. This saves the time spent wandering from one source to another. Fight the temptation to go online shopping without having completed this portion of the strategy.

Write down your strategy. Writing will assist you in remembering the search and omitting repetitive start-up time if you get interrupted. Writing the preliminary issue statement, Step 3, is particularly important because it will help you to decide where to start and how to focus your research throughout the process.

To maximize your efficiency, use a range of online tools as part of a larger research strategy rather than relying on one tool or system. Whatever tool you are using, understand both how it works generally and what its limitations are, because each has nuanced tools and paths. However you use electronic services, remember that they are not error proof and cannot solve all research problems. It is up to you to frame a good question because the better the prompt or question, the better the results. And always adapt your strategy to fit each research project.

Before you look at sources.

1. Collect the facts.

    Just as a journalist does, make sure you know the *who*, *what*, *where*, *when*, *why*, and *how* of the facts. You may want to create a template for collecting these facts, which you can then adapt for use on each project. You can collect the facts by reading the complete file or transcript, taking notes during a client interview, doing your own discovery, and talking directly to the client.

2. Analyze the facts and create search terms.

    Using whatever system you prefer or have, group the facts into general legal categories. If you do not know enough about the area of law to identify all these categories, consult a secondary authority to provide the needed background and terms. You can use categories such as *parties*, *places*, *objects*, *basis*, *defense*, *relief* or *things*, *acts*, *persons*, *places*. Or you can invent your own categories, depending on the kind of law you practice. Brainstorm at this stage; avoid editing. Give each category a page or a column, and then think of possible SYNONYMS and ANTONYMS in order to get accurate search terms.

3. Formulate preliminary Questions Presented and prioritize them.

    Brainstorm again, thinking of all the possible questions. If you are not familiar with this area of the law, do some background reading in SECONDARY SOURCES, in appropriate web sources, or in artificial intelligence (AI) searches. Look particularly at TERMS OF ART and verbs to determine how scholars and decision makers address the topic and state results. Research the precise vocabulary that addresses the topic you are researching. Write out your questions in a way that includes the legally significant information, such as the following three-step formula.

> ***Under*** **[the governing legal source, such as *Nebraska's motor vehicle statute*],**
>
> ***did*** **[the legal question, such as *did a driver take due care*]**
>
> ***when*** **[the LEGALLY SIGNIFICANT FACTS, such as *when she drifted out of her lane while texting*]?**

The first part of the question tells you what sources to use, such as the Nebraska statutory materials. The second part tells you what topic to find or what search terms to use, such as *due care*. The third part tells you how to filter through the summaries of the sources you read if you are looking for factual comparisons. For example, you would look for sources involving drivers who drift or otherwise lose control of their vehicles. You can eliminate those cases whose summaries do not indicate a similarity to these legally significant facts or to related principles

Then organize the issues logically, putting threshold issues first, such as *standing*, and substantive issues later such as *whether X assaulted Y*. For related information, see PROMPTS; QUESTIONS PRESENTED, LEGALLY SIGNIFICANT FACTS, and ISSUES.

4. Verify jurisdiction.

Make sure you know whose law applies. You can look at court filings in a case to make sure you know what court or even what judge is hearing the case. If there is a potential conflict-of-laws question, or a question about whether federal or state law applies or what treaties govern an international question, make resolving the jurisdiction question the first issue when you begin your research.

Decide whether to target a resource up front or to use filters to manage your results after searching broadly. For example, even if you routinely start with a natural language search, you may sometimes find it more efficient to start with a known statute and update it. Most databases search across a wide variety of available information on that database. Exclude from your search all the irrelevant materials right away. For example, if you want federal cases, pre-select federal cases as your parameter before searching, thereby excluding all the other material that could clog your search results. Make sure you know which jurisdiction's law will apply and therefore which database you wish to search. For related information, see SCOPE.

5. Formulate an effective query or PROMPT.

   (a) Choose terms from the list you made in Step 2 and identify the search words most important to your issue, concentrating on terms a court might have used, such as *consideration*, rather than more general terms, such as *payment*.

   (b) Formulate the query or prompt accordingly so that it follows your question in Step 3.

   (c) Carefully limit your query. Consider first the scope of the topic. If it is wide, try to use more specific language to narrow the results or limit it by jurisdiction. If the scope is narrow, you may want to broaden your question to get a more useable range of research results.

   (d) You may want to experiment with low- or no-cost resources first to find useful search terms. If you are completely lost, your research system may have available experts to help you to formulate an effective query or prompt.

6. Make a research plan, using a three-way approach.

Map out your research strategy, depending on what sources you already have and what sources you would like to search. Decide where you will go first, second, third, and why. Make a plan that you can keep track of even if you get interrupted and prepare to keep track of where you are in your strategy, such as using a checklist or your own notation system.

You may want to go to several more places, but make sure that you approach your research from at least three different starting points, whether they are subscription or free databases, websites, or artificial intelligence sources. Rather like the Mercedes symbol, legal research often requires a query to follow three starting points before the circle is complete. It is crucial to think through this three-way approach before you start researching to avoid wasting time wandering from source to source. It is also crucial to know the differences among the quality and weight of the results you find, such as whether they are persuasive or mandatory authority, primary or secondary references, and frequently cited or rarely used.

One general approach is to begin on Lexis, then research the same question on Westlaw and a state database. Another is to begin with American Law Reports (A.L.R.), then check an administrative law source and the statutes annotated. For example, after you look through the Nebraska statutes, you might plan to update the statute to get relevant cases, then check the Nebraska Patterned Jury Instructions and update them. Plan to cover all the relevant materials, moving back and forth from primary to secondary sources using features such as citing references and controlled vocabulary search functions. Again, remember to check more than one source, so you do not risk missing materials that were categorized slightly differently by other publishers, which use different algorithms for categorizing legal materials.

In addition, have your own system ready for taking effective NOTES. If you are also using an online note-taking program, know its features and options. For example, make sure you know how to save your research for a later time, how to move between the researching function and your own notes, and how to save excerpts and exceptions to rules. Then make that research yours by meshing it with your own note-taking system. For example, you may be using an outline feature, a spreadsheet, or folders for topics and subtopics. Whatever you use, be systematic. Avoid having too many browser tabs open at the same time because you can get lost. If you are working collaboratively, determine the best place to save your work and share it.

Finally, as you create an efficient strategy, include in your calculation the costs of using various electronic sources. The way a source bills for its use can often affect your research plan. Understand the charges for various actions so you avoid unnecessary expense. If you do not have unlimited access to the source, be especially aware of your time, so you can minimize the time charged to your client or office. One useful shortcut is to save the cases to your computer to be studied when you are not paying to use that expensive source.

As you research.

7. Enter your query or prompt.

The more specifically you can locate the law in your artificial intelligence (AI) program, the more likely you are to get accurate results. For the legal question, use verbs drawn from the TERMS OF ART in that statute, regulation, or case. Precise subjects, verbs, and SUBJECT-VERB COMBINATIONS in your prompt will generate more precise results. If you do not know the specific terms, using AI may help you locate those terms.

Determine the LEGALLY SIGNIFICANT FACTS and KEY BACKGROUND FACTS and incorporate those into your prompt so that you can find information similar to those facts. In a separate prompt, one option may be to use ANTONYMS to find the situations that your opponents will find. As noted in #1, review and understand the LLM's privacy settings before entering any facts that might be confidential. See how many sources you find. If it is a usable amount, continue your search; if not, edit your query or prompt.

8. Find the law.

The purpose of this step is to make sure you find all relevant sources, particularly statutes, cases, and regulations. Your query or prompt may generate a range of sources, some of which are relevant to your analysis or document, others of which look interesting but will not be useful. To analyze a document's relevance, ask the following:

(a) Is the source PRIMARY AUTHORITY?

Is it a relevant statute?

Is it a relevant case?

Is it a relevant regulation?

Have I updated it? Remember that the citing references you see lead to other types of results tied to your citation.

(b) Is the source MANDATORY AUTHORITY?

Is it in my jurisdiction?

Has it been used by decision-makers in my jurisdiction?

Have I updated it?

(c) Is it a secondary source?

If SECONDARY SOURCES can lead you to a cluster of primary authority in your jurisdiction, use them to get you there. But if it is not within the SCOPE of the document you are writing, make a note to read it later if you have time. For example, you may read an overview of the subject in such places as American Law Reports (A.L.R.), Corpus Juris Secundum (C.J.S.), American Jurisprudence (Am. Jur.), or the Restatements, and so on.

(d) Does the source answer, amend, or advance your question?

Does it answer the question? For example, it might be a relevant statute in your jurisdiction or a holding in a case that specifically suggests an answer to the question or a relevant regulation the makes the statute's application more specific.

Does it amend the question? For example, the statute or regulation might provide a more specific verb or phrase with which to frame the question or narrow the scope of your broad question. Or the law itself may have changed so that the question needs to be reframed. Or the law may provide more specific TERMS OF ART to narrow or the question.

Does it advance the question? For example, the source may reveal that your question was too specific or addressed an issue that is part of a broader field or inquiry. You may need to ask a different question or shift to a more pertinent question.

Read each source carefully to see how it responds to the question you framed in Step 3 to keep the scope of your research under control. Keep tying your source to your question and letting your thinking evolve.

9. Read the law to make sure it is relevant. Avoid the procrastination method of saving and downloading or printing now and reading later.

   (a) Evaluate internally.

   - Statute. Evaluate the language of the statute itself.

     Is there a general factual similarity to this case?

     Is there AMBIGUITY in the legislative intent that favors this case?

     Does the statute's context give it a focus applicable to this case?

     Does the statute's legislative history illuminate its meaning?

     How do the CANONS OF CONSTRUCTION augment the statute's meaning?

   - Case. Evaluate the pertinent language of the case.

     Is there a factual similarity to this case?

     Is the RULE pertinent and useful?

     Do the HOLDINGS help define the RULE's parameters and terms?

     Is there a general similarity that is useful if any aspects of the case are accurately recharacterized?

     Does the POLICY provide a useful basis for argument?

   (b) Evaluate the law externally.

   - Current status.

     Has the statute been invalidated, repealed, or amended?

     Are these subsequent interpretations of cases useful to this case?

   - Possible future status.

     Can a new rule or innovative twist be formulated?

     Is the statute a codification or a departure from previous rules?

     Has a novel policy or doctrine emerged?

10. Update the law.
    (a) Use tools such as *KeyCite* or *Shepard's*. See UPDATING THE LAW.
    (b) Check other possible sources, such as news articles, for recent opinions or references to the source, noting their quality and being aware of any DISINFORMATION or MISINFORMATION problems.
    (c) When you see the same core sources coming up repeatedly, stop. For related information, see WHEN TO STOP.
11. Take effective NOTES.
    (a) Have a system and write out the plan as described in step 6.
    (b) Reread your preliminary issues periodically to maintain your focus.
    (c) Record full CITATIONS in proper form. If your source is electronic, be alert to LINK ROT.
12. Ask or call.

    Sometimes information is not easily available, or your library does not have it. You may then find it more useful and efficient to ask specific questions of your librarian, the supervising attorney, another associate who has worked on similar cases, or an expert in the field. You may also find it more efficient to call sources, such as agencies that have set up a number for asking questions.

For related information, see ARTIFICIAL INTELLIGENCE AND RESEARCH; ARTIFICIAL INTELLIGENCE AND WRITING; DEADLINES, MEETING THEM; GETTING STARTED; ORGANIZE, HOW TO; ORGANIZATION FOR THOSE WHO CAN'T OUTLINE; OUTLINES; PREWRITING; PRIORITIES WITHIN A PROJECT; PROMPTS; REASONING, PRESENTING IT; RECORDS, KEEPING THEM; RESEARCH AS WRITING; RESEARCH PROCESS CHECKLIST; TIME MANAGEMENT; UPDATING THE LAW; WHEN TO STOP; and WRITING PROCESS.

RESPECTIVELY

Some writers like to use *respectively* because it is concise and makes it easier to express a comparison. It does not, however, usually make the sentence easier to read. If you use the term, make sure you are not making the comparison more difficult for the reader to understand. For example, avoid placing *respectively* after the comparison, which forces the reader to reprocess the sentence when reaching the word *respectively*. Place *respectively* before the comparison.

Mr. Eldridge received a performance review and disciplinary review on, respectively, June 12 and 21.

rather than

Mr. Eldridge received a performance review and disciplinary review on June 12 and 21, respectively.

This earlier placement, while clearer, may sound awkward to you. If so, consider rewording the sentence without *respectively*.

Mr. Eldridge received a performance review on June 12 and a disciplinary review on June 21.

Also avoid adding *respectively* when it adds no information.

The meetings occurred on March 21 and April 13, respectively.

Over time, you are likely to find that you write more clearly when you avoid using *respectively* in comparisons.

RESPONDENT

Respondent can be used as either a proper noun or a generic description, like *Appellant*, *Defendant*, and *Plaintiff*. When used as a proper noun, it should be capitalized and used without an article.

Respondent objects to Appellant's characterizing the case as a simple one.

When used generically, it should not be capitalized, and the article should be used.

The respondent filed the brief well within the time limits.

Lawyers use *respondent* both ways, so check the conventions of your office or particularly of your audience. If your readers have no preference, choose whatever you prefer, but be consistent throughout the document. Avoid choosing the proper noun solely for conciseness; omitting *the* will shorten your document slightly but may create a telegraphic or harsh tone.

RESTRICTIVE PHRASES

See *THAT* OR *WHICH*?

REVISING

Revising follows REWRITING in the WRITING PROCESS. During rewriting, you settled the document's legal correctness, completeness of content, and coherent and logical organization; during revising, you are then free to concentrate on the expression of the content. In this stage, you are making sure that wording and the relationship among sentences accurately conveys the legal meaning. Revising includes refining small-scale organization, SENTENCE STRUCTURE, TRANSITIONS, PARAGRAPHS, and PUNCTUATION. The varied nature of these revision concerns precludes making all the changes needed on one pass in any but the simplest documents. To revise efficiently, you need to make multiple passes through longer documents, focusing in each pass on just a few aspects of revision. To do this efficiently, you need a checklist. Over time, you may develop one of your own, but you may start with the one included in REVISING CHECKLIST.

For example, you may want to begin with several passes checking accuracy, such as checking your presentation of the law for consistent and precise wording. Check the wording of your ISSUES or the places where legal terms or relations are defined. Make sure the legal phrases are accurately stated throughout the document. Check the places where you connect the law to the facts and use precise terms for doing so.

Then you may turn to concerns of clarity, reviewing the topic sentences alone on one pass and reviewing transitions on another. Replace overly general language such as *clearly* or *obviously* with terms that demonstrate more accurately the logical steps. In contracts, settle on precise terms and make sure they are used consistently throughout the document. Move sentences within paragraphs to convey accurate legal relationships. Omit modifiers unless they are legally significant. Match legal substance to syntax with accurate use of devices such as PARALLEL STRUCTURE and antithesis.

Additional passes can focus on the POINT OF VIEW, and READABILITY. For example, make sure the level of formality is consistent and the VOICE is unified and appropriate. Check for deviations in TONE.

You may be able to use artificial intelligence (AI) in REVISING to help with specific edits, such as minimizing use of PASSIVE VOICE, increasing READABILITY, or achieving CONCISENESS. For help using AI at this stage of the writing process, see REVISING CHECKLIST.

Remember three things about revising.

1. Do not revise while you write.

   Trying to combine both tasks slows down both the writing and the revising processes. When you are writing, concentrate solely on expressing your ideas, no matter how unpolished your writing may seem. Revise later.

2. Do not revise while you rewrite.

   Rewriting involves adding, deleting, and moving content. Revising before you rewrite often means you spent time refining a passage you later end up deleting. Work out your organization and get everything in place before you start revision.

3. Revise in stages.

   It is exhausting and inefficient to try to revise on every level at once. For help with this, see REVISING CHECKLIST or the checklist appropriate to your specific document.

REVISING CHECKLIST

When your document is legally correct, complete, and coherent, you are ready to move from rewriting to REVISING. In this stage of the WRITING PROCESS, you focus on revising paragraphs, sentences, and phrases for accuracy and readability. The following list may seem long, but it can actually help you complete the revision efficiently and with much less stress. Because each step is focused, the whole process can move quickly. Additionally, when you have completed the process, you can have confidence that your document has moved several notches higher in quality. For related information, see ORGANIZATION, SMALL-SCALE.

1. Is the content communicated accurately?

   (a) Is the wording of the law accurate? Could any words be misinterpreted because of ambiguity? See AMBIGUITY, WAYS TO AVOID.

   (b) Are TERMS OF ART and key terms used accurately in all places in the text?

   (c) Is each PARAPHRASE accurate?

   (d) Is the name and status of each party accurate?

   (e) Does the wording of the application accurately convey the logical parallels?

   (f) Are legally significant facts worded accurately?

2. Does the wording convey the organization and content clearly?

   (a) Are paragraphs coherent? Is the logical flow from sentence to sentence conveyed clearly? Do clear and precise transitions connect paragraphs and sentences? See CONNECTIONS, MAKING THEM; PARAGRAPH BLOCKS; PARAGRAPHS; and TRANSITIONS.

   (b) When read apart from the text, do HEADINGS present the message and structure of the document? Are those headings parallel in meaning and grammatical structure?

   (c) Does the topic sentence of each paragraph give the overall message of that paragraph, and do those topic sentences usually appear at the beginning of the paragraph? See SUBJECT-VERB COMBINATIONS and TOPIC SENTENCES.

(d) Do topic sentences, when read consecutively and without the intervening text, reveal the progression of the document's logic to the readers?

(e) Are KEY TERMS echoed throughout the document in strategic positions, such as headings and topic sentences? See PARALLEL STRUCTURE, POSITIONS OF EMPHASIS, and SUBJECT-VERB COMBINATIONS.

3. Is the POINT OF VIEW unified throughout the document?

(a) Is the tone and level of formality appropriate and consistent? See FORMALITY, LEVEL OF.

(b) Is VOICE unified throughout the document?

4. Is the document easy to read?

(a) Are subjects and verbs close together?

(b) Is passive voice used only when needed?

(c) Is the text free of excessive quotations, string citations, and JARGON?

(d) Are sentences free of unnecessary NOMINALIZATIONS?

(e) Are unnecessary MODIFIERS eliminated, such as *clearly* and *obviously*?

(f) Is sentence length appropriate throughout? Is it varied for interest? See SENTENCE STRUCTURE.

(g) Are lists clearly structured? See LISTS, STRUCTURE OF.

(h) Are sentences free of unnecessary prepositions and prepositional phrases?

(i) Is the text generally concise? See CONCISENESS.

5. Are all valid criticisms from reviewers systematically incorporated throughout the paper, changing PARAGRAPH STRUCTURE, SENTENCE STRUCTURE, WORD CHOICE, TONE, and overall STYLE appropriately?

REVISING THE WRITING OF OTHERS

See EDITING and MANAGING WRITERS.

REWRITING

Rewriting, as used in this text, follows the writing stage in the WRITING PROCESS. When rewriting, you focus on matters of legal accuracy and correctness, completeness of content, and coherent and logical organization. It is useful to distinguish rewriting from revising because each of these two tasks deserves its own attention, and each requires a different focus. This is the stage where criticism takes over from creativity and the text starts moving from a writer-oriented first draft toward a reader-oriented final draft.

By separating rewriting from the other stages in the writing process, you can concentrate on the content rather than its expression. Use this stage to do any needed shifting of large sections, focusing on priorities appropriate for the document.

Check the document to make sure the content is correct and complete. For example, review contract provisions to make sure all are present and not repeated. In opinion communications, check that all strengths and weaknesses are presented so that the reader can make a decision. In memos or briefs, check the law, facts, issues, and answers to make sure they are correct, complete, and address the reader's concerns. Make sure you have stated all the steps in the reasoning, the relative strength of the various legal points, and the conclusions you need to make. Then check to make sure you have omitted any tangents.

To achieve coherence, review the organization to make sure all details of the document are congruent. For example, check the headings and subheadings to make sure that each indicates how that part factors into the whole. Review thesis sentences to make sure that the presentation flows logically and does not skip or repeat steps. These checks will refine your large-scale organization.

You may use several different techniques to review the document. For example, it may be helpful to move between the outline and the overall document, comparing them with your THEME to make sure each section furthers that theme. You may print out your document to facilitate your ability to move back and forth through the document when you are considering the sequence of the content. You may even find it helpful to physically cut and paste sections if the organization needs to be redone, moving it in the electronic version only after you have settled on your reorganization. This change in medium can also help you give the document a fresh reading. Or you may want to read aloud any sections that are not working and listen for shifts in wording, organization, or ideas that would be jarring to readers. You may hear problems that you cannot see.

Avoid making small edits at this stage. Only when you are satisfied that everything needed is accurate, present, and in an overall logical order are you ready to move to REVISING.

For specific questions to ask yourself, see REWRITING CHECKLIST. See also ORGANIZATION, LARGE-SCALE. For more ideas about reviewing your document at this stage, see PRINCIPLES OF GOOD LEGAL WRITING. For advice on specific documents such as CONTRACTS, WILLS, motions, and the like, see the entry for the particular document. For related information, see DESIGN; LEGAL ANALYSIS; ORGANIZE, HOW TO; PURPOSE; and REASONING, PRESENTING IT.

REWRITING CHECKLIST

After you have completed a full initial draft of your document, you are ready to begin the work of REWRITING. In this stage, you focus on legal correctness, completeness of content, and coherent and logical organization. For legal readers, these are the most important aspects of the document. For legal writers, these are not easily achieved, so they deserve their own focus, which this stage provides. When these elements are in place, you can move on to the details involved in REVISING and POLISHING. For the broader view of all the stages, see WRITING PROCESS. For information about reviewing specific documents, see the entry for the specific kind of drafting you are doing, such as COMPLAINTS; CONTRACTS; CORPORATE DOCUMENTS; LEGISLATION; MOTIONS; NOTICE OF MOTION; or WILLS.

1. Is the document legally correct?
   - (a) Does the document meet its purpose?
   - (b) Are the issues, answers, or theses precisely framed?
   - (c) Are the facts precisely stated?
   - (d) Is the law accurately stated?
   - (e) If needed in this document, are citations included to support legal statements?
2. Is the document legally complete? Are there any holes in the reasoning, unnecessary repetition, or tangents?
   - (a) Does the document include all needed facts? For details see BACKGROUND FACTS, EMOTIONALLY SIGNIFICANT FACTS, and LEGALLY SIGNIFICANT FACTS.
   - (b) Does it include all relevant legal issues?
   - (c) Is the law complete? Does it include all relevant constitutional provisions, statutes, cases, regulations? Is irrelevant law omitted?
   - (d) Does it address the strengths and weaknesses of all options or arguments as needed?
   - (e) Does it communicate which points are stronger, where appropriate?
   - (f) Does it include all steps in the reasoning?
   - (g) Does it include the prediction, remedy, result, or practical steps, where appropriate?

(h) Are tangents omitted?

(i) Does it state a specific CONCLUSION to the logic?

3. Is the document's organization coherent?

(a) Is the structure congruent with the substantive law as it applies to my client's situation?

(b) Are the points in my analysis connected throughout the document so that the audience understands the reasons for reaching the conclusions?

(c) Do the topic sentences, when read without the intervening text, convey the essential points of the document?

(d) If applicable, are threshold issues first?

(e) Are key terms used consistently throughout the document?

(f) In a persuasive document, are the issues arranged in the most persuasive order?

(g) Do the headings and subheadings convey the logical content and organization of the whole document?

(h) Can any reader follow the order?

- Does the REASONING move in a recognizable way?
- Does the organization match the PURPOSE?
- Does the organization meet the AUDIENCE's needs?

For more on presenting reasoning, see DESIGN; REASONING, ANALOGICAL; REASONING, DEDUCTIVE; REASONING, INDUCTIVE; REASONING, MODERN; REASONING, POSTMODERN; REASONING, OTHER; and REASONING, PRESENTING IT.

(i) Do the thesis sentences, when read without supporting information, communicate the paragraphs' information and convey the logical flow of the text?

RHETORICAL QUESTIONS

Avoid them in legal writing. Rhetorical questions, which have either an obvious answer or no answer, usually irritate legal readers and invite them to question your point. Ask questions only in your ISSUES or QUESTIONS PRESENTED; give the answers to those questions in your ARGUMENT SECTION or DISCUSSION SECTION. To make a rhetorical point, state it in declarative sentence form.

RHYMES

Avoid them in legal writing unless you intend to be humorous and the humor is appropriate to the content and all READERS. For related information, see ALLITERATION.

ROUGH DRAFTS

See WRITING and WRITING PROCESS.

RULES

This entry discusses legal rules used as part of legal analysis. If you are looking for guidance writing administrative rules, see LEGISLATION.

Legal rules are statements of law that provide the basis for legal analysis. They are often general principles that can be applied to several situations, such as constitutional provisions or statutes. Sometimes they are derived from cases, where a judge has used a common law principle as the basis for the analysis. When a rule is not explicitly stated in a case, the writer must derive that rule by examining the court's foundation for its reasoning, formulating a statement of the rule used in that case, and then synthesizing that rule with the rules from multiple cases to establish the general rule.

In the broader sense, *rule* refers to the law that you will be applying in a given situation, rather than to a particular statement. For related information, see SYLLOGISM, SYNTHESIS, and HOLDINGS.

Rules fall into a hierarchy of authority. Thus, if a constitutional provision is involved in your issues, it is usually discussed first because the constitution supersedes all other law. If a statute is involved, it often comes next, or first if no constitutional provision is involved. Rules construing the statute may come next to show how the law is being enforced by the executive branch. Case law or agency decisions usually come last because they provide the governing principles when there is no statute or rule covering the issue, or they provide the definitions of terms in the constitution or statute.

Consider the following in presenting the rules.

1. Present rule structure at the beginning of your analysis.

   When legal rules provide the structure for your analysis or argument, present the rules at the beginning of your analysis because this overview of the rules foreshadows the structure of your analysis.

   All citizens are protected from unreasonable searches not only in their homes, but wherever they have a right to be. Wash. Const. art. I, § 7.

and

The plaintiff's recovery is barred when the plaintiff's negligence exceeds the defendant's negligence. Or. Rev. Stat. § 18.470 (2025).

and

Jury misconduct occurs when a juror supplies information to other jurors that is outside the recorded evidence of the trial and not subject to the protections and limitations of court proceedings. Salverson v. Anderson, 99 Wash. 2d 746, 752, 913 P.3d 827, 830 (2025).

Legal readers need to know the sources from which you have drawn the rules, so cite thoroughly and accurately. It is not usually sufficient to cite extensively from one source and put only one citation at the end of a paragraph, because that leaves the reader guessing about how much of the information is attributable to the cited source. Instead, cite after each relevant statement that provides new information. Often, this means you will include a citation after every sentence when presenting a rule unless a statement directly follows another in the source itself.

2. Decide whether case law presents a rule.

   You may find a rule from case law in any of three ways.

   (a) A case may explicitly state the definitive rule; if so, you may cite the case singly as the source of that rule.

   (b) Several cases may be synthesized to form the rule; if so, you must cite those cases separately, each standing for a proposition that contributes to the rule.

   (c) Several cases may provide a rule plus exceptions; if so, you should cite the case giving the rule first, with the cases giving exceptions after.

To state a cause of action, a plaintiff must prove that the defendant either intended his actions to inflict severe emotional distress or knew that there was a high probability of his actions causing severe emotional distress. Public Business Corp., 60 N.E.3d at 661 (Ill. 2024). It is not enough that the defendant acted with a tortious or criminal intent; the defendant must intend the severe emotional distress or know that it will result from his actions. Gau v. Lee, 374 N.E.3d 157, 164 (Ill. 2025). In order for Ms. Hudson to sustain a

claim for this tort, she must allege that Mr. Crowe intended or knew that his act of arson would cause her severe emotional distress.

3. As you construct your rule from statutes and cases, synthesize when needed.

Synthesizing a rule means pulling pieces from several cases together to explain the rule for the particular issue. Courts do not always state these general rules because they decide specific factual situations and thus do not need to pull the larger rule together. You must therefore synthesize it yourself. To do this, step back from the pieces and try to see the larger picture. (For help with this, see REASONING, PRESENTING IT.) Then characterize that picture in your own words as a topic sentence. (See TOPIC SENTENCES.) Follow this sentence with the sections of the cases that create this picture, and give appropriate citations. Then explain enough about each case to show the reader how that piece fits into your big picture of the rule.

Although VARA is contained within the copyright title of the U.S. Code, rights under VARA are not analogous to those historically protected by copyright. Turcan v. Nichols, 250 F. Supp. 3d 393, 399 n.10 (N.D.N.Y. 2025). Rather, VARA protects moral rights that are independent of rights under the general meaning of the copyright statutes. Quality Queen Distributors, Inc. v. Alliance Global Research, Inc., 942 U.S. 643, 659 (2025). Congress created this independence when it decided to distinguish moral rights from the economic rights that copyrights traditionally protect. Padilla v. Calibre Associates, 610 F. Supp. 3d 436, 452 (S.D.N.Y. 2024) (citing H.R. Rep. No. 211–987, 21 (2024)). VARA consequently has the purpose of protecting the moral rights of "integrity" and "attribution," even after an artist has given up the legal title to a work. See e.g., Hussein v. Pandan Companies, Inc., 589 F.3d 102, 104–09 (9th Cir. 2025); Cheong v. Dutro-Alther, Inc., 422 F.3d 52, 59 (2d Cir. 2025). To succeed in bringing a claim under VARA, then, Williams must be able to show that "Zenith" is a work protected by the statute, that the alterations Bates made violate Williams's rights to integrity and attribution in his work, and that these alterations damage his reputation as an artist.

4. When constructing a rule from cases, include exceptions.

Remember that any rule may have exceptions so, after making sure that the rule and its source are clear to the reader, follow with the exceptions. If you know that the opposing side will raise a question, you know you must deal with it. For ways to address these points in persuasive writing, see COUNTERARGUMENTS, HOW TO HANDLE.

> **"[T]he Fourth Amendment incorporates the common-law requirement that police officers entering a dwelling must knock on the door and announce their identity and purpose before attempting forcible entry." Caine v. Mutiny, 999 U. S. 123 (2025). But the "flexible requirement of reasonableness should not be read to mandate a rigid rule of announcement that ignores countervailing law enforcement interests," id. at 134, so the Court leaves "to the lower courts the task of determining the circumstances under which an unannounced entry is reasonable under the Fourth Amendment." Id. at 936. Thus the knock-and-announce requirement can, for example, give way "under circumstances presenting a threat of physical violence," or "where police officers have reason to believe that evidence would likely be destroyed if advance notice were given." Smith v. Jones, 999 U.S. 341, 344.**

5. Check for accuracy and logical links.

Your presentation of the law outlines the structure of your entire analysis, argument, or explanation, so make sure the rules are accurately presented. Check for logical links between subparts, so that the reader knows exactly how the rule works when applied. Then you are ready to follow this logic in applying the rules to the facts of your analysis.

> **Under the Kansas Prevention of Assisted Suicide Act, it is a crime to intentionally and purposefully assist in another person's suicide or suicide attempt by knowingly "providing the physical means ... or participating in a physical act by which another person commits or attempts to commit suicide." Kan. Stat. Ann. § 52–2507(2) (Supp. 2025). The statute's language therefore establishes three elements necessary to prove the crime of assisted suicide: (1) the existence of a suicide or an attempted suicide by another person, (2) a person's intent to assist a suicide**

> **or attempted suicide, and (3) the physical act of assistance to the suicide or attempted suicide. See id. The absence of binding precedent construing the Kansas Prevention of Assisted Suicide Act requires a closer examination of the facts of Mrs. Pernitz's situation and their fit with the statutory language. The prosecution also carries the burden of proof beyond a reasonable doubt: "A defendant is presumed to be innocent until the contrary is proved. When there is reasonable doubt as to his guilt, he must be acquitted." Kan. Stat. Ann. § 52–9821 (2025).**

RULES, ADMINISTRATIVE

Administrative rules, regulations, procedures, orders, and decisions are created by the executive branch to enforce laws created by Congress or state legislatures. In legal analysis, administrative rules may be part of the broader legal foundation for an analysis. For help writing rules, see LEGISLATION.

RUN-ON SENTENCES

Run-on sentences, in the narrow sense, are sentences that join two independent clauses without using a period, semicolon, or conjunction. Most often, the writer has used a comma rather than the punctuation mark needed.

> The statute does not apply to motorized wheelchairs, it was meant for vehicles not allowed in buildings.

Also called a *comma splice*, this kind of run-on sentence is a grammatical error and must always be fixed.

> **The statute does not apply to motorized wheelchairs; it was meant for vehicles not allowed in buildings.**
>
> or
>
> **The statute does not apply to motorized wheelchairs because it was meant for vehicles not allowed in buildings.**

In a broader sense, readers sometimes incorrectly use this term to refer to any sentence that goes on too long, even one that is grammatically written, such as the following sentence.

> Because motorized wheelchairs were not part of the intended class of vehicle for which these safety rules were enacted, this statute does not apply to motorized wheelchairs, but was meant for vehicles not allowed to be used in buildings, such as self-balancing scooters, motor scooters, motorcycles, go carts, and other small

motorized vehicles that have been created for recreational use rather than for necessity and have been intended for use in the outdoors.

This incorrect use of *run-on sentence* can cause some confusion for lovers of literature, who are used to the long sentences in Faulkner or Dickens, and who have probably worked very hard to keep their long sentences grammatical. Nevertheless, in legal writing, this kind of lengthy sentence should generally be revised for READABILITY.

Because they are not part of the intended class covered by these safety rules, this statute does not apply to motorized wheelchairs. Rather, the statute covers vehicles not allowed to be used in buildings, such as self-balancing scooters, motor scooters, and other small, motorized vehicles intended for outdoor use.

SAID

Substitute *this, that,* or a more detailed description.

This document was signed by the plaintiff.

rather than

Said document was signed by the plaintiff.

Arcane legal language includes *said* as an adjective; do not use it that way. Similarly, *said* was once used in legal documents to say, *I mean the one mentioned above, in contrast to any mentioned below or elsewhere.* But often no other one was mentioned, so *said* was nonsensical. When you need to distinguish one item from another, simply repeat the designation used earlier.

the 2024 contract

rather than

the said contract

For related information, see SUCH.

SALUTATIONS

The salutation is the line beginning with *Dear* that traditionally introduces the text of a letter. Salutations are often included in email, too. There are three common questions about salutations: (1) whether to include them, (2) how to write them when you do not know the sex of the reader, and (3) whether to punctuate them with commas or semicolons.

1. Including or omitting the salutation.

   In general, include the salutation in letters. Include the salutation in email to create a more courteous, formal, or businesslike effect. Some writers omit the salutation in business letters, substituting instead a subject line. Omitting the salutation, however, may in some situations make the letter or email seem rather abrupt and impersonal, which may not be the tone you intend. For more on this generally, see COMMUNICATIONS, TONE OF.

2. Writing the salutation.

   If you do not know the preferred address form of the person to whom you are writing, substitute the name without a title of *Mr.* or *Ms.* If appropriate, you may also choose to use the person's name only.

   Dear D. A. Young:

   or

   Dear Terry Holmes:

   or

   Terry,

   If you do not know the name, use the person's title or some appropriate generic term when you are writing a letter.

   Dear Administrator:

   or

   Dear Client:

   If you believe you must include a salutation, but you cannot come up with a generic term, you may use the following, but you risk sounding too formal.

   To Whom It May Concern:

   At this point, it may be better to omit the salutation. For alternatives to salutations, see SUBJECT LINES.

3. Choosing commas or colons.

   Using colons in business writing is more formal than using commas. Colons are often used after general salutations, such as *To Whom It May Concern.* Depending on what TONE you want to create, be aware that this punctuation contributes to the overall effect.

SARCASM

Do not use sarcasm in legal writing; it is too easy for the reader to take it literally. Even if the reader catches your sarcastic tone, that tone is usually inappropriate in legal writing. In general, sarcasm is only effective when writing to readers who already whole-heartedly agree with your position. Dry humor may occasionally be used, because the content will still be literally correct. Many of your readers, however, will miss the humor altogether, so you risk losing them or having them misinterpret your meaning.

SAYING *NO*

Saying *no* to requests to do additional work may be hard for you, as it is for many lawyers. But maintaining good quality in your writing will require you to learn how to do it. Taking on all requests eventually forces you to do mediocre work, which will damage your credibility and reputation. In contrast, saying *no* when appropriate keeps the quality of your work high and may win you respect. To help you know when you cannot take on more tasks, stay aware of your deadlines and workload.

Depending on the professional posture you choose to project, you can refuse gently (*I would love to, but I don't think I can do a good job.*), firmly (*I cannot do that for you. I'm sorry.*), with limits (*Yes, I can do that for you, but not until six weeks from now.*), or you can flatter (*Of all the people I enjoy working with, you are the one I enjoy most. But I cannot do it for you this time. Please ask again.*).

If you know that your refusal will cause you problems or create tension, try asking to be used as a back-up (*This is very inconvenient for me right now. Can you find someone else? If not, then get back to me.*) or give a long-term *no* (*I will do this last project for you, but I cannot be called upon with such short notice in the future.*) Find ways that work best with your personality and that of your associates. For related information, see CREDIBILITY, PROFESSIONAL LANGUAGE AND PRESENTATION, and TIME MANAGEMENT.

SCARCELY

Scarcely is an adverb that can mean either *barely* or *assuredly not.* It has a negative meaning, but it is not as obvious as *no* or *not.* This makes it easily misread, and thus it is best to avoid this term. Because *scarcely* has a negative meaning, it should not follow another negative.

The defendant could scarcely deny the charges.

rather than

The defendant couldn't scarcely deny the charges.

Place *scarcely* just before the word or group of words that it modifies.

The defendant heard the pronouncement of sentence with scarcely a change in demeanor.

rather than

The defendant heard the pronouncement of sentence scarcely with a change in demeanor.

SCHOLARLY WRITING

Scholarly articles differ from other forms of legal writing because many of the factors involved in writing an article are more complex. Not only are you expected to do extensive, original research on a timely topic, but you are also expected to create a paper that joins the scholarly conversation on that topic. This requires rethinking all aspects of the project. The SCOPE of scholarly articles is generally broader and deeper than in other forms of writing, which requires more steps in every stage of your writing process. However, the scope cannot be so broad and deep that the article becomes a tome. This sometimes requires adjusting the THEME until the topic and scope are congruent.

Readers of scholarly writing expect a thorough treatment of the topic. They want enough information to be able to evaluate the merit of the article's reasoning and enough citations to allow them to find all the sources used to support that reasoning. Readers also cover a wide range, from experts to novices, scholars to practitioners. Keep these diverse readers in mind as you identify your purpose and synthesize the substance of the paper.

Just as a scholarly paper is read by several readers, it may also serve a range of purposes. That range can include suggesting changes in the law, clarifying issues across jurisdictions, or inventing creative solutions for new legal problems, among many others. This rich complexity of purposes liberates creative thinking for both writers and readers. To keep your document unified, decide on a primary purpose and then carefully include underlying purposes.

Scholarly articles have a much broader scope than most legal documents, so decisions about what to include are usually more complex, and you have to relate each point to your overall purpose. Here tangents are more tolerated if they lead the reader to interesting research that explores a related topic, but those ideas must still be related to the THESIS STATEMENT. The extensive research also requires meticulous FOOTNOTES.

Finally, scholarly articles provide writers with the opportunity to be more original and expressive. Unlike briefs or memos, an article allows wide latitude in using figurative meaning, emotional language, and a personal persuasive style. Because the article may be a commentary, it also may allow for a wider range in tone. That style and tone must not, however, range so far that that it lessens the writer's credibility. For an explanation of these terms, see EMOTIONAL LANGUAGE, EMPHASIS, FIGURATIVE MEANING, and IMAGERY. For relevant techniques, see TONE.

For more help in writing a scholarly article, see SCHOLARLY WRITING PROCESS and SCHOLARLY WRITING PROCESS CHECKLIST. For related information, see CITATIONS, STRING; FORMALITY, LEVEL OF; NOTES; and RESEARCH AS WRITING. For related information, see PROCESS AND PRODUCT COMPARED. For using artificial intelligence, see ARTIFICIAL INTELLIGENCE AND RESEARCH, ARTIFICIAL INTELLIGENCE AND WRITING, PROMPTS, and RESEARCH STRATEGY GUIDE.

SCHOLARLY WRITING PROCESS

When working on a scholarly paper, your writing process will likely change. This happens because many factors differ: time, purpose, scope, research, audience, and need for originality. Your purpose is determined by interest in a topic, rather than the needs of a client, and you may not be given a topic. Thus you will need to add steps in the process for preliminary research to identify your topic. Your research will be more comprehensive, your writing will include more detail, and your rewriting may require more reorganization because of the paper's broader scope and audience. The good news is that you will often have a much longer period of time to write a scholarly work than to write other documents.

Rather than approaching this as just another writing assignment, always write with publication in mind. Doing this will make the paper more creative and thorough and will sharpen your focus on the features of the document, reader expectations, and content. To adapt comfortably to these differences, you might want to include the following steps in your process.

Prewriting

1. Set your deadlines.

   Writing a scholarly article is a big, complicated process, so you need to put both your final and interim deadlines into your calendar early. You may also want to set deadlines for selecting the topic, doing a preemption check, completing research, completing notes, outlining, drafting, doing further research, rewriting, revising, sending to others, updating footnotes, and submitting the final version. Be aware that things usually take much longer than you anticipate, so give yourself a lot of breathing room as you create your calendar. Take time to consider how this project will blend with your other work so that you can keep balance in your schedule. Treat the dates respectfully, because legal scholarship requires steady work and cannot all be done at the end like an undergraduate paper. For related information, see DEADLINES, MEETING THEM; and TIME MANAGEMENT.

2. Select a PURPOSE and topic, and estimate the project's SCOPE.

To determine what areas need exploring, read the news for current legal topics, find the latest article on your topic and see what questions are not answered, or consult with an expert in that field. You may want to use artificial intelligence (AI) to give you an overview of your topic, investigate current research, and discover potential approaches. For help doing this, see ARTIFICIAL INTELLIGENCE AND RESEARCH, ARTIFICIAL INTELLIGENCE AND WRITING, PROMPTS, and RESEARCH STRATEGY GUIDE.

After you find a topic of interest, narrow it until it fulfills a scholarly purpose and is timely, useful, and interesting. Check recent cases on the topic because courts leave questions unanswered or create splits on certain issues, and those may need clarifying. For more information about the range of purposes, see PURPOSE and SCHOLARLY WRITING.

Identify the topic that interests you and write down a sentence or two hypothesizing what you think you would say about that topic. Then use that statement, modifying it as needed, to maintain your focus as you research, write, revise, and work through footnotes throughout the prewriting stage. As you select a topic, keep in mind the question *So what?* This question will help you relate each point to the overall purpose and connect your message to your range of readers.

A scholarly paper may serve several purposes, so list and evaluate the range of those purposes. For a clearer focus, one of those purposes must be uppermost. Although one of the purposes may be to secure tenure or build your professional profile to add clients, that usually will factor into the selection of a topic rather than be the primary purpose of the specific article. As the following list illustrates, some of the purposes of the paper may be

- to organize a confusing array of issues;
- to expand a field of knowledge by offering a new direction;
- to predict developments in the law; or
- to suggest changes in the law or advocate a plan of action.

This primary purpose will guide research and decisions about what content to include so that the scope does not get too broad.

Write down a target page length; that number may help to keep your scope manageable. Research can quickly get out of hand, so keep focused on your purpose and your developing THEME. Then ask yourself whether or not you can achieve your stated purpose in this amount of space.

As part of this process, you will need to check technical details such as the required citation form and any length or format requirements. Doing this at the beginning of the process will save you time and avoid frustration later. For more ideas, see FOOTNOTES, NOTES, PREWRITING, and RESEARCH STRATEGY GUIDE.

3. Refine your preliminary topic and purpose statement to state the THEME of your article.

   Try to refine your initial sentences to state this theme in one sentence. Include a meaningful subject and verb, even if you do not use this exact statement in the paper. The difference between a topic and a theme is the verb, which should indicate what you intend to say about the topic. Including a *because* phrase can further enhance your statement by showing the direction of your reasoning. While this theme will likely evolve as you research and analyze further, keeping focused on it should prevent you from going too far afield in your research or drafting. Refer to your evolving theme throughout prewriting, writing, and rewriting. For related information, see SUBJECT-VERB COMBINATIONS and WRITING PROCESS.

4. Consider your audience and adapt your purpose, topic, and theme as needed.

   Your readers expect a thorough treatment of the topic with enough analysis to evaluate the article's reasoning and enough citations to allow them to find all the sources used to support that reasoning. Beyond that, the readers differ, including any of the following:

   - experts in the field who expect accuracy and exhaustive research;
   - practitioners who want practical answers to specific questions;
   - judges who want to be brought up to date on this topic;
   - nonlawyers who want to understand this topic;
   - prospective future employers looking for excellent analysis and good writing;
   - faculty committees evaluating you for tenure, who also require innovative thought; and
   - future scholars looking for examples of creative analysis and thorough research.

Keep these diverse readers in mind as you refine your purpose and synthesize the substance of the paper.

To do this, you can try any of several approaches, choosing the one that best fits with your personal writing process. First, you can copy the list given above and, under each group of readers, list the content they would expect to see. Considering each group individually can make the process seem less intimidating because it breaks the thought process into simpler tasks. Second, you can relay your working THESIS SENTENCE to colleagues, asking them to list what questions this statement raises. This can be an excellent way to get yourself thinking outside the box of your own analysis. Their questions can often suggest an organization of the content as well. Third, you can try to imagine all your potential readers gathered in one room; then create the tone, organization, style, and thesis that will satisfy both the most confused and critical readers' needs. For related information, see AUDIENCE.

A fourth approach is to choose one primary reader and write for that reader through the first draft and first stages of rewriting. Then, in later stages of rewriting, adjust to accommodate your other, secondary readers. Thus in rewriting you might

- insert paragraphs that answer questions these readers may raise;
- replace technical terms or add definitions of some terms of art;
- change your organization or headings; or
- move some extensive technical details to tables, footnotes, or subsections so the readers who want to can easily skip over this detail and still follow your article.

5. Do a preemption check and modify the topic, purpose, and scope as needed.

Check to make sure your topic has not been preempted by another writer. This check requires an exhaustive search of scholarly materials. Artificial intelligence (AI) may help at this stage, but make sure you verify its results. Plan for a sufficient amount of time to do this, knowing that time will be well invested. The search will complete the research you started in your topic search and focus the research you will use in your paper.

If someone has come close to your topic, modify it so yours adds something new. For example, you may have to create a theory, propose a statute, or offer a new synthesis. You may need to shift your angle on the subject or modify your focus. Often other scholars will help by raising questions at the ends of their articles that suggest further research. If you cannot add anything new, abandon the topic and try another.

When you have secured and sufficiently modified your thesis, consider the scope that your thesis dictates. Narrow or broaden your thesis so that your readers will easily comprehend your message, the relevance of your research, and the originality of your commentary. Remember that part of the paper's scope is including and refuting arguments that do not support your thesis. Then relate your ideas to your thesis throughout the process. You may also want to recheck your revised thesis with various legal readers.

6. Make a research plan.

Before you launch into any additional research, plan your approach. In the long run, this will save you time and reduce the potential for confusion. Make sure to research materials addressing and leading to this topic. You may need to divide the plan by jurisdictions, points of view, strings of arguments, or historical developments, depending on your topic. Aim for a plan that researches all points of view on the topic so that you can analyze and predict accordingly. One thing quickly leads to another, so use your thesis to stay alert to how ideas relate to one another. For help doing this, see RESEARCH STRATEGY GUIDE.

7. Learn the technical details.

Become familiar with your citation guide's current edition. This will enable you to record the full citations correctly as you find them. Having to return to the sources solely for citation information is time-consuming and irritating. If you plan on publishing, research the page length and requirements for the range of publications you are considering.

8. Take accurate notes from the beginning of your research process.

Researching a scholarly article is a long and complex process; do not plan to rely on your memory of what you have and have not researched or what you have or have not found. Record meticulously both content and the dates of your research so that you can keep track of the materials and your developing analysis of them. In particular, note TERMS OF ART, phrases that contribute to the development of your proof or criticism, and arguments that need refutation. Use the terms you capture in your notes to develop and refine the language of your thesis sentence.

If you can, note relationships between concepts and sketch how they relate to each other. Build logical connections between the research and your thesis. Refer to your purpose to decide why things are in a particular order and refer to your scope to keep the article's length in check.

9. Organize.

After you have revised your thesis sentence to better express the originality of your contribution to the topic, create an organization that flows from that thesis. For example, if you want to criticize the oblique language of business prospectuses, start with a quotation of that language and show what problems it creates; then give your solutions. If you want to suggest the best resolution of a circuit split, characterize the split, group together circuits that agree, and then show which is better and why. Beware of following a standard format for scholarship because the topics and subtopics are numerous, varied, and complex. If you are having trouble seeing new options, using artificial intelligence (AI) may offer some different approaches to organization. Read these approaches critically. Take time to arrange your topics and subtopics in a way that best fits the materials and suits your purposes. This is a good time in your process to get feedback, so you might want to go over the resulting outline with your editor or professor. For related information, see ORGANIZE, HOW TO; ORGANIZATION, LARGE-SCALE; OUTLINES; and PARAGRAPHS.

Writing

10. Make a drafting plan.

You may want to draft in pieces, concentrating fully on each piece, or draft in one sitting. For example, if you have a historical background section, you might want to draft that in one sitting. Or if you are developing your argument, you might want to draft that without stopping. You may even want to draft the whole article all at once so you are forced to synthesize the document fully. Your topic can change so much that it loses its force and integrity, so be flexible enough to change your plan to suit the paper but realistic enough to meet your deadline.

11. Begin drafting early so that your thinking can develop.

Because of its detail and length, scholarly writing requires more time. For example, you will need more time to decide what to include because you will have so many sources. When in doubt, include it. Allow yourself to overwrite at this stage as needed to keep your mind free. You can edit for conciseness and unity in later stages of the process. Keep uppermost in your mind the idea that you need to get a draft completed and get your thoughts on paper so you can refine and revise them later. Beware of procrastination at this point. If you are having trouble writing, see PERFECTIONISM, PROCRASTINATION, WRITING, and WRITING BLOCK.

Keep relating your writing to your theme statement and include information not just because you found it but because it advances or supports your theme. Show how it does that. When in doubt, leave in your thoughts because they are hard to recreate later.

Allow yourself more latitude in using figurative meaning, emotional language, and your own persuasive style than you would in briefs or memos. Because the article is your commentary on a given subject, also allow your style and tone wider range. Do not, however, range so far that you lessen your CREDIBILITY. For an explanation of these terms, see EMOTIONAL LANGUAGE, EMPHASIS, FIGURATIVE MEANING, and IMAGERY. For relevant techniques, see TONE.

If you feel stuck or overwhelmed and want to try using AI, try using it for smaller sections such as historical summaries, definitions, or explanations. Then you can rewrite them to fit your overall organization, THEME, PURPOSE and point of view. For more help here, see ARTIFICIAL INTELLIGENCE AND WRITING.

12. Use footnotes wisely.

Use footnotes to acknowledge, educate, and substantiate. Use footnotes to acknowledge the sources of your points. This attribution, and the manner in which you present it, is key to the value given your scholarship. Also use footnotes to educate readers about valuable historical or background information and about sources a future researcher would need for reference.

If you are doing traditional scholarly writing, use footnotes for any of the following three purposes:

- to cite authority for all unoriginal propositions,
- to expand on authority by offering several other sources, or
- to add supporting details.

Avoid using footnotes to write another paper within this text, to argue with yourself, to record irrelevant sources, or to substitute for deciding where to put some information or analytical point. Footnotes should enhance the paper, not salve the writer's frustration at researching an unused source. Above all, do not diminish the impact of your analysis by making individual footnotes longer than the content justifies.

You may want to write the paper first, noting where footnotes belong and putting in enough information to remember what the footnote will contain. Then you can go back and put them all in proper citation form with appropriate signals. Or you may choose to write the footnotes as you go, which can offer you a respite from the larger ideas. The latter choice takes longer and can distract from the document's overall coherence, so find a balance that allows you to write fluidly and document your resources accurately. For more information, see FOOTNOTES.

Rewriting

13. Plan for multiple redrafts.

Plan to make multiple passes through your draft so you can focus on a manageable number of concerns on each draft. This can make the overall process less stressful and often more efficient. Whenever you are feeling overwhelmed, consider breaking the rewriting process into several steps. For ideas on how to do this, see REWRITING, REWRITING CHECKLIST, and SCHOLARLY WRITING PROCESS CHECKLIST, subsection 3.

Remain aware of the final deadline and pace yourself so you can redraft as much as necessary to develop the topic comfortably and get the content and organization to fit your purpose and message. Make sure all parts of the paper support the thesis with research and footnotes. Determine where to state your thesis and then make sure that the headings support and advance the thesis. Check that all relevant views on the topic are presented accurately. Eliminate extraneous material and rearrange sections if there is a better way to support the thesis.

If you were thinking of one primary reader when you drafted, you can now adjust your organization and headings or add footnotes to accommodate your other, secondary readers. You might do that by inserting paragraphs that answer questions these readers may raise; replacing technical terms or add definitions of some terms of art; or moving some extensive technical details to tables, footnotes, or subsections so the readers who want to can easily skip over this detail and still follow your article. For related information, see AUDIENCE and FOOTNOTES.

14. State the theme and purpose early.

Tell the reader your point at the beginning of the article, by the end of the introduction, rather than building up to it at the article's end. Most legal readers like to know what they are reading about and then see the explanation because they can then follow and evaluate the writer's reasoning that leads to that point. Even if the readers are likely to question your position, you are more likely to convince them if they read your article with questions in mind other than *Where is this article going?* You may state your point at the end of your introduction or in the very first sentence of the article. For related information, see ORGANIZE, HOW TO; ORGANIZATION, LARGE-SCALE; and PARAGRAPHS.

15. Refine the paper's organization to convey the message and maintain the theme.

    Make sure that your organization reflects the substance of your piece. You may discover another, better structure. For example, you might want to convey that *international law does not adequately address human rights in newly formed countries*. To convey that message, you might structure your presentation by explaining which international law may apply, demonstrating how that law works in some other countries, explaining its weaknesses, and finally demonstrating how those weaknesses keep it from being effective in newly formed countries. Alternatively, you might select a structure that begins with a scenario from a particular country, giving details of human rights violations. You could then invoke the international law that might apply and demonstrate how it is inadequate. Construct creatively but carefully.

    Once you decide on the best structure, check your headings and content. Make sure that the HEADINGS convey that structure clearly. Any headings or subheadings should be helpful signals, not merely a parroting of traditional format. Try using sentences or phrases that communicate your argument from a consistent point of view, rather than just depending on words like *Introduction* or *Historical Background*. Make sure the structure is congruent with your content, so that readers understand your message not just from the words but also from the structure. You may also discover that you have extraneous material that can be removed.

    Similarly, you may want to check your THESIS SENTENCES to make sure you have one in most paragraphs and that they connect logically with each other and with the content of the paragraph. As part of this back-and-forth process, you may find yourself dividing paragraphs differently, revising thesis sentences, or moving content.

16. Refine the proportion of information as it relates to the thesis.

    Check each point in relation to the thesis to make sure that you are not using too much space for an irrelevant point and too little for a major point. While this is not a literal rule, you can mislead readers if the proportions contradict the point's relevance to your thesis. Once you are happy with the content and organization overall, check specifically for this balance among authorities, arguments, and your own analysis.

Revising

17. Plan for multiple revisions.

    As with rewriting, expect this stage to require more passes than you plan for in other writing projects. Consider revising at least once for each major concern, such as small-scale organization and clarity, which include such matters as TONE, VOICE, READABILITY, and EMPHASIS. You may, for example, revise the whole draft with a focus on thesis and language furthering the thesis. Or you may revise for SENTENCE STRUCTURE only, saving other concerns for earlier or later drafts. Try to break the revision task into small enough units to allow you to keep moving and resist the urge to procrastinate. For more ideas, see REVISING.

18. Create a concise presentation.

In articles, honor the same fundamental of legal writing that you do in briefs: make every word count. It is tempting to say more than is necessary in articles, but giving in to that temptation can lose readers. For related information, see SCHOLARLY WRITING PROCESS CHECKLIST. Artificial intelligence (AI) may be able to suggest revision ideas, such as minimizing use of PASSIVE VOICE and attaining CONCISENESS.

19. Ask for comments and criticisms on the paper.

To gain specific advice, select carefully the readers who have an eye for what the paper needs at this point. You may want to send a cover memo with the paper asking questions about the draft and how to handle particularly troublesome places. The reader, by responding to your specific questions and adding other comments, will offer valuable evidence of audience reaction. Then you can adjust the draft to make it clearer. If you have more than one reader, compare suggestions and pay special attention to the common points. Attend to the problems the readers see; if you disagree with their solutions, fashion one that is better. Not only will the paper be better, but you will also become a better writer. For ideas on how readers may react, see EDITING.

Polishing

20. Check the details.

Check for smoothness and elegance, making sure that headings are consistent, emphatic techniques reinforce the content, and no phrases are overused or distract from the content. When you have finished making all the edits you want on your paper, read it just for technical details. This will take much longer than you think, and you may tire quickly. So work in short spurts, perhaps jumping among various sections, and check for one thing at a time, such as citation form or format or consistent wording for key concepts. As you do this, resist the urge to consider possible revisions, so you can focus on the smallest details rather than moving back into revision. To help with this, you might want to work backward or on the second half of the paper first, where there are usually more mistakes.

Reread, perhaps converting to 200% size in your viewer, to make sure that punctuation is correct. Particularly watch for extra spaces or changes made by the grammar checker that do not conform to the style rules you are using.

Review your notes on accurate citation usage and make sure that every citation is accurate and correct. Check numbers for accuracy, including all pinpoints. Run your spellchecker, grammar checker, and other artificial intelligence (AI) tools that are helpful. Proofread for WORDS SPELLCHECKERS MAY NOT CATCH. For more techniques, see POLISHING. For a list of details to check, see SCHOLARLY WRITING PROCESS CHECKLIST.

SCHOLARLY WRITING PROCESS CHECKLIST

As you work on your scholarly paper, you may want to create your own checklist for the document. Creating a checklist can help you find your way through the complicated process of scholarly writing. Checklists can be particularly useful for the parts of the scholarly writing process where you tend to feel overwhelmed. Dividing those parts of the process into smaller steps can reduce your stress and save you time. Additionally, checklists can help you to verify any results obtained from using AI. For more explanation, see SCHOLARLY WRITING and SCHOLARLY WRITING PROCESS.

You can use the following questions to get started, but make the checklist your own.

1. When PREWRITING.
   (a) Have I set deadlines for the following tasks?
      - Appropriately original and narrow topic selected?
      - Preemption check completed?
      - Research completed?
      - Notes completed?
      - Outline drafted, sketched, or assembled?
      - First draft completed, with footnotes?
      - Further research completed?
      - Draft rewritten for organization, content, and scope?
      - Draft sent to editor or other reader?
      - Draft revised?

- Second to the last draft completed?
- Footnotes checked for accuracy and citation form?
- Final draft completed?
- Deadlines coordinated with other projects and deadlines?

(b) Have I determined required technical matters, such as page length, citation format, and so on?

(c) Have I determined my overall thesis and purpose?

- Have I written the thesis in one sentence that includes my original idea and *because* to explain why it is important?
- Have I decided on my primary purpose:
    - to organize a confusing array of issues,
    - to expand a field of knowledge by offering a new direction,
    - to predict developments in the law.
    - to suggest changes in the law or advocate a plan of action, or
    - other?
- Do I keep asking *So what?* so that I can keep relating each point to the overall purpose?
- Am I thinking about publication, which will sharpen my focus?

(d) Have I considered the SCOPE of the paper?

- Have I written down a target page length?
- Do I have a sense of how much research I need to gather so that readers can evaluate the merit of the article's reasoning?
- Am I ready to capture all relevant sources and cite them?

(e) Have I considered the range of readers and accounted for what they need?

(f) Have I completed my preemption check?

(g) Have I ascertained the technical details for citation form and publication?

(h) Have I made a research plan?

- To research materials addressing and anticipating this topic?
- To incorporate all relevant points of view on the topic?
- To establish the importance of this topic?

- To develop an original thesis about this topic and predict or analyze accordingly?

(i) Have I taken accurate notes throughout the process?

- Have I recorded meticulously both content and the dates of my research?
- Have I kept track of the materials and my developing analysis?
- Have I noted terms of art, phrases that develop my proof or criticism, and arguments that need refutation?
- Am I using the terms captured in my notes to develop and refine the language of my thesis sentence?

(j) Have I created an organization that is appropriate for the topic, not just standard?

2. When WRITING.

(a) Do I have a drafting plan, that is, what sections I will draft first, second, and so on?

(b) Do I keep moving rather than allowing myself to bog down in one troublesome area?

(c) Am I developing my analysis of the topic?

(d) Am I keeping track of sources and securing them in draft footnotes?

(e) Am I allowing myself to be original and revise my thesis statement as my thinking evolves?

3. When REWRITING.

(a) Have I allowed time for multiple passes through the draft?

(b) Content.

- Do the THEME and PURPOSE appear early enough to satisfy the reader?
- Have I accounted secondary readers in both content and organization?
- Do all parts of the paper support the thesis?
- Have I deleted extraneous or unhelpful material?
- Are all relevant views on the topic presented accurately?
- Do the headings all relate to the theme and the purpose?
- Do most paragraphs have a thesis sentence?

- Do the thesis sentences, when read without the supporting content, convey the logical flow of the document?
- Does each section and paragraph relate directly to both the thesis sentence and relevant heading? See SCHOLARLY WRITING.
- Is the document's point of view clear? (See POINT OF VIEW, OBJECTIVE TO PERSUASIVE.)
- Does the paper include, in either text or footnotes, all the information needed by all intended readers to understand the thesis and its support? For information on various readers, see AUDIENCE, CONTEXT-INDEPENDENT WRITING, and SCHOLARLY WRITING. Also see UNOBTRUSIVE DEFINITIONS.
- Do FOOTNOTES acknowledge, educate, or substantiate, and are they properly placed? For example, does each do one of following:
    - cite authority for all unoriginal propositions;
    - expand on one authority by offering other, related sources;
    - add detail, explanation, or definitions needed by an audience;
    - add detail for the reader using the paper as a scholarly tool; or
    - give the text of a statute, regulation, quotation, or specific source being discussed?

(c) Large-Scale Organization.

- Does the structure flow from substance?
    - Is my current organization the best one for carrying my thesis? Is there a better alternative?
    - Do the HEADINGS connect with each other to reveal the steps in your analysis?
    - Do the THESIS SENTENCES, when read without the supporting text, reveal the logical flow?
        - Does each paragraph have a thesis sentence that states the point of the paragraph?
        - Is the content of each paragraph sufficient to support the point made in the thesis sentence?

- Is each section's relationship to the thesis statement clearly reflected by its order in the organization?
- Are the parts congruent with the overall logical rationale? For example, do they use one of the following:
  - parts used in previous cases,
  - parts used in a statute,
  - parts used in other legal documents,
  - parts of an overall process, or
  - different causes of one effect?
- Is the amount of information and analysis proportional to its importance to the thesis?
- Does the paper use headings, footnotes, or PARAGRAPH BLOCKS so that the reader can easily identify each part's role in the whole? See ORGANIZATION, LARGE-SCALE.

4. When REVISING.

(a) Have I allowed time for multiple drafts to revise well?

(b) Small-Scale Organization.

- Does the introduction present a blueprint for the paper? That is, are points presented in the same order used in the body of the article? Are the same terms used for key concepts that are used later in the article?
- Is each section connected accurately and clearly both to the thesis and to previous and subsequent points?
- Do the first sentences of each paragraph, when read without the intervening text, accurately and clearly convey their points? See TOPIC SENTENCES.
- Is the logical connection between each of these first sentences clearly communicated? See CONNECTIONS, MAKING THEM.
- Are sentences organized logically, e.g., subordinate ideas are subordinated, main ideas appear in main clauses, and PARALLEL STRUCTURE is used to present like ideas?

(c) CLARITY.

- Are TOPIC SENTENCES worded so they read as a smooth summary of the content? Are their SUBJECT-VERB COMBINATIONS effective? Are TRANSITIONS used effectively? For help here, see CONNECTIONS, MAKING THEM.

- Will the reader, at any point, not misunderstand the content? For related information, see AMBIGUITY, WAYS TO AVOID.
- Is the wording for key concepts consistent throughout the document?
    - Is phrasing clear?
    - Is word choice precise?
    - Is plain English used rather than jargon or legalese?
    - Do the subject-verb combinations carry your message, remind the reader of the thesis?
    - Are nominalizations minimized or avoided?
- Is the text readable?
    - Is there only one main point per sentence?
    - Are topic sentences generally the first sentences of paragraphs?
    - Are subjects and verbs close together?
    - Is passive voice avoided unless needed?
- Is the emphasis effective?
    - Does phrasing emphasize key points?
    - Are key points made in positions of emphasis?
    - Is repetition used effectively where appropriate?
    - Does parallel structure reveal parallel ideas?
    - Do short sentences make emphatic points or catch reader's attention? See SENTENCE LENGTH and SENTENCE STRUCTURE, subsection 1.

5. When POLISHING.

(a) Smoothness and elegance.

- Are no phrases or techniques overused, so that they draw the writer's attention to the phrase itself?
- Are all HEADINGS in consistent format?

(b) Mechanics.

- Have I run the spellchecker and grammar checker?
- Have I reread once, perhaps aloud, to make sure the grammar checker has not missed anything?
    - Do subjects and verbs agree?

  - Is punctuation correct?
  - Are there extra spaces?
  - Are there any WORDS SPELLCHECKERS MAY NOT CATCH?

(c) Citations.

- Are the citations in correct form?
  - Are the case and statute names correct?
  - Are the abbreviations correct?
  - Are the numbers correct?
  - Is the spacing correct?
- Are the signals accurate?
- Are parentheticals used correctly?

6. When finished, have I allowed time for criticism and comments and suggested revisions?

SCOPE

Scope describes what your document covers, its length and depth. You can measure scope in part by content and page limit. Scope in content refers to the amount of material and the level of detail you use. For example, you may be analyzing a narrow tort issue within one state, so your scope is derived from that state's mandatory authority on that issue, your discussion about that mandatory authority, and its application to your situation. If the mandatory authority is not sufficient to address the issue, you will expand your scope to include persuasive authority from another jurisdiction.

Scope in page limit refers to either the official page limit for a document, such as a brief, or to the unofficial page limit generated by the circumstances. If you are writing a brief on that tort issue, the court may have a limit on the number of pages you can write. You will limit your analysis accordingly, concentrating on the mandatory authority and legally significant facts, adding salient points about persuasive authority only if necessary. If you are writing a memo on the tort issue, you may discuss the mandatory authority in more detail and add a small range of persuasive authority showing how other states assess the situation. The challenge in doing this occurs because many legal issues lend themselves to the proportions of a scholarly article. You could, for example, discuss each bit of mandatory authority in great detail and add persuasive authority from dozens of states, all of which might have something to say about that tort issue. That is usually too much.

Scope is interrelated with AUDIENCE and PURPOSE. Before you begin researching, assess the appropriate scope for the situation, determining as closely as you can how much your reader will read and what purpose you want to achieve. You may even ask your readers directly. The answer can determine how much research you do and how you design the document.

For example, while the scope of the document discussed in OUTLINES may seem logical and appropriate, it may be too long for some readers and for the purpose of a memo, such as obtaining custody of the children for the mother. So, before you write, you may regroup the presentation to show what elements are not in dispute, then focus in one section on the elements most favorable to the mother, and demonstrate in another section how the father cannot meet the best interests standard, as demonstrated in the subsequent examples in that entry. This will shorten the document and heighten its persuasive impact. As you research and rewrite, reassess scope periodically; most readers appreciate conciseness in design, perhaps more than conciseness in sentences.

SCRUBBING ELECTRONIC DOCUMENTS

See METADATA REMOVAL.

SECONDARY SOURCES

Secondary sources bring together primary law and commentary on a specific topic or field of law, such as tax, copyright, or environmental law. These collections integrate information from several sources, including courts, executive agencies, scholars, and practitioners. Secondary sources can provide overviews of specific issues, offer related information, and give a general context or understanding of an area of law. These tools are especially valuable when you are working on a project in an unfamiliar area of law because you can read for context, timeliness, and general background. For related information, see ARTIFICIAL INTELLIGENCE AND RESEARCH, PROMPTS, MANDATORY AUTHORITY, PERSUASIVE AUTHORITY, RESEARCH STRATEGY GUIDE, and UPDATING THE LAW.

SECTION

Section should always be spelled out when it begins a sentence. In text, also spell out *section* except when referring to a U.S. Code provision or a federal regulation. Use the § symbol in footnotes and citations. Use *s.* or *sec.* only if your jurisdiction permits.

SELF- OR *SELF*?

Use *self-* when adding it as a prefix to another noun: *self-interest*, *self-serving*, and *self-sufficient*. Use *self* as the first syllable in words such as *selflessness*, *selfish*, and *selfsame*. For related information, see HYPHENS.

SEMICOLONS

Semicolons have two uses: (1) as an end mark between two closely related clauses and (2) as a super comma.

1. As an end mark between two clauses.

You may use a semicolon instead of a period between two sentences if those sentences are closely related logically but could each stand as complete sentences.

The Plaintiff did not intend to destroy another's property; he broke the window only because he saw flames inside the house.

Avoid using semicolons without clarifying the logical relationship of your points.

This action violated Tremont's rights to both freedom of speech and due process.

rather than

This case involves not only freedom of speech, but also due process; each of these issues indicates that Tremont's rights were violated.

Use a semicolon rather than a comma between two independent clauses when there is no conjunction, such as *and*, following the comma. This error occurs frequently when *however* connects two clauses.

Cutts denied being at the scene of the crime; however, he admitted having been there two hours earlier.

rather than

Cutts denied being at the scene of the crime, however, he admitted having been there two hours earlier.

2. As a super comma.

You must use a semicolon, instead of a comma, at the end of each element in a list when a comma occurs within any one element in the list.

The Company warrants for one year that its compressors (1) are free from defects in material and

> **workmanship; (2) have the capacities and rating set forth in the Company's catalogs, provided that no warranty is made against corrosion, erosion, or deterioration; and (3) meet all relevant federal safety standards.**
>
> **The Company is not liable for any delay in performance due to any of the following:**
>
> **(1) any act of God, including but not limited to floods, epidemics, fires, storms, or earthquakes;**
>
> **(2) any acts of others beyond the reasonable control of the Company, including but not limited to strikes or other labor disturbances, riots, wars, acts of civil or military authority, or acts of the Customer; and**
>
> **(3) any cause beyond its reasonable control, including but not limited to delays in transportation, inability to obtain necessary materials or components, or labor shortages.**

The semicolon is needed because a comma is no longer sufficient to show the reader where each item on the list begins and ends.

Do not use a semicolon at the end of each element in a list solely because the list is tabulated rather than run in text. Commas are still sufficient if there are no commas within any of the items listed.

> **"Remanufacturing equipment" included the following processes:**
>
> **(1) disassembly to a predetermined standard established by the Manufacturer for each model,**
>
> **(2) cleaning,**
>
> **(3) refinishing,**
>
> **(4) inspecting and testing to new machine test standards,**
>
> **(5) installation of all retrofits, and**
>
> **(6) operational testing.**

For related information, see HOWEVER; LISTS, STRUCTURE OF; and TRANSITIONS.

SENTENCE FRAGMENTS

Sentence fragments are phrases that could be part of a sentence, but as worded do not make up a complete sentence. To be a complete sentence, the phrase must have a subject and verb, which makes it a clause.

subject verb

Any vendor who supplies the University must file this document.

rather than

Any vendor who supplies the University.

and

subject verb verb

Even if the work is derivative, parts of it may still be copyrightable.

rather than

Parts still copyrightable.

If there is a sentence fragment, most legal readers will assume you have not polished the document. Some will assume that you did not know better. Although fragments can be used for emphasis, their effect in legal writing can be summed up as follows.

Probably too dramatic.

The previous fragment may have caught your attention, but it is too informal for legal writing. Thus, even in persuasive writing, be careful. Make sure your fragment is unambiguously intentional if you use it. While you could use the following version if you are beginning a paragraph that leads directly to it, it is a judgment call.

Not so here.

You might better preserve your credibility by writing the following.

That is not what happened here.

For other ways to create emphasis, see EMPHASIS.

SENTENCE LENGTH

In general, avoid making sentences longer than three-and-one-half lines of text. The one exception to this is sentences containing lists, which are easier to read because of their more obvious structure.

A doctor may forgo disclosure to a patient if any of the following situations occur: (1) if the patient is unconscious, incompetent, or otherwise incapable of understanding the information; (2) if the patient is a minor; (3) if in the

doctor's opinion the information would have a disproportionately adverse effect on the patient's ability to make a rational decision; or (4) if an emergency exists which allows no time to safely consult with the patient.

One handy way to check sentence length is to scan several pages of your text and draw slashes after each period, which you can do without actually reading the text. Then look at the slashes. If you see several sentences in a row that run more than four lines, try to shorten at least one.

Similarly, if you see several sentences in a row that are only one line long, see if you should combine two of them or make some other changes to avoid a choppy tone. Occasionally, however, you may want this choppy effect.

The major purpose of the trial court's established procedure is to give the litigants a fair opportunity to address their claims and have them resolved by a court of law. That purpose was met here. The litigants had eight years of opportunity. In this context, their arguments on appeal are particularly specious.

For related information, see REVISING CHECKLIST; SENTENCE STRUCTURE; and TOUGH, SOUNDING THAT WAY.

SENTENCE, PARTS OF

Knowing the parts of a sentence can help you understand sentence structure, which in turn can help you write sentences that convey your meaning and emphasize your points effectively. If you have trouble identifying such things as verbs or indirect objects, this quick overview may help.

1. Verb.

Each sentence has at least one verb. The verb expresses either an action, such as *hit* or *received*, or a state of being, such as *is* or *seemed*. The verb may be one word, such as *signed* or *appeared*, or more than one word, such as *must complete* or *will have been signed*. When the verb contains more than one word, it is called a *verb phrase*.

The following verbs express an action.

Faulkner signed a waiver of rights.

All nonresidents living in Illinois for more than three months of a calendar year must complete the following section.

The defendant agreed.

The contract will have been signed by that date.

The trial court determined that the defendant's statements were voluntary and admitted them at trial.

The following verbs express a state of being.

The settlement seems reasonable in light of the facts.

The plaintiff is a former employee of Stills, International.

In this case, nevertheless, the problem exists.

For common problems, see VERBS. For more information on specific kinds of verbs, see DIFFERENT TENSES IN THE SAME SENTENCE; VERBS, AUXILIARY; VERBS, IRREGULAR; VERBS, LINKING; VERBS, MOODS; VERBS, PARTICIPLES; VERBS, TENSES; and VOICE, ACTIVE OR PASSIVE?

2. Subject.

Each sentence has at least one subject. The complete subject is the person, thing, or idea about which the verb speaks, and may be one word or many.

Faulkner signed a waiver of rights.

All nonresidents living in Illinois for more than three months of a calendar year must complete the following section.

The defendant agreed.

The contract will have been signed by that date.

The trial court determined that the defendant's statements were voluntary and admitted them at trial.

The settlement seems reasonable in light of the facts.

The plaintiff is a former employee of Stills, International.

The defendant's statements were voluntary.

The simple subject is the main word in the complete subject.

All nonresidents living in Illinois for more than three months of a calendar year must complete the following section.

3. Predicate.

Each sentence has a predicate. The predicate is the part of the sentence that says something about the subject.

All nonresidents living in Illinois for more than three months of a calendar year must complete the following section.

The defendant agreed.

The contract will have been signed by that date.

The trial court determined that the defendant's statements were voluntary and admitted them at trial.

The settlement seems reasonable in light of the facts.

The plaintiff is a former employee of Stills, International.

The defendant's statements were voluntary.

Every predicate includes at least one verb, and it may include any or all of the following: direct objects, indirect objects, prepositional phrases, and participial phrases.

4. Direct Object.

A direct object is the person, object, or idea receiving the action of the verb.

The plaintiff built the house with his own hands.

Faulkner signed a waiver of rights.

The defendant's action destroyed that right.

All sentences have a subject and predicate, but not all have a direct object.

The defendant testified at trial.

5. Indirect Object.

An indirect object receives the direct object, rather than the action of the verb.

The plaintiff gave the defendant the house when she agreed to cohabit.

Here, *the defendant* received the house, and thus is the indirect object. *The house* is the direct object, because it was the object of the verb, *gave*. Not all sentences have an indirect object.

6. Prepositional Phrase.

A prepositional phrase is a group of words that work together to show the relationship of a noun or pronoun to the rest of the sentence. This noun or pronoun is called the object of the preposition. A PREPOSITION, which is always the first word in a prepositional phrase, shows how the rest of that phrase is logically related to the sentence. Examples of prepositions are *of, to, on, off, between, through, in, at, without, over,* and *under*. The following examples of prepositional phrases illustrate the variety of information they can convey.

He built the house with his own hands.

All nonresidents living in Illinois for more than three months of a calendar year must complete the following section.

The contract will have been signed by that date.

The settlement seems reasonable in light of the facts.

7. Participial Phrase.

A participial phrase is a group of words that work together to show the relationship of some action to the rest of the sentence. A participle, which is always the first word in a participial phrase, is either the *-ed* or *-ing* form of a regular verb (*followed, following, covered, covering*) or the past tense or *-ing* form of an irregular verb (*held, holding*). The following examples illustrate how participial phrases can be used in a sentence.

The boat, built by Mr. Tremat, should not be considered community property.

The attorney focused her argument on this issue, building carefully on these facts.

Covered by snow, the edge of the ditch was not visible.

The statute covering this issue is unambiguous.

This right, held inviolate since the founding of our country, must not now be extinguished.

Any court holding on this issue must address the elements of the statute.

8. Clause.

A clause is a group of words that includes both a subject and a predicate.

subject predicate
The trial court determined this issue.

In contrast, a phrase does not necessarily include both a subject and a predicate.

a case of first impression

determining this issue

There are two kinds of clauses: independent (or main) and dependent. An independent clause can be set off as a sentence by itself.

> **The defendant knew or should have known this.**
>
> **The company gave a free water heater to residential customers.**

Every sentence must include at least one independent clause.

A dependent clause cannot by itself form a sentence because it is logically dependent on an independent clause.

> **that the plaintiff would not be aware of the stock market usage of the phrase "passed its dividends"**
>
> **who installed electric space heating**

This logical dependence is signaled by the conjunction that introduces the dependent clause, which is called a subordinating conjunction. For related information, see SUBORDINATION.

Make sure all dependent clauses are part of a larger sentence including an independent clause.

> **The defendant knew or should have known that the plaintiff would not be aware of the stock market usage of the phrase "passed its dividends."**
>
> rather than
>
> The defendant knew or should have known. That the plaintiff would not be aware of the stock market usage of the phrase "passed its dividends."
>
> and
>
> **The company gave a free water heater to residential customers who installed electric space heating.**
>
> rather than
>
> The company gave a free water heater to residential customers. Who installed electric space heating.

For related information, see SENTENCE STRUCTURE and SYNTAX.

SENTENCES, MAIN

See TOPIC SENTENCES.

SENTENCE STRUCTURE

Mastering the basics of sentence structure provides a valuable tool for effective writing. After you learn how to change the structure of a sentence, you can use that skill to emphasize or deemphasize points, to increase readability, to change tone, and to clarify transitions between paragraphs and sentences.

What follows are explanations of four basic sentence structures (subsections 1–4) and examples and explanations of ways you can exploit those basics to create sentences that are both readable and effective (subsections 5–7). For help identifying the grammatical parts of a sentence, see SENTENCE, PARTS OF. For related information, see SYNTAX.

1. Simple Sentence.

Grammatically, this sentence includes only one set of subjects and verbs, although either the subject or verb may include more than one entity and the sentence may have many modifying phrases.

sub. verb
This case addresses three issues.

subject subject verb
Mr. Smith and his attorney will confer on the matter tomorrow.

subject sub. verb
The defendant and his wife ransacked the house and

verb
took items worth $3,000.

Strategically, use a simple sentence that has only a few words, usually fewer than ten, if you want the dramatic impact that a simple sentence can have.

The Court of Appeals refused to consider this argument because it "was not properly . . . presented to the trial court." The court did not elaborate.

2. Compound Sentence.

This structure includes two or more independent clauses joined by a conjunction, semicolon, or colon. An independent clause could be set off as a sentence by itself.

subject verb conjunction
There can be no negligence without duty, and in this

sub. verb
case there is no duty.

subject verb semicolon
There can be no negligence without duty; in this case,

sub. verb
no duty exists.

subject verb colon
In this case, one element of negligence is missing:

sub. verb
there is no duty.

This structure can create a one-two punch. This effect will be stronger if the second of the joined sentences is short. For related information, see COLONS; SEMICOLONS; and SENTENCE, PARTS OF.

3. Complex Sentence.

(a) Definition.

In a complex sentence, one or more dependent clauses have been inserted into another sentence, which is the independent clause.

dependent clause
Because more married women entered the labor market as second earners,

independent clause
more married couples were subject to the tax penalty.

The independent clause includes the main subject, verb, and object of the sentence. Because this is the structural heart of the sentence, you want to put your main information here.

More married couples were subject to the tax penalty.

Often you will want to use dependent clauses to add some background information, elaboration, or other less important points to the sentence. A dependent clause cannot by itself form a sentence because it begins with a subordinating word, and thus it is logically dependent on an independent clause.

because more married women entered the labor market as second earners

(b) Advantages and disadvantages of this structure.

The complex sentence is useful because it allows the writer to show the logical relationship of two or more points while giving more emphasis to one point. As a result, the complex sentence is common in legal writing. To use it effectively, however, you must keep the complex sentence readable and logically structured.

independent clause
This court interpreted the statute broadly in previous cases,

dependent clause
when it applied the statute to parents of minor children, trustees of the estates of handicapped adults, and foster parents.

rather than

subject dependent clause
This court, when it in previous cases applied the statute to parents of minor children, trustees of the estates of handicapped adults, and foster parents,

verb
interpreted this statute broadly.

Avoid using complex sentences exclusively; also exploit the strengths of simple and compound sentences. Too many complex sentences make the text less interesting. For a related topic, see VARIETY. If all your sentences are complex, try restructuring some important points into simple sentences.

Also avoid overdoing the complexity of the sentence. In general, do not insert more than two dependent clauses in one sentence; doing so gives the reader a bite too big to chew. If you decide you must show the logical interrelationship of more actions, try putting those actions in separate sentences and using a connecting word or phrase that explains that logical interrelationship.

Waivers of constitutional rights not only must be voluntary; they must also be knowing, intelligent acts done with sufficient awareness of the relevant circumstances and likely consequences. <u>Breckenridge v. United States</u>, 900 U.S. 321, 323 (2025). Furthermore, waiver of the right to counsel cannot be presumed from a silent record. <u>Kelstad v. Karney</u>, 969 U.S. 506, 516 (2025).

For more on the use of the complex sentence, see subsections 6 and 7. For help connecting two sentences, see CONNECTIONS, MAKING THEM; and TRANSITIONS.

4. Inverted sentence.

One final structure you can use occasionally is the inverted sentence. In this structure, some part of the predicate, such as the object of the verb, comes before the subject.

S V
Imprudent it was, but not illegal.

rather than

S V
It was imprudent, but not illegal.

In the inverted version of this sentence, the predicate adjective *imprudent* is placed before the subject *it*, rather than after the linking verb *was*. The inverted sentence is dramatic precisely because the parts of the sentence are out of their usual order. It is so dramatic, however, that it is hard to find an occasion to use it in legal writing without sounding self-conscious, as would be the case if someone said, *While coming to work today, an old friend I saw.*

5. Using subjects and verbs effectively.

Put your main point in the main subject and verb in your sentence. Conversely, deemphasize points by putting them in dependent clauses. For example, the following sentence emphasizes *he had slowed and was not accelerating* by making that the main subject and verb.

Although the defendant had not come to a full stop at the official stop sign, he had slowed to less than five miles per hour and was not accelerating at the time of the accident.

6. Matching substance and structure.

Consciously design your sentences to reinforce the legal analysis. Never use a sentence structure that goes against the logical structure of your content. To do so is tantamount to signaling that you plan to move to the right lane on a freeway and then moving to the left lane instead. Even if the reader manages to keep up with you, that reader will be distrustful and unhappy.

Put your main point in the main SUBJECT-VERB COMBINATION in each sentence, moving subordinate ideas to subordinate clauses. For example, you can deemphasize unimportant or unfavorable information, such as facts that embarrass your client, by placing them in a subordinate clause at the end or in the middle of a sentence. When you have a point you want to emphasize that can stand alone, put it in a short sentence. You can be accurate and add the emphasis you want by consciously designing your sentences.

Although the unmodified, simple sentence is strong and effective, you will usually need to add more to the sentence because you need to add more information. There are three places where these extra phrases can be inserted.

(a) Inserting extra phrases after the independent clause.

This inflationary effect was especially marked for two-earner married couples, whose income is aggregated for tax purposes.

Triavil offered no treatment or cure for tension headaches, as testified by Dr. Paul Wyles (R. 1159).

The minority arrived at the same conclusion, although for different reasons.

This structure is the mainstay of communication because it is the easiest for the reader to follow. For example, in the following sentence you understand the point immediately because you get the independent clause right away, before getting the elaboration.

I saw an old friend while coming to work today.

As such, this structure is useful for presenting routine information that needs no special emphasis.

This inequity affected more people in the early eighties, when more married women entered the labor market.

It is also useful for presenting information that is complex and thus must be presented in a simple form.

Unmarried individuals paid substantially greater taxes than married individuals between 1948 and 1969, in some cases more than 40% in excess of a married individual's tax on an identical income.

(b) Inserting extra phrases before the independent clause.

Until recently, others have supported inserting legislative veto provisions in statutes covering most agency rulemaking.

Despite the difficulty of this test, the gravity of the situation required that it be done.

This structure, a mainstay of storytellers, is useful when you want to create a touch of suspense. For example, after reading the following sentence, you expect more after hearing the introductory phrase.

While coming to work today, I saw an old friend.

The change in structure alone tells the reader that this is the beginning of a story. You might use this touch of suspense to present either facts or an argument.

Pointing the gun at the teller, the defendant ordered her to fill the bag with cash.

Because there was no timely notice, this opportunity for hearing provided no opportunity at all.

Additionally, placing information before the independent clause is a useful way to provide a transition at the beginning of a paragraph. In the following example, the information placed at the beginning of the paragraph both reminds the reader of the topic of the previous paragraph and shows the reader how that topic relates to this paragraph.

Environmental Impact Studies could be handled similarly, without delaying the hearing.

Even if there were some delay, that delay would present no procedural difficulties.

Finally, placing a dependent clause before the independent clause can signal to the reader that the added information is less important than the independent clause.

Although there are three kinds of marital status discrimination, this comment focuses only on the marriage penalty.

This structure can be useful when you need to include an unfavorable fact and you want to make that fact seem as unimportant as possible.

Although Mr. Allerton was in the room during the signing of the will, he was there only because it was his habit to sit in the living room while reading the evening paper.

(c) Inserting extra information in the middle of the independent clause.

Anorexics, by failing to eat, passively expose themselves to harm.

This structure, a tool of orators, creates a very formal tone. For example, the following sentence sounds rather stuffy.

I, while coming to work today, saw an old friend.

This structure is harder to read because to understand the main point the reader must remember the first part of the sentence, read the interrupting clause, and then mentally reunite the last part of the sentence with the first. Therefore, avoid using the structure in sentence after sentence; give the reader breathing space between these difficult sentences. Also, avoid allowing the interruption to exceed seven or eight words. If the interruption is longer, the reader would have to reread the sentence to get the point.

The burden is on the defendant to show not just that the tax is excessive, but also that the defendant was taxed for more than its fair share.

These issues, controversial but crucial, must be resolved by this court.

Dr. Yu, who attended the plaintiff immediately after the accident, has testified that her internal injuries were caused by the faulty seatbelts.

For information about problems associated with long interruptions, see AGREEMENT, SUBJECTS AND VERBS.

7. Varying your sentence structure.

In general, vary your sentence structure to keep your reader engaged. Balance content and variety carefully. After you are sure that the syntax is accurately carrying the substance, check for readability. Avoid using several long sentences in a row. Read important passages of text aloud so you can note the rhythm created by the text. Sometimes the content is good, but the repetition of a rhythmic pattern lulls the reader to sleep. A judicious amount of variety keeps the reader alert and interested. For more information on how to do this, see CONNECTIONS, MAKING THEM; CLARITY; PARAGRAPHS; READABILITY; TONE; and TRANSITIONS.

SENTENCES WITH *AND*

See *AND*; COMMA, OXFORD; LISTS, STRUCTURE OF; and SENTENCE STRUCTURE.

SETTLEMENT LETTERS AND EMAIL

A settlement letter is written to encourage a party to settle a case. It is usually written by one client's attorney and directed to the other client's attorney. A settlement letter is designed to inform the reader of the writer's argument and to persuade the reader to accept that argument. While this kind of action can be taken by email, the ramifications are so great that many lawyers prefer the paper form. Check with your colleagues to determine the correct medium. Consider the following when writing either a letter or email intended to settle a case.

1. Choose the approach you think is most likely to influence the other attorney.

   For example, if you think the attorney and client can be persuaded gently, you might want to begin with a friendly opening, show you have considered the other side, and then build your argument, leading to the settlement offer. If you think this attorney and client would be more convinced by a stronger opening, start with the offer of settlement. For related information, see AUDIENCE.

2. Make sure the attorney knows that you understand the other client's position.

   For example, if the client and attorney have already offered a settlement, remind them that you are aware of that offer and of how much it was, and that you appreciate the offer.

3. Choose a tone appropriate to the method of persuasion.

   This tone might be tough if you expect unreasonable opposition, or friendly if you want them to be convinced that your offer is fair. When determining the tone of a letter, consider what will be most effective rather than choosing what satisfies your own feelings, which might for example be frustration, exasperation, or uncertainty. For more information, see COMMUNICATIONS, TONE OF.

4. Follow a format that includes the following, adjusting the order and content to suit your purpose, tone, and audience:

   (a) a heading;

   (b) a salutation or subject line;

   (c) an introduction that identifies the purpose of settling;

   (d) your terms for settlement and the reasoning behind them;

   (e) a course of action on the settlement matter;

   (f) a specific directive to the attorney to call you or answer your offer of settlement, including a deadline, if applicable; and

   (g) a closing. For help here, see CLOSINGS FOR LETTERS AND EMAIL.

See also COMMUNICATIONS, CLOSINGS FOR; COMMUNICATIONS, ELECTRONIC; COMMUNICATIONS, INTERNATIONAL; COMMUNICATIONS, OPENINGS FOR; COMMUNICATIONS, PERSUASIVE; COMMUNICATIONS, TONE OF; EMAIL; PROFESSIONAL LANGUAGE AND PRESENTATION; SOCIAL MEDIA; SUBJECT LINES; WRITING, PERSUASIVE; WRITING TO ATTORNEYS; and WRITING TO CLIENTS.

SEXIST LANGUAGE, WAYS TO AVOID

When you are referring to a specific person who uses *he* or *she* for gender identity, it is legitimate to use *he* or *she*. This is often the situation in briefs or memos. When you are referring to a person who uses *they* as a personal pronoun, use that term unless it creates a legal problem, as it might in a will, trust, or contract. Only when your governing jurisdiction accepts any new term or usage can you trust that usage to be interpreted as you intended. If you are writing to a court that you know dislikes this use of *they,* consult with your client before making your decision about what term to use, and use what is in the best interest of your client.

Sometimes, however, you will be discussing general principles that apply to all persons. In those situations, use one of the following options.

1. Reword the phrase to omit the pronoun. This takes some thought, but is often the most effective option.

   Anyone desiring a position with this firm should submit a résumé at the interview.

   rather than

   Anyone desiring a position with this firm should submit his or her résumé at the time of his or her interview.

2. Substitute *one* throughout the text.

   One cannot apply for a loan if one does not have collateral.

   rather than

   A person cannot apply for a loan if he or she does not have collateral.

   This technique is hard to use gracefully without creating an unwanted TONE, but at least it would be accurate.

3. Refer to people in the plural so that you can accurately substitute *they* for the outdated *he or she.*

   All attorneys must adjust their trial strategies in response to this ruling.

   rather than

   Each attorney must adjust his or her trial strategies in response to this ruling.

   or

   Each attorney must adjust their trial strategies in response to this ruling.

This is often the easiest approach when discussing broader ideas, as is common in scholarly articles.

Be careful, however, about using a plural pronoun to refer to a singular noun in legal writing.

Anyone desiring a position should submit a résumé.

rather than

Anyone desiring a position should submit their résumé.

This use of the plural pronoun *they* to replace *he or she* is used in general speech, but it is often ambiguous in legal drafting. For example, *each child shall inherit an equal share of the land as long as they live* could result in confusion about what happens if only one of the children dies. Do not resort to using *s/he*. It is outdated and awkward for the reader, who will stumble slightly over the term, substituting *he or she* to read the sentence.

If you find that nothing you try sounds graceful, choose *the person* or some other accurate noun. In time, social custom may offer other acceptable choices. In legal writing, a conflict between accuracy and elegance should be resolved in favor of accuracy. For avoiding sexist language when beginning a business letter, see SALUTATIONS, subsection 2; and SUBJECT LINES. For related information, see GENDER IN WRITING.

SHALL

In all legal writing except LEGISLATION, use *must* instead of *shall* to state that something must be done; use *may* when stating something that may be done. Legislation traditionally treats *shall* as establishing a requirement, and therefore *shall* is not ambiguous in that context.

Taxes shall be filed on April 15 or the next business day each year.

The general public, however, does not necessarily give *shall* this more specific meaning. To them, *shall* is often an archaic or fancy version of *will*. They also may read *shall* as meaning either *must* or *may*, and thus it can be ambiguous.

I shall attempt to go over Niagara Falls in a barrel.

For this reason, *must* is usually the more precise choice.

S/HE

See GENDER IN WRITING and SEXIST LANGUAGE, WAYS TO AVOID.

SHEPARD'S CITATIONS

See UPDATING THE LAW.

SHORT SENTENCES

Short sentences provide one of the most effective ways to emphasize a point.

This was an error.

He failed to do so.

The Court of Appeals refused to consider this argument because it "was not properly . . . presented to the trial court." The Court did not elaborate.

Several short sentences in a row also create a clipped, no-nonsense tone.

My client, Ms. Ambrose, does not intend to pay this bill. She has no reason to pay this bill. She did not receive any software from your company. She did not order any software from your company. Until receiving your bill, she did not know your company existed.

Avoid creating any unintended emphasis by avoiding short sentences for unimportant points or using several short sentences in a row, unless you want a clipped or exasperated tone. For related information, see TOUGH, SOUNDING THAT WAY; and WRITING, PERSUASIVE, subsection 4(f). For a broader context, see SENTENCE STRUCTURE.

SHOULD

Should has several meanings, and thus can create some ambiguity. In the following sentence, for example, it could mean *ought*, *must*, or *may*.

The affidavit should be in our office at least five days before the scheduled hearing.

In general, legal writing needs the meaning of *must*; use *must* whenever that is your meaning.

The affidavit must be in our office at least five days before the scheduled hearing to ensure that the proceeding goes forward.

Should can be useful when you want to imply that something was not done that should have been.

The police should have read him his Miranda rights before searching his car.

Should is sometimes used to imply doubt that something will happen in the future. But avoid this use, because this implication is ambiguous and thus may not be inferred by the reader.

The contract should arrive in our office by next Thursday.

You may consider using *should* for tact when the statement is an indirect request, although *ought* may actually be the precise choice.

To ensure that the proceeding goes forward, the affidavit ought to be in our office at least five days before the scheduled hearing.

The safer route may be to make a direct request.

Please send the affidavit to our office at least five days before the scheduled hearing to insure that the proceeding goes forward.

When the statement is a comment on what may happen, use *may* rather than *should.*

The affidavit may arrive in our office several days before the actual hearing.

To increase readability, avoid using *should* at the beginning of a sentence when you really mean *if.* While *if* is precise because it can only mean that what follows is an *if . . . then* situation, *should* is less precise because it can introduce either a question or an *if . . . then* situation. For related information, see VERBS, AUXILIARY.

SIC

This is a Latin word that means *thus* or *so.* Use it within quotations to inform the reader that the error in the text was in the original, rather than an error you made when copying the quotation. *Sic* is surrounded by brackets and not italicized.

The police read defendant his Mirenda [sic] rights.

When the error is minor and obvious, as in the previous example, consider whether just correcting it would be a courtesy to the original writer. This might be appropriate when citing a case to the court who wrote the case, for example. For related information, see QUOTATIONS, HOW TO PUNCTUATE.

SIGNALS

See CITATIONS, SIGNALS.

SIMPLE SENTENCE

A simple sentence includes only one set of subjects and verbs, although it may have many modifying phrases.

subject verb
This case involves three issues.

subject subject verb
Mr. Smith and his attorney will confer on the matter tomorrow.

subject subject verb verb
The defendant and his wife ransacked the house and took items worth $3,000.

Strategically, use a simple sentence that has only a few words, usually fewer than ten, if you want the dramatic impact that a simple sentence can have.

The Court of Appeals refused to consider this argument because it "was not properly . . . presented to the trial court." The court did not elaborate.

For related information, see SENTENCE STRUCTURE and SHORT SENTENCES.

SIMPLICITY

Simplicity has gained status in legal writing over the years, mostly because of the universal overload under which lawyers and judges operate; most legal readers want to finish the job and go home. Confine your presentation to the information essential to your case, nothing more and nothing less. Achieving the delicate balance between thoroughness and simplicity in your writing will win you respect and credibility.

To achieve simplicity, concentrate on

- using terms of art and other key terms in subjects and verbs,
- focusing issues specifically,
- using clear and logical organization,
- revising for conciseness, and
- using plain English, rather than jargon or flowery language.

For specific suggestions, see CONCISENESS; CREDIBILITY; FLOWERY LANGUAGE; ISSUES; JARGON; LEGALESE; PARAGRAPHS; READABILITY, subsections 3 and 4; REPETITION; TERMS OF ART; and WORD CHOICE.

SINCE OR *BECAUSE*?

See *BECAUSE* OR *SINCE*?

SINGLE QUOTATION MARKS

See QUOTATION MARKS, SINGLE.

SINGULAR OR PLURAL?

When deciding whether to use the singular or plural form, you will usually determine your choice on the basis of ACCURACY. You may have several accurate options, however. Whatever choice you make, be consistent throughout.

Each petitioner must sign that petitioner's full legal name.

or

Petitioners must sign their full legal names.

rather than

Each petitioner must sign their full legal names.

In everyday speech, *they* is commonly used as a singular term to avoid having to make a gender choice or use the unpronounceable *s/he*, or the outdated *he or she*. But *they* is still also the plural form of the third person pronoun, so in legal writing sometimes it creates ambiguity when used as a singular term. In that situation, see subpoint 6 below. Although there have been several attempts to create gender neutral singular pronouns, none has yet become familiar enough or standard enough to be acceptable in legal writing.

When you may accurately use either singular or plural, consider the following guidelines. Use the plural *they* for any of the following three reasons.

1. Avoiding using *he or she*.

   Attorneys must file their complaints by the fourth day of the month in which they are requesting a hearing.

   rather than

   An attorney must file his or her complaint by the fourth day of the month in which he or she is requesting a hearing.

2. Stating a point that applies logically to a class of people or a concept, rather than an individual.

   The asbestos victims in this class action request monetary damages for three reasons. First, they . . . .

3. Distancing the reader from the idea or persons the term represents.

   Injured plaintiffs must file their claims before the statute of limitations runs.

Use the singular and repeat the relevant noun for any of these reasons, when doing so does not cause distracting repetition.

4. Pulling the reader closer to the idea or persons the term represents.

   Each defendant must be held accountable for that defendant's part in this tragedy.

5. Stating a point that applies logically to a concern for an individual rather than a class of people or a concept.

   Unlike an older child, a toddler cannot describe a parent's abusive actions. But that child can feel the results of the abuse and may be permanently harmed.

6. Avoiding ambiguity caused by the plural form.

   Each beneficiary must be identified by that beneficiary's full legal name.

   rather than

   All beneficiaries must be identified by their full legal names.

For related information, see GENDER IN WRITING and SEXIST LANGUAGE, WAYS TO AVOID.

SLANG

Avoid using slang in legal writing because it is too informal, too emotional, and often too imprecise.

SLANTED LANGUAGE

See EMOTIONAL LANGUAGE.

SLASH

The only time you should use a slash (/) in legal writing is when you are writing a form in which the person signing is to mark out the inappropriate word, as in *Mr./Ms./Mrs./Miss*. For related information, see *AND/OR* and GENDER IN WRITING.

SMOOTHNESS

See COHERENCE, EMPHASIS, LOGICAL LINKS, and READABILITY.

SO

So has several different meanings and thus must be used carefully to avoid potential ambiguity. For example, when used as a conjunction, *so* can introduce a clause stating a consequence of the point stated before *so*.

The defendant was in the hospital at the time, so he could not have been at the meeting.

When *so* introduces a clause stating a consequence, substitute *and as a result* or *and therefore* if *so* could be ambiguous.

The defendant was in the hospital at the time, and as a result he could not have been at the meeting.

or

The defendant was in the hospital at the time and therefore could not have been at the meeting.

So can also introduce a clause stating the purpose of the point stated before *so*.

Mrs. Williamson asked for the check to be mailed to her mother's home so her husband could not intercept it.

To avoid ambiguity, substitute *so that* when you are introducing a clause stating a purpose.

Mrs. Williamson asked for the check to be mailed to her mother's home so that her husband could not intercept it.

So may also intensify an adjective or adverb.

So serious was the oversight that, had it not been caught by Ms. Abrahams, it would have cost the company millions of dollars.

or

The car moved so slowly that it created a traffic hazard.

SOCIAL MEDIA

Social media can include a variety of platforms for communicating with colleagues, clients, and classmates. The operative word for lawyers is *social*. Avoid using social media as a substitute for official documents or emails carrying substantive or confidential information. While protections for social media communications are developing, they are not yet reliable; err on the side of caution. Check your state laws and office practices for guidelines on safe and appropriate use of these digital platforms. For related information, see EMOJIS, TEXTING UNDER THE TABLE, and ELECTRONIC MESSAGING.

SOMEBODY

Use *someone* instead in formal legal writing because *somebody* sounds informal. Like *someone, somebody* is singular and takes a singular verb.

Someone claims to have seen the defendant elsewhere that night.

SOMEDAY OR *SOME DAY*?

Someday means at *some future time*; *some day* means a *day in the past or the future.*

SOMEONE

Someone is singular and uses a singular verb and a singular pronoun.

If someone needs to contact me, that person should call this number.

Or, only if the reader accepts this form, you might be able to write the following.

If someone needs to contact me, they should call this number.

SOMETIME OR *SOME TIME*?

Use *sometime* to refer to an indefinite point in time.

This question will reoccur sometime in the future.

Use *some time* to refer to an indefinite quantity of time.

We need to spend some time identifying all the options we have when the question does arise.

SO WHAT?

You may have encountered this comment on your paper, or you may be feeling it about a point you are trying to make. Most legal readers ask *So what?* whenever they read legal documents. Those readers have been taught to question each authority, each premise, and each idea. They expect explanations, yet they also expect no extraneous information.

So what? usually indicates that the opposite has occurred: the reader has encountered an idea that is not fully developed or is extraneous. Or it may only seem so because it is inadequately connected to the overall message, to the previous point, or to the next point.

Make *So what?* work for you. Ask yourself that question during PREWRITING, as you decide what to include; during REWRITING, as you decide what is and is not essential to the analysis; and during REVISING, as you check your expression for accuracy. Answering the question throughout the document will ensure that no one in your audience will have to ask it. For a broader context, see WRITING PROCESS.

SPACING BETWEEN SENTENCES

Sources are still divided, sometimes vehemently, on the question of whether to put one or two spaces at the end of a sentence after the period or other end punctuation mark. The general use in books, newspapers, and other publications is now one space; the usual argument is that this convention avoids wasting space. The U.S. Supreme Court, however, uses two spaces; the usual argument for this convention is that it helps the reader distinguish the ends of sentences more quickly. Adjust your spacing to your reader's preferences. Or, as in our case, adjust to your publisher's.

SPECIFICITY

See PRECISION.

SPELLING PROBLEMS

See MISSPELLINGS, HOW TO AVOID; and WORDS SPELLCHECKERS MAY NOT CATCH.

SPELLCHECKERS

See MISSPELLINGS, HOW TO AVOID; and WORDS SPELLCHECKERS MAY NOT CATCH.

SPLIT INFINITIVES

An infinitive consists of *to* plus the verb. Some readers believe a split infinitive is grammatically incorrect; it is not, but avoid splitting an infinitive when writing for readers who may still think it is a grammar error.

> **to move afterwards**
>
> rather than
>
> to afterwards move

On rare occasions, a split infinitive will avoid ambiguities.

> **The mayor agreed to only suggest the alternative if the matter came up in committee meeting.**

In this case, putting *only* before *to* would communicate that this was the only thing to which the mayor agreed.

The mayor agreed only . . . .

Putting *only* after *suggest* would communicate that this is the only alternative the mayor would suggest.

suggest only this alternative . . . .

When forced to make a choice like this, choose the clarity of the split infinitive over the elegance of the ambiguous unsplit version. You may often find, however, that you can avoid the problem by restructuring the sentence altogether.

The mayor agreed that she would only suggest the alternative if the matter came up in the committee meeting. She would refrain from requesting it.

This is the safest route; your revised version will offend no one and still avoid ambiguity. If you choose to boldly split with this tradition, consider whether this minor rebellion will cost you CREDIBILITY with your reader, and then decide. For related information, see AMBIGUITY, WAYS TO AVOID; and PRECISION.

SQUINTING MODIFIERS

A squinting modifier could be called shifty-eyed because its gaze shifts indecisively between two different terms. Because it could be modifying either term, it creates ambiguity.

The point the appellant is making logically applies to the Fourth Amendment claim.

Logically, as it is currently placed, could modify either *making* or *applies*. Often the phrase's position creates the ambiguity, and reordering solves the problem.

The point the appellant is making applies logically to the Fourth Amendment claim.

At other times clearer verbal signals may be needed.

The point, which the appellant has logically presented, applies to the Fourth Amendment claim.

STANCE

See POINT OF VIEW, OBJECTIVE TO PERSUASIVE.

STANDARD OF REVIEW

The standard of review is the standard by which appellate courts and other reviewing bodies measure errors made by lower courts and decision makers on specific legal issues. When researching an appellate issue, ascertain the standard of review early in your researching process, for it will guide the structure of your whole brief. If you are using artificial intelligence, be particularly vigilant that it has identified the correct standard of review.

When writing an appellate brief, make sure you state the standard of review for the issue you are appealing. You can place the discussion of the standard of review at the beginning of each main section, right after the point heading, or in your argument. In some jurisdictions, you can use a separate section for the standard of review. The standard of review differs for each legal issue, even within the same brief, so research each issue specifically and ascertain the relationship among the standards.

One way to think about standard of review is to see it on a spectrum from most restrictive to least restrictive, as illustrated by some of the standards here.

MOST RESTRICTIVE STANDARD

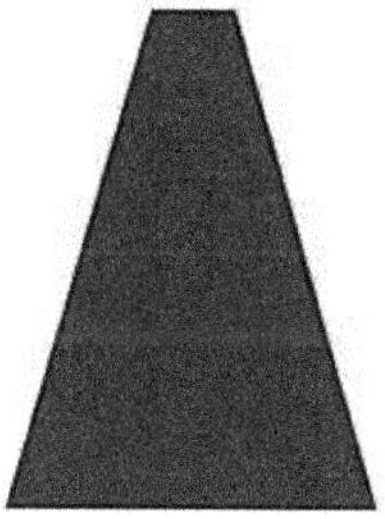

Arbitrary and Capricious

Gross Abuse of Discretion

Abuse of Discretion

Clearly Erroneous

Erroneous

de novo

LEAST RESTRICTIVE STANDARD

The most restrictive standard, at the top of this list, means that the reviewing court will overturn a lower court's decision only if it finds that the decision below was arbitrary and capricious. This standard, for example, is often used in reviewing administrative agency decisions, which are more technical. Overturning under this narrow standard happens very rarely. At the bottom are the standards that give the court greater latitude in reviewing facts, issues, and procedure. Under a *de novo* review, for example, the court may review all aspects of the case below, as in constitutional cases that affect fundamental rights.

As you research, pay particular attention to your jurisdiction. In one jurisdiction, the appellate court might reverse the lower court in a particular situation only if the findings are *clearly erroneous*. In a similar case in another jurisdiction, the appellate court might reverse the lower court only if the lower court *manifestly abused* its discretion. Use your jurisdiction's language to frame your issues so that you frame your analysis as the court will.

Derive the specific definition of the standard of review for your issues by examining significant cases in that subject area and determining the exact circumstances under which the court was willing to reverse the trial court. Find the language the court uses to define the standard of review or analyze the standard they seem to be using if they do not articulate it. If, for example, the court reviews the facts and analysis anew, they are using a *de novo* standard, even if they say they are using *abuse of discretion*. The latter would analyze the lower court's treatment of the case, not all of the law and facts.

The same approach to standard of review holds true of other reviewing bodies, such as international arbitration tribunals: find the language of the standards by which decisions are determined and use that language to frame your ISSUES and ARGUMENTS.

For related information, see BRIEFS; BRIEFS, APPELLATE; BRIEFS, AMICUS; and POINT HEADINGS.

STARE DECISIS

Stare decisis, which is Latin for *to stand by things decided*, describes a legal concept. It does not, however, replace the need for an explanation of legal reasoning. Thus, when explaining how a line of common law applies to a new case, do not assume that you have supported your case adequately just because you have used the term, as in the following example.

> Under *stare decisis*, this five-year-old child is incapable of forming any intent.

Instead, explain your reasoning fully by making comparisons and demonstrating the conclusions that should be drawn from those comparisons.

Conceptually, *stare decisis* also presents at least two other problems. First, cases are rarely exactly similar, so analogizing leaves room for different interpretations. Thus a six-year-old may be similar enough, but a nine-year-old may not, and such inexact comparisons can be considered weak. Second, legal analysis is in the process of pulling away from *stare decisis*, beginning with the legal realism movement in the early twentieth century and continuing through postmodern legal analysis in the early twenty-first century. Courts use *stare decisis* as only one of several ways to analyze a problem, so outcomes are less predictable and more complicated. Lawyers have a greater array of analytical choices now, which allows more possibilities for designing arguments and assisting clients.

For more information on this, see HOLDINGS; REASONING, ANALOGICAL; REASONING, DEDUCTIVE; REASONING, INDUCTIVE; REASONING, MODERN; REASONING, OTHER; REASONING, POSTMODERN, REASONING, PRESENTING IT; and RULES.

STATEMENT OF FACTS

The Statement of Facts is one section in an objective memo or brief. Its purpose is to explain concisely the facts that gave rise to the legal issues, so the Statement of Facts tells the reader why the document exists. It may be placed either after the caption; after the Question Presented and Brief Answer in a memo or the Issue in a brief; or as part of the Introduction to a brief or memo.

1. What to include.

   The Statement of Facts must contain all the legally significant facts: those facts that, if changed, would change the outcome of the analysis. The Statement of Facts must also include any background facts or emotional facts needed to orient the reader to the information being analyzed in the memo. The reader should not encounter any new facts in the other parts of the memo.

   Generally, it is difficult to determine precisely what the Statement of Facts should include until you have finished writing the Issues and Discussion Section. For that reason, either wait to write the Statement until you have completed the analysis or argument or plan to revise your Statement after completing the other parts of the memo. Check to be sure that all the facts you used later in the memo do indeed appear in the Statement of Facts.

   Despite this need for completeness, the Statement of Facts should be concise. Thus, after you have checked for completeness, revise the facts again for conciseness. Omit any facts that you now see as unneeded. Beyond those deletions, do not remove content. Instead, use more concise phrasing and reduce lengthy transitions. For ways to do this, see CONCISENESS.

2. How to organize.

   You may organize the facts in any way that assists your analysis or argument. Two common ways people think of organizing facts are chronologically or topically. When the factual sequence is legally significant or when the facts are simple and the issues unified around one area of law, you may organize chronologically. Often, however, chronological is not the best solution.

   Many readers prefer topical organization because it often matters little when something occurred, just that it did. Grouping together facts that give rise to specific legal issues allows the reader to plan for the analysis while reading the facts. When the procedural history is complex, you may combine these two organizational patterns, pulling facts into several topical groups of paragraphs and then organizing chronologically within that group. When the events leading to the case occurred at several different locations or involve several distinct concerns, you may group the facts by those locations or concerns and organize chronologically within those groups. If the facts are extremely long and complex, you may even add subheadings. You can modify a straight topical or chronological organization by adding an opening paragraph that overviews the situation or presents a central event before launching into the strict chronology.

Whatever organization you choose, remember that you are explaining how the client has reached this point and how these issues arose. Remembering this approach can help you explain or advocate naturally and directly, and the reader will be grateful. For related information, see BACKGROUND FACTS; EMOTIONAL FACTS; GENDER IN WRITING; LEGALLY SIGNIFICANT FACTS; NARRATIVE WRITING; ORGANIZATION, CHRONOLOGICAL; ORGANIZATION, TOPICAL; and WRITING, OBJECTIVE.

STATEMENT OF THE CASE

The Statement of the Case is the section in a persuasive legal document that crafts the facts to make the reader see the common-sense justice in the client's position. The Statement of the Case, or its equivalent, appears in such legal documents as Memoranda of Points and Authorities, pretrial briefs, trial briefs, appellate briefs, and settlement letters. Judges and litigators agree that it is a crucial part of any brief, and some believe it is the most important part. The Statement of the Case should leave the court wanting to find in favor of your client, while the Argument should leave the court believing that such a finding is legally justified. The Statement of the Case is written persuasively and contains legally significant facts, along with relevant background and emotional facts.

The Statement of the Case needs to be clearly organized without becoming lifeless. Begin by dividing the procedural details from the facts leading to the trial. Then you can prepare your fact statement in three steps.

1. Present the procedure.

   You may want to emphasize certain aspects of the procedure. If you represent the Appellant, you may emphasize aspects of the procedure that were in error, perhaps tying the effect of this error to the outcome. This may work best in a topical organization. If you represent the Respondent, you may want to explain how the procedure worked as it should. Often this works best in a chronological organization, with an air of normalcy and with little particular emphasis. Sometimes you may want to emphasize aspects of the procedure that compensated for the error and made it harmless, if you cannot directly show that no error occurred. Choose the organization that best suits your persuasive goals. In appellate briefs, this section may be quite detailed and may need to be set apart with a separate heading, such as *Procedural History*.

2. Present the facts.

   How much you emphasize particular facts leading up to the trial depends on your brief's purpose. If the merits of the case favor your client but some procedural anomalies occurred, then you may want to emphasize the facts so that the judge is less eager to let a procedural technicality upset the judgment. You might achieve this, for example, by using more concrete and specific words, active voice, and subtly favorable verbs. If, however, the facts do not favor your client, you may want to state them more generally, allowing the procedural facts to become the clearer picture in the judge's mind. For related information, see WRITING, PERSUASIVE.

   Group the facts chronologically if the story is simple or the chronology itself is legally significant or compelling. But you may find it most effective to group the facts topically if the events occurred at several different locations or involve several distinct concerns. Within each group of events, you can then organize chronologically. When the facts are extremely long and complex, you may want to add subheadings. Remember that you are telling a story, just as a movie or novel does. Just as they use different organizations, flashbacks, settings, and framing to tell a story, you can use these techniques to help the reader see the facts from your client's point of view.

3. Revise for emphasis.

   After your basic organization is in place and you have drafted your Argument, revise the facts for emphasis. This revision will breathe life and drama into your Statement of the Case. After reviewing for completeness and conciseness (for help here, see REWRITING and REVISING), choose two or three facts that you want to emphasize. These facts should be the ones that you want to stay in the reader's mind throughout the reading of your brief, the facts that are most likely to make the reader want to find in favor of your client. When you have chosen these facts, revise your sentence structure and SUBJECT-VERB COMBINATIONS to make them stand out in the statement. Rather than emphasizing every fact you can, focus the reader's attention on these key facts. For techniques to achieve this, see EMPHASIS.

   When you have restructured these emphasized facts, revise the rest of the statement so that the emphasized facts fit in smoothly and naturally. Build around these facts just as a composer builds music around the dramatic highlights of a symphony. For help doing this, see READABILITY; and SENTENCE STRUCTURE, subsections 6 and 7.

For related information, see BACKGROUND FACTS; BRIEFS; BRIEFS, AMICUS; BRIEFS, PRETRIAL; BRIEFS, TRIAL; BRIEFS, REPLY; EMOTIONAL FACTS; GENDER IN WRITING, LEGALLY SIGNIFICANT FACTS; NARRATIVE WRITING; ORGANIZATION, CHRONOLOGICAL; ORGANIZATION, TOPICAL; and WRITING, PERSUASIVE.

STATES, ABBREVIATIONS OF

See ABBREVIATING DATES, NAMES, STATES, AND TITLES.

STATING CONDITIONS

See CONDITIONS, STATING THEM.

STATISTICS

Whenever you use statistics, be sure they are logically connected to your legal reasoning, are well documented, and advance the point you are making. Do not allow them to distract from your main purpose.

Statistics are most often useful to support an explicit contention. For example, you could support an assertion that a faulty taillight rarely causes injury with statistics on the number of accidents in which a faulty taillight was cited as a cause. To make its significance clear, you would then explain the significance of the statistic to your case. Thus statistics are usually best placed in the middle of a paragraph or paragraph block. Unless their significance is striking and intuitively clear, statistics are not as effective as opening or summary sentences.

Also consider your readers and their particular reactions to statistics, if you can predict it. Statistics stir varied responses in readers. Although some readers revere statistics, others have a reaction similar to that credited to Disraeli: "There are three kinds of lies: lies, damned lies, and statistics." Thus their persuasive power is uncertain. For information related to presenting statistics, see GRAPHICS, WHEN TO USE and GRAPHICS, HOW TO USE.

STATUTES, DRAFTING

See LEGISLATION.

STORYTELLING

See NARRATIVE WRITING.

STRING CITATIONS

See CITATIONS, STRING.

STRUCTURE

See DESIGN; ORGANIZATION, LARGE-SCALE; ORGANIZATION, SMALL-SCALE; ORGANIZE, HOW TO; OUTLINES; or SENTENCE STRUCTURE.

STUFFY LANGUAGE

See FLOWERY LANGUAGE, JARGON, LEGALESE, PLAIN ENGLISH, and TONE.

STYLE

Style is used to refer to three different concepts:

(1) choices made in writing, including syntax patterns, word choice, verb phrases, usage, methods of presentation, and other choices;

(2) level of objectivity or persuasiveness; and

(3) conformity to or violation of standard rules.

1. Choices made in writing.

Your personal writing style is communicated through the habitual choices you make in your wording, sentence structures, paragraph structures, sentence rhythms, and other structural facets of writing. As clothes reflect your personal tastes, so your written product inevitably reflects your personal level of formality, your choice of tone, and your patterns of organization. Your point of view or professional posture determines your sentence structure and language choices. For example, you may use active voice, and short sentences for emphasis. You may use long introductory phrases to build the reader's anticipation, or you may use particular sentence rhythms, such as long-long-short-long. To illustrate the effect of style, consider the following three versions of the same opening to a paragraph.

> **Section III(c) is still more illogical and unsound. In devising a new monthly fee for the company, the government arbitrarily assumed that the company included thirty-five minutes each of peak and off-peak air time in its proposed monthly fee access.**
>
> or
>
> **Even more surprising is Section III(c). There, the government's new monthly fee plan is based**

> **arbitrarily and mistakenly on a false assumption: that the company included thirty-five minutes each of peak and off-peak air time in its proposed monthly fee access.**
>
> or
>
> **In devising a new monthly fee for the company under Section III(c), the government arbitrarily assumed that the company included thirty-five minutes each of peak and off-peak air time in its proposed monthly fee access, an assumption not based in fact, law, or practice.**

Your personal legal writing style will develop over time. To develop a style you like, study the syntax and writing patterns used by other writers. Keep a list of the kinds of phrases, syntax patterns, word choice, and overall structures that appeal to you and note why you like them. Determine which techniques are appropriate in different contexts. Experiment with different techniques as you develop your legal writing voice. Study, imitate, experiment, and discover. Using your observations, build your own style repertoire.

To actively change your personal style, focus on one aspect or incorporate one new technique at a time until you become comfortable with it. Begin with the basic components of style: sentence structure and word choice. As versatility develops with these basics, add other skills. Gradually, these skills will merge into a pattern that is your own style.

Do not, however, become preoccupied with the problem of developing or losing your personal style. Instead, focus on mastering the various aspects of good writing. From this seed of individual mastery, your personal style will blossom naturally and inevitably.

However your style develops, you will need to vary it according to your document's purpose. You may choose a quiet, standard legal style for form letters or email. You may choose an elaborate style for a short appellate brief, or a blunt style for a trial brief. For a discussion of aspects of writing that frequently influence your style, see POSITIONS OF EMPHASIS; PROFESSIONAL LANGUAGE AND PRESENTATION; SENTENCE STRUCTURE; TONE; VERBS, TENSES, and WORD CHOICE. For related information, see CHOICES IN LEGAL WRITING.

2. Level of objectivity or persuasiveness.

Objective and persuasive writing are more like points on a continuum than separate categories. Depending on your audience and your purpose, you will place each document at a different point along this continuum. Legal research memos, for example, are usually written in an objective style. This means that they focus equally on the strengths and weaknesses of any particular argument. The memo's purpose is to provide the reader with all the information that reader needs to make a decision, more than to advocate for a particular decision. In contrast, briefs written to a court are written in a persuasive style. Although these briefs often do address weaknesses in the writer's position, they do so only to explain how those weaknesses do not defeat the writer's purpose, which is to persuade the reader to make a particular decision in favor of the client. Settlement letters may lie closer to the middle of the continuum as they capture the terms of the agreement with a force that stops attempts to negotiate further.

Many documents fall closer to the mid-point of the objective-persuasive continuum. For example, an opinion letter that answers a client's question may explain why one action is preferable to another, but it always fully informs the client of the options. The opinion letter finally leaves the decision to the client. Similarly, a Complaint filed with a trial court presents facts rather than making persuasive arguments. Nevertheless, the purpose of the Complaint is to establish to the judge that the plaintiff does indeed have a claim for which legal relief exists.

For concerns related to objectivity or persuasiveness, see the entry for the particular document you are writing, such as BRIEFS; BRIEFS, AMICUS; BRIEFS, APPELLATE; BRIEFS, PRETRIAL; BRIEFS, TRIAL; MEMOS; OPINIONS, LEGAL; and PLEADINGS. For more about the concepts involved in style, see AUDIENCE; POINT OF VIEW, OBJECTIVE TO PERSUASIVE; PURPOSE; TONE; and VOICE. For how-to techniques, see COMMUNICATIONS, PERSUASIVE; COMMUNICATIONS, TONE OF; READERS; WRITING, OBJECTIVE; and WRITING, PERSUASIVE.

3. Conformity to or violation of standard rules.

Legal writing is generally more formal than other kinds of English. As part of that formality, it is more conservative in its observation of rules, as discussed throughout this book. With the complexity of most legal topics, legal writing can become dangerously unreadable when created without attention to standard grammatical and punctuation rules. Study the writing within your legal community for patterns, norms, and expectations. Once you have mastered those, experiment with how much you can stretch within those rules, or stretch the rules themselves. For example, a deliberately fashioned sentence fragment may draw attention to a critical point in a trial brief. A short, thematic sentence may set a dramatic tone in the opening of a Summary of Argument. In contrast, contractions may be appropriate in an informal email. Make sure you know the rules before you break them; then break them for calculated and successful effect. For concerns related to standard rules, see BENDING THE RULES. For help with particular rules, see the entry for the relevant topic, such as SEMICOLONS, VERBS, or SUBJECT-VERB AGREEMENT.

SUBHEADINGS

See POINT HEADINGS and HEADINGS.

SUBJECT

See SENTENCE, PARTS OF, subsection 2.

SUBJECT LINES

The subject line offers a good opportunity to make sure your reader gets your message, no matter how hurried the reader may be. This is true whether the subject line appears in an email, a research memo, or a letter. To make the most of this opportunity, phrase your subject line to include the specific essence of your content, as in the following examples. Consider using a complete sentence when needed for clarity.

In email, use

Your hearing will be Friday, November 12, at 10:00 a.m.

rather than

important!

In a research memo, use

H. Jakobsen Workers' Comp Claim against McGinnis Manufacturing

rather than

Workers' Comp Claim.

In a letter to a client, use

RE: Proposed estate plan for you and your spouse

rather than

RE: response to your request.

SUBJECT-VERB AGREEMENT

Sometimes, when the subject and verb are far apart in a sentence, the writer accidentally uses a plural verb with a singular subject, or a singular verb with a plural subject.

In the interviews, each of the many therapists currently finding their practice restricted by these recent holdings is [not *are*] **less likely to be willing to treat these patients.**

If you receive any comments about agreement from your readers, take the comment seriously. Take steps immediately to remedy the problem. Even though it may happen only occasionally, subject-verb agreement is considered a basic language skill in English, and even occasional errors in this area substantially erode the reader's opinion of the writer's ability.

To check your subject-verb agreement, underline the subject and verb in each sentence throughout your document or a section that has been giving you trouble. Then read just those subjects and verbs. You will then expose any agreement problems immediately, and you can fix them. One good way to avoid making these errors is to avoid putting more than seven words between your subject and verb. This will not only help you avoid agreement problems but will make your writing more readable. See READABILITY, subsection 5.

SUBJECT-VERB COMBINATIONS

Subject-verb combinations help move the legal reader along when they are specific and concrete; they halt the reader when they are vague and abstract. Because the subject and verb are the main part of the sentence, try to place important information in your subjects and verbs; often this information is best expressed by terms of art and key facts. Do not waste subjects and verbs on information that is unimportant to the reader.

subject verb

The show-up I.D. negated the effect of capturing the defendant one block from the crime.

rather than

subject verb

The court stated that the show-up I.D. negated the effect of capturing the defendant one block from the crime.

In this example, the legal point is more important than the narration that the court stated it. Use a citation to give that information.

Minimize use of combinations like *it is*, *there is*, or *there were*. Use nouns instead of those pronouns, specific verbs instead of those verbs of being.

subject verb

False imprisonment occurs when a person is restrained without consent.

rather than

sub. verb
There is false imprisonment when a person is restrained without consent.

For related information, see CONCISENESS, subsection 4; KEY TERMS; READABILITY, subsection 5; and TERMS OF ART.

SUBJUNCTIVE TENSES

See VERBS, MOODS.

SUBORDINATING CONJUNCTIONS

See CONJUNCTIONS and SUBORDINATION.

SUBORDINATION

You are subordinating information when you make one point in a sentence depend structurally on another point.

Although our client did not look both ways immediately before stepping into the street, this fact alone is not enough to constitute contributory negligence.

The writer here subordinates a fact that works against the client's case by placing it in a dependent clause beginning with *although*. Similarly, the following sentence downplays an unfavorable fact by putting it in a dependent clause beginning with *even though*.

Even though he had not come to a full stop at the stop sign, the defendant had slowed to less than five miles per hour and was not accelerating at the time of the accident.

See also SENTENCE, PARTS OF, subsection 8 and EMPHASIS.

SUBSTANTIVE OR *PROCEDURAL*?

See *PROCEDURAL* OR *SUBSTANTIVE*?

SUCH

Avoid using *such* as an unnecessary adjective, which is sometimes used in arcane legal writing. Substitute *this*, *that*, or a more detailed description.

This document was signed by three witnesses.

rather than

Such document was signed by three witnesses.

SUMMARY OF THE ARGUMENT

The Summary of the Argument is a separate section used in long briefs to state the gist of the writer's arguments without referring to specific authority. The section appears just before the Argument. The purpose of this section is to pull together the writer's arguments without stopping the flow with references to details of authority. Thus at one glance the reader can understand the writer's argument.

A general guide for writing summaries is to use one paragraph per issue. Make sure you state the Summary of the Argument in your own words, as if you were making an oral presentation, rather than solely quoting. For related information, see PARAPHRASE.

As a process matter, writing a Summary of the Argument can be a good way of getting started. Even if this summary is not included in the final product, it can help you focus issues, answers, and explanations. For related information, see BRIEFS; BRIEFS, AMICUS; and BRIEFS, APPELLATE.

SUPPORT

The legal reader generally does not believe any assertion unless it is backed by authority such as case law, statutes, or regulations. Therefore, support your assertions more thoroughly in legal writing than you might in other situations. In a brief, for example, if you are illustrating why your client should have been able to breach a restrictive covenant, give examples of cases where others have breached a restrictive covenant and show the legal, factual, economic, or policy similarities that explain why the same legal principles should apply in your case.

When stating your rule, show the legal reader that you have stated each rule correctly by including pinpoint citations to the page in a case where the rule is stated. (See CITATIONS, PINPOINT.) When explaining what a rule means, show that your reasoning is valid by paraphrasing the court's reasoning and again giving pinpoint citations. (See LEGAL ANALYSIS.) When including a case that you believe is relevant to your client's situation, prove your point by telling the reader the relevant aspects of the precedent case. (See RULES.) When synthesizing the rule from various sources, make sure the connections among the sources are evident. (See SYLLOGISMS and SYNTHESIS.) When explaining how that case applies to your client's situation, prove your point by explaining the common qualities or common legal issues your case and the precedent cases share. (See REASONING entries.)

Do not expect your reader to fill in the gaps for you. When rewriting, make sure you have not made assertions that are not connected to authority, to your issue, and to each other. For other related information, see PARAGRAPHS, REWRITING, and REVISING.

SYLLOGISMS

A syllogism is a form of deductive reasoning that consists of a major premise, a minor premise, and a conclusion. It moves from general to specific.

Major premise: **All men are mortal.**

Minor premise: **Socrates is a man.**

Conclusion: **Therefore Socrates is mortal.**

Syllogisms in some form are used in legal writing when the analysis proceeds from the general to the specific. The major premise is derived from the law itself, and it states the rule governing the specific situation, such as the general rule that *All men are mortal*. The minor premise expresses the intersection of the rule, *man*, and the facts of the situation, *Socrates*. The conclusion is validly derived when, among other things, the term in common, *men-man*, appears in the first two premises and not the last. In legal writing, the conclusion states the logical outcome of applying the rule to the situation. That conclusion may be a prediction, as in a memo; a holding, as in an opinion; or a request for relief, as in the argument of a brief.

You may find the syllogism a useful reference for designing your document's structure because you can use it as a device to expose each step in your reasoning. More often, you may find it helpful for reading other documents and trying to test the validity of their reasoning. Your notes may look like this.

Major premise: **Delay between the commission of an offense and the initiation of prosecution is a violation of defendant's due process rights.**

Minor premise: **The conduct of the State is a delay between this defendant's commission of the robbery and the State's initiation of prosecution.**

Conclusion: **Therefore, the conduct of the State is a violation of defendant's due process rights.**

or

Major premise: **A party entitled to judgment as a matter of law is a party who can receive a directed verdict.**

Minor premise: **This party is entitled to judgment as a matter of law.**

Conclusion: **Therefore, this party is a party who can receive a directed verdict.**

Remember that few legal propositions present themselves so neatly. Instead, the premises in legal arguments are often in dispute, so analyze those premises first. Furthermore, most legal reasoning involves a complex interaction of premises, each of which must be untangled and analyzed, as in the following examples.

First level of reasoning about lack of consent.

Major premise: **Entries into a home without evidence establishing consent are entries into a home without consent.** [*Not explicitly stated by the court*]

Minor premise: **The officers' entry into defendant's home was entry into a home without evidence establishing consent.**

Conclusion: **Therefore, the officers' entry into defendant's home was entry into a home without consent.**

Second level of reasoning about lack of consent renders entry illegal.

Major premise: **Entries into a home without consent are illegal entries.**

Minor premise: **The officers' entry into defendant's home was entry into a home without consent.**

Conclusion: **Therefore, the officers' entry into defendant's home was an illegal entry.**

Third level of reasoning about late consent as unreliable.

Major premise: **Consents to searches given after illegal entries are consents that are not reliable.**

Minor premise: **Defendant's consent was consent to search after an illegal entry.**

Conclusion: **Therefore, defendant's consent was a consent that was not reliable.**

Fourth level of reasoning about unreliable consent requires warrant.

Major premise: **Searches made pursuant to consents that are not reliable are searches that require warrants.**

Minor premise: **The officers' search was a search made pursuant to consent that was not reliable.**

Conclusion: **Therefore, the officers' search was a search that required a warrant.**

When reading cases, make sure that you yourself understand the connection among all three parts of the syllogism and the interconnection among the syllogisms. If the connections are faulty, these holes in the reasoning may allow you to distinguish the case from your client's situation; you can then fill the holes according to your own reasoning and perhaps reach a different result.

When writing, make sure your reader understands the connection among the parts of each syllogism and the interconnection of the syllogisms. If you are looking for syllogisms or trying to create them, make sure to account for other types of reasoning. For related information, see REASONING, ANALOGICAL; REASONING, DEDUCTIVE; REASONING; INDUCTIVE; REASONING, MODERN; REASONING, OTHER; REASONING, POST-MODERN; and REASONING, PRESENTING IT.

SYMBOLS IN EMAIL

Keep your use of symbols to a minimum in professional email. Resist the urge to use emojis or any other symbols. Also avoid using any stylistic symbols that may not translate correctly when opened by your reader's email server. For example, tabulations, bullets, or italics can create unreadable messages when they are received by a different email system. For this reason, keep all formatting simple and minimal in email. For more on this, see EMOJIS.

SYNONYMS

A synonym is a word or phrase with a meaning nearly the same as another word or phrase in the same language. For example, *attorney* is a synonym for *lawyer*, *proceeding* is a synonym for *trial*, and *agreement* can be a synonym for *contract*. Be careful not to use synonyms within the same written analysis because legal readers may think you are talking about a different document, as in the third example. If you choose to use *contract*, keep using that term throughout your analysis. If you have used generative artificial intelligence (AI), verify carefully the results because AI may incorporate synonyms for legal terms, which can create imprecision. For related information, see ANTONYMS; HOMONYMS; RESEARCH STRATEGY GUIDE, section 3; and WORD CHOICE.

SYNTAX

Syntax is the grammatical term for the rules that govern how words and phrases can be put together in a given language. The phrase *syntax error* means that something has been written that does not conform to the rules of the language. Each language has certain acceptable patterns of syntax. For example, English commonly uses the subject-verb-object organization, such as *the judge issued a ruling*, while Arabic syntax sometimes allows the expression of complete ideas without verbs. English syntax also dictates the order of modifiers describing a noun, such as *three big, leather-bound, legal casebooks.* For people whose first language is English, these rules are usually intuitive; for those learning the language later, the rules must be learned.

In legal writing, sensitivity to syntax can be used to increase accuracy and emphasis. For example, the order of the words communicates meaning in English, as is illustrated by the difference between *dog bites man* and *man bites dog*. On a subtler level, the independent clause in English is structurally more important in a sentence than the dependent clauses. You can use this syntax rule to underscore a point.

dependent clause

Although the father claims he spent time with the

independent clause

children, he was absent for 110 days in a row last year.

rather than

independent clause dependent clause

The father claims he spent time with the children even though he was absent for 110 days in a row last year.

Here, using a dependent clause for a subordinate idea deemphasizes the idea in both language and structure. Placing the main argument in the main, independent clause emphasizes that idea. If you are arguing for custody for the mother, you may want to use the first example. To make the best use of English syntax, always try to put your main point in the main subject, verb, and object of the sentence's independent clause. For more examples and techniques, see SENTENCE, PARTS OF; and SENTENCE STRUCTURE.

Similarly, careful placement of words can add emphasis because the beginning and end of a sentence usually get more emphasis than the middle.

Only under exigent circumstances may police enter a house without a warrant. [cite]

rather than

The court held that only under exigent circumstances may police enter a house without a warrant.

For more on this, see POSITIONS OF EMPHASIS. By consciously matching the syntax with the meaning, you are increasing clarity and precision. For related information, see CLAUSES; SENTENCE, PARTS OF; SENTENCE STRUCTURE; and WRITING, PERSUASIVE.

SYNTHESIS

Synthesis, as the term is used in law, describes using several separate elements to create a unified presentation of a larger point. This term is often used to refer to the process of common law analysis where several holdings or other components of previous holdings are combined to form a current rule or synthesis of the law. In a strictly common law analysis, this synthesis often appears at the beginning of an analysis in a Discussion or an Argument. In statutory analysis, several holdings are often synthesized to define statutory terms. To synthesize accurately, you must recognize common themes and logical connections among the components you are synthesizing. Use your own language to demonstrate the connections among the parts so that the reader understands how the pieces make a whole. Do not simply state the separate elements and assume the reader will reach the conclusion you want. Instead, explain the common theme and its significance to your legal reasoning. For related information, see DESIGN; ORGANIZE, HOW TO; ORGANIZATION, LARGE-SCALE; LEGAL ANALYSIS; REASONING, ANALOGICAL; REASONING, DEDUCTIVE; REASONING, INDUCTIVE; REASONING, MODERN; REASONING, OTHER; REASONING, POSTMODERN; REASONING, PRESENTING IT; and TRANSITIONS.

TABLE OF AUTHORITIES

The Table of Authorities is required in many briefs. It documents all the legal authorities used in the brief, which allows the reader to see the brief's legal SCOPE at a glance and to locate referenced authorities as desired. Check the court rules to determine if a Table of Authorities is required and, if so, how it should be assembled. Some courts specify the order in which the authorities should be presented, such as statutes, rules, cases, and secondary authorities.

To prepare the Table of Authorities, find directions online for your type of computer and software. After the brief is written, you can use these directions to prepare your table quickly and accurately. There may be an electronic system or artificial intelligence (AI) tool that will help with this task. For related information, see APPELLATE BRIEFS; ARTIFICIAL INTELLIGENCE AND RESEARCH; ARTIFICIAL INTELLIGENCE AND WRITING; and TABLE OF CONTENTS.

TABLE OF CONTENTS

A Table of Contents is required in many BRIEFS. It organizes the contents of your brief so that your reader can see your brief's overall SCOPE and organization and easily choose specific sections to read. In the Argument, the Table of Contents displays your POINT HEADINGS so that the reader can see your Argument's structure at a glance. Check the court rules to determine if a Table of Contents is required, being sure to note and follow any format requirements the court has listed.

You may want to include a Table of Contents even if not required because it offers easy entry into longer documents. After the brief or longer document is written, you can prepare your table by using the appropriate software tool. Even if you do not include the Table of Contents in the final document, creating one is an excellent way to test your organization. For related information, see BRIEFS, APPELLATE; ORGANIZE, HOW TO; and TABLE OF AUTHORITIES.

TABLES

See GRAPHICS, WHICH FORM TO USE, subsection 5. For related information, see TABLE OF CONTENTS or TABLE OF AUTHORITIES.

TABULATION

See ENUMERATION and LISTS, STRUCTURING THEM, subsection 8.

TACT

See BAD NEWS, SOFTENING IT; COMMUNICATIONS, TONE OF; FORMALITY, LEVEL OF; GRACE UNDER FIRE; PROFESSIONAL LANGUAGE AND PRESENTATION; and TONE.

TAKING NOTES

See NOTES.

TECHNOLOGY

See WRITING AND TECHNOLOGY.

TENSES

See VERBS, TENSES.

TERMS OF ADDRESS FOR COURTS

See JUDGES, HOW TO ADDRESS.

TERMS OF ART

Terms of art are those terms used specifically in the law to describe legal theories, rules, or doctrines. They are the words that carry the most weight in legal writing and the words on which the legal reader focuses. Because of their importance to the legal reader, terms of art should often be used as subjects and verbs in the sentences in which they appear.

The Parol Evidence Rule prevents admission of this evidence.

Terms of art should also be placed at positions of emphasis, such as the beginnings or ends of sentences.

Plaintiff brought an action under the theory of *res ipsa loquitur*.

and

The police escaped the strict requirements of the search and seizure rule by claiming that they were operating under exigent circumstances.

and

Washington is one of a minority of states to use the Family Car Doctrine.

Terms of art should generally be used in the legal question parts of Questions Presented or Issues. Make sure they are used precisely as intended under the authority specific to them. If you are quoting key language from a statute, you may want to identify that fact by putting the term of art in quotation marks.

Under the exigent circumstances exception to the Fourth Amendment, were police in "hot pursuit" when defendant had sold drugs to an undercover officer four hours before the search and had not left the premises?

and

Under Washington tort law, can a five-year-old commit an "intentional tort" when he pulls a chair away from an elderly lady who is in the process of sitting down?

Use Latin terms when they are terms of art, such as *res ipsa loquitur*. Do not, however, use them when they can be replaced by plain English. For example, use *on its own* rather than *sua sponte*. Similarly, terms such as *hereinafter* or *aforesaid* are legalese, not terms of art. For related information, see ISSUES, LEGALESE, POSITIONS OF EMPHASIS, QUESTIONS PRESENTED, and RULES.

TERTIARY DEGREE TITLES

See ABBREVIATING DATES, NAMES, STATES, AND TITLES.

TEXTING AND INSTANT MESSAGING

For effective use, see ELECTRONIC MESSAGING.

TEXTING UNDER THE TABLE

Resist the temptation to text under the table during meetings with clients, colleagues, or anyone else when you are working, even during online video conferences. You may feel that you are multi-tasking brilliantly, but your companions are likely to think that you are being rude and inattentive. They can see you. This is rather like typing email responses while you are talking to someone on the phone. They can hear the keyboard and they notice the time lag it takes for you to respond to their comments, so avoid that activity, too. Distinguish yourself by being the person that is 100% attentive to one thing at a time, a key component of good time management. For more information on efficiency, see MULTI-TASKING, PROFESSIONAL LANGUAGE AND PRESENTATION, and TIME MANAGEMENT.

THAT NEEDED?

Omit *that* only if doing so will not confuse the reader.

Mr. Salovar agreed he would pay the overtime costs.

or

Mr. Salovar agreed that he would pay the overtime costs.

But retain *that* when needed.

The court decided that the ruling was an abuse of discretion.

rather than

The court decided the ruling was an abuse of discretion.

The confusion occurs when the noun after the verb could be a DIRECT OBJECT, as would be true with *the key* in the following sentence.

The prosecution found the key here was the defendant's own admission.

That is needed to avoid the temporary confusion, as an aid to readability.

The prosecution found that the key here was the defendant's own admission.

In the following example, however, *his safety procedures* could not be the direct object of *believed*, so *that* may safely be omitted.

The defendant believed his safety procedures were adequate.

For related concerns, see *THAT* OR *WHICH*?

THAT OR *WHICH*?

In legal writing, especially legal drafting, it is useful to maintain a distinction between *that* and *which*. This remains true in law even though many writers in other fields use these terms interchangeably.

1. Use *that* when you are adding a phrase to narrow the range of items covered by a word.

   All cars that remain in the lot after 10 p.m. will be towed.

   [R]emain in the lot after 10 p.m. narrows the range of cars under discussion, so *that* should introduce the phrase. Do not put commas before or after this narrowing phrase, called a *restrictive phrase*. This punctuation rule is important because even general writing still observes this distinction.

2. Use *which* when you are adding a phrase that does not limit the range of items covered by the word it modifies, called a *nonrestrictive phrase*.

   Your car, which was still in the lot at midnight, was towed.

   The range included in *your* car is not limited by the following phrase, so *which* is the correct word to begin the phrase. Put commas both before and after a *which* phrase. The commas work like parentheses, showing that the phrase could be lifted from the sentence without changing the essential meaning. Another way to think about the distinction is that if you need commas, use *which*; if you do not need commas, use *that*.

3. For ACCURACY, use both commas and *which* to distinguish non-limiting phrases from limiting ones. If you do not, your sentences may suffer from AMBIGUITY.

   The taxes, which have been paid, should not appear on this statement.

or

The taxes that have been paid should not appear on this statement.

rather than

The taxes which have been paid should not appear on this statement.

In the first version, all the taxes have been paid. In the second, some of the taxes have been paid. In the last version, however, you are not sure whether all or part of the taxes have been paid.

4. *Which* can be substituted for *that* when two *that*'s appear in a row.

That which is good is not always pleasant; that which is pleasant is not always good.

rather than

That that is good is not always pleasant; that that is pleasant is not always good.

When possible, however, revise to avoid *that which,* which is rather awkward to read.

THE

Do not omit *the*, *a*, or *an* solely to gain conciseness.

The owner of the car gave the keys to Hendricks, who was supposed to move the car to a legal parking spot.

rather than

Owner of car gave keys to Hendricks, who was supposed to move car to legal parking spot.

Omitting these articles will give the text an abrupt tone, like a telegram, and will decrease the text's READABILITY.

THEIRS OR *THEIR'S*?

Theirs, always.

THEME

Theme in legal writing is a term that describes the message you intend to convey in your document. It is the document's essential meaning. It should tell your reader the document's essential *what* and *why*.

Laffon violated Barker's moral right because he altered the sculpture so significantly that any reasonable viewer would misinterpret Barker's original message.

or

Current ethics rules are inadequate to handle conflicts that arise in public interest practice.

or

The police arrested the wrong person because they relied on a faulty show-up ID.

Usually you can state the theme in one sentence, although you need not include that exact sentence in your document. If you cannot contain it in one sentence, you may have too many subthemes instead of one overarching message. In memos, the theme is usually in the Brief Answer; in briefs, it is in the opening paragraph or Summary of Argument; in email or letters, it is usually in the opening paragraph.

Draft a preliminary version of your theme to assist you when getting started on your draft because the theme is sometimes clearer to you before you get immersed in researching or drafting. Adjust the theme as you work on your issues and Questions Presented; there it emerges as you match question and answer. Finally, use the theme to test your document's coherence. Review it and make sure it is the message you wish to convey. As you rewrite and revise, note where you state the theme and subthemes and how you relate them to each other. Alter the theme if needed to unify the document. For related information, see PURPOSE, ISSUES, QUESTIONS PRESENTED, and SCHOLARLY WRITING.

THEORY OF THE CASE

Your theory of the case unifies your brief. *Theory of the case* refers to the legal, factual, and contextual principles that underlie your approach. These principles are founded first in the law: its history, purposes, use, and context. Those principles are then combined with the specific facts and context of your case. Together, these create a unique, unifying theory to persuade decision makers. As such, the theory leads to the THEME, STANCE, ORGANIZATION, and PROPORTION of your argument.

Develop your theory by drawings on law, facts, subarguments, legal reasoning, and practical circumstances. Take all of these into account to capture the driving thought that summarizes your position. Even when the arguments are not obviously connected, a good theory of the case can unify the brief's purpose and direction. Formulating a theory of the case forces you to connect all parts of the brief and avoid creating a list of unrelated arguments.

For example, you may have a theory of the case that *the court should release this incarcerated woman early because she is pregnant.* If, however, she became pregnant after she escaped from a low-security facility, you may decide that a theory of the case emphasizing her behavior may not be persuasive. Instead, you may be more likely to prevail if you choose a theory of the case that emphasizes the child, namely, *it is in the best interests of the child for the court to release this incarcerated woman early*. The theory can be quite general and never stated in the brief.

A deal is a deal.

The police overdid it this time.

This is not an appropriate situation for an injunction.

Alternatively, the theory can be more specific, appearing in the wording of the INTRODUCTION and POINT HEADINGS.

Groups that promote violence, such as this one, should not be allowed access to school facilities.

Property can be taken for use by the public, but only in rare circumstances, which is not the case here.

In this state, the greater public good outweighs one private owner's needs, especially when that owner has repeatedly disregarded the public good.

If possible, develop the theory during PREWRITING as you develop possible arguments. You may develop the theory as you see trends in your research, such as patterns of strict statutory interpretation, the court's reluctance to push the law's boundaries, procedural limitations, or obstacles in the standards of review. Thus, instead of arguing over *offer and acceptance* in a motion for summary judgment, you may develop a theory of the case that *there is a dispute as to the material facts*; instead of arguing over application of regulatory standards, you may be required to develop a theory that *the decision is arbitrary and capricious* because of the standard of review; or you may have a choice to develop one of a range of theories, one of which may appeal more to you, your client, or your assigning attorney. Sometimes your theory may emerge as you draft any portion of your brief if a particular aspect of the case emerges as central to the analysis. For related matters, see BRIEFS; BRIEFS, APPELLATE; BRIEFS, AMICUS; BRIEFS, TRIAL; BRIEFS, PRETRIAL; LEGAL ANALYSIS; POINT HEADINGS; and THEME.

THEREBY

Avoid using this term unnecessarily because it is legalese.

The judge sentenced the defendant to seven years, and so closed the case.

rather than

The judge sentenced the defendant to seven years, thereby closing the case.

For related information, see LEGALESE.

THEREFORE OR *THEREFOR*?

Use *therefore*, or you risk sounding arcane or archaic.

THERE IS OR *THERE ARE*?

The answer to this question depends on the word that follows the verb, the PREDICATE adjective. If it is plural, use *are*.

There are twelve members on each jury in this state.

If it is singular, use *is*.

There is one alternative we have not yet discussed.

Sometimes the choice is not so obvious with more abstract nouns. For example, either of the following sentences is correct.

There are precedents for this line of reasoning, although they address different factual situations.

or

There is precedent for this line of reasoning, although the cases establishing this precedent address different factual situations.

If you use this phrase frequently, consider more concise alternatives. For more on this, see SUBJECT-VERB COMBINATIONS. For related information, see SINGULAR OR PLURAL? and *NONE*, SINGULAR OR PLURAL?

THERE IS . . . THAT

Omitting this phrase when you can do so creates a more concise sentence.

No cases address this issue directly.

rather than

There are no cases that address this issue directly.

Similarly, revise to omit *it is . . . that* and *there are . . . that*. For more examples, see CONCISENESS, subsection 10.

THESIS SENTENCES

In this text, the terms *thesis sentence* and *topic sentence* both refer to a sentence that is clear enough to communicate both the point that the paragraph supports and its logical connection to the whole of the text. See TOPIC SENTENCES.

THESIS SENTENCES OR *TOPIC SENTENCES*?

These terms are usually interchangeable, and that is how we use them in this text to minimize confusion. However, some readers and writing teachers distinguish between them. In some writing texts, *topic sentence* is used to identify a sentence that introduces a general subject but does not say much about that subject. This kind of topic sentence is often too general to provide an effective opening to a legal writing paragraph, so *topic sentence* used in this way is an unfavorable description.

This issue is addressed in a recent Minnesota case.

In contrast, those writing texts use *thesis sentence* to identify a sentence that introduces a subject and states the point, or the thesis, to be supported in the body of the paragraph. This usually should be the first sentence of the paragraph.

> **In Minnesota, medical technicians are protected under the Good Samaritan statute. Colon v. Makagon, 99 N.W.2d 99, 100 (Minn. 2025).**
>
> or
>
> **A causal connection can be established even when another actor was involved in the accident.**

Whether you use *topic sentence* or *thesis sentence* to identify this key part of a paragraph, make sure your version includes enough substance to avoid the criticism of being *just a topic sentence.* For related information, see PARAGRAPH BLOCKS, PARAGRAPHS, POSITIONS OF EMPHASIS, and TOPIC SENTENCES.

THEY AS GENDER NEUTRAL

Using *they* instead of *he or she* or *she or he* is common enough that it has become acceptable to most people in conversation, and might be acceptable by your AUDIENCE in oral legal presentations and emails. When *they* is the pronoun chosen by the person referred to and when no legal consequences arise from using *they,* that term is safe to use. Its literal meaning is still a plural pronoun, however, and therefore this substitution is not precise enough for some legal documents. In that situation, when accuracy trumps the individual's choice, try using a definite article or repeating the noun to avoid using any PRONOUN.

> **Vee Chalmer agrees to reimburse Allison Day for any travel expenses Day incurs while acting as Chalmer's purchasing agent under the terms of this contract.**

rather than

Vee Chalmer agrees to reimburse Allison Day for any travel expenses she incurs while acting as their purchasing agent under the terms of this contract.

Although new constructions have been proposed as alternatives to the longer phrase or as alternatives to a binary gender term, none has as yet become standard or, more important, legally defined. For now, it may be easier to learn techniques that minimize the need for *he or she.* See GENDER IN WRITING and SEXIST LANGUAGE, WAYS TO AVOID.

THEY OR *HE OR SHE*?

Although using *they* to replace the outdated *he or she* is commonly used in speech, it is often unworkable in legal writing, where ACCURACY is a paramount concern. When choosing between the plural or singular form, first determine whether one of the two forms is required for accuracy. Then, if the singular form is required, repeat the noun to avoid *he or she* or *they.*

If a member chooses to go forward with a grievance, that member must explain that grievance in writing.

rather than

If members choose to go forward with a grievance, they must explain that grievance in writing.

The second version could be read to exclude an individual from bringing a grievance, and so would be unclear.

If accuracy does not limit you, you may use the plural form.

The members had the opportunity to air their concerns at the November meeting.

Whichever form you choose, use it consistently throughout the text. For related information, see GENDER IN WRITING and SEXIST LANGUAGE, WAYS TO AVOID.

THIS

This frequently creates ambiguity because it can refer to any idea or object and because it often starts a sentence. To avoid ambiguity, add the noun after *this* when it begins a sentence.

You must ultimately make a judgment about the weight of the evidence. This judgment will help you decide what the verdict should be.

rather than

> You must ultimately make a judgment about the weight of the evidence. This will help you decide what the verdict should be.

In the second version, it is not clear whether *this* refers to *judgment* or *evidence*. For related information, see AMBIGUITY, WAYS TO AVOID, subsection 2.

THOROUGHNESS

Even when writing under time constraints, a legal writer must always include the support and information sufficient to accomplish the document's PURPOSE. In your effort to be concise, do not omit any needed information. For example, a COMPLAINT must include enough information to withstand a motion to dismiss for failure to state a claim. A MEMO must contain enough analysis for your reader to disagree with the result. A request for information from a client must include enough information to ensure that the client knows what is needed, why, and how to comply.

A closely related need is for the content to be clear enough to be understood by the READER. For example, when writing instructions, make them clear enough to be followed correctly, or you may have to write a second time.

One way to attain thoroughness is to develop checklists for different legal documents that you write frequently, to help you check for needed content under time pressure. Also see SCOPE. For broader, related information, see PRINCIPLES OF GOOD LEGAL WRITING, PRIORITIES, and REWRITING CHECKLIST.

THOUGH OR *ALTHOUGH*?

See *ALTHOUGH* OR *THOUGH*?

TIME MANAGEMENT

Writing well often involves managing your time, particularly when you have several projects to work on simultaneously. If the load becomes unmanageable, it can reduce the quality of your professional and personal life. When you develop a more efficient approach to time management that is realistic given your own writing process, you can enhance your ability to meet professional demands without sacrificing personal life. You want to make sure you are running the project, rather than the project running you.

To increase your writing efficiency and effectiveness, follow three important principles:

(1) compartmentalize,

(2) concentrate, and

(3) condense.

Then you can add more techniques as you become more adept:

(4) record directions,

(5) prioritize items immediately,

(6) say *no*,

(7) delegate,

(8) percolate,

(9) use the calendar and the clock, and

(10) choreograph your day.

1. Compartmentalize.

Break your work into compartments by content or type of task. Keep the compartments small: *writing the brief* is too big; so is *researching the memo. Writing the introduction* is a small compartment, as is *researching the Seventh Circuit on this issue.*

Pull together similar tasks, such as researching specific jurisdictions on several short projects, drafting emails, or polishing outgoing documents. If there are some tasks that artificial intelligence (AI) can help with, decide what those are, when you will use it, and how long it will take to verify the results.

As much as you can, do similar tasks in one block of time. For example, set aside time for reading electronic correspondence and emails and responding and filing them, rather than reading each as soon as it comes in. Allocate some time periodically throughout your day to check these sources, so you respond quickly enough without allowing them to consume too much time. Then set aside different compartments for drafting short segments of documents, holding meetings, and so on. This approach eliminates unnecessary changeover time, and your mind can remain focused on the tasks within each compartment. For related information, see EMAIL, HOW TO MANAGE.

2. Concentrate.

Now that you have compartmentalized tasks, devote all of your attention to the compartment in front of you. The smaller the compartment, the higher your concentration will be. You should find that your mind works more easily and quickly when you give it only one task at a time.

3. Condense.

After you have created compartments and increased your concentration, try to decrease the quantity of time you spend without jeopardizing the quality of the product. Unmonitored research or writing will expand to fill any amount of time available. Become more alert to ways that increase speed without causing unnecessary stress. Sometimes changing the medium will help: you might use voice-to-text to dictate letters rather than type them, revise drafts by finding patterns rather than reading page by page, or write the theme and subthemes by hand to own the document's message and structure. When reviewing email, scan the names and subject lines to determine which mail to open when. When time is short, perform triage; open important email and leave others to be opened later.

When you have taken command of these three tasks, you can then move on to improve your overall approach to managing your time. For example, you may want to add some of the following goals to your list.

4. Record directions.

If you have had trouble understanding what is wanted of you, try recording directions when you receive them, with permission. Then, if you have a question, you can refer to your recording or notes rather than contact your supervisor or retrace your steps. Take your laptop or device with you to meetings and initial assignment discussions. Take your own list of questions so that you are actively recording directions, not just passively listening. Similarly, if you give directions, send them by email. Then, when you are busy, the person to whom the task has been delegated can continue to work without having to interrupt you. Writing precise directions can save hours of volleying between attorneys. It also saves start-up time spent reminding yourself where you should be going on the project.

5. Prioritize items immediately.

Try to avoid shuffling documents, emails, or messages too much. Give each item a home by filing it immediately, marking a deadline on it, or forwarding it to the person who should take action. For related information, see TRIAGE.

For example, within the time you have set aside to deal with email, assess the complexity of the needed response. Try to delete or discard on the spot what you can. For those emails that can be answered quickly, dictate or write needed responses. Mark emails that need some thought before answering and decide when you are going to respond. Finally, store and label documents systematically, which will make finding them faster and easier.

6. Say *no*.

   Know your own capacity as a researcher and writer, and try to decline projects that will overwhelm you or interfere with the quality of other projects. If you are under particular pressure from a supervisor, choose a gentle way to say *no* or set aside time to meet with that person in the future to discuss reasonable workload. See SAYING *NO* for specific suggestions.

7. Delegate wherever you can.

   Ask others to do tasks that they can and save your time for matters only you can do. This can be a hard adjustment to make, especially if you are used to doing everything for yourself. For ways to do this, see COLLABORATION, EDITING, and MANAGING WRITERS. You may be able to use artificial intelligence (AI) to help with some tasks, such as revising for conciseness or creating a TABLE OF CONTENTS; use what you can without letting it substitute for your own thinking.

8. Percolate, don't procrastinate.

   Rather than putting a project aside when you receive it, consider doing some preliminary work immediately. Take a few minutes to gather facts, hypothesize some issues, and note a possible research strategy. Create a file, label it, and write your opening thoughts, so you will not wonder later what that inspiration was. Then stop; leave those ideas while you work on another compartment. Percolating usually allows your mind to create better ideas than immersing does. In fact, it is often necessary to good legal analysis because it allows time for your ideas to steep. See PERFECTIONISM, PROCRASTINATION, and RESEARCH STRATEGY GUIDE.

9. Use the calendar and the clock.

   Remain aware of your major deadlines and pace yourself accordingly. Use the clock as a helpful friend who reminds you when your mind is wandering unnecessarily, when the meeting you are conducting is lasting too long, or when you are tempted to research longer than you should. In your meeting room, try to place a clock where you can check it subtly or have a system in place to stop on time. Writing tasks often take longer than you anticipate, so set a realistic ending time before you begin.

10. Choreograph your day.

    Use your high energy times for the most critical tasks or those you like least; use your low energy times for the least critical or those you like most. When your energy wanes, answer calls, hold meetings, or do other activities that will keep you awake. Then your day will become more even, rather than clustered around least favorite and most favorite moments.

Although you may see many changes you want to make in managing your writing time, implement changes gradually. This minimizes upset to either your own balance or that of your associates. You might start by changing your approach to one major writing project or by trying one new technique for a period. For more on this, see WRITING PROCESS. At the end of that project or period, assess the success of the change and revise your writing process as needed. If the change worked, try it next on two projects at once. Gradually, you can fold your new techniques into your schedule; give yourself a year or more to transform yourself into an efficient and effective writer.

For more ideas on making time management decisions, see ARTIFICIAL INTELLIGENCE AND RESEARCH, ARTIFICIAL INTELLIGENCE AND WRITING, DEADLINES, MEETING THEM; PRIORITIES WITHIN ONE PROJECT, and RESEARCH STRATEGY GUIDE.

TITLES, ABBREVIATIONS OF

See ABBREVIATING DATES, NAMES, STATES, AND TITLES.

TITLES OF JUDGES

See JUDGES, HOW TO ADDRESS.

TO BE

To be, in its various forms, communicates a continuing state of being. When used appropriately, this verb does not add unnecessary words to the language. Additionally, the past tense of *was* is also a useful linking verb and is not in itself PASSIVE VOICE. Therefore do not try to avoid using *was*, *were*, *are*, or *is*; instead avoid their overuse. *To be* has three main uses: (1) as a linking verb, (2) as a helping verb, and (3) as a statement of existence.

1. As a linking verb.

   This is its most recognized use, where it often is the only verb in the sentence.

   Strict interpretation of this statute is essential to the preservation of this doctrine.

   The problem with using this and other linking verbs is that they create a sentence without action. When used frequently, the writing itself stagnates and becomes uninteresting to read. To avoid this problem, use action verbs whenever it is logical to do so.

The motor stalled immediately after the plaintiff engaged the gear.

rather than

The motor was immediately inoperable after the driver engaged the gear.

2. As a helping verb.

Used as a helping verb with the *-ing* form of another verb, a form of *to be* shows that an action occurred over a period of time.

The witness was operating a lawn mower at the time he reported hearing the scream.

Often this communication of relative time is legally significant. This use of *to be* is needed, not wordy; it is also past progressive tense, not passive voice, so you need not avoid it for that reason.

To be does create the passive voice, however, when used as a helping verb with the *-ed* past participle form of the main verb.

The lawn mower was operated by the witness.

Passive voice is harder to understand and requires more words, so use it only when it is needed. For more on this, see PASSIVE VOICE.

3. As a statement of being.

This is the use seen least in legal writing.

She is.

It may occasionally be useful, however, for EMPHASIS in WRITING, PERSUASIVE.

The witness has repeatedly testified that, since the attack, she is terrified by sudden noises. She is.

For related information, see VERBS, TENSES.

TONE

Tone communicates the writer's point of view or attitude toward the reader and the subject matter. Choose a tone appropriate for the medium, such as matter-of-fact for office memos, friendly for informative client letters, or stern for tough settlement letters. Then choose words and sentence structures to convey that tone. After choosing your tone, make sure you hold that tone consistently; otherwise, you are likely to confuse the reader and sound unprofessional.

Tone is established and conveyed through attention to details of word choice and sentence structure. As the following subsections explain, you can convey tone through

(1) word choice

(a) by choosing the appropriate subjects, verbs, and modifiers;

(b) by choosing appropriate terms of address;

(c) by choosing words that have the appropriate emotional overtone and level of formality;

and through

(2) sentence structure

(a) by making effective use of active and passive voice and positions of emphasis, and

(b) by choosing appropriate sentence length, subject-verb combinations, and various kinds of sentence structure.

1. Conveying tone through word choice.

(a) Choose appropriate subjects, verbs, and modifiers.

For example, in memos, when you want to convey an objective and businesslike tone, use terms of art as subjects and verbs to keep the text focused on the issue being analyzed rather than the people involved.

The Family Car Doctrine holds parents liable for their child's negligence.

rather than

Under the Family Car Doctrine, John Applegate may face some liability for his daughter's negligence.

Keep modifiers to a minimum, and then use only factual, specific information. This creates a businesslike, unemotional tone and makes your writing more concise.

Jamison grasped Hendricks by the arm and led him to the door.

rather than

Jamison rudely grasped the unfortunate Hendricks by the left arm and inexorably led him slowly to the battered wooden door.

For related information, see MODIFIERS and TERMS OF ART.

In briefs, when you want to convey a persuasive and more assertive tone, retain terms of art as subjects and verbs to help the reader focus on your point. But also use stronger subjects and verbs when stating favorable facts, that is, subjects and verbs that give the reader a vivid picture of those facts.

> **Jamison grasped Hendricks' left arm and pulled him slowly toward the door.**

When stating unfavorable facts, use weaker, more abstract subjects and verbs.

> **The defendant then took Hendricks by the arm and moved to the door.**

Also use modifiers with subtle emotional connotations that favor your position.

> **Muttering threats, Jamison grasped Hendricks' bruised arm and pulled him toward the door.**

But do not overdo, or you may hamper your credibility. For more specific information, see WRITING, PERSUASIVE.

(b) Choose the appropriate terms of address.

In a memo or brief, you want to avoid terms of address that refer to yourself or the reader because the focus should be on the legal issues and the parties rather than on the attorneys or judges.

> **Granting a summary judgment is not justifiable in this case.**
>
> rather than
>
> You must not grant a summary judgment because we think these facts preclude it.

In an email or letter to a client, however, you will often want to refer to yourself and the reader because you are indeed speaking as one person to another.

> **At our meeting on Tuesday, April 11, you asked me to give you a legal opinion on whether. . . .**
>
> rather than
>
> In response to the request made on Tuesday, April 11, for an opinion on whether. . . .

If you avoid all personal references in email and letters, you create a distant, cold tone. You may want to use this cold tone occasionally, as in a tough settlement letter, but it is not wise to use it with your current clients. For related information, see TOUGH, SOUNDING THAT WAY; and TONE IN LETTERS.

(c) Choose the appropriate level of formality.

In general, use more formal language in official documents, such as briefs or opinion letters, because you want to sound respectful and serious. Use less formal language in other writing, such as memos or general communication, where you want to be readable and avoid being stuffy. Be careful, however, of becoming too informal in email. For example, you might say the following in a conference with another attorney.

> **Helen Thomas bought her computer at the local Apex store.**

But you might write it this way in a brief,

> **Ms. Thomas purchased her computer at Apex Computers, located at 417 Cherry Street.**

or this way in an email.

> **You bought your computer at your neighborhood store.**

Avoid creating a stuffy tone by using overly formal language, especially when describing everyday concepts.

> **the trash truck**
>
> rather than
>
> the refuse management vehicle

For more explanation and examples, see FORMALITY, LEVEL OF.

2. Conveying tone through SENTENCE LENGTH and structure.

(a) For a clipped, no-nonsense tone, use shorter sentences.

> **My client, Ms. Ambrose, does not intend to pay this bill. She has no reason to pay this bill. She did not receive any software from your company. She did not order any software from your company. Until receiving your bill, she did not know your company existed.**

(b) For a more conversational tone, use longer sentences with the subject and verb near the beginning of the sentence.

> **You asked me to research the possibility of recovering part or all of your down payment on a hot tub you later decided not to purchase.**

rather than

In our phone conversation, you stated that, after some consideration, you wanted to recover . . . .

or

You asked me to research a question for you. Specifically, you want to know if you can recover part or all of a down payment. The down payment was made for. . . .

For more information, see the entry for the specific kind of document you are writing.

(c) For a more formal tone, use some interrupting phrases in your sentence structure.

Anorexics, by failing to eat, passively expose themselves to harm.

This sentence structure is harder to read because to understand the main point the reader must remember the first part of the sentence, read the interrupting clause, and then reunite the last part of the sentence with the first. Therefore avoid using it in sentence after sentence; give the reader breathing space between these difficult sentences. Finally, do not allow the interruption to exceed seven or eight words. After a longer interruption, the reader would have to reread the sentence to understand the point.

For related information, see BAD NEWS, SOFTENING IT; COMMUNICATIONS, TONE OF; FORMALITY, LEVEL OF; GENDER IN WRITING; POINT OF VIEW, OBJECTIVE OR PERSUASIVE; PROFESSIONAL LANGUAGE AND PRESENTATION; STANCE; TOUGH, SOUNDING THAT WAY; WRITING, OBJECTIVE; and WRITING, PERSUASIVE.

TONE IN LETTERS AND EMAIL

See COMMUNICATIONS, TONE OF and GENDER IN WRITING.

TOPICAL ORGANIZATION

See ORGANIZATION, TOPICAL.

TOPIC SENTENCES

Topic sentences, sometimes called thesis sentences, deserve particular attention in legal writing because they convey the main points of paragraphs. Topic sentences are most effective at POSITIONS OF EMPHASIS. For example, use a topic sentence at the beginning of a paragraph to state the conclusion the paragraph supports. Alternatively, use it to create a question in the reader's mind and then explain the answer in the body of the paragraph. In either situation, the topic sentence sets up an expectation that the body of the paragraph fulfills.

> **Although the 2019 Act eased the singles penalty, it did so at the expense of married couples.**

The questioning legal reader will ask, "Okay, so how exactly did the Act disadvantage married couples?" If this is the point the paragraph explains, the topic sentence has prepared the reader for the paragraph's content.

An effective topic sentence not only communicates the thesis of the paragraph, but also signals the relationship of that thesis to the content that came before or after. This signal is often subtle, but it is always present in writing that flows smoothly and logically. The signal may be a TRANSITION word or phrase, such as *nevertheless* or *in this situation*. Often it is the repetition of a key word from the previous thesis sentence. For example, the following phrase might open the paragraph that follows the previous example topic sentence.

> **Married couples under this act received no . . . .**

When these connections work, the reader can skim the topic sentences of a document and understand the logical flow as well as the content of the document. REWRITING your topic sentences to achieve this flow is a powerful tool, especially in persuasive writing. For more on how to do this, see CONNECTIONS, MAKING THEM.

Occasionally you may use a topic sentence at the end of a paragraph to summarize or conclude; remember, however, that busy legal readers may skip to the end or get impatient about any suspense created by waiting for the point. Therefore use this delaying technique rarely in legal writing. It is more likely to be workable at the end of an introductory paragraph in a law review article or long brief, and then only when the previous sentences engage the reader enough to pique that reader's curiosity.

For related information, see *THESIS SENTENCES* OR *TOPIC SENTENCES*?, and PARAGRAPHS.

TOPIC SENTENCES OR *THESIS SENTENCES*?

See *THESIS SENTENCES* OR *TOPIC SENTENCES*?

TOTALLY

See *COMPLETELY* and HYPERBOLE.

TOUGH, SOUNDING THAT WAY

Try the following techniques to sound tough.

1. Use shorter sentences, perhaps several in a row.

    This creates a clipped, no-nonsense tone.

    My client, Ms. Ambrose, does not intend to pay this bill. She has no reason to pay you. She did not receive any software from your company. She did not order any software from your company. Until receiving your bill, she did not know your company existed.

2. Use objective language.

    If you use emotional words (*unabashedly, horrendous, outrageous*), you will sound angry, but not tough. Tough people stay in control. Persuade with careful use of POSITIONS OF EMPHASIS and SENTENCE STRUCTURE.

3. If appropriate, explain the options the reader has and the results of those options.

    This puts the responsibility clearly in the reader's lap. If the reader is at all inclined to feel guilty, this explanation makes the reader squirm. If the reader has no sense of guilt, the explanation will still make your position clear, so you have lost nothing.

4. Never threaten idly.

    The people with whom you most likely need to get tough are often those people who have heard many threats in their lives and have learned to ignore them. They may be experienced enough, however, to recognize a genuine threat that is well presented.

For related information, see BAD NEWS, GIVING IT; BAD NEWS, SOFTENING IT; COMMUNICATIONS, ELECTRONIC; COMMUNICATIONS, INTERNATIONAL; COMMUNICATIONS, OPENINGS FOR; COMMUNICATIONS, PERSUASIVE; EMAIL; TONE OF; PROFESSIONAL LANGUAGE AND PRESENTATION; SOCIAL MEDIA; WRITING TO ATTORNEYS; and WRITING TO CLIENTS.

TRANSITIONS

Some of the most useful ways to communicate the logical connection between two points are to use headings, sentences, phrases, or words. These devices signal the relationship between the content of one section, paragraph, or sentence and the next. To make these connections clear, choose accurate, exact transitions that reveal the nature of the connection. There are two kinds of transitions you can use: (1) repetition of previous key terms, with or without parallel structure, and (2) transitional words.

1. Repetition of key terms with or without parallel structure.

   Use this technique in headings between sections. Because they are farther apart in the text, the stronger transition with both parallel structure and repetition of key terms is likely to remind the reader of distant content rather than appearing too repetitious.

   I. POLICE VIOLATED DEFENDANT'S FOURTH AMENDMENT RIGHTS FIRST WHEN THEY ENTERED HER HOME WITHOUT A WARRANT.

   and

   II. POLICE VIOLATED DEFENDANT'S FOURTH AMENDMENT RIGHTS AGAIN WHEN THEY SEIZED EVIDENCE THAT WAS NOT IN PLAIN VIEW.

   You can repeat key terms to connect paragraphs with strong topic sentences.

   Plaintiff was a holder in due course because she took the check in good faith.

   and

   Plaintiff took the check in good faith because she knew the vendor and had worked with him before.

   and

   As a holder in due course, Plaintiff is now entitled to the value of the check.

   You can also use repetition in a subtler form to dovetail sentences within a paragraph.

   Plaintiff was a holder in due course because she took the check in good faith. This good faith was evident in. . . .

2. Transitional words.

   Transitional words connect sentences, and when used accurately can effectively guide the reader through a paragraph and larger text. There are, however, a few hazards to guard against. When using transitional words between paragraphs or sentences, you may find that you use only one or two transition words most of the time, perhaps repeating one word three or four times on a page. This overuse can signal several problems. Sometimes, overuse of one transition signals organization problems. For example, if you use *however* frequently, check to see if you are combining points that could better be presented in separate paragraphs. Other times, overuse of one transition may mean that you are using the word out of habit rather than out of conscious choice. If so, some other word will probably be more precise. For example, *similarly* may be more precise for a comparison than *additionally*.

To help you choose the most accurate transition quickly, consult the following list of transitions grouped by their logical functions.

(a) Signaling similarity.

- *similarly*
- *analogously*
- *as*
- *accordingly*

(b) Signaling contrast.

- *not . . . but, not only . . . but also*
- *but*
- *in contrast, conversely, on the contrary*
- *however*
- *nevertheless*
- *on the one hand . . . on the other hand*
- *while, yet*

(c) Introducing conditions.

- *although, even though, though*
- *if, only if, but only if*
- *provided that, unless*
- *when, whenever*
- *while*
- *whereas*

(d) Introducing results.

- *if . . . , then; when . . . , then*
- *accordingly, consequently*
- *therefore, thus*
- *as a result, hence*
- *so, so that*

(e) Introducing reasons for a result.

- *because*

(f) Introducing examples.

- *as if, as though*
- *for example*
- *specifically*
- *namely*
- *that is*
- *such as*
- *including, including but not limited to*
- *i.e.*

(g) Signaling a list.

- *first, second, third, etc.*
- *both . . . and*
- *either . . . or, neither . . . nor*
- *and, also, additionally*
- *furthermore*
- *or, nor*
- *last, finally, in conclusion*

(h) Showing time relationships.

- *after, afterward, later, once*
- *during, while, meanwhile, concurrently, at the same time*
- *as, as long as, simultaneously*
- *before, earlier, since*
- *then, until*
- *when, whenever*
- *now*

(i) Showing relationship of place.

- *where*
- *wherever*
- *near, nearby*
- *beside, behind, before, in front of*

(j) Summarizing.

- *finally*

- *in conclusion*
- *in summary*

For other ways to make transitions, see CONNECTIONS, MAKING THEM.

TRIAGE

Borrowed from the medical field, *triage* describes an approach that is useful in writing emergencies as well as medical ones. When you find yourself with inadequate time to finish a document to the quality level you want, it is time to practice triage. To do this, create a comfortable system. For example, you can quickly write out a list of all the tasks remaining to finish the document to the quality you desire. Then determine why each task is needed. If the task is needed for ACCURACY or to make the document legally and functionally sufficient, label it with an *A*. If the task is needed to make the document more readable or easier to use by the reader, label it with an *R*. If the task is needed to add professional polish or for any reason other than those previously listed, label it with a *P*.

Then complete all the tasks labeled with an *A*. These must be completed before the document leaves your hands. When those are finished, determine how much time, if any, you have left to work on readability issues, and use that time to work on the tasks labeled *R*. When that time is up, begin working on the tasks labeled *P*. While this triage may not result in a perfect document, it is likely to give you the best results you can achieve given the time you have. More important, it is likely to prevent you from omitting any tasks that are necessary to avoid serious problems.

For related information, see DEADLINES, MEETING THEM; GETTING STARTED; NOTES; ORGANIZE, HOW TO; PERFECTIONISM; PROCRASTINATION; PRIORITIES WITHIN ONE DOCUMENT; and TIME MANAGEMENT.

TRIAL BRIEFS

See BRIEFS, TRIAL.

TRUSTS

See WILLS.

TYPEFACE SIZE

See FONT SIZE.

UNCLEAR MEANING

This comment on your writing could be triggered by problems in any of several areas. For help, see AMBIGUITY, WAYS TO AVOID; APPLICATION; LEGAL ANALYSIS; MODIFIERS, DANGLING; PRECISION; and REASONING, PRESENTING IT.

UNDERLINING

Underlining is used in practitioners' legal writing:

(1) to add emphasis to terms or phrases in quotations,

(2) to identify case names and components of a legal record, and

(3) to identify foreign words or phrases.

To avoid confusion, (4) underlining should not be used solely to recreate the emphasis a word would be given in speech.

1. Adding emphasis to terms and phrases in quotations.

Underline to add emphasis to important terms in quotations, such as in a rule or holding. When you underline part of a quotation, add *(emphasis added)* after the citation following the quotation.

> **As this court itself has stated, "[T]he court must intervene because <u>the issue of mutuality</u>, not to mention that of duress, requires that the court examine <u>the parol evidence surrounding the signing</u> of the contract." <u>Durant v. Colt</u>, 945 F. Supp. 3d 641 (D.D.C. 2025) (emphasis added).**

Similarly, underline to add emphasis to key phrases in quotations long enough to be indented and single-spaced in the text. Underlining may encourage the legal reader to read the quotation by making the single spacing more palatable. When you underline, add *(emphasis added)* after the citation on the first line of text following the indented quotation, not within the indented quotation itself. The phrase *(emphasis added)* within a quotation would signal that that phrase was present in the original.

> **The court in this case addressed the issue of mutuality.**
>
> > **Despite the defendant's emotional plea regarding the centrality of upholding contracts to the free working of a democracy, we cannot ignore the plaintiff's complaint. In this case, the court must intervene because <u>the issue of mutuality</u>, not to mention that of duress, <u>requires that the court examine both</u>**

the contract's wording and the parol evidence surrounding the signing of that contract.

Durant v. Colt, 945 F. Supp. 3d 641 (D.D.C. 2025) (emphasis added).

2. Identifying case names and components of a legal record.

Underline cases in citations in text. Do not underline the comma.

Peabody v. Hart, 958 F.3d 391 (7th Cir. 2025).

Underline references to the record if your jurisdiction so requires. Check for local practice about whether or not to underline the period.

Defendant failed to use his turn signal. Tr. 17.

3. Identifying foreign words or phrases.

Underline phrases from other languages if they are not commonly incorporated into English. Often, however, the phrase you use will have been incorporated, such as Latin phrases that are terms of art.

The court appointed a guardian ad litem.

but

In France, this right is known as the droit moral.

4. Not underlining to replace the emphasis of speech.

Do not use underlining to replace the emphasis you would give a word when speaking. This use of underlining is acceptable in casual writing, such as in an email to a friend or an informal memo to a coworker, but it is less effective in briefs or research memos for several reasons. First, the use of underlining can be confusing. Often the legal reader's first reaction to underlining is to assume you are highlighting a quotation or indicating one of the other specific uses of underlining in legal writing. Second, legal readers may think you are resorting to the obvious, which can make you seem less in control of the text. To avoid this problem, use positions of emphasis and sentence structure techniques instead of underlining. For ways to do this, see EMPHASIS. For related information, see CITATIONS; and QUOTATIONS, HOW TO PUNCTUATE.

UNDERSTANDABILITY

See CLARITY and READABILITY.

UNDOUBTEDLY

Avoid the term. The point is probably not undoubted by all legal readers. If it is, you do not need to tell the reader this. If you must use *undoubtedly*, do not spell it *undoubtably*. See MODIFIERS.

UNINTERESTED OR *DISINTERESTED*?

See *DISINTERESTED* OR *UNINTERESTED*?

UNIQUE

Unique means that the item or idea referred to is the only one of its kind, or without an equivalent. *Unique* is not preceded by qualifying adverbs. For example, do not say *the most unique* or *rather unique* or *somewhat unique*. If it is unique, it is *unique*.

UNITY

See COHERENCE.

UNLESS

Use *unless* with care because it is easily misread. *Unless* is actually a negative, like *not* or *no*, but often readers do not realize this. As a result, readers may miss the negative and think the *unless* phrase means the opposite of what the writer intended. To avoid this ambiguity, substitute another word for *unless* when possible.

Come to the hearings only if you are subpoenaed.

rather than

Come to the hearings unless you are not subpoenaed.

and

A signature on an absentee ballot must be notarized. The only exception to this is a military member's signature on an absentee ballot.

rather than

Notarize a signature on an absentee ballot unless the absentee voter is a member of the military.

UNOBTRUSIVE DEFINITIONS

Unobtrusive definitions are short, conveniently placed explanations of technical terms that may not be completely familiar to the reader. Include these when you think any of your readers may not be aware of the term. The reader who understands the term can skip over the definition easily because it is structurally identifiable as a definition. The reader who needs the definition, however, will read it and thus understand your point. There are three ways to include unobtrusive definitions:

(1) include an appositive,

(2) insert an explanatory sentence, or

(3) include a definition section.

1. Include an appositive.

Include an appositive, or a few words in a phrase inserted immediately after the term being defined, when the definition is short and will not make the overall sentence too long.

The tortfeasor, or the person committing the tort, may be . . . .

For related information, see APPOSITIVE.

2. Insert an explanatory sentence.

When a longer definition is needed, insert an explanatory sentence right after the sentence using the phrase.

At least 80% of the net tax should be paid during the tax year. Net tax is the tax remaining after all deductions have been included.

Sometimes these definitions are placed in PARENTHESES. But avoid overusing parentheses because they can become a visual distraction to the reader.

3. Include a definition section.

If you need to insert many definitions, you can include an alphabetical list of those definitions in a separate section, such as the definition sections in statutes, contracts, or trusts. Save this approach for times when it is necessary. Use a definition section only when needed; a separate section is inconvenient for the reader.

If you are afraid you will offend sophisticated readers by defining legal terms, reanalyze your text in relation to your audience. Readers are often more frustrated by undefined terms than by excessive definitions. For example, a judge may be frustrated by *a logic flow schematic of an example embodiment of the present invention* if that judge has not done patent cases for a while. Similarly, clients may be frustrated by *tortfeasor* if they are not sure exactly what the word means. When in doubt, give your readers the definitions for any key terms or terms of art that may be unfamiliar. For related information, see JARGON, LEGALESE, PRECISION, READABILITY, and TERMS OF ART.

UNTIL SUCH TIME AS

Substitute *until*; you will gain conciseness with no loss in precision.

UNTO

Just use *to*. *Unto* means *to*; it does not mean *onto*.

UPDATING THE LAW

There are several systems for updating legal sources, and all can be useful in this indispensable step of thorough research. If possible, use at least two approaches to updating to make sure your law is good, because you may get different results from different systems. Some citators are created by human editors, such as those at WESTLAW and LEXIS, and others are algorithmic based, so there will be variations in results that are worth comparing. Some are subscriber based, and some are free or of low cost, such as those provided by state bar associations. Be sure to ascertain which sources they update and the scope of their services.

Each updating system has its own supplementary method of updating legal sources. These systems not only update the sources but also help you find other relevant legal sources. They are the main services you can use to determine whether the source you are using has been overturned, distinguished, endorsed, or modified in any way. In other words, these services let you know if your source is still usable. LEXIS, for example, offers an electronic updating service patterned on *Shepard's Citations*, which is the book form once indispensable for updating the law. WESTLAW offers a service called *KeyCite*, which performs many of the same services offered by *Shepard's* on LEXIS. The displays are similar, as is the information provided. Both services give researchers timely and accurate information regarding the history of legal sources. Be aware, however, that both services use their own analysts and interpreters; the information they provide is their interpretation only. You must go directly to the sources they describe to verify their interpretations.

There are several approaches to updating. One way is to follow these steps.

1. Log in and bring up a citator page in an updating system, such as *Shepard's* or *KeyCite*. After you have entered the system, enter your citation. If your case has parallel citations, you may enter any of the citations to access the same information. Alternatively, you may begin by clicking on the link to the case you are reading.
2. The service will provide you with the previous and subsequent history of your source, as well as references to other cases and secondary sources that cite your source. You can examine those cases and secondary sources directly from the display.
3. Note if, according to that system's analysis, a case was subsequently overturned, distinguished from other cases, dissented from, and so forth. The notations differ for cases, statutes, regulations, law review

articles, court rules, city charters, and constitutions. Inspect the display for specific notations on your source and make sure you know what those notations mean.

4. If necessary, restrict the citations that the system generates according to your research needs. For example, you can restrict or narrow your search by jurisdiction, headnote, positive or negative treatment, and type of citation, such as a case or a law review article.
5. Repeat this process, using the other citator system, if you have access to it.

For related broader contexts, see RESEARCH STRATEGY GUIDE.

UPON OR *ON*?

Upon means *on the surface*; *on* means *in support of*, among other things. While the words are sometimes interchangeable, in legal writing use *upon* for the literal and more formal meaning, and *on* for either the literal or the figurative.

He placed the gargoyle upon the exhibit table, mistakenly assuming that it could support the gargoyle's weight.

but

Counsel assured the defendant he was on the defendant's side.

UTILIZE

Substitute *use*, which is precise, readable, and not suggestive of JARGON.

Please use this form to provide the information requested.

rather than

Please utilize this form to provide the information requested.

UTTERLY

Omit this word; in legal writing, it almost always strikes the reader as an overstatement that weakens the statement rather than strengthening it. To emphasize a point, try using a short, direct statement rather than adding *utterly*.

The plaintiff's statement is false.

rather than

The statement made by the plaintiff is utterly false.

For related information, see LITERAL MEANING.

VAGUE WORDS

See AMBIGUITY, WAYS TO AVOID, subsection 3; PRECISION, subsection 2; and WORD CHOICE.

VARIETY

The word *variety* has three different meanings relevant to writing. *Variety* is sometimes used as a noun meaning a *collection of various things*. As such, it is too general to be useful in legal writing. If there is a variety, that variety will usually have to be explained.

Variety is also sometimes a goal in word choice. But in legal writing, avoid varying nouns or verbs solely for the sake of variety. Legal readers look for consistency, particularly in terms of art and key terms. For more on this, see ACCURACY, subsection 1; KEY TERMS; SYNONYMS; and TERMS OF ART.

Finally, *variety* in sentence length and sentence structure, is a goal for legal writing, but let it arise naturally from the logical relations of your content. For ways to achieve this, see SENTENCE STRUCTURE and EMPHASIS. Also vary your choice of transition words by using those that reflect the precise relationship of ideas. For help with this, see TRANSITIONS. For related information, see CONNECTIONS, MAKING THEM.

VERBAL OR *ORAL*?

See *ORAL* OR *VERBAL*?

VERBOSITY

See CONCISENESS.

VERBS, AUXILIARY

Auxiliary verbs, or *helping verbs*, are added to the basic verb to change verb tenses and to add specific shades of meaning. Choosing the correct auxiliary verbs, therefore, can help you be more precise and persuasive. The following list explains how to use specific auxiliary verbs. Subsections 1–10 explain how different auxiliary verbs add subtle shades of meaning. Subsection 11 lists all the other auxiliary verbs, which form different verb tenses and which should be used for accuracy rather than to nuance the meaning.

1. *Should.*

Should implies that some action was preferable but was not in fact taken. For example, it can be useful for suggesting a breach of duty.

The defendant should have set the emergency brake, but he did not.

2. *Could.*

Could implies the capacity to do something but suggests that the action will not or has not been done.

The defendant could have set the emergency brake; his arm was not broken.

3. *Would.*

Would implies that an action would have been taken had conditions been different.

The defendant would have set the emergency brake had he not been rushing to assist the people in the other car.

4. *Can.*

Can implies capacity to do something, although the action may not have been taken.

When weighing the evidence, the jury can take into account the witness's apparent intelligence and the clarity of the witness's memory of the event.

5. *Might.*

Might implies possibility.

The district attorney might prosecute.

Often *might* suggests *if facts were otherwise.*

If the will disinherits one of the children, that child might challenge the legality of the will.

6. *May.*

May implies permission to do something.

If the Seller fails to comply with the nondiscrimination clauses of this contract, the Seller may be declared ineligible for further government contracts.

May also implies the possibility of something happening.

The grand jury may subpoena you.

Because it has two possible meanings, watch for potential ambiguities when using *may* in drafting. Sometimes, but not always, the meaning of *may* will be clear in context. When ambiguity is possible, use *might* for possibility and add a phrase like *if the client chooses* for permission.

7. *Must.*

   Must implies a requirement to do something or to refrain from doing something.

   The Seller must not in any manner advertise, without first obtaining the Buyer's written consent, that the Seller has contracted to furnish goods to the Buyer.

8. *Shall.*

   Shall can imply a requirement, and is used to mean this in legislation.

   All Petitioners shall file . . . .

   But in general writing *shall* also implies the future tense.

   The Williams opera shall premiere in December, if all goes as planned.

   Therefore, *shall* can be ambiguous; whenever ambiguity is possible, use *must* for requirements and *will* for future tenses.

9. *Do* or *does.*

   Do adds emphasis. It often indicates a positive answer when a negative one is expected.

   On the contrary, I do plan to attend the hearings.

10. *Do not* or *does not.*

    Do not or *does not* denies an action.

    My client does not know of any such plans.

11. *Am, are, is, was, were, has, had, have,* and *been.*

    These auxiliaries combine with the main verb to form other tenses, either the progressive or perfect form of the present or past tenses.

    I am meeting with the client today.

    We are considering the matter.

    The defendant is planning to testify.

    We were considering the matter, but decided it was not worth further pursuit.

The defendant was planning to testify before this evidence came to light.

Ms. Wiley had considered settling out of court.

Both attorneys have filed pretrial motions.

They have been planning this banquet for months.

For an explanation of how tenses are formed, see VERBS, TENSES.

VERBS, EFFECTIVE USE OF

Verbs, which are words expressing an action or a state of being, focus the legal reader more than any other part of speech. In legal writing, verbs play a particularly vital role in outlining the contours of legal analysis. The following five guidelines can help you use verbs effectively. For grammar guidance related to verbs, see SENTENCES, PARTS OF; and VERBS, TENSES. For more information about specific kinds of verbs, see VERBS, IRREGULAR; VERBS, LINKING; VERBS, MOODS; or VERBS, PARTICIPLES.

1. Make sure subjects and verbs agree.

Sometimes when the subject and verb are far apart in a sentence, you may accidentally use a plural verb with a singular subject, or a singular verb with a plural subject. One effective way to avoid having this happen is to avoid putting more than seven words between your subject and verb. This will not only help you avoid agreement problems but will also make your writing more readable.

Each of the therapists interviewed was less willing to treat these patients after finding that recent holdings restricted their practice.

rather than

In the interviews, each of the many therapists currently finding their practice restricted by these recent holdings were less willing to treat these patients.

For related information, see READABILITY, subsection 5.

2. Use specific verbs.

Verbs help the reader focus when they are specific. Try to state important action in the verb, rather than wasting this part of the sentence on information less important to the reader.

The show-up I.D. negated the effect of capturing the defendant one block from the crime.

rather than

The court stated that the show-up I.D. negated the effect of capturing the defendant one block from the crime.

In this example, the legal point is more important than the fact that the court stated it. Use a citation to give that information.

Avoid abstract combinations like *it is*, *there is*, or *there were*. Use nouns instead of those pronouns, specific verbs instead of those verbs of being.

Lerner intentionally distorted Faber's work of art when he replaced a central part of the sculpture.

rather than

There is intentional distortion when a person replaces the central part of a sculpture.

For related information, see THERE IS . . . THAT.

3. Use active voice.

Active voice describes an action done by the subject.

The jury decided that the defendant was guilty of manslaughter.

rather than

It was decided that the defendant was guilty of manslaughter.

Active voice is easier to read and more concise. It also adds precision because it makes clear who did what. Therefore, use active voice unless the writing requires passive voice for effect. For more help here, see ACTIVE VOICE and PASSIVE VOICE.

4. Use the auxiliary verb that best expresses your shade of meaning.

Careful use of auxiliary verbs can clarify the exact meaning of your verb. For example, if you wanted to communicate that the defendant had the capacity to do something but did not, use *could*.

The defendant could have set the emergency brake.

Conversely, if you want to communicate that the defendant had good reason for not setting the brake, use *would have*.

The defendant would have set the emergency brake had he not been rushing to assist the people in the other car.

For specific information about this use of verbs, see VERBS, AUXILIARY.

5. Split infinitives when required for accuracy.

Past standard wisdom has been to avoid splitting infinitives at all times, although that was never a grammatical requirement.

to move afterwards

rather than

to afterwards move

Because some of your readers may still favor keeping infinitives together, you may want to avoid splitting them when possible.

Split the infinitive, however, when necessary to avoid ambiguities.

The mayor agreed to only suggest the alternative if the matter came up in committee meeting.

In this case, putting *only* before *to* would communicate that this was the only thing to which the mayor agreed.

The mayor agreed only to suggest . . . .

Putting *only* after *suggest* would communicate that this is the only alternative the mayor would suggest.

The mayor agreed to suggest only this alternative. . . .

When forced to make a choice like this, choose the clarity of the split infinitive over the elegance of the ambiguous unsplit version. You may find, however, that you can avoid the problem by restructuring the sentence altogether.

The mayor agreed that she would only suggest the alternative if the matter came up in the committee meeting. She would refrain from requesting it.

This is the safest route; your revised version will offend no one and still avoid ambiguity. For related information see *ONLY*, WHERE TO PLACE. For a definition of infinitives, see VERBS, TENSES.

VERBS, INFLECTIONS

See VERBS, MOODS.

VERBS, IRREGULAR

Irregular verbs are verbs that do not form their past participles in quite the same way that regular verbs do, although the future tense usually does not vary from the standard form of regular verbs. Irregular verbs are old verbs; they predate the time when English moved to the standardizing pattern of adding an *-ed* to the end of the verb to form the past tense. They include *to be, to go, to have, to eat, to sit, to run, to see,* and *to hold,* among others.

Regular verb

Present: I finish, you finish, it finishes

Past: I finished, you finished, it finished

Future: I will finish, you will finish, it will finish

Irregular verbs

Present: I am, you are, it is

Past: I was, you were, it was

Future: I will be, you will be, it will be

Present: I hold, you hold, it holds

Past: I held, you held, it held

Future: I will hold, you will hold, it will hold

For more information, see VERBS, PARTICIPLES; and VERBS, TENSES.

VERBS, LINKING

Linking verbs, such as *to be* or *to seem* link a subject and a predicate but show no action. They are roughly equivalent to equal signs. They are not the same as PASSIVE VOICE. Avoid overusing linking verbs because they are not as emphatic, interesting, or precise as active verbs.

The court reasoned that . . . .

rather than

The court's reasoning was that . . . .

Use linking verbs, however, when they accurately state the point. Often linking verbs are needed when TERMS OF ART are the subjects of the sentence.

Awarding custody to the mother is in the best interests of the children.

and

The standard of care is higher here because of this fiduciary duty.

For a clarification of active and passive voice and linking verbs, see VOICE, ACTIVE OR PASSIVE?

VERBS, MOODS

Mood refers to changes made in the form of the verb to indicate whether the action described by the verb happened in fact. These changes in the form of the verb are called inflections and create four moods. These moods are important conveyors of meaning in legal writing.

1. Indicative.

   The indicative mood refers to actions that have in fact happened, are happening, or will in fact happen. This mood is used most often in legal writing and can be used with any tense.

   The defendant filed a motion for failure to state a claim.

   The buyer is agreeing to assume this responsibility.

   The legislature will consider the matter in the next session.

2. Subjunctive.

   The subjunctive mood refers to actions that will not necessarily happen but are being discussed hypothetically. This can be particularly useful when ARGUING IN THE ALTERNATIVE.

   If I were you, I would file a claim.

   If the defendant were younger, such an assault might have been possible.

   The subjunctive mood can be used with any verb tense, as the following list illustrates.

   (a) Past Subjunctive.

   If the legislature intended for the law to exempt owner-operated bars, it would have stated so in the law itself.

   (b) Past Progressive Subjunctive.

   If the legislature had been planning to exempt owner-operated bars, documentation of that plan would have appeared somewhere in the legislative history of the law.

   (c) Past Perfect Subjunctive.

   If the legislature had intended for the law to exempt owner-operated bars, it would have stated so.

(d) Future Subjunctive.

If the legislature were to exempt owner-operated bars, it would create a suspect classification.

(e) Future Progressive Subjunctive.

If the legislature were planning to exempt owner-operated bars, local bar owners' associations would surely be made aware of that plan.

(f) Future Perfect Subjunctive.

If the legislature were to have exempted owner-operated bars, they certainly were not aware of that intention when they drafted the law.

For related information, see VERBS, TENSES.

3. Imperative.

The imperative mood states commands directly to the reader.

In preparation for this meeting, please complete this questionnaire and bring it with you to the meeting.

This direct address creates a more personal tone, and so it must be used appropriately. For example, direct address is natural for a request in a letter.

For our next meeting, please (1) bring all documents relating to the previous sale of your house and (2) collect all tax information for 2022.

You could also naturally use it in a written request to someone you supervise.

When researching the DuBois case, check the statutes for any provisions relating to previous sales.

But it is not used in formal court documents, such as a pleading. There, use the third person.

The plaintiff respectfully requests that this court overturn the trial court's ruling.

It may also be inappropriate in a note to a superior or colleague, for reasons of TONE. In that situation, use the question form if adding *please* is not sufficiently deferential.

Could you please provide me a copy of the client's letters that address her preferences for the will?

4. Emphatic.

The emphatic mood is formed by adding *do* to the verb. Some sources call this use of *do* by other grammatical names, including classifying it as a tense. Whatever its classification, you may use the emphatic mood to underscore a positive or negative response, particularly when the opposite answer is the one the reader might expect.

He does plan to pursue the matter.

She does not consider this offer acceptable.

VERBS, PARTICIPLES

Participles are the forms of verbs that combine with auxiliary verbs to form different verb tenses. There are two kinds of participles: present and past.

1. Present participle.

This participle ends in *-ing*, such as *deciding, continuing, being, losing,* and *going*. It is used to form progressive tenses.

The trial is continuing to draw much attention from the media.

The children were playing near the pool when the accident happened.

The Court will be deciding this issue next month.

In contrast, this *-ing* form is called a gerund when it is used as a noun. (Also see GERUND.)

Seeing is believing.

Reversing lower court decisions seems to be this judge's mission.

2. Past participle.

This form ends in *-ed*, such as *decided* and *continued*. The past participles of irregular verbs such as *been, lost,* and *gone* do not end in *-ed*. Past participles are used to form past and perfect tenses.

The attorneys had already decided how to proceed when the settlement offer came.

The defendant has lost on appeal but is going to pursue other possible actions.

Participles can also be used to introduce phrases, which are then called *participial phrases*. These participles modify a noun, so make sure that noun is in the main clause, or you risk creating ambiguity.

The defendant tried to put out the flames with a blanket but was forced back, coughing and gasping for air.

Discouraged by this lack of response, Allen decided to leave the organization.

rather than

Discouraged by this lack of response, the organization no longer seemed relevant to Allen.

For more on using participles accurately, see MODIFIERS, DANGLING; and MODIFIERS, SQUINTING. Also see VERBS, IRREGULAR.

VERBS, TENSES

Verb tenses tell the reader how the actions in the text relate to each other. The rule about using verb tenses is to be accurate, not just to use the same tense throughout a document. You will usually need to use different tenses to communicate how actions relate to each other. Do not, however, shift tenses without a logical reason for doing so. Verb tenses can also be used to add shades of meaning, if accuracy is not lost.

Depending on the grammar source you read, English has between three and a dozen tenses. The following list takes a moderate approach, listing nine tenses and the infinitive form. The following subsections also explain ways you can use tenses to your advantage in legal writing. For more on similar techniques, see VERBS, AUXILIARY; and VERB TENSES, WHICH TO USE?

1. Simple Present Tense.

   Use the simple present tense for a current or habitual action.

   I handle all the estate planning in the firm.

   Its main use in legal writing is for referring to statutes or other rules currently in effect.

   False imprisonment occurs when . . . .

   This statute requires all nonresidents to . . . .

   Use the present progressive tense, not the present tense, in situations where you do not want to imply that this is a habitual action.

   Our client is complaining that Jones Corporation . . . .

   rather than

   Our client complains that Jones Corporation . . . .

2. Present Progressive Tense.

Use the present progressive tense for actions currently in progress. This tense is formed by *am*, *are*, or *is* and the *-ing* participle.

The client is suing the Jones Corporation.

Also use the present progressive tense for actions going on during or in the context of some other present action.

Even as we are debating the issue here, the courts face the same issue in Colson v. Perry.

3. Present Perfect Tense.

Use the present perfect tense for actions now completed but related to a current action. The present perfect tense is formed by *have* or *has* plus the past participle.

After the testator has executed the will, the will becomes valid.

When used in context with another action, that action is usually stated in the present tense, as in the previous example. The present perfect tense is useful for showing that a current action is logically subsequent to a previous recent action.

After the offeree has relied to the offeree's detriment upon the offer, the contract is enforceable.

4. Simple Past Tense.

Use the simple past tense for actions completed before the current writing.

The court decided to review the case.

The past tense is useful for suggesting an action is finished and cannot be changed.

The Supreme Court resolved this issue in . . . .

5. Past Progressive Tense.

Use the past progressive for actions completed before the current writing but going on over a period of time in relation to some other past action.

Mr. Jones was changing a flat tire when Mr. Smith's car struck him.

The past progressive tense is formed by *was* or *were* and the present participle, or the *-ing* form of the verb. When used with another action, the other action is usually stated in the past tense, as in the previous example.

The past progressive tense is useful for showing the context in which some past action happened, and thus it can suggest mitigating circumstances.

So bad was Julia's health that, even though he was battling cancer at the time, Colonel Hart insisted that Julia never be left alone.

6. Past Perfect Tense.

Use the past perfect tense for actions completed before some other past action took place.

Because Anderson had accepted the original offer, the contract was legally valid.

The past perfect is formed by *have* or *had* and the past participle. When used in context of another action, that other action is usually stated in the past tense, as in the previous example.

The past perfect is useful for expressing a previous past action that logically led to a subsequent past action.

Since the tenant had given the landlord permission to enter the apartment to repair the faucet in the kitchen, the landlord assumed she could also repair the broken latch on the bedroom closet door.

7. Simple Future Tense.

Use the future tense for actions not yet done.

We will send you a draft of your new trust so that you can review it before our next conference.

The future tense is formed by *will* and the same form of the verb that would go after *to* in the infinitive verb, such as *send, finish,* or *be.*

The future tense suggests that the action will in fact happen, even though it has not yet happened. It is useful for suggesting a result is certain.

Judge Roland Hausler will win reelection.

If you want to suggest that the future action may not be done, use *would* instead. For more on this, see VERBS, AUXILIARY, subsection 3; and WOULD.

8. Future Progressive Tense.

Use the future progressive tense for actions that will be going on over a period of time in the future.

This action will be pending for many years before the court reaches a decision.

The future progressive is formed by *will be* plus the present participle, or *-ing* form of the verb. When used in the context of another action, that action is usually stated in the present tense, as in the previous example.

9. Future Perfect Tense.

Use the future perfect tense for actions that are not yet completed but will have been completed before some other action.

The company will have bound itself legally to the contract when it accepts the offer.

The future perfect tense is formed by *will have* and the *-ed* form of the verb. When used in the context of another action, that other action is usually stated in the present tense, as in the previous example.

This tense is useful for showing the logical consequence of future possible actions.

If the court accepts the plaintiff's reasoning, then it will have opened the door to unharmed plaintiffs seeking to recover damages.

10. Infinitive Verbs.

Although the infinitive is not technically a tense, it can be used to clarify sequence and meaning like a tense. The infinitive form is not tied to any person or time. It consists of *to* plus the verb, and often functions like a noun.

To appeal may be too expensive.

It is useful when you want to suggest that the point you are making is always true, rather than focusing particularly on the present instance.

To say that one idea cannot be expressed in print is to say that all ideas are subject to potential censorship.

VERB TENSES, DIFFERENT ONES IN THE SAME TEXT

The governing rule here is to use the accurate tense. Doing this will often require you to use different tenses within a passage of text and even within a sentence. When these changes are not required for accuracy, however, keep the verb tense consistent throughout your text. For example, use simple past tense in both of the main verbs in the following sentences.

The trial court found that the defendant had made a good faith effort to inform the plaintiff of the impending problems meeting deadlines. The court also stated that the plaintiff had ignored the defendant's requests.

rather than

The trial court found that the defendant had made a good faith effort to inform the plaintiff of the impending problems meeting deadlines. The court also states that the plaintiff had ignored the defendant's requests.

Use of two different tenses within the same sentence is often necessary to keep the time relationship of two actions clear.

present perfect

Because the court has determined that state law applies

present

rather than federal, it now can address the question of jurisdiction.

and

past

Although the plaintiff argued his case under a theory of

present

restitution, he now requests what are in effect punitive damages.

In contrast, the following version, which uses a consistent tense, is inaccurate because the events did not occur at the same time.

past perfect

Although the plaintiff has argued his case under a theory of restitution, he

past perfect

has requested what are in effect punitive damages.

Thus in the previous examples, two different tenses are used within each sentence: the simple past and the past perfect. These shifts in tense tell the reader that one action was completed before the other past action.

VERB TENSES, WHICH TO USE?

Use the tense that accurately conveys the meaning of the verb, always. Occasionally people will tell you that you must use a consistent tense throughout a document; what they mean to say is that you must use tense accurately. These guidelines should help you do that.

Use the present tense when talking about law that is currently in effect. Constitutions, statutes, rules, and cases that are still good law can all be stated in the present tense.

False imprisonment occurs when . . .

and

The statute of limitations tolls when . . .

and

Employers must provide notice to employees when . . .

If the law is not in effect, then use the verb tense that accurately states the point. For example, in a sentence talking about a law that was not passed, use the following.

Had the bill passed, it would have required employers to provide notice to employees when. . .

But in a law that is no longer in effect, use the past tense.

The previous Act excluded non-resident aliens; the current Act includes them.

When synthesizing the law for the reader of the current law, use the present tense for CONCISENESS. This structure helps unify the synthesis by translating statements about the current law into the present tense, so that the reader understands that the sources are good law. Use appropriate citations to communicate the sources of that law in place of *the court held* or *the statute stated.*

Rather than using the narrow interpretation of the term "public use," the supreme court interprets it to "include public utility, benefit, and advantage." LVDA v. Prince, 76 P.3d 1, 9 (Nev. 2025). To qualify as a "public use," condemned property need not be physically utilized by the public; it may just benefit them. A "public purpose" benefits the public and satisfies the state constitutional "public use" obligation. Id. Nevada's eminent domain statute, which requires that the land be put to "public purpose," is consistent with both the federal and state constitutional "public use" requirements. Nev. Rev. Stat. § 58.22 (2025).

rather than

The Nevada Supreme Court rejected the narrow interpretation of "public use" and interpreted it to "include public utility, benefit, and advantage." LVDA v. Prince, 76 P.3d 1, 9 (Nev. 2025). They stated that, to qualify as a "public use," condemned property did not need to be physically utilized by the public, just benefit them. Id. A "public purpose" benefited the public, and satisfied the state constitutional "public use" obligation. Id. Nevada's eminent domain statute, which required that the land be put to "public purpose," was deemed by the legislature to be consistent with both the federal and state constitutional "public use" requirements. See Nev. Rev. Stat. § 58.22 (2025).

For related matters, see VERBS, EFFECTIVE USE OF; VERBS, TENSES; and VERB TENSES, DIFFERENT ONES IN THE SAME TEXT.

VERIFICATION

A verification is sometimes included at the end of a COMPLAINT, after the attorney's signature.

Plaintiff asserts that the facts stated above are true.

____

[Plaintiff's name typed under the signature]

Adding a verification helps drive home the importance of being truthful, which is useful especially when the attorney is taking the client's word for the truthfulness of key facts.

VERSATILITY

The legal writer must develop versatility for maximum effectiveness, because lawyers must write to a nonlegal as well as a legal audience and because the legal audience is varied in both background and needs. To develop this versatility, learn how different writing techniques work so you have the tools and understanding you need. For help doing this, study examples of others' writing, particularly those who are your primary readers. Exchange ideas with others about strategy, theory, and practical recommendations; then practice varying your approach to organization and style. For related information, see SENTENCES, STRUCTURE OF and HABITS.

Practice adapting to different readers' needs. Your own writing will improve as you add to your repertoire the successful structures, approaches, writing patterns, and styles of others. If you are working for a supervisor who sees a different theory or structure to your document, try to compose the document that way, even if you disagree about why. Similarly, if you are working for a judge who prefers terse expression, or even a partner who demands flowery language, try imitating those styles. With these additions, you will become more adept in your ability to choose the expression and approach you want.

For specific situations, see EDITING, GHOST WRITING, GRACE UNDER FIRE, MANAGING WRITERS, and PRIORITIES WITHIN ONE DOCUMENT. For general concepts, see AUDIENCE; DESIGN; HABITS, WRITING; MULTI-TASKING; STYLE; THEORY OF THE CASE; and TRIAGE. For how-to information, see DEADLINES, MEETING THEM;

ORGANIZATION, LARGE-SCALE; ORGANIZATION, SMALL-SCALE; READERS; and TIME MANAGEMENT.

VERY

Avoid overusing *very*. It adds little meaning, and often it detracts from the word it modifies, rather than emphasizing it.

This issue is crucial.

rather than

This issue is very important.

For related information, see MODIFIERS.

VIRGULE

The only times you should use a virgule, or slash, in legal writing are when you are writing fractions or when writing a form in which the person signing is to mark out the inappropriate word, as in *Mr./Ms./Mrs./Miss.* For related information, see AND/OR and S/HE.

VIRTUALLY

Virtually means *essential to all purposes* or *in effect*. It contrasts with *literally*.

The exceptions have virtually swallowed the rule.

Often *virtually* can be omitted with no loss of accuracy, unless you want to explicitly distinguish the meaning from LITERALLY. Also see MODIFIERS.

VIZ.

Viz., or *videlicet*, is unnecessary because there are clear English equivalents. Use *namely*, *that is*, or *that is to say* instead. For related information, see LEGALESE.

VOICE

Voice is a literary term for the way you transmit an impression when writing a particular document. Voice is created by many components: favored sentence structures, levels of formality, preferred word choices, and preferred organizational patterns, both large- and small-scale. Your voice is, then, a collection of your habits or preferences. As you develop your legal voice, you may expand or shift some of those preferences, depending on the context of your writing, just as your voice shifts when you talk to your spouse or your boss. As a legal writer, your voice might be that of a bill collector asking a client to pay an overdue bill, an advocate trying to change a judge's mind, or an apologetic bearer of bad news. But in all situations, the shift lies within a professional and temperate range.

Voice is alive and well in legal writing. From Holmes to Cardozo to Ginsburg, legal writers have carved out specific laws, persuaded readers, and stopped detractors short by the use of their voices. As you read and hear legal voices, you may accept or reject certain features. Eventually, you can combine features and generate others to create your own legal voice, which will develop over time. You need not lose your past writing voice because you have entered the law. You will, however, need to adapt the voice to the constraints of legal writing. To do this, analyze its features and decide what transfers well into legal writing. You will decide what to use or drop. You will also decide when to use your legal voice strongly and when, instead, to soften that voice for the sake of your readers. And there will be times when you need to imitate literally another's voice. For a discussion of this, see GHOST WRITING. For a discussion of various components of personal style, see SENTENCE STRUCTURE, TONE, and WORD CHOICE.

VOICE, ACTIVE OR PASSIVE?

Voice is a verb form that indicates the relation between the subject and the action expressed by the verb. In active voice the subject does the action; in passive voice the subject receives the action.

> **The boy hit the ball.** [Active voice]
>
> **The ball was hit.** [Passive voice]
>
> and
>
> **The defendant assaulted the victim.** [Active voice]
>
> **The victim was assaulted.** [Passive voice]
>
> and
>
> **The court held the identification evidence admissible.** [Active voice]
>
> **The identification evidence was held admissible.** [Passive voice]

1. Uses of active voice.

   Using active voice instead of passive voice usually eliminates extra words. Using active voice also eliminates the ambiguity that might be caused by abstract verbs, such as *consists of* or *concerns* or *involves*.

   > **Petitioner filed the motion on time.**

Section 436 requires taxpayers to notify the IRS of any changes.

2. Uses of passive voice.

Passive voice is useful in four specific situations. In legal writing, use it consciously and for these reasons only; otherwise, use active voice.

(a) Passive voice is useful for deemphasizing unfavorable facts or law. For example, the attorney for the defense might want to write the following.

The plaintiff was assaulted by the defendant.

The attorney for the prosecution, however, might write the following.

The defendant assaulted the plaintiff.

(b) Passive voice is useful for hiding the identity of the actor.

A decision was made to cut your salary.

Here, passive voice avoids telling who made the decision.

(c) Passive voice is also useful when the subject is very long. In this situation, passive voice creates a more readable sentence by keeping the subject and verb closer together.

This action is required by statutory law, by the common law principle of due care, and by a general sense of justice.

rather than

Statutory law, the common law principle of due care, and a general sense of justice require this action.

(d) Finally, passive voice is useful when the subject is much less important than the object.

Freedom of speech cannot be encumbered by concerns of propriety.

rather than

Concerns of propriety cannot encumber freedom of speech.

VOICE MAIL

When you want to communicate by phone but find you have to leave a message, make the most of that opportunity. Try to capture the purpose of your call and the tone you want to establish in a short, appropriate message. Leave your name, number, and your available times so that you can start to establish useful parameters for connecting.

When you must leave someone a substantive message that is best not put in writing, remember that voice mail may be recorded, transcribed, and forwarded. Use voice mail instead to set up a face-to-face meeting.

WAS OR *WERE*?

See *THERE IS* OR *THERE ARE*? or VERBS, MOODS.

WE

We is a special problem in legal writing because you may, by using *we*, inadvertently speak for your whole law office or organization. Never use *we* when you really mean *I*; use *we* only when you are speaking officially for the organization of which you are a part, as one judge may do when drafting an opinion for the whole bench.

> **We [the members of the firm] suggest you try to settle the case.**
>
> rather than
>
> We [I, but I don't want to admit it] think the merits of the case are too weak.
>
> or
>
> We [who?] now move on to the next issue.

For related information, see ANTECEDENTS and PRONOUNS.

We can also be used in constructions where a verb is implied. For example, *as well as we* implies *as well as we are*, and *such as we* implies *such as we are.*

> **I am sorry to inform you that the defendant's firm is unwilling to discuss a settlement with lawyers such as we.**

WELL OR *GOOD*?

See *GOOD* OR *WELL*?

WHEN AM I DONE?

See WHEN TO STOP.

WHEN OR *IF*?

Use *when* to refer to a relationship of time; use *if* to refer to a logical relationship. See also *WHEN* OR *WHERE*?

WHEN OR *WHERE*?

When indicates a point in time; *where* indicates a physical place. In Questions Presented and Issues, often you should use *when* because it is more precise, describing events in time. Use *if*, however, when referring to a logical relationship rather than the relative timing of two different events.

WHEN TO STOP

The purpose of this section is to help you overcome any tendencies you may have to fiddle with a document forever, miss your deadlines, frustrate your coworkers, or drive yourself crazy with uncertainty about your writing. Ideally, each document you produce would be perfect. Realistically, that is not possible. It is seldom possible to get even one document perfect, let alone all that you write. You therefore must make some decisions about which documents are worth pushing closer to perfection and which must be turned in sooner.

The following guidelines can help you make these difficult decisions at each stage of the writing process. But also use your common sense and revise the list as needed to suit your circumstances.

1. When to stop PREWRITING.

    (a) When to stop researching.

    Stop when you keep finding the same sources. Stop when mandatory authority is sufficient to answer the question. Stop when you have the appropriate research to answer the question within the scope of the project. Wherever you begin your research, including using ARTIFICIAL INTELLIGENCE AND RESEARCH, save time by following the RESEARCH STRATEGY GUIDE and by completing all updating. Do not waste time looking for the fictitious smoking gun, or the case exactly like yours; concentrate instead on the sources that turn up repeatedly or appropriately address the question.

    Stop when you have the essential sources appropriate to the document's SCOPE. Although there may be numerous other sources to answer the question, your AUDIENCE may not need all of them. If you can, ascertain the appropriate level of detail necessary to answer the question before you begin researching. Then you can choose the essential sources and eliminate the others as you read. If you can answer the question using MANDATORY AUTHORITY, you may be able to stop; if not, you may need to use PERSUASIVE AUTHORITY. For further detail, see PREWRITING CHECKLIST.

(b) When to stop outlining.

If you tend to linger at this stage so long that you have inadequate time for the later stages of the writing process, stop when you have completed enough of an outline to give shape to your general ideas and when you have listed specific points under each general idea. In general, however, allow plenty of time for this stage; it will prevent time-consuming errors at later stages. If you use artificial intelligence (AI) to find sample outlines, stop when you have three or four possibilities. Then be sure to allow enough time to evaluate them and use them to create your own. For help if you are stuck, see OUTLINES and ORGANIZATION FOR THOSE WHO CAN'T OUTLINE.

2. When to stop WRITING.

The critical factor here is to stop rewriting, revising, and polishing when you are writing this first draft. Let your ideas flow, unedited. If you sense holes in your reasoning, let them pass for now; fill them in later in the rewriting stage. If you sense awkward phrases, let them pass also; you can revise them later. You will thus stop when you have a complete draft, not a perfect one. Save that for the next stages.

3. When to stop REWRITING.

Stop when you have the large-scale ideas in place, the paragraphs in a logical order, the topic sentences in place, and all needed content and explanation in the text. Make sure the organization is correct, complete, and coherent enough to be followed by any legal reader. Also make sure any unneeded information is omitted. Then move on to revising. For help focusing on rewriting tasks, see REWRITING CHECKLIST.

4. When to stop REVISING.

The key here is to do first things first. You are still looking for accuracy in content, but now in the terminology and precision of HEADINGS, SUBJECT-VERB COMBINATIONS, and TOPIC SENTENCES. Make sure paragraphs and sentences are readable and connected. Check your POSITIONS OF EMPHASIS and TRANSITIONS for accuracy. And make sure POINT OF VIEW and TONE are consistent. You may want to use artificial intelligence (AI) tools in revising to help with specific edits, such as minimizing use of PASSIVE VOICE, increasing READABILITY, or achieving CONCISENESS. For more guidance, see REVISING CHECKLIST.

5. When to stop POLISHING.

This phase takes longer than you think. Rather than read from start to finish (you will tire midway), read for the things that catch the reader's eye right away. Check first for format. Then proof just the citations all the way through. Then check numbers. Then names. Then quotations. Sweep through the document, concentrating on just one thing in each pass. Finally, proofread the text for typographical, grammatical, and punctuation errors. Make sure to incorporate on the list your own frequent errors. When this is done, if you have time left, you may go back and check any other concerns that you wish. If you have no time left, at least you can take comfort in the fact that you have avoided major writing errors and that the document is even throughout, not perfect at the beginning and sloppy at the end. For more help, see POLISHING CHECKLIST. You may also find artificial intelligence (AI) useful in POLISHING to proofread or check for format consistency, but do not end with AI tools; begin with them and verify the results by using the techniques above. For related information, see PRIORITIES, TIME MANAGEMENT, WORDS SPELLCHECKERS MAY NOT CATCH, and WRITING BLOCK.

WHERE OR *WHEN*?

See *WHEN* OR *WHERE*?

WHETHER

Whether is a subordinating conjunction that introduces a dependent clause.

Whether the court will address this question is unknown.

Therefore a *whether* clause by itself cannot be a complete sentence.

whether the court will address this issue

In legal writing, however, *whether* is often used to introduce QUESTIONS PRESENTED and ISSUES. If you use the *whether* form of a Question Presented or an Issue, end it with a period, not a question mark.

To avoid writing your Issue or Question Presented as an incomplete sentence, see if you can reformulate it as a question, leaving out *whether*.

Did the trial court err in awarding custody of both children to a mother when . . . ?

rather than

Whether the trial court erred in awarding custody of both children to a mother when . . . .

WHETHER OR *WHETHER OR NOT*?

Use *whether* for most legal readers, many of whom have dropped the *or not* in all but the most formal writing. Use *whether or not* when you want the reader to pause and measure two options equally.

The court considered whether or not to impose the death penalty.

WHICH OR *THAT*?

See *THAT* OR *WHICH*?

WHITE PAPERS

A white paper is a reference paper that lays out a principle, theory, or analysis to inform readers on a specific topic. A white paper is often objective but may also take the issuing body's point of view on the topic. Unlike legal scholarship, it does not present the writer's specific point of view. For information on how to write them, see INFORMATIVE ARTICLES. For related information, see AUDIENCE; DESIGN; and POINT OF VIEW, OBJECTIVE TO PERSUASIVE. For techniques related to producing a white paper, see SCHOLARLY WRITING, SCHOLARLY WRITING PROCESS, and SCHOLARLY WRITING PROCESS CHECKLIST.

WHOEVER OR *WHOMEVER*?

Use *whoever* as you would use *who*; use *whomever* as you would use *whom*. Thus, use *whoever* as the subject of a sentence, *whomever* as the object of a verb or preposition. Each means *any person whatever*, but the choice of where to place these relative pronouns depends on the word's grammatical placement, as with *who* and *whom*.

Whoever talked to the client on Tuesday neglected to report the details of the discussion to the partner.

and

I will give the tickets to whomever.

Some of the confusion occurs when the pronoun appears to be the object of a preposition but is actually the subject of a dependent clause.

I will give the tickets to whoever calls first.

but

You may invite whomever you want.

WHO OR *WHOM*?

Although this distinction is fading from common speech, it is not gone yet from formal English. Getting it right adds precision and polish to professional writing. Use *who* as a subject, *whom* as an object. Thus, use *whom* whenever it is the object of a preposition.

To whom did you present the question about the gun?

Use *whom* as the object of a verb.

Whom did you see on the night of the incident?

Or use *whom* when it introduces a clause that identifies a person who is the object of a linking verb that acts as the direct object of the verb.

The defendant is the person whom the plaintiff saw on the night of the crime.

Use *who* as a subject of a sentence.

Who took my shoes?

Also use *who* as the subject of a clause.

You are the person who called me yesterday.

When you do this, use the verb ending that matches the word *who* replaces.

It is I who am interested in this matter.

and

It is he who is interested in this matter.

WILLS

The principles for writing wills are much the same as those for writing contracts. As with contracts, you might want to use forms to help you get started. For help here, see FORMS, USE OF. In addition to the principles listed under CONTRACTS, also focus on these important tasks.

1. Ascertain the client's needs and the jurisdiction's requirements.

   Interview the client thoroughly, so that you are clear about the client's desires and concerns. Ascertain the details you need about matters such as assets, legal domicile, and beneficiaries and other relatives. Ask the client to identify alternative beneficiaries and personal representatives. But while concentrating on getting all the needed information, also pay attention to your client's sensibilities. For many people, preparing a will is an emotional event; the client will appreciate a sensitive interviewer.

   Next, research your jurisdiction's statutory and procedural requirements for wills. If your jurisdiction's requirements are less stringent than other states, consider creating a will that conforms to the higher standards. For example, even if your jurisdiction requires only two witnesses to the will, include three witnesses so that the will would also be recognized in other states.

In your research, consider also the tax and property ownership consequences. Anticipate potential problems in transferring ownership of various properties. Consider what happens to debts incurred by the testator. Prepare for possible challenges to the will. Allow sufficient time for this critical planning.

2. Choose and organize the document's content.

Generally, wills include at least the following parts:

(a) an introductory clause naming the testator,

(b) what to do with anything left over (the residuary clause),

(c) general and specific bequests,

(d) appointment of personal representatives,

(e) a place for the testator's signature (the testimonium), and

(f) a place for witnesses to sign, saying that the will was properly executed.

Some wills also include trust arrangements, instructions to pay burial expenses, instructions to pay just debts, statements of disinheritance, naming of guardians for minors, and other special clauses. Adding these special clauses can create problems as well as prevent them, depending on the specific circumstances. Therefore, make sure you have researched the ramifications of each provision you decide to include. Also make sure you state each provision clearly. For help here, see CONDITIONS, STATING THEM. Finally, check your jurisdiction's requirements, rather than relying on this list alone.

3. Revise the document for accuracy and clarity.

The will must stand up to legal scrutiny, but the client and executor must also understand all the particulars of the will. Rewrite and revise with these two goals in mind. As when drafting a contract, plan to make many passes through the document. On separate passes, check for consistent and unambiguous language, specific references, and absence of legalese. Identify all needed terms of art and make sure that you have explained them to the client. Never include a single word or phrase that you yourself do not understand. You must be able to explain this document to the client, so you must be able to answer any questions about it. Even more important, the document must stand under the ultimate scrutiny of a wide legal and nonlegal audience. For related information, see AUDIENCE, LEGALESE, and TERMS OF ART.

4. Adjust language for tone if needed.

   Use flowery language only if your client prefers this because of the seriousness of the situation. Never sacrifice PRECISION. For more explanation, see FLOWERY LANGUAGE.

5. Polish with great care.

   Revise painstakingly for grammatical accuracy and correct punctuation. Mistakes in these areas can translate into thousands of dollars, as the following phrases show.

   my daughter's share of the estate

   or

   my daughters' share of the estate

   or

   divided equally among my nephew, my son, my daughter, and my son-in-law

   rather than

   divided equally among my nephew, my son, my daughter and my son-in-law

6. Near the end of the process, look again at the will as a whole and make sure it accomplishes your client's wishes and is legally sound.

   The detail work necessary to drafting can temporarily blind you to the effectiveness of the whole.

WOMAN, LADY, OR *FEMALE*?

Use *woman* unless the context requires one of the alternatives. For more on this, see GENDER IN WRITING.

WORD CHOICE

Choose words carefully because every word counts in legal writing. When selecting the right word, give priority to PRECISION, but within that framework focus on READABILITY. When writing to persuade, also adjust your level of abstraction to create sympathy or emotional distance as needed. When writing to create a specific TONE, choose words that keep your level of formality consistent. See FORMALITY, LEVEL OF and PROFESSIONAL LANGUAGE AND PRESENTATION for ways to balance friendliness and professionalism.

The following list provides an overview of the major concerns involved in effective word choice.

1. Unless you intend to be vague, use specific nouns and verbs rather than abstract ones. This will help focus the reader on your main points.

   The defendant moves to dismiss the case under Fed. R. Civ. P. 12(b)(6).

   rather than

   This concerns the defendant's motion to dismiss.

   Use the most specific term possible. For example, do not say *involves* when you mean *is liable.* Use more general terms only when you need to be ambiguous for some reason, or when the context requires them. For related information, see AMBIGUITY, WAYS TO AVOID, subsection 3. For a discussion of situations where you may need to be vague or ambiguous, see WRITING, PERSUASIVE, subsection 4(b). For related information, see WRITING, PERSUASIVE, subsection 4; and EMPHASIS.

2. Use terms of art or key terms, but avoid unneeded verbiage, such as legalese.

   The defendant moves to dismiss the case under Fed. R. Civ. P. 12(b)(6).

   rather than

   This action prays to the court to dismiss the plaintiff's cause of action on the grounds that the said plaintiff has failed to state a case for which relief can be granted by the court as required under Federal Rules of Civil Procedure.

   For definitions, see KEY TERMS, LEGALESE, and TERMS OF ART. For related information, see CONCISENESS and READABILITY.

3. Use modifiers only for essential information.

   An alcoholic father cannot serve the best interests of his children.

   rather than

   A habitually alcoholic father clearly cannot serve the best interests of his unfortunate children.

   For related information, see MODIFIERS and CONCISENESS, subsection 7.

4. Use accurate transitions to convey the logical links between ideas.

    The litigation may cost more than the amount our client could recover if she wins the suit. Nevertheless, she has chosen to pursue her claim.

    rather than

    The litigation may cost more than the amount our client could recover if she wins the suit, and she has chosen to pursue her claim.

    For more examples and explanation, see TRANSITIONS.

5. Use consistent wording.

    To avoid confusion, use the same term for the same concept throughout the document; do not change it just for variety.

    The defendant proposes that his repair of the water heater was adequate. This proposal, however, ...

    rather than

    The defendant proposes that his repair of the water heater was adequate. This suggestion, however, ...

    For related information, see ELEGANT VARIATION and REPETITION.

6. Make sure all pronouns are unambiguous.

    For example, if two or more women are mentioned in a text, then *she* is likely to be ambiguous. Therefore, check each pronoun.

    Ms. Jones did not ask Ms. Wilson to doublecheck the amount because Ms. Wilson routinely checked all the amounts listed.

    rather than

    Ms. Jones did not ask Ms. Wilson to doublecheck the amount because she routinely checked all the amounts listed.

    Also make sure each *this* is unambiguous. *This* is the pronoun most likely to cause inaccuracies. *This* can refer to an idea or a thing, one word or a whole sentence; as a result, you must make sure that the reader always knows what *this* means. If there is any question, add the appropriate noun after *this*.

    The court reasoned that the difference among experts on the antique armoire's provenance was not the determining factor. This reasoning . . . .

    For more examples, see AMBIGUITY, WAYS TO AVOID, subsection 2; and THIS.

WORDINESS

See CONCISENESS.

WORDS SPELLCHECKERS MAY NOT CATCH

The following table lists some common words that can cause problems in legal writing not because they are misspelled, but because they are not the words you meant. Add to this list any of your own typical misspellings and always check the words on your list to avoid embarrassment. You may be able to avoid some problems by deleting the offending words from your spellchecker, but you will not be able to delete all of them. Proofreading will remain a necessity.

Sample Words That a Spellchecker Often Misses

What you meant	What you got
advise	*advice*
assess	*asses*
but	*butt*
causal	*casual*
discrete	*discreet*
fact	*fart*
facts	*fats*
fare	*fear*
from	*form*
hello	*hell*
may	*my*
mediation	*meditation*
nonsensical	*nonsexual*
not	
public	*pubic*
or	*of*
rare	*rear*
scared	*scarred*
some	*come*
statute	*statue*
trial	*trail*

What you meant	What you got
undue	*undone*
united	*untied*

For related information, see DEADLINES, MEETING THEM; PERFECTIONISM; PROOFREADING; TIME MANAGEMENT; and WRITING AND TECHNOLOGY.

WORDY PHRASES

For general information, see CONCISENESS. For a discussion of specific phrases, see those entries. For a quick fix, try the shorter phrase in the right column.

Wordy Phrase	**Concise Alternative**
at this point in time	***now, currently***
at the time that	***when***
during the time that	***while***
for the period of	***during***
in absence of	***without***
in question	***this***
it is . . . that	***[start with the word after that]***
prior to	***before***
there are . . . that	***[start with the word after that]***
until such time as	***until***

Try to omit the following words and phrases because they lengthen the prose and raise more questions than they answer.

as a matter of fact
clearly
it is said that
obviously
of course
really
the fact of the matter is
the fact that
to all intents and purposes
undoubtedly
utterly
very

WOULD

Would implies that something should have been done but was not in fact done. Thus it can be useful in Statements of the Case when you are explaining the reason behind an unfavorable fact.

> **The defendant would have set the emergency brake had he not been rushing to assist the people in the other car.**

It can also be useful in Arguments to express hypotheticals or dicta.

> **The assumption would be valid if the defendant had intended to purchase the property, thus showing some interest in its transfer. But she made no such purchase.**

But do not use *would* if you mean to imply that something will be done or if you do not want to imply that it should have been done. For general information, see VERBS, AUXILIARY.

WRITER'S BLOCK

See WRITING BLOCK.

WRITING

Writing the first draft of a document, which is the second stage in the overall WRITING PROCESS, is a creative act rather than a critical one. It involves capturing your thoughts and understanding of the content of your document so that you can later evaluate and shape them into something the reader can understand. When you reach this stage, allow your creative voice to write without stopping to correct errors: don't get it right, just get it written. Later, in the rewriting and revising stages of the overall process, your critical voice will get it right.

The most common mistake many writers make, one that costs hours and adds stress, is to write, rewrite, and revise simultaneously. Some writers even try to polish while writing the first draft. This approach forces the id of creative thought to clash with the super-ego of correction, an impossible and insufferable pairing. The result is often writer's block. No wonder.

One way to avoid writer's block is to keep your words flowing onto the screen as though you are writing an exam or giving an opening argument. If you get stuck on a point because you are suffering from writing block, either skip that part or break it down into smaller pieces, but try not to stop. If necessary, write out your frustration, such as *I can't remember the source but I know it's here somewhere!*, and keep writing. When you finish, leave the draft and catch your breath. Let the draft breathe, too, before you begin rewriting. Then, when you return to your first draft, remember that rough drafts, although necessary, are not final drafts. Expect to rewrite and revise extensively. For more on ways to do this, see DICTATION, REWRITING, and REVISING.

Other ways to keep writing creative, rather than critical, include changing the medium you use to write, writing before you outline rather than after, and writing a middle section first rather than starting at the beginning. For example, you might try dictating rather than writing the first draft. You might write a draft as a means of brainstorming before you outline. Or you might begin by writing about the point most familiar to you.

Although you may want to use artificial intelligence (AI) to generate a preliminary draft, be aware of its limitations. The draft AI generates will not be specific to you, your client's situation, and your unique reasoning. For example, when writing your prompt, you must be vigilant about your client's specific information. Before you enter that information, check all pertinent confidentiality and privacy requirements as well as whether the AI system you are using retains and publishes this information. AI may also be too indiscriminate about legal content. For example, AI may not discern between MANDATORY AUTHORITY and PERSUASIVE AUTHORITY and may not focus on the analytical patterns most appropriate to your case. For help with this, see ARTIFICIAL INTELLIGENCE AND RESEARCH, ARTIFICIAL INTELLIGENCE AND WRITING, and PROMPTS.

There is no one right method to use; the right method is the one that helps you get the document written. For more help, see GETTING STARTED, WRITING BLOCK, and WRITING PROCESS. For help with each of the other stages of writing, see PREWRITING, REWRITING, REVISING, and POLISHING.

WRITING AND TECHNOLOGY

Technology can either devour your time and energy or save it, depending on how you use it. For example, you may spend time fussing over technicalities and neglect paying attention to the overall logic of the document. Stay flexible in your writing and use technology to your best advantage.

Technology can also change qualities in your writing. For example, you may write faster and with more conversational quality. Or, because you are tempted to cut and paste your research, your writing may become wordier, more literal, and less personal. You may forget to check your headings because the software has made an outline of your work, not you. Then your document, like the leaning Tower of Pisa, may look fine layer by layer but may in fact be tilting precariously.

To maximize the usefulness of technology to you as a writer, remember these general principles.

1. Keep your technologies functionally up to date.

   Resist the temptation to limit yourself to the same technology you were using ten years ago simply because you do not want to learn a new system. With the rapid development of new technologies, you may be unwilling to explore new options. Nevertheless, you need to know how to use what your readers expect and can use. As much as possible, time your acquisition of new software so that you can give yourself enough time to learn them. Be realistic, expecting to have a sometimes painful learning curve. Remember that, in the long run, you will reap the benefits of the improved technology.

2. Know when technology is helping or hindering.

   Writing technology can allow ideas to develop rapidly because of its ease of use. Using artificial intelligence can help you to jump start your research or discover potential approaches to your analysis, for example. Other technologies maximize sharing documents and editing among many writers. Proofreading technologies may catch errors you do not see. For related information, see ARTIFICIAL INTELLIGENCE AND RESEARCH, ARTIFICIAL INTELLIGENCE AND WRITING, COMMUNICATIONS, ELECTRONIC; SOCIAL MEDIA; PROMPTS; and WORDS SPELLCHECKERS MAY NOT CATCH.

   But those advantages also create liabilities that can hinder your work, especially the quality of your thought itself. Your analysis and writing process must always be your focus. For example, jumping into research without framing an issue or developing search terms can result in hours spent not finding the right sources. In contrast, a conversation with an expert might be more fruitful, whether a supervising attorney or librarian. Consulting a reliable source that specializes in the relevant area of law may also help you focus accurately and quickly. Writing themes, headings, or conclusions by hand may give you time to evaluate them more carefully.

   Technological writing aids are likely to be most helpful at the beginning or end of your writing process. For example, voice-to-text software may help you get all your thoughts written down in your notes or your first draft. Spelling and grammar checkers can help you reduce the number of errors as you begin polishing a document, leaving fewer errors for you to catch in proofreading. For more practical tips, see DICTATION; HEADINGS; NOTES; ORGANIZE, HOW TO; ORGANIZATION FOR THOSE WHO CAN'T OUTLINE; OUTLINES; and THEME.

3. Beware of false COHERENCE.

Own the structure and analytical integrity of your document. Do not be deceived by a pretty Table of Contents or outlining function. These are useful tools for revealing your thinking, but they can also appear to be more coherent than they are. Study them as a way of developing and then rewriting your document. Software is very helpful for generating Tables of Contents or outlines; it also helps you to conform to format requirements. But screens can lure you into thinking the writing is solid because it looks polished. A neat appearance does not compensate for unreadable sentences and poor logic. Learn when it is best for you to move away from the screen and analyze what you are doing. What is the document's message? Is each heading related to that message? Do the headings relate to each other? Do they carry the analysis to the conclusion? For more tips on training yourself to use technology wisely, especially in prewriting, see NOTES, RESEARCH STRATEGY GUIDE, and UPDATING THE LAW. For related information, see REWRITING.

4. Consider using voice-to-text technology.

Your voice, literally, may strengthen your PREWRITING and WRITING. To see if this improves your writing, try using a software program that enables your device to type while you speak. This method can give your fingers a rest and allow your thoughts to emerge.

When using this program, do not look at the screen as you speak, for that would lead you to start revising. Instead, speak as though you were speaking to your readers. Prepare ahead of time as you would for an oral presentation. Then dictate your document. After you get accustomed to this method and adjust for your own speech habits, you may become faster and better at speaking your analysis. For more help, see DICTATION; DICTION; FORMALITY, LEVEL OF; and VOICE.

5. Cut and paste before you fix sentences.

This phrase, now a metaphor, refers to cutting large sections out of documents or moving large sections to better places in the document. To do this effectively, keep a copy of your original version so you can later check to see that no essential information was omitted. Then copy your headings and first sentences and put them in a new document sequentially. Do they work? If not, reorder them until they fit the logic that best carries your message. Then return to the document and move the large sections accordingly. You can omit repetition this way and fuse sections that work together. It is often hard to do this as you are composing the document. Rewriting in this way helps you to see the larger picture and condense the document appropriately. For more help, see COHERENCE, LOGIC, REWRITING, and SYLLOGISMS.

6. Find and replace your bad habits.

   Use technology to help you fix patterns in writing that are not working for you. For example, use the "Find" function to locate key phrases in your document and see where they are placed. Are they in headings, topic sentences, or main verbs? If not, move them so that key parts of your analysis are not buried in subordinate clauses or middles of paragraphs. Or, to reduce your use of passive voice, you may use a grammar checking program to locate it in your text, so you can make revisions as needed. For more ideas on what to find and replace, see PATTERNS; STYLE; TRANSITIONS; and VERBS, EFFECTIVE USE OF. For more ways to use grammar checkers to improve your writing, see CONCISENESS and POLISHING CHECKLIST.

For related information, see ELECTRONIC FILINGS, ELECTRONIC MESSAGING, and RECORDS, KEEPING THEM.

WRITING BLOCK

Writers may suffer from writing blocks at any stage of the writing process, but usually they happen when the writer feels overwhelmed by the task, believes the written product must be perfect, feels inadequate to the task, or experiences all of the above. Almost all writers suffer from writing blocks occasionally; some endure them on almost every project. Fortunately, writing blocks can usually be overcome by using any or all of the following techniques.

1. Divide and conquer.

   Break the writing task into smaller steps, and keep breaking it down until you see a step that does not look overwhelming. Never mind if the list of steps is pages long; each of those steps may go rather quickly. These small tasks may be boring, but they will not be overwhelming. Then order the steps and start doing them. To gain a sense of progress, check each one off as you finish. For example, if the whole project seems overwhelming, start by listing all the tasks involved, such as

   (a) research,

   (b) outline,

   (c) write,

   (d) rewrite,

   (e) revise, and

   (f) polish.

   Then break each one of those down. For example, you might break *outline* into

(b) outline,

- list all possible points,
- group those points somehow,
- summarize each group, and
- decide which group goes first, second, etc.

If this is still overwhelming, you can break *list all possible points* into

- list all possible points,
    - o list all points that make sense to me,
    - o list all points mentioned in any analogous cases, and
    - o identify all points that occur on both lists.

2. Start somewhere else.

If you are stuck on a particular writing task, set it aside and work on something else. For example, if you cannot decide how to organize the facts section of a memo, leave it and begin writing the issues. If you cannot write the issue, try writing the conclusion. You need to complete many tasks in any writing project, but you need not complete them in any particular order.

3. Try something else.

Vary your approach. You might try voice-to-text technology for taking NOTES or generating your draft. You may need to take a walk or talk to someone about the project. You may want to use artificial intelligence to generate ideas in PREWRITING. For more help here, see ARTIFICIAL INTELLIGENCE AND RESEARCH, ARTIFICIAL INTELLIGENCE AND WRITING, and PROMPTS.

4. Separate the essential from the desirable.

To be efficient, focus on quality and accuracy first. For example, when revising, focus on essentials, such as accurate facts and clear organization, before you tackle desirables, such as emphasis and tone. For help doing this, see WRITING PROCESS. If you are finding it hard to get started, see GETTING STARTED. If you are having trouble finishing, see WHEN TO STOP. For related information, see DEADLINES, MEETING THEM; PERFECTIONISM; and TRIAGE.

WRITING HABITS

See HABITS, WRITING.

WRITING, OBJECTIVE

Objective is the term often used to refer to legal writing that informs and predicts, using a relatively neutral point of view. For example, objective memos can inform the reader of the current status of the law; objective opinion letters can inform the reader of the most likely outcome of litigation. In either situation, the reader is looking for a relatively unbiased assessment of the circumstances. The legal reader may also expect objective writing to include a prediction of the outcome of the case. This prediction should be based on an unbiased analysis of the law that explains and weighs the strengths and weaknesses of the client's position. Objective writing does not minimize the weaknesses of one side's argument, as persuasive writing does.

> **Most state statutes of limitation allow at least five years for this issue; only four states have drawn the line earlier.**
>
> rather than
>
> Not one, not two, but four states of the fifty have statutes of limitation that prevent bringing these actions after three years.

Many lawyers believe that objective writing does not exist because even a neutral assessment of the circumstances requires the analyst's point of view. And many legal readers will expect this assessment to be strongly informed by the writer's individual analytical abilities. Nevertheless, the term *objective writing* has come to refer to most forms of legal writing that are not formally persuasive, such as BRIEFS.

Consider the following checklist when preparing any objective writing, such as a memo or an opinion letter. These tools should help you keep an objective point of view.

1. Carefully identify the facts: *who, what, where, when, why,* and *how,* as suggested in the RESEARCH STRATEGY GUIDE. This separation allows you to evaluate the scope and interrelationship of the KEY FACTS and background information before connecting it to the law.
2. As you read the law, frame the issues carefully and take notes not only on the holdings and facts of each case, but also on the law's parameters, history, and trends. This will allow you to develop and evaluate the arguments available to all parties involved in the situation. For more detail, see CASE BRIEFS, HOLDING, NOTES, QUESTIONS PRESENTED, and RULES.
3. As you report on the law, frame it so that the reader sees how the law works, regardless of the upcoming arguments. For example, you may report a statute's specific language relevant to your facts, or you may synthesize a general rule of law from several cases. Report what the law or the status of the case is by giving an objective summary of the

law. For more elaboration, see DESIGN; DISCUSSION SECTION; LEGAL ANALYSIS; REASONING, ANALOGICAL; REASONING, DEDUCTIVE; REASONING, INDUCTIVE; REASONING, MODERN; REASONING, OTHER; REASONING, POSTMODERN; REASONING, PRESENTING IT; and SYLLOGISMS.

4. Clarify both the strengths and weaknesses of the client's arguments. Make sure the information in the memo is complete, despite your personal bias; do not omit unfavorable points the other side may raise. Account for them and work them into your analysis. For more on this, see ARGUING IN THE ALTERNATIVE; and COUNTERARGUMENTS, HOW TO HANDLE.

5. Weigh the merits of those strengths and weaknesses against each other. That is, evaluate the relative weight that such matters as the law, precedent, practical circumstances, social and legal trends, economics, general policy, and overall equity should be given in this situation.

6. Offer the reader your assessment of how you think the situation will be interpreted and why. The reader is usually interested in your synthesis of all the information, arguments, and possibilities.

7. Avoid overuse of MODIFIERS, because they often add interpretation more than analysis; objective writing informs but does not persuade. Concentrate instead on precise use of nouns and verbs. Specific facts, such as numbers or descriptions, are more convincing than general characterizations. When using modifiers, avoid those that argue, such as *unjust* or *unmistakably*; use only those modifiers that are factually based, such as *unsettled* or *previously*. For more information, see ADJECTIVES and ADVERBS.

For related information, see OBJECTIVITY; and POINT OF VIEW, OBJECTIVE TO PERSUASIVE. For explanations of related concepts, see EQUITY and POLICY.

WRITING OPINIONS

See OPINIONS, JUDICIAL; OPINIONS, LEGAL; WRITING TO CLIENTS; and WRITING TO ATTORNEYS.

WRITING, PERSUASIVE

Writing persuasively is writing to create a desired outcome with a specific audience. In legal writing, you may be persuading a trial court to rule positively on a motion, persuading an appellate court to remand a case, or persuading an agency board that your client should get relief. When designing a persuasive document, use the following steps. For examples of how to apply these principles in specific situations, see BAD NEWS,

GIVING IT; BAD NEWS, SOFTENING IT; COMMUNICATIONS, ELECTRONIC; WRITING TO ATTORNEYS; and WRITING TO CLIENTS. For related concepts, see COMMUNICATIONS, TONE OF; TONE; and VOICE.

1. Clarify your PURPOSE.

   Your overall purpose will guide your choices throughout the writing process, from choosing content, strategy, and organization to revising for emphasis. Generally, your overall purpose will be to engage the reader's cooperation in some way, whether that means having a judge rely on the law you set out or having a party settle a claim out of court. Your secondary purposes may include retaining a client, clarifying the law, or identifying a legal trend no one else has noticed. Analyze the relationship among these purposes to determine organization, point of view, and TONE. Focus on the project's goals so that you do not include personal vendettas into your decision-making, regardless of what the other side has provoked.

2. Focus on your AUDIENCE and frame the issues.

   Choose the strategy and content that will persuade the various individual readers you are addressing. For example, when writing a brief, ask yourself what questions this court will ask and how the law supports resolving those questions in your client's favor. Also consider what a potential court would look at upon review if the outcome is appealed. As you choose your THEORY OF THE CASE, consider the broadest range of possible approaches. For example, if you were arguing that an incarcerated woman should be released early because she is pregnant, but she became pregnant after she escaped from a low-security facility, you would not be likely to find a winning argument by focusing on her. However, if you focused on what was in the best interest of the child, you might be able to prevail.

   Do not assume that the exact arguments that prevailed at one level in the court system will prevail at the next. For example, trial courts often emphasize precedent, appellate courts focus on legal errors, and courts that review constitutional issues may consider long-term effects, precedent, or public policy. So when deciding a criminal case, a trial court might be convinced by a careful comparison of your client's facts to the facts of previous cases. But an appellate court reviewing the same case might be convinced only by arguments that the trial court made a procedural error. To frame issues, see ISSUES, QUESTIONS PRESENTED, and STANDARD OF REVIEW. To research and take effective notes, see CASE BRIEFS, NOTES, and RESEARCH STRATEGY GUIDE. To assess analytical choices, see LEGAL ANALYSIS. For planning persuasive letters or email, see

COMMUNICATIONS, ELECTRONIC; COMMUNICATIONS, TONE OF; WRITING TO ATTORNEYS; and WRITING TO CLIENTS.

3. Structure your Argument to convince your readers.

(a) Order your presentation logically.

Choose the structure that is most coherent and convincing to your readers. When ordering your issues, begin with the threshold issue if there is one; do not violate the readers' sense of logical progression, especially when writing to a court. But if issues are independent, then begin with your most compelling argument. This order creates a strong first impression. If one of three arguments is weaker than the others, place it between the other two so it is not in a POSITION OF EMPHASIS.

When stating and presenting each issue in a legal argument presented to a court, begin with an affirmative statement of your position.

> **The plaintiff provided adequate warning. Twice he tried to reach the defendant by telephone before leaving messages when no one answered.**

Avoid letting your opponent's arguments dictate your structure; use the structure that best suits your position. See ARGUING IN THE ALTERNATIVE; and COUNTERARGUMENTS, HOW TO HANDLE. For ways to organize, see DESIGN; DISCUSSION SECTION; LEGAL ANALYSIS; ORGANIZATION, LARGE-SCALE; OUTLINES; REASONING, ANALOGICAL; REASONING, DEDUCTIVE; REASONING, INDUCTIVE; REASONING, MODERN; REASONING, OTHER; REASONING, POSTMODERN; REASONING, PRESENTING IT; and SYLLOGISMS.

(b) Communicate your structure.

Within paragraphs and paragraph blocks, subordinate the arguments through careful use of subordinate clauses, subheadings, or paragraphs placed in a larger paragraph block. Retain your focus on your client's position. Although you may need to refer to your opponent's position during your Argument, do not dwell on it. Thus if the opposition is arguing that your client did not provide adequate warning, you might write the following.

> **The plaintiff gave adequate warning. She telephoned repeatedly and left messages on the defendant's answering machine on two occasions.**

> rather than

> The defense argues that plaintiff gave no warning. This is not the case, however, because the plaintiff left

messages on the defendant's answering machine on two occasions.

Beginning with a statement of the opposition's position would create a defensive tone and make your organization dependent on the other side's position. For related organizational strategies, see BAD NEWS, SOFTENING IT; COUNTERARGUMENTS, HOW TO HANDLE; ORGANIZATION, SMALL-SCALE; and TRANSITIONS.

4. Revise with persuasion in mind.

Revising for persuasion entails the use of many specific techniques, none of which alone makes an obvious difference but all of which, when working in harmony, create a masterful piece of persuasion. Each of these techniques takes practice to master. Therefore, choose two or three from the following list, practice and master those techniques, and incorporate them into your writing habits:

(a) use subjects and verbs for specific effect,

(b) use specific and concrete words,

(c) choose the most appropriate term of address,

(d) repeat key words,

(e) repeat sentence or phrase structures,

(f) adjust sentence length,

(g) insert information into a sentence with care,

(h) place key phrases at the beginning or end of a paragraph or a sentence,

(i) use subtly emotional language rather than overly emotional,

(j) play one persuasive technique against another, or

(k) avoid overdoing.

Each of these techniques is discussed in the following subsections. Study them and choose the techniques that you understand now. Then, as you master those, add new ones to your repertoire.

(a) Use subjects and verbs for specific effect.

Put your main point in the main subject and verb in your sentence. Conversely, deemphasize points by putting them in dependent clauses. For example, the following sentence emphasizes *he had slowed and was not accelerating* by making that the main subject and verb.

Although the defendant had not come to a full stop at the official stop sign, he had slowed to less than

five miles per hour and was not accelerating at the time of the accident.

Use auxiliary verbs carefully to shade your meaning. For example, you may use *did* to counter an argument.

The plaintiff did provide adequate warning.

You may use *can* to remind the reader that some action is possible under the law, or *must* to remind the reader that it is required.

Intent can be inferred from the defendant's actions.

and

The driver must come to a complete stop.

For more about this technique, see VERBS, AUXILIARY.

Use active or PASSIVE VOICE strategically. When you want to create a focus on the entity taking an action, use ACTIVE VOICE.

The Supreme Court has consistently upheld . . . .

When you want to focus on the act but not the actor, or when you want to hide the actor, use passive voice.

The court's discretion is not limited by . . . .

(b) Use specific and concrete words.

Specific and concrete words create clearer images in the reader's mind than general, abstract ones, and those clearer images are more memorable. For example, *a recent model silver Lamborghini* is more memorable than *vehicle*. This tool is especially useful in drafting fact situations for briefs, because you can use concrete words for facts that favor your client and abstract ones for facts that you want to deemphasize. For example, if you are deemphasizing the illness of a testator and the medications she was taking, you might write the following.

Because Julia Easley had a history of arthritic and cardiovascular diseases, she was taking a variety of medications.

If, however, you were trying to emphasize the illness and the medications, you might write the following.

Julia Easley's health was poor. She suffered from excruciating tension headaches (R. 92), and during the past year she experienced increasing cardiovascular problems, cataracts, arteriosclerosis, and other problems (R. 92-96). She was also on

> **a large and complex daily regimen of drugs (R. 97). Daily she took three kinds of barbiturates: Tuinal (R. 115–16), Fiornal (R. 113), and Fiornal with Codeine (R. 113–14). Additionally, she took greater-than-normal daily dosages of Triavil (R. 114–15), a specialized compound tranquilizer formulated and normally prescribed for mental depression (R. 148–49).**

For related information, see COUNTERARGUMENTS, HOW TO HANDLE.

(c) Choose the most appropriate term of address.

This choice is related to the choice of concrete or abstract nouns. In a brief, if you have a situation where your client is a sympathetic figure and the opposition is not, use names such as *Ms. Jones* or *Julia Easley*, for both parties. This will gently remind the reader of the real people involved here. If the facts are not sympathetic to your client and you are making an argument based more on the impersonal logic of the relevant law, then use generic terms, such as *Plaintiff* and *Defendant*. Use the same kind of term for both sides, however; using *Ms. Jones* for the defendant but then using *Plaintiff* would be too confusing and too obviously biased, even if it seemed appropriate. If you are addressing an agency in a persuasive letter, follow the same guidelines. But if you are persuading another lawyer or your client, use the term of address that you normally use, whether it is a first name or more formal title.

(d) Repeat key words for emphasis.

If you want to emphasize a word, repeat it. This is most often useful in the Argument of a brief.

> **The defendant abused the privileges offered him; he abused the procedures designed to protect him.**

When repeating a term, however, make sure that the idea represented by the term is indeed one you do want to emphasize. For example, repeating *clearly* will create a distraction, not effective emphasis.

Also remember that the effect of a repeated word grows exponentially, rather than linearly. That is, if you use a word twice, it is given perhaps four times the emphasis, not just two. So do not overdo it. This is a place where reading it aloud may be a disservice; you may hear yourself repeating a theme like the master orator Martin Luther King, Jr., did, but your reader, not hearing your impassioned pauses and intonations, may instead find it amusing or distracting. Let your eye and common sense guide you.

(e) Repeat sentence or phrase structures to underscore parallels.

This tool is particularly useful when analogizing cases (see COMPARISON) and is also useful and subtly dramatic in conclusions and sometimes in fact sections. Repetition of structure creates a sense of rhythm and anticipation. To some extent, it telegraphs to the reader what is coming, so that the reader gets a sense of completion when the expected information arrives.

> **At best, the City confused its argument by trying to do too much without a full explanation. At worst, the City contradicted itself by misinterpreting the law.**

But this expectation can turn to boredom, so again avoid overdoing it. See also REPETITION.

(f) Adjust sentence length.

Short sentences are emphatic. Therefore use them for points you want to emphasize, but do not use them for unimportant points. This tool is particularly useful in fact situations, where tools involving word choice are more limited.

> **Julia was uniformly described by all the witnesses who had personally known her as a strong-willed, positive, and independent woman. The plaintiff himself called her "independent and abrupt."**

It is also useful in Arguments.

> **The major purpose of the trial court's established procedures is to give the litigants a fair opportunity to address their claims and have them resolved by a court of law. These petitioners had eight years of opportunity. Therefore, their current procedural arguments . . . .**

Several short sentences in a row create a choppy, rather impatient or angry tone. Sometimes this can have a useful effect.

> **The major purpose of the trial court's established procedure is to give the litigants a fair opportunity to address their claims and have them resolved by a court of law. That purpose was met here. The litigants had eight years of opportunity. In this context, their arguments on appeal fail. Never, in those eight years, did they make one move to resolve these claims.**

Four sentences are as far as you should push the series. Any more and the court might sense an intemperate tirade. After a series of short sentences, return to sentences of normal length and make a scrupulously objective statement of your reasoning. See also SHORT SENTENCES.

(g) Insert information into a sentence with care.

If you want to use a point to set the stage for a punch line, put that point in an introductory phrase at the beginning of a sentence.

> **Despite the difficulty of this test, the gravity of the situation required that it be done.**

This technique becomes more dramatic when the introductory phrase is relatively long and the main clause is rather short.

> **Frightened by the approaching figure and seeing no means of escape, she fired.**

If you want to deemphasize a point, put it in an added phrase at the end of the sentence, like an afterthought.

> **The minority arrived at the same conclusion, although for different reasons.**

When you do this, make sure that the word at the end of the sentence is not one you want to deemphasize. For examples and more details on this technique, see SENTENCE STRUCTURE, subsection 6.

(h) Place key phrases at the beginning or end of a paragraph or a sentence.

In general, words at the beginning or end get more attention than those in the middle. In legal writing, things at the beginning have a slight edge because you are never sure the busy and often-interrupted legal reader will finish reading your document with care. While revising, scan your topic sentences to see if the first half-line of each paragraph includes the key terms of the paragraph. Avoid starting a paragraph with dates or case names unless you have a reason to emphasize that date or name.

> **Evidence of this concern showed up in the defendant's letter dated January 12, 2025, which stated . . . .**
>
> rather than
>
> On January 12, 2025, the defendant wrote a letter that showed evidence of this concern when it stated . . . .

For related information, see POSITIONS OF EMPHASIS.

(i) Use subtly emotional language, rather than overly emotional.

Emotional language should persuade, not lose, the reader. Therefore, choose words precisely to fit the persuasive approach you are taking. Emotional words are not just positive or negative; instead, each word falls somewhere on a continuum between extremely positive and extremely negative. For example, one person who decided to maintain a position on an issue could be described as *ever-faithful*, *steadfast*, *unwavering*, *unchanging*, *stubborn*, or *pigheaded*. In legal writing, choose words that fall closer to the center of the continuum to color your meanings and avoid the extremes. For example, if trying to show that someone was overmedicated and thus not capable of making a will, write the following.

Julia Easley was on a large and complex daily regimen of drugs, including . . . .

rather than

Julia Easley was drugged into a vegetative state daily.

Also avoid overly emotional language because it draws the reader's attention to the emotional level of the writing itself, rather than to the content of the persuasive argument. For example, many extremely emotional words, such as *blockhead, horrendous,* or *disaster*, can impair the writer's credibility in court, where another lawyer can point out the silliness of the overstatement.

Finally, avoid overly emotional language because it may be limited by the constraints of legal writing. For example, many words with emotional overtones, such as *derelict* or *nuisance*, are also terms of art that must be used with precision, whether or not the emotional overtone is appropriate.

(j) Play one persuasive technique against another.

As you are using these tools, you may find some contradictions; applying one principle means you violate another. Practice playing these techniques against each other to get just the effect you want.

(k) Avoid overdoing any technique.

Any of these persuasive techniques can be overdone. If you tend to overdo, use Marilyn Monroe's technique to solve the problem. This may be apocryphal, but it has been said that Marilyn tended to over accessorize. To compensate for this, she kept a full-length mirror in her entry. Before she left the house, she would walk away from the mirror and then turn quickly to look at her image. She would then take off the first accessory that caught her eye. Similarly, as you read over your last draft of a persuasive piece, take out the most obvious persuasive tools you have used. After all, it worked for Marilyn. Few would have called her overdressed.

WRITING PROCESS

The writing process is the entire creative, analytical, and critical experience that begins with an idea or assignment and ends with a finished document. The process as we see it incorporates five stages: PREWRITING, WRITING, REWRITING, REVISING, and POLISHING. You can save a great deal of time and become much more effective throughout the process by understanding each of these stages. Use the ideas in this entry to make writing more comfortable and efficient; your writing process is personal and should be comfortably fitted to your own temperament and work habits.

Your process must also be productive, building on your strengths while compensating for your weaknesses. Thus you may want to evaluate your process and adapt changes that improve it. You may find it useful to write your own process out as a checklist, so that you can focus on one step at a time, which can be more efficient and less stressful. The key to success in streamlining your writing process is breaking it into pieces and fixing one piece at a time. Over time, your techniques will work into a smooth process that is strictly yours. For help developing your checklists, see PREWRITING CHECKLIST, REWRITING CHECKLIST, REVISING CHECKLIST, and POLISHING CHECKLIST.

The following suggestions can help you make your writing process both more efficient and more effective.

1. Identify the point in the process with which you are most comfortable.

   For example, you might like research but hate revising, or you might feel comfortable correcting mechanics and citations but very uncomfortable in writing. You are probably fastest at that point where you feel most comfortable, so you can allocate less time for that step when you establish your schedule.

2. Identify where you are least comfortable.

   For example, you may dislike revising because you are not sure of grammatical structures and how to fix them, so you get bogged down in miscellaneous questions. Or you may dislike writing because you feel each sentence should be perfect before you go on to the next one.

3. Focus on the least comfortable task and break it into subtasks so you can concentrate on each subtask.

For example, if you dread writing the first draft, try to write without allowing yourself to delete ideas you think may be weak, reorganize sentences, check spelling, or revise awkward phrases. Trust yourself to edit the document for those concerns later. At this time, just get all your ideas written, as though you were writing an exam answer. Alternatively, if you dislike revising, try not to revise all of every sentence all at once. Instead, revise the whole text once just for one aspect of the revising process. For help identifying these aspects, see REVISING and REVISING CHECKLIST. These smaller, focused read-throughs can be done in between other tasks during the day. Additionally, by giving them your full concentration, you can complete them effectively in a minimal amount of time. In general, when you are uncomfortable with a writing task, consider whether you are trying to do too many things at once. Review the checklist for the relevant stage of the writing process and choose one smaller task to focus on. For additional help here, also see WRITING.

4. Consider using technology to assist in your thinking process.

You may consider using artificial intelligence (AI) at three points in the WRITING PROCESS. First, you might want to use AI in PREWRITING either to jump start your research or to discover potential approaches to your analysis. For help doing this, see PROMPTS, QUESTIONS PRESENTED, and RESEARCH STRATEGY GUIDE. Second, you may want to use AI in REVISING to help with specific edits, such as minimizing use of PASSIVE VOICE, increasing READABILITY, or achieving CONCISENESS. For help using AI at this stage, see REVISING CHECKLIST. Third, you may find AI useful in POLISHING to proofread or check for format consistency. For help here, see POLISHING CHECKLIST.

Using AI to generate an initial draft, however, may be less useful because it may be too generic. Confidentiality and privacy requirements may restrict your use of specific client information, so a draft may be too general to be useful. AI may also be too indiscriminate about legal content. For example, AI may not discern between MANDATORY AUTHORITY and PERSUASIVE AUTHORITY and may not focus on the analytical patterns most appropriate to your case. If you do use AI for a preliminary draft, be sure to review and revise it thoroughly to make it your own. See REWRITING CHECKLIST.

5. Incorporate into your process your deadlines and the constraints they represent.

Start with your deadline and work backwards toward the starting point, setting interim deadlines for each stage of the process. By allocating the most time for the place that is the least comfortable and the least time for the place that is the most comfortable, you can set a more realistic schedule that you will be more likely to meet. For an example of organizing to meet deadlines, see DEADLINES, MEETING THEM.

6. Reevaluate your writing process periodically.

   You will probably find yourself outgrowing your old process as your experience and skill increase.

7. Concentrate on breaking bad habits by conquering one bad habit at a time.

   For example, if you are weak on transitions, concentrate primarily on transitions in the revision process on one paper. Keep working on transitions on subsequent assignments until you feel comfortable with them; then move on to another bad habit. Perhaps you might concentrate next on better sentence structure.

8. Work chronologically.

   When you want to make changes in your writing process, work through your process chronologically, because improvement in the early stages of the process may change the later stages automatically. For a starting point, see PREWRITING, WRITING, REWRITING, REVISING, and POLISHING.

WRITING TO ATTORNEYS

When you correspond with other lawyers, you can enjoy to some extent the shorthand developed by the profession. This shorthand may include using legal terms without explanation or using common analytical forms without the added details that would be needed when corresponding with clients. Or you might dwell on analysis and interpretation more than description. You can often relax your correspondence style when writing to these readers because they share your profession and may be personal friends.

But be sure to make the communication context independent. Other lawyers are busy, too, and sometimes the shorthand may leave them guessing about the issues, law, or current thinking on this case. Also do not relax so much that you lose ACCURACY or lessen your professionalism. Especially watch for the pitfalls of becoming too relaxed in writing email or any electronic communications. For related information, see BAD NEWS, GIVING IT; BAD NEWS, SOFTENING IT; EXECUTIVE SUMMARY; GENDER IN WRITING; PROFESSIONAL LANGUAGE AND PRESENTATION; COMMUNICATIONS, TONE OF; SOCIAL MEDIA; and WRITING TO CLIENTS.

The subsections below outline how writing for legal readers differs from writing for nonlegal readers in word choice, tone, and level of detail.

1. Word choice.

You may use technical legal vocabulary and terms of art more frequently with legal readers, as a shorthand for expressing a point. But use a term only when you are sure the reader will understand it readily. For example, you might write the following sentence to another attorney in your firm.

> **Our client was probably a holder in due course because he took the check in good faith without any notice.**

In contrast, the following sentence, written for your client, would use fewer legal terms.

> **You are probably entitled to keep the check because you had no idea that Mr. Hobbs had forged it.**

2. TONE.

Tone conveys your relationship to the reader and the situation, apart from the literal content of the document. As that relationship varies, your tone will vary. For example, when writing an informational memo to a close colleague, you may use more personal phrases or more informal, direct language.

> **Jane, I'll be writing my first brief for Judge Chang next week. I know you have a lot of experience in her court—got any helpful hints about writing for her?**

Alternatively, you may use a more formal tone to a colleague you do not know.

> **Dear Mr. Morton:**
>
> **You and I will be representing the plaintiffs in Carolet v. McCartney. To coordinate our strategies, I would like to meet with all the plaintiffs' attorneys. I suggest that the meeting be during the second week in February. Please call my office this week to arrange a mutually convenient time.**

Maintain your professional image in all situations, even casual ones. Use your correspondence to establish your professional image and develop relationships with colleagues over time. Avoid intemperate or sarcastic communications, no matter how tempted you may be. Keep the long view; even if intemperate tirades are common in communications from others, they are not going to appear professional in the long run. In a world where all communications may appear in public someday, avoid writing anything you may regret later.

3. Level of detail.

Include as much detail as your reader needs to understand your point. Beyond that, adjust the level of detail to make your reader comfortable. Some attorneys prefer that all memos be kept as brief as possible, while others feel uneasy if not fully informed of the thought or research behind a point. If possible, ask the reader about preferences for including copies of cases, short summaries of legal conclusions, or the middle route of the standard memo. When beginning to write for a new employer, ask that employer for good examples you can review. The more you learn about your reader, the more effective, efficient, and comfortable writing will be for you. For related information, see AUDIENCE, READERS, SCOPE, TONE, and WORD CHOICE.

4. Confidentiality.

Before sending anything, doublecheck the confidentiality and privacy restrictions appropriate to the document and situation. Make sure the list of recipients includes only those appropriate for this communication. Also make sure the content does not reveal any proprietary information. For example, if your office has an in-house, secure artificial intelligence (AI) program, you may be able to use it within the office to research and communicate your analysis. But before you communicate with attorneys outside the office, make sure you have cleansed the document of any confidential information that should not reach their eyes or be discoverable. For more on this, see ARTIFICIAL INTELLIGENCE AND RESEARCH, ARTIFICIAL INTELLIGENCE AND WRITING, METADATA REMOVAL, and PROFESSIONAL LANGUAGE AND PRESENTATION, PROMPTS, and REPLY TO ALL.

For how-to information, see COMMUNICATIONS, CLOSINGS FOR; COMMUNICATIONS, ELECTRONIC; COMMUNICATIONS, INTERNATIONAL; COMMUNICATIONS, OPENINGS FOR; COMMUNICATIONS, PERSUASIVE; EMAIL; PROFESSIONAL LANGUAGE AND PRESENTATION; and TEXTING UNDER THE TABLE. See also OPINIONS, LEGAL.

WRITING TO CLIENTS

Writing to clients is so important that sometimes only the most experienced lawyers are allowed to do it. This importance, along with the frequent need to respond to correspondence quickly, means you need to approach this writing task both effectively and efficiently. You also need to decide what format to use. For help on this, see EMAIL OR MEMO?

This important endeavor is not a task to delegate to artificial intelligence. Instead, take on the task yourself by focusing on your PURPOSE, SCOPE, and READERS.

1. Identify the communication's primary PURPOSE.

   Whether this document is part of a series of short exchanges or is something more extensive, it usually has one of the following purposes:

   (a) answering or making requests,

   (b) delivering information,

   (c) delivering bad news, or

   (d) advising the reader.

   To focus on the purpose of your correspondence, you might first jot down in one sentence the main point. Be bluntly honest; this is for your private use, not for inclusion. For example, your point might be any of the following.

   Here is your revised will.

   You may need to change your method of keeping tax records.

   There is no way your lawsuit can succeed.

   Then decide which kind of correspondence this purpose requires. When you have identified the primary purpose, you can begin with the standard organization described in the subsection below, which you can then adapt as needed to fit your situation and any secondary purposes. This helps you determine what your message is and get started quickly organizing your content.

   Often the correspondence with a client will be a cover memo for a formal legal document, such as a will, contract, or a brief. For those and any such documents, refer to the relevant specific entry and begin the cover memo with the appropriate organizing format from those described below.

   (a) Answering or making requests.

   If the document is delivering requested information (as in the first example: *Here is your revised will.*), you may simply refer to the request and then respond.

   At our conference on January 23, you asked me to help you make several changes in your will. I have subsequently drafted a new will incorporating these changes and am including a copy of this draft with this letter.

   Take a moment to pay attention to tone. Sometimes a very blunt, concise opening may be off-putting.

Per your request, below please find . . . .

Elaborate or explain as needed in the second paragraph.

Please review this draft carefully. Specifically, consider the following questions:

(1) . . . ,

Then close politely in the last paragraph.

If you have any questions or wish to make any further changes in the will, do not hesitate to call. I will have the final will prepared and you may come to the office to execute it on February 22, as we have scheduled.

When making a routine request, one which the reader will not think twice about answering, determine whether the context of the request needs to be explained. If not, simply begin with a polite request.

To help us prepare your estate plan, please send me . . . .

If some context is needed, summarize that briefly with the request.

A few technical points need to be clarified to enable us to begin your lawsuit. Please provide answers to the following questions.

If there is any chance the reader will feel uncomfortable about fulfilling your request, or if the reader will hesitate at all, you may want to add reasoning as described in subsection (d).

(b) Delivering information.

In an FYI (For Your Information) message (as in *You may need to change your methods of keeping tax records.*), start with a statement of the point.

As your attorney, I want to notify you of some recent changes in the tax law that may require a change in your record-keeping practices.

If needed, include this opening in a brief description or explanation of why you are writing. In subsequent paragraphs, elaborate as needed.

Specifically, the new law requires you to keep a log of your use of the computer, so that you can document . . . . Additionally, the law requires . . . .

In the final paragraph, close politely.

Please feel free to call to set up an appointment if you have any questions about this or other tax matters.

(c) Delivering bad news.

If the correspondence is delivering bad news (as in *There is no way your lawsuit can succeed.*), try organizing it in three parts that do the following: (1) set the tone, (2) deliver the bad news, and (3) reestablish the tone.

- Set the tone.

In the first paragraph, establish the tone you want to take with the reader. For example, you will likely want to communicate that you have carefully considered what the client wanted.

I have reviewed your potential claim and certainly understand why you would want to bring a suit to rectify this unjust situation.

You may choose to be warm and personal.

Thank you for inviting me to speak at your organization's annual meeting. Regrettably, ...

Rarely, you may need to be more distant, without appearing unfeeling.

As you requested, I have researched the potential rationales you might use to request a reduction in your child support payments in light of current Maryland laws.

If answering a request, you may want to restate the request in more detail, so that the reader knows you paid attention to the request before saying no. This added explanation may seem unneeded, but it can be helpful to reassure the client that the request was taken seriously. It can also help clarify the request, in case there is any chance of misunderstanding about the subject.

In your email dated March 3, 2025, you requested a restructuring of your payment schedule for the land contract on . . . . Your reasons were that . . . .

- Deliver the bad news.

At the beginning of the second paragraph, state the bad news plainly so that the reader cannot misinterpret what you are saying. Follow this statement with your reasons, if appropriate. This paragraph will be unemotional and matter of fact, no matter what the tone of the other paragraphs. This section may also extend for several paragraphs if needed.

> **I have reviewed your potential claim and certainly understand why you would want to bring a suit to rectify this unjust situation. The loss of. . . .**
>
> **Under local zoning laws and state law regarding city removal of trees, the city was within its legal rights when removing the tree from the easement at the rear of your property. As a result, a lawsuit against the city would not prevail. . . .**

- Reestablish the tone.

  In the final paragraph, reestablish your tone while you state closing technicalities. For example, you may suggest that the reader call if questions remain.

> **If you have any questions concerning this situation, please feel free to call me at (500) 555–1234. And if there is any other legal matter that we can help you with, ...**

If you are being kind, you may wish the reader some sort of relevant good fortune.

> **The theme for your organization's annual meeting is interesting to me and particularly relevant now. I regret being unable to participate.**

For related information, see BAD NEWS, SOFTENING IT.

(d) Advising the client.

Advising a client can take many forms and will usually require more thought and organizing effort than the previous purposes. Generally, your professional responsibility will require you to focus on informing your client, even though it may feel like persuasion at times. As you are focusing on the client's best interest, you may want to be sure you present the information in a way that helps that client make the best decision. Informing the client, however, must include explaining all sides of the decision so that the client can see the relative strength of each possible decision and perhaps disagree with you. Focusing on your client's best interests may require you to consider factors outside the legal situation itself. For example, you may find it appropriate to include other nonlegal concerns, such as financial outlay or exposure to publicity or loss of personal time to the legal effort. Thus focus on fully and clearly informing your client, including not just the reasons you see as favoring a particular decision, but also those reasons that may be important to the client and the possible outcomes.

In general, use an unemotional, polite tone. you will usually want to present yourself as a logical, reasonable person who, is making a coherent and logical argument. For a discussion of related points, see WRITING, PERSUASIVE.

2. Determine the SCOPE of the correspondence.

When you work with a client, you may often have multiple subjects or purposes, and it can be tempting to combine these into one email. Before you do that, however, consider whether combining multiple topics may cause problems. For example, one topic may be appropriate to forward to a broader audience, while another may need to remain private and thus trigger confidentiality or discovery issues. One topic may need immediate attention, while others may be simply for-your-information matters. Additionally, multiple varying responses to multiple concerns can cause you to lose control of the communication about each separate legal matter. Finally, record-keeping issues may be complicated if multiple legal problems are included in one email.

Because of these concerns, limit the scope of your correspondence as much as you reasonably can to focus on specific issues and purposes, thus avoiding any distracting information that may complicate the conversation. If the content of your correspondence can be stated simply and does not require a complex format, then you may be able to include it in the body of an email. However, if the format is complex and essential to the document's integrity and you are sending the correspondence via email, include the document as an attachment in a protected file.

If you need to include multiple purposes, make that fact clear by including the other content in a separate paragraph or section and indicate that this is another point in the opening of the sentence, perhaps by simply adding an introductory phrase that conveys the change in topic, such as *Regarding the second issue of . . .* or adding *Additionally.*

3. Consider your reader's potential responses.

Your reader's response to all correspondence, regardless of its purpose, is affected by your choices regarding two components: (a) tone of the correspondence, and (b) openings and closings.

(a) Use the appropriate TONE.

Tone is especially important in correspondence. As the tone of your voice creates an impression in the mind of the listener, so the tone of your email creates an impression in the mind of the reader. Thus your tone in various correspondence may range from friendly to businesslike. A chatty tone will seem slightly unprofessional in all but purely personal correspondence. A tirade will also seem unprofessional, even if the client sympathizes with your position.

Additionally, email crafted too quickly can create an abrupt tone and, over time, a series of such emails can impair your credibility. Within these limits, however, you must make your own choices, based on what is appropriate to the situation and what suits your personal communication style.

When considering tone, first consider the client, who is your primary reader. Consider all the possible responses your reader might have to the wording of the text. For example, consider the client's familiarity with the legal terms and likely emotional responses to the content. This focus should help you avoid the Scylla and Charybdis of either condescending by explaining more than needed or alienating by using language that is bureaucratic or beyond the client's understanding.

Another concern may be what pronoun to use with clients who do not identify as *he* or *she*. That can usually be settled by using the term the client prefers. While using *they* may cause ambiguity in some legal documents, it is not likely to do so in correspondence addressed specifically to the client. For more on gender terms, see GENDER IN WRITING.

Then consider your potential broader AUDIENCE and adjust the content as needed. Is this correspondence discoverable? Is it likely to be forwarded or reviewed by other attorneys? For example, you may need to warn the client to refrain from forwarding this document. For more on this concern, see EMAIL and REPLY TO ALL. Or you may need to use technical legal terms with which the client may not be familiar. If so, you can include appropriate definitions or explanations. For help here, see UNOBTRUSIVE DEFINITIONS.

Using tone effectively in correspondence involves three tasks:

- choosing the appropriate tone,
- creating that tone through word choice and sentence structure, and
- keeping the tone consistent.

By focusing on each of these tasks separately, you can manage tone more efficiently.

- Choosing the appropriate tone.

You may choose to be polite and businesslike or, if appropriate, you may choose a friendly tone.

> **Regarding your request for an estimate of how much it would cost to revise your will, I am including . . . .**
>
> or
>
> **I would be happy to update your will for you if you wish; the cost would be determined by the amount of . . . .**

- Creating the appropriate tone through word choice and sentence structure.

Choosing your words carefully is one effective way to establish your tone. For example, if you want to create an informal and friendly tone, use less formal words, such as *talk* and *meeting.* If you want to create a more formal tone, use more formal words, such as *confer* and *discussion.* For more on this, see FORMALITY, LEVEL OF.

Avoid, however, using formal words to the point that your email becomes hard to read or stuffy. For more on this, see LEGALESE.

> **Regarding this question, I have conferred with Ms. Jamison's attorney, who explained that . . . .**
>
> rather than
>
> In pursuit of this query, I have held consultations with counsel for Ms. Jamison, who elucidated the point by stating that . . . .

Another way to avoid a stuffy tone is to avoid inappropriately using the third person, such as *this attorney,* when the first person, *I,* is accurate. In general, correspondence is addressed from one person to another, and so the use of *I* is appropriate, or *we* if you are speaking officially for a group of people, such as a whole law office. See PERSON: FIRST, SECOND OR THIRD?

You may also establish your tone by using appropriate sentence structure. For example, if you want to create a friendly, informal tone, use longer sentences rather than terse ones.

> **Thank you for your kind invitation to speak at your annual banquet honoring outstanding alumni from the law school.**
>
> rather than
>
> Thank you for the invitation to speak at the law school alumni banquet.

Short sentences, while effective for emphasis, can create a terse, impatient tone if used extensively in correspondence.

- Keeping the tone consistent.

Inconsistent tone occurs most often when a letter or email includes words that are noticeably more formal or informal than the rest. So avoid using a formal phrase, such as *please be advised that,* in an otherwise informal email. Similarly, avoid using a colloquialism, such as *ripped off,* in an otherwise businesslike correspondence. For more on this point, see PROFESSIONAL LANGUAGE AND PRESENTATION.

Uneven tone also may occur when sentence structure changes markedly. For example, a reader might be taken aback by a series of three SHORT SENTENCES near the end of an otherwise friendly letter. Similarly, a reader might be put off by a long, complex sentence in an otherwise informal email. Therefore check your sentence structure for consistent tone.

For more help in choosing the appropriate tone, see the following more specific entries: REQUESTS FOR PAYMENT or TOUGH, SOUNDING THAT WAY. For related information, see WORD CHOICE and SENTENCE STRUCTURE.

(b) Choose the appropriate opening and closing.

- Including or omitting SALUTATIONS.

In general letter and email writing, include a salutation. Some writers omit the salutation, substituting instead a subject line, and this is not technically wrong. Omitting the salutation, however, can make the correspondence seem abrupt and impersonal, which is not usually the tone you want when writing to a client. In email, you may want to use the salutation to create a friendlier and more courteous opening, although it is technically redundant because email is presented in a memo format.

- Writing gender-free openings.

  Use the title your client prefers. If your client is nonbinary and has not communicated preferred titles, you may be able to substitute the name. For more on this, see GENDER IN WRITING.

  Dear D.A. Young:

  or

  Dear Terry Holmes,

- Choosing commas or colons for salutations.

  Using colons in business writing is more formal than using commas. Colons are often used after general salutations, such as *To Whom It May Concern*. Depending on what TONE you want to create, be aware that this punctuation contributes to the overall effect.

- Choosing an appropriate closing.

  Choose the standard closing that suits your writing STYLE and the tone of your correspondence. If the tone of your letter or email is businesslike and yet friendly, use *Sincerely* or *Sincerely yours*. If your tone is more formal, use *Yours truly* or *Very truly yours*. Use these or other comfortable closings in email to create a courteous ending. Do not worry about seeming insincere; these closings are not taken literally.

4. Consider your professional responsibilities.

Before you send it, remember to check for privacy, confidentiality, discoverability, and proprietary concerns. Also remove any technical data you do not want others to see. For help here, see METADATA REMOVAL and REPLY TO ALL.

For specific situations, see COMMUNICATIONS, ELECTRONIC; COMMUNICATIONS, INTERNATIONAL; COMMUNICATIONS, PERSUASIVE; EMAIL; OPINIONS, LEGAL; SOCIAL MEDIA; TEXTING UNDER THE TABLE; and WRITING TO ATTORNEYS. For how-to information, see COMMUNICATIONS, TONE OF; EXECUTIVE SUMMARY; and PROFESSIONAL LANGUAGE AND PRESENTATION.

YET

Yet, a conjunction, can be used in legal writing to indicate *nevertheless* or *despite this.* Like *but, yet* can be an effective transition to show contrast and opposing ideas.

Plaintiff still claims my client is guilty, yet she has failed to meet her burden to prove that guilt.

and

Most commentators rely on this reasoning. Yet none has provided adequate authority on which to base that reasoning.

For related information, see TRANSITIONS.

YOU

Use the second person, *you,* to address the audience directly, when appropriate. For example, you may use *you* in correspondence when you want to sound as though you are talking to a person face to face.

You asked that I write to you about the legal consequences of your automobile accident.

You may also use *you* in consumer contracts or other situations when you need to tell someone clearly what that person can or cannot do.

If you choose to change attorneys, you must notify . . . .

Do not, however, use *you* in BRIEFS to the court. In those situations, you are focusing on the argument itself, rather than on a one-to-one conversation.

Equity requires consideration of this issue.

rather than

You must consider this issue.

ZWEURGET

Zweurget (pronounced somewhat like *tsvoirgit*) is a rather esoteric noun that expresses the confidence, accomplishment, and giddy exuberance one feels upon completion of any arduous, lengthy, and complex task. Thus it readily describes a writer's feeling at the end of any major writing project.

The authors basked in the *zweurget* they felt when they finished the manuscript.

While it aptly explains the feeling, *zweurget* is an unfamiliar term, and thus should be avoided in legal writing. You may, however, want to use it with your friends to let them know how you feel when you finish a project.

Alphabetical Index of Entries

A

ABBREVIATING DATES, NAMES, STATES, AND TITLES 1
ABBREVIATIONS IN TEXT 4
ABHORRENCE OF OR *ABHORRENCE FOR*? 5
ABOVE 5
ABSTRACT NOUNS 5
ACCURACY 5
ACTIVE VERBS (See ACTIVE VOICE.) 8
ACTIVE VOICE 8
ACTUALLY 10
AD HOC 11
ADJECTIVES 11
ADJECTIVES AFTER A LINKING VERB 12
ADJUSTING TO A NEW WRITING SITUATION 13
A.D. OR *C.E.*? 14
ADVERBS 14
AFFECT OR *EFFECT*? 15
AFORESAID 15
AFRICAN AMERICAN OR *AFRICAN-AMERICAN*? 15
AGES 15
AGREEMENT, SUBJECTS AND VERBS 16
AGREEMENTS, WRITTEN (See CONTRACTS.) 16
AGREE TO OR *AGREE WITH*? 16
ALL AROUND OR *ALL-ROUND*? 17
ALLITERATION 17
ALL READY OR *ALREADY*? 18
ALL RIGHT OR *ALRIGHT*? 18
ALL, SINGULAR OR PLURAL? 18
ALL TOGETHER OR *ALTOGETHER*? 18
ALTERNATIVE 18
ALTHOUGH OR *THOUGH*? 18
ALTOGETHER OR *ALL TOGETHER*? (See *ALL TOGETHER* OR *ALTOGETHER*?) 19
ALWD GUIDE TO LEGAL CITATION 19
A.M. 19
AMBIGUITY, WAYS TO AVOID 20
AMENDMENT CAPITALIZED? 22
AMICUS BRIEFS (See BRIEFS, AMICUS.) 23
AMONG OR *BETWEEN*? 23

ANALOGICAL REASONING, PRESENTING IT (See REASONING, ANALOGICAL; REASONING, INDUCTIVE; and REASONING, PRESENTING IT.) 23
ANALOGOUS CASES 23
ANALYSIS (See LEGAL ANALYSIS and REASONING, PRESENTING IT.) 24
AND 24
AND/OR 24
ANIMAL—*HE*, *SHE*, OR *IT*? 25
ANSWERS TO COMPLAINTS 25
ANTECEDENTS 27
ANTE- OR *ANTI-*? 27
ANTONYMS 27
ANYBODY, SINGULAR OR PLURAL? 28
ANYONE, SINGULAR OR PLURAL? 28
A OR *AN*? 28
APOSTROPHES 28
APPEAL 31
APPELLATE BRIEFS (See BRIEFS, APPELLATE.) 31
APPENDIX 31
APPLICATION 32
APPOSITIVE 33
ARGUING IN THE ALTERNATIVE 33
ARGUMENT HEADINGS (See POINT HEADINGS.) 34
ARGUMENT SECTION 34
ARTICLES, GRAMMAR 39
ARTICLES, PUBLISHED (See SCHOLARLY WRITING, SCHOLARLY WRITING PROCESS, and SCHOLARLY WRITING PROCESS CHECKLIST.) 39
ARTIFICIAL INTELLIGENCE AND RESEARCH 39
ARTIFICIAL INTELLIGENCE AND WRITING 41
AS 45
AS A MATTER OF FACT 45
AS IF OR *AS THOUGH*? 45
AS OR *LIKE*? 45
AS PER 45
ASSONANCE 46
ASSURE, *ENSURE*, OR *INSURE*? 46
ASTERISKS 47
AS THOUGH OR *AS IF*? 47
AS TO 47
AT THE TIME THAT 47
AT THIS POINT IN TIME 47
ATTORNEY OR *LAWYER*? 48
AUDIENCE 48

AUDIENCE OR *READER*? ... 50
AUXILIARY VERB (See VERBS, AUXILIARY.) ... 50

B

BACKGROUND FACTS ... 50
BAD NEWS, GIVING IT ... 51
BAD NEWS, SOFTENING IT ... 54
BAD OR *BADLY*? ... 56
BAR GRAPHS (See GRAPHICS, WHICH FORMS TO USE, subsection 2.) ... 56
BASED ON ... 56
BASICALLY ... 57
B.C. OR *B.C.E.*? ... 57
BECAUSE OR *SINCE*? ... 57
BEGINNING ... 58
BEING THAT ... 58
BENCH MEMOS ... 58
BENDING THE RULES ... 61
BEST OR *BETTER*? ... 61
BETWEEN OR *AMONG*? (See *AMONG* OR *BETWEEN*?) ... 62
BETWEEN YOU AND ME OR *BETWEEN YOU AND I*? ... 62
BILLS, WRITING THEM (See LEGISLATION or REQUESTS FOR PAYMENT.) ... 62
BLACK ... 62
BLUEBOOK ... 62
BOLDFACE TYPE ... 62
BOTH ... 63
BOTH . . . AND ... 63
BRACKETS ... 63
BREAKING THE RULES (See BENDING THE RULES.) ... 64
BRIEF ANSWERS ... 64
BRIEFS ... 65
BRIEFS, AMICUS ... 68
BRIEFS, APPELLATE ... 69
BRIEFS, BENCH (See BENCH MEMOS.) ... 72
BRIEFS, CASE (See CASE BRIEFS.) ... 72
BRIEFS, PRETRIAL ... 72
BRIEFS, REPLY ... 72
BRIEFS, TRIAL ... 73
BULLET POINTS ... 74
BUSINESS EMAIL OR LETTERS (See COMMUNICATIONS.) ... 75
BUT ... 75

C

CAN 75
CAN HARDLY OR *CAN'T HARDLY*? 76
CANNOT OR *CAN NOT*? 76
CANONS OF CONSTRUCTION 76
CAN OR *COULD*? (See VERBS, AUXILIARY, subsections 2 and 4.) 76
CAN OR *MAY*? 76
CAPITALIZATION 77
CAPTIONS 79
CASE 81
CASE BRIEFS 81
CASE NAMES, UNDERLINE OR ITALICIZE? 84
CASUAL LANGUAGE (See COLLOQUIALISM.) 85
C.E. OR *A.D.*? (See *A.D.* OR *C.E.*?) 85
CERTAIN OR *CERTAINLY*? 85
CHARTS 85
CHOICES IN LEGAL WRITING 86
CHRONOLOGICAL ORGANIZATION (See ORGANIZATION, CHRONOLOGICAL.) 86
CIRCUMLOCUTION (See CONCISENESS, subsection 2.) 86
CITATIONS 86
CITATIONS, BASIC FORMATS 88
CITATIONS, ELECTRONIC 89
CITATIONS, PARALLEL 90
CITATIONS, PINPOINT 91
CITATIONS, SIGNALS 91
CITATIONS, STRING 92
CITATIONS, VARYING FORMATS 93
CLARITY 93
CLAUSES 94
CLEANSING ELECTRONIC DOCUMENTS (See METADATA REMOVAL.) 95
CLEARLY 95
CLEAR WRITING (See CLARITY and READABILITY.) 95
CLICHÉ 95
CLIENT CORRESPONDENCE (See WRITING TO CLIENTS.) 96
CLOSINGS FOR LETTERS AND EMAIL (See COMMUNICATIONS, CLOSINGS FOR.) 96
COHERENCE 96
COLLABORATION 96
COLLECTIVE NOUNS 100
COLLOQUIALISM 100
COLONS 101
COMBINING WORDS 102

COMMA BEFORE *AND*? (See COMMA, OXFORD; and LISTS, STRUCTURE OF, subsection 3.) 103
COMMA, OXFORD 103
COMMAS 104
COMMA SPLICE 109
COMMON NOUN (See NOUNS.) 109
COMMON SENSE 109
COMMUNICATIONS, CLOSINGS FOR 110
COMMUNICATIONS, ELECTRONIC 111
COMMUNICATIONS, EMAIL (See EMAIL and EMAIL OR MEMO?) 112
COMMUNICATIONS, INTERNATIONAL 112
COMMUNICATIONS, OPENINGS FOR 114
COMMUNICATIONS, PERSUASIVE 115
COMMUNICATIONS, REAL-TIME 118
COMMUNICATIONS, TO ATTORNEYS (See WRITING TO ATTORNEYS.) 119
COMMUNICATIONS, TO CLIENTS (See WRITING TO CLIENTS.) 119
COMMUNICATIONS, TONE OF 119
COMPARE AND CONTRAST 122
COMPARE TO OR *COMPARE WITH*? 122
COMPARISON 122
COMPLAINTS 124
COMPLETELY 126
COMPLEMENT OR *COMPLIMENT*? 126
COMPLEX SENTENCES 126
COMPOUND SENTENCES 127
COMPOUND WORDS, WHEN TO HYPHENATE (See HYPHENS.) 127
CONCISENESS 127
CONCLUSIONS 130
CONCLUSORY 132
CONCRETE NOUNS (See ABSTRACT NOUNS.) 132
CONDITIONS, STATING THEM 132
CONFORM TO, *CONFORM WITH*, OR *CONFORM IN*? 133
CONJUNCTIONS 133
CONNECTING WORDS (See TRANSITIONS.) 135
CONNECTIONS, MAKING THEM 135
CONNECTORS (See CONNECTIONS, MAKING THEM; and TRANSITIONS.) 136
CONNOTATION 136
CONTACT 136
CONTEND 137
CONTEXT, CLARIFYING 137
CONTEXT-INDEPENDENT WRITING 138
CONTINUAL OR *CONTINUOUS*? 139
CONTRACTIONS 139

CONTRACTS 140
CONTRAST 142
CORPORATE DOCUMENTS 142
CORPORATIONS, *THEY* OR *IT*? 144
CORRELATING CONJUNCTIONS (See CONJUNCTIONS and READABILITY, subsection 7.) 144
CORRESPONDENCE See COMMUNICATIONS, CLOSINGS FOR or COMMUNICATIONS, OPENINGS FOR.) 144
CORRESPOND TO OR *CORRESPOND WITH*? 144
COULD 144
COULD CARE LESS OR *COULDN'T CARE LESS*? 144
COULD OR *CAN*? 145
COUNSEL 145
COUNSELING CLIENTS 145
COUNTERARGUMENTS, HOW TO HANDLE 146
COURTS, HOW TO ADDRESS (See JUDGES, HOW TO ADDRESS.) 147
COURTS, *THEY* OR *IT*? 147
CRAC 147
CREDIBILITY 148
CUTTING CORNERS 149
CYBERSECURITY 149

D

DANGLING MODIFIERS (See MODIFIERS, DANGLING.) 149
DASHES 149
DATA 151
DATES, ABBREVIATIONS OF (See ABBREVIATING DATES, NAMES, STATES, AND TITLES.) 151
DEADLINES, MEETING THEM 151
DEEM 156
DEFINITELY 156
DEFINITIONS, WHEN AND HOW TO INCLUDE 156
DEGREES AFTER NAMES (See ABBREVIATING DATES, NAMES, STATES, AND TITLES.) 156
DEMAND FOR PAYMENT (See REQUESTS FOR PAYMENT.) 156
DEPENDENT CLAUSES 157
DESIGN 157
DESPERATION (See HELP.) 159
DICTA 159
DICTATION 159
DICTION 160
DIFFERENT FROM OR *DIFFERENT THAN*? 161
DIGRESSION 161
DIRECTING OTHERS' WORK (See EDITING; INSTRUCTIONS, GIVING THEM; and MANAGING WRITERS.) 162

DIRECTIONS, GIVING THEM (See EDITING; INSTRUCTIONS, GIVING THEM; and MANAGING WRITERS.) 162
DIRECT OBJECTS (See SENTENCE, PARTS OF, subsection 4.) 162
DISCUSSION SECTION 162
DISINFORMATION 164
DISINTERESTED OR *UNINTERESTED*? 164
DO 164
DOCUMENT CHECKLIST 164
DOVETAILING (See CONNECTIONS, MAKING THEM.) 167
DRAFTING 167
DRAFTS 167
DUE TO 167
DUNNING LETTERS (See REQUESTS FOR PAYMENT.) 168
DURING THE TIME THAT 168

E

EACH 168
EDITING 168
EDITING QUOTATIONS 172
EFFECT OR *AFFECT*? 173
E.G. (See SIGNALS.) 173
ELECTRONIC ETIQUETTE 173
ELECTRONIC FILINGS 173
ELECTRONIC MESSAGING 174
ELECTRONIC RESEARCH (See RESEARCH STRATEGY GUIDE.) 175
ELEGANT VARIATION 175
ELLIPSES 175
EM OR EN DASH? (See HYPHENS and DASHES.) 176
EMAIL 176
EMAIL, HOW TO MANAGE 180
EMAIL OR MEMO? 181
EMINENT OR *IMMINENT*? 182
EMOJIS 182
EMOTIONAL FACTS 183
EMOTIONAL LANGUAGE 183
EMPHASIS 184
EMPHASIS ADDED (See QUOTATIONS, HOW TO PUNCTUATE, subsection 6.) 186
END RESULT 187
ENGLISH AS A SECOND LANGUAGE 187
ENGLISH IN INTERNATIONAL SITUATIONS (See COMMUNICATIONS, INTERNATIONAL; and ENGLISH AS A SECOND LANGUAGE.) 190
ENSURE, INSURE, OR *ASSURE*? (See *ASSURE, ENSURE,* OR *INSURE*? 190

ENUMERATION 190
EQUITY 190
ETC. 190
EVERYBODY 190
EVERYONE 191
EVIDENCE 191
EX- 191
EXACTNESS (See WORD CHOICE.) 191
EXCLAMATION 191
EXECUTIVE SUMMARY 192
EXCLAMATION POINTS 192
EXPLANATIONS, WHEN AND HOW MUCH? 192
EXPLANATORY PHRASES 193
EXPOSITORY WRITING 193
EXTENDED QUOTATIONS 195

F

FACT OF THE MATTER, THE 196
FACTS 196
FACT SHEETS 197
FACT THAT, THE 197
FALLACIES (See LOGICAL FALLACIES.) 197
FARTHER OR *FURTHER*? 197
FAXING 198
FEEL 198
FEWER OR *LESS*? 198
FIGURATIVE MEANING 199
FIND 199
FIND, HOLD, OR *REASON*? 199
FLOWERY LANGUAGE 200
FOCUS 200
FONT CHOICES 201
FONT SIZE 202
FOOTNOTES 202
FOR 203
FOR ALL INTENTS AND PURPOSES 203
FORCEFUL WRITING (See EMPHASIS and POSITIONS OF EMPHASIS.) 203
FOREGO OR *FORGO*? 204
FORMALISM 204
FORMALITY, LEVEL OF 204
FORMAT 206
FORMS 206
FORM CONTRACTS 207
FORMER 208

FOR THE PERIOD OF 208
FURTHER OR *FARTHER*? (See *FARTHER* OR *FURTHER*? 208
FUTURE PERFECT TENSE (See VERBS, TENSES, subsection 9.) 208
FUTURE PROGRESSIVE TENSE (See VERBS, TENSES, subsection 8.) 208
FUTURE TENSES (See VERBS, TENSES, subsections 7–9.) 208

G

GENDER IN WRITING 208
GENERAL CORRESPONDENCE LETTERS AND EMAIL (See COMMUNICATIONS.) 211
GENERALLY 211
GERUNDS 211
GETTING ORGANIZED 212
GETTING STARTED 212
GHOST WRITING 214
GIVEN THAT (See BEING THAT.) 217
GLOBAL ENGLISH (See COMMUNICATIONS, INTERNATIONAL.) 217
GOOD OR *WELL*? 217
GRACE UNDER FIRE 217
GRAMMAR 218
GRAPHICS AND SYMBOLS IN EMAIL (See SYMBOLS IN EMAIL.) 218
GRAPHICS, HOW TO USE 218
GRAPHICS, WHEN TO USE 222
GRAPHICS, WHICH FORM TO USE 223

H

HABITS, WRITING 227
HALLUCINATIONS 228
HANGED OR *HUNG*? 229
HARDLY 229
HEADINGS 229
HEADNOTES 230
HELP 230
HELPING VERBS (See VERBS, AUXILIARY; and VERBS, TENSES.) 230
HE OR SHE? 230
HEREBY 231
HE/SHE, WHEN TO USE 231
HOLD 231
HOLDING 231
HOLDING OR *RULE*? 232
HOMONYMS 233
HOPEFULLY 233
HOWEVER 233
HUMOR 235

HUNG OR *HANGED*? (See *HANGED* OR *HUNG*? 235
HYPERBOLE 235
HYPHENS 235

I

I 238
IDIOM 238
I.E. 239
IF 239
IF AND WHEN 239
IF OR *WHEN*? 240
IMAGERY 240
IMMINENT OR *EMINENT*? (See *EMINENT* OR *IMMINENT*?) 241
IMPACT 241
IMPERATIVE MOOD (See VERBS, MOODS, subsection 3.) 241
IMPLY OR *INFER*? 241
IN ADVANCE OF 241
INCLUDING, BUT NOT LIMITED TO 242
INDENTED QUOTATIONS OR QUOTATION MARKS? 242
INDENTING (See QUOTATIONS, HOW TO PUNCTUATE.) 242
INDEPENDENCE IN LEGAL WRITING 242
INDEPENDENT CLAUSE (See CLAUSES or SENTENCE, PARTS OF, subsection 8.) 243
INDICATIVE MOOD (See VERBS, MOODS, subsection 1.) 243
INDIRECT OBJECTS (See SENTENCE, PARTS OF, subsection 5.) 243
INFER OR *IMPLY*? (See *IMPLY* OR *INFER*? 243
INFINITIVE VERBS (See VERBS, TENSES, subsection 10.) 243
INFORMAL LANGUAGE (See COLLOQUIALISM.) 243
INFORMATIVE ARTICLES 243
-ING WORDS (See GERUNDS.) 245
IN, INTO, OR *IN TO*? 245
INITIALS 245
IN ORDER TO OR *TO*? 246
IN QUESTION 246
INSERTED PHRASES (See INTRUSIVE PHRASES.) 246
INSTANT MESSAGING (See ELECTRONIC MESSAGING and SOCIAL MEDIA.) 246
INSTRUCTIONS TO THE JURY (See JURY INSTRUCTIONS.) 246
INSTRUCTIONS, WRITING THEM 246
INSURE OR *ENSURE*? (See *ASSURE, ENSURE*, OR *INSURE*?) 249
INTERJECTIONS 249
IN TERMS OF 249
INTERVIEWING CLIENTS 249
INTERNATIONAL LEGAL WRITING (See COMMUNICATIONS, INTERNATIONAL.) 250

INTRODUCTIONS 250
INTRUSIVE PHRASES 253
INVERTED ORDER (See SENTENCE STRUCTURE, subsection 4.) 254
IRAC 254
IRREGARDLESS OR *REGARDLESS*? 254
ISSUES 255
IT 259
ITALICS 259
IT IS SAID THAT, IT WOULD SEEM THAT, IT MIGHT BE SAID THAT 261
IT IS . . . THAT 261
IT OR *THEY*? 261
ITS OR *IT'S*? 261

J

JARGON 262
J.D. OR *JD*? (See ABBREVIATING DATES, NAMES, STATES, AND TITLES, section 1; and JUDGES, HOW TO ADDRESS.) 262
JUDGES, HOW TO ADDRESS 262
JUDGMENT 262
JUDICIAL OPINIONS (See OPINIONS, JUDICIAL; and OPINIONS, READING THEM.) 262
JUDICIAL OR *JUDICIOUS*? 263
JUMP CITATIONS (See CITATIONS, PINPOINT.) 263
JURISDICTION 263
JURY INSTRUCTIONS 264
JURY, PLURAL OR SINGULAR? 267

K

KEYCITE (See UPDATING THE LAW.) 267
KEY TERMS 267

L

LARGE-SCALE ORGANIZATION (See ORGANIZATION, LARGE-SCALE.) 268
LATIN PHRASES 268
LATTER (See FORMER.) 268
LAW REVIEW ARTICLES (See SCHOLARLY WRITING, SCHOLARLY WRITING PROCESS, and SCHOLARLY WRITING PROCESS CHECKLIST.) 268
LAWYER OR *ATTORNEY*? (See *ATTORNEY* OR *LAWYER*? 268
LAY OR *LIE*? 269
LEAD OR *LED*? 269
LEGAL ANALYSIS 269
LEGALESE 275

LEGALLY SIGNIFICANT FACTS 276
LEGAL OPINIONS (See OPINIONS, LEGAL.) 277
LEGAL WRITING CHECKLIST (See DOCUMENT CHECKLIST or PRINCIPLES OF GOOD LEGAL WRITING.) 277
LEGISLATION 277
LENGTHY QUOTATIONS (See EXTENDED QUOTATIONS.) 279
LESS OR *FEWER*? (See *FEWER* OR *LESS*?) 279
LETTERS 279
LIE OR *LAY*? (See *LAY* OR *LIE*?) 280
LIKE OR *AS*? (See *AS* OR *LIKE*?) 280
LIMITS OF PROOFREADING (See PROOFREADING and WORDS SPELLCHECKERS MAY NOT CATCH.) 280
LINKING VERBS (See VERBS, LINKING.) 280
LINK ROT 280
LISTS, STRUCTURE OF 281
LISTS, WHEN TO USE 286
LITERAL LANGUAGE 287
LITERALLY 287
LITERAL MEANING 288
LOGICAL FALLACIES 288
LOGICAL LINKS 288
LONG QUOTATIONS (See EXTENDED QUOTATIONS.) 288
LUCIDITY (See ACCURACY and READABILITY.) 288
-LY OR NOT? 289

M

MAIN SENTENCES (See TOPIC SENTENCES.) 289
MANAGING WRITERS 289
MANDATORY AUTHORITY 292
MATHEMATICAL SYMBOLS 293
MATTER OF FACT, AS A (See *AS A MATTER OF FACT.*) 294
MAY 294
MAY OR *CAN*? (See *CAN* OR *MAY*?) 294
MAY OR *MIGHT*? 294
MEANING OF WORDS 294
MEMORANDUM OF POINTS AND AUTHORITIES 295
MEMOS 295
MERELY 301
METADATA REMOVAL 301
MIGHT 302
MIGHT OR *MAY*? (See *MAY* OR *MIGHT*?) 303
MISINFORMATION 303
MISSPELLINGS, HOW TO AVOID 303
MODELS (See FORMS.) 304
MODIFIERS 304

MODIFIERS, DANGLING 305
MODIFIERS, MISPLACED 305
MODIFIERS, SQUINTING 306
MOODS (See VERBS, MOODS.) 306
MOST IMPORTANTLY 306
MOTIONS 306
MS., *MRS.*, OR *MISS*? 307
MULTI-SENTENCE ISSUES 307
MULTI-TASKING 308
MUST 308
MUST OR *SHOULD*? 309

N

NAMES 309
NAMES, ABBREVIATIONS OF (See ABBREVIATING DATES, NAMES, STATES, AND TITLES.) 310
NAMES OR GENERIC DESCRIPTION? 310
NAMES WITH TITLES (See ABBREVIATING DATES, NAMES, STATES, AND TITLES.) 311
NARRATIVE WRITING 311
NEGATIVES 312
NEITHER 313
NEWSLETTERS 313
NOBODY 313
NOMINALIZATION 314
NONE, SINGULAR OR PLURAL? 314
NO ONE 314
NON OR *NON-*? 315
NONRESTRICTIVE PHRASES 315
NONVERBAL SYMBOLS 315
(See EMOJIS, MATHEMATICAL SYMBOLS, or GRAPHICS.) 315
NOR 315
NOT 316
NOTES 316
NOTICE OF MOTION 319
NOT . . . BUT 320
NOT ONLY . . . BUT ALSO 321
NOT SO MUCH . . . AS 321
NOUNS 322
NOUN STRING 324
NUMBERS (See NUMERALS.) 325
NUMERALS 325

O

OBJECT (See SENTENCE, PARTS OF, subsections 4 and 5.) 326
OBJECTIVE WRITING (See WRITING, OBJECTIVE.) 326
OBJECTIVITY 326
OBJECT OF A PREPOSITION (See PREPOSITIONS and SENTENCE, PARTS OF, subsection 6.) 327
OBLIVIOUS OF OR *OBLIVIOUS TO*? 327
OBVIOUSLY 327
OF COURSE 327
OK, O.K., OR *OKAY*? 327
OMITTING WORDS FROM QUOTATIONS 328
ONE 328
ONE-SENTENCE PARAGRAPHS 328
ON LINE, ONLINE, OR *ON-LINE*? 328
ONLY, WHERE TO PLACE 329
ON THE CONDITION THAT OR *WITH THE CONDITION THAT*? 329
OPENINGS FOR LETTERS 329
OPINION LETTERS AND EMAIL (See OPINIONS, LEGAL.) 330
OPINION OR ADVICE? 330
OPINIONS, JUDICIAL 330
OPINIONS, LEGAL 332
OPINIONS, READING THEM 338
OPTIMAL OR *OPTIMUM*? 340
OR 340
ORAL OR *VERBAL*? 341
ORAL PRESENTATIONS 341
ORDERS 345
ORDINANCES (See LEGISLATION.) 346
ORGANIZATION, CHRONOLOGICAL 346
ORGANIZATION FOR THOSE WHO CAN'T OUTLINE 346
ORGANIZATION, LARGE-SCALE 349
ORGANIZATION, SMALL-SCALE 352
ORGANIZATION, TOPICAL 353
ORGANIZATIONS, *THEY* OR *IT*? 353
ORGANIZE, HOW TO 353
ORNATE LANGUAGE (See FLOWERY LANGUAGE.) 357
OTHERWISE 357
OUTLINES 357
OVERDONE (See FLOWERY LANGUAGE, MODIFIERS, and EMOTIONAL LANGUAGE.) 365
OVERREFINEMENT 365
OXFORD COMMA (See COMMA, OXFORD; and COMMAS, subsection 7.) 365

P

PADDING 365
PAPERLESS PRACTICE 365
PAPER, USING IT 367
PARAGRAPH BLOCKS 367
PARAGRAPH LENGTH 368
PARAGRAPHS 369
PARALLEL CITATIONS (See CITATIONS, PARALLEL.) 370
PARALLELISM (See EMPHASIS; LISTS, STRUCTURE OF; and PARALLEL STRUCTURE.) 370
PARALLEL STRUCTURE 370
PARAPHRASE 372
PARENTHESES 373
PARENTHETICALS 375
PARTICIPLES (See VERBS, PARTICIPLES.) 376
PARTS OF A SENTENCE (See SENTENCE, PARTS OF.) 376
PARTS OF SPEECH 376
PARTY 376
PASSIVE OR ACTIVE VOICE? (See PASSIVE VOICE and VOICE, ACTIVE OR PASSIVE?) 377
PASSIVE VERBS (See PASSIVE VOICE.) 377
PASSIVE VOICE 377
PAST PARTICIPLES 379
PAST PERFECT TENSE (See VERBS, TENSES.) 379
PAST PROGRESSIVE TENSE (See VERBS, TENSES.) 379
PAST TENSE (See VERBS, TENSES.) 379
PATTERNS 379
PEOPLE OR *PERSONS*? 381
PER 381
PERCENT, %, OR *PER CENT*? 381
PERFECTIONISM 382
PERFECT TENSES (See VERBS, TENSES.) 383
PERIOD OR QUESTION MARK? (See QUESTION MARKS.) 383
PERIODS 383
PERSONALITY IN LEGAL WRITING 384
PERSONAL REFERENCES 385
PERSON: FIRST, SECOND, OR THIRD? 385
PERSONS OR *PEOPLE*? (See *PEOPLE* OR *PERSONS*?) 386
PERSUASIVE AUTHORITY 387
PERSUASIVE CORRESPONDENCE (See COMMUNICATIONS, PERSUASIVE; and WRITING, PERSUASIVE.) 387
PERSUASIVE WRITING (See WRITING, PERSUASIVE.) 387
PHENOMENA OR *PHENOMENONS*? 388
PHRASES 388

PIE CHARTS (See GRAPHICS, WHICH FORM TO USE, subsection 1.) 388
PINPOINT CITATIONS (See CITATIONS, PINPOINT.) 388
PLAGIARISM 388
PLAIN ENGLISH 389
PLAIN MEANING 389
PLEADINGS 389
PLEAD, *PLEADED*, OR *PLED*? 391
PLURALS OF NAMES 391
P.M. 392
POINT HEADINGS 392
POINT OF VIEW, OBJECTIVE TO PERSUASIVE 393
POLICY 394
POLISHING 394
POLISHING CHECKLIST 395
POSITIONS OF EMPHASIS 397
POSSESSIVES 398
POWERPOINTS 399
PRECISION 401
PREDICATE (See SENTENCE, PARTS OF.) 404
PREFIXES, WHEN TO HYPHENATE (See HYPHENS, *EX*-, and *SELF*- OR *SELF*? 404
PREPOSITIONAL PHRASES 404
PREPOSITION, ENDING A SENTENCE WITH 404
PREPOSITIONS 405
PRESENT PARTICIPLES (See VERBS, PARTICIPLES; and VERBS, TENSES, subsections 5 and 8.) 407
PRESENT PERFECT TENSE (See VERBS, TENSES, subsection 3.) 407
PRESENT PROGRESSIVE TENSE (See VERBS, TENSES, subsection 2.) 408
PRESENT TENSE (See VERBS, TENSES, subsections 1–3.) 408
PRETRIAL BRIEFS (See BRIEFS, PRETRIAL.) 408
PREVIOUS TO 408
PREWRITING 408
PREWRITING CHECKLIST 410
PRINCIPAL OR *PRINCIPLE*? 411
PRINCIPLES OF GOOD LEGAL WRITING 411
PRIORITIES COORDINATING MULTIPLE PROJECTS (See TIME MANAGEMENT.) 417
PRIORITIES WITHIN ONE PROJECT 418
PRIOR TO 419
PRIVACY 419
PROCEDURAL OR *SUBSTANTIVE*? 420
PROCESS AND PRODUCT COMPARED 420
PROCRASTINATION 421

PROFESSIONAL LANGUAGE AND PRESENTATION 422
PROFESSIONAL POSTURE (See PROFESSIONAL LANGUAGE AND PRESENTATION.) 424
PROFESSIONAL TONE (See PROFESSIONAL LANGUAGE AND PRESENTATION and TONE.) 425
PROGRESSIVE TENSES (See VERBS, TENSES.) 425
PROMPTS 425
PRONOUN REFERENCE (See AMBIGUITY, WAYS TO AVOID, subsection 2.) 427
PRONOUNS 427
PROOFREADING 430
PROPER NOUNS 431
PROVIDED THAT 431
PUNCTUATING LISTS (See LISTS, STRUCTURE OF.) 431
PUNCTUATION 431
PURPOSE 432
PURSUANT TO 433

Q

QUALITY AS A MODIFIER 433
QUESTION MARK OR PERIOD? (See QUESTION MARKS.) 433
QUESTION MARKS 433
QUESTIONS PRESENTED 435
QUOTATION MARKS 436
QUOTATION MARKS IN LEGISLATION (See LEGISLATION.) 437
QUOTATION MARKS OR INDENTED QUOTATIONS? (See QUOTATIONS, HOW TO PUNCTUATE, subsections 1 and 2.) 437
QUOTATION MARKS, SINGLE 437
QUOTATIONS, HOW TO PUNCTUATE 438
QUOTATIONS, LONG (See EXTENDED QUOTATIONS.) 445
QUOTATIONS, WHEN TO USE 445
QUOTATION WITHIN A QUOTATION (See QUOTATIONS, HOW TO PUNCTUATE, subsection 5.) 446

R

RAMBLING 446
RE 446
READABILITY 446
READERS 450
READING LEGAL SOURCES EFFICIENTLY 452
READING OPINIONS (See CASE BRIEFS; NOTES; OPINIONS, JUDICIAL; READING LEGAL SOURCES EFFICIENTLY.) 454
REALLY 454
REASONED (See *FIND*, *HOLD*, OR *REASON*?) 454
REASONING, ANALOGICAL 454

REASONING, DEDUCTIVE 455
REASONING, INDUCTIVE 456
REASONING, MODERN 457
REASONING, OTHER 457
REASONING, POSTMODERN 458
REASONING, PRESENTING IT 459
RECOMMENDATIONS, JOB-RELATED 466
RECOMMENDATIONS, LEGAL 467
RECORD, CITING TO IT 467
RECORDS, KEEPING THEM 468
RECUR OR *REOCCUR*? 470
REDUNDANCY (See CONCISENESS. For related information, see REPETITION.) 470
REFERENCES (See CITATIONS; FOOTNOTES; and RECORD, CITING TO IT.) 470
REFERENTS (See ANTECEDENTS.) 470
REGARDLESS OR *IRREGARDLESS*? 470
REGULATIONS, DRAFTING (See LEGISLATION.) 470
REJECTION LETTERS (See BAD NEWS, SOFTENING IT and BAD NEWS, GIVING IT.) 470
REPETITION 470
REPETITION OF SOUNDS (See ALLITERATION and ASSONANCE.) 471
REPLY BRIEFS (See BRIEFS, REPLY.) 472
REPLY TO ALL 472
REQUESTS FOR PAYMENT 472
RESEARCH 473
RESEARCH AS WRITING 473
RESEARCH PROCESS CHECKLIST 475
RESEARCH STRATEGY GUIDE 476
RESPECTIVELY 483
RESPONDENT 484
RESTRICTIVE PHRASES (See *THAT* OR *WHICH*?) 484
REVISING 484
REVISING CHECKLIST 486
REVISING THE WRITING OF OTHERS (See EDITING and MANAGING WRITERS.) 487
REWRITING 487
REWRITING CHECKLIST 489
RHETORICAL QUESTIONS 490
RHYMES 491
ROUGH DRAFTS (See WRITING and WRITING PROCESS.) 491
RULES 491
RULES, ADMINISTRATIVE 495
RUN-ON SENTENCES 495

S

SAID 496
SALUTATIONS 496
SARCASM 497
SAYING *NO* 498
SCARCELY 498
SCHOLARLY WRITING 499
SCHOLARLY WRITING PROCESS 500
SCHOLARLY WRITING PROCESS CHECKLIST 510
SCOPE 516
SCRUBBING ELECTRONIC DOCUMENTS (See METADATA REMOVAL.) 517
SECONDARY SOURCES 517
SECTION 517
SELF- OR *SELF*? 518
SEMICOLONS 518
SENTENCE FRAGMENTS 520
SENTENCE LENGTH 520
SENTENCE, PARTS OF 521
SENTENCES, MAIN (See TOPIC SENTENCES.) 525
SENTENCE STRUCTURE 525
SENTENCES WITH *AND* (See *AND*; COMMA, OXFORD; LISTS, STRUCTURE OF; and SENTENCE STRUCTURE.) 532
SETTLEMENT LETTERS AND EMAIL 532
SEXIST LANGUAGE, WAYS TO AVOID 534
SHALL 535
S/HE 535
SHEPARD'S CITATIONS (See UPDATING THE LAW.) 536
SHORT SENTENCES 536
SHOULD 536
SIC 537
SIGNALS (See CITATIONS, SIGNALS.) 537
SIMPLE SENTENCE 538
SIMPLICITY 538
SINCE OR *BECAUSE*? (See *BECAUSE* OR *SINCE*?) 539
SINGLE QUOTATION MARKS (See QUOTATION MARKS, SINGLE.) 539
SINGULAR OR PLURAL? 539
SLANG 540
SLANTED LANGUAGE (See EMOTIONAL LANGUAGE.) 540
SLASH 540
SMOOTHNESS (See COHERENCE, EMPHASIS, LOGICAL LINKS, and READABILITY.) 540
SO 541

SOCIAL MEDIA 541
SOMEBODY 542
SOMEDAY OR *SOME DAY*? 542
SOMEONE 542
SOMETIME OR *SOME TIME*? 542
SO WHAT? 542
SPACING BETWEEN SENTENCES 543
SPECIFICITY (See PRECISION.) 543
SPELLING PROBLEMS (See MISSPELLINGS, HOW TO AVOID; and WORDS SPELLCHECKERS MAY NOT CATCH.) 543
SPELLCHECKERS (See MISSPELLINGS, HOW TO AVOID; and WORDS SPELLCHECKERS MAY NOT CATCH.) 543
SPLIT INFINITIVES 543
SQUINTING MODIFIERS 544
STANCE (See POINT OF VIEW, OBJECTIVE TO PERSUASIVE.) 544
STANDARD OF REVIEW 544
STARE DECISIS 546
STATEMENT OF FACTS 547
STATEMENT OF THE CASE 548
STATES, ABBREVIATIONS OF (See ABBREVIATING DATES, NAMES, STATES, AND TITLES.) 550
STATING CONDITIONS (See CONDITIONS, STATING THEM.) 550
STATISTICS 550
STATUTES, DRAFTING (See LEGISLATION.) 550
STORYTELLING 550
STRING CITATIONS (See CITATIONS, STRING.) 551
STRUCTURE (See DESIGN 551
STUFFY LANGUAGE (See FLOWERY LANGUAGE, JARGON, LEGALESE, PLAIN ENGLISH, and TONE.) 551
STYLE 551
SUBHEADINGS (See POINT HEADINGS and HEADINGS.) 554
SUBJECT (See SENTENCE, PARTS OF, subsection 2.) 554
SUBJECT LINES 554
SUBJECT-VERB AGREEMENT 554
SUBJECT-VERB COMBINATIONS 555
SUBJUNCTIVE TENSES (See VERBS, MOODS.) 556
SUBORDINATING CONJUNCTIONS (See CONJUNCTIONS and SUBORDINATION.) 556
SUBORDINATION 556
SUBSTANTIVE OR *PROCEDURAL*? (See *PROCEDURAL* OR *SUBSTANTIVE*?) 556
SUCH 556
SUMMARY OF THE ARGUMENT 557
SUPPORT 557
SYLLOGISMS 558

SYMBOLS IN EMAIL 560
SYNONYMS 560
SYNTAX 560
SYNTHESIS 562

T

TABLE OF AUTHORITIES 562
TABLE OF CONTENTS 563
TABLES (See GRAPHICS, WHICH FORM TO USE, subsection 5.) 563
TABULATION (See ENUMERATION and LISTS, STRUCTURING THEM, subsection 8.) 563
TACT (See BAD NEWS, SOFTENING IT.) 563
TAKING NOTES (See NOTES.) 563
Technology (See WRITING AND TECHNOLOGY.) 563
TENSES (See VERBS, TENSES.) 563
TERMS OF ADDRESS FOR COURTS (See JUDGES, HOW TO ADDRESS.) 564
TERMS OF ART 564
TERTIARY DEGREE TITLES (See ABBREVIATING DATES, NAMES, STATES, AND TITLES.) 565
TEXTING AND INSTANT MESSAGING 565
TEXTING UNDER THE TABLE 565
THAT NEEDED? 565
THAT OR *WHICH*? 566
THE 567
THEIRS OR *THEIR'S*? 567
THEME 567
THEORY OF THE CASE 568
THEREBY 569
THEREFORE OR *THEREFOR*? 570
THERE IS OR *THERE ARE*? 570
THERE IS . . . THAT 570
THESIS SENTENCES 570
THESIS SENTENCES OR *TOPIC SENTENCES*? 571
THEY AS GENDER NEUTRAL 571
THEY OR *HE OR SHE*? 572
THIS 572
THOROUGHNESS 573
THOUGH OR *ALTHOUGH*? (See *ALTHOUGH* OR *THOUGH*?) 573
TIME MANAGEMENT 573
TITLES, ABBREVIATIONS OF (See ABBREVIATING DATES, NAMES, STATES, AND TITLES.) 577
TITLES OF JUDGES (See JUDGES, HOW TO ADDRESS.) 577
TO BE 577
TONE 578

TONE IN LETTERS AND EMAIL (See COMMUNICATIONS, TONE OF and GENDER IN WRITING.) 582
TOPICAL ORGANIZATION (See ORGANIZATION, TOPICAL.) 582
TOPIC SENTENCES 582
TOPIC SENTENCES OR *THESIS SENTENCES*? (See *THESIS SENTENCES* OR *TOPIC SENTENCES*?) 583
TOTALLY (See *COMPLETELY* and HYPERBOLE.) 583
TOUGH, SOUNDING THAT WAY 583
TRANSITIONS 584
TRIAGE 588
TRIAL BRIEFS (See BRIEFS, TRIAL.) 588
TRUSTS (See WILLS.) 588
TYPEFACE SIZE (See FONT SIZE.) 588

U

UNCLEAR MEANING 589
UNDERLINING 589
UNDERSTANDABILITY (See CLARITY and READABILITY.) 590
UNDOUBTEDLY 590
UNINTERESTED OR *DISINTERESTED*? (See *DISINTERESTED* OR *UNINTERESTED*? 591
UNIQUE 591
UNITY (See COHERENCE.) 591
UNLESS 591
UNOBTRUSIVE DEFINITIONS 591
UNTIL SUCH TIME AS 592
UNTO 593
UPDATING THE LAW 593
UPON OR *ON*? 594
UTILIZE 594
UTTERLY 594

V

VAGUE WORDS (See AMBIGUITY, WAYS TO AVOID, subsection 3; PRECISION, subsection 2; and WORD CHOICE.) 595
VARIETY 595
VERBAL OR *ORAL*? (See *ORAL* OR *VERBAL*?) 595
VERBOSITY (See CONCISENESS.) 595
VERBS, AUXILIARY 595
VERBS, EFFECTIVE USE OF 598
VERBS, INFLECTIONS (See VERBS, MOODS.) 600
VERBS, IRREGULAR 600
VERBS, LINKING 601
VERBS, MOODS 602
VERBS, PARTICIPLES 604

VERBS, TENSES 605
VERB TENSES, DIFFERENT ONES IN THE SAME TEXT 608
VERB TENSES, WHICH TO USE? 609
VERIFICATION 611
VERSATILITY 611
VERY 612
VIRGULE 612
VIRTUALLY 612
VIZ. 612
VOICE 612
VOICE, ACTIVE OR PASSIVE? 613
VOICE MAIL 614

W

WAS OR *WERE*? (See *THERE IS* OR *THERE ARE*? or VERBS, MOODS.) 615
WE 615
WELL OR *GOOD*? (See *GOOD* OR *WELL*?) 615
WHEN AM I DONE? (See WHEN TO STOP.) 615
WHEN OR *IF*? 615
WHEN OR *WHERE*? 616
WHEN TO STOP 616
WHERE OR *WHEN*? (See *WHEN* OR *WHERE*?) 618
WHETHER 618
WHETHER OR *WHETHER OR NOT*? 619
WHICH OR *THAT*? (See *THAT* OR *WHICH*? 619
WHITE PAPERS 619
WHOEVER OR *WHOMEVER*? 619
WHO OR *WHOM*? 620
WILLS 620
WOMAN, *LADY*, OR *FEMALE*? 622
WORD CHOICE 622
WORDINESS (See CONCISENESS.) 625
WORDS SPELLCHECKERS MAY NOT CATCH 625
WORDY PHRASES 626
WOULD 627
WRITER'S BLOCK (See WRITING BLOCK.) 627
WRITING 627
WRITING AND TECHNOLOGY 628
WRITING BLOCK 631
WRITING HABITS (See HABITS, WRITING.) 632
WRITING, OBJECTIVE 633
WRITING OPINIONS (See OPINIONS, JUDICIAL; OPINIONS, LEGAL; WRITING TO CLIENTS; and WRITING TO ATTORNEYS.) 634

WRITING, PERSUASIVE 634
WRITING PROCESS 643
WRITING TO ATTORNEYS 645
WRITING TO CLIENTS 647

Y

YET 657
YOU 657

Z

ZWEURGET 657